October 7–12, 2012
Tampere, Finland

I0038163

**Association for
Computing Machinery**

Advancing Computing as a Science & Profession

CASES'12

Proceedings of the 2012 ACM International Conference on

Compilers, Architectures and Synthesis for Embedded Systems (co-located with ESWEEK)

Sponsored by:
ACM SIGMICRO, ACM SIGBED, and ACM SIGDA

Technical Supporters:
IEEE Computer Society, IEEE Circuits and Systems Society, and IEEE Council on Electronic Design Automation

Supporters:
IFIP, IEEE Finland Section, and Federation of Finnish Learned Societies

**Association for
Computing Machinery**

Advancing Computing as a Science & Profession

The Association for Computing Machinery
2 Penn Plaza, Suite 701
New York, New York 10121-0701

Notice to Past Authors of ACM-Published Articles

ISBN: 978-1-4503-1423-7 (Digital)

ISBN: 978-1-4503-1424-4 (Print)

Additional copies may be ordered prepaid from:

ACM Order Department
PO Box 30777
New York, NY 10087-0777, USA

Phone: 1-800-342-6626 (USA and Canada)
+1-212-626-0500 (Global)
Fax: +1-212-944-1318
E-mail: acmhelp@acm.org
Hours of Operation: 8:30 am – 4:30 pm ET

ACM Order Number: 618122

Printed in the USA

Welcome Message

On behalf of the Organizing Committee and the committees of our participating conferences - CASES, CODES+ISSS, and EMSOFT - we would like to welcome you to Embedded Systems Week - ESWEEK 2012 - in Tampere, Finland. 2012 marks the 8th edition of ESWEEK. Earlier meetings were held in Jersey City, Seoul, Salzburg, Atlanta, Grenoble, Scottsdale and Taipei. This meeting has grown from two conferences and a handful of workshops to three conferences and ten workshops and symposia. ESWEEK is now widely recognized as the premier technical event in embedded computing.

The combined programme of the three conferences will offer three plenary keynotes, an industry day, and over 100 technical paper presentations. ESWEEK will also offer a number of half-day tutorials that cover hot topics of general interest to the embedded systems community. Additionally, this year, the International Symposium on System-on-Chip (SoC) will be co-located with ESWEEK. First of all, special thanks go to the technical programme chairs of the three conferences: Vincent Mooney, Rodric Rabbah, Franco Fummi, Naehyuck Chang, Florence Maraninchi, and John Regehr. This year, Embedded Systems Week includes ten workshops featuring outstanding contributions on specific topics. We especially wish to thank the workshop organisers: Aviral Shrivastava, Wolfgang Ecker, Wolfgang Mueller, Shahrokh Daijavad, Sumedh Sathaye, Seraphin Calo, Dimitrios Serpanos, Jian-Jia Chen, Maurizio Palesi, Nikil Dutt, Jason Xue, Jeff Jackson, Peter Marwedel, Kenneth Ricks, Fabiano Hessel, Jérôme Hugues, Frédéric Rousseau, Rolf Ernst and Alberto Sangiovanni-Vincentelli.

A complex event such as ESWEEK is a team effort that requires a dedicated group of volunteers to manage the success of the conference's growth in scale and offerings. We wish to thank every member of the organizing committee for their dedicated efforts in making the event a success. In particular, special thanks go to the following people for managing critical aspects of the conference organization: Jari Nurmi and Irmeli Lehto for local organization; David Atienza for finances; Suzanne Lesecq for publications; Francescantonio Della Rosa and Aviral Shrivastava for the conference website; Edward Chu and Frédéric Pétrot for electronic media and the paper submission system; Sungjoo Yoo, Tapani Ahonen and Yuan Xie for industry liaison; Gabriela Nicolescu, Jian-Jia Chen and Roberto Airoldi for workshops; Saddek Bensalem for tutorials; Henri-Pierre Charles, Xiaobo Sharon Hu and Hamaguchi Kiyoharu for publicity; Enrico Macii for coordinating the best paper award selections; Rolf Ernst for panels and special sessions; Hiroto Yasuura and Hiroyuki Tomiyama for handling the Asia liaison; Luigi Carro and Fabiano Hessel for handling Latin America liaison; Rajesh Gupta, Alex Orailoglu, Marilyn Wolf, Naehyuck Chang and Donald Thomas for professional society liaisons.

We also thank the Steering Committee members and the Technical Programme Committee members of each conference and workshop for selecting papers of the highest quality. Finally, we thank our sponsoring societies: ACM (SIGBED, SIGDA, SIGMICRO), IEEE (CAS, Computer, CEDA), and the cooperation with IFIP.

Tampere – the SoC city – is situated in the heart of beautiful Finnish Lakeland. The banks of the Tammerkoski rapids still feature old traditional industrial buildings which have now been converted to house pleasant restaurants, pubs or high-tech companies. Tampere is also a city of theatres, arts, sciences, sport and modern industrial culture. We therefore invite you to attend ESWEEK 2012 to learn about the latest in embedded system technologies, and also discover the beauty, culture and technological miracles of Finland.

Ahmed Jerraya   **Luca Carloni**
ESWeek 2012 General Chair   *ESWeek 2012 General co-Chair*
CEA, France   *Columbia University, USA*

Message from the Program Co-Chairs

Welcome to the 2012 Conference on *Compilers, Architectures and Synthesis for Embedded Systems – CASES'12*! We are very pleased to continue the *CASES* tradition of bringing a unique focus on the intersection of compilers and architectures to *Embedded Systems Week (ESWEEK)*. CASES has served this purpose since 2006 when it first formed part of the three core conferences that comprise ESWEEK.

This year, the program emphasizes a number of trends in compilation technology, architectures and memory systems. Some highlights include the keynote presentation from Professor Satnam Singh who explores the programming challenges we face as the well-established concept of the instruction set architecture (ISA) erodes with the emergence of heterogeneous architectures. Two invited papers further this dialogue by exploring new roles compilers and auto-tuners serve in the context of increasingly parallel and heterogeneous architectures.

Several of the other sessions address old and new challenges in the context of memory systems. Among the latter is an especially important emphasis on security in memory. As the number of embedded systems per person shows no signs of slowing its dramatic increase over the past ten years, many predict that, in the next ten years, security will become as critical of an issue as energy consumption and power have come to be. It is for this reason we decided to open the conference with an invited paper on this topic.

The *CASES* program committee accepted 18 out of 60 papers. All submissions received at least four reviews and half received five reviews. Every paper was discussed online, and the committee reached a number of decisions using online dialogue. This process allowed the committee to focus on a small number of papers at the face-to-face meeting where the program was finalized. This meeting was collocated with the *Design Automation Conference (DAC)* and held on June 3 in San Francisco, CA.

The program this year consists of eight sessions and will follow a format established last year where each two-hour session has three papers and a final half-hour poster session. The poster session worked well in the past and we believe it affords a closer interaction between the authors and the attendees. We encourage you to take advantage of this format to have all of your questions answered!

CASES is excited to be in Tampere, Finland – home to Nokia, one of the largest producers of mobile phone technology. Finland also serves as an important link between Europe and Russia. It is exciting to have an opportunity to learn more about Finnish culture and technology. Several keynote speakers, a packed industrial session, and an excellent technical program will provide significant insight into the state of the art in embedded systems and the emerging challenges ahead. Finally, we would like to thank the many volunteers – especially the *CASES* program committee and the ESWEEK local arrangements chairs, whose kind and dedicated effort make the conference possible.

Vincent John Mooney III   **Rodric Rabbah**
CASES'12 Program Chair   *CASES'12 Program Co-Chair*

Table of Contents

Session 3: Optimizing Heterogeneous Multicore Systems

Session Chair: Brett Meyer *(McGill University)*

Session 4: Frontline Challenges in Versatile Computing

Session Chair: Muhammad Shafique *(Karlsruhe Institute of Technology)*,

Session 5: Static and Dynamic Energy Management

Session Chair: Henri-Pierre Charles *(CEA-LIST)*

Session 6: Software/Hardware Techniques for Cache Management

Session Chair: Oliver Bringmann *(Forschungszentrum Informatik)*

Session 7: New Advances in Microfluidic Chips

Session Chair: Fadi Kurdahi *(University of California, Irvine)*

Session 8: Memory Management

Session Chair: Frank Mueller *(North Carolina State University)*

Tutorial 1

Tutorial 2

Author Index

ESWEEK 2012 Organizing Committee

General Chairs: Ahmed Jerraya *(CEA-Leti, France)*
Luca Carloni *(Columbia University, USA)*

Conference Programme Chairs: CASES
Vincent Mooney *(Georgia Institute of Technology, USA)*
Rodric Rabbah *(IBM, USA)*

CODES+ISSS
Franco Fummi *(University of Verona, Italy)*
Naehyuck Chang *(Seoul National University, Korea)*

EMSOFT
Florence Maraninchi *(Grenoble INP, France)*
John Regehr *(School of Computing, University of Utah, USA)*

Finance Chair: David Atienza *(EPFL, Switzerland)*

Local Arrangements Chairs: Jari Nurmi *(Tampere University of Technology, Finland)*
Irmeli Lehto *(Tampere University of Technology, Finland)*

Workshop Chairs: Gabriela Nicolescu *(Polytechnique Montréal, Canada)*
Jian-Jia Chen *(Karlsruhe Institute of Technology, Germany)*
Roberto Airoldi *(Tampere University of Technology, Finland)*

Publication Chair: Suzanne Lesecq *(CEA-Leti, France)*

Awards Chair: Enrico Macii *(Politecnico di Torino, Italy)*

Tutorials Chair: Saddek Bensalem *(Université Joseph Fourier, France)*

Panels & Special Sessions Chair: Rolf Ernst *(TU Braunschweig, Germany)*

Web Chairs: Aviral Shrivastava *(Arizona State University, USA)*
Francescantonio Della Rosa *(Tampere University of Technology, Finland)*

Electronic Media Chairs: Edward Chu *(National Yunlin University of Science and Technology, Taiwan)*
Frederic Pétrot *(Grenoble INP, France)*

Publicity Chair Europe: Henri-Pierre Charles *(CEA-List, France)*

Publicity Chair North America: Xiaobo Sharon Hu *(University of Notre Dame, USA)*

Publicity Chair Asia Pacific:	Hamaguchi Kiyoharu *(Osaka University, Japan)*
Industry Liaison Asia Pacific:	Sungjoo Yoo *(Postech, Korea)*
Industry Liaison Europe:	Tapani Ahonen *(Tampere University of Technology)*
Industry Liaison North America:	Yuan Xie *(Pennsylvania State University, USA)*
Latin America Liaison Chairs:	Luigi Carro *(Federal University of Rio Grande do Sul, Brasil)* Fabiano Hessel *(PUCRS, Brasil)*
Asia Liaison:	Hiroto Yasuura *(Kyushu University, Japan)* Hiroyuki Tomiyama *(Ritsumeikan University, Japan)*
IEEE CEDA/CAS Liaison:	Rajesh Gupta *(University of California, San Diego, USA)*
IEEE CS Liaison:	Alex Orailoglu *(University of California, San Diego, USA)*
IFIP Liaison:	Marilyn Wolf *(Georgia Tech, USA)*
ACM SIGDA Liaison:	Naehyuck Chang *(Seoul National University, Korea)*
ACM SIGBED Liaison:	Donald Thomas *(Carnegie Mellon University, USA)*
Steering Committee:	CASES Joerg Henkel *(Karlsruhe Institute of Technology, Germany)* Vinod Kathail *(Xilinx, Synfora, USA)* CODES+ISSS Reinaldo Bergamaschi *(Odysci, USA)* Don Thomas *(Carnegie Mellon University, USA)* EMSOFT Insup Lee *(University of Pennsylvania, USA)* Lothar Thiele *(ETH Zurich, Switzerland)*

CASES 2012 Conference Organization

Program Co-Chairs: Vincent Mooney *(Georgia Institute of Technology)*
Rodric Rabbah *(IBM Research)*

Steering Committee: Erik Altman *(IBM Research)*
Jorge Henkel *(Karlsruhe Institute of Technology)*
Vinod Kathail *(Xilinx)*
Krishna Palem *(Rice University & Nanyang Tech. U.)*

Program Committee: M. Balakrishnan *(Indian Institute of Technology Delhi)*
Oliver Bringmann *(Forschungszentrum Informatik)*
Srihari Cadambi *(NEC)*
John Cavazos *(University of Delaware)*
Henri-Pierre Charles *(CEA-LIST)*
Bruce Childers *(University of Pittsburgh)*
Henk Corporaal *(Tech. Univ. Eindhoven)*
Adam Donlin *(Xilinx)*
Heiko Falk *(Ulm University)*
Björn Franke *(University of Edinburgh)*
Tony Givargis *(University of California at Irvine)*
Ann Gordon-Ross *(University of Florida)*
Rajiv Gupta *(University of California at Riverside)*
Jörg Henkel *(Karlsruhe Institute of Technology)*
James Hoe *(Carnegie-Mellon University)*
Amir Hormati *(Microsoft)*
Michael Hübner *(Karlsruhe Institute of Technology)*
Andreas Krall *(Vienna University of Technology)*
Anshul Kumar *(Indian Institute of Technology Delhi)*
Ronny Krashinsky *(Nvidia)*
Rakesh Kumar *(University of Illinois at Urbana-Champaign)*
Rabi Mahapatra *(Texas A&M University)*
Scott Mahlke *(University of Michigan)*
Brett Meyer *(McGill University)*
Tulika Mitra *(National University of Singapore)*
Jaime Moreno *(IBM Research)*
Frank Mueller *(North Carolina State University)*
Stephen Neuendorffer *(Xilinx)*
Walid Najjar *(University of California at Riverside)*
Laura Pozzi *(University of Lugano)*
Anand Raghunathan *(Purdue University)*
Muhammad Shafique *(Karlsruhe Institute of Technology)*
Tim Sherwood *(University of California at Santa Barbara)*
Sunil Shukla *(IBM Research)*

Program Committee

(continued): Aviral Shrivastava *(Arizona State University)*
Michael Taylor *(University of California at San Diego)*
Lothar Thiele *(ETH Zurich)*
Weng-Fai Wong *(National University of Singapore)*
Jiang Xu *(Hong Kong University of Science and Technology)*
Jingling Xue *(University of New South Wales)*
Sami Yehia *(Intel)*

Additional reviewers:

Tosiron Adegbija	Ryan Moore
Ahmed Amin	Roger Moussalli
Hussam Amrouch	Abhinav Parvathareddy
Gogul Balakrishnan	Viktor Pavlu
Gerg Barany	Maurice Peemen
Micha Borrmann	Musfiq Rahman
Andreas Burger	Marisha Rawlins
Kiran Chandramohan	Semeen Rehman
Ting-Shuo Chou	Sebastian Reiter
Thomas Ebi	Arash Rezaei
Min Feng	Pooja Roy
Christoph Gerum	Abhik Sarkar
Volkan Gunes	Dongrui She
Robert Halstead	Stefan Stattelmann
Janmartin Jahn	Yulei Sui
Usman Khan	Wai-Teng Tang
Nikolai Kim	William Thies
Ratna Krishnamoorthy	Aalap Tripathy
Hugh Leather	Chundong Wang
Cheng-Hong Li	Yan Wang
Changhui Lin	Hui Wu
Manmohan Manoharan	Wei Zang
Mojtaba Mehrara	Christopher Zimmer

ESWEEK 2012 Sponsors & Supporters

Sponsors:

Technical Supporters: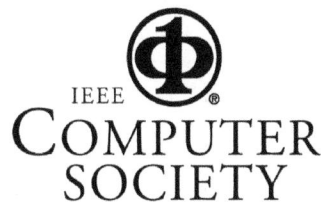

Supporters:

Wireless Innovations for Smartphones

Hannu Kauppinen
Nokia Research Center,
Helsinki, Finland
hannu.kauppinen@nokia.com

ABSTRACT

The ever increasing demand for fast mobile internet connectivity continues to set challenges for research in radio communications. On one hand the capacity demand can be served by offloading data traffic to local networks. On the other hand using more bandwidth, and possibly dynamically allocating spectrum in a flexible way, will improve the usage of the available spectrum. The future of wireless access continues to be defined by the 3GPP and IEEE standards setting bodies. Radios can also provide innovative features that offer new functionalities for consumers, such as ultra-fast local connectivity, sensing and positioning. This talk will present examples of various radio, sensing and multimedia innovations for smartphones.

Categories and Subject Descriptors

H.4.3 [**Information Systems Applications**]: Communications Applications

General Terms

Design.

Keywords

Radio connectivity, mobile internet connectivity, dynamic spectrum allocation.

BIOGRAPHY

Dr. Hannu Kauppinen is currently holding the position of Vice President, Head of Nokia Research Center. In this capacity he is responsible for the long term research of mobile technologies that will secure product differentiation and long-term profitable growth for Nokia. Hannu Kauppinen has a strong track record in bringing research innovations to products.

Hannu Kauppinen joined Nokia Research Center in 1997 has since then held key leadership positions in Nokia's wireless research. He has contributed to and overseen research in cognitive radio systems, cellular systems, wireless local connectivity, networking technologies, software defined radios, RF and antenna design, as well as sensing and positioning radios. During 2007-2008 and 2010-2011 Hannu Kauppinen was the Director of the Radio Systems Laboratory in Nokia Research Center. He was responsible for the research for 3GPP and IEEE radio standards as well as the research for cognitive and sensor radios to ensure innovativeness and competitiveness of wireless communication solutions in Nokia's products.

Hannu Kauppinen holds a PhD degree in Physics from the Helsinki University of Technology (1997) and an Executive MBA from the Helsinki School of Economics (2007).

Computing Without Processors

Satnam Singh
Technical Infrastructure division,
Google
1600 Amphitheatre Parkway
Mountain View, CA 94043
s.singh@acm.org

ABSTRACT

The duopoly of computing has up until now been delimited by drawing a line in the sand that defines the instruction set architecture as the hard division between software and hardware. On one side of this contract Intel improved the design of processors and on the other side of this line Microsoft developed ever more sophisticated software. This cozy relationship is now over as the distinction between hardware and software is blurred due to relentless pressure for performance and reduction in latency and energy consumption. Increasingly we will be forced to compute with architectures and machines which do not resemble regular processors with a fixed memory hierarchy based on heuristic caching schemes. Other ways to bake all that sand will include the evolution of GPUs and FPGAs to form heterogeneous computing resources which are much better suited to meeting our computing needs than racks of multicore processors. This presentation will highlight some of the programming challenges we face when trying to develop for heterogeneous architectures and a few promising lines of attack are identified.

Categories and Subject Descriptors

D.1.0 [**Programming Techniques**]: General

General Terms

Algorithms, Design.

Keywords

HW/SW frontier, programming, heterogeneous architecture.

BIOGRAPHY

Prof. Singh works in the Technical Infrastructure division of Google in Mountain View, California and focuses on the configuration management of Google's data-center services. Previously Prof. Singh worked on the design of heterogeneous systems at Microsoft Research in Cambridge UK and on parallel programming techniques at Microsoft's Developer Division in Redmond USA. He has also worked on re-configurable computing and formal verification at Xilinx in San Jose, California and as an academic at the University of Glasgow. He also currently holds a part-time position as the Chair of Reconfigurable Systems at the University of Birmingham.

ESWEEK 2012 Keynote Talk

A Standards-Based, Fully-Open Software Platform for Smart Embedded Systems

Jong-Deok Choi
Samsung Electronics
Suwon, Gyeonggi-Do, Korea
jd11.choi@samsung.com

ABSTRACT

There has been an explosion of smart mobile devices over the last few years. These smart devices, such as smartphones and tablets, have changed many aspects of modern life. They have also enabled whole new industries to grow up that develop and manufacture "companion products" of the smart devices. These companion products, however, are mostly built around the smart devices, instead of being tightly integrated into them, and fail to utilize the full capabilities of the smart devices. The main cause for their failure is that the software platforms these smart devices are built on are not fully open. This hinders efforts by device manufacturers or software developers to create innovative new products or product categories based on those software platforms.

In this talk, we present Tizen (www.tizen.org), which is a "fully open" software platform for embedded systems. Tizen allows for everyone involved in building and using devices built on it to freely define, invent, add new features or business models, or create new device categories. Tizen offers an industry leading HTML5-based application APIs, the preferred development environment for apps and services for the future. The HTML5-based APIs make it easy for developers to create applications that run across various categories of devices such as mobile, in-vehicle infotainment (IVI), Digital TV, netbooks, health and medical devices, etc. In this talk we also present Tizen's optimization technologies that enable HTML5-based applications to enjoy performance comparable to that of native applications. We also describe how Tizen balances the trade-offs between performance and power consumption, which is of extreme importance for mobile devices.

Categories and Subject Descriptors

D.3.3 [**Programming Languages**]: Language Constructs and Features – *frameworks.*

General Terms

Languages.

Keywords

Tizen, HTML5, smart device, software platform.

BIOGRAPHY

Dr. Jong-Deok Choi is an Executive Vice President at Samsung Electronics in Korea, and is currently in charge of the Software Platform Team within Samsung's Software Research Center. Before joining Samsung Electronics, he worked at IBM T. J. Watson Research Center as a Research Staff Member and Manager.

While working at IBM Research, he contributed to optimizing Java Webservices applications, the JikesRVM open-source Java virtual machine (JVM), the PTRAN parallelizing-compiler project, and others.

Dr. Choi has published over 50 technical papers in top journals and conferences on various fields in computer science, and holds over 20 US patents. He has served as a program (co-)chair, conference steering-committee member, and program-committee member for numerous technical conferences.

Dr. Choi received his Ph.D. and M.S. in Computer Sciences from University of Wisconsin - Madison, USA, in 1989 and 1985, respectively; M.S. in Electrical Engineering from KAIST, Korea, in 1981; and B.S. in Electronic Engineering from Seoul National University (SNU), Korea, in 1979.

Internet-of-Energy: Combining Embedded Computing and Communication for the Smart Grid

Randolf Mock
Siemens AG
Munich, Germany

Moritz Neukirchner, Rolf Ernst
TU Braunschweig
Braunschweig, Germany

Ruud Wijtvliet
Centrosolar Group
Hamburg, Germany

Michael Huetwohl
Lantiq GmbH
Munich, Germany

Pascal Urard
ST Microelectronics
Crolles, France

Ovidiu Vermesan (organizer)
Sintef ICT
Oslo, Norway
Ovidiu.Vermesan@sintef.no

ABSTRACT

Driven by increasing cost of energy and by the inclusion of re-newable but time variant sources of energy on the production side, and by new requirements from electromobility, building and home automation on the consumption side, the energy grid has moved in the focus of research, industry and infrastructure development. One of the key challenges is the interaction of the numerous em-bedded systems controlling energy producing and consuming devices using an "internet of energy."

This session will provide different views on this development towards a smart energy grid. The first talk given by a leading provider of energy grid equipment will give an overview on the new developments and challenges in modeling and simulating local grid behavior. The second talk discusses building energy management at the interface between home automation and the smart grid, both from the application and the embedded platform perspective. The third talk addresses home automation which serves many objectives, besides being a terminal network of the smart grind. Last not least, the fourth talk presents new development in wireless sensor devices as an important component of future home and energy networks.

Categories and Subject Descriptors

J.7 [**Computer Applications**]: COMPUTERS IN OTHER SYS-TEMS – *Command and control; Process control; Real time.*

Keywords

Design, Measurement, Performance, Reliability, Verification, Smart Energy, Smart Grid.

1. Interactions of Large Scale EV Mobility and Smart Grids - Chances and Challenges of Grid Infrastructure Simulations

Randolf Mock, Siemens, Germany

The complex interactions between electric mobility on a large scale with the electric distribution grid constitute a considerable challenge regarding the feasibility, the efficiency and the stability of smart electric distribution grids. Grid infrastructure simulations which take into account the details of these interactions and which are backed by comprehensive demonstrators may help to shed light on crucial aspects of both energy and information exchange between the traffic and the electric energy infrastructure regime. This will be highlighted by selected topics which intend to shed light on the scope and the challenges inherent in this area of simulation.

2. Reliable Building Energy Management in the Smart Grid

Moritz Neukirchner, Rolf Ernst, TU Braunschweig; Ruud Wijtvliet, Centrosolar, Germany

Reliable building energy management must guarantee a variety of services, support of local network control for grid stability and optimization, access for remote device maintenance and diagnosis, tamperfree metering, security against attacks targeting the building or network operations. The talk discusses applications, derives embedded platform requirements, and shows first solutions based on virtualization and self-protection.

3. Home Networks for the Smart Grid and Other Future Applications

Michael Huetwohl, Lantiq, Germany

The number of connected devices in our daily live has significantly increased. And it will continue to further increase x-fold in the near future. IPv6 is the key enabler. The huge social-economic challenges like the transition to renewable energy sources or the aging society are the drivers for this development. The devices and related applications will have a wide spread of different requirements: data rates from kbit/s to Gbit/s, Qualtity of Service, security and reliability will be of significant importance. In order to support these requirements a powerful Home Network and smart, easy-to-use, interoperable communication devices will be needed. The current status of Home Networks is not adequate and needs improvement.

4. Wireless Sensor Components (Draft title)

Pascal Urard, ST Microelectronics, France

Abstract not available at time of publication.

ESWEEK 2012 Special Presentation
CASES'12, CODES+ISSS'12, EMSOFT'12,
Oct. 7–12, 2012, Tampere, Finland.
ACM 978-1-4503-1424-4 & 978-1-4503-1426-8
 & 978-1-4503-1425-1/12/09.

Trends in Automotive Embedded Systems

Dan Gunnarsson
BMW Group
Munich, Germany

Stefan Kuntz
Continental Corp.
Regensburg, Germany

Glenn Farrall
Infineon
Bristol, UK

Akihiko Iwai
Denso Corp.
Kariya-shi, Japan

Rolf Ernst *(organizer)*
Technische Universität Braunschweig
Braunschweig, Germany
r.ernst@tu-bs.de

ABSTRACT

Automotive embedded systems have developed from single controllers to networked embedded systems integrating an ever growing variety of distributed applications. New features for driving assistance, improved safety, motor and energy management, and infotainment lead to shorter innovation cycles for software architectures, network technologies, and hardware architectures. While, e.g., the new FlexRay bus standard has just been introduced, next generation Ethernet is already at the edge of introduction. The 4 talks in this session present OEM, 1st tier supplier and semiconductor vendor views from leading automotive companies and suppliers.

Categories and Subject Descriptors

C.3 [**Computer Systems Organization**]: Real-time and embedded systems.

Keywordss

Design, Economics, Performance, Reliability, Security, Verification, Automotive electronics.

1. Trends and new Challenges in Automotive E/E Architectures

Dan Gunnarsson, BMW, Germany

Over the last decades integrated systems, where functions are partitioned on several ECUs, connected with data communication networks has evolved. During this development new communication methods and principal have been introduced, starting with system with low to moderate complexity moving to highly complex systems. Current requirements on the E/E Architecture are increasingly complex e.g. through the introduction of new and more advanced driver assistance systems where new use-cases like transmission of video streams with real-time requirements are becoming more common. To meet these requirements Ethernet is currently being introduced as an automotive network. This means that new challenges with regard to gateways and the transition between different protocols and networks have to be mastered. To cope with these increasingly complex tasks new modeling and analysis capabilities are needed.

2. New Challenges in HW and SW Integration

Stefan Kuntz, Continental, Germany

The continuing increase in/of functionality and density of functions in embedded distributed real-time systems within the automotive industry, as well as the importance of satisfying safety and security requirements in such systems require new approaches in managing the resulting complexities. Namely the integration of hardware and software is a concern and faces new challenges with the advent of multicore and manycore systems in the automotive domain. This presentation identifies the main challenges and sketches out some directions to tackle those challenges utilizing model based development and methodologies.

3. Virtualisation Support for an Embedded Automotive Environment

Glenn Farrall, Infineon, UK

Virtualisation is now a well established and relied upon technology for many environments - servers, cloud computing and even some environments that can be considered embedded. There is a difference however between soft-real time or multimedia embedded environments and systems in the safety and the hard-real time application space. This presentation covers some of the differences in the Automotive arena making the problem both easier and harder in various aspects and some of the features and solutions provided in the AURIX(r) multicore devices to address these issues.

4. Software Engineering for the next-generation automotive systems

Akihiko Iwai, Denso, Japan

Nowadays automotive E/E systems are getting large and complex due to its growing needs for new functionalities. The source of such new functionalities include active safety applications using vehicle to infrastructure communication, telematics services cooperating with services on cloud, vehicle to grid/home energy management applications. In this talk, while introducing some cooperative works in Japanese embedded systems industries, we will talk about current works and some technical issues of automotive software development.

ESWEEK 2012 Special Presentation
CASES'12, CODES+ISSS'12, EMSOFT'12,
Oct. 7–12, 2012, Tampere, Finland.
ACM 978-1-4503-1424-4 & 978-1-4503-1426-8
& 978-1-4503-1425-1/12/09.

Research Issues in Smart Phones, Notepads and Related Services

Petri Liuha
Nokia
Finland

Kari Pehkonen
Renesas Mobile
Finland

Juhani Rummukainen
ST-Ericsson
Finland

Veli-Pekka Vatula
Intel
Finland

Tatu Koljonen *(organizer)*
VTT
Finland
Tatu.Koljonen@vtt.fi

ABSTRACT

Networked embedded systems are building intelligence to every-place. There are more and more incentives to open proprietary data and interfaces for free to third party service developers. This development called "ubiquitous communication" or "internet of things" requires new dominant design for user interfaces, interoperability and contextuality. In the user interface design, for example, we have witnessed the growth of the smartphone display, which today is at about 5 inches. Developing the new dominant designs is part of the "ecosystem war", where the most attractive platforms are getting the most developer, users and profits. The four speakers of today represent companies that have entered the competition with different platforms, assets and strategies and hence have different research challenges to be solved..

Categories and Subject Descriptors

C.3 [**Computer Systems Organization**]: Real-time and embedded systems.

General Terms

Design, Economics, Performance, Reliability, Security, Verification.

1. Challenges in Building Smart Spaces (Draft title)

Petri Liuha, Nokia, Finland

2. Role of Wireless in Networked Embedded Systems (Draft title)

Kari Pehkonen, Renesas Mobile, Finland

3. Enable Coolest, Richest, Affordable Devices (Draft title)

Juhani Rummukainen, ST-Ericsson, Finland

4. Expanding from Chips to Handset (Draft title)

Veli-Pekka Vatula, Intel, Finland

Side Channel Attacks and the Non Volatile Memory of the Future

Zoya Dyka

Christian Walcyk
Damian Walczyk
Christian Wenger

Peter Langendoerfer

IHP
Im Technologiepark 25
15236 Frankfurt (oder), Germany
+493355625350
{dyka|langendoerfer}@ihp-microelectronics.com

ABSTRACT
In this paper, we describe a new non-volatile memory, based on metal-insulator-metal that provides performance benefits compared to standard Flash memory. In addition and more importantly, it comes with some advantages with respect to side channel attacks, i.e., its structure prevents by default optical analysis.

Categories and Subject Descriptors
B.3.1 Semiconductor Memories

Keywords
Side channel attacks, new memory structures.

1. INTRODUCTION
Wireless sensor networks (WSNs) are becoming an essential building block in application fields such as critical infrastructure protection, industrial automation and telemedicine to name a few areas in which security plays a central role. Potential attackers of those applications will most probably attack the most vulnerable part of the overall systems, i.e., the WSNs. The wireless sensor nodes can be attacked by "standard" network based approaches but also by physical means if they are left unattended in remote sites which is, after all, the preferred application for WSN. We are convinced that protecting the wireless sensor nodes is essential since compromised nodes put the whole system at risk. While much research effort has been spent on improving the network security of WSN, the protection of the nodes and especially their protection against physical attacks has gained only little attention up to now. The problem with protecting WSNs from physical attacks is that the key management in WSNs is extremely difficult, i.e., key exchange or revocation of keys. As a consequence, most of the nodes share a common key, i.e., if the key is extracted from a single sensor node a significant part of the network is compromised. While most of the cipher algorithms provide good security against standard crypt-analysis approaches,

most implementations come with some weaknesses that can be exploited. The maybe most straight forward attack is directly extracting the key from the memory if the sensor node can be physically accessed. The following successful attacks against non-volatile re-programmable memory have been reported in the literature in the recent past:

- Optical fault injection attacks [1]: These attacks exploit sensitivity of the floating gate memories to light or especially to UV light. The goal of such attacks can be the extraction of the secret data, for example of the cryptographic key [2]. Another goal is to prevent the change of the memory content with the goal to disrupt the normal functionality of the devices [3].

- Local heating attacks [4]: The content of EEPROM and Flash memory cells can be modified via locally heating up of memory cells using lasers.

- Extraction of information from EEPROM memory cells via charge measurements [5], [6]: the floating gate potential can be probed directly using electrical scanning probe microscopy to retrieve the stored content.

A potential countermeasure is the use of new types of non-volatile memory, e.g., metal-isolator-metal structures.

2. MIM Memory
Numerous Metal–Insulator–Metal (MIM) systems show electrically induced resistive switching effects and have therefore been proposed as the basis for future non-volatile memories.

The typical unit cell used for this kind of memory is a simple capacitor-like structure (MIM) with a functional material sandwiched between those two conductive electrodes. In our case, the MIM structure consists of TiN/Ti/HfO$_2$/TiN. The inclusion of a Ti layer as the reactive buffer seems to greatly improve the performance of the device [7]. The microstructure of the MIM memory devices was investigated by cross-sectional transmission electron microscopy (XTEM) shown in Fig. 1a, where the Ti/TiN is a polycrystalline film with grain boundaries. Recently, MIM memory devices in a 1 transistor – 1 resistor (1T-1R) architecture were integrated in a modified Si CMOS technology, Fig. 1b [8], [9], which improves the capability of controlling the switching parameters.

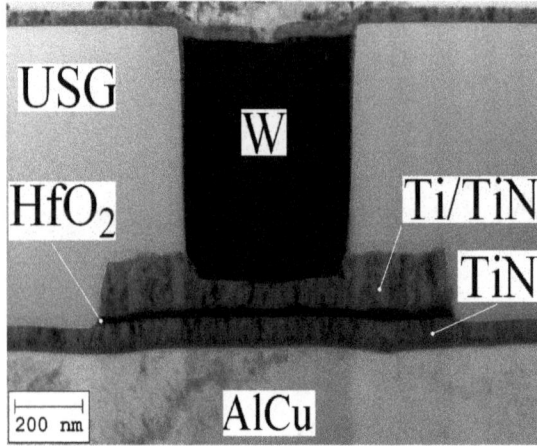

(a) MIM cell

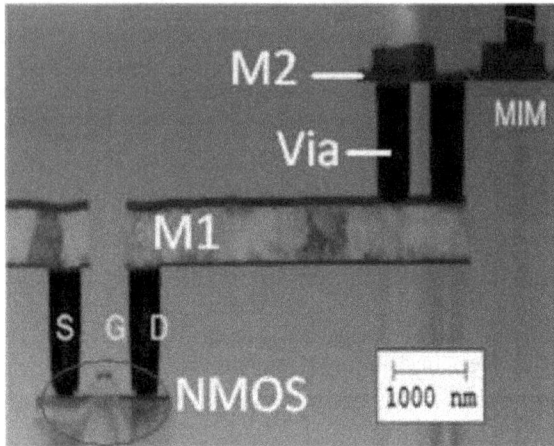

(b) MIM cell with a NMOS access transistor (1T-1R architecture)

Figure 1: XTEM image of a TiN/HfO$_2$/Ti/TiN MIM device with a cell size of 1×1 μm^2

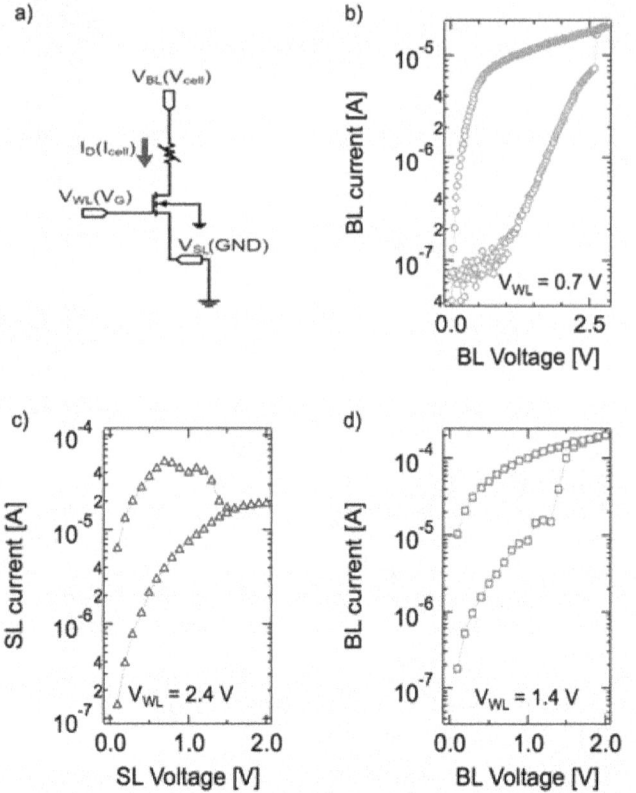

Figure 2: In the 1T-1R architecture, NMOS transistors with W/L = 1.14μm × 0.24μm are connected in series with MIM devices (a). I-V characteristics: Typical forming (b), reset (c), and set process (d).

As is necessary for memories, the structures are characterized by two distinct resistance states: ON state (with low resistance, a binary 1) and OFF state (with high resistance, a binary 0). The so-called electroforming process, which consists in the application of a bit line (BL, MIM connected to the drain pin) voltage sweep to VBL = 2.5 V, is required to initiate the resistive switching behavior in the 1T-1R devices (Fig. 2(b)). The reset operation changes the device to the OFF-state by applying a voltage to source line (SL) and 0 V to BL. The set operation changes the RRAM device from a high-resistive state to a low-resistive state by applying a voltage to BL and 0V to SL. Fig. 2(c) and (d) show an example of the reset/set process. First, the reset process was performed, which starts at VSL = 0.8 V (5.6 × 10^{-5} A), whereas the set operation occurs at VBL = 1.4 V (2.4 × 10^{-5} A). For reading the information from the MIM storage cell its control transistor is biased with voltage VSL=0.2V. If the current via the MIM structure is small (<10^{-6}A) the MIM cell contains a binary '0'; otherwise i.e. if the current is larger (>10^{-6}A) a binary '1' is stored and retrieved in the reading process.

In order to evaluate the potential of RRAM and to ramp-up in product maturity level, a 4 Kbit memory device array with the associated control circuitry was specified and designed at IHP [10].

3. Security Analysis of the MIM

RRAM has shown promising scalability, non-volatility, multiple state operation, 3D stackability, and CMOS compatibility. Furthermore for embedded applications it is mandatory to achieve low-power dissipation, fast access time, bit alterability, high reliability at room and higher temperatures, resistivity towards radiation. Fig. 3 shows typical performance parameters - access time for Read/Write 50 ns, latency < 20 ns, bandwidth >200 Mbps, endurance > 10^5, retention > 10 years, energy dissipation < 10pJ/operation, and cell size < 0.5 μm^2.

These advantages of RRAM already make it a very promising candidate for the next generation of memory, i.e., to replace Flash especially in wireless sensor networks where available energy is very limited. Moreover, the concept of RRAM provides good security properties by its design, i.e., these are intrinsic features and nothing added after security issues have been observed. This is due to the fact that the exploited storage effect is not based on charge storage and thus prevents attacks by directly probing potentials [5].

Also optical imaging and fault injection attacks can be avoided using RRAM. As it can be seen in Fig. 1b, the layout consists of Metal 2 (M2), the MIM structure with $1 \times 1 \ \mu m^2$ area, vertical tungsten interconnects, and Metal 3 (M3), i.e. the insulator of the MIM cell is placed between M2 and M3. The optical analysis of the insulator of the MIM cell impossible because it is protected by its own structure: the metal-insulator-metal structure. The access to the MIM structure from the back side is very tricky, since in a more advanced design than the one shown in Fig. 1(b) the MIM structure will be placed directly on top of the transistor. This reduces the area and can make the local heating attacks inefficient. All these suggestions have to be proved.

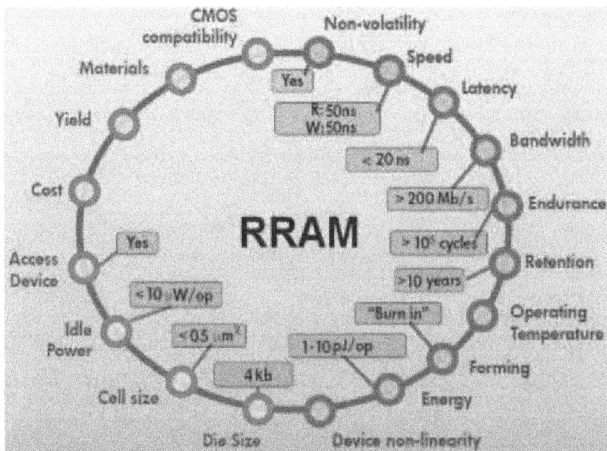

Figure 3: Performance parameters for RRAM

4. Conclusions

In this paper we have discussed the use of MIM based non-volatile memory. This new type of memory has significant advantages compared to today's technologies, especially when applied for wireless sensor nodes:

- Reduced power consumption for read/write operations, increased number of write cycles

- Improved security features, the structure itself prevents optical analysis and the new type of storage capability helps to prevent simple probing attacks.

To summarize MIM provide very interesting new features that help to improve reliability and security of wireless sensor networks in the future, but its security features need thorough investigation which we plan to do in the future.

5. ACKNOWLEDGMENTS

This work was partially funded by the EU as part of the TAMPRES project.

6. REFERENCES

[1] S. P. Skorobogatov: Semi-invasive attacks - a new approach to hardware security analysis, Computer Laboratory, University of Cambridge, Technical report ACAM-cl-tr-630, 2005

[2] S. P. Skorobogatov: Flash memory 'Bumping' attacks. In: S. Mangard, F.-X. Standaert, (eds.) CHES 2010. LNCS, vol. 6225, pp. 158–172. Springer, Heidelberg (2010), http://www.springerlink.com/content/57775039411561x1/

[3] S. P. Skorobogatov: Optical Fault Masking Attacks," Fault Diagnosis and Tolerance in Cryptography, FDTC 2010, pp. 23–29, 2010

[4] S. P. Skorobogatov: Local Heating Attacks on Flash Memory Devices, Hardware-Oriented Security and Trust (HOST-2009) Workshop, San Francisco, USA, 27 July 2009, http://ieeexplore.ieee.org/

[5] Ch. De Nardi, R. Desplats, Ph. Perdu, F. Beaudoin, J. L. Gauffier: EEPROM Failure Analysis Methodology: Can Programmed Charges Be Measured Directly by Electrical Techniques of Scanning Probe Microscopy?, Proceedings of the 31 International Symposium for Testing and Failure Analysis November 6–10, 2005, McEnery Convention Center, San Jose, California, USA

[6] D. I. Konopinski, A. J. Kenyon: Data recovery from damaged electronic memory devices, Department of Electrical and Electronic Engineering, University College London, http://www.ee.ucl.ac.uk/lcs/previous/LCS2009/NEMS/Konopinski.pdf

[7] P.-S. Chen, H.-Y. Lee, Y.-S. Chen, P.-Y. Gu, F. Chen, and M.-J. Tsai, "Impact of engineered Ti layer on the memory performance of HfOx- based resistive memory," Electrochem. Solid State Lett., vol. 13, no. 12, pp. H423–H425, 2010.

[8] Ch. Walczyk, D. Walczyk, T. Schroeder, T. Bertaud, M. Sowinska, M. Lukosius, M. Fraschke, D. Wolansky, B. Tillack, E. Miranda, and C. Wenger: "Impact of Temperature on the Resistive Switching Behavior of Embedded HfO_2-based RRAM devices", IEEE Trans. Electron Devices, 58, 3124, 2011,

[9] D. Walczyk, Ch. Walczyk, T. Schroeder, T. Bertaud, M. Sowinska, M. Lukosius, M. Fraschke, B. Tillack, Ch. Wenger: "Resistive switching characteristics of CMOS embedded HfO_2-based 1T1R cells", Microelectronic Eng. 88, 1133, 2011, http://www.sciencedirect.com/science/article/pii/S0167931711003820

[10] D. Walczyk, T. Bertaud, M. Sowinska, M. Lukosius, M. A. Schubert, A. Fox, D. Wolansky, A. Scheit, M. Fraschke, G. Schoof, Ch. Wolf, R. Kraemer, B. Tillack, R. Korolevych, V. Stikanov, Ch. Wenger, T. Schroeder, and Ch. Walczyk: "Resistive switching behavior in TiN/ HfO_2/Ti/TiN devices", to be presented at the 2012 ISCDG.

A Cost-Effective Tag Design for Memory Data Authentication in Embedded Systems

Mei Hong
School of Computer
Science and Engineering
University of New South Wales
Sydney, NSW 2052, Australia
meihong@cse.unsw.edu.au

Hui Guo
School of Computer
Science and Engineering
University of New South Wales
Sydney, NSW 2052, Australia
huig@cse.unsw.edu.au

X. Sharon Hu
Department of Computer
Science and Engineering
University of Notre Dame
Notre Dame, IN 46556, USA
shu@cse.nd.edu

ABSTRACT

This paper presents a tag design approach for memory data integrity protection. The approach is area, power and memory efficient, suitable to embedded systems that often suffer from stringent resource restriction. Experiments have been performed to compare the proposed approach with the state-of-the-art designs, which demonstrate that the approach can produce a memory data protection design with a low resource cost - achieving overhead savings of about 39% on chip area, 45% on power consumption, 65% on performance, and 12% on memory cost while maintaining the same or higher security level.

Categories and Subject Descriptors

C.3 [**Special-purpose and Application-based Systems**]: Real-time and Embedded Systems; C.1 [**Processor Architectures**]: General

General Terms

Design, Performance, Security

Keywords

tag design, memory data authentication, low on-chip cost, embedded systems

1. INTRODUCTION

Security becomes increasingly critical in embedded systems. Most embedded systems consist of secure processor chips and insecure off-chip memory components. To protect the system from intentional attacks on the insecure components, data in the off-chip memory often need to be encrypted and authenticated. Use of data tagging is a common approach to protect data integrity, where data is attached with a tag and the tag value is checked each time the data

is used; if the tag value is changed, the data is deemed as tampered and invalid.

Unlike the tag design in network communication, where data are immediately authenticated upon arrival at the destination - hence no tag storing is needed, the tag for memory data should be saved since the data will only be authenticated some time later when they are fetched by the processor. Therefore, apart from the performance overhead, the tag design for memory data encounters more challenges: 1) high memory cost for tag storage, which can be very prohibitive because huge number of tags are often used; and 2) increased security risk since the tag can be attacked during its prolonged life in the memory.

In terms of tag design, there are two basic data protection design paradigms, as illustrated in Figure 1. In the first design shown in Figure 1(a), the tag value is generated *independently* from the data (D). The data is earmarked by the tag via encryption (denoted as Enc in the figure). The encrypted data and tag, $Enc(D\|tag)$, are transmitted and stored in the insecure memory. Due to the diffusion feature of the encryption operation, a change to $Enc(D\|tag)$, will very likely alter the tag value after decryption (i.e. the output, tag', of Dec in the figure); hence the change can be detected during authentication. This design requires the original tag be stored on the processor chip.

The second design given in Figure 1(b) computes the tag based on the data, namely, the tag is *dependent* on the data value. The authentication compares the tag calculated from the received data with the provided tag value. The tag in this design can be stored either on-chip or off-chip.

Since the first design (data-independent tag) takes the tag value as part of the input data to be encrypted (which increases the amount of encryption operations), and requires both that the tag be saved on-chip (consuming precious on-chip resources) and that the data authentication be performed after the decryption (namely, wasteful decryption is performed for invalid data), we focus on the second design paradigm - design with a data-dependent tag. Specifically, the tag is generated based on encrypted data; The encrypted data and their tags are stored in the off-chip memory. **We aim to develop a cost effective tag design to counter physical attacks on the insecure off-chip memory and its buses.**

The main contributions made in this paper are

- a simple security evaluation model based on the avail-

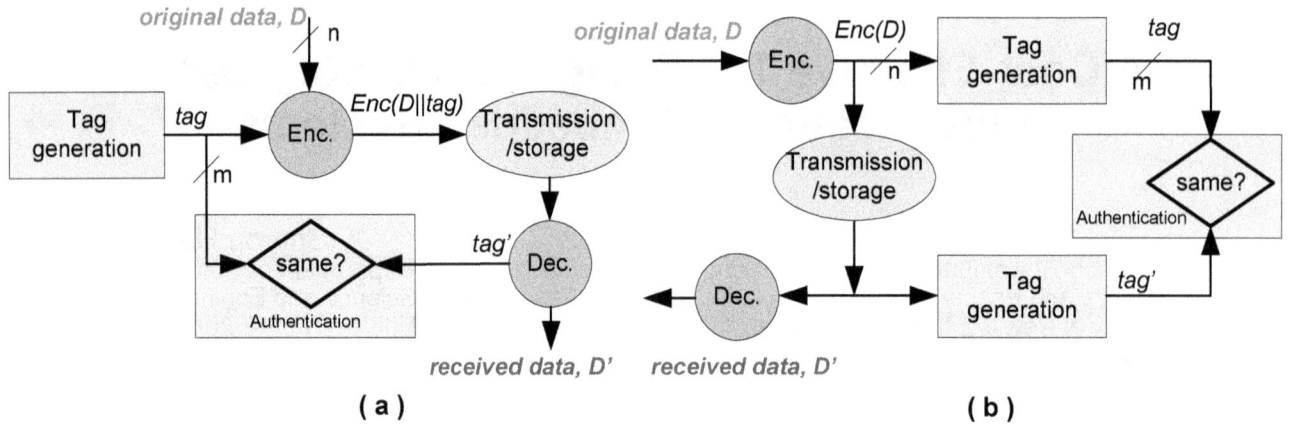

Figure 1: Two Memory Data Protection Design Paradigms (a) with Data-Independent Tag (b) with Data-Dependent Tag

able search spaces of sensitive values that are used in the design. The model builds on the premise that uniformly distributed values lead to high-level of security and allows efficient evaluation of different tag design approaches;

- an innovative tag generation approach (based on a statistic *inverse transform* scheme). The approach offers a parameterized security design, with a design space that can be explored for trade-off between security, on-chip overhead (e.g. area, power consumption) and off-chip memory cost;

- a novel technique for prudently selecting the tag size to achieve a maximal level of security with small off-chip memory overhead (due to tag storage).

- an evaluation platform that incorporates the memory protection design with a processor system and can estimate both the software execution time and the design hardware cost.

Both the tag generation approach and the tag size selection method enable effectively protecting data integrity for embedded systems.

The rest of the paper is organized as follows. Section 2 reviews some existing works related to data authentication and tag design. Our tag design approach is presented in Section 3. The experiment results to show the effectiveness of our approach are given in Section 4, and the paper is concluded in Section 5.

2. RELATED WORK

Authentication was initially introduced to messages communicated between a sender and a receiver over the network so that tampering with messages (forgery, unauthorized modifications, reordering, etc.) can be detected. The fundamental idea of message authentication is to use a checksum (a.k.a message digest, or tag) calculated from the original message by the sender such that any change to the message will lead to a different checksum. The checksum is appended to the message on transmission. At the receiver side, the checksum is re-computed from the received message and is compared with the original checksum that comes with

the message. If they match, the message is authenticated; otherwise, the message is considered to be corrupted.

Blum et al. in [1] discussed possible attacks to the memory contents, demonstrating the need of authentication for memory data even if they are in an encrypted format.

XOM (eXecution Only Memory) [2], proposed by Lie et al., is a hardware-based design for authenticating application code from insecure external memory. In this design, applications are encrypted and stored in separate memory sections. Each of these sections has a unique and fixed numerical identifier and the identifier is used to generate a data-dependent tag for the code in the memory section. When an application is executed, the tag (computed based on the fetched data from the memory) is compared with the tag stored in a secure table. If they are the same, the execution is allowed to continue, otherwise, an exception is generated and the execution is disabled. By this way, applications are isolated and protected from each other. This design uses static data-dependent tags, suitable to read-only memory data; it is not effective for protecting dynamic read-write data from replay-attacks (a form of attack in which a current data value is maliciously replaced with a previously used and valid value).

To protect dynamic data, Suh et al. [3] proposed a design, called AEGIS (Architectural EnGines for Information Security), for tamper-evident and tamper-resistant processing.

Since on-chip memory is very limited and expensive, to reduce on-chip memory cost, Suh et al. [4] applied a hash tree proposed by Merkel[5]. The tree leaves are memory content blocks, and the nodes are hash values of their immediate children in the tree. The tree captures the integrity state of all memory contents. In their design, only the root node is stored on-chip that is inaccessible by the adversary; Other nodes are stored off-chip. On a memory read, a path of tree nodes from the leaf (that is associated with the requested memory block) to the root will be re-calculated. If the resulting root matches the reference root stored on-chip, the memory contents are validated; otherwise, the contents are invalidated. The tree is updated from leaf to root on a memory write operation. Since the node path recalculation/update involves heavy computation and multiple memory accesses, long delays will be incurred. To reduce the delay, Gassend et al. [6] proposed to save tree nodes that have been previously authenticated in a fast on-chip cache.

With the node caching, the path nodes re-calculation process will stop as soon as it hits a cached node and the authentication can be completed earlier by just comparing the cached tree node with the newly computed node. Elbaz et al. [7] further improved the hash tree design by constructing a Tamper-Evident Counter tree (TEC-tree) where both authentication and tree update processes are parallelizable. Rather than waiting for lower level nodes' calculation from the memory data, the tree allows for calculation of nodes from counter values at different tree levels simultaneously .

The above designs can be categorized as using a Generic Composition (GC) approach, where encryption on the plain memory data is performed first, followed by the tag generation for data authentication.

Since both encryption and authentication are often computationally intensive, the sequential execution of the two processes in GC designs has a significant impact on the system performance. Some authenticated-encryption (AE) algorithms have, therefore, been proposed [8] [9] [10]. AE algorithms usually use the block cipher and mode operations for encryption and authentication. Since the mode operations are parallelizable, the performance overhead can be moderated. Moreover, instead of in two sequential execution steps, AE algorithms mix encryption and authentication in one step, enabling further parallel operations for performance improvement.

In [11], Yan et al. applied an AE algorithm, Galois Counter Mode (GCM) [9], which was initially proposed for message authentication, for general-purpose processor computing systems. With their design, the memory authentication is done in parallel with encryption. Nonce values are used in generating authentication tags; A nonce is formed by a non-repeated counter and memory address. Tags are updated when memory contents are modified to resist the old tag replay attacks. Tags are placed in off-chip memory, and counters are maintained in a counter tree, with only the root counter stored on-chip to save on-chip memory. Each time a nonce is used for memory data authentication, its counter value is retrieved from the counter tree. Maintaining a counter tree is more resource efficient than that for the tag tree, since counters usually have a small size and low computation overhead.

Rogers et al. [10] used a similar tag generation approach as proposed by Yan et al. in [11]. Unlike Yan's approach, where GCM is used, Roger's design applies a Parallel Message Authentication Code (PMAC) algorithm [8] that allows for using a single hardware encryption component for both encryption and authentication, hence it is computing-resource wise and cost effective.

In [12], Elbaz et al. proposed an Added Redundancy Explicit Authentication (AREA) scheme, which eliminates tag calculation during authentication. AREA is an AE approach in a sense that both encryption and tag generation are completed in one step. The principle of the AREA scheme is to insert a tag as redundancy into the plaintext before encryption and to check it after decryption. The memory address and nonce are used to form the tag. Because of the diffusion property of encryption function, the tag and data are mingled in encrypted bit string. Any change to the bit string could cause change to the tag after decryption. This method requires nonces be stored on-chip. In order to save on-chip memory cost, the scheme treats Read Only (RO) memory

contents and Read Write (RW) memory contents differently. For RO memory data, which is never changed during runtime, no nonce is needed and only memory address is used in the tag. For the RW data that may change during execution, a nonce and its memory address are used in the tag.

In this paper, we focus on the tag design to protect the off-chip memory data integrity for embedded systems. On the one hand, embedded systems are increasingly demanding security due to their fast-growing application domains; On the other hand, the strict restriction of resources in embedded system makes most existing design approaches ineffective. Our work aims to reduce both on-chip resource overhead and off-chip memory cost incurred by the memory data integrity protection.

Our approach is similar to Yan's and Roger's approaches in that all are AE algorithm based, the tag generation is nonce-controlled, and tags are saved off chip. But there are major differences: 1) Both Yan's and Roger's approaches use an existing algorithm (GCM, PMAC) originally developed for message authentication, which is computation-intensive and consumes large hardware resources, and 2) None of the two works address customization of the tag size, which has a great impact on memory consumption and system security. Since most embedded systems are application specific, we can customize the design to achieve high security while at a low cost. Specifically, we customize the tag size and tag generation algorithm to achieve an optimal tradeoff between security and the design overhead.

3. DESIGN APPROACH

We target an embedded system that has a secure processor chip and insecure off-chip memory. The processor chip also contains cache and components for encryption/decryption and tag generation/data authentication. Here, we first present an overview of our tag design, which leads to the related design techniques detailed in the second part of this section.

3.1 Overview

Given such a system with secure processor chip and insecure off-chip memory, for a cache line to be written to the off-chip memory, a tag is first generated on the processor chip, then the tag together with the encrypted data is transferred to and stored in the off-chip memory. When the data is later required and fetched into the processor chip, a tag value of the fetched data is calculated and compared with the tag obtained from the memory. If both values are the same, the data is authenticated and can be further decrypted for use. Otherwise, the data should be discarded.

Figure 2 illustrates the flow of tag movement in our target system, where the bus and off-chip memory can be under physical attacks. The tag (T), together with the encrypted cache line ($Enc(L)$), basically can go four stages, as shown in dashed blocks: 1) generated on the processor chip, $Enc(L)\|T$, 2) transmitted over the bus to memory, $Enc^{(1)}(L)\|T^{(1)}$, 3) stored in the off-chip memory, $Enc^{(2)}(L)\|T^{(2)}$, and 4) transmitted back from memory to the processor chip, $Enc^{(3)}(L)\|T^{(3)}$.

For a cache line L, its encrypted data $Enc(L)$ and related tag, T, can be tampered in three circumstances: 1) on the bus during transmission to the memory (denoted as **bus attack**), where $Enc(L)$ is replaced with $Enc^{(1)}(L)$ and/or

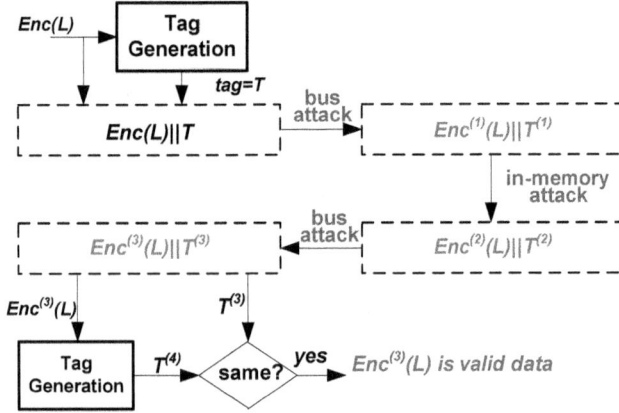

Figure 2: Tag Movement and Possible Attack Places in the Target System

T is replaced with $T^{(1)}$; 2) in the memory (denoted as **in-memory attack**, where the data and tag can be changed to $Enc^{(2)}(L)$ and $T^{(2)}$); and 3) on the bus when the data is fetched from the memory to the processor (with altered $Enc^{(3)}(L)$ and $T^{(3)}$ for the memory data and the related tag).

Based on Figure 2, a data alteration can escape authentication (i.e. the attack succeeds) if the tag ($T^{(4)}$) of the fetched memory data ($En^{(3)}(L)$) and the tag value from the memory ($T^{(3)}$) are the same, which allows for the following types of attacks:

- *Type A* Replacement Attack, with random and known values. $En^{(3)}(L)$ is randomly selected or purposely picked, and the tag for $En^{(3)}(L)$ is guessed correctly (namely, $T^{(3)} = T^{(4)}$).

- *Type B* Replacement Attack, with known value and tag pairs. $En^{(3)}(L)$ and $T^{(3)}$ are a valid copy of a different memory location.

- *Replay Attack.* $En^{(3)}(L)$ and $T^{(3)}$ are a copy of a previously observed valid data and tag pair at the same memory location.

To perform a type A replacement attack, a brute-force approach can be applied to explore a correct tag value. For the type B replacement attack and replay attack, they basically *replay* valid data and can be easily implemented since the encrypted cache line and tag are accessible to the adversary through buses and the off-chip memory.

Therefore, the guidelines below should be followed for an effective tag design:

- The tag possesses a strong resistance to the type B replacement attack and the replay attack. The tag value will change with the data memory location and the time when the data was accessed.

- The tag is highly sensitive to a change on the data, and is difficult to be guessed correctly.

- The tag design is easy to implement, with low hardware, performance and power overheads, especially as low memory consumption as possible.

To meet the above requirements, in our design approach, we

- apply a nonce to tag generation. The nonce value is memory location and access specific, to counter replay related attacks;

- ensure high randomness of the tag value and the operations used in the tag generation process, to resist replacement (type A) based attacks;

- use a small yet effective logic for tag generation to reduce the on-chip hardware implementation overhead and use an as small tag as possible to tag a larger cache line data, to reduce the off-chip memory overhead for tag storage.

The tag design is elaborated in next section.

3.2 Tag Generation

The tag generation process is to produce a tag value for each encrypted cache line. High quality encrypted data tend to be uniformly distributed since the uniform distribution offers the highest randomness, making deciphering the data difficult [13]. Hence we assume that the encrypted cache line is uniformly distributed. For high security, we want its tag to be a uniform random number as well. Therefore, we utilize a statistic *inverse transform* method [14] in our tag design - **generating a uniformly distributed random tag from a uniformly distributed random encrypted cache line**.

To develop such an inverse transform function, we have investigated a set of operations to see whether they can result in a uniform random output given a uniform random input. We summarize our finding in Table 1, where X, Y, I, J are uniform random variables and c is a constant.

As can be seen from the table, a few operations can convert a uniform random value to another value that is also uniformly distributed. We call such operations, *Uniform Convert (UC)* operation. To ensure the tag value is uniformly distributed, we use UC operations in generating tags. Which specific UC operations are used depend on several considerations and will be discussed below.

One critical requirement for the tag generation process is its speed. Besides choosing fast and low-overhead UC operations, we partition each cache line into multiple blocks so that each block can be processed in parallel. However, the block-operation based design may invite the slicing attack (an attack that replaces a block in the original data with a known block). Hence, we apply a shuffle operation on the input data. The shuffle operation mixes the bits in the original data and makes the slicing attack difficult.

Figure 3 illustrates our tag generation scheme. It consists of three steps: The encrypted cache line is first shuffled and then evenly divided into multiple blocks. The block size is the same as the tag size. Each block is next transformed through a permutation function. The results of the transformed blocks are finally XORed to form the tag. Both the shuffle and permutation steps are controlled by a nonce value, which is random and unique to each memory cache line access. The designs for line shuffle, block random permutation and nonce values are explained below.

The security and hardware cost of the shuffle design depend on the level of shuffle granularity and the number of

function	function description	uniform rand?
$X + c$	add with constant	yes
$X + Y$	add with variable	no
cX	multiply with constant	yes
$X * Y$	multiply with variable	no
$X << c$	logic shift with constant bits	no
$X << Y$	logic shift with variable bits	no
$X\ RS\ c$	rotate shift with constant bits	no
$X\ RS\ Y$	rotate shift with variable bits	yes
$X\ AND\ Y$	bitwise logic AND	no
$X\ OR\ Y$	bitwise logic OR	no
$X\ XOR\ Y$	biswise logic XOR	yes
$NOT\ X$	bit inverse	yes
$Swap(X, I, J, n)$	swap two n-bit sections in X	yes

Table 1: The Output Behavior of Selected Functions for Uniformly Distributed Random Input Data

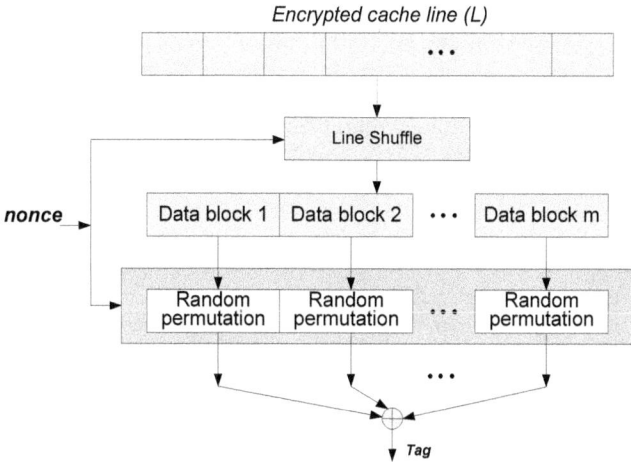

Figure 3: Tag Generation Design Overview

Figure 4: Costs of a Typical Shuffle Design

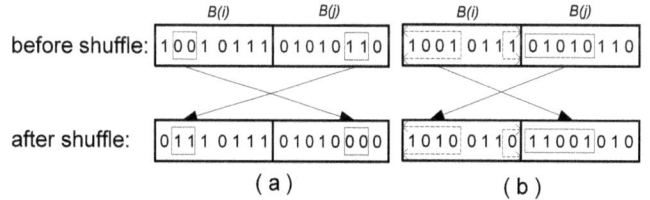

shuffle rounds applied. To increase the security, we want the shuffle as thorough as possible, for example, at the bit level and with sufficient shuffle rounds.

Figure 4 shows the hardware cost, execution time, and energy consumption of a design under different granularities for one round shuffle. As can be seen from the plots, the costs of the shuffle design increases exponentially as the granularity (i.e. unit size) in the shuffle decreases.

Based on our experimental study, we choose a simplified shuffle design. The cache line is first partitioned into blocks of the same size as the tag; the shuffle is performed between blocks and only a segment from each block participates in one shuffle (we call it **segment shuffle**). The size of the segment in the shuffle varies and is randomly determined by the nonce value. For each shuffle operation, a random block pair are selected, and the location of the block segment and its size are also varied over their value range. Each block is treated as wrapped so that shuffles of different segment sizes are possible.

Figure 5 shows two examples of the shuffle operation between block i, $B(i)$, and block j, $B(j)$, with the size of shuffle segments being 2 bits and 5 bits, respectively. For the 5-bits segment shuffle, the segment in $B(i)$ is wrapped; and the segment value "11001" is replaced by "01010" from $B(j)$.

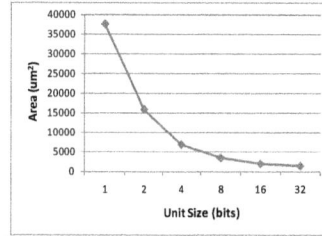

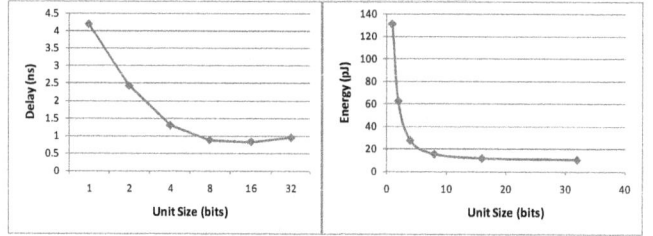

Figure 5: Segment Shuffle between Blocks of Different Segment Size (a) 2 bits (b) 5 bits

After the line shuffle, a permutation is performed on each of the new blocks. The rotate-shift operation is used for permutation. Each block is left rotate-shifted by a random number of bits, which is controlled by the nonce value.

Both the shuffle and permutation steps use a nonce as a control variable. The nonce is an encryption of a unique value that has three fields, as shown in Figure 6: 1) memory cache line address, associated with the memory location of the data encrypted, 2) random value, for high unpredictability of the unique value, and 3) the counter, for a different access to the same memory cache line.

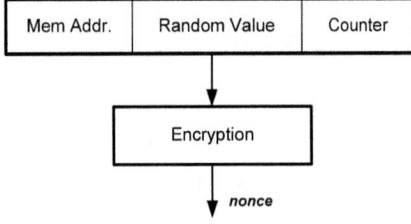

Figure 6: Nonce Construction

With the nonce constructed in this way, the same data value at different memory locations or different accesses to even a same memory location, will have a different tag. Therefore, replaying any previous observed data and tag pair in the attack will be detected during the authentication. In addition, the encryption operation randomizes the nonce such that its values are uniformly distributed, which is required in our tag generation.

Algorithm 1 Tag Generation

/* Input: a cache line L, n (cache line size), m (tag size), β (total number of shuffle rounds), and α (upper bound on shuffle segment size).
Output: Tag */

/* determine the number of blocks, q */
$q = n/m$;
$V = GetNonce(n, q, \beta)$;
/* divide the cache line, L, into blocks */
$L = B(1)\|B(2)\ldots\|B(q)$;
/* shuffle the cache line β rounds*/
for *each round $k, k \in \{1, \beta\}$* **do**
    /* get the round control */
    $v(k) = GetShuffleControl(V, k)$;
    /* select indices of two random blocks; */
    $(i, j) = Get2Blocks(v(k))$;
    /* get the size of the segment for shuffle operation, in the range of $[0, \alpha]$*/
    $segSize = GetSegSize(v(k))$;
    /* get the segment position pos_a, pos_b for block $B(i)$ and $B(j)$, respectively. */
    $(pos_a, pos_b) = GetSegPosition(v(k))$;
    /* swap the segments between $Block(i)$ and $Block(j)$ */
    $BsegSwap(B(i), B(j), pos_a, pos_b, segSize)$;
end for
/* left rotate-shift each block */
for *each block, $B(i), i \in \{1, q\}$* **do**
    /* get the number of bits to be shifted from V */
    $shiftAmount = GetShiftAmount(V, i)$;
    $LeftRotateShift(B(i), shiftAmount)$;
end for
/* Bit-XOR all blocks to obtain the tag value */
$tag = B(1)$;
for *each block, $B(i), i \in \{2, q\}$* **do**
    $tag = tag \oplus B(i)$;
end for

The entire tag generation process is given in Algorithm 1. In the algorithm, the `GetNonce` function employs a standard encryption function (such as AES) and creates a nonce, V. The nonce value is divided into bit-sections; the number of sections and the size of each section are determined by n, q, and β. The value of each section in V is used to control one type of operations for the line shuffle or block permutation, and they are retrieved by the following different `Get-` functions. The `GetShuffleControl` function

reads a bit section $v(k)$ from V for one round shuffle. Functions `Get2Blocks`, `GetSegSize`, and `GetSegPosition` obtain, respectively, a pair of block indices, a segment size, and the segment position in each of the two blocks, from $v(k)$; `BsegSwaP` swaps the segments between the two selected blocks. For block permutation, `GetShiftAmount` obtains a shift amount from V for the left rotate-shift operation, which is performed by function `LeftRotateShift`. Given the shuffle round number β, and the upper bound of shuffle segment size α, under the control of a nonce value, the algorithm can generate a tag for an encrypted cache line, where the tag size is given and assumed to be smaller than the cache line size.

Since the tag size will ultimately affect the memory consumption, on-chip cost, and level of security, we propose a tag selection scheme which is explained in the next subsection.

3.3 Tag Size Selection

We want the tag size to be small for low memory usage, yet effective for high security. Here security is measured in terms of the resistance to brute-force attacks. There are two ways that a brute-force attack can be applied: on the tag value, and on the tag generation process.

Since the tag and the random values used in the tag generation process are uniformly distributed, we can use the size of the search space of the two brute-force attacks for security evaluation. The **search space**, or simply **space**, of a brute-force attack represents the number of values to be tried by the brute-force attack. The bigger the space, the more secure the design. The space for the tag value and the tag generation process is derived below.

We first discuss the space for the tag generation process. The size of this space mainly depends on the ranges of the random variables used in the two operations, i.e., line shuffle and block permutation.

Assume that the cache line size is n and the tag size is m, then the number of blocks in the cache line is n/m. The shuffle space with β shuffle rounds is

$$S_{shuffle} = (C_{n/m}^2 \cdot m^2 \cdot \alpha)^\beta \quad (1)$$

where C_a^b is the combinatorial function of choosing b from a, α and β are, respectively, used for controlling the segment size and shuffle round. The values of α and β affect the $S_{shuffle}$ value and also influence the design complexity for tag generation logic. High α and β lead to high hardware cost. The permutation space is

$$S_{permutation} = m^{n/m}. \quad (2)$$

The entire search space for tag generation through Algorithm 1 is

$$
\begin{aligned}
S_{tag\_G} &= S_{shuffle} \cdot S_{permutation} \\
&= (n(n-m)/2 \cdot \alpha)^\beta \cdot m^{n/m}. \quad (3)
\end{aligned}
$$

On the other hand, the search space for the tag value is

$$S_{tag\_V} = 2^m. \quad (4)$$

Therefore, the effective search space of the tag attack is

$$S = \min\{S_{tag\_G}, S_{tag\_V}\}. \quad (5)$$

It can be easily seen from Formula (4) that S_{tag_V} increases with the tag size. In addition, from Formula (3), we have

$$\frac{dS_{tag\_G}}{dm} = k[\frac{n(n-m)(1-\ln m)}{m^2} - \beta], \qquad (6)$$

where k is a constant value, ln the natural logarithm function. As can be seen from Formula (6), $\frac{dS_{tag\_G}}{dm} < 0$ when m is greater than the natural value $e(= 2.718282)$ (which is often the case). Therefore, S_{tag_G} is monotonically decreasing as m increases. Since S_{tag_V} is monotonically increasing as m increases, S must occur when $S_{tag\_G} = S_{tag\_V}$. Using this equation, for a given α and β value, we can determine the optimal m value that results in the largest search space (hence, the highest security)[1].

By using the above analytical model, one can adjust the tag generation algorithm and customize the tag size for given security and design requirements.

4. EXPERIMENTAL EVALUATION

To access the effectiveness of our design approach, we have developed an evaluation platform and compared our design with the most related and state-of-the-art tag designs.

4.1 Evaluation Platform

Figure 7 shows the overall evaluation platform. It consists of a processor system, tag generation and authentication logic for data protection, and a set of simulation tools for evaluating application performance and hardware cost.

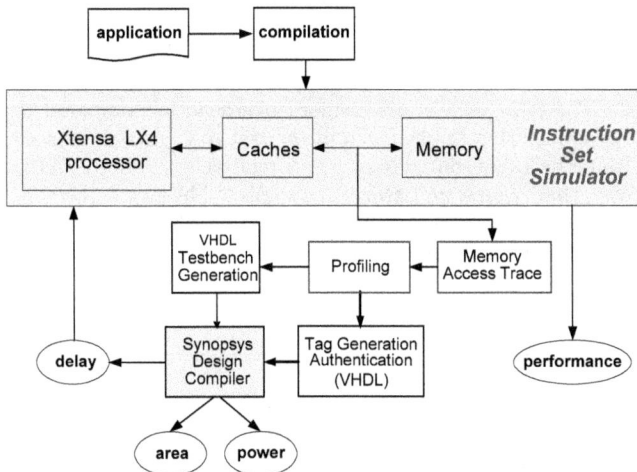

Figure 7: Evaluation Platform

The baseline processor system is built based on an Xtensa $LX4$ embedded system processor from Tensilica [15]. The processor system can be configured with different instruction set, clock speed, memory hierarchy, and related cache/memory access time. The system configuration parameters and their values used in our experiment, are listed in Table2.

Eight applications are selected from the embedded system benchmark suite MiBench [16]. The C codes of these applications are compiled with the Xtensa XCC compiler and simulated on the Xtensa cycle-accurate Instruction Set Simulator (ISS).

---

[1]There may be no algebra solution for $S_{tag\_G} = S_{tag\_V}$, and only the numeric result is available.

Parameter	Value
Core Speed	694 MHz
I-Cache	2KB
D-Cache	2KB
Cache Line	256 bits
Cache Access Time	1.44ns
System RAM	1MB
System ROM	4MB
Memory Access time	25.92ns (18ccs)
Instruction Bus Width	4B
Data R/W Bus Width	4B

Table 2: Xtensa Base Processor Configuration

Our design for tag generation and data authentication is modeled in VHDL at RTL level. It is simulated with Model-Sim [17] for the functional verification and is synthesized by the Synopsys Design Compiler [18] with the $65nm$ technology library. The Design Compiler provides the area, power consumption and delay of the design. The extra delay incurred by the tag generation/data authentication logic is then incorporated back to the software simulation for the overall application performance.

We compare our design with other two closely related memory authentication approaches, Yan's work [11] and Rogers' work [10]. All three works use the block cipher encryption: we use the block cipher encryption for creating nonce values and they use the block cipher encryption in their tag generation process. To be fair, we apply a same encryption function, AES [19], for the block cipher in each design. The three designs also utilize a similar approach: storing tags off-chip to save on-chip memory costs.

4.2 Simulation Results

The experiment results about the tag selection and the overhead savings are presented in the following two subsections.

4.2.1 Tag Selection

From Section 3.3, we know that the tag search space is related to two parameters: α and β. Due to the page limit, Table 3 shows part of simulation results (based on Formulas (3)(4) and (5)) that demonstrate how the search space sizes of S_{tag_G}, S_{tag_V}, and S vary with the tag size (listed in the first column) under two sets of α and β values. The size of the search space is measured by the number of different values in the space. The tag value search space S_{tag_V} is purely determined by the tag size and is given in the second column. The space S_{tag_G} from the tag generation process and the effective search space S with different tag generation designs are given in Columns 3 & 4 and 5 & 6, respectively.

As can be seen from Table 3, a large tag size may not result in a large search space (S) for high security; similarly, a sophisticated and expensive tag generation algorithm can be totally nullified by a small size tag. For example, for the tag generation design with $\alpha = 16$ and $\beta = 1$, a tag size of 48 bits is the optimal selection, with a maximum of 2.81E+14 values in the search space S; A smaller tag will reduce the search space, hence security. On the other hand, for the same 48-bit tag size, use of the design with $\alpha = 32$ and $\beta = 2$ will bring no security enhancement, rather than consuming more on-chip resources. For $\alpha = 32$ and $\beta = 2$, the best tag size is 64 bits, as has been highlighted in the table.

Given a value pair of α and β, we can find an optimal tag size. Similarly, for a given tag size, we can tune α and β for a largest tag search space, hence achieving as high security as possible.

4.2.2 Overhead Savings

Neither Yan's nor Roger's work includes any investigation on how the tag size should be selected, and they use a fixed tag size in their designs. In Yan's design, the 64-bit tag size is adopted, while the tag size used by the Rogers's design is 128 bits.

For comparison, we create two separate designs: one with the tag size of 64 bits, and another 128 bits. In each design, we tune α and β values to make the given tag size optimal (namely $S_{tag\_G} = S_{tag\_V} = S$)[2], for a maximal search space. With the 64-bit tag design, we have $\alpha = 4$ and $\beta = 3$; While for the 128-bit tag, we have $\alpha = 32$ and $\beta = 6$.

With such α and β values, our design guarantees that the actual search space is the same as (or most close to) that determined by the tag size. For the other two existing methods, their search spaces cannot be great than the tag value space. Therefore, the security level of our design cannot be worse than those by the other two.

Based on such same tag-size designs, we then compare the design overhead between our approach with each of the two existing approaches.

Table 4 gives hardware resource overheads of the tag generation designs from the three design approaches. Each design is modeled in VHDL, and their area cost, power consumption and delay are obtained from the Synopsys Design Compiler. For the designs from our and Yan's approaches with the 64-bit tag, the overheads are given in Rows 3 & 4; For the 128-bit tag, the overheads of our and Rogers' designs are presented in Rows 6 & 7. The relative overhead savings of our design as compared to each of the existing designs are given in Rows 5 and 8, respectively. As can be seen from the table, our design incurs less on-chip resource overhead in area, power and delay as compared to each of the existing designs.

		Area (μm^2)	Power (μW)	Delay (ns)
64-bit tag	Ours	309970.50	1151.52	99.95
	Yan's	508423.50	2365.60	207.42
	Overhead Saving	39%	51%	52%
128-bit tag	Ours	355407.14	1320.45	100.12
	Rogers'	582367.00	2131.40	280.50
	Overhead Saving	39%	38%	64%

Table 4: On-Chip Overhead

Based on the tag generation design, we derive the extra clock cycles incurred by the tag generation logic for each

[2]The equation may result in non-integer solutions. In our experiment, we choose integer values for α and β such that $|S| = |S_{tag\_v}|$ and the discrepancy $|S_{tag\_G}| - |S|$ is as small as possible.

memory access, and re-run application programs with the delay overhead in the instruction set simulator for execution time.

It is worth to point out that the extra clock cycle value is calculated based on the given processor speed. The impact of the tag generation delay on the overall system performance can change when the processor speed is different.

Table 5 shows the normalized execution time (based on the baseline system without any data protection logic). As can be seen from Table 5, our design incurs much smaller performance overhead than the Yan's and Rogers' designs.

Application	Ours	Yan's	Rogers'
adpcm	28.19%	88.25%	77.11%
dijkstra	261.59%	814.19%	711.73%
jpeg	170.97%	533.50%	466.28%
qsort	220.94%	695.35%	607.38%
rijndael	362.27%	1123.87%	982.65%
sha	109.37%	347.83%	303.61%
stringsearch	260.41%	712.55%	622.76%
susan	114.04%	354.82%	310.17%
Average	190.97%	583.80%	510.21%

Table 5: Performance Overhead

We calculate the memory consumption of the tag off-chip storage, which can be determined by the tag size and the code and data footprint in the memory. For comparison, we also calculated the off-chip memory consumption for Yan's and Rogers' designs. Table 6 shows the memory overhead, measured in kilo bytes (KB), of the three designs for each application. The size of each application is given in Column 2. The relative average memory overhead as compared to the application size is given in the last row. As can be seen from the table, our design has a relatively smaller off-chip cost than Yan's and Rogers' designs. The extra memory costs from their designs are due to storing some tree nodes required in their tag generation.

Application	Total Size (KB)	64-bit tag		128-bit tag	
		Ours	Yan's	Ours	Rogers'
adpcm	308	77	88	154	178
dijkstra	436	109	124	218	251
jpeg	759	190	216	380	438
qsort	403	101	115	202	232
rijndael	334	84	95	167	193
sha	301	75	86	151	174
stringsearch	295	74	84	148	170
susan	459	115	131	230	265
Average		25%	29%	50%	58%

Table 6: Memory Overhead (KB)

Figure 8 summarizes the relative overhead savings in terms of on-chip area, power consumption, delay, application performance, and off-chip memory cost; Each relative saving value is calculated by $(y-x)/y$, where y is the overhead from the existing design and x the overhead from ours. Compared to Yan's design, our design saves 39% area, 51% power, an average of 67% execution time, and 12% off-chip memory. The savings can also be found when comparing with Rogers'

Tag Size (bit)	S_{tag_V}	$\beta{=}1$, $\alpha{=}16$		$\beta{=}2$, $\alpha{=}32$	
		S_{tag_G}	S	S_{tag_G}	S
8	2.56E+02	4.02E+34	2.56E+02	8.18E+40	2.56E+02
16	6.55E+04	9.07E+24	6.55E+04	1.78E+31	6.55E+04
24	1.68E+07	2.51E+20	1.68E+07	4.76E+26	1.68E+07
32	4.29E+09	5.04E+17	4.29E+09	9.26E+23	4.29E+09
40	1.10E+12	7.92E+15	1.10E+12	1.40E+22	1.10E+12
48	2.81E+14	3.94E+14	**2.81E+14**	6.72E+20	2.81E+14
56	7.21E+16	4.02E+13	4.02E+13	6.58E+19	7.21E+16
64	1.84E+19	6.60E+12	6.60E+12	1.04E+19	**1.04E+19**
72	4.72E+21	1.51E+12	1.51E+12	2.28E+18	2.28E+18
80	1.21E+24	4.43E+11	4.43E+11	6.39E+17	6.39E+17
88	3.09E+26	1.56E+11	1.56E+11	2.15E+17	2.15E+17

Table 3: Tag Exploration Space

design, with 39%, 38%, 63%, and 13% reductions in area, power consumption, execution time, and off-chip memory, respectively.

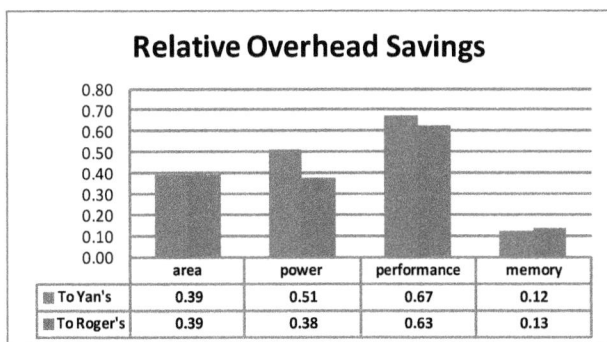

Figure 8: Overhead Savings over Yan's and Rogers' Designs

5. CONCLUSIONS

Use of tag for memory data integrity protection is an effective approach for secure embedded system design. This paper addresses the cost issue related to the tag design, which is critical to resource constrained embedded systems.

We have presented an inverse transform method based on the UC (Uniform Convert) operations to generate the tag that is uniformly distributed to achieve a maximum randomness of the tag value; The uniform random distribution is also realized for the operations of tag generation process. The high randomness of both the tag value and the tag generation offers the system a high ability to counter brute-force attacks, and also allows us to build an analytical model for security evaluation. With the security evaluation model, we proposed a tag selection method to find an optimal tag size such that the maximal security level can be achieved with the on-chip resource overhead and off-chip memory cost as small as possible.

Experiments have been conducted to evaluate our design, which shows that our design is more cost effective than the existing state-of-the-art designs, the significant overhead savings - on average, 39% on area, 45% on power, 65% on performance, and 12% on off-chip memory - can be achieved.

It is worth to note that the UC operations studied in this paper can be extended by considering other operations for completeness and the inverse conversion design can have many different forms, which will be investigated in future.

It is also worth to restate that the security evaluation model used in this paper is based on the premise that uniformly distributed values lead to high-level of security. Further theoretical study would enrich the design approach.

6. REFERENCES

[1] M. Blum, W. Evans, P. Gemmell, S. Kannan, and M. Naor. Checking the correctness of memories. In *Algorithmica*, pages 90–99, 1995.

[2] D. Lie, C. Thekkath, M. Mitchell, P. Lincoln, D. Boneh, J. Mitchell, and M. Horowitz. Architectural support for copy and tamper resistant software. In *9th International Conference on Architectural Support for Programming Languages and Operating Systems (ASPLOS)*, pages 168 – 177, 2000.

[3] G. E. Suh, D. Clarke, B. Gasend, M. van Dijk, and S. Devadas. AEGIS: architecture for tamper-evident and tamper-resistant processing. In *International Conference on SuperComputing*, 2003.

[4] G. E. Suh, D. Clarke, B. Gasend, M. van Dijk, and S. Devadas. Efficient memory integrity verification and encryption for secure processor. In *36th International Symposium on Microarchitecture*, 2003.

[5] R.C. Merkle. Protocols for public key cryptosystems. In *Proceedings of the 1980 Symposium on Security and Privacy*, pages 122 – 34, 1980.

[6] B. Gassend, G.E. Suh, D. Clarke, M. van Dijk, and S. Devadas. Caches and hash trees for efficient memory integrity verification. pages 295 – 306, 2003.

[7] R. Elbaz, D. Champagne, R.B. Lee, and L. Torres. Tec-tree: a low-cost, parallelizable tree for efficient defense against memory replay attacks. In *Cryptographic Hardware and Embedded Systems (CHES)*, pages 289–302, 2007.

[8] P. Rogaway, M. Bellare, J. Black, and T. Krovetz. OCB: a block-cipher mode of operation for efficient authenticated encryption. In *ACM conference on Computer and communications Security*, 2001.

[9] D.A. McGrew and J. Viega. The galois counter mode of operation (GCM). Technical report, Submission to

operation	First Four Most-Fit Distributions				Fitting Rank of Four Typical Distributions			
	1st fit	2nd fit	3rd fit	4th fit	Normal	Lognormal	Exponential	Uniform
x+6	Uniform	Error	Johnson SB	Power	12	37	46	1
4*x	Uniform	Error	Gen. Pareto	Johnson SB	9	34	37	1
x/8	Uniform	Error	Johnson SB	Gen. Pareto	5	34	35	1
x mod 16	Uniform	Error	Johnson SB	Gen. Pareto	6	33	27	1
x+y	Cauchy	Johnson SB	Error	Normal	4	32	15	53
x*y	Triangular	Error	Logistic	Normal	4	22	31	32
NOT x	Uniform	Error	Gen. Pareto	Johnson SB	9	33	36	1
x AND y	Log-Logistics	Dagum	Frechet	Gen. Pareto	29	7	33	49
x OR y	Kumarsawamy	Pareto 2	Exponential	Expoential (2P)	24	34	3	53
x XOR y	Uniform	Error	Johnson SB	Gen. Pareto	8	33	36	1
RT x ≫ y	Uniform	Error	Johnson SB	Gen. Pareto	7	32	35	1
swap	Uniform	Error	Johnson SB	Gen. Pareto	9	33	38	1

Table 7: Distribution Fitting

National Institute of Standards and Technology, Federal Information Processing Standards, 2004.

[10] A. Rogers and A. Milenkovic. Security extensions for integrity and confidentiality in embedded processors. *Microprocessors and Microsystems*, 33(5-6):398 – 414, 2009.

[11] C. Yan, B. Rogers, D. Englender, D. Solihin, and M. Prvulovic. Improving cost, performance, and security of memory encryption and authentication. In *33rd International Symposium on Computer Architecture*, 2006.

[12] C Fruhwirth. New methods in hard disk encryption. Technical report, Institute for Computer Languages, Theory and Logic Group, Vienna University of Technology, 2005.

[13] C. Meyer and S. Matyas. *Cryptography: A New Dimension in Computer Data Security.* John Wiley & Sons, 1982.

[14] J. Banks and B. L. Nelson. *Discrete-event system simulation.* Prentice Hall, 2010.

[15] Tensilica. Xtensa customizable processor. http://www.tensilica.com.

[16] M.R. Guthaus and J. S. Ringenberg. Mibench: a free, commercially representiative embedded benchmark suite. In *IEEE 4th Annual Workshop on Workload Characterization*, 2001.

[17] Mentor Graphics Corp. http://www.mentor.com.

[18] Design compiler. Synopsys Inc. (http://www.synopsys.com).

[19] FIPS Pub. 197. Specification for the advanced encryption standard (AES). Technical report, National Institute of Standards and Technology, Federal Information Processing Standards, 2001.

[20] EasyFitXL. Easyfitxl. http://www.mathwave.com/articles/fit-distributions-excel.html.

APPENDIX

A. UC OPERATIONS FOR UNIFORMLY DISTRIBUTED OUTPUTS

We developed some C code to generate results for a set of operations on the random inputs that are uniformly dis-

tributed. The distribution of those results are then examined under a distribution fitting scheme with the EasyFit distribution-fit tool [20]. Table 7 shows the results. For each operation listed in Column 1 (where X and Y are uniform random variables, and RT represents rotate for shift operations), its four most-fit distributions are given in Columns 2 & 5. The last four columns provide the fitting rank for four typical distributions (Normal, Lognormal, Exponential and Uniform) for each type of operations. For example, for the operation of X plus a constant as shown in Row 3, the first four best fit distributions are: Uniform, Error, Johnson SB and Power; if the results of $X + c$ are fitted to the Normal distribution, the fitting rank will be 12, as given in Column 6 in this row.

UC operation	Uniform Distribution Fit Error
4*x	0.00658
6+x	0.00565
x/8	0.03001
x mod 16	0.05293
NOT x	0.00526
x XOR y	0.00731
rotate shift	0.00855
swap	0.00685
Average	0.0153925

Table 8: Random-Distribution Fit Error of *UC* Operations

From Table 7, we can see that multiplication, addition, AND, OR of two uniform random variables do not generate a uniform random result. But for other operations, their results best fit to the uniform distribution, and such functions are denoted as *UC* operation that enables the conversion from a uniform rand variable to another uniform random value. The fitting errors of the *UC* operations are given in Table 8, which shows small fitting errors, about 0.015 on average.

Static Secure Page Allocation for Light-Weight Dynamic Information Flow Tracking

Juan Carlos Martínez
Santos[*]
Northeastern University
Boston, Massachusetts
jcmartin@ece.neu.edu

Yunsi Fei
Northeastern University
Boston, Massachusetts
yfei@ece.neu.edu

Zhijie Jerry Shi
University of Connecticut
Storrs, Connecticut
zshi@cse.uconn.edu

ABSTRACT

Dynamic information flow tracking (DIFT) is an effective security countermeasure for both low-level memory corruptions and high-level semantic attacks. However, many software approaches suffer large performance degradation, and hardware approaches have high logic and storage overhead. We propose a flexible and light-weight hardware/software co-design approach to perform DIFT based on secure page allocation. Instead of associating every data with a taint tag, we aggregate data according to their taints, i.e., putting data with different attributes in separate memory pages. Our approach is a compiler-aided process with architecture support. The implementation and analysis show that the memory overhead is little, and our approach can protect critical information, including return address, indirect jump address, and system call IDs, from being overwritten by malicious users.

Categories and Subject Descriptors

D.3.4 [**Programming Languages, Processor, Compilers**]: Memory management; K.6.5 [**Computing Milieux**]: Security and Protection

Keywords

Dynamic Information Flow Tracking; Static Control Flow Analysis; Security Attacks

1. INTRODUCTION

Software security has been a critical consideration for computer systems. A series of software vulnerabilities, e.g., buffer overflows and format string vulnerabilities [32], can be exploited by adversaries to corrupt a program's memory space with malicious code and data. Many countermeasures have been devised to prevent code injection attacks or to

---

[*]Currently on leave from Universidad Tecnológica de Bolívar, Cartagena, Colombia.

address certain vulnerability, such as StackGuard, StackGhost, and RAD [5, 9, 4]. In addition to low-level memory corruption attacks, high-level semantic attacks, such as cross-site scripting, SQL injection, and Java Script hijacking are emerging as another major category of security threats [12]. One common root cause of both low-level and high-level software attacks is that untrusted external data, like user input, is used in an illegitimate way to hijack the normal program control flow. For example, because of lack of input boundary checking, the memory next to the region intended for the user input can be corrupted by a buffer overflow. At higher levels, when the user inputs are not appropriately filtered, the inputs may be taken as statements or commands rather than regular data.

Recently, the dynamic information flow tracking (DIFT) technique has been presented to defend against these software attacks by differentiating sources of data (trusted or untrusted), tracking the data flow at run-time, and checking the usage of different kinds of data. Each data is associated with a taint, which is usually a one-bit field that tags the data as trusted (0) or untrusted (1). Data taints are initialized according to their input sources - data from trusted sources, like local disks, starts out as trusted, and data from untrusted sources that can be utilized by malicious users, like networks and keyboards, starts out as untrusted. Taints are then propagated along the program execution and stored in memory and registers temporally. To detect software attacks, critical control instruction sites are checked to prevent the use of tainted data, e.g., address for function returns, system call IDs, or control-flow transfer target addresses.

There has been many DIFT implementations in software (at both static and run time) [17, 34, 23, 16], and hardware [29, 6, 33, 30, 25]. In general, software-based approaches are flexible with taint propagation and checking policies. However, static software approaches incur large code (memory) overhead and performance degradation and could not handle cases like self-modifying code, just-in-time compilation, and multi-thread applications [31]. Dynamic software approaches support dynamic code generation, but the performance overhead due to the instrumentation limits their applicability. Hardware-based approaches address these drawbacks and reduce the performance degradation, but require a drastic redesign of the processor core for taint storage and processing (including propagation and checking). They are often limited by certain pre-set rules to avoid false alarms and cannot neutralize new emerging attacks. Most of the hardware-assisted DIFT schemes couple the taint storage tightly with the data, e.g., extend the width of memory, cache, and register file to accommodate the extra taint bits. Moreover, taints can also be stored in a dedicated memory region without changing the storage and communication bus, incurring memory overhead and execution slowdown.

We present a novel hardware/software co-design approach for efficient dynamic information flow tracking using secure page allocation. Our approach differs from previous DIFT approaches in three ways. First, rather than tracking the information and tainting data at run-time, i.e., updating the taints of both registers and memory, our approach identifies taints of memory data statically. The compiler allocates trusted/untrusted information into different memory pages. In this case, the run-time taint propagation and updating is only for registers. Second, instead of associating each data value to a taint bit, we aggregate data according to their taints, i.e., putting trusted data in trusted memory pages, and untrusted data in untrusted memory pages. The whole page has only one taint bit stored in the page table that reduces the memory space overhead significantly. Finally, our approach requires less hardware augmentation to do DIFT taint processing compared to hardware approaches, demands less OS support for taint handling, and more importantly, does not require double memory access (one for the data and the other one for the tag). As a result, the performance overhead is lower. This work includes not only the design of page-level tainting, but also the implementation of secure page allocation in a compiler, and the validation of the approach. We find that static analysis at compile-time and memory reallocation at run-time have to work in conjunction to implement the page-level tainting effectively and efficiently.

The rest of the paper is structured as follows. Section 2 reviews the related work on DIFT for low-level memory-corruption security attacks. Section 3 and 4 describe our approach at design time and run-time in details. Section 5 and 6 present the security analysis and the experimental results. Section 7 discusses more about our approach, and Section 8 concludes the paper.

2. RELATED WORK

A lot of research work has been done for enforcing secure program execution through DIFT on computer systems. In most cases, four aspects of the system may get involved or require modifications to different extents: application, operating system (OS), compiler, and hardware.

Software approaches allow much flexibility in policies for taint propagation and checking, and cover most of the known vulnerabilities [17, 34, 23, 1, 16, 22, 26]. However, they suffer a significant performance slowdown, e.g., as shown in Securifly [17] with 37% execution overhead, 76% in Taint-enhanced [34], 363% in LIFT [23], and 35% in GIFT [16]. In addition, they cannot track information flow inside binary libraries or system call functions [34, 22], and do not support multi-threaded code [17, 23]. To reduce the amount of information that must be tracked and also the size of extra code, [1] uses static analysis and a declarative annotation language to associate symbolic tags with data at run-time. In [22], a value-range propagation algorithm is combined with taint analysis to help programmers apply an effective boundary-aware programming style. In [26], static taint analysis and program transformations are performed at compile-time to guarantee that program execution is free of unauthorized flow.

Hardware-assisted approaches address the problems of software approaches by introducing changes inside the processor core for taint storage and processing. The changes include widening the memory, register file, and buses, and introducing logic to initialize, propagate, and check the taints [29, 7, 3, 15, 10]. The taint initialization could be done by the Operating System [29, 15], or by new instructions [7]. The policies for propagation and checking could be set up at the beginning of the execution [29], or reconfigured at run-time [7]. Some approaches use a special memory region to store the taints [31, 3] instead of widening the memory and buses. They may introduce more latencies for cache misses when the processor needs to retrieve the taint for data from the memory.

There also exists some hardware/software co-design work that utilizes the inherent processor architectural features without changes to the processor or memory system. An approach presented in [2] leverages the speculative execution hardware support in modern commodity processors, like the *Itanium* processor, for DIFT. They utilize the *deferred exception* mechanism, using the exception token bit extended on each general-purpose register for the taint bit. However, they have to set up a bitmap for data memory for their taints. They use software-assigned policies to specify security violations, and software techniques for taint propagation.

To reduce the performance degradation of DIFT process, one recent tendency is to run separately the normal application and the DIFT process on different cores utilizing multi-core architecture [21, 3, 24, 11]. In [21], on one core, the application runs speculatively without any security check. On the other one, the application runs with DIFT. The system checks if the results of the two cores are the same. If they differ from each other, the system will roll the application back to the previous checkpoint. In [3], one core is used as a centralized *lifeguard* of the whole system, responsible for propagating the taints and checking the usage of them while the other cores are executing the applications. In [24], a Log-Based Architecture (LBA) system provides hardware support for logging a program trace and delivering it to the monitoring processors. In [11], a memory-layout diversification technique and an efficient delta execution are used to reduce the overhead associated with executing several replicas.

The closest techniques to our page-level tainting are presented in [36, 35, 19]. The idea of splitting data onto multiple stacks and heaps based on their types was first proposed in [36, 35], where their data types are an attribute easy to retrieve from the source code. Work in [19] presents the basic concept of page-level tainting by manually assigning variables onto pages based on profiling. Our approach is much more sophisticated, and implements the automatic taint analysis and page allocation process in a compiler with moderat hardware support. Our hardware/software co-design approach works efficiently and effectively for dynamic information flow tracking. Table 1 summarizes the comparison between our approach and other DIFT implementations.

In summary, we propose a hardware/software co-design solution to perform DIFT based on compile-time static taint analysis and secure page allocation with minimal hardware changes. Our approach reduces the memory overhead significantly by aggregating data according to their taints and using only one taint bit in the page table for each page. We

Table 1: Comparison between different DIFT techniques.

DIFT Steps	Software	Hardware-assisted	Our approach
Initialization	application extension/compiler	OS support	compiler
Propagation	application extension	extra HW logic	extra HW logic
Storage	dedicated memory region	widened memory or dedicated region	page table
Checking	application extension	extra HW logic	extra HW logic

demonstrate that our approach can reach the same security level as hardware-assisted approaches, i.e., addressing self-modifying code, JIT compilation, third-party libraries, as long as the attributes (trusted or untrusted) of the sources of these codes are known a prior. Different from software approaches that annotate the code and add extra code to be executed, our approach only involves system software, including compilation passes and OS support, without re-programming the applications. Therefore, the performance degradation of application execution is very small.

3. OUR APPROACH

We propose a novel approach to taint the memory at the granularity of page, normally at the size of 4KB, and allocate data to memories according to their attributes, *trusted* (TR) or *untrusted* (UTR), at compile-time.

3.1 General Idea

In our approach, the attributes of data are obtained from a static taint analysis of the source code at compile-time first. The compiler then divides all the data into two categories: *trusted* (TR) and *untrusted* (UTR). At loading time, the *loader* (an OS service) stores the data variables in different types of pages and initializes the page tag. At execution time, when a data is accessed, the *Memory Controller* (another OS service) retrieves the taint from the data address. In addition, the *Memory Controller* also allocates dynamic pages according to the attributes. Fig. 1 shows the mapping of the virtual address space to physical memory, which is managed by the page table where a tag is set for each page. By default, the text segment, containing instructions, is trusted (TR). The data segment, the stack, and the heap are divided into two types of regions, according to the data that they will keep. At run-time, trusted/untrusted information will be allocated into trusted/untrusted pages accordingly. As a result, the overhead for storing/accessing taints is basically zero in our approach.

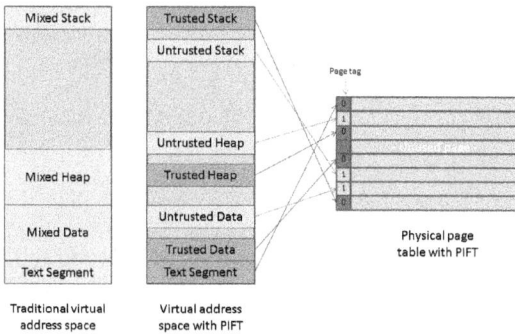

Figure 1: Virtual address space and page table

To propagate taints between the off-chip memory and on-chip register file, we have to augment the processor architec-

ture slightly [1]. The register file is widened by one bit to hold the taint. We also include logic to calculate the propagation of the taints. Many propagation rules, e.g., those in [7], can be employed and selected through a configuration register. We adopt the OR-rule on all the involved operands. Note that different rules just require different taint propagation logic.

Different from other DIFT approaches, our approach statically ensures that untrusted data will not be stored in a trusted page and vice versa. Thus, at run-time, our approach checks this condition along with program taint propagation. Violations of such a condition may indicate possible memory corruption attacks, and the processor will raise an exception which allows the OS or other service routines to examine the violation further. By allocating the critical information, like the return address and system call IDs, into trusted pages and enforcing the taint checking policy, our approach protects the memory systematically. Our solution eliminates the need to check these control sites at run-time, e.g., function return and system call. However, indirect jump sites need taint checking, where the target addresses in registers must be trusted.

3.2 Compilation Stage

At this stage, our approach does static taint analysis and memory map generation, which includes data attribute assignment, instruction duplication, and data duplication.

Fig. 2 shows the basic code transformations done by a modified compiler. Our approach does not change the source code. Instead, it changes the compiler *front-end* to add annotations to each variable of the program in the Static Single Assignment (SSA) representation. These annotations contain the taint information for each variable and are used by newly added passes in the *middle-end* to do static taint analysis for all the variables. We define five attributes: *UNINITIALIZED*, *UNKNOWN*, *NOT_TAINTED*, *TAINTED*, and *BOTH*. The static analysis checks the statements one by one. If a variable is only declared, as in `#define INDEX`, the initial attribute is *UNKNOWN*. If the variable is declared and an immediate value is assigned, as in `#define MAX_SIZE 128`, the initial attribute is *NOT_TAINTED*. Sometimes, the analysis finds variables that are used without a formal declaration, and it sets the attribute as *UNINITIALIZED*. Later, when these variables are declared, the attribute will be updated. Function arguments, inside the function, are set by default as *UNKNOWN*. This attribute is used during the intra-procedural analysis, and gets updated at the function call sites when the attribute of the passed in arguments is known. The objective of the static analysis is to find the final attribute (*TAINTED*, *NOT_TAINTED*, or *BOTH*) for all variables. The taint information is held during all the compiler optimization passes, and it is passed on to the *back-end* to generate the reordered memory map.

---

[1] Details about architectural changes are given in Section 4.

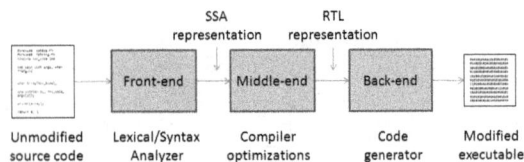

Figure 2: Code transformations at compile-time

When identifying the data sources and consequently, the initial taint values, our approach also does annotations for critical C standard library functions, which are found vulnerable to memory corruption attacks [32]. Although the vulnerable function is given as a black box, each time it is invoked, the compiler checks how the taints of the arguments affect the taints of the return results (if available). For example, function *malloc (size)* returns a pointer to a newly allocated block, *size* bytes long, and we let the attribute of the returned pointer depend on the taint of variable *size*.

3.2.1 Memory Map and Data Attribute

The application memory space is divided into four segments: text, data, heap, and stack. We handle each segment to support dynamic information flow tracking specifically, adhering to certain overwriting policies that we set for memory integrity protection. We adopt a run-time policy that data is only allowed to be exchanged between pages with the same taint. Our static transformation ensures it at compiler time. We show later in Section 5 by enforcing this policy various memory corruption attacks are caught by our checking mechanism.

By default, the text or code segment is set up as trusted. Therefore, when it is loaded, the memory page taints are trusted. In general, this segment is read-only for program instruction fetching. However, in the case of applications with dynamically generated code (i.e., self-modifying code), the text segment could be overwritten. In these scenarios, the new code must be from trusted sources (i.e., trusted Java's bytecode). If a piece of code is invoked from another section (i.e., the stack segment), a similar policy is applied. The code in all cases must be trusted.

The data segment normally contains initialized data used by the program (constants and global variables) and the BBS segment[2]. The constants are known at compile time and will keep their values throughout the execution. Hence, they are tagged as trusted and allocated on trusted memory pages. In contrast, although global variables may be initialized to some values, the values may change, and their attributes could be either trusted or untrusted at different execution times. If the different data stored in a global variable have the same attribute throughout program execution, the compiler fixes the tag value and allocates the global variable to a proper page. If the static taint analysis shows that a global variable can have both attributes, our approach duplicates the global variable, one copy for trusted uses and the other for untrusted uses.

Our approach implements intra- and inter-procedural data flow analysis at the compiler *middle-end* to get a list of

variables and their attributes, and then identify which global variables need to be declared twice. The duplication results in data overhead and slight code size increase. However, it helps us to protect critical information, like data pointers in the data segment, from being overwritten by malicious untrusted information.

Heap segment is a memory section dynamically allocated to store temporary information. If the information comes from a trusted source, a trusted page (or pages) will be allocated. Otherwise, untrusted pages will be allocated. The taints are associated with the pages until the pages are released. At compile-time, the *linker* (the last step in the compiler *back-end*) assigns the right attribute to each heap chunk, and therefore the Operating System (OS) can allocate the heaps on different pages.

In addition to dynamic data, the heap also holds critical metadata used by the Memory Management Unit (MMU) for memory chunks. Attackers can exploit programming errors to overwrite the metadata, like forward and backward pointers that link to available memory chunks, to change the execution flow. If the MMU stores these critical pointers in a trusted page, our approach can avoid the possibility that they are corrupted by a heap overflow or double free. In [35], it shows that by modifying the *Memory Controller* (an OS service) and using a lookup table, the heap's metadata can be separated and located in a different memory region. We propose to hold the metadata in trusted pages.

The last segment, stack, requires special considerations. At the beginning of the *back-end* code generation, some variables are assigned to the stack, and some are mapped onto registers. The stack variables could be function arguments, local variables, and special registers. Hence, the stack segment can hold both trusted and untrusted information. For example, frame pointer and return address are trusted. However, the attributes of function arguments and local variables depend on the static analysis, and they may need to be allocated on different pages. In order to separate trusted data from untrusted data, we modify the way how the compiler allocates each variable on the stack. By default, each variable on the stack is indirectly addressed through the stack pointer and a relative offset (calculated at compile-time based on the position where the variables will be held). In our modified compiler, trusted variables and untrusted variables are allocated with a different offset. The offset is large enough to avoid stack overlapping, and is page-aligned as well. This modification helps to protect critical data, including return address, system call IDs, and function call pointers. The idea of multiple stacks has been presented in the previous work [36], where data is placed on different stacks according to their types, like array, integer, etc. Here we use attributes to differentiate them.

3.2.2 Code Duplication

As mentioned above, our compiler specifies the attribute of each variable and stores it in an appropriate memory page. In the cases where a variable must be duplicated, the compiler has to generate a new statement to use the duplicated variable. Fig. 3 shows an example using the GIMPLE[3] representation. In the example, the system identifies that the attribute of variable c_3 can be trusted and untrusted, so instead of merging c_1 and c_2 in c_3 (by the *phi()* operator),

---

[2]The BSS segment, also called Block-Started-by-Symbol, includes all uninitialized variables declared at the file level as well as uninitialized local variables declared with the `static` keyword.

[3]GIMPLE representation is a tree based intermediate language used during *middle-end* compiler optimization.

it keeps both copies. Subsequently, the system duplicates an keeps both d_1 and d_2, one trusted (dependent on c_1) and the other untrusted (dependent on c_2). Due to statement duplication, the size of the code can increase. In Section 6, we present the experimental results.

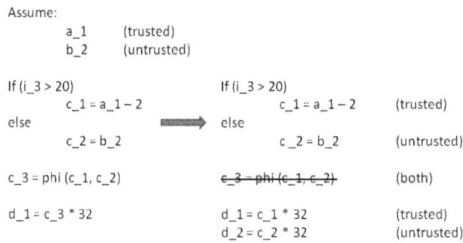

Figure 3: Example of code duplication

There is an issue with function calls because the arguments' attributes may be trusted or untrusted at different sites. Fig. 4 shows an example. When an argument has different attributes at different call sites, as shown in Fig. 4 for $var1$ and $var3$, the function needs to be duplicated, and the function call sites need to be modified. During the static analysis, the system finds that the attribute for argument 1 is *BOTH*. Thus, the system duplicates the function and propagate both attributes *NOT_TAINTED* and *TAINTED*. Although the statement duplication suggests an exponential increase of the code, our static taint analysis shows that function duplication is a rare condition. In most of the cases, the *BOTH* attribute is masked by the OR rule propagation, when this variable is operated with a *TAINTED* variable.

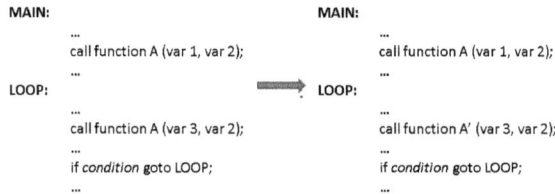

Figure 4: Function argument at execution time

4. ARCHITECTURAL AUGMENTATION

In the above sections, we explain how the compiler sets the variable attributes and how the variables are aggregated to different kind of pages. In this section, we show how the OS, especially the memory controller, should handle each segment of the memory map at run-time. We also describe what changes are needed inside the processor to support taint propagation and checking in order to detect security attacks on the application.

Fig. 5 shows the architecture design. Our approach allows the compiler to aggregate data based on their taints, i.e., trusted data and untrusted data will be put in different pages. At run-time, when the Operating System (OS) allocates memory for the current process, it initializes the page taint accordingly in the *Page Table* (in memory). Each time the processor fetches an instruction from the memory, the *Memory Management Unit* (managed by the OS) retrieves the *Page Taint* from the *Page Table*. The taint for the instruction has to be trusted in order to prevent ma-

licious code injection and execution. This is ensured by a *Taint Checking* module at the IF stage.

During instruction execution, the tag is propagated inside the processor by the *Taint Propagation* module. There are two locations for such modules. One is at the ID stage where the taints of the source operand registers are known, and the current instruction is decoded. The other is at the MEM stage where the taint of memory data (e.g., for LOAD instruction) is retrieved from the page table.

For taint checking, the *Memory Management Unit* module ensures that when data is being written to the memory (in the MEM stage), the combination of taints for the source and destination is allowed by the overwriting policy. In addition, the *Taint Checking* module checks that the jump target address is always trusted (in the MEM stage). Otherwise, an exception is raised.

Details about architectural changes are given below.

4.1 Wider Register File

Each register is widened by one bit to hold the taint. For taint propagation between registers or between memory and registers, we include glue logic to read and write these taints. "OR" operations are performed on the source taints except several special cases. For example, when the instruction has only one source operand, the taint is propagated directly without any operation. Another case is when a destination register is cleared using the XOR instruction ($xor\ r1, r1, r1$) or the AND instruction ($and\ r1, r1, 0$), the register's taint is trusted independent, of the source operands taints. In addition, when an instruction loads an immediate value ($movl\ \$10, (\%esp)$), the destination register or variable is always trusted. These special cases are all considered in the *Taint Propagation* module, as shown in Fig. 5.

4.2 Memory Taint Bit Retrieval

During taint propagation between registers and memory, the taint associated with a variable (in fact, with the memory page that holds the variable) should be retrieved on any LOAD or STORE instruction. At sites of LOAD instructions, when the memory address is used to look up the data memory/cache for data, it is used to look up page table for taint as well. At sites of STORE instructions, the taint for the memory location is retrieved in a similar manner, and the overwriting policy of no trusted/untrusted data moved to untrusted/trusted page is enforced with security alarms raised on violations.

In systems that support virtual memory, the page table has to be looked up for any memory-access instruction for data retrieval anyway. Therefore, there is no extra overhead for retrieving the taint bit stored in the page table.

At compile time, the static analysis assigns the tag for each memory segment. At run-time, when the OS loads the program, all the page attributes are set, and the tag information is kept in the page table. If the page table is full and a new page request arises with a page fault, a victim page has to be chosen and swapped out from the memory to disk. Correspondingly, its entry in the page table also has to be deleted. However, its taint has to be saved in memory (some special region) for later reuse. When data on this victim page is needed again, the page will be swapped of the memory, and its taint will be recovered from the special memory region into the page table. Note that this page taint memory is managed by the OS, and the page fault handling

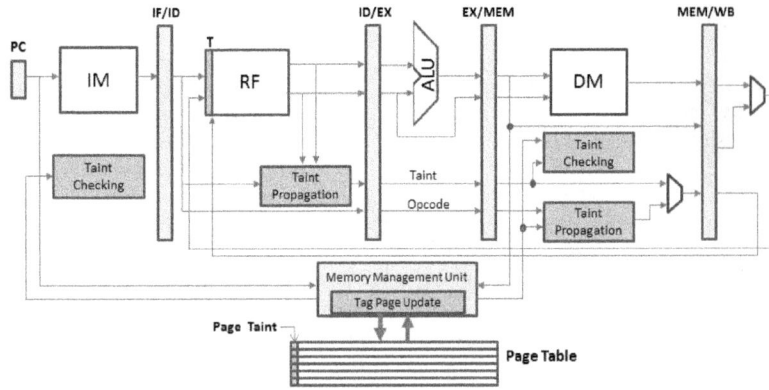

Figure 5: Architecture design

5. SECURITY ANALYSIS

There are two considerations in evaluating the effectiveness of our approach. First, the approach should not produce false alarms when no attack is launched upon the system. Second, the approach should be able to detect attacks that attempt to overwrite critical information.

To evaluate the false alarms, we run several SPEC CINT2000 benchmarks [28]. For each application, the source code is compiled twice, one with a regular compiler and the other with our modified compiler. The obtained functionality is the same, and the applications run without false alarms. Details about how our compiler affects the execution are given in Section 6.

To evaluate the security effectiveness of our approach, we use three micro-benchmarks to test if our system can detect overwrites of critical memory positions by untrusted information. These benchmarks were used in [33] to show the effectiveness of DIFT. To simulate dynamic information flow tracking at run-time, we used a modified version of *tracegrind*, an instrumentation framework to track the flow of tainted data, which is a plug-in for Valgrind [20] developed by Avalanche project [13].

5.1 Protecting the Stack from Buffer Overflow

The first micro benchmark intends to experiment with stack buffer overflow attacks. As shown in Fig. 6, it reads and prints an array of 10 elements (by definition). Because the function *fscanf* does not check the input size, the program can read more elements and overwrite the stack of function `main`. As a result, the stack can be smashed, and the return address can be overwritten. In our approach, the overwriting is avoided because the return address and other trusted variables are put on a trusted page while *array* is put on an untrusted page. The buffer overflow cannot affect the return address. Details of the attack are shown in Fig. 7. The Memory Management Unit (MMU) allows *array* to grow, but only within untrusted pages. When it continues to overwrite an adjacent trusted page, the MMU will halt the execution, and the OS will take control of the application. In an X86 architecture, the attack is detected at this point because the taint attributes of the *Source Index Register*

(ESI) and the *Destination Index Register* (EDI) differ, which are used by the system call, *fscanf*, to perform copying a chunk of data in a memory region.

```
#define MAX_SIZE 10

int loadInputFile(char filename [], int array[]) {
  FILE * file = fopen(filename, "rt");
  int i = 0;
  fscanf(file, "%d\n", array + i);
  while(!feof(file)) {
     i++;
     fscanf(file, "%d \n", array + i); }
  fclose(file);
  return i; }

int main ( int argc, char ** argv) {
  int array[MAX_SIZE];
  int size = loadInputFile(argv[1], array);
  … }
```

Figure 6: Micro benchmark for stack buffer overflow

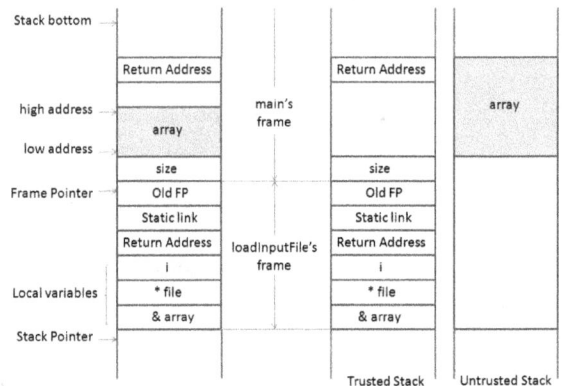

Figure 7: Defending against stack buffer overflow

5.2 Avoiding Format String Exploitation

The second micro benchmark, shown in Fig. 8, demonstrates how to exploit the format string vulnerability when the function *printf* is invoked incorrectly. This vulnerability allows an attacker to send a format string like "1111 %p" (in *array*), to reveal information on the process' memory. With other format strings like "1111 %n" in *array*, the attacker can even overwrite the process' memory.

32

Our approach catches the attack when the system tries to use the format directive %p. In normal conditions, the format directive %p is stored in a register that is used by the function *printf* to handle the formatted printing. With our implementation, the attribute of this register is untrusted because the content comes from the user input. The taint of the format directive register gets to propagate to a register used by a conditional jump in the *printf* function, and our checking policy does not allow untrusted target address.

```
#include <stdio.h>
#include <string.h>
#define MAX_SIZE 100

int main (int argc, char **argv) {
    char array[MAX_SIZE];
    snprintf(array, MAX_SIZE, argv[1]);
    printf(array);
    return 0; }
```

Figure 8: Micro-benchmark for format string vulnerability

5.3 Protecting the Heap

The third micro benchmark, shown in Fig. 9, shows a heap corruption attack. Two arrays of eight elements, *array* and *p*, are allocated. One of them, *array*, is used to hold an untrusted string. Because the function *scanf* does not check the size of input, an attacker can introduce more elements and overwrite critical information (forward and backward link pointers) held in the memory next to *array*.

At static time, the compiler cannot determine where *p* and *array* will be allocated. The exact position is only determined at run-time. However, the static analysis can determinate the attribute during compilation. The attribute of each chunk of memory is passed to the MMU when the program is loaded. When a new chunk of memory is needed, the MMU will allocate it in the right page. In this example, *array* is used to hold untrusted data from *scanf* function. Details are shown in Fig. 10.

Our approach prevents the attack because *array* is now put in an untrusted page without the possibility of overwriting the critical meta-data or any trusted chunk of memory.

```
#include <stdio.h>
#include <string.h>
#define SIZE 8

int main () {
    char * array;
    char * p;
    array = malloc(SIZE);
    p = malloc(SIZE);
    scanf("%s", array);
    free(array);
    return 0; }
```

Figure 9: Micro-benchmark for heap corruption

5.4 Defending Against other Attacks

For system calls and *return-to-libc* attacks, our approach is also effective because the system ensures that the IDs for system calls are always stored in a trusted page. Our approach prevents the attacker from invoking an arbitrary

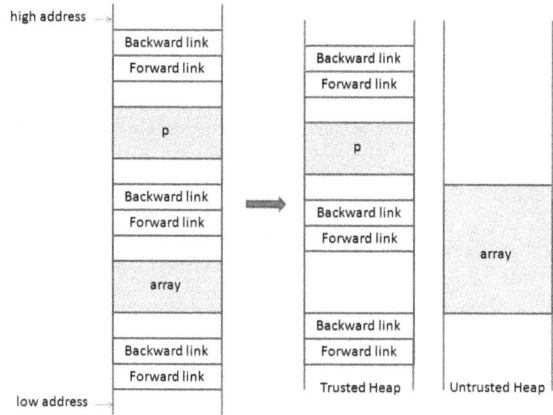

Figure 10: Detail of heap corruption attack

system call, but it does not prevent the attacker from requesting a system call with untrusted corrupted arguments.

For high-level semantic software attacks, e.g. XSS [4] attacks, the security weakness is the failure to validate properly inputs from the user. Our approach will be useful as well because the system ensures that only code from a trustworthy source can be executed. In addition, our approach will detect any attempt to corrupt trusted information by an untrusted source.

Overall, our approach can detect the attacks that intend to take control of the application by overwriting critical information like return address, system call IDs, and function pointers or by intending to execute untrusted code. Although the attacker can still overwrite some memory positions, no crucial information will be changed due to different page allocation and security policies. Our approach can be complemented with other techniques that watch the run-time execution of a program for abnormality [18].

5.5 Testing Our Approach with a Real Attack

Fig. 11 shows the code of the widely used SSH server authentication. Function *packet_read* has a bug, allowing attackers to overwrite the memory [8]. The SSH server relies on the function *do_authentication*() to authenticate remote users. A stack variable *auth* is defined to indicate whether the user has succeeded in the authentication. The initial value of *auth* is 0. While not authenticated, the vulnerable function is called to read the password. At this point, the attacker can overwrite the *auth* variable to 1. Hence, the server lets the attacker to login even with a wrong password.

Our approach addresses this problem by allocating the *auth* variable on the trusted stack page, so the attacker cannot overwrite it.

6. EXPERIMENTAL RESULTS

6.1 Software Implementation

At compile-time, our implementation includes two parts: static taint analysis (that includes variable, code, and function duplication) and memory map generation.

Our compiler is built on top of Vulncheck [27], an extension of GCC 4.2.1 for detecting code vulnerabilities. Instead

---

[4]Cross-site scripting (XSS).

33

```
void do_authentication(char *user, ...)
{   int auth = 0;
    ...
    while (!auth)
    { /* Get a packet from the client */
      type = packet_read();
      switch (type)
      { ...
        case SSH_CMSG_AUTH_PASSWORD:
          if (auth_password(user, password))
            auth =1;
        case ...
      }
      if (auth) break;
    }
    /* Perform session preparation. */
    do_authenticated(…); }
```

Figure 11: A real attack

of detecting vulnerabilities, our approach does taint analysis to initialize and propagate variable taints.

6.2 Static Memory Overhead

There are two sources of memory overhead: global variable and statement duplication. Fig. 12 shows that the overhead for global variable duplication is 6% on average. Small variable duplication results in small statement duplication, as shown in Fig. 13. The average code overhead is less than 1%.

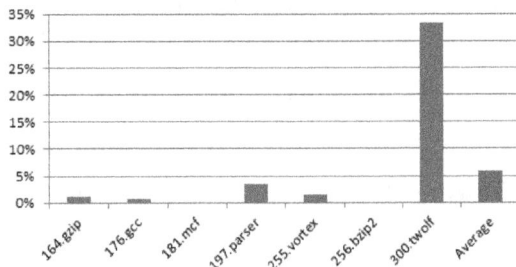

Figure 12: Global variable overhead

In general, the total amount of memory used for global variables is less than a hundred bytes. Thus, getting 6% in global variable duplication in a program with several hundreds of kilobytes is a very small overhead. Nevertheless, how the variable duplication affects the code size is more important. The results show that 6% of the global variables (less than ten bytes) leads to a code increase of 1%, around 10 kilobytes for a program of 1 megabyte.

6.3 Dynamic Memory Overhead

The static analysis reveals that no program requires heap duplication, just separation. However, that is not the case for stack. Using drd, a Valgrind tool for monitoring the process behavior [20], we measured how much each stack grows during execution. Fig.14 shows the result. For some applications, the stack is just split into two orthogonal stacks (untrusted and trusted). The overall effective size is the same, so that the overhead is zero, like 176.gcc and 197.$parser$. For some applications, the majority of the stack needs to

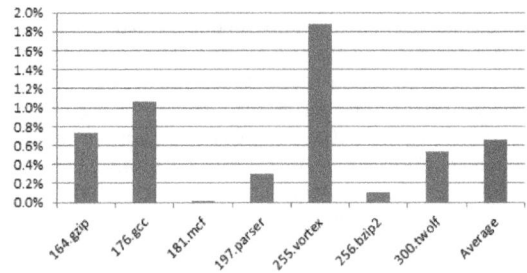

Figure 13: Code overhead

be duplicated (e.g., local variables that are trusted and untrusted at different usages), and the overhead is near 100%, e.g., 164.$gzip$, 181.mcf, 255.$vortex$, and 300.$twolf$. For other applications, it is a mix of separation and duplication, and the overhead depends on the composites of stacks, e.g., 256.$bzip2$.

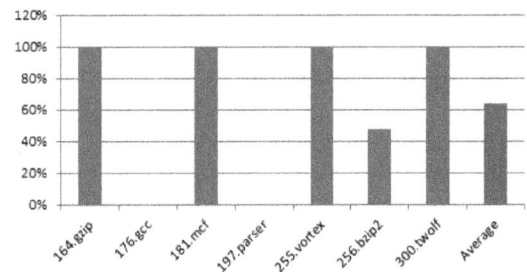

Figure 14: Stack overhead

The stack size for the applications that need stack duplication is on average 8 kilobytes. Thus, 8 kilobytes over a few megabytes (for code size) is a small overhead.

6.4 Execution Overhead

To measure the performance impact of our approach, we simulate a set of SPEC CINT2000 applications on $cachegrind$, a Valgrind tool for cache and branch-prediction profiling. The architecture parameters for the simulator are listed in Table 2.

Table 2: Parameters for Simulations.

Parameter	Value
CPU Model	Pentium 4 D
Frequency	2.80GHz
I1	16KB, 8-way, 32 byte line size
D1	16KB, 8-way, 64 byte line size
L2	2MB, 8-way, 64 byte line size
Conditional Branch Predictor	16,384 2-bit saturating counters
Branch Target Address	512 entries
L1 access latency	10 cycles
L2 access latency	200 cycles
Mispredicted Branch latency	20 cycles
Simulator	Cachegrind

In order to evaluate performance, we run two sets of program simulations and compare their number of cycles. One set is compiled and executed without any modifications, and the other set is compiled with our enhanced compiler. Fig. 15 shows the effect on performance degradation, less

34

than 2% on average, which is negligible. The execution overhead is caused by an increase in the cache misses due to the memory duplication. When data with different attributes are allocated into different pages, the original spatial locality is reduced, and hence there will be more capacity-limit cache misses. At the same time, code size may get larger and average memory access time to code pages may increase as well.

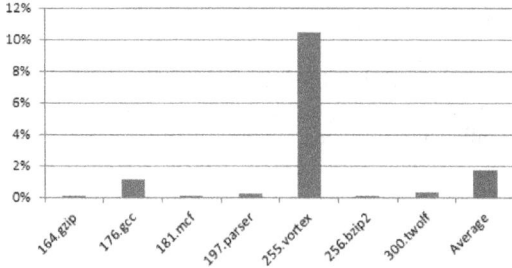

Figure 15: Execution cycle overhead

7. DISCUSSIONS

7.1 Summary of Our Approach

Using a taint bit for each page helps us check data structure boundaries indirectly. We enforce that trusted memory cannot be overwritten by untrusted data and vice versa. In this way, data read from local disk like program instructions, initialized variables, and constant tables are trusted, and the attacker cannot overwrite it with data obtained from untrusted sources, like input/output (I/O) ports.

Although splitting the memory pages into trusted and untrusted does not avoid attacks like buffer overflows, our proposed approach can protect critical information which otherwise could be used to take control over the application. The critical information, *return address, system call IDs*, etc., is stored in trusted pages. The attackers may attempt to modify them, but the input sources are usually untrusted, and our approach detects the attacks by enforcing the overwriting policy. For each control flow instruction, our approach makes sure that the target address is trusted. The system will either raise an exception or stall the execution directly if there are attempts to violate the above policies.

7.2 Generalization and Limitation

Our approach can support self-modifying code and executable stack. However, the instructions must come from a trusted page. A more flexible approach may allow the execution of untrusted code that does not invoke an untrusted system call or try to overwrite trusted data/output ports.

The implementation of our approach is based on C programs. However, it can be extended for other languages like C++, because the taint analysis is done when the code is in GIMPLE representation, which is a common intermediate representation. When applying our approach to different architectures, some consideration should be taken into account. For example, how arguments are passed from the caller function to the callee, how the stack memory is laid out, etc.

One limitation of the approach is that it cannot detect decision data attack, which is to change critical untrusted

local data for making decision (i.e., the data that determines whether to jump or fall through at a branch site). This kind of attacks requires control flow validation [18], which can work in conjunction with our solution.

7.3 Application on Multi-core Architectures

For applications running on multi-cores, there is extra performance degradation due to the necessity of maintaining the atomicity between data and metadata for shared memory, i.e., eliminating the possibility that a processor accesses a modified data with an old metadata. In [14], an enhanced cache coherency protocol tracks the order of data updates and enforces the same order on meta-data operations. Using our approach, the system does not need to access the memory twice, nor need to modify the current coherency protocol. Our solution does not require updating data taints at run-time, which are preset and embedded in the page table. However, this approach requires more efforts at static time because the compiler would need to split and duplicate shared data if they are dual-tagged.

8. CONCLUSIONS

In summary, we propose a flexible, efficient, and lightweight hardware/software co-design solution for Dynamic Information Flow Tracking with compile-time page allocation. It achieves the same level of security as hardware-assisted DIFT, with less hardware augmentation. The overhead for taint storage is reduced almost to zero. The little memory and hardware overhead for implementing the proposed page-level taint processing yield a negligible performance overhead for the system.

9. ACKNOWLEDGEMENTS

We would like to thank the anonymous CASES reviewers for their comments and feedback on the ideas in this paper. This work was supported by National Science Foundation under CAREER grant - CNS 0845871.

10. REFERENCES

[1] W. Chang, B. Streiff, and C. Lin. Efficient and extensible security enforcement using dynamic data flow analysis. In *Proc. Conf. Computer & Communications Security*, pages 39–50, Oct. 2008.

[2] H. Chen, X. Wu, L. Yuan, B. Zang, P.-c. Yew, and F. T. Chong. From speculation to security: Practical and efficient information flow tracking using speculative hardware. In *Proc. Int. Symp. Computer Architecture*, pages 401–412, June 2008.

[3] S. Chen, M. Kozuch, T. Strigkos, B. Falsafi, P. B. Gibbons, T. C. Mowry, V. Ramachandran, O. Ruwase, M. Ryan, and E. Vlachos. Flexible hardware acceleration for instruction-grain program monitoring. In *Proc. Int. Symp. Computer Architecture*, pages 377–388, Jun. 2008.

[4] T.-C. Chiueh and F.-H. Hsu. RAD: A compile-time solution to buffer overflow attacks. In *Proc. Int Conf. Distributed Computing Systems*, pages 409–417, Apr. 2001.

[5] C. Cowen, C. Pu, D. Maier, H. Hinton, J. Walpole, P. Bakke, S. Beattie, A. Grier, P. Wagle, and Q. Zhang. StackGuard: Automatic adaptive detection

and prevention of buffer-overflow attacks. In *Proc. USENIX Security Symp.*, pages 63–78, Jan. 1998.

[6] J. R. Crandall, S. F. Wu, and F. T. Chong. Minos: Architectural support for protecting control data. *ACM Tran. Architecture & Code Optimization*, 3(4):359–389, Dec. 2006.

[7] M. Dalton, H. Kannan, and C. Kozyrakis. Raksha: A flexible flow architecture for software security. In *Proc. Int. Symp. Computer Architecture*, pages 482–293, June 2007.

[8] S. Focus. Ssh crc-32 compensation attack detector vulnerability, 2001. http://http://www.securityfocus.com/bid/2347/.

[9] M. Frantzen and M. Shuey. StackGhost: Hardware facilitated stack protection. In *Proc. USENIX Security Symp.*, pages 55–66, Aug. 2001.

[10] A. Ho, M. Fetterman, C. Clark, A. Warfield, and S. Hand. Practical taint-based protection using demand emulation. In *EUROSYS '06*, 2006.

[11] R. Huang, D. Y. Deng, and G. E. Suh. Orthrus: efficient software integrity protection on multi-cores. *Comput. Archit. News*, 38(1):371–384, 2010.

[12] Imperva. Securesphere and owasp 2010 top ten most critical web application security risks, 2010. http://www.imperva.com/docs/TB_SecureSphere_OWASP_2010-Top-Ten.pdf.

[13] I. K. Isaev and D. V. Sidorov. The use of dynamic analysis for generation of input data that demonstrates critical bugs and vulnerabilities in programs. *Programming and Computer Software*, 36(4):225–236, Sept. 2010.

[14] H. Kannan. Ordering decoupled metadata accesses in multiprocessors. In *Proc. Int. Symp. Microarchitecture*, pages 381 –390, Dec. 2009.

[15] S. Katsunuma, H. Kurita, R. Shioya, K. Shimizu, H. Irie, M. Goshima, and S. Sakai. Base address recognition with data flow tracking for injection attack detection. In *Proc. Pacific Rim Inter. Symp. Dependable Computing*, pages 165 –172, Dec. 2006.

[16] L. C. Lam and T.-c. Chiueh. A general dynamic information flow tracking framework for security applications. In *Proc. Annual Computer Security Applications Conf.*, pages 463–472, Dec. 2006.

[17] B. Livshits, M. Martin, and M. S. Lam. Securifly: Runtime protection and recovery from web application vulnerabilities. Technical report, Stanford University, 2006.

[18] J. C. Martinez Santos and Y. Fei. Leveraging speculative architectures for run-time program validation. In *Proc. Int. Conf. Computer Design*, pages 498–505, Oct. 2008.

[19] J. C. Martinez Santos, Y. Fei, and Z. J. Shi. Pift: Efficient dynamic information flow tracking using secure page allocation. In *Proc. WkShp on Embedded Systems Security*, pages 6:1–6:8, Oct 2009.

[20] N. Nethercote and J. Seward. Valgrind: a framework for heavyweight dynamic binary instrumentation. In *Proc. Conference on Programming Language Design & Implementation*, pages 89–100, Jun. 2007.

[21] E. B. Nightingale, D. Peek, P. M. Chen, and J. Flinn. Parallelizing security checks on commodity hardware. In *Proc. Int. Conf. Architectural Support for Programming Languages & Operating Systems*, pages 308–318, Mar. 2008.

[22] D. Pozza and R. Sisto. A lightweight security analyzer inside gcc. *Proc. Int. Conf. Availability, Reliability & Security*, pages 851–858, 2008.

[23] F. Qin, C. Wang, Z. Li, H. seop Kim, Y. Zhou, and Y. Wu. LIFT: A Low-Overhead Practical Information Flow Tracking System for Detecting Security Attacks. In *IEEE/ACM Int. Symp. on Microarchitecture*, pages 135–148, Dec. 2006.

[24] O. Ruwase, P. B. Gibbons, T. C. Mowry, V. Ramachandran, S. Chen, M. Kozuch, and M. Ryan. Parallelizing dynamic information flow tracking. In *Proc. Annual Symp. Parallelism in Algorithms & Architectures*, pages 35–45, Jun. 2008.

[25] W. Shi, J. Fryman, G. Gu, H.-H. Lee, Y. Zhang, and J. Yang. InfoShield: A security architecture for protecting information usage in memory. *Int. Symp. on High-Performance Computer Architecture*, pages 222–231, Feb. 2006.

[26] I. Sophia, A. Méditerranée, and S. Antipolis. Secure slices of insecure programs categories and subject descriptors. In *Language*, pages 112–122, Mar. 2008.

[27] A. Sotirov. *Automatic vulnerability detection using static source code analysis*. PhD thesis, University of Alabama, 2005.

[28] SPEC. SPEC CINT 2000 Benchmarks, 2000. http://www.spec.org/cpu2000/CINT2000/.

[29] G. E. Suh, J. W. Lee, D. Zhang, and S. Devadas. Secure program execution via dynamic information flow tracking. In *Proc. Int. Conf. on Architectural Support for Programming Languages & Operating Systems*, pages 85–96, 2004.

[30] N. Vachharajani, M. J. Bridges, J. Chang, R. Rangan, G. Ottoni, J. A. Blome, G. A. Reis, M. Vachharajani, and D. I. August. RIFLE: An architectural framework for user-centric information-flow security. In *Proc. Int. Symp. Microarchitecture*, pages 243–254, 2004.

[31] G. Venkataramani, I. Doudalis, Y. Solihin, and M. Prvulovic. Flexitaint: A programmable accelerator for dynamic taint propagation. In *Proc. Int. Symp. High-Performance Computer Architecture*, pages 173–184, Feb. 2008.

[32] J. Wilander and M. Kamkar. A comparison of publicly available tools for static intrusion prevention, 2002.

[33] J. Xu and N. Nakka. Defeating memory corruption attacks via pointer taintedness detection. In *Proc. Int. Conf. on Dependable Systems & Networks*, pages 378–387, 2005.

[34] W. Xu, S. Bhatkar, and R. Sekar. Taint-enhanced policy enforcement: a practical approach to defeat a wide range of attacks. In *Proc. USENIX Security Symp.*, pages 121–136, July-Aug. 2006.

[35] Y. Younan, W. Joosen, and F. Piessens. Efficient protection against heap-based buffer overflows without resorting to magic. In *Proc. Int. Conf. on Information & Communication Security*, Dec. 2006.

[36] Y. Younan, D. Pozza, F. Piessens, and W. Joosen. Extended protection against stack smashing attacks without performance loss. In *Proc. Annual Computer Security Applications Conf.*, pages 429–438, Dec. 2006.

From Sequential Programming to Flexible Parallel Execution

Arun Raman
Intel Labs
Santa Clara, USA
arun.a.raman@intel.com

Jae W. Lee
Sungkyunkwan University
Suwon, Korea
jaewlee@skku.edu

David I. August
Princeton University
Princeton, USA
august@princeton.edu

ABSTRACT

The embedded computing landscape is being transformed by three trends: growing demand for greater functionality and enriched user experience, increasing diversity and parallelism in the processing substrate, and an accelerating push for ever-greater energy efficiency. For programmers, these trends give rise to three challenges: writing code for a potentially heterogeneous architecture, extracting parallelism in software, and maximizing a multivariate (performance, power, energy, etc.) fitness function of user satisfaction which may vary with time. To meet these challenges, clarion calls have been issued for programmers to start writing software in new *parallel* programming models. Fundamentally, however, these proposals detract programmers from delivering new features and enriched user experience in the shortest time possible. This paper proposes to attract embedded systems programmers to a vertically integrated approach, comprising extensions to the sequential programming model, a parallelizing compiler, and an optimizing run-time system, to enable them to tackle all three challenges.

Categories and Subject Descriptors

D.3.4 [**Programming Languages**]: Processors—*Compilers, Run-time environments*

General Terms

Design, Performance

Keywords

adaptivity, code generation, compiler, embedded, flexible, GPGPU, heterogeneous, multicore, optimization, parallel, parallelization, performance portability, run-time, tuning

1. INTRODUCTION

In mainstream computing, a heterogeneous multicore architecture comprising a mixture of multiple, different, types of computational elements is becoming the predominant processor design. Heterogeneity is *de rigueur* in embedded systems, but there is also a definite push towards consolidating multicore CPUs, multicore GPUs, and various accelerators onto a single chip. The primary obstacle to effective use of these ostensibly powerful computational substrates is the difficulty in programming them. Two predominant schools of thought exist to overcome this obstacle.

The first school exhorts programmers to write code using new parallel programming models or libraries [1, 5, 6, 11]. These, however, burden the programmer with the need to reason about complex thread interleavings and concurrency control mechanisms, or serialize execution between different computational elements. Often, these models force the programmer to specify a fixed parallelization strategy (e.g. data parallel, pipeline parallel), fixed split of functionality across heterogeneous computational elements (e.g. a CPU program with GPU "kernels"), and fixed concurrency control strategy (e.g. locking, transactions) [7]. This *early binding* of function to form breaks the abstraction between software and hardware, resulting in suboptimal performance when workload or resource availability changes [3, 9].

The second school promises to unburden the programmer of the onerous task of (re-)writing parallel programs, by having the compiler automatically extract parallelism from the program [4, 10]. However, in practice, the widespread use of sequential programming to implement algorithmic specifications imposes severe constraints on the compiler's ability to extract scalable parallelism. As with manual parallel programming, most compilers perform early binding, leading to suboptimal parallel execution in a variety of scenarios [9].

To overcome challenges evident in both approaches, this paper argues for a three-pronged approach consisting of:

- Extensions to the sequential programming model, which relax the constraints on instruction ordering by enabling programmers to specify commutativity relationships between sets of instructions and weaker data consistency requirements. By using these extensions, the programmer does not specify parallelism, but rather *enables* automatic parallelization. Additionally, the programmer embeds hints in code blocks indicating the natural affinity of that code block to a computational unit (to a particular accelerator, for example). However, the system may choose to ignore the hints.

- A parallelizing compiler, which uses the relaxations and hints specified by the programmer to extract multiple types of parallelism from the sequential program, generate multiple code versions to target a heterogeneous architecture, and encode the program configuration space induced by parallelization and code versioning in a small set of tunable parameters. Programs created thus are called *flexible parallel programs*.

- An optimizing run-time system, which monitors program performance and system events, such as launches of new programs and resource availability change, and determines the best configurations (settings of the tunable parameters exposed by the compiler, and the dynamic mapping of code to computational element) of all concurrently executing flexible parallel programs. The optimization objective is specified by the user, may vary with time, and may be composed of latency and throughput requirements with constraints on power, memory, energy, temperature, etc.

The remainder of this paper describes synergistic advances in the above three areas, which together may restore the embedded system developer's focus to delivering exciting new features and applications.

2. PROPOSED APPROACH

Figure 1 shows the proposed programming model and execution architecture. Note the strong separation of concerns; offloading parallelism extraction and tuning away from the programmer to an automatic system reduces time to market of new systems and features.

2.1 Relaxed Sequential Programming

For many applications, there is no single required order of execution or even a single correct output. Semantically, a multitude of execution orders and outputs may be equally correct. However, a side effect of expressing the algorithm in a sequential programming model is the implicit declaration of an arbitrary single order and single output as correct. Consider the code in Figure 2. The dependency on the `seed` variable across invocations of `random` prevents a compiler from scheduling iterations of the loop in `main` to execute concurrently and without synchronization[1]. However, if the programmer marks the function as *Commutative*, indicating that invocations of `random` may happen atomically in any order, then the compiler is free to apply DOANY parallelization [13], which schedules iterations for concurrent execution and ensures consistency of `seed` state by making calls to `random` atomic. Recent work demonstrates how scalable parallelism of different types can be obtained via a generalized commutativity framework [7].

Some data structures offer sequential semantics to programs that may work correctly even with relaxed semantics. For example, in many iterative convergence algorithms, ignoring flow dependencies and allowing reads of stale values (earlier versions of a memory location) unlocks parallelism by enabling iterations of a loop to execute in parallel [12]. Respecting the dependencies improves algorithmic convergence time, but breaking the dependencies unlocks parallelism which in several cases compensates the former.

---

[1] Sophisticated parallelization algorithms can extract some forms of parallelism from the loop [10].

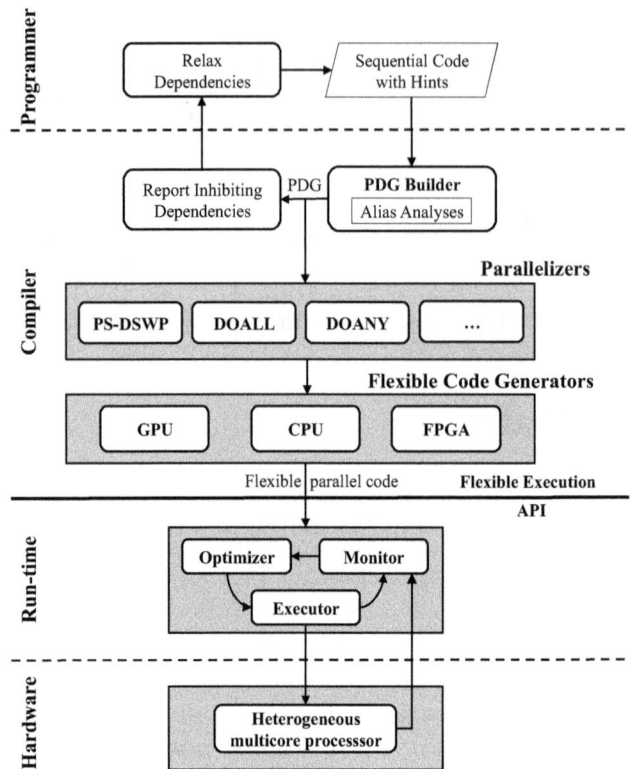

Figure 1: **Programming and Execution Architecture**

2.2 Parallelizing Compiler

The compiler identifies parallelizable regions in a sequential program and applies multiple parallelizing transforms to each region, generating multiple versions of *flexible parallel code*. The generated flexible code can be paused during its sequential or parallel execution, reconfigured, and efficiently resumed by the run-time task executor. The compiler also inserts profiling hooks into the generated code for the run-time monitor to observe program behavior.

Referring to Figure 1, the compiler discovers parallelism by building a Program Dependence Graph (PDG) of the hottest outermost loop nest. The compiler processes the programmer-specified order and data consistency relaxations to remove some dependencies (while inserting appropriate synchronization where necessary). The compiler then applies multiple parallelizing transforms, such as DOALL [2], DOANY [13], and PS-DSWP [10], to the PDG of a loop nest. The framework can accommodate additional, new transforms. Each transform extracts a distinct form of thread-level parallelism—data parallelism, pipeline parallelism, and task parallelism—encapsulated in code packages called *tasks*. The original, sequential version of the loop is also maintained as a task. Dynamic instances of a task may either execute sequentially or in parallel, depending on the task's dependency pattern. Note that parallel execution may involve communication or synchronization.

Flexible parallel execution entails dynamic scheduling of task instances across different types of cores, execution of parallel tasks by a dynamically varying number of cores, and pausing a set of tasks followed by resumption of a possibly different set of functionally equivalent tasks. To facili-

```
1  @Commutative
2  int random() {
3      int temp = seed / 127773L;
4      seed = 16807L * (seed − temp * 127773L)
5          − (temp * 2836L);
6      if (seed < 0)
7          seed += 2147483647L; // (2<<31)−1
8      return seed;
9  }
10 int main() {
11     for(i=0; i<N; i++) {
12         int seed = random();
13         work(seed);
14     }
15 }
```

Figure 2: *Commutative* **annotation allows multiple calls of** random **to execute out of order, unlocking loop level parallelism**

tate such execution, the compiler uses the flexible code generation algorithm [9] to generate multiple versions of code suited to the different components of the heterogeneous architecture [3], and parameterizes the code on a relatively small set of variables whose values are dynamically tuned to optimize for any given execution environment [9].

An embedded system developer knows that certain code blocks may execute efficiently on specific accelerators. The developer can share this knowledge with the compiler by tagging code blocks with affinity hints. The compiler uses the hints to suggest initial program configurations in different program phases to the run-time system.

2.3 Optimizing Run-time System

Workload, platform, and available resources constitute a program's execution environment. Recent work demonstrates the effectiveness of an optimizing run-time system in improving system performance by adapting program configuration to change in execution environment [9].

While deploying an embedded system, the developer specifies an optimization objective; for example, a real-time latency requirement under specified peak power constraint and average energy constraint. Given this objective, the run-time system drives the embedded program through a series of program configurations to identify the optimal configuration. A program configuration may consist of: (1) the specific set of tasks chosen to implement desired functionality; (2) the Degree of Parallelism (DoP), the varying number of cores allocated to every parallel task; and (3) the mapping of tasks to the different types of computational units available. The initial program configuration may be the one generated by the compiler using the programmer's affinity hints. The run-time system records statistics/characteristics of flexible execution and the hardware platform by using monitoring interfaces provided by the hardware. Different control and optimization techniques, both open loop and closed loop, use the gathered run-time information to converge upon the optimal program configuration [8].

Severe resource constraints in embedded systems shrink the configuration space of a flexible parallel program significantly. While this reduces the slack available to a run-time optimizer, it also reduces the size of the search space potentially leading to quicker convergence. Tight memory budget

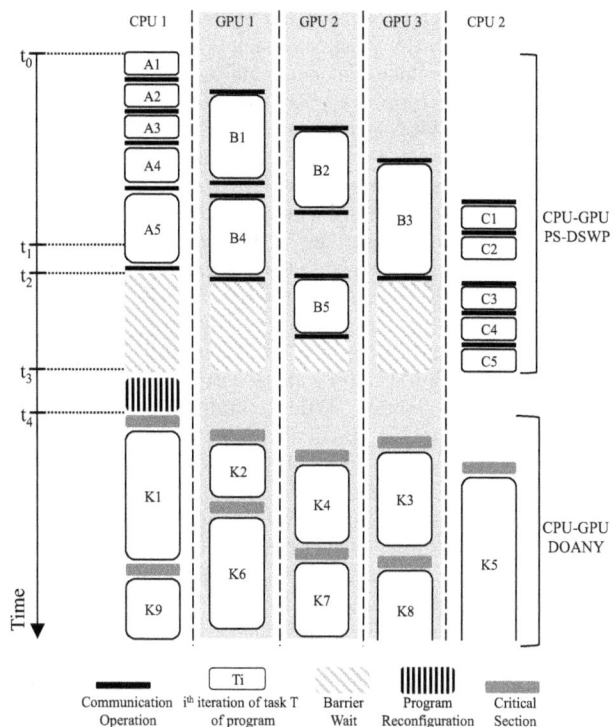

Figure 3: **Flexible Execution: Run-time system adapts program configuration including task-to-core mapping to suit execution environment**

and smaller address space may make some parallelization schemes impractical. Moreover, extreme demands for energy efficiency prevent adoption of parallelization schemes with relatively high constant overhead such as speculative parallelization. Consequently, the design of an efficient and flexible run-time optimizer for embedded systems requires additional research.

2.4 Flexible Parallel Execution

Figure 3 shows an example of the proposed execution model on a hypothetical machine with two CPU cores and three GPU cores. GPU core lanes are shaded grey. A parallel region consists of a set of concurrently executing tasks. (The inscription inside each box indicates the task and its dynamic instance; e.g., $B5$ represents the fifth dynamic instance of task B.) At time t_0, the program is launched with a pipeline parallel configuration (PS-DSWP [10], which splits a loop body across stages and schedules them for concurrent execution) having three stages corresponding to tasks A, B, and C. A and C are executed sequentially by the CPU cores whereas B is executed in parallel by three GPU cores as determined by the run-time system. Note that a single parallel region is executed on both the CPU *and* GPU, with the appropriate code packages compiled for the CPU and GPU, respectively, being dispatched. This is in contrast to models where execution on the CPU and GPU is serialized and orchestrated statically. The run-time system measures the performance of this configuration and tries alternative configurations to avoid a local maximum. At time t_1, the run-time system signals the program to pause. The core receiving this signal (CPU 1) acknowledges the signal at time

t_2 and propagates the pause signal to the other downstream cores. At time t_3, the program reaches a known consistent state[2], following which the run-time system determines a new allocation of resources. At time t_4, the run-time system launches a data-parallel configuration (DOANY [13], which schedules loop iterations for parallel execution while synchronizing shared data accesses by means of critical sections). Task K and the associated critical section implement the same functionality as tasks A, B, and C combined. While the example execution shows some cores idling at a barrier prior to reconfiguration, the barrier wait can be eliminated in common reconfiguration scenarios [8].

In the flexible parallel execution model, task serialization is enforced only by the dependency structure of the algorithm and global resource hazards, and not by artificial local hazards created by the inflexibility of a programming model. For instance, in OpenMP, a parallel region and its continuation are serialized. By contrast, in flexible parallel execution, the continuation may be launched on any available computation unit, even if the unit does not match the affinity hint that may have been specified by the programmer for the continuation code block.

Finally, researchers have demonstrated that synergistic use of extensions to the sequential programming model, a parallelizing compiler, and an optimizing run-time system for flexible parallel execution, unlocks scalable parallelism and leads to efficient execution of a wide variety of programs. One study improved the response time and throughput of various benchmarks from the SPEC and PARSEC benchmark suites by 136% (geomean) over their original manual parallel implementations. The study also maximized performance under a variety of power and energy constraints. Further, in the context of a multiprogrammed system, the study improved system-wide performance while reducing energy consumption [8, 9].

3. CONCLUSIONS

To overcome the challenges of software development for emerging embedded system platforms, this paper describes a novel tightly integrated approach that has shown promise on mainstream computing platforms. Applications are developed in the sequential programming model (including legacy applications) and are automatically enhanced to execute flexibly on heterogeneous multicore platforms. The run-time system holistically optimizes the execution of multiple flexible parallel programs executing simultaneously.

While the effectiveness of this approach has been demonstrated on mainstream computing platforms, research is yet to be done to deploy this approach on embedded systems with their unique challenges. However, the multidimensional nature of performance objectives and constraints in the embedded domain makes the manual, static development process untenable, and makes an approach of the kind described in this paper absolutely essential.

4. ACKNOWLEDGEMENTS

We thank Nick Johnson for his feedback. This material is partly based on work supported by National Science Foundation Grant 1047879. Jae W. Lee was supported by the Korean IT R&D program of MKE/KEIT KI001810041244.

---

[2] An analysis can identify points at which the program can be efficiently paused [8].

5. REFERENCES

[1] The OpenMP API specification. http://www.openmp.org.

[2] R. Allen and K. Kennedy. *Optimizing Compilers for Modern Architectures: A Dependence-based Approach.* Morgan Kaufmann Publishers Inc., 2002.

[3] J. Auerbach, D. F. Bacon, I. Burcea, P. Cheng, S. J. Fink, R. Rabbah, and S. Shukla. A compiler and runtime for heterogeneous computing. In *Proceedings of the 49th ACM/IEEE Design Automation Conference (DAC)*, 2012.

[4] S. Campanoni, T. Jones, G. Holloway, V. J. Reddi, G.-Y. Wei, and D. Brooks. HELIX: Automatic parallelization of irregular programs for chip multiprocessing. In *Proceedings of the Annual International Symposium on Code Generation and Optimization (CGO)*, 2012.

[5] NVIDIA Corporation. *NVIDIA CUDA Programming Guide 4*, April 2011.

[6] The OpenAcc API specification for accelerators. http://www.openacc-standard.org.

[7] P. Prabhu, S. Ghosh, Y. Zhang, N. P. Johnson, and D. I. August. Commutative set: A language extension for implicit parallel programming. In *Proceedings of the 32nd ACM SIGPLAN Conference on Programming Language Design and Implementation (PLDI)*, 2011.

[8] A. Raman. *A System for Flexible Parallel Execution.* PhD thesis, Department of Computer Science, Princeton University, Princeton, New Jersey, United States, December 2011.

[9] A. Raman, A. Zaks, J. W. Lee, and D. I. August. Parcae: A system for flexible parallel execution. In *Proceedings of the 33rd ACM SIGPLAN Conference on Programming Language Design and Implementation (PLDI)*, 2012.

[10] E. Raman, G. Ottoni, A. Raman, M. Bridges, and D. I. August. Parallel-stage decoupled software pipelining. In *Proceedings of the Annual International Symposium on Code Generation and Optimization (CGO)*, 2008.

[11] J. Reinders. *Intel Threading Building Blocks.* O'Reilly & Associates, Inc., 2007.

[12] A. Udupa, K. Rajan, and W. Thies. ALTER: Exploiting breakable dependences for parallelization. In *Proceedings of the 32nd ACM SIGPLAN Conference on Programming Language Design and Implementation (PLDI)*, 2011.

[13] M. Wolfe. DOANY: Not just another parallel loop. In *Proceedings of the 4th International Workshop on Languages and Compilers for Parallel Computing (LCPC)*, 1992.

A Hybrid Just-In-Time Compiler for Android

Comparing JIT Types and the Result of Cooperation

Guillermo A. Pérez
National Tsing Hua University
Hsinchu, Taiwan
gaperez64@
sslab.cs.nthu.edu.tw

Chung-Min Kao
National Tsing Hua University
Hsinchu, Taiwan
klozesk@
sslab.cs.nthu.edu.tw

Yeh-Ching Chung
National Tsing Hua University
Hsinchu, Taiwan
ychung@cs.nthu.edu.tw

Wei-Chung Hsu
National Chiao Tung University
Hsinchu, Taiwan
hsu@cs.nctu.edu.tw

ABSTRACT

The Dalvik virtual machine is the main application platform running on Google's Android operating system for mobile devices and tablets. It is a Java Virtual Machine running a basic trace-based JIT compiler, unlike web browser JavaScript engines that usually run a combination of both method and trace-based JIT types. We developed a method-based JIT compiler based on the Low Level Virtual Machine framework that delivers performance improvement comparable to that of an Ahead-Of-Time compiler. We compared our method-based JIT against Dalvik's own trace-based JIT using common benchmarks available in the Android Market. Our results show that our method-based JIT is better than a basic trace-based JIT, and that, by sharing profiling and compilation information among each other, a smart combination of both JIT techniques can achieve a great performance gain.

Categories and Subject Descriptors

D.3.4 [**Programming Languages**]: Processors—*Compilers, Interpreters, Code generation, Optimization, Parsing, Retargetable compilers*

General Terms

Performance, Design, Experimentation, Languages

Keywords

Method-Based, Trace-Based, JIT, Android, Dalvik VM

1. INTRODUCTION

Interpreted and Dynamic languages have been on the rise for several years now. These programming languages are not compiled and translated into native instructions like classical programming languages are. Instead, a program written using them is read line by line and executed by an intermediate engine or virtual machine. The process of fetching each instruction and the execution of it can be much slower than how a native program is usually ran. This problem has traditionally been dealt with by adding a Just-In-Time (JIT) Compiler to the virtual machine [25] [4]. A JIT Compiler is a compiler that takes a code sequence or code block and translates it into native code during run time in order to improve its execution time.

The Java language is an example of an interpreted language which runs on top of Oracle's Java^{TM} Virtual Machine (JVM). Java allows developers to write a program once and run it on any platform that implements a JVM [30]. Developers might choose to write computationally intensive code using a different programming language (C and assembler are the most common choices) and communicate with the JVM using Java's Native Interface (JNI) [28]. This approach, however, requires that the developer provide the target user with a library compiled for the user's hardware. The use of JNI to interface with the virtual machine is also a problem because of the overhead required to change from the interpreted to the native environment and back [20]. It is also possible to compile an application written in Java to a native binary file using Java to native compilers [9] [32] but the resulting binary and the libraries needed to execute it need to be compiled for the user's platform as well, making this and the previous approaches less portable than the JVM and Google's Dalvik virtual machine. Because of these reasons most Java applications are written using mostly Java and are therefore benefited by a VM's JIT compiler. As of Java 1.3, the standard HotSpot became the default Sun Java Virtual Machine [29]. The HotSpot virtual machine included a method-based (MB) JIT compiler to analyze the program's performance for hot spots (frequently executed instructions) and compile them.

Recently, trace-based (TB) JIT compilers have become more popular than it's MB counterpart because of its ability to define traces that range from one method to another and therefore extend the scope of what is being considered for compilation and optimization. TB JIT compilers can also take dynamically typed languages and compile them to optimized native code that handles the variables' types being observed during run time [10]. As is explained in section 4.1.1, Java is not actually a dynamically typed language and therefore such an optimization does not completely apply to the Dalvik VM. Nevertheless, short instruction sequence compilation can result in smaller memory footprint and still improve performance by selecting the few most executed instructions for JIT compilation. Because of these reasons, and also because of the speed at which a simple TB JIT can start delivering performance improvements, Google chose to implement a TB JIT compiler for their Android operating system for mobile devices [6]. However, with the advantage of method structures as basic block delimiters and considering that Android's TB JIT, currently does not have the ability to create traces containing code from more than one method, it is not really clear and no one has really studied if a MB JIT would have the same effect or achieve even better performance.

Both JIT compiler types have their own strengths and outperform the other in terms of memory usage or delivered code quality depending on the situation and the platform's resources. Simple TB JIT compilers, such as Dalvik's, might seem better suited for resource-constrained devices such as cellphones because of their ability to avoid compiling cold code and their fast compilation times. However, more robust TB JIT compilers or MB JIT compilers, although slower and even though they might have a bigger memory footprint, deliver faster, more efficient, code. This paper compares the performance of the code generated by a limited TB JIT compiler and a MB JIT compiler running on a mobile device and suggests the usage of a fast, incomplex JIT compiler combined with a slow JIT compiler capable of delivering better optimized code.

In this work we propose a MB JIT compiler based on the Low Level Virtual Machine (LLVM) [22] compiler framework and API to deal with methods that can be further optimized by considering them as a whole block instead of focusing merely on the hot traces they contain, like the current TB compiler does. Our resulting JIT framework has been shown to improve the execution speed of commonly used benchmarks to test the speed of Java Virtual Machines by up to 4 times compared to Android's mainstream, unmodified Dalvik VM. We show that a MB JIT compiler can provide similar results to those a static compiler could while having the advantage of run-time profiling information and taking a relatively small toll on resource usage compared to the performance gain. Finally, we propose a sharing environment in which information resulted from the TB JIT profiling and subsequent compilation of code can be useful for our MB compiler and vice versa in order for each compiler to complement each other's weaknesses and harness their own advantages.

2. OVERVIEW

2.1 Method-Based JIT Compiler flow

Every time an application is launched in Android a new copy of the Dalvik VM is spawned from the system Dalvik zygote. Each DVM acts as an application sandbox with its own Garbage Collection and Compiler Threads. The new DVM opens the application file (called a dex file) and loads into memory the contents of it. In order to speed up the execution of interpreted instructions, a TB JIT compiler checks for hot traces while the program is being run. Any instruc-

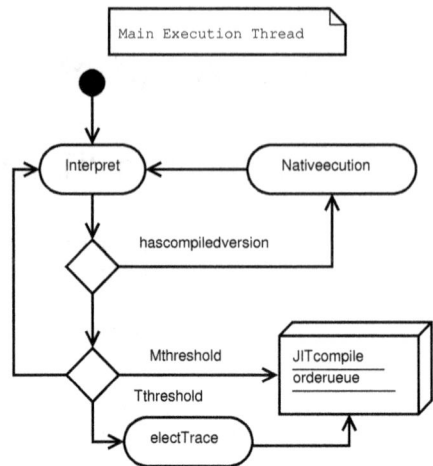

Figure 1: Main Thread State Diagram

tion executed a certain amount of times can trigger a trace selection phase inside the interpreter and then a trace compile order will be emitted for the compiler to transform the trace into native code. Our work adds a second threshold to the process. The new threshold applies only for invocation opcodes and is tuned to allow the TB JIT to run as the base JIT compiler to allow for fast optimization of the application by means of short traces being compiled while the MB compiler delivers faster, heavily optimized compiled methods afterwards. When the threshold for invocation instructions is reached, there is no need for a trace selection phase so the compile order is emitted quicker than a trace compile order. Figure 1 depicts the first profiling phase for our MB JIT and how it appends to the existing JIT profiling technique. This thread profiling phase is simpler than Dalvik's JIT because there is no need to build a trace before submitting a method compile order.

In recent times, the tendency has been to create software that can be executed in parallel on multi-core processors. This is often allowed by processes spawning new child processes or by processes being further divided internally as threads. Java virtual machines provide a mechanism to create, handle and kill additional threads apart from the main execution thread [28]. Threads can be created and started using the `Runnable` interface or the `Thread` class and the virtual machine is in charge of creating a new thread and executing the code in the class' implementation of the run method [27]. In the case of the Dalvik VM, this threads are provided via POSIX [17] threads and the corresponding API. The invocation of the `run()` method is not profiled by Dalvik's TB JIT because it is directly invoked from the virtual machine. We propose an additional Class-level profiling phase to be able to select when the `run()` should be considered for MB JIT compilation. Having Class-level profiling information might enable us to consider related methods from the same Class or related Classes for JIT compilation. This kind of semantic information is not being utilized, at the moment, by the JIT compiler framework.

The Compiler Thread works by emptying the compile order queue and processing every trace one at a time. Trace orders are handled by Google's Dalvik VM TB JIT compiler. At this moment, the only methods considered for inlining by the TB JIT compiler are simple methods that fit the profile

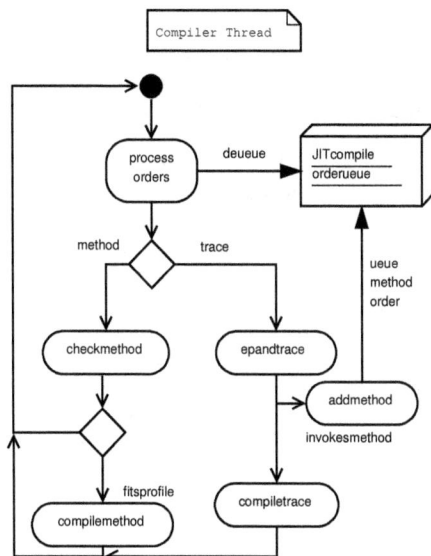

Figure 2: Compiler Thread State Diagram

of `getters` or `setters`. When presented with invocations to other methods then inlining is not realized. In our proposed framework we consider the case in which a method is not inlined counter productive for the JIT compiler's goal. Therefore we add a call to our MB compiler to avoid having a compiled trace call an interpreted method and then return to the native environment because of the overhead that this would mean (interfacing native code with interpreted usually implies the use of JNI or another bridge) [20]. This is the third way a method can be scheduled for MB compilation. We chose to append our MB JIT compiler to the same compiler thread because this, when the profiler is tuned to favor the TB JIT as the base JIT, allows for traces to be compiled first. In this manner, the TB compiler thread does not compete with the MB compiler thread for CPU time, because they are handled by one single compiler thread, and together deliver quicker native versions of traces while the slower method compilations are left for later. The assumptions and derivations we followed for the tuning of our profiler are explained in section 3.2. Figure 2 shows all the states in which the compiler thread can find itself. It also shows the method level profiling phase of our proposed JIT.

A second advantage of our decision to use the same compiler thread is that Dalvik's original security scheme is left unmodified. Every application still runs inside its own virtual machine and every virtual machine has its own compiler thread that has access to its own native compiled code. The only difference is that, for method work orders, after some transformations are applied to the DEX code, the MB JIT is called instead of the original TB JIT.

2.2 The Compiler

The compiler itself uses LLVM's framework to translate optimized DEX instructions directly into LLVM bitcode. Although a trace is not provided for the compiler to work on, the object oriented structures created by the DVM to hold classes, objects and such provide access to the DEX code without having to reload the dex file from the application. The reasons for having chosen LLVM as the compiler's back-

bone and the benefits that this meant, and ones yet to exploit, are explained in section 4.2.

Using a third party developed compiler such as LLVM's allows us to focus on the comparison and cooperation between JIT types. The idea of building a JVM using third party components had already been fathomed by Geoffray et al. [11] to reduce the expertise needed to implement any of its main components. The JIT compiler is just another one of a JVM's components and its job is to take an intermediate representation (IR), be it DEX code or LLVM bitcode, and generate native code. The compiler thread (its state diagram shown in figure 2) is in charge of calling the right JIT compiler for each work order. The Dalvik VM later sets the jump point from interpreted code to the newly compiled one.

3. PROFILING APPROACH

3.1 Existing Profiling Tools

Google provides a tool called traceview to profile the execution of applications on the Dalvik Virtual Machine. Wang's previous work on an Ahead-Of-Time-Compiler (AOTC), Icing [35], bases its profiling model on information provided by traceview available after the application has been ran once. The information is then considered at static time to determine which methods are good candidates for static compilation previous to repackaging the Android application. The situation for a JIT is a bit different since run time information is readily available and more valuable than any sort that could be obtained ahead-of-time. In most cases user behavior will affect which methods and which code sections are executed more often, this is something that can only be determined during run-time. Further differences with similar compilers and their approaches are discussed in section 6.

Dalvik's TB JIT compiler keeps track of the amount of times most instructions from a program have been called. This information is stored in a hash table and is updated any time a candidate trace entry point is about to be interpreted. The choice of a hash table is definitely based on the need for the interpreter to be able to continue its job without much overhead being added by the TB JIT. Once the amount of times an instruction has been called passes the threshold set for the TB JIT to kick in then the entry in the hash table is reset and the Interpreter goes through a series of steps to decide where the trace should stop, taking into account a parametrized maximum length for any given trace. The trace is later dispatched as a work order for the Compiler Thread to take care of the JIT compilation and attachment of the compiled code where the Interpreter is able to call it. The compiled code, however, is not called until the execution threshold is once again passed; at this moment the interpreter checks if the code has already been compiled, and if it has, then jumps to the native compiled code. At this point we notice that, not only are trace compile orders dispatched earlier, but they will also be called earlier (given the fact that the TB JIT threshold, $thresh_T$, is low enough). With a different tuning, the profiler would easily be able to make the MB JIT the base JIT because the MB compile orders take less time to build and they do not depend on the invocation threshold being passed twice for the native code to be installed.

3.2 Profiling for our Method-Based JIT

We took advantage of the existing profiling mechanism and for every method called we check if a specific MB threshold had been reached. Once the threshold is passed then a work order is submitted to the Compiler Thread for the method to be compiled and made available for future calls. The method is marked so that, in the future, it will not be considered for MB JIT orders and rather be taken into consideration only for trace compilations. This way we avoid re-evaluating rejected methods. Since the native version of the method will replace the invocation to a interpreted method for an invocation to a native one, this only affect in the case that the method was considered not fit for the MB JIT. The modifications we added to this profiling stage are executed in constant time and account for a minimum amount of time in the whole compilation process. The interpreter only needs to check a hash table and update the counter stored in it.

In order to obtain an initial setting for the profiling model thresholds we followed a simple derivation. We defined a `Method` as a finite sequence of instructions: $Method = \{i_0, i_1, i_2, ...\}$; and a `Trace` as a subsequence of instructions $Trace \subseteq Method$ so if we set our MB JIT threshold, $thresh_M$, to any value such that $thresh_M > 1$, the hot traces of instructions inside a method's instruction sequence are sure to be dispatched as trace compile orders if there is a flow control structure inside the method such that the TB JIT's threshold is reached. Actually, although loops, recursive method calls and repetitive event inputs are all examples of situations that might cause an instruction to be ran several times, only loops do not implicitly include the invocation of a method (which would be profiled for the MB JIT as well). With this setting then, an instruction can be called a certain amount of times before the compiler's behavior degenerates into compiled traces being outdated by complete native methods. Consider $exec(i)$ to be the expected amount of times an instruction $i \in Method = \{i_0, i_1, i_2, ...\}$ is to be executed per method call. We can now say that the degenerate case occurs when we have the following conditions:

- $\exists i \in Method \mid exec(i) \geq thresh_T / thresh_M$

- calls to $Method$ exceed $thresh_M$

This means that an optimal tuning should consider low MB thresholds compared to the numerator, otherwise the degenerate case might occur too often. The usual TB threshold for Dalvik (around 40) proved to be a good setting in combination with a relatively small MB one (around 2 or 5). If the TB threshold is increased too much then the speed boosts will be delivered too late for some benchmarks and probably for short-lived applications as well. Of course, the TB maximum trace length and the MB minimum instruction count for consideration also play a role in avoiding attempts to compile a method that has already have most of its instructions or opcodes translated by the TB JIT. However, we depend on the above formulation for the case in which a method is worth being compiled completely even if it contains a loop that might trigger the TB beforehand.

A compiled trace is also called earlier because the process of building the trace itself and then compiling it takes two passes over a $length_{Trace} = |Trace|$ instructions long trace. Our previous derivations imply that $length_{Method} = |Method| \geq length_{Trace}$. For most cases, at the very least in our tests, this is enough time for the trace to be ready the

next time $thresh_T$ is reached. The compilation of a method also takes two passes over the instruction sequence but we devised a simple optimization (described in section 4.3) so that we can avoid having to wait for the threshold to be met again until the native version of the method is put in place.

When the compiler thread is faced with a method compilation work order it has to determine whether a compiled version of it will help increase performance or not. First of all, the method should contain no instructions that will indicate a need to jump from native to interpreted environment. In the case of DEX instructions, invocations of non-inlineable methods would end up being compiled to a call to the interpreter to execute the method. Instructions requiring access to fields in order to retrieve or save values can be provided because the JIT sends a reference to the method's owner, be it an Object or a Class, and therefore do not have to be banned. Second, the method instruction count should amount or surpass a threshold set to avoid small methods, that usually only set, get or return a value, from being compiled. The described types of methods would only result in native code islands and would probably only increase the amount of environment jumps between interpreted and native code and would not be benefited from MB JIT compilation, they should instead be inlined.

3.3 Trace-Based vs. Method-Based JIT

Android's TB JIT for the Dalvik Virtual Machine focuses on the hot parts of a method's code and compiles them into native code that is linked to the first instruction from the original trace. Methods with loops and other flow control constructs that cause instructions to be executed repeatedly, will trigger this behavior and cause a trace compilation work order to be emitted. However, if an invocation to a method is included in a hot trace or if a method is being invoked too often, it is probably better to compile all of the method into native code instead of calling an interpreted method and then shift to native code once inside the method and possibly back into interpreted code (if the trace does not extend until the end of the method) before returning. The situation looks even more complicated when a trace containing a method invocation is compiled and the method's code includes a compiled trace of its own. Consequently, we decided that a trace compilation work order including an invocation instruction should also trigger a method compilation order so as to avoid unnecessary environment jumps.

Most literature indicates that loops can be exploited so that observed variable types are used for further optimized code generation [10]. Short traces that are executed for a long period of time over and over again constitute the perfect target for Dalvik's standard JIT. The difference with most dynamic programming languages that are sped up by TB JIT compilers and DEX code is that, although being indeed a type-less registered based intermediate representation, most DEX code opcodes reveal hints as to what the registers' types could be. Translating the registers to LLVM bitcode, which has to indicate variables' types explicitly, is hard but not impossible if we handle registers as 32 or 64 bit integers when only their type size is known. When a later executed instruction reveals the real type of a register it can be casted using the `bitcast` instruction [22]. When we are done with the translation, we are left with an SSA representation of the method, with information regarding all of the variables' types and many options for optimizations.

4. THE METHOD-BASED COMPILER

We based our JIT compiler on LLVM, translating Dalvik's DEX code into LLVM bitcode to be able to use its method-based JIT. LLVM provides libraries and APIs for the translation of any source language into bitcode IR, LLVM's lingua franca, and manipulate the resulting bitcode in many forms.

4.1 DEX code to LLVM bitcode

The Dalvik VM is a register based Virtual Machine. Registers have no type and can be assigned many times through the execution of any given method. LLVM bitcode, on the other hand, has to comply with SSA form and has to load and store values to and from memory if the same variable is to be assigned more than once. Every method compile work order is handled by translating every DEX instruction in the original method to a sequence of IR instructions equivalent to it. The translation is dealt with in two passes: *1)* search for backward branching targets and opcode filtering; and *2)* code translation.

The first pass deals with labeling of backward branch targets and making sure that the method contains no banned opcodes (examples of undesired opcodes for MB JIT compilation are mentioned in section 3.2). The first pass also makes sure the amount of instructions that will be translated exceeds the instruction count threshold for the method to actually benefit from being JIT compiled. Finally, if the method contains only desired instructions then the second pass will translate all DEX instructions into LLVM IR, validate and compile it to memory.

4.1.1 Typing the Typeless

Although Java is a statically typed language, Google's dx tool [12] translates Java bytecode into a typeless register based represensation, DEX code. This presents a problem when translating into LLVM bitcode because all operations on LLVM bitcode have to be executed on operands with strictly the same type. Most DEX opcodes present hints as to what type of data a register holds, but sometimes it is necessary to infer the data from assignment operations or such. To overcome this problem and to avoid having many versions of the same register name, we translate every DEX register into variables representing the register name and their type, i.e. `v5_INTEGER`, and since the variables, in most cases, are references to memory in order to preserve the SSA constraint, any register could represent a number of different variables in its LLVM bitcode translation and have many memory addresses related to it.

4.2 LLVM Advantages

LLVM provides an API to run several transformations through code represented using its bitcode. Once the translation from DEX code to bitcode is done, we can optimize the resulting code using these transformations and optimization passes to get different levels of optimized code. LLVM also provides many ways of running the code. One of them, conveniently for us, is a JIT compiler that returns the address of the memory location of the compiled method. Aside from the obvious reason of convenience, we chose LLVM to build our compiler because of Google's own decision to include it into Android with the Renderscript [34] execution engine. Although our compiler uses the mainstream execution engine to create the JIT compiled code, it can be slimmed down to have a smaller footprint on the operat-

ODEX Instruction	Original Instruction
`iget-quick offset`	`iget id`
`iput-quick offset`	`iput id`
`invoke-virtual-quick offset`	`invoke-virtual id`
`invoke-super-quick offset`	`invoke-super id`

Table 1: Optimized opcodes

ing system, just like libbcc (Renderscript's execution engine) was. The other option would be to modify libbcc to allow for it to compile methods for Dalvik. The latter would not be too hard a modification to our work since our translation to bitcode would only have to call a different library for the last phase, native code emission. The benefits of using libbcc include caching of compiled code (faster applications without having to recompile methods) and the use of a common LLVM execution engine throughout Andoid, which roughly translates to less space on disk.

In our experiments, code compiled using LLVM's JIT compiler performs better than code compiled by Dalvik's TB JIT compiler in part because of it's use of ARM's floating point architecture VFP [24]. The standard version of Google's Dalvik VM and its JIT compiler don't use vfp instructions by default and require device manufacturers to modify Android to have the JIT compiler emit different specialized instructions specific for their platforms. LLVM takes care of generating specialized code depending on the platform it was set up for.

4.3 Optimizations

4.3.1 Quick Field Access

Usually native code called from Java has to go through the Java Native Interface in order to have access to fields inside objects or classes even if the address to the container has been passed as an argument to the method. We avoid the situation in which we have to call back into the interpreted environment at all costs, so instead we take advantage of Dalvik's optimized instructions, which have the offset of every field to speed up the retrieval of them. Just as the interpreter uses the optimized opcodes to get fields by adding the base address with the offset of any field, we use LLVM's API to manage pointers to addresses and are able to load fields in constant time. Examples of instructions that are optimized by `dexopt` [33] are shown in table 1.

4.3.2 Installing the Compiled Method

Dalvik's JIT delegates the job of linking the compiled code to the interpreted trace to the main execution thread. After the execution count for an instruction exceeds the *thresh$_T$* then the translation cache is checked to verify that a native translation of the trace exists. It is then called instead of the interpreter continuing normally. In our case we are changing a whole method from interpreted to native, the easiest way is to change the method's attributes to tell the interpreter that it requires a call to native code and allow for a Java Native Interface (JNI) call. However, changing the method's attributes would allow for bugs during the execution if there are more than one thread trying to call the method (i.e. one thread calls the native method but the address has not yet been updated) so we modified the `Method`

45

structure inside Dalvik to be able to have additional information and additional checks so that no bugs are introduced. This also allows for faster calls to native code, avoiding some checks and parameter conversion routines that JNI does before calling native code. The result is that our native code pinning process is quicker than how the TB JIT does it and allows for additional information to be available to the native code, compared to what would normally be for a JNI compliant native method, while making sure that regular security checks are still applied to external native code being called by the Java Native Interface (effectively giving special treatment to internal native code).

4.3.3 Invocation to System Libraries

Finally, our choice of LLVM as our MB JIT compiler framework has the advantage that it seamlessly links external function calls to the standard library (i.e. sine or cosine) without any additional library having to be added, resulting in less memory wasted. This allows for static invocations into standard Java libraries to be translated to static native calls. DEX code tries to cope with this by using an opcode (`execute-inline`) to inline common static system routine calls, so we translate both static invocations and inlined invocations to the `java\lang\*` library into external method calls that LLVM deals with.

5. RESULTS

The following tests, mentioned in this section, were ran on a Galaxy Nexus [14] phone running our modified image of Google's latest version of the Android - Ice Cream Sandwich operating system [13]. This platform has a 1.2 GHz TI OMAP 4460 ARM Cortex-A9 dual-core processor and a 304 MHz PowerVR SGX540 (Underclocked from 384MHz) GPU, as wel as 1 GB of memory. Note that the platform does have hardware-based floating point operation support (ARM's Floating Point Architecture - VFP [24]).

5.1 CaffeineMark 3.0 Benchmark

To test our own implemented MB JIT compiler and to provide information we could use to compare it to the TB JIT and existing ahead-of-time compilers for Java, we targeted two of the most commonly used benchmarks for Java virtual machines. The calculation of the number π (pi) up to a specific number of digits and a series of mathematical tests whose execution is counted versus a given amount of time are the main tasks carried out by the BenchmarkPi and CaffeineMark 3.0 Android applications. Both have been used by Google to test their JIT compiler and by Wang et al. [35] to prove the potential of a MB AOTC. The mathematical tests executed by the CaffeineMark benchmark include the Sieve of Erathosthenes, the execution of many code branches, loops and floating point calculations.

Our tests suggest that methods compiled using our MB JIT compiler can be almost twice as fast as methods that have only been optimized by Dalvik's standard JIT. Figure 3 shows how the Sieve, Loop, Float and Logic tests from the CaffeineBenchmark3.0 are faster when ran on our proposed hybrid JIT. Float, Loop and Logic tests being the ones that enjoy the most benefits from being compiled using the MB JIT. The figure also shows that the MB JIT by itself appears to be better then the proposed hybrid JIT framework (Loop and Logic tests). This is due to the fact that the TB and MB JIT compilers by themselves create less compile orders and

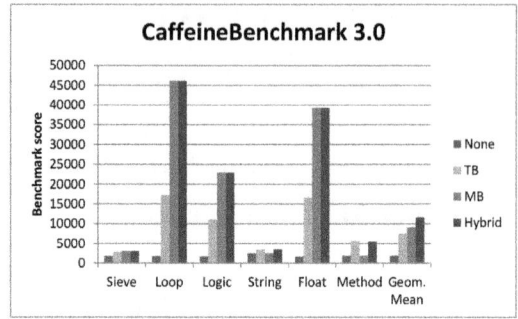

Figure 3: CaffeineMark 3.0 benchmark results (the higher the better)

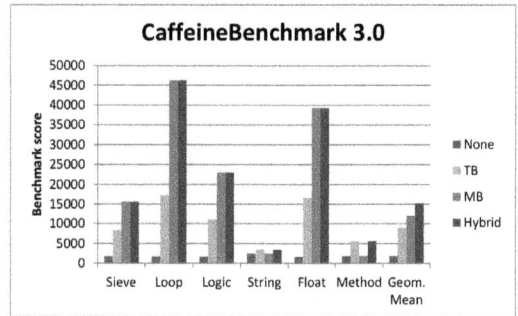

Figure 4: CaffeineMark 3.0, second run

so the native versions of the traces or methods are delivered and consequently used earlier, resulting in the native code providing earlier perceivable performance gain. However, the proposed hybrid JIT, because of our profiling choices, delivers performance gain almost as good or sometimes even better than that of the TB JIT on initial runs and much better on following ones.

Since our modifications to Dalvik's profiling system create an extra flow of work into the compiler thread, it is to be expected that some of the compilation orders are not attended at the very start. The profiler settings can be tuned to allow for compile orders to be dispatched earlier but this would rather be a problem if the compiler thread becomes overwhelmed and neither type of JIT would deliver on time. This behavior is not unique to our proposed hybrid JIT, Android's standard TB JIT also exhibits better performance results during the second run (especially for the first tests that were run by the benchmark, i.e. Sieve). Figure 4 shows how some of the tests in the CaffeineMark3.0 benchmark are much quicker during a second execution of the application since the compiler thread has dealt with all the compile orders in queue. Code as much as twice as fast as the one delivered by the TB JIT is observed for the Sieve test and, although not as easily visualized on the graph, for the Logic test after executing it more than once.

In both figure 3 and figure 4 it is also evident that the Method and String tests were rejected by one of the MB JIT profiling phases. Their score is almost as good as the one corresponding to the TB and the virtual machine with no JIT compiler (the first compared to the hybrid JIT and the latter compared with the MB JIT alone). Although the MB compilation of these tests has been rejected, the additional

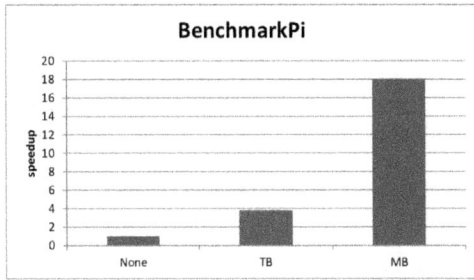

Figure 5: Pi Benchmark results

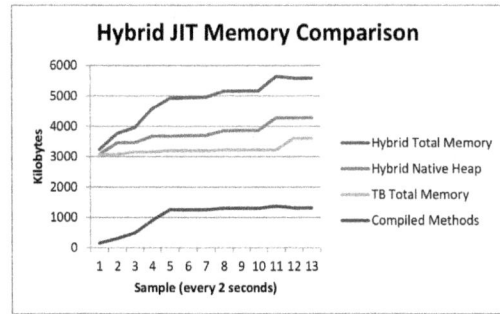

Figure 6: Hybrid versus trace-based JIT memory overhead (Hybrid Total Memory is the sum of its Native Heap and Compiled Methods)

lag introduced by our proposed profiling techniques is almost non-existent, even though the first run of this application generates many compile orders (both traces and methods) for the compiler thread to handle all at once. Although we do not expect our present profiling tuning to be perfect for all situations, we observe that there at least exists such a configuration for applications behaving similar to the ones we tested.

5.2 BenchmarkPi

Another well-known benchmark used by Google to benchmark their JIT is the BenchmarkPi [31]. The benchmarks computes the number π up to a specific amount of digits and times the computation. Our results show that performance improvement achieved by our hybrid JIT framework can obtain similar results to those of an Ahead-Of-Time-Compiler such as Wang et al.'s Icing [35]. Figure 5 shows how fast the benchmark can be ran once both TB and MB JIT compilers have done their work compared to having only a TB JIT. Our results show that a MB JIT outperforms Android's TB JIT by almost a factor of 4 in such computation-intensive applications. MB JIT compilers are expected to outperform simple TB JIT compilers on such computations but the huge difference in performance is mainly due to LLVM's advantages previously mentioned in section 4.2.

5.3 Memory Overhead

Our proposed hybrid JIT compiler framework transforms complete methods into a faster native version, but in doing so requires more memory than a TB JIT compiler which would only translate a subset of the method's instructions. This compilation of both hot code and cold code in methods is also the reason why compiling methods takes longer than compiling traces, which consist only of the hot code. The memory overhead in which we incur by compiling whole methods is proportional to the amount of instructions each compiled method contains. Figure 6 shows both the TB JIT and hybrid JIT compilers and their memory usage behavior throughout one of our tests. The memory usage of the hybrid JIT is made up of its native heap and compiled methods, both shown on the graph. As is expected, compiling methods is costly and therefore has to be done smartly and sparingly. This reaffirms the importance of our framework's profiler having to be tuned in order to provide good performance without having to exhaust the system's resources. It also confirms that the decision to keep the default TB JIT compiler as the base JIT compiler for a hybrid framework is the best idea for a resource constrained device.

6. RELATED WORK

During Google I/O 2010 [6], Google announced that the TB JIT they now provide for Android was only the initial step towards improving their application platform. The compiler's code reveals hints that plans for extensions towards making the trace analysis include complete methods have been considered, and the outline for a basic MB compiler is also laid out but not fully implemented. Their proposed MB compiler scheme includes an SSA transformation stage, register allocation as well as translation phases to two intermediate representations before generating native instructions (all of which LLVM provides to our proposed framework without the need for more than one intermediate representation). Google also fathomed the idea of both JIT types coexisting in Android but there have been no further comments or developments on this project.

Other authors have tried to compare mature MB compilers with their own TB JIT compilers [18] but haven't done so in a resource constrained environment. Nor have they measured a limited TB JIT's capabilities versus a MB JIT. The cooperation between a limited TB compiler, like the one provided by Google for the DVM, and our proposed MB JIT delivers a speed boost quickly after starting an application and replaces slow, hot methods with fast and optimized native ones after they have been invoked a few times. It does so without having to compile all the DEX code and whithout replacing Android's TB JIT as the base JIT compiler because it is more mature in the Android operating system. It is also worth mentioning that the work by Inoue et al. [18] does talk about a TB compiler and its advantages over a regular MB one but refers to a compiler that has the ability to analyze traces that span more than one method and therefore is not comparable to our study.

6.1 Disassemblers

There are many tools available for the disassembly of DEX code or complete Android packaged applications into text files containing DEX source code. Most of them read the dex file format and obtain all the strings from the constant pool and the opcodes for each instruction in order to construct a stream of human readable dex code. Smali and Baksmali [19] as well as Android's DexDump [12] tool are some of the most popular. Baksmali can even be used to reconstruct an application from modified DEX source files. However, all of these tools go through an unnecessary step by transforming DEX opcodes into readable text, which our compiler does not need, and therefore are not suited for a fast DEX IR to LLVM IR transformation like the one we implemented.

DEX disassembler programs are able to output human readable code after parsing DEX code. Disassembler applications are similar to our DEX to LLVM IR translator because they also decode DEX code and transform it into another format, plain text. Understanding of the DEX code format is necessary to be able to read the instructions correctly from the DEX file, be able to group them using a common format and finally translate them (a similar process is used by the DexDump tool).

6.2 Method-Based Compilers

The Icing Ahead-Of-Time-Compiler [35] provides a fairly good attempt at profiling the Dalvik VM's behavior and determining which methods are better off being completely native instead of just having traces compiled. Our profiling model is based on parts of their work, such as the avoidance of excessive environment jumping and attempting to access object fields directly from object pointers. However, the impasses prompted by the use of the Java Native Interface are no longer present in a run time compiler and cooperation with the TB JIT compiler makes it possible for easier method inlining and a more accurate decision on which methods can be considered hot.

6.2.1 Zero and Shark

Zero and Shark [5] are an implementation of a Java Virtual Machine using zero architecture dependent code. The project aimed at delivering a more portable version of the Virtual Machine that could be used by Linux on other architectures besides x86. This zero-machine code OpenJDK port is profiled by a MB JIT that works on top of the LLVM framework. Shark, the JIT compiler, has dealt with all the issues involved with plugging a JIT into a Java VM. Most issues include dealing with the Garbage Collector and the way references are deemed unused. Our work takes some ideas from their implementation, but the Dalvik VM internals differ a lot from regular Java virtual machines, and so most of their insights are not of much use for the Android application platform.

6.3 Combined JIT Frameworks

Most attempts at combining both trace and MB JIT compilers have been on the field of JavaScript engines. During the past few years most web browser companies have developed a fairly good combination of a quick MB JIT compiler to avoid having to interpret, sometimes at all, and a slower TB compiler that applies aggressive optimizations and is supported by run time information to replace initially compiled code with several versions of heavily optimized traces. Our approach is quite different since we propose the MB JIT compiler to be the one with heavy optimization settings and leave early speed boosts up to Android's TB JIT compiler, the latter providing a few optimization considerations but not as complete as static compilers and others have to offer.

The work by Lee et al. [23] provides good insight regarding whether JavaScript engines should put so much effort into compiling all the script to avoid interpretation. Benchmark software exhibit many opportunities for hot traces to be compiled into extremely efficient native code but real web pages' JavaScript code does not necessarily contain so many

instructions being called again and again. Their work concludes that a good interpreter matched with a JIT compiler that is used only when the situation really calls for it, is often better than trying to compile everything. Google has already adopted this idea with their quick interpreter being optimized only when necessary by their TB JIT. Additionally, our hybrid framework builds on top of the same idea by compiling methods only when certain conditions are met.

6.3.1 Chrome's V8

Google's JavaScript execution engine V8 [15] translates most of the script into native code as soon as it is downloaded. The JavaScript is translated using a MB compiler initially. It then uses a TB JIT to optimize the code being executed so that loops, and run time observed types can be used to compile faster versions of portions of the code.

6.3.2 JaegerMonkey

Firefox's mature JavaScript execution engine, SpiderMonkey, has been upgraded to TraceMonkey and more recently to JaegerMonkey [26] to allow the code to enjoy an initial quick boost from the MB JIT. The TB JIT then applies late improvements to hot loops and other traces with additional run time information.

7. CONCLUSIONS

First and most importantly, this work proves that a limited TB JIT compiler is still no match for a robust MB JIT such as the one provided by the LLVM compiler framework. More specifically, most advantages one could achieve by favoring the implementation of a TB JIT over a MB one are minimized by the properties of DEX code, which can be "lazily" transformed back into a typed representation. Although type specialization and various versions of optimized code might not be good optimization approaches for DEX code, it turns out that the TB JIT works really well for considerably long loops, especially if the trace does not invoke other methods. Other DEX code properties might later be studied to reveal further optimization opportunities available to either JIT compiler type.

7.1 JIT Type Comparison

Dalvik's TB JIT compiler achieves performance boost quickly by compiling instruction sequences that are being called too often, hot traces. When possible, it inlines small methods being invoked by the instructions contained in the trace. In contrast, the MB JIT compiler we designed is capable of compiling most methods, as long as they pass the profiling steps. The compiler is able to apply optimizations regarding the "liveness" of variables and other optimization techniques that are only possible because the whole method is being taken into consideration. Further transformations similar, if not the same as, GCC's O3 and O2 battery of optimizations [8], are also available to our MB JIT compiler through LLVM's clang [3] and jello [21] projects. Although our MB JIT does incur on more memory usage than a basic TB JIT, and the average compilation time for a method might be up to one-hundred (100) times that of a small trace, when hot methods are chosen correctly (and this can be fine-tuned depending on the platform system), performance can be greatly improved.

7.2 JIT Behavior

From our tests we have also come to the conclusion that both TB and MB JIT compilers become idle after an application has been executing for some time. A benchmark is a good example of this situation, when the same methods are ran several times and not much changes between runs. We believe this idle time can be used for further aggressive optimizations and even some unsound optimizations, as categorized by Guo and Palsberg [16], could be attempted in order to increase the execution speed of the program under the current observed state as long as a side-exit [10] is made available. The previously described behavior could be proposed for devices that are currently connected to a fixed power source, and therefore in a state where further resource usage can be afforded without compromising the battery's life. Google had proposed the introduction of a dynamically adjustable profiling approach [6], but right now Dalvik's JIT's behavior does not adapt much to the hardware's state.

7.3 Relevance

Our proposed hybrid JIT compiler takes ideas from what current web browsers are trying to do to speed up the interpretation of a scripted language. Java and .NET technologies, however, do not output a script but instead transform code into an intermediate representation, which could be stack or register based and that is easily transformed into machine code by the respective implementations of their virtual machines for all the architectures they support. Each intermediate representation has been conceived with specific features that may allow a TB or MB JIT to compile it easily into native code. As we have proven in our work, hybrid JIT compilers can be easily tuned depending on how fast performance gain is needed and code behavior. Although our test platform is a resource constrained device running an Android operating system, different systems run programming languages that are stored as intermediate representations and so these systems could possibly benefit from the inclusion of a similar tool.

8. PROJECT STATUS AND FUTURE WORK

8.1 Tool Status

Many methods have been successfully compiled using our MB JIT but not all methods can be successfully emitted into memory as native instructions by LLVM's current JIT. All previous phases (namely translation, transformations and optimizations) are completed correctly and promptly but the JIT's support for ARM is limited and probably buggy or broken in some parts. To overcome this problem with some methods the profiler indicated had to be processed by the MB JIT, we were forced to execute the last step (compiling from assembler to native code) manually using LLVM's static compiler. The LLVM team is currently working on a new version of the compiler, MCJIT [2], and will deprecate the current JIT framework.

Our framework also supports memory petitions to the Dalvik VM from MB JIT compiled code, and therefore requires that we handle garbage collection in an efficient manner. We currently yield to the garbage collection thread every time we have a request for virtual machine managed memory. This is necessary because the Dalvik VM does not pause threads running on native mode to allow garbage collection. If we did not yield at this moment an interpreted heap memory request might be denied because of yet uncollected garbage, even if there is unused memory. This technique, however, is an overly simplistic solution. Since the benchmarks used to measure the performance of our framework did not result on compilation of memory requests, further testing of our approach to manage native and the virtual machine's memory has to take place before being able to conclude anything relevant on the matter.

8.2 Future Work

There are many other benchmark applications available in Android's application market that can be tested to get more conclusive results on how TB and MB JIT compilers behave. There are even different versions of the CaffeineBenchmark which include image, graphics and other tests which are not included in the version used for our experiments [7]. Moreover, the effect of using our hybrid JIT approach on real applications, apart from benchmarks, is still unknown. In order for further tests to be conducted more DEX opcodes have to be translated into LLVM bitcode.

Although the cooperation between both types of JIT compiler has been shown to improve performance and each one has covered many of the other's weaknesses, these compilers are far from finished. Google's TB JIT for the Dalvik VM still lacks support for traces spanning through more than one method. The implementation of this feature would mean that the profiling model proposed in section 3.2 would have to be reevaluated. The TB JIT could also be extended to profile MB JIT compiled code and attach optimized versions of hot traces inside hot methods as was proposed by Bala et al. [4]. This extension to the TB JIT could work on top of a native version of the method as well as its original DEX code. In this case the TB JIT would also be able to inline native code invocations, like those done through the Java Native Interface, which previous work on the Dynamo project [4] indicate would increase performance.

Another possibility for future comparisons would be splitting the compiler thread into a MB JIT thread and a TB JIT thread. This would probably result in optimized compiled methods being delivered earlier but would definitely make it more difficult to avoid the problem of compiling a trace only to later compile the whole method. Finally, we propose testing different methods of communication between the interpreted and native parts of the code. Google has already designed Renderscript [34] with a parallel thread in charge of the execution of the compiled script and Asghar et al. also describe an alternative way, A-JUMP [1] for parallel applications using multiple programming languages. Such techniques could reduce the amount of time wasted in environment jumps and would allow both environments to communicate more often without having to avoid it for performance's sake [20].

9. REFERENCES

[1] S. Asghar, M. Hafeez, U. A. Malik, A. ur Rehman, and N. Riaz. A-jump, architecture for java universal message passing. In *Proceedings of the 8th International Conference on Frontiers of Information Technology*, FIT '10, pages 34:1–34:6, New York, NY, USA, 2010. ACM.

[2] C. S. D. at the University of Illinois at Urbana-Champaign. The llvm target-independent code generator. `http://llvm.org/docs/CodeGenerator.html#mc`, 16 January, 2012.

[3] C. S. D. at the University of Illinois at Urbana-Champaign. clang: a c language family frontend for llvm. `http://clang.llvm.org/`, 2012.

[4] V. Bala, E. Duesterwald, and S. Banerjia. Dynamo: a transparent dynamic optimization system. *SIGPLAN Not.*, 35(5):1–12, May 2000.

[5] G. Benson. Zero and shark: a zero-assembly port of openjdk. `http://today.java.net/pub/a/today/2009/05/21/zero-and-shark-openjdk-port.html`, 2009.

[6] B. Cheng and B. Buzbee. A jit compiler for android's dalvik vm. `http://dl.google.com/googleio/2010/android-jit-compiler-androids-dalvik-vm.pdf`, 2010.

[7] P. S. Corporation. Caffeinemark 3.0 benchmark. `http://www.benchmarkhq.ru/cm30/`, 1997.

[8] I. Free Software Foundation. Gcc, the gnu c compiler. `http://gcc.gnu.org/`, 05 March, 2012.

[9] I. Free Software Foundation. Gcj - the gnu compiler for the java programming. `http://gcc.gnu.org/java/`, 2012.

[10] A. Gal, B. Eich, M. Shaver, D. Anderson, D. Mandelin, M. R. Haghighat, B. Kaplan, G. Hoare, B. Zbarsky, J. Orendorff, J. Ruderman, E. W. Smith, R. Reitmaier, M. Bebenita, M. Chang, and M. Franz. Trace-based just-in-time type specialization for dynamic languages. *SIGPLAN Not.*, 44:465–478, June 2009.

[11] N. Geoffray, G. Thomas, C. Clément, and B. Folliot. A lazy developer approach: building a jvm with third party software. In *Proceedings of the 6th international symposium on Principles and practice of programming in Java*, PPPJ '08, pages 73–82, New York, NY, USA, 2008. ACM.

[12] Google. Android developer tools. `http://developer.android.com/guide/developing/tools/index.html`, 2007.

[13] Google. Google android - an open handset alliance project. `http://code.google.com/android/`, 2008.

[14] Google. Galaxy nexus. `http://www.google.com/nexus/`, 2011.

[15] Google. V8 javascript engine. `http://code.google.com/p/v8/`, 2011.

[16] S.-y. Guo and J. Palsberg. The essence of compiling with traces. *SIGPLAN Not.*, 46(1):563–574, Jan. 2011.

[17] T. IEEE and T. O. Group. Posix.1-2008: The open group base specifications issue 7. `http://pubs.opengroup.org/onlinepubs/9699919799/`, 2001 - 2008.

[18] H. Inoue, H. Hayashizaki, P. Wu, and T. Nakatani. A trace-based java jit compiler retrofitted from a method-based compiler. In *Code Generation and Optimization (CGO), 2011 9th Annual IEEE/ACM International Symposium on*, pages 246 –256, april 2011.

[19] JesusFreke. smali/baksmali: An assembler for android's dex format. `http://code.google.com/p/smali/`, 2009.

[20] D. Kurzyniec and V. Sunderam. Efficient cooperation between java and native codes âĂŞ jni performance benchmark. In *In The 2001 International Conference on Parallel and Distributed Processing Techniques and Applications*, 2001.

[21] C. Lattner, M. Brukman, and B. Gaeke. Jello: a retargetable just-in-time compiler for llvm bytecode, 2002.

[22] C. A. Lattner. Llvm: An infrastructure for multi-stage optimization. Technical report, 2002.

[23] S.-W. Lee and S.-M. Moon. Selective just-in-time compilation for client-side mobile javascript engine. In *Proceedings of the 14th international conference on Compilers, architectures and synthesis for embedded systems*, CASES '11, pages 5–14, New York, NY, USA, 2011. ACM.

[24] A. Ltd. Arm: Floating point architecture. `http://www.arm.com/products/processors/technologies/vector-floating-point.php`, 2012.

[25] J. McCarthy. Recursive functions of symbolic expressions and their computation by machine, part i. *Commun. ACM*, 3(4):184–195, Apr. 1960.

[26] Mozilla. Jaegermonkey. `https://wiki.mozilla.org/JaegerMonkey`, 2010.

[27] S. Oaks and H. Wong. *Java Threads*. O'Reilly Media, Inc., 2004.

[28] Oracle. Java se specifications. `http://docs.oracle.com/javase/specs/`, 2012.

[29] Oracle. Openjdk's hotspot vm. `http://openjdk.java.net/groups/hotspot/`, 2012.

[30] Oracle. Oracle. `http://www.java.com/en/about/`, 2012.

[31] V. K. Polychronis. Benchmarkpi - android benchmarking tool. `http://androidbenchmark.com/`, 2009.

[32] T. A. Proebsting, G. Townsend, P. Bridges, J. H. Hartman, T. Newsham, and S. A. Watterson. Toba: Java for applications - a way ahead of time (wat) compiler. In *In Proceedings of the 3rd Conference on Object-Oriented Technologies and Systems*, pages 41–53, 1997.

[33] T. A. O. S. Project. Dalvik optimization and verification with dexopt. `http://www.netmite.com/android/mydroid/dalvik/docs/dexopt.html`, 2008.

[34] G. Tim Bray. Renderscript. `http://android-developers.blogspot.com/2011/02/introducing-renderscript.html`, 09 February, 2011.

[35] C.-S. Wang, G. Perez, Y.-C. Chung, W.-C. Hsu, W.-K. Shih, and H.-R. Hsu. A method-based ahead-of-time compiler for android applications. In *Proceedings of the 14th international conference on Compilers, architectures and synthesis for embedded systems*, CASES '11, pages 15–24, New York, NY, USA, 2011. ACM.

LLBT: An LLVM-based Static Binary Translator

Bor-Yeh Shen
National Chiao Tung University
Hsinchu, Taiwan, R.O.C.
byshen@cs.nctu.edu.tw

Jiunn-Yeu Chen
National Chiao Tung University
Hsinchu, Taiwan, R.O.C.
jiunnyeu@cs.nctu.edu.tw

Wei-Chung Hsu
National Chiao Tung University
Hsinchu, Taiwan, R.O.C.
hsu@cs.nctu.edu.tw

Wuu Yang
National Chiao Tung University
Hsinchu, Taiwan, R.O.C.
wuuyang@cs.nctu.edu.tw

ABSTRACT

Lack of applications has always been a serious concern for designing machines with a new but incompatible ISA. To address this concern, binary translation is one common technique to migrate applications from one legacy ISA to new ones. In the past, dynamic binary translation (DBT) has been more widely adopted for migrating applications since it avoids some challenging problems for binary translation such as code discovery for variable length ISA and code location issues for handling indirect branches. Static binary translation (SBT) is usually regarded as a less general solution and has not been actively researched on. However, SBT has advantages of performing more aggressive optimizations, which could yield more compact code and greater code quality. In general, SBT translated applications are likely to consume less memory, processor cycles and power, and can be started more quickly. All the above advantages are more critical for embedded systems than for general systems. Therefore, we believe that even though SBT is not as general as DBT, it has a unique role to play for migrating applications in embedded systems.

In this paper, we designed and implemented a new portable SBT tool, called LLBT, which translates source binary into LLVM IR and then retargets the LLVM IR to various ISAs by using the LLVM compiler infrastructure. Using the LLVM compiler infrastructure, LLBT successfully leverages two important functionalities from LLVM: the comprehensive optimizations and the retargetability. For example, most DBTs map guest architecture states into the host registers to minimize accessing guest architecture states with memory operations, but must deal with guest architecture state saving/reloading at trace/block entry/exit points. LLBT can treat the complete application binary as a single function and uses the global register allocation optimization in LLVM to consistently map guest architecture states in host registers so as to avoid the costly state saving and reloading at trace/block exits.

In this paper, we have shown our ARM-based LLBT can effectively migrate EEMBC benchmark Suite from ARMv5 to Intel IA32, Intel x64, MIPS, and other ARMs such as ARMv7. On the Intel i7 based host systems, the LLBT generated code can run 3 to 64 times faster than emulating with QEMU, which uses the DBT technique.

Categories and Subject Descriptors

D.3.4 [**Programming Languages**]: Processors—*Code generation, Optimization, Retargetable compilers*

General Terms

Design, Languages, Performance

Keywords

Static binary translation, compiler, retargeting, intermediate representation

1. INTRODUCTION

Binary Translation (BT) techniques have been actively studied and developed for the past two decades [19, 3]. They have been widely adopted in many different areas such as fast simulation, software security enforcement, application profiling [16], and system virtual machine implementations [20], and have become a standard approach for migrating application binaries directly from one ISA to another. For example, Apple developed Rosetta [4], which dynamically translates PowerPC programs into Intel X86 binaries, Hewlett-Packard developed Aries [22], which dynamically translates PA-RISC executables to IA-64 architecture, and DEC developed FX!32 [7] to make X86 Win32 applications runnable on Windows NT/Alpha platforms.

ARM pretty much dominates the embedded-system market, especially in smartphones and tablets. In order to share the fast growing market, many system vendors have ported popular embedded operating systems onto their own ISA based processors such as MIPS and Intel Atom. However, they may not have the large number of popular applications ready to run on their processors as ARM does. Consider the Android, for example, it has become the worldwide best selling OS in the smart phone market in just a few years. And with the release of the Honeycomb and Ice Cream Sandwich, it is further positioned to take control of the tablet market in 2012. For simplicity of deployment, Google has been targeting ARM based systems for the Android market.

Although this may be Google's strategy to quickly get into the smart phone and tablet market, it has created some issues with expanding support to other ISA (Instruction Set Architecture)s. One of the main concerns for system vendors is that many popular application codes on Android are ARM-dependent. The above statement may seem odd since the majority of these applications should be based on Java, and therefore supposed to be ISA independent. However, for performance reasons or for easy-porting reasons, many applications on Google Play do contain native libraries in ARM code in their .APK package. The dependence on such native library codes makes some of the popular applications not available for system vendors using ISA different from ARM. Without removing such dependencies associated with ARM natively compiled applications, system vendors with different ISAs are at a disadvantage when competing with ARM-based systems.

One way to get away from such ISA dependences is to migrate such native code components to new ISAs using BT techniques. Software-based binary translation systems can be roughly classified in two categories: static binary translation (SBT) and dynamic binary translation (DBT) [11, 2]. On desktops or workstations, most application binary migrations are based on DBT systems because both the code discovery and the code location problems [20] can be easily handled. However, DBT has its own limitations, such as the overhead of runtime translation, the lack of optimizations for translated binaries, and the increased memory usage. Although such shortcomings may not be a serious issue for general purpose computing environments, they are unacceptable for embedded computing where the application start-up time, the power consumption, and memory footprint are primary concerns

On the other hand, SBT must deal with the code discovery, the code location and the Self-Modifying Code (SMC) issues effectively before being considered for a real solution. The code discovery problem refers to the difficulty to precisely decode the source binary since data and instructions may be mixed in some sections of the elf object file. With variable length instruction ISA, such as x86, once a section of data is decoded as instructions, the decoder lost track of the address of each valid instruction and therefore, the translated code can be totally wrong and lead to incorrect execution. For fixed instruction size ISA, this is less an issue, since even if data are mis-interpreted as instructions, all instruction boundaries will still be clearly identified and correctly translated. Although some data sections are translated into bogus code, they will not get executed at runtime anyway. The code location problem refers to the handling of indirect jumps where the jump target address must be mapped to the address in the translated code. Both the code discovery and code locations problems can be less complex when dealing with fixed-length instructions, or variable length instructions with very limited lengths, such as only 16 bits (short) and 32 bits (long). RISC processors, such as ARM, are usually based on fixed length instructions. Although ARM/Thumb-1 and Thumb-2 are also variable length ISA, but they support only two sizes: 16 bits and 32 bits, so it is easier to handle than the completely variable length ISA, such as x86. In this paper, we have effectively solved the issues for handling the short/long mixed instruction issue for ARM/Thumb-1. Another well-known limitation of SBT is its inability to handle self-modifying code (SMC). How-

ever, SMC is not common on embedded applications. We have analyzed over ten thousand applications downloaded from online software stores, and failed to find any application that contains SMC. Therefore, we believe that the well-cited problems for SBT do not really affect its usability to binary migration in embedded systems.

In application binary migration, DBT is often regarded as more transparent since the translation step is hidden by the runtime system. However, this issue may not be applicable to the embedded system world. First, most of embedded applications are pre-installed by system vendors. For mobile devices, such as smartphones and tablets, third-party applications are usually downloaded from online software stores (such as Apple's App Store or Google Play). These applications can be translated either on the server side according to the client's architecture before downloading or on the client side during installation. Therefore, the translation step can also be hidden from users.

In this paper, we present an LLVM-based static binary translator, LLBT, which leverages the LLVM infrastructure and translates ARM-based binaries to many different ISAs supported by LLVM, such as ARM, X86-32, X86-64, and MIPS. Compared to QEMU [6], which adopts a retargetable dynamic binary translation approach, code generated by LLBT can run 3 to 64 times faster on the EEMBC benchmark suite. In summary, this work makes the following contributions:

- We are the first to build a robust retargetable static binary translator that can be reliably used in comparing the performance of static and dynamic binary translation approaches for embedded environments. The results show that LLBT generated code yields significantly higher performance and uses less memory than a retargetable dynamic binary translation approach.

- LLBT effectively solves the code location problem. It does not need an interpreter or emulator for handling indirect branches. We have proposed and evaluated innovative address table optimizations to more effectively handle indirect branch look-ups for compiler-generated code.

- This paper also provides engineering details on how to translate an instruction set to a target-independent compiler IR.

The rest of this paper is organized as follows. Section 2 and Section 3 discuss related work and give an overview of LLBT. Section 4 provides the implementation details. Section 5 presents and discusses our experiments results. Section 6 summaries and concludes the paper.

2. RELATED WORK

This section describes related static and dynamic binary translation systems, and gives a brief overview of the LLVM compiler infrastructure.

2.1 Static binary translators

FX!32 [7] is a dynamic profiling and static translating binary translation system, which translates X86 Win32 applications to run on Windows NT/Alpha platforms. Initially, X86 applications will be interpreted to gather some execution profiles. The collected profiles will be used to guide a static binary translator to generate native Alpha code. In subsequent runs of the same application, previously generated Alpha native code could be used instead of interpretation. The interpreter in FX!32 plays an important role in handling code discovery as well as possible SMC issues.

UQBT [9, 12] is a retargetable SBT tool which translates source binaries into a high-level intermediate language, called HRTL, then HRTL will be further translated into various forms depending on the translation purposes. For example, the forms can be low-level C code, object code, and VPO RTL. However, UQBT still relies on a runtime interpreter for handling indirect register calls that can not be discovered at static translation time. Besides, the lack of debugging support of HRTL makes it difficult to debug and verify the translated code

In the embedded system area, there is an ARM-based SBT system [14] which migrates executables from ARM to MIPS-like architecture and apply some optimizations to make the translated executable as efficient as the source executable. Compare to LLBT, a direct ISA-to-ISA translation may expose more optimization opportunities for handling specific cases, however, a direct ISA-to-ISA translation lacks the retargetability provided by LLBT. For instance, it took us only two person-weeks to port the ARM-to-x86 LLBT to ARM-to-MIPS LLBT. Furthermore, LLBT leverages rich machine independent and machine dependent optimizations developed in LLVM. It is very time consuming to develop, test and verify such optimizations for a direct ISA-to-ISA binary translator.

2.2 Dynamic binary translators

QEMU [6] is a fast and portable dynamic binary translator, which supports both user-mode and full-system emulations. The initial QEMU implementation translates source binary instructions into a sequence of micro operations, each micro operation is implemented by a small piece of C code and the C code is pre-compiled by GCC into target binary. At runtime, each micro operation is replaced by the pre-compiled binary. Newer versions of QEMU use TCG (Tiny Code Generator) to turn source binaries into IRs and translate IRs into different target native code. There are DBTs such as DynamoRIO, Aries [22], and Rosetta [4] which may generate higher quality target code than QEMU's DBT, however, QEMU is retargetable and a very widely used system emulator for embedded systems. Therefore, it is more related to this work, and is selected for performance comparison.

UQDBT [21] and Walkabout [10] also support retargetability through the use of specifications of the syntax and semantics of target machine instructions. Strata [17] is another retargetable binary translator which defines a reconfigurable target interface. In Strata, only the target-specific functions required by the target interface need to be implemented when retargeting to a new platform. The above retargetable binary translators are all dynamic translators, and they are not designed for embedded environments.

Some DBT systems focused on minimizing the dynamic translation and runtime optimization overheads. HP's Aries [22], IBM's BOA [13], and Walkabout [10] combined an interpreter with their DBT systems to collect runtime profile information and limit the scope of dynamic translation to a block or a trace of instructions. This requires additional interpretation before dynamic translation to identify

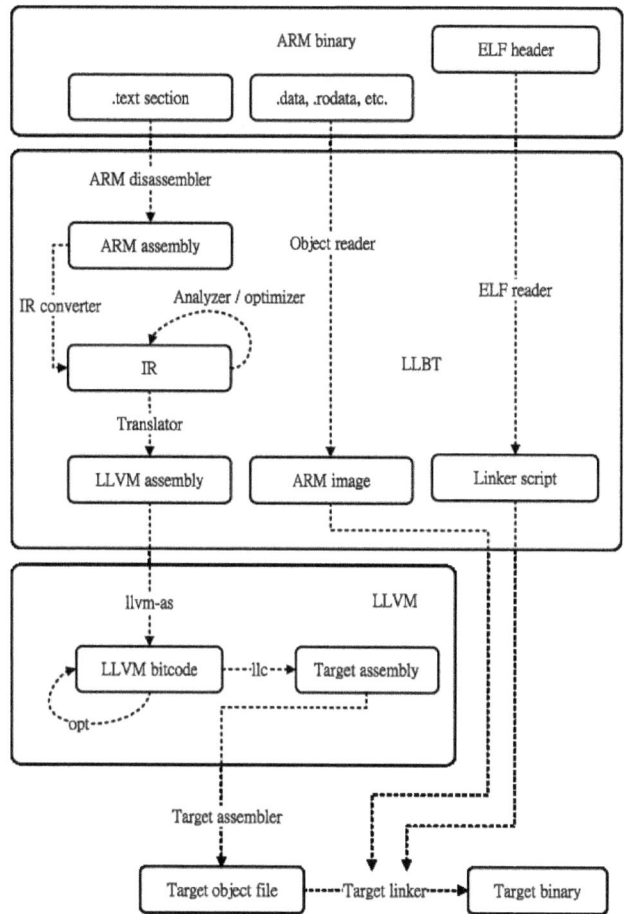

Figure 1: The architecture of LLBT.

frequently executed code. Similarly, IA-32 Execution Layer [5] adopted a two-phase translation design which translates cold code first with minimal optimizations and uses instrumentations to gather profiles for later optimizations on hot code. Such DBT systems are also not suitable for embedded environments since most embedded applications are client-side programs, which have relatively short execution time. For short running applications, these adaptive DBT systems may end up with either full interpretation or fast translated code with minimal optimizations.

2.3 LLVM

LLVM [15] is an open source project began at the University of Illinois. It designs a SSA-based instruction set and provides a collection of reusable compiler components for supporting both static and dynamic compilation. With the rapid development of the LLVM compiler framework in recent years, there have been various advanced optimizations and analysis phases added to the LLVM infrastructure. The relatively robust infrastructure and the rich optimizations available in LLVM have inspired us to build a portable binary translator on top of LLVM.

3. LLBT OVERVIEW

In order to fit the requirements of embedded systems and system vendors, some design decisions are made on our SBT tool. One of the important concerns is development cost. Crafting a binary translator from scratch requires extraordinary effort, especially in the design and verification of various optimizations. Moreover, since binary translators are highly target-machine-dependent, most of the efforts may not be leveraged if we wish to switch to a different target machine, which is very common in the embedded world. Therefore, retargeting a binary translator to a different platform, especially when serious optimizations are required, has been a highly desirable but challenging task.

To come up with a retargetable binary translator, we took the general approach of portable compilers which separate the translation process into target-dependent and target-independent parts, interfaced by intermediate representation (IR) forms. The front-end of a SBT compiler would translate the executable of the source architecture into IR forms and then the backend translates the IR forms into binaries of the target architecture. However, instead of designing a new target-independent IR and implementing a code generator for various architectures, we tended to leverage an existing compiler infrastructure to build a high-performance and retargetable binary translator.

LLBT is targeted for application-level translation. It can translate executables or shared libraries which run on top of the Linux operating systems. LLBT was developed with two goals in mind: avoiding runtime translation and going after more aggressive code optimizations. In addition, in order to leverage development effort for different target architectures, we prefer the translator to be portable. Therefore, LLBT selects the LLVM infrastructure as the base for its implementation. Currently, we have implemented an ARM-based LLBT which takes an ARM binary file in ELF format as its input. It translates the ARM instructions into LLVM IR and invokes the LLVM optimizer and the LLVM static compiler to produce optimized code for different target architectures. LLBT also provides a set of target-independent APIs which can be reused for building a new frontend for other architectures. Figure 1 shows the whole translation process which is summarized as follows:

1. An ARM input binary is disassembled to an assembly file, and then an IR converter will translate these ARM assembly instructions into LLBT's internal IR.

2. Some analysis and optimization passes, such as finding PC-relative data and jump table recovery, will be performed by LLBT on its internal IR before generating the corresponding LLVM instructions.

3. The LLVM assembly generated by the LLBT translator is assembled to a bitcode representation by the LLVM assembler (`llvm-as`).

4. LLVM optimizations and required analysis passes are selectively performed by using the LLVM optimizer (`opt`).

5. The LLVM static compiler (`llc`) performs some target-specific optimizations and transforms the optimized bitcode to a target assembly file.

6. After generating a target object file, the target linker reads a linker script, which contains the information about the memory layout, and links the object files with the ARM image to create a target binary.

```
define i32 @main(i32 %argc, i8** %argv,
                           i8** %envp) nounwind {
entry:
    ; Initialize ARM registers and stack.
    ......
    ; Set the entry point address of the source
    ; binary to PC.
    store i32 33024, i32* %ARM_pc, align 4
    ; Branch to the corresponding address of the
    ; source entry point.
    br label %L_00000009
    ; Start of the source instruction translation.
    ......
L_00000009:
    ......
    ; End of the source instruction translation.
address_translation_table_stub:
    ; The address mapping table.
    ......
    ret i32 0
}
; Prototypes of external functions.
......
; Metadata.
......
```

Figure 2: An overview of LLVM IR generated by LLBT.

4. IMPLEMENTATION

The ARM-based LLBT frontend (including the object reader and the disassembler) was modified from the GNU binutils [1]. In this section, we will mainly cover the implementation details of the translator in LLBT. Figure 2 gives an overview of the LLVM IR generated by the LLBT translator. The `main` function contains all LLVM instructions translated from the source binary. Before the execution jumps to the entry point (i.e., %L_00000009 in Figure 2), the `main` function has to allocate local variables for the simulated ARM architectural state and the source stack. In order to handle command-line arguments and Linux environment variables, we copy the addresses of arguments and environment variables from the target stack to the source stack. The entry point address of the source binary (i.e., 33024 in Figure 2) is extracted from the ELF header of the source binary.

4.1 Code Discovery

Normally, ARM toolchain produces some special symbols which can help discover ARM, Thumb, and PC-relative data in the binary. These symbols includes $a, $t, and $d, each represents begin of ARM instruction region, Thumb instruction region, and PC-relative data region. Along with special symbols, every word in the binary can be disassembled correctly. For handling pure ARM binaries, we can disassemble instructions correctly because every instructions are 32 bits. LLBT can disassemble input binaries from the begin of the text section smoothly. However, in ARM binaries with 16-bit Thumb-1 instructions, the disassembly result may be wrong because the opcode encoding of ARM and Thumb-1 ISA are overlapping. A word could be disassembled as either a 32-bit ARM instruction or two 16-bit Thumb-1 instructions.

This problem can be handled easily if input binaries contain special symbols. However, stripped binaries do not have symbol table, which means the programs lack of special symbols and can not distinguish the ARM and Thumb-1 regions in a binary. To figure out the ARM/Thumb-1 regions, LLBT

(a): ARM Instructions:

```
andsne r1, r1, r2
```

(b): LLVM Instructions:

```
Conditional execution check.
 1. L_1:
 2.    %CPSR_z_1 = load i32* %CPSR_z
 3.    %PASS_z_1 = icmp eq i32 %CPSR_z_1, 0
 4.    br i1 %PASS_z_1, label %L_2, label %L_3
Instruction body.
 5. L_2:
 6.    %OP1_1 = load i32* %ARM_r1
 7.    %OP2_1 = load i32* %ARM_r2
 8.    %RESULT_1 = and i32 %OP1_1, %OP2_1
 9.    store i32 %RESULT_1, i32* %ARM_r1
Conditional flags update.
10.    ; Update the N flag.
11.    %OP1_2 = load i32* %ARM_r1
12.    %RESULT_2 = lshr i32 %OP1_2, 31
13.    store i32 %RESULT_2, i32* %CPSR_n
14.    ; Update the Z flag.
15.    %OP1_3 = load i32* %ARM_r1
16.    %CMP_1 = icmp eq i32 %OP1_3, 0
17.    %RESULT_3 = select i1 %CMP_1, i32 1, i32 0
18.    store i32 %RESULT_3, i32* %CPSR_z
The next instruction.
19. L_3:
```

Figure 3: The mapping of the ARM ands (Logical AND) instruction with the NE (Not Equal) condition.

```
Instruction
    ANDS Rd, Rd, Rm
Operation
    Rd = Rd AND Rm
    N Flag = Rd[31]
    C Flag = unaffected
    Z Flag = if Rd == 0 then 1 else 0
    V Flag = unaffected
```

Figure 4: The operation of the ands instruction [18].

tectural state. This is because LLVM IR is in SSA form and the architectural state will be updated many times. Therefore, LLBT declares ARM registers and condition flags as local variables, which use alloca instructions in LLVM. Since these alloca instructions only have loads and stores in our translated IR, they will be promoted to LLVM registers later by the LLVM optimizer.

Ideally, we would like each LLVM register which represents an ARM register to be mapped to a real register in the target architecture. This is relatively easy if the target architecture has more than 16 registers, such as typical RISC machines and the IA64 architecture. Mapping ARM's general purpose registers to the target architecture registers can significantly reduce the number of memory operations generated to read/write the ARM architectural state. In LLBT, this mapping is determined by the LLVM register allocator. Typically, the LLVM register allocator will allocate frequently used variables to target architecture registers. However, if the number of target registers is fewer than 16, such as the X86 architecture, some of the LLVM registers must be spilled to memory.

4.3 Instruction Translation

The instruction translation is a one-to-many mapping process between ARM and LLVM instructions. The process can be divided into three parts:

Conditional execution check is a mechanism to check the current program status (the four flags stored in the CPSR register) to determine whether the instruction should be executed. In the ARM ISA, almost all instructions can be conditionally executed. As shown in Figure 3, LLBT translates a conditional execution instruction into three parts. The first part is checking the status.

Instruction body contains all the corresponding instruction mapped to the ARM instruction excluding condition-related checks and updates.

Conditional flags update is usually required for comparison instructions, such as cmn (Compare Negative), cmp (Compare), teq (Test Equivalence), and tst (Test), etc. In addition, some other arithmetic, logical, and move instructions with the S qualifier [18] will also update the condition flags. For the aforementioned ARM instructions, LLBT generates instructions for updating the condition flags.

Figure 3 shows an example of the ARM ands instruction and the corresponding LLVM IRs. The detailed operations of the instruction are listed in Figure 4. In Figure 3(b), lines 1-4 check whether the Z flag in CPSR register satisfies the specified condition (i.e., NE). If true, the instruction

requires a set of entries as start points of code discovery. In a stripped binary, these entries can only be fetched from program entry or global functions. The program entry is preserved as program start point, and the global functions are preserved for dynamic linking. The ISA type can determined by the last bit of the entry address. Zero means the entry is belong to ARM ISA, and one belongs to the Thumb-1 ISA. With the entries, LLBT can discover ARM/Thumb-1 region by following two steps: 1) enclose a region for each entry 2) discover more entries through enclosed region.

To enclose a region for an entry, LLBT will check each instruction which is fall through from the entry until a unconditional branch is found. This branch is considered the end of the region begin by the entry. Since all the instructions in the region can be fall through from the entry, the instructions in the region must belong to the same ISA. Once a region is discovered, the direct branches in the region can help to search more entries with the same ISA as current region. The two steps will be repeated until no new entry is found. In our experiment, this code discovery mechanism can help identifying more than 90% ARM/Thumb-1 regions of ARM binaries with Thumb-1 instructions. For those unknown regions, LLBT will translate them as ARM region and Thumb-1 region both to ensure the correctness. For the discovered region, translating single ISA improve the time and space efficiency.

4.2 Register Mapping

The ARM architectural state includes general-purpose registers and condition flags. In the ARM user mode, there are 16 general-purpose registers and a current program status register (CPSR), which contains 4 condition flags (i.e., Negative, Zero, Carry, and Overflow). Although LLVM IR provides infinite virtual registers, we can not map each ARM register to an LLVM register for maintaining the ARM archi-

ARM Instructions:

```
mov pc, r3
```

LLVM Instructions:

```
%0 = load i32* %ARM_r3
store i32 %0, i32* %ARM_pc
br label %address_translation_table_stub
```

Figure 5: An example of indirect branches.

```
address_translation_table_stub:
  %address = load i32* %ARM_pc
  switch i32 %address, label %look_up_failure [
    i32 32120, label %L_00007d78
    i32 32160, label %L_00007da0
    ....
    i32 46360, label %L_0000b518
  ]
look_up_failure:
  ......
```

Figure 6: An example of the address mapping table stub.

body (i.e., lines 5-9) will be executed and the condition flags will be updated (i.e., lines 10-18), otherwise a direct branch which jumps to the next instruction (i.e., line 19) will be taken.

4.4 Handling Indirect Branches

Unlike direct branches, the target address of an indirect branch is not known until run time. In order to handle indirect branches at translation time, LLBT prepares an address mapping table which maps each source address of an indirect branch target to the corresponding target address of the translated code, and generates a jump for the indirect branch instruction. The jump instruction transfers control to a stub which searches the address mapping table for the target address. A naive address mapping table will be very large because it must include an entry for every ARM instruction.

In order to minimize the address mapping table, LLBT does not keep entries for all source instructions. Instead, it maintains only entries for the source instruction can possibly be the target addresses of an indirect branch, which includes function entry points, return addresses, function pointer addresses, and addresses in virtual method tables.

- Function entries can be found in the symbol table of the input binary. If the symbol table is stripped off, the instruction that immediately follows a **return** instruction will be considered as a function entry and its address will be included in the address mapping table. If there is PC-relative data that immediately follows a **return** instruction, it will be skipped and the next data is considered recursively. Besides, we also look at the call instructions to find function entries.

- A return address is the address of the instruction that a function returns to. It is the address of the instruction that immediately follows a function call instruction.

- A function pointer address is usually stored as a piece of PC-relative data in the input binary. We examine all

```
address_translation_table_stub:
  %address = load i32* %ARM_pc
  %tmp = lshr i32 %address, 3
  %key = and i32 %tmp, 15
  switch i32 %key, label %look_up_failure [
    i32 0, label %table_0
    i32 1, label %table_1
    ......
    i32 14, label %table_14
    i32 15, label %table_15
  ]
table_0:
  switch i32 %address, label %look_up_failure [
    i32 33536, label %L_00008300
    i32 33412, label %L_00008284
  ]
......
table_15:
  switch i32 %address, label %look_up_failure [
  ]
look_up_failure:
  ......
```

Figure 7: An example of address mapping table with a runtime dispatcher.

the PC-relative load instructions in the ARM binary. If the loaded data is an address located at the code segment, it is included in the address mapping table.

- A virtual method table is a mechanism used to support dynamic dispatch for some programming languages, such as C++. The table is usually stored in the read-only data (.rodata) section of input binaries. For binaries written in such languages, we examine the data in the .rodata section. If the data is an address located at the code segment, it is included in the address mapping table.

While our method seems incomplete for arbitrary binaries created from an assembly program, it is reasonable for code generated by a compiler. Figure 5 and Figure 6 show an example of indirect branches and the address mapping table stub respectively. LLBT will update the value of **ARM_pc** and jump to **address_translation_table_stub** if the instruction is an indirect branch. The address mapping table is implemented by the LLVM **switch** instruction. If the value of **ARM_pc** can be found in the switch cases, the program will jump to the corresponding destination (i.e., the target address of the **ARM_pc**). Otherwise, the control flow will be transferred to a default destination, **not_found**, and a runtime exception will be raised.

The LLVM **switch** instruction may be implemented in different ways, depending on target machines and the instruction context. Typically, since the address mapping table consists of sparse case values, LLVM is likely to translate the **switch** instruction into a series of chained conditional branches. Such an implementation may substantially decrease the performance of table lookup, especially when the table is large. Therefore, in order to speed up the table search time, we currently use a runtime dispatcher to hash the source address (i.e., **ARM_pc**) to one of many small address mapping tables. Figure 7 shows an example of the address mapping table with a runtime dispatcher.

4.5 Jump Table Recovery

Compilers usually generate a jump table for switch state-

(1) ARM Instructions:

```
83ec:        cmp      r5, #4
83f0:        ldrls    pc, [pc, r5, lsl #2]
83f4:        b        8454
83f8:        .word    0x0000840c
83fc:        .word    0x00008414
8400:        .word    0x00008424
8404:        .word    0x00008434
8408:        .word    0x00008444
......
```

(2) LLVM Instructions:

```
...... (update/check condition code)

L_000083f0:
    %0 = load i32* %ARM_r5
    %1 = shl i32 %0, 2
    %2 = load i32* %ARM_pc
    %3 = add i32 %2, %1
    switch i32 %3, label %L_00008454 [
        i32 33784, label %L_0000840c
        i32 33788, label %L_00008414
        i32 33792, label %L_00008424
        i32 33796, label %L_00008434
        i32 33800, label %L_00008444
    ]
```

Figure 8: An example of a switch statement in (1) C Language, (2) the corresponding ARM instructions, which is a jump table, generated by GCC, and (3) the LLVM switch instructions recovered by LLBT.

ments. For example, Figure 8.1 is a jump table generated by GCC. An indirect branch is usually used to access the branch targets from the jump table. As shown in Figure 8.1, the target of each case in the switch statement is stored as PC-relative data. Typically, the address mapping tables generated by a SBT should include each address in the jump table because it is a branch target of an indirect branch. However, it is possible to recover a jump table back to a switch statement. Cifuentes [8] proposed a technique to recover jump tables in a machine-independent way which can find more than 90% of addresses in jump tables. In LLBT, we employ a different approach that uses a few patterns in ARM assembly code to recover all jump tables generated by GCC back to LLVM switch instructions. Figure 8.2 shows the LLVM switch instruction recovered from Figure 8.1 by LLBT. Once the jump tables are recovered, the target addresses of indirect branches will be limited to function entries and function return points. This would significantly reduce the number of entries to be placed in the address mapping table. In addition, this transformation can also speedup the address mapping table lookup and enable LLVM to generate a jump table in target binaries.

4.6 PC-relative Data Inlining

Compilers typically place constant values in a literal pool and generate a PC-relative data load instruction to move the constant from the literal pool into a register when the constant is too large to be encoded within an instruction. However, a constant that can not be encoded in an ARM instruction may be able to be encoded in a target instruction if the target ISA supports for larger immediate values. Therefore, LLBT will inline all PC-relative data load instructions into LLVM instructions. This transformation provides an opportunity for the LLVM to encode more con-

ARM Instructions:

```
81ec:        ldr      r0, [pc, #44]
......
8220:        .word    0x0000d3e0
```

LLVM Instructions:

```
store i32 54240, i32* %ARM_r0
```

Figure 9: An example of inlining PC-relative data.

ARM Instructions:

```
bl __aeabi_idiv
```

LLVM Instructions:

```
%0 = load i32* %ARM_r0
%1 = load i32* %ARM_r1
%2 = sdiv i32 %0, %1
%3 = srem i32 %0, %1
store i32 %2, i32* %ARM_r0
store i32 %3, i32* %ARM_r1
```

Figure 10: Integer division helper replacement.

stants in target instruction. Figure 9 shows an example of inlining PC-relative data.

With the help of PC-relative data inlining and jump table recovery, we do not have to keep the text section of input binaries in the target binaries. This is because all instructions in the text section have been translated and all data in the text section have been inlined/recovered to LLVM instructions. This optimization can also save the code size and memory for embedded systems. On the other hand, DBTs have to keep the text section in memory because source instructions are translated at runtime.

4.7 Helper Function Replacement

When hardware floating point support is not available, the compiler resorts to software floating point helper functions. This happens when the ARM code generation is targeted for ARMv5TE ISA since many ARMv5 implementations do not have a FPU. In order to maintain portability, applications usually use a software floating point library to emulate floating point operations. For a similar reason, the ARMv5TE does not provide an integer division instruction, compilers usually generate a sequence of code that invokes an external helper function for handling integer division. For example, GCC provides a low-level runtime library, libgcc, that contains helpers for emulating floating point and integer division operations on ARM platforms. Since other CPUs may have integer division or floating point instructions, these helpers are usually target-specific. Therefore, if we migrate an ARM binary to other targets, we have to either (1) translate each ARM instruction in the helpers or (2) implement these helpers using target instructions. LLBT selects the second approach for the performance reason. In our ARM-based LLBT, each call instruction that invoke integer division or floating point helpers will be replaced by a sequence of LLVM instructions. Figure 10 shows an ARM instruction that invokes the integer division helper and the corresponding LLVM instructions that replace the helper call. After the helper function replacement, LLVM could generate integer divide and/or FP instructions directly on the target machine.

5. EXPERIMENTAL RESULTS

We used the industry standard EEMBC 1.1 and the CoreMark embedded benchmark suites to evaluate the implementation of the retargetable LLBT. The ARM binaries (i.e., source binaries) of the benchmarks were all compiled using the GNU GCC 4.4.6 compiler with the -O2 optimization setting. The cross compiler is configured to generate ARMv5TE instructions with software floating point by default since this is the most commonly used setting on current embedded systems. The LLVM version used in LLBT is 3.0 and the target binaries translated by LLBT use the LLVM default optimization setting (i.e., -O2).

5.1 SBT vs. DBT

We first compare the performance between static and dynamic binary translations. Figure 11 shows the experimental results of EEMBC benchmark suites run on (a) Intel Xeon E5506 (2.13GHz) and (b) Ingenic JZ4760 MIPS processor (528Mhz). We translate the EEMBC benchmark suites from ARM to X86 and MIPS binaries by using our LLBT. We then compare the performance of such translated binaries running on respective systems (Intel E5506 and Ingenic JZ4760 MIPS) to the execution of ARM binaries on the QEMU on the same platforms. The QEMU used in our experiments is version 1.0. The performance comparison results show that the LLBT generated code can run from 3X to 64X faster than using QEMU with DBT. The performance differences between X86 and MIPS on the same benchmark could be affected by the specific implementation of X86 and MIPS backend in QEMU and LLVM. Some benchmarks, such as a2time01, basefp01 and matrix01, SBT can result in 20 times speedup over DBT. The outstanding performance improvement is because there are many integer division or floating point operations in these benchmarks. In ARM binaries, those operations are implemented by calling external helpers in libgcc. In SBT, our LLBT replaces these helper calls to corresponding LLVM instructions to enable LLVM generating integer division and floating point instructions on X86 and MIPS target platforms. In addition, the helper function replacement also reduces function call overhead. On average (i.e. by geometric mean), LLBT generated code can run about 7.14 and 7.35 times faster than QEMU on X86 and MIPS, respectively.

Figure 12 shows the experimental results of CoreMark run on Intel Xeon E5506 (2.13GHz). The X86 binaries were translated under different optimization levels to show the power of LLVM optimizations. The LLVM optimizer (i.e., opt) and the LLVM static compiler (i.e., llc) can perform target-independent and target dependent optimizations under LLVM IR respectively. In the first configuration, LLBT uses no optimizations at all on the translated IR. However, the translated code is still a little faster than the QEMU runs because DBT systems would have runtime translation and management overhead. In the second configuration, we turn on the LLVM optimization level 3 to enable several time consuming optimizations.

The result shows that LLBT translated code can now be 2.5 times faster than DBT runs. In this configuration, the LLVM static compiler used local register allocation and a fast instruction selection algorithm to speed up code gener-

ation. This behavior is somewhat similar to many DBT systems where they typically use a basic block as a translation unit and have to load/store the architectural state at the translation block boundaries. In the final configuration, we turn on all target-dependent optimizations and also enable global register allocation on the whole translated IR. The result shows that the performance of our static binary system can now be more than 6 times faster than the DBT run. DBT generated code are executed in the code cache. So we look further into how the execution time is divided among different components in QEMU. By using the Perf, performance counters subsystem in Linux, we found that only 40 percent of execution time spent in the code cache. About 40% of time spent in QEMU, including interpretation, translation and runtime management. Another 20 percent of time spent on shared libraries. This shows more than half of the execution time is wasted on overhead and this is quite typical for migrating short running applications with DBT. We believe this is the more common scenario for embedded systems. In summary, SBT translated binaries run faster than DBT translated binaries for two main reasons: 1) DBT has runtime overhead, including interpretation, translation and runtime management. This overhead is more apparent for programs with relatively short run time. 2) DBT performs much less code optimizations since optimization time is part of runtime. For long running applications, where the translation overhead can be amortized, the main difference in performance would be due to the quality of translated code. QEMU does not perform cross block optimizations, while LLVM is rather strong in global optimizations. This gap might be reduced in the future since many new DBT has started to adopt trace based code generation and optimizations rather than one-block-at-a-time approach used by the current QEMU.

5.2 Startup Time

A fast startup is important for embedded applications. We compare the startup time of a static translated program to start time of a dynamic translated one in this subsection. Instead of measuring the startup time until the beginning of the main function, we measured the startup time until the process can actually provide some real services. The benchmark we choose is lighttpd, a lightweight webserver which is feasible for embedded systems. We measured the execution time until the lighttpd starts as a daemon and waits for connection requests from the clients. The translated lighttpd runs on a MIPS processor (Ingenic JZ4760) with Linux version 2.6.32, and the dynamic translator we use to compare the startup time is QEMU version 1.0. Figure 13 shows the startup time of the two approaches. As shown in the figure, lighttpd emulated by QEMU on MIPS platform requires about 6.48 times of the execution time of the SBT translated lighttpd. The gap between the two is caused by large amount of translation overhead at the beginning of a process. After profiling by using Perf, we found that the translation time occupied almost half of the startup time, but it only spends 3.9% of the execution time on in the code cache. The high translation overhead at the beginning of the process implies that there might be no hot spots in the execution paths at the startup time, this is also typical in applications. DBT often takes advantage of hot spots to minimize translation and optimization time, however, lack of hot spots in the execution paths making SBT

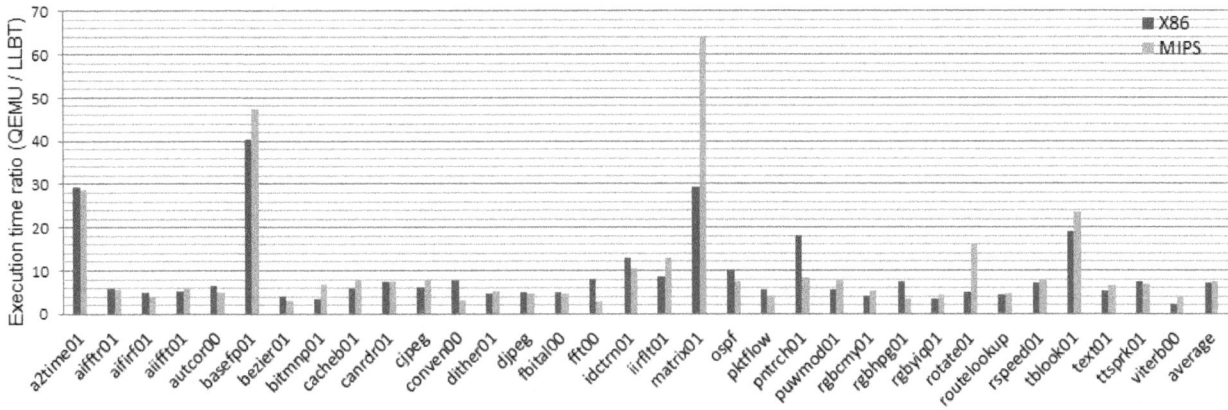

Figure 11: Execution time ratio of "QEMU / LLBT" on translating EEMBC benchmark suites from ARM to (a) X86 and (b) MIPS.

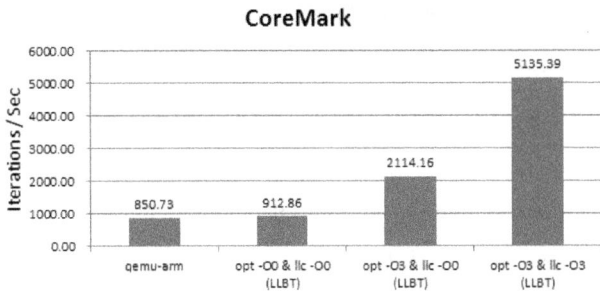

Figure 12: Comparing the performance of CoreMark running on QEMU with the translated CoreMark in different LLVM configurations.

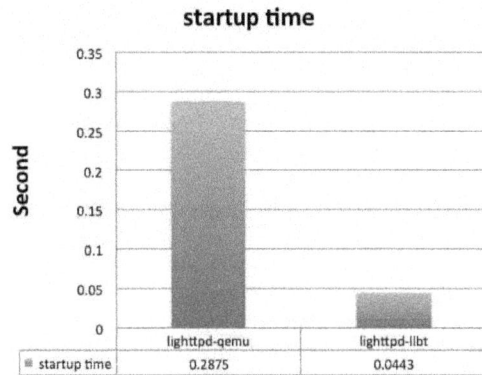

Figure 13: Comparing the startup time of (a) `lighttpd` running on QEMU and (b) `lighttpd` translated by LLBT.

a more attractive solution when the short startup time is a major concern.

5.3 Address Mapping Table

A naive implementation of the runtime address mapping table could significantly increase the memory requirement of SBT generated code. In the worst case, every ARM instruction could possibly be the target of an indirect branch, thus may require one entry in the address mapping table. In LLBT, we pay extra attention on the address mapping table design to minimize the memory usage. LLBT generates a smaller table if the input ARM binaries contain symbol table information since we can explicitly know which instruction addresses are function entries. Otherwise, if the symbol tables of the input binaries are stripped, LLBT have to include any possible addresses which might be function entries in the address mapping table. With the help of symbol table information, there are only 7.55% of instruction addresses on average are actually included in the address mapping on the EEMBC benchmark suite. However, when no symbol tables are available, our heuristics will add only 2-7% more instruction addresses into the address mapping table.

6. CONCLUSIONS

This paper presents a portable static binary translation tool, called LLBT, which translates ARM binaries to LLVM

IR and leverage the LLVM compiler infrastructure to generate binaries for different target architectures. DBT is usually the top choice for migrating application binaries from one ISA to another. However, for embedded systems, the startup time, the memory usage and the power efficiency are all important considerations. SBT can be far more efficient than DBT when migrating relatively short running applications. However, in the past, SBT has been downplayed because the challenges in code discovery issues, code location handling and issues like SMC. To migrate ARM based binaries to other ISAs, we have devised various techniques to get away from code discovery problems such as jump table recovery and PC-relative data inlining. To handle indirect branches, a large address mapping table is typically used in SBT. Since we target at compiler generated code rather than hand-crafted binary, we could narrow down the possible target addresses for the addressing table. With our minimization, the address mapping requires only 7% of all ARM instruction addresses as entries in the table. SMC rarely happens in all the applications available in Google Play. Hence, we believe using SBT for migrating applications under Android for embedded systems could be a viable solution.

In this paper, we have discussed issues related to generating code in terms of register mapping, conditional execution translation, indirect branch handling, PC-relative data inlining, jump table recovery, and helper function replacement, in order to enable LLBT to be an effective and efficient retargetable binary translator. Our experiments show that LLBT translated code can run more than 7 times faster, on average, than DBT runs on the two public embedded benchmark suites: EEMBC and CoreMark. With the help from the comprehensive optimizations in LLVM, LLBT can effectively support migrating applications to new architectures, especially for the embedded environments. We have demonstrated the retargetability by translating ARM binaries to X86 and MIPS, on real hardware, with high migration efficiency.

7. ACKNOWLEDGMENTS

The work reported in this paper is partially supported by National Science Council, Taiwan, Republic of China, under grants NSC 100-2218-E-009-010-MY3 and NSC 100-2218-E-009-009-MY3.

8. REFERENCES

[1] Gnu binutils. http://www.gnu.org/software/binutils/.

[2] E. Altman, D. Kaeli, and Y. Sheffer. Welcome to the opportunities of binary translation. *Computer*, 33(3):40–45, March 2000.

[3] K. Andrews and D. Sand. Migrating a cisc computer family onto risc via object code translation. In *Proceedings of the fifth international conference on Architectural support for programming languages and operating systems*, ASPLOS-V, pages 213–222, New York, NY, USA, 1992. ACM.

[4] Apple. Rosetta. http://www.apple.com/rosetta/.

[5] L. Baraz, T. Devor, O. Etzion, S. Goldenberg, A. Skaletsky, Y. Wang, and Y. Zemach. Ia-32 execution layer: a two-phase dynamic translator designed to support ia-32 applications on itanium-based systems. In *Proceedings of the 36th annual IEEE/ACM International Symposium on Microarchitecture*, MICRO 36, pages 191–, Washington, DC, USA, 2003. IEEE Computer Society.

[6] F. Bellard. Qemu, a fast and portable dynamic translator. In *Proceedings of the annual conference on USENIX Annual Technical Conference*, ATEC '05, pages 41–41, Berkeley, CA, USA, 2005. USENIX Association.

[7] A. Chernoff, M. Herdeg, R. Hookway, C. Reeve, N. Rubin, T. Tye, S. B. Yadavalli, and J. Yates. Fx!32: A profile-directed binary translator. *IEEE Micro*, 18:56–64, March 1998.

[8] C. Cifuentes and M. V. Emmerik. Recovery of jump table case statements from binary code. In *Proceedings of the 7th International Workshop on Program Comprehension*, IWPC '99, pages 192–, Washington, DC, USA, 1999. IEEE Computer Society.

[9] C. Cifuentes and M. V. Emmerik. Uqbt: Adaptable binary translation at low cost. *Computer*, 33:60–66, March 2000.

[10] C. Cifuentes, B. Lewis, and D. Ung. Walkabout: a retargetable dynamic binary translation framework. Technical report, Mountain View, CA, USA, 2002.

[11] C. Cifuentes and V. M. Malhotra. Binary translation: Static, dynamic, retargetable? In *Proceedings of the 1996 International Conference on Software Maintenance*, ICSM '96, Washington, DC, USA, 1996. IEEE Computer Society.

[12] C. Cifuentes, M. Van Emmerik, N. Ramsey, and B. Lewis. Experience in the design, implementation and use of a retargetable static binary translation framework. Technical report, Mountain View, CA, USA, 2002.

[13] M. Gschwind, E. R. Altman, S. Sathaye, P. Ledak, and D. Appenzeller. Dynamic and transparent binary translation. *Computer*, 33:54–59, March 2000.

[14] C. S. Jiunn-Yeu Chen, Wuu Yang and W. C. Hsu. A static binary translator for efficient migration of arm based applications. In *Proceedings of the 6th Workshop on Optimizations for DSP and Embedded Systems*, April 2008.

[15] C. Lattner and V. Adve. Llvm: A compilation framework for lifelong program analysis & transformation. In *Proceedings of the international symposium on Code generation and optimization: feedback-directed and runtime optimization*, CGO '04, pages 75–, Washington, DC, USA, 2004. IEEE Computer Society.

[16] C.-K. Luk, R. Cohn, R. Muth, H. Patil, A. Klauser, G. Lowney, S. Wallace, V. J. Reddi, and K. Hazelwood. Pin: building customized program analysis tools with dynamic instrumentation. In *Proceedings of the 2005 ACM SIGPLAN conference on Programming language design and implementation*, PLDI '05, pages 190–200, New York, NY, USA, 2005. ACM.

[17] K. Scott, N. Kumar, S. Velusamy, B. Childers, J. W. Davidson, and M. L. Soffa. Retargetable and reconfigurable software dynamic translation. In *Proceedings of the international symposium on Code generation and optimization: feedback-directed and runtime optimization*, CGO '03, pages 36–47, Washington, DC, USA, 2003. IEEE Computer Society.

[18] D. Seal. *ARM Architecture Reference Manual*. Addison-Wesley Longman Publishing Co., 2000.

[19] R. L. Sites, A. Chernoff, M. B. Kirk, M. P. Marks, and S. G. Robinson. Binary translation. *Commun. ACM*, 36:69–81, February 1993.

[20] J. Smith and R. Nair. *Virtual Machines: Versatile Platforms for Systems and Processes*. Morgan Kaufmann, 2005.

[21] D. Ung and C. Cifuentes. Machine-adaptable dynamic binary translation. In *Proceedings of the ACM SIGPLAN workshop on Dynamic and adaptive compilation and optimization*, DYNAMO '00, pages 41–51, New York, NY, USA, 2000. ACM.

[22] C. Zheng and C. Thompson. Pa-risc to ia-64: Transparent execution, no recompilation. *Computer*, 33:47–52, March 2000.

Power Agnostic Technique for Efficient Temperature Estimation of Multicore Embedded Systems

Devendra Rai, Hoeseok Yang, Iuliana Bacivarov and Lothar Thiele
Computer Engineering and Networks Laboratory
ETH Zurich, 8092 Zurich, Switzerland
firstname.lastname@tik.ee.ethz.ch

ABSTRACT

Temperature plays an increasingly important role in the overall performance and reliability of a computing system. Multi- and many-core systems provide an opportunity to manage the overall temperature profile by cleverly designing the application-to-core mapping and the associated scheduling policies. An uncontrolled temperature profile may lead to an unplanned performance loss, since the system activates protective mechanisms such as voltage and/or frequency scaling to cool itself. Similarly, deep thermal cycles with high frequency lead to severe deterioration in the overall reliability of the system. Design space exploration tools are often used to optimize binding and scheduling choices based on a given set of constraints and objectives, thus motivating the need for fast and accurate temperature estimation techniques. We argue that the currently available techniques are not an ideal fit to design space exploration tools, and suggest a system level technique which is based on application fingerprinting. It does not need any information about the processor floorplan, the physical and thermal structure, or about power consumption. Instead, its temperature estimation is based on a set of application-specific calibration runs and associated temperature measurements using available built-in sensors. We show that a given application possesses a unique thermal signature on the system it executes on, which provides a computationally fast method to calculate accurate temperature traces. Extensive experimental studies show that our technique can estimate temperature on all cores of a system to within $5^\circ C$, and is three orders of magnitude faster than state of the art numerical simulators like *Hotspot*.

Categories and Subject Descriptors

I.6 [**Simulation and Modeling**]: Model Development

Keywords

power, temperature, modeling

1. INTRODUCTION

High temperature has become a first order concern in recent microprocessors due to significantly higher power densities, see [1, 2]. Managing the temperature profile of a system is critical, specially in safety critical applications, like embedded electronic control units (ECUs) in a modern car. These ECUs are generally mounted in areas where ambient temperature is already high, such as in the vicinity of the engine. This creates a situation where thermal affects of applications running on the ECU must be carefully analyzed, and controlled to achieve reliable and consistent computational performance, see [3].

Different applications stress a given processor core differently, thereby giving rise to different temperature profiles over time. Excessively high temperatures may also lead to "thermal runaway" causing physical destruction of the computing hardware, see [4]. A core experiencing a dangerously high temperature automatically triggers dynamic temperature control techniques like DFVS, or may shutdown, leading to an unplanned loss of quality-of-service, see [5, 6, 7]. Such performance disruptions make it hard to provide end-to-end performance guarantees about the system; and can be avoided if one can ensure that the set of applications mapped to the cores of a multiprocessor, along with the scheduling algorithms used on each core, will never lead to a temperature increase beyond the critical values. Even if dynamic power reduction techniques are applied, the availability of a proper thermal analysis methodology will allow for a combined temperature and performance analysis that can be used to explore alternative mapping, scheduling and thermal management mechanisms.

Beyond the analysis and control of the maximal temperature, it is also important to investigate thermal cycles: the magnitude and frequency of temperature variations on a processor influences its reliability, see [8, 9].

Embedded multiprocessor embedded systems generally do not have spare computational power for online computation of suitable task mappings and scheduling so that all temperature and performance metrics are met. Thus, a potentially large design space needs to be explored offline using temperature-aware exploration tools, to evaluate various mappings and select the one which best suits the optimization criteria at hand.

The overall objective of this work, therefore, is to develop a fast and yet accurate temperature estimation framework, which can be used in design space exploration iterations. The problem of correctly estimating the temperature profile of all cores in a given multiprocessor has traditionally been solved by using two common approaches. One solution is to use a low-level thermal simulator, like *Hotspot* which requires detailed knowledge of the floorplan and electrical characteristics such as technology node, rail voltage, materials used, and power consumption of each micro-architectural unit in the processor, just to name a few, see [10]. This information is not easily available, requiring designers to approximate the physical and electrical characteristics of the processor, which may lead to unacceptable inaccuracies in the estimated temperature traces. Numerical simulators also tend to be too slow to be used in an iterative design-space exploration tool.

It is possible to get total power consumption of the processor by using the measuring technique described in [11]. On the other hand, without detailed circuit and hardware implementation information, it is not possible to get an accurate breakdown of the total power amongst the micro-architectural units (power density distribution). Consequently, abstract temperature models have been reported in [12] which attempt to estimate the temperature profile as a function of total power consumption of each core. Such abstract models can be computed quickly, but are relatively inaccurate, since these consider only a few observable parameters to calculate temperature, e.g. the total power consumption of a processor. We argue that it is not possible to build a sufficiently accurate thermal model by using such coarse-grained abstractions.

1.1 Motivational Example

The approach used in this work is unique, since it does not abstract away power density distribution information as a given application executes on a core of a multiprocessor, which may lead to inaccurate temperature estimates as illustrated in this section. To motivate the discussion, a commonly used hardware architecture is used, which allows us to clearly identify deficiencies of current approaches. Please note that new techniques that will be described in later sections do not need information about hardware details like floorplan or power-density information.

1.1.1 Correct Temperature Trace Estimation

Consider a four-core chip-multiprocessor (CMP) on which three applications: *producer*, *FFT* and *consumer*, are running, see Figure 1. The *producer* is in charge of creating data for the *FFT* application, which in turn supplies the results to the *consumer* for display. Both, *producer* and *consumer*, are I/O intensive applications with data caches dominating the total power consumption. On the other hand, *FFT* is a compute-intensive application and the ALU will dominate the power consumption of the corresponding processor core. All three applications consume the same total amount of power.

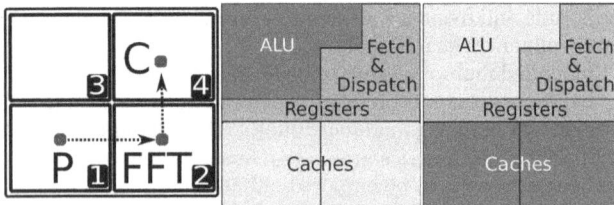

Figure 1: Producer (P), FFT and Consumer (C) applications on a CMP. The power density distribution on cores 1 and 2 is shown, where lighter shades show areas with higher power consumption.

The left floorplan shows the power consumption on core 1 when *producer* is running, while the right floorplan shows the power distribution on core 2 when FFT executes. The temperature sensor is located near the upper left corner of the processor. hence, it is more sensitive to the heat generated by the computational units of the processor.

Coarse grained temperature estimation techniques (see [12, 13]) estimate temperature as a function of total power consumption of a core i according to

$$T_i(t) = f_i\left(\mathcal{P}_1(t), \ldots, \mathcal{P}_n(t)\right) \qquad (1)$$

where $\mathcal{P}_i(t)$ denotes the total power consumption of processor core i in the CMP at time t.

The temperature trace on the cores 1, 2 and 4 is shown in Figure 2. The temperature simulation was performed on Hotspot using the Alpha 21264 thermal model as supplied with Hotspot. Power numbers were generated from the Wattch/ Simplescalar tool chain [14]. Temperature influence from cores to their neighbors has been accounted for. All applications execute in lock-step, i.e. cores 1, 2, and 4 have the same total power trace over time. Communication between cores is implemented using FIFO buffers. In such a scenario, a simple coarse grained model such as in (1) can not be expected to yield accurate results since it is oblivious to the power density distribution in the cores. The model will predict the same temperature trace for cores 1, 2 and 4, which may be similar to *one* of the temperature traces shown in Figure 2, depending on how f_i is constructed.

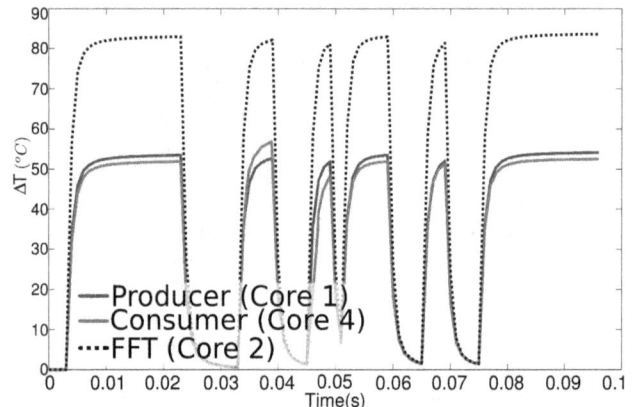

Figure 2: Temperature trace on four cores due to running applications *Producer, Consumer* and *FFT*.

We can conclude that ignoring the power density distribution between the micro-architectural units can lead to large errors in the temperature estimates. Knowledge of power distribution information requires detailed circuit level and physical models, which are rarely available for modern processors.

1.1.2 Computation Time

The temperature trace in the previous example was calculated using Hotspot at a temporal resolution of $1ms$, requiring 6 hours for a relatively short trace of $100ms$. Clearly, numerical simulators, due to their long run time are not suitable for design space exploration tools, since potentially hundreds of mappings may need to investigated. Instead, an ideal temperature estimation technique for design space exploration must be *reasonably* accurate, sufficiently fast, and must not rely on often unavailable information such as detailed power, layout, physical and thermal models.

1.2 The Problem

Based on the above discussion, the problem that needs to be solved can be described as follows:

Given a possibly heterogeneous chip multiprocessor system S and a set of applications $\mathcal{A}$: estimate the temperature trace on all cores of S with sufficient speed and accuracy as required for design space exploration. The method should not depend on prior availability of power, layout, physical and thermal models of the hardware platform.

As we will see below, the fingerprinting approach as proposed in this paper replaces the detailed knowledge about platform internals by a limited set of calibration runs where applications are executed on the platform and temperature traces from the internal sensors are recorded.

1.3 Our Contribution

It is clear that an ideal temperature estimation framework for DSE will need to rely on an abstract thermal model, which provides sufficient speed and accuracy such that many mappings of $\mathcal{A}$ onto $\mathcal{S}$ can be quickly evaluated. In this work, we demonstrate a technique to build a thermal model relying on the results of a limited set of calibration runs including temperature measurements. This model is combined with mapping and scheduling information and results in the desired estimated temperature traces.

Specifically, our contribution is a temperature evaluation framework which:

- Correctly determines a correct temperature trace even when two applications running on the CMP consume the same total power but exercise different micro architectural units;
- Does not require knowledge of power traces, and does not assume that all cores of the CMP are homogeneous;
- Can model and evaluate temperature effects of various mapping policies in terms of peak temperature, dynamic temperature range both in space and time;
- Does not depend on prior knowledge of details about the hardware platform;
- Allows for fast and accurate temperature estimation to be reliably used in DSE loops.

2. RELATED WORK

Temperature estimation has been recent focus of research, due to the reasons discussed above. Overall, the estimation techniques are based on numerical simulation, or based on abstract relationships between power and temperature such as (1).

Numerical simulators model the entire multiprocessor as a complex resistor-capacitor network (eg, Hotspot) and calculate temperature by numerically solving a large set of differential equations. These simulators depend on knowledge of the exact power consumption of each micro-architectural unit within each core. These power numbers may be obtained for certain processors using the Wattch/Simplescalar toolchain. For other processor designs, a generally accepted method has been to use hardware sniffers, which calculate the number of times a micro-architectural unit has been accessed by an application, see [15]. However, this requires setting up special registers using software or hardware methods that record the accesses of all micro-architectural entities in the processor, which may not be always possible. In addition, unless dedicated hardware is used, the measurement of access counts may disturb the behavior of the profiled application itself, leading to an inaccurate model. The combination of large computational power required for numerical simulators, in addition to detailed knowledge of the hardware as well as software make this approach unfeasible for design space exploration. A System-C based thermal simulator has recently been reported, but suffers from the same basic limitation as other simulators: the level of detailed information required for setting up the model is not easily available, see [16].

Computationally fast simulators based on first-order differential equations have been used in [12], but their applicability to modern CMP systems is not clear since the thermal model is too simplistic to take all important temperature dynamics into account, like differences in utilization of core's

micro-architectural units. Li et al. propose an abstraction based approach, which builds a thermal model based on total power consumption of the processor, for calculating temperature traces for given applications, see [17]. Li'a approach is oblivious to the power density distribution of applications, i.e., two applications consuming the same total power but targeting different micro-architectural units are indistinguishable. Such an abstraction can lead to large errors in the estimated temperature of cores, as already discussed in Section 1.1.

A look-up table based approach involves building resistor-capacitor (RC) models for $\mathcal{S}$, and recording tables of time-temperature relationship for the set of applications, $\mathcal{A}$, see [18]. The resulting estimation methods are fast, but again, they assume that a unique total power consumption always implies a unique temperature distribution. Separate databases are created for temperature increments and decrements (when an application raises or lowers the temperature of the CMP, respectively). Since temperature changes depend on the current temperature of a core, it is not clear as how to how much data is required to model all possible switching scenarios.

Thus, conventionally available solutions either assume the availability of hard to get information (numerical simulators based approach) or are too abstract for estimating correct temperature traces (abstract power-model based models).

3. SETUP AND NOTATIONS

In the following sections, we assume an arbitrary chip multiprocessor $\mathcal{S}$ consisting of $\mathcal{N} \in \mathbb{N}$ cores $\mathcal{S}_j \in \mathcal{S}$. It is not necessary that all cores in $\mathcal{S}$ are homogeneous. A core, for instance may be of type graphics processor (GPU), a floating point processor (FPU), a RISC processor etc. Thus, we have available a set of processor types, $\mathcal{C} = \{GPU, FPU, RISC, ...\}$ available on $\mathcal{S}$. A function $\mathcal{T} : \mathcal{S} \rightarrow \mathcal{C}$ maps the set of cores in $\mathcal{S}$ to their types. Also available is the set of applications $\mathcal{A}$ that may execute on $\mathcal{S}$. The ith application in $\mathcal{A}$ is referred to as $\mathcal{A}_i$. The approach taken in the work treats each application $\mathcal{A}_i \in \mathcal{A}$ as a black-box to be run on $\mathcal{S}$. Thus, this approach can be used to estimate temperature for an arbitrary given set of applications. All applications bound to a given core may be scheduled according to a scheduling policy such as *earliest deadline first* (EDF), *round-robin* (RR), *least laxity first* (LFF) or *rate-monotonic* (RM).

$P(\mathcal{A}_i, \mathcal{S}_j)$ denotes the instantaneous total power consumption of core $\mathcal{S}_j$ due to an application $\mathcal{A}_i$. $\mathcal{P}(\mathcal{A}_i, \mathcal{S}_j)$ refers to time trace of instantaneous total power consumption of core $\mathcal{S}_j$ due to the application $\mathcal{A}_i$; henceforth referred to as 'power trace'. We suppose that an application consumes constant power as long as it is running. The utilization alphabet, $\mathcal{U} \in \{0, 1\}$ represents the utilization of a core by an application for a time interval with length t_s. In other words, if an application is running then its utilization is 1, otherwise 0. The time-trace of an application $\mathcal{A}_i$ is given by $\sum_\mathcal{U} \mathcal{A}_i$, which is a tuple whose elements are in $\{0, 1\}$. The set of all tuples is denoted by $\sum_\mathcal{U}^*$. In other words, $\sum_\mathcal{U} \mathcal{A}_i$ is the time-trace of the utilization of application $\mathcal{A}_i$, specified with a given time-resolution t_s.

If $\mathcal{S}$ has a square or a rectangular physical footprint, the location of a core in $\mathcal{S}$ can also be specified in Cartesian coordinates <x,y>, with the origin located at the lower left corner of $\mathcal{S}$. In this case, two cores with co-ordinates <x,y> and <x',y'>, respectively, are said to be k hops apart, if $k = \max\{|x' - x|, |y' - y|\}$.

A set of temperature sensors $\mathcal{R}$ is available on $\mathcal{S}$. Temperature for core $\mathcal{S}_j$ is available from $\mathcal{R}_j$. It is assumed that a reading from $\mathcal{R}_j$ represents the temperature for that core. Logging of temperature trace is done only during the construction of the thermal model.

We also define the severity of thermal cycles experienced by the chip multiprocessor. Thermal cycles are periodic changes in temperature experienced by a core $\mathcal{S}_j$, when a given subset $\mathcal{A}' \subseteq \mathcal{A}$ of applications execute on it. Large variations in temperature are said to be worse for hardware reliability, as compared to small ones. The hardware is designed to withstand a certain maximum number of such temperature cycles, before it fails, see [19]. Therefore, a core $\mathcal{S}_j$ has a fixed "thermal-cycle budget", and the entire system's budget is simply the sum total of the thermal-cycle budgets for each core. Based on this concept, a simple metric that measures the "expenditure" from the total thermal-cycle budget, is $\mathcal{V}$:

$$\mathcal{V} = \sum_{i=1}^{\mathcal{N}} (\Delta T_i) \times f_i \qquad (2)$$

ΔT_i is the maximum temperature variation experienced by a core $\mathcal{S}_i$; f_i is the frequency of this variation and '$\times$' is the multiplication operator. A mapping with smaller $\mathcal{V}$ is preferable.

4. APPLICATION FINGERPRINTING

This section describes the construction of the thermal model of chip multiprocessor $\mathcal{S}$, given a set of applications, $\mathcal{A}$. We call this technique "application fingerprinting". Application fingerprinting assumes that the thermal model of $\mathcal{S}$ is linear. It has been shown that a thermal model of a processor can be constructed by using only passive electrical components, such as a resistor and a capacitor, which therefore forms a linear circuit, see [20, 10, 21].

The overall idea of application fingerprinting is to determine the thermal impulse response, $H(\mathcal{A}_i, \mathcal{S}_p, \mathcal{S}_q) \, \forall \, i, p, q$ such that the temperature trace $T(\mathcal{A}_i, \mathcal{S}_p, \mathcal{S}_q)$ due to $\mathcal{A}_i$ can then be calculated easily:

$$T(\mathcal{A}_i, \mathcal{S}_p, \mathcal{S}_q) = \sum_{\mathcal{U}} \mathcal{A}_i \otimes H(\mathcal{A}_i, \mathcal{S}_p, \mathcal{S}_q) \qquad (3)$$

where $H(\mathcal{A}_i, \mathcal{S}_p, \mathcal{S}_q)$ is the required thermal impulse response for the application $\mathcal{A}_i$, when it executes on core $\mathcal{S}_p$ and the resulting temperature change is calculated for core $\mathcal{S}_q$. The symbol $\otimes$ is the convolution operator. Notice that power trace is not used in (3). The utilization trace, $\sum_{\mathcal{U}} \mathcal{A}_i$, the impulse response, and the calculated temperature trace are all given at the time resolution of t_s.

Presented next are two claims that enable the calculation of accurate temperature traces, without requiring any knowledge of the power density distribution in a core, or its power trace. Data extracted from the Simplescalar/Wattch simulator is used to support the claims being made on the the relationships between total power, temperature and power-densities, due to an application such as $\mathcal{A}_i$.

4.1 Non-Unique Relationship between Total Power Trace and Temperature Trace

A power trace associated with an application $\mathcal{A}_i$, executing on a core $\mathcal{S}_j$, does not automatically imply a unique temperature trace, on any core in the chip multiprocessor $\mathcal{S}$. The power density distribution in the core determines the net flow of heat between various parts of the core, and hence, the overall temperature trace. Multiple applications can have the same total power consumption, but different power density distributions, causing a different overall temperature trace. An example was already discussed in section 1.1. Thus, a correct thermal model must not calculate temperature traces

S.No	Application	#Runs	ΔP_{max}	Instructions Executed
1	FFT	10	4%	64, 892 354, 675
2	I-JPEG	10	2.7%	6.2×10^6 119.6×10^6
3	Matrix-Multiplication	10	1.2%	85, 910 107.6×10^6
4	GSM-Encoder ("toast")	10	0.8%	5.6×10^6 19.6×10^6

Table 1: Power distribution statistics of selected benchmarks.

solely as a function of various power traces when the set of applications $\mathcal{A}$ execute on the system $\mathcal{S}$.

In summary, given a temperature trace $T(\mathcal{A}_i, \mathcal{S}_p, \mathcal{S}_q)$, the application $\mathcal{A}_i$ may not be unique. However, the following relationship is deterministic: given $\mathcal{A}_i$ executes on core $\mathcal{S}_p$, its power trace is always $\mathcal{P}(\mathcal{A}_i, \mathcal{S}_p)$.

4.2 Unique Relationship between application and Relative Power Distribution

An application $\mathcal{A}_i$ executing on core $\mathcal{S}_p$, consumes a constant total instantaneous power, $P(A_i, \mathcal{S}_p)$. Furthermore, a given $P(A_i, \mathcal{S}_p)$ uniquely determines the relative distribution of this total power amongst the core's micro-architectural units. This unique relationship between an application and its power distribution holds well for typical embedded applications, which are often subjected to similar inputs over their lifetime. We suppose that a particular application, such as a 16-point FFT, will run through the same sequence of steps, irrespective of the inputs. We show that such an assumption is a reasonable abstraction. In case the input to this application varies, these sequence of steps are repeated appropriately. Such repetitions also cause the number of accesses to each of $\mathcal{S}_p$'s micro-architectural units to scale appropriately.

This claim was validated using several benchmarks from the MiBench Embedded Systems benchmarks suite, see [22]. The results for selected benchmarks are shown in Table 1. These benchmarks were run with varying inputs, which is reflected in the number of instructions executed (column 5, minimum vs maximum number of instructions executed). The variation in instantaneous total power consumption of an application executing under varying inputs is minimal. For instance, the maximum variation for the FFT application was only 4%, with inputs ranging from single-digit values to six-digit values. Similar results are obtained for other benchmarks.

In addition, power consumption per instruction for each of these benchmarks was also evaluated after making suitable modifications to the Wattch simulator. The results for FFT and GSM-Encoder ("toast") application are shown in Figure 3. The same conclusions apply for other applications. It can be seen from the figure that the mean power consumption in all micro-architectural units in the core remains almost constant even under significant input variations. Almost all the difference in any total power consumption can be attributed to the variation in power consumed by the clock. Statistical parameters such as mode, median and standard-deviation are also shown in Figure 3. It can be observed that these statistical parameters also remain relatively constant.

From the preceding discussion, the following conclusions can be drawn:

- The instantaneous total power consumption of $\mathcal{A}_i$ exe-

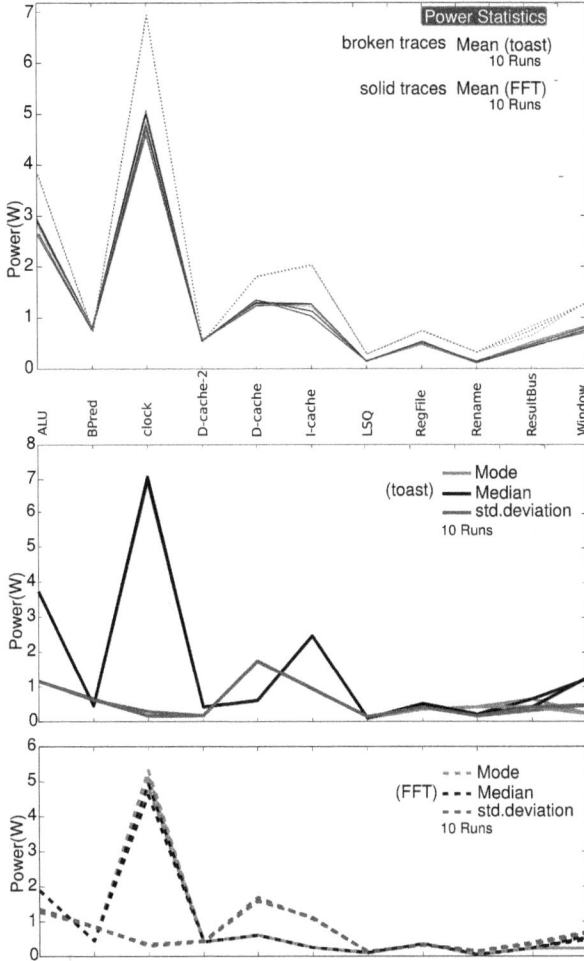

Figure 3: Statistics on power consumption for major micro-architectural units. Results from the "toast" and "FFT" applications are presented.

cuting on core $\mathcal{S}_p$ is:

$$\begin{cases} P(\mathcal{A}_i, \mathcal{S}_p) & : \quad \mathcal{U} = 1 \\ 0 & : \quad \mathcal{U} = 0 \end{cases} \qquad (4)$$

- For an application $\mathcal{A}_i \in \mathcal{A}$, executing on core $\mathcal{S}_p$, its utilization trace, $\sum_\mathcal{U} \mathcal{A}_i$ also determines its power trace, one varying from the other only by a scalar. Specifically:

$$\mathcal{P}(\mathcal{A}_i, \mathcal{S}_p) = s(\mathcal{A}_i, \mathcal{T}(\mathcal{S}_p)) \times \sum_\mathcal{U} \mathcal{A}_i \qquad (5)$$

where $s(\mathcal{A}_i, \mathcal{T}(\mathcal{S}_p))$ is scalar depending on $\mathcal{A}_i$, and the type of processor core $\mathcal{T}(\mathcal{S}_p)$.

- Assume a thermal impulse response $H'(\mathcal{A}_i, \mathcal{S}_p, \mathcal{S}_q)$ determined from power-trace $\mathcal{P}(\mathcal{A}_i, \mathcal{S}_p)$ and temperature trace $T(\mathcal{A}_i, \mathcal{S}_p, \mathcal{S}_q)$. Also assume another impulse response $H(\mathcal{A}_i, \mathcal{S}_p, \mathcal{S}_q)$, determined from $\sum_\mathcal{U} \mathcal{A}_i$ and $T(\mathcal{A}_i, \mathcal{S}_p, \mathcal{S}_q)$. Requiring that the temperature traces calculated using either impulse responses must be equal:

$$\sum_\mathcal{U} \mathcal{A}_i \otimes H(\mathcal{A}_i, \mathcal{S}_p, \mathcal{S}_q) = \mathcal{P}(\mathcal{A}_i, \mathcal{S}_p) \otimes H'(\mathcal{A}_i, \mathcal{S}_p, \mathcal{S}_q)$$
$$= \{s(\mathcal{A}_i, \mathcal{T}(\mathcal{S}_p)) \times \sum_\mathcal{U} \mathcal{A}_i\} \otimes H'(\mathcal{A}_i, \mathcal{S}_p, \mathcal{S}_q)$$
$$= \sum_\mathcal{U} \mathcal{A}_i \otimes \{s(\mathcal{A}_i, \mathcal{T}(\mathcal{S}_p)) \times H'(\mathcal{A}_i, \mathcal{S}_p, \mathcal{S}_q)\} \qquad (6)$$

Therefore, we find:

$$H(\mathcal{A}_i, \mathcal{S}_p, \mathcal{S}_q) = s(\mathcal{A}_i, \mathcal{T}(\mathcal{S}_p)) \times H'(\mathcal{A}_i, \mathcal{S}_p, \mathcal{S}_q) \qquad (7)$$

and:

$$T(\mathcal{A}_i, \mathcal{S}_p, \mathcal{S}_q) = \mathcal{P}(\mathcal{A}_i, \mathcal{S}_p) \otimes H'(\mathcal{A}_i, \mathcal{S}_p, \mathcal{S}_q)$$
$$= s(\mathcal{A}_i, \mathcal{T}(\mathcal{S}_p)) \times \sum_\mathcal{U} \mathcal{A}_i \otimes H'(\mathcal{A}_i, \mathcal{S}_p, \mathcal{S}_q))$$
$$= \sum_\mathcal{U} \mathcal{A}_i \otimes \{s(\mathcal{A}_i, \mathcal{T}(\mathcal{S}_p))) \times H'(\mathcal{A}_i, \mathcal{S}_p, \mathcal{S}_q))\} \qquad (8)$$

In other words, (5), (7) and (8) taken together show that the impulse response $H(\mathcal{A}_i, \mathcal{S}_p, \mathcal{S}_q))$ determined using the temperature trace, $T(\mathcal{A}_i, \mathcal{S}_p, \mathcal{S}_q)$ and the utilization trace, $\sum_\mathcal{U} \mathcal{A}_i$ can be used to estimate correct temperature traces, without requiring any power trace information.

4.3 Estimating Impulse Responses

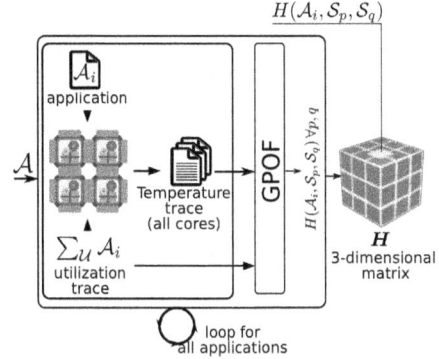

Figure 4: Overview of the application fingerprinting technique

Figure 4 shows the overview of the application fingerprinting technique. The technique starts with taking the set of applications, $\mathcal{A}$ and the system $\mathcal{S}$, for estimation of impulse responses, $H(\mathcal{A}_i, \mathcal{S}_p, \mathcal{S}_q) \forall i, p, q$. Each application $\mathcal{A}_i \in \mathcal{A}$ is run individually on $\mathcal{S}_p$ using a known utilization trace, $\sum_\mathcal{U} \mathcal{A}_i$. As the application $\mathcal{A}_i$ executes, temperature traces from all other cores are $\mathcal{S}$ recorded. The estimation of impulse responses is based on the *Generalized Pencil-of-functions* (GPOF) technique, see [23]. Our estimation approach is summarized in Algorithm 1. All impulse responses are collected in a three dimensional matrix, H.

Notice that the procedure for estimation of impulse responses is different from Li's approach, see [17]. Li requires power trace information, whereas we require only utilization traces and corresponding temperature traces from $\mathcal{S}$. Impulse responses are estimated for each application $\mathcal{A}_i \in \mathcal{A}$, making it possible to account for different power density distributions, even when there are multiple applications consuming the same total power. As a consequence, it is possible to avoid incorrect calculations of temperature traces, as discussed in section 1.1. Note that since impulse responses are calculated using the utilization trace of an application and the corresponding temperature trace, the scalar, $s(\mathcal{A}_i, \mathcal{T}(\mathcal{S}_p))$ is automatically accounted for. Once all impulse responses are available, the correct temperature trace can be calculated for any candidate mapping consisting of applications from $\mathcal{A}$, executing on $\mathcal{S}$. Subsequent temperature trace calculations require the knowledge of only the utilization trace, $\sum_\mathcal{U} \mathcal{A}_i$ of the core on which the application $\mathcal{A}_i$ executes. Note that power traces are not required for the temperature estimation step.

Algorithm 1 Algorithm to determine $H(\mathcal{A}_i, \mathcal{S}_p, \mathcal{S}_q)$

```
1:  begin
2:    A: set of applications
3:    |A|: cardinality of A.
4:    T(A_i, S_p, S_q): temperature trace of application A_i running on core S_p,
      with temperature measured on core S_q
5:    ∑_U A_i: utilization trace of application A_i running on core S_p.
6:    do for i = 1 : |A| // Iterate over all applications
7:      do for p = 1 : N //Iterate for all cores in S
8:        Run A_i on core S_p
9:        H(A_i, S_p, S_q) = GPOF(∑_U A_i, T(A_i, S_p, S_q)), ∀q
        //s(A_i, T(S_p)) is automatically accounted for
10:     end
11:   end
12:   Procedure: GPOF(PowerTrace, TemperatureTrace)
13:     // Calculates impulse response from utilization trace and temperature
        trace based on the generalized pencil-of-functions algorithm.
14:     // returns the estimated impulse response.
15:  end
```

5. TEMPERATURE AWARE DESIGN SPACE EXPLORATION

DSE tools are already available, which, given a set of applications, and a set of abstract hardware properties (number of cores, type of cores etc, but not the detailed floorplan) calculate various mappings subject to a set of constraints and objectives, see [24]. However, such tools usually are not temperature aware. However, once all required impulse responses are available, temperature-aware design space exploration can now be performed, using applications from the set $\mathcal{A}$, on the system $\mathcal{S}$.

A temperature aware DSE loop is shown in Figure 5. The DSE tool accepts the following parameters:

1. Abstract architectural properties: available computing resources, their types etc;
2. Set of mapping constraints and objectives;
3. Set of applications, $\mathcal{A}$;
4. Evaluated temperature traces for a given mapping, $\mathcal{M}$. A mapping $\mathcal{M}$ provides the following information:
   - Binding for all applications in $\mathcal{A}$, i,e., each application in $\mathcal{A}$ is provided with a core to execute on;
   - Scheduling policy for each *core*, such as EDF, RR, LFF etc.

A candidate mapping generated by the DSE tool is evaluated using the temperature evaluation component. The detailed algorithm for calculation of temperature traces is presented in the next section. Based on the feedback of the temperature evaluation component, the DSE tool may modify its internal parameters to rule out combinations that lead to unacceptable temperature profiles on $\mathcal{S}$. Or, the DSE tool may successively refine mappings that are deemed to be favorable in terms of temperature. A simple approach used in successive refinement of mappings is simulated annealing, which successively transforms an initial mapping $\mathcal{M}_0$, by moving applications between cores, and recalculating temperature traces at each step. The DSE tool also evaluates different scheduling policies for each core. The process continues till the required performance objectives are met (viz., minimizing peak temperature, minimizing thermal cycles).

5.1 Temperature Trace Calculation from a given Mapping

The linearity property of the thermal model of $\mathcal{S}$ allows us to use the superposition principle for determining the overall temperature trace due a given mapping, $\mathcal{M}$. Algorithm 2 presents the procedure to calculate detailed temperature traces.

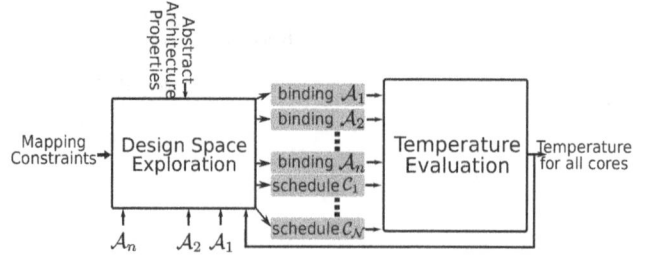

Figure 5: Temperature aware DSE Loop.

Algorithm 2 Temperature estimation for $\mathcal{S}$, given a mapping $\mathcal{M}$

```
1:  begin
2:    M: a mapping from DSE.
3:    M_B(A_i): Core to which A_i is bound
4:    |M(A)|: total number of applications bound to S.
5:    U ∈ (∑_U)^|M(A)|: Array of utilization traces. Contains |M(A)| traces.
6:    U(A_i) ∈ ∑_U*: Utilization trace for A_i.
7:    S_q ∈ S: Core in S on which temperature is to be estimated.
8:    T_q: Temperature trace on core S_q.
9:    U = Cheddar(M)
10:   init: T_q = 0 ∀q
11:   do for i = 1 : |M(A)| //Iterate for all applications
12:     do for q = 1 : N //Iterate for all cores
13:       →T_q = →T_q + H(A_i, M_B(A_i), S_q) ⊗ U(A_i)  //Calculate
        temperature trace on S_q due to A_i on core M_B(A_i).
14:     end for
15:   end for
16:
17:   function Cheddar(M)
18:     Return utilization trace for each application in M, using libraries from
        Cheddar project.
19:  end
```

Temperature trace calculations start with a candidate mapping provided by the DSE. For a given core $\mathcal{S}_p$, its scheduling policy determines the utilization trace for each application bound to $\mathcal{S}_p$. The Cheddar project provides for automating the construction of such utilization traces, see [25].

Referring to Algorithm 2, lines 2-8 define the required variables. Line 11 initializes a loop to iterate over all applications to be run on $\mathcal{S}$. Line 12 iterates over each core in $\mathcal{S}$, calculating the temperature trace due to $\mathcal{A}_i$, on all cores of $\mathcal{S}$ (Line 13). The algorithm loops till all applications have been accounted for, and the overall temperature trace on each core due to mapping $\mathcal{M}$ is calculated by superposition.

5.2 Sources of Inaccuracies

5.2.1 Inexact Impulse Responses

Estimation of the impulse response from a given utilization trace and an associated temperature trace measurement is often an approximate process. Further, the order of the thermal model of $\mathcal{S}$ is limited to avoid dealing with overly complex impulse responses, thereby saving some computational effort. In this work, the accuracy of estimated impulse response, $H(\mathcal{A}_i, \mathcal{S}_p, \mathcal{S}_q)$ is specified as *Quality of Fit* (QoF):

$$QoF_{H(\mathcal{A}_i, \mathcal{S}_p, \mathcal{S}_q)} = 100 \left[1 - \frac{N}{D} \right] \qquad [\%] \qquad (9)$$

Where:

$$N = ||T(\mathcal{A}_i, \mathcal{S}_p, \mathcal{S}_q)_m - T(\mathcal{A}_i, \mathcal{S}_p, \mathcal{S}_q)_e||$$

$$D = ||T(\mathcal{A}_i, \mathcal{S}_p, \mathcal{S}_q)_m - \overline{T(\mathcal{A}_i, \mathcal{S}_p, \mathcal{S}_q)_m}||$$

$T(\mathcal{A}_i, \mathcal{S}_p, \mathcal{S}_q)_m$ is the measured temperature trace, due to a known utilization trace, $\sum_{\mathcal{U}} \mathcal{A}_i$. The mean value of the measured temperature trace is given by $\overline{T(\mathcal{A}_i, \mathcal{S}_p, \mathcal{S}_q)_m}$. The temperature trace, $T(\mathcal{A}_i, \mathcal{S}_p, \mathcal{S}_q)_e$ is calculated using the esti-

Algorithm 3 Worst Case Error Estimate.

```
 1: begin
 2:   k: hops beyond which temperature affect of an active core is ignored.
 3:   S_p: A core in S.
 4:   O_{c, c'}: Observer core with location c, c', at the center of S.
 5:   A: set of applications. A_i: i^{th} application in A.
 6:   |A|: cardinality of A.
 7:   E*: Maximum error in temperature estimation, observed at O_{c, c'}.
 8:   H^k = {C_{x', y'} | (|y' − c'| = k) ||(|x' − c| = k)} //set of all cores k
       hops away.
 9:   L is the largest hop distance in the S, w.r.t. O_{c, c'}.
10:   // From all applications in A, determine which one leads to highest
       temperature rise.
11:   do for i = 1: |A|
12:     T*(i) = FV(H(A_i, S_p, S_p))
13:   end for
14:   A*: application that leads to highest T*(i) ∀i.
15:   do for i = k+1:L // go over all hop distances from k + 1 outwards
16:     do for j=1:|H^i| // go over cores at this hop distance
17:       E* = E* + FV(H(A*, H^i_j, O_{c, c'}))// H^i_j ∈ H^i, is j^{th} core in
         set H^i.
18:     end for
19:   end for
20:
21:   Procedure FV(H(A_i, S_p, S_q))
22:     Return steady-state temperature on core q due to A_i running on S_p.
23:     //Calculated using final-value theorem. Steady-state temperature is
       the highest temperature any core will experience due to A_i running
       continuously.
24: end
```

mated impulse response, and the utilization trace $\sum_{\mathcal{U}} \mathcal{A}_i$. A QoF of 100% indicates a perfect impulse response. The QoF depends on the p, q, $\mathcal{A}_i$, on the order of the thermal model, and on the utilization trace $\sum_{\mathcal{U}} \mathcal{A}_i$. The QoF reported in the experiments section is the worst QoF calculated over several utilization traces, ranging from $\sum_{\mathcal{U}} \mathcal{A}_i = [1, 1...1]$ (i.e., always executing) to $\sum_{\mathcal{U}} \mathcal{A}_i = [1, 0, 1, 0...]$ (start-stop execution with period t_s).

5.2.2 Under-estimating the impact of a hot core on a distant neighbor

Due to high lateral thermal resistance, the temperature on a core drops rapidly with distance from the temperature hotspot, see [26]. If from section 4.3, it is determined that the lateral thermal resistance of $\mathcal{S}$ is very high, it becomes tempting to ignore the temperature effects of an active core on cores far away from itself. This reduces the effort for the computation of temperature traces, but at the cost of accuracy. In this case, the maximum possible error that can be incurred in temperature calculations must be determined. Assuming that we would like to ignore the temperature affects due to an active core beyond distances of k hops, the resulting worst case error in temperature estimates is calculated from Algorithm 3.

Referring to Algorithm 3, the worst case error is estimated at an 'observer core', $O_{c,c'}$, at the center of $\mathcal{S}$. Since the temperature affect of an active core reduces with the hop distance from itself, a centrally located core will have maximum 1-hop neighbors, maximum 2-hop neighbors and so on. Further, uniform cooling over $\mathcal{S}$ is assumed, ensuring that the worst case error in temperature estimate is not missed. Final Value theorem for transfer functions is used to determine the maximum possible temperature influence of an active core on its neighbors. Line 12 determines the steady-state temperature due to application $\mathcal{A}_i$, running on a core $\mathcal{S}_p$. Any core $\mathcal{S}_p$ within $\mathcal{S}$ may be chosen. Line 14 determines the application $\mathcal{A}*$ which leads to the highest steady-state temperature on core $\mathcal{S}_p$. Line 17 then calculates the error by calculating the accumulated influence of all cores beyond k hops from $O_{c,c'}$.

The algorithm assumes that all cores which lie more than k hops from $O_{c, c'}$ are running $\mathcal{A}*$. The values of $E*$ with respect to hop distance are shown in Figure 6.

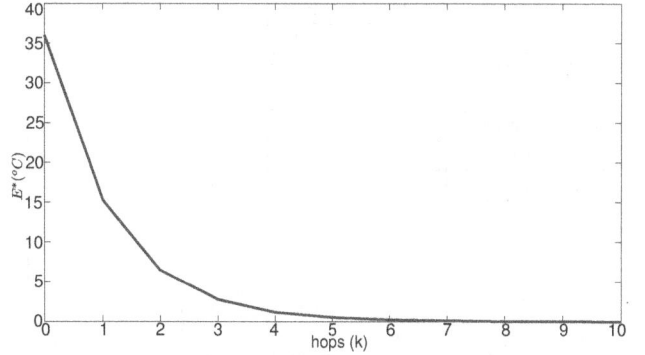

Figure 6: Maximum error in temperature estimate at $O_{c, c'}$ with hop-distance beyond which it is assumed that an active core produces no temperature affect.

The values in Figure 6 are specific to our experimental platform, but the nature of the curve is expected to remain the same for any chip-multiprocessor platform. The results clearly show the risk associated with making any uncalculated simplifications on the impact of a hot core on its neighbors.

6. EXPERIMENTS AND RESULTS

Our approach was validated using Hotspot, with the specification of $\mathcal{S}$ was taken from Magma project, which provides a variety of multicore floorplans consisting of 2 core- through 64 core- layouts, see [27]. Each core is an appropriately scaled version of the Alpha 21264 processor. The knowledge of physical arrangement of cores on the chip multiprocessor is required, only if the user intends to apply approximations discussed in section 5.2.2. Such approximations were not made in our experiments. Although our technique does not require that all cores of $\mathcal{S}$ be homogeneous, the floorplans available in the Magma project consist of only homogeneous cores, and thus we report results for a system with homogeneous cores. Furthermore, no power traces were used, neither in the estimation of impulse responses, nor in the calculation of any temperature traces. The scalability of our technique is demonstrated using a floorplan consisting of an 8x8 arrangement of cores. The following sections describe results relating to the QoF of estimated impulse responses, the accuracy of estimated temperature traces and the speedup due to our model, as compared to Hotspot. The time resolution t_s is 1 ms.

6.1 Accuracy of Estimated Impulse Responses

The order of the thermal model was limited to 10, at which the QoF achieved was greater than 90%. Further gains in QoF with increase in the order of the model were insignificant ($< 0.1\%$). The net effect of thermal resistance and thermal capacitance becomes increasingly complex, with the hop distance between two given cores, resulting in a QoF drop. However, due to high lateral thermal resistance, the absolute error in temperature estimates remains small ($5^0 C$). The results are summarized in Table 2. Only the worst QoF per hop is reported for summary.

6.2 Speedup

A total of sixty mappings were evaluated, using applications from Table 2. The scheduling policy used on each core was varied between EDF, LFF, RM and RR. For each mapping, temperature traces were calculated using our model, as

Application	0-hop	1-hop	2-hop	3-hop	> 3 hops
splitstream*	99	99	95	89	83
splitframe*	99	99	94	84	84
iqzigzagidct*	99	99	92	89	83
mergestream*	99	99	91	90	85
mergeframe*	99	98	94	85	82
Trigger*	99	98	91	91	86
susan†	99	99	95	88	84
qsort†	98	94	85	84	81
toast†	99	98	95	85	84
untoast†	99	99	96	90	87
FFT†	99	98	95	90	86
bitcount†	99	98	94	87	82
basicmath†	99	98	92	88	84
adpcm†	99	99	94	90	85
LAME†	99	99	95	87	83
Matrix Multiplication‡	99	98	90	89	83
Producer‡	98	98	92	87	80

Table 2: *QoF* of impulse responses. *: Motion-JPEG application split in 6 sub-applications[28], †: MiBench Embedded Benchmark [22], ‡: Internal benchmark.

Parameter($\downarrow$)	Our Model	Hotspot	Speedup
Mean Time (s)	24.853	29517	1187x
Maximum Time (s)	24.984	30057	1203x
Minimum Time (s)	24.795	27525	1110x
Standard Deviation (s)	0.054	547	

Table 3: Speedup achieved using our approach, as compared to Hotspot.

well as Hotspot. The average time for calculations using our model was ~ 24.9 seconds, while Hotspot averaged ~ 6 hours, see Table 3. Further speedup is expected upon porting our algorithms to C/C++ from Matlab/Java environment.

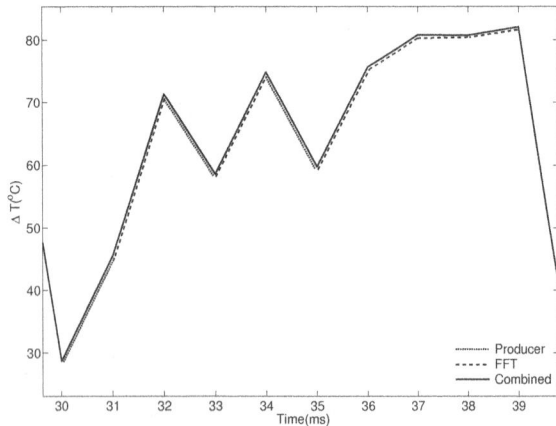

Figure 7: Section of temperature trace on core <4,4>. Both FFT and Producer applications have the same total power consumption, but lead to different temperature traces.

6.3 Accuracy of Estimation

We consider a mapping in which all applications are bound to cores located in a close spatial neighborhood. The temper-

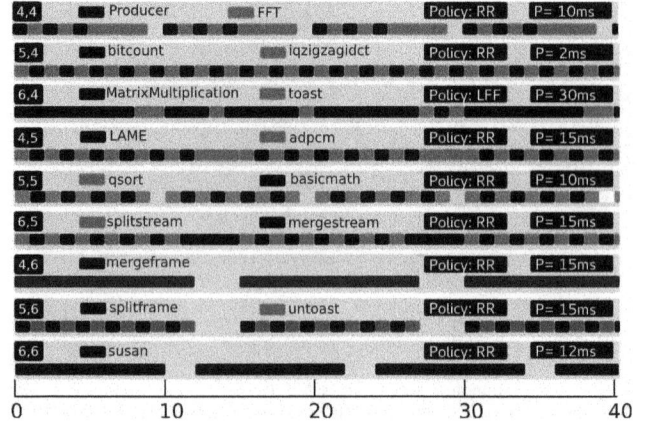

Figure 9: Schedule for nine cores. Time scale in ms. Letter 'P' shows the period of each schedule.

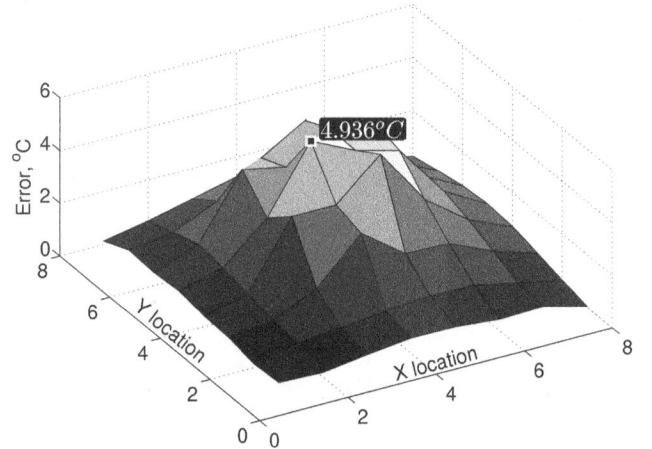

Figure 10: Maximum error in prediction over entire S. Errors in absolute values.

ature of each active core in thus significantly influenced by all other active cores. Further, all active cores in this mapping are scheduled according to round-robin (1-ms quantum) policy, where possible, leading to significant number of context switches, and rapid variations in temperature over time. Such a mapping provides a good test for demonstrating the accuracy of temperature traces estimated using our technique.

The mapping is shown in figure 9. Taking the core with <5,5> as the center, applications are mapped on the immediate 1-hop neighborhood, totaling 9 heat generating cores. All other are idle. The results are shown is shown in Figures 8. It is clear that the mapping in Figure 9 led to large changes in temperature on almost all active cores. Our thermal model was able to calculate correct temperature traces for all cores, well within the accuracy goal set up in the introductory section of this paper, see Figure 10.

In section 1.1, the applications *producer* and *FFT* consume the same total power, but differ in their respective power density distributions. Both these applications were mapped onto core <4,4>, see Figure 9. Our model was able to accurately capture the effect of differences in power density distribution between *producer* and *FFT*, leading to the trace in Figure 8, showing temperature variations as each application executes. Figure 7 shows a section of temperature trace for core <4,4> from Figure 8 for more clarity.

Other mappings, in which active cores are not immediate neighbors were also evaluated, and the prediction error was

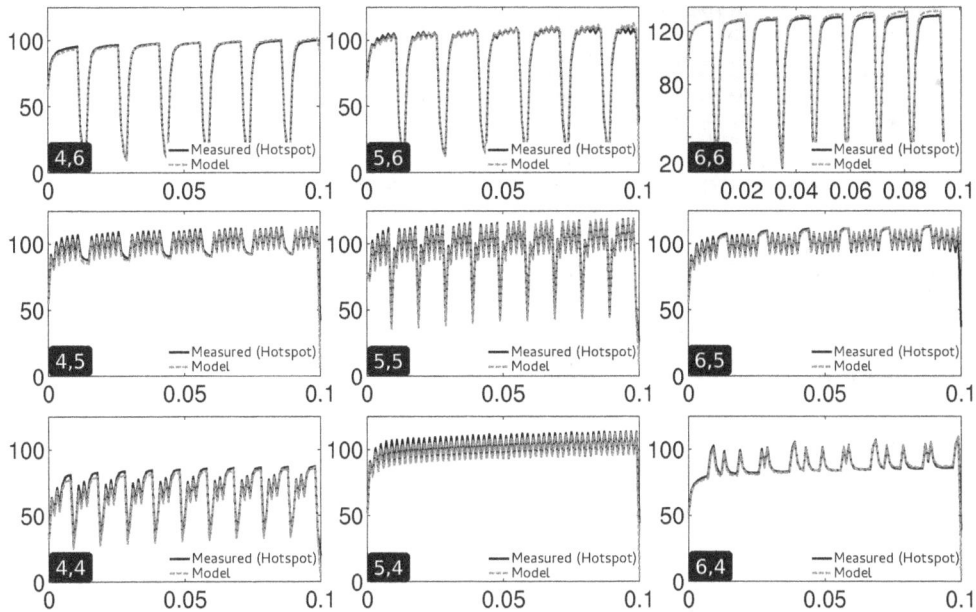

Figure 8: Measured temperature vs estimated temperature for nine active cores. Horizontal axes is time in seconds, vertical axes is $\Delta T (^{\circ}C)$. $\mathcal{V} = 47.7$.

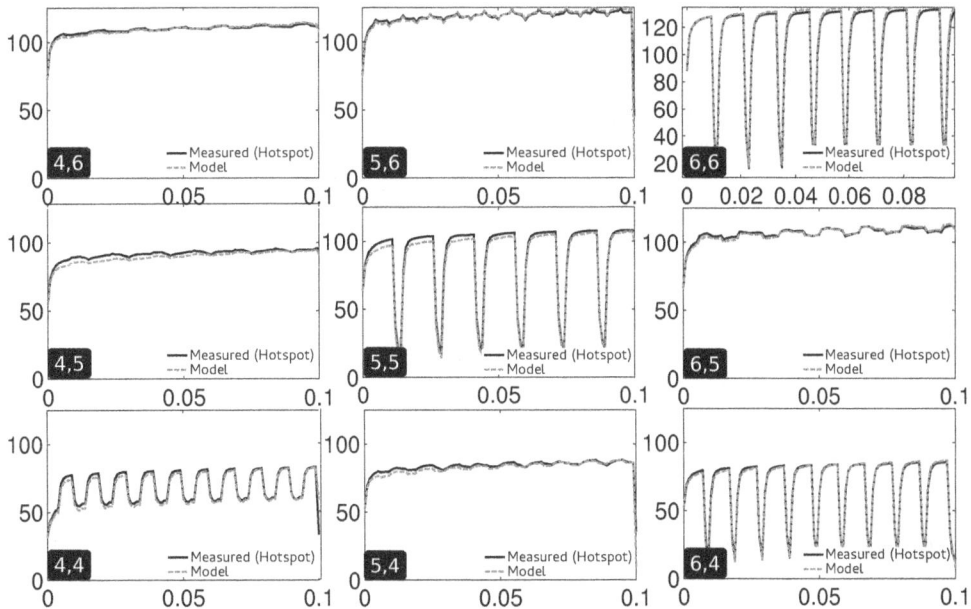

Figure 11: Reduction of thermal cycles by changing bindings of applications. Horizontal axes is time in seconds, vertical axes is $\Delta T (^{\circ}C)$. $\mathcal{V} = 25.1$

lower than what is reported in Figure 10. This is because an active core was not significantly influenced by its neighbors. Under such circumstances, estimation errors due to relatively low QoF were limited by high thermal resistance, see Table 2.

The speedup gained due to our approach allowed us to experiment with a lot of different mappings using the design space exploration loop. For instance, it was possible to reduce thermal cycles experienced by $\mathcal{S}$ by changing the binding and scheduling policies of a few applications, as shown in Figure 12, resulting in temperature traces shown in Figure 11. Notice that the total work done by each application remains unchanged. For instance, LAME executes for a total of 6ms, with a period of 15ms in both mappings. The overall error in estimated temperature is similar to the result shown in Fig-

ure 10; with the maximum error being $4.7^{\circ}C$. It is not always possible to reduce thermal cycles by changing the bindings of applications, for a feasible scheduling policy for all cores may not exist.

7. VARIATIONS AND OPTIMIZATIONS

It is not necessary to estimate impulse responses for all cores, if the given system has thermal symmetry. In this case, all cores are first classified into a set of thermally different locations (TDLs), see [18]. During the calibration step, applications need to be executed on only one distinguished core in each TDL. The calculation of thermal effect of an active core $\mathcal{S}_p$ on core $\mathcal{S}_q$ then proceeds in two steps. First, a sequence of transformations is determined which translates $\mathcal{S}_p$ to a core in one of the TDLs. Next, the same sequence of transforma-

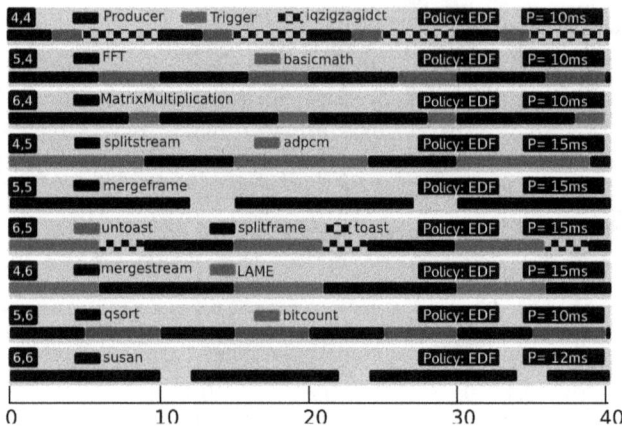

Figure 12: New mapping derived from the mapping in Figure 9.

tions is applied to core S_q, preserving the relative location of cores S_p and S_q. Temperature trace calculation then proceeds normally. Thermal symmetry reduces the memory space required to store H, and a one-time effort required for its calculation. However, if large errors in temperature estimates are to be avoided, the computational effort may not change much, see section 5.2.2.

The affect of caches on temperature was factored in during the impulse response estimation step. All caches are "clean" before executing an application in order to collect associated temperature traces. Thus, even when multiple applications execute on the same core, the impulse responses already account for the effect of inevitable cache misses. Consequently, our approach is thermally safe since temperature traces estimated using our approach will be slightly higher than actual measurements.

8. CONCLUSIONS

The paper presented a new calibration based approach for estimating accurate temperature traces. A compact thermal model was built using a small set of mappings and associated temperature trace measurement. The speed and accuracy of our approach enables exploration of a large set of mappings using the design space exploration loop. The highlight of our approach is that it does not require any power-trace information, or the hard-to-obtain details about hardware, such as the detailed floorplan. Our technique can also account for differences in power densities on a core due to an application, even when the total power consumed by two or more applications is the same. This makes our technique applicable to any given set of embedded applications and hardware.

APPENDIX
A. ACKNOWLEDGMENTS

This work was supported by EU FP7 project EURETILE under grant number 247846.

B. REFERENCES

[1] C. Meenderinck and B. Juurlink, "(when) will cmps hit the power wall?" Delft University of Technology, Tech. Rep., 2008.

[2] E. Nowak, T. Ludwig, et al., "Scaling beyond the 65 nm node with finfet-dgcmos," in *Custom Integrated Circuits Conference*, sept. 2003, pp. 339–342.

[3] S. Park, J.-J. Chen et al., "Dynamic thermal management for networked embedded systems under harsh ambient temperature variation," in *ACM/IEEE International Symposium on Low-Power Electronics and Design*, aug. 2010, pp. 289–294.

[4] A. Vassighi and M. Sachdev, "Thermal runaway in integrated circuits," *Device and Materials Reliability, IEEE Transactions on*, vol. 6, no. 2, pp. 300–305, june 2006.

[5] Y. Wang, K. Ma et al., "Temperature-constrained power control for chip multiprocessors with online model estimation," in *Proc. 36th annual international symposium on Computer architecture*, ser. ISCA '09, pp.314–324.

[6] S. Herbert and D. Marculescu, "Analysis of dynamic voltage/frequency scaling in chip-multiprocessors," in *Low Power Electronics and Design (ISLPED), ACM/IEEE International Symposium on*, aug. 2007, pp. 38–43.

[7] K. Choi, R. Soma et al., "Fine-grained dynamic voltage and frequency scaling for precise energy and performance trade-off based on the ratio of off-chip access to on-chip computation times," in *Proc. Design, automation and test in Europe - Volume 1*, DATE '04.

[8] J. Srinivasan, S. Adve et al., "The impact of technology scaling on lifetime reliability, in *Dependable Systems and Networks, 2004 International Conference on*, june-july 2004, pp. 177–186.

[9] A. Coskun, T. Rosing et al., "Static and dynamic temperature-aware scheduling for multiprocessor socs," *Very Large Scale Integration (VLSI) Systems, IEEE Transactions on*, vol. 16, no. 9, pp. 1127–1140, sept. 2008.

[10] K. Skadron, M. Stan et al., "Temperature-aware microarchitecture," in *30th Annual International Symposium on Computer Architecture*, june 2003, pp. 2–13.

[11] W. L. Bircher and L. K. John, "Complete system power estimation using processor performance events," *Computers, IEEE Transactions on*, vol. 61, no. 4, pp. 563–577, april 2012.

[12] D. Rai, H. Yang, et al., "Worst-case temperature analysis for real-time systems," in *Design, Automation Test in Europe Conference Exhibition (DATE)*, march 2011, pp. 1–6.

[13] Z. Wang and S. Ranka, "A simple thermal model for multi-core processors and its application to slack allocation", in *Parallel Distributed Processing (IPDPS), IEEE International Symposium on*, april 2010, pp. 1–11.

[14] D. Brooks, V. Tiwari et al., "Wattch: a framework for architectural-level power analysis and optimizations," in *Proc. 27th annual international symposium on Computer architecture*, ISCA '00.

[15] K.-J. Lee and K. Skadron, "Using performance counters for runtime temperature sensing in high-performance processors," in *Proceedings of the 19th IEEE International Parallel and Distributed Processing Symposium (IPDPS'05)*.

[16] T. Wegner, C. Cornelius et al., "Simulation of thermal behavior for networks-on-chip," in *NORCHIP, 2010*, nov. 2010, pp. 1–4.

[17] D. Li, S. X.-D. Tan et al., "Architecture-level thermal behavioral characterization for multi-core microprocessors," in *Proc. Asia and South Pacific Design Automation Conference*, ASP-DAC '08.

[18] J. Cui and D. Maskell, "High level event driven thermal estimation for thermal aware task allocation and scheduling," in *Design Automation Conference (ASP-DAC) 15th Asia and South Pacific*, jan. 2010, pp. 793–798.

[19] E. Karl, D. Blaauw et al., "Reliability modeling and management in dynamic microprocessor-based systems," in *Design Automation Conference, 43rd ACM/IEEE*, pp. 1057–1060.

[20] K. Skadron, T. Abdelzaher et al., "Control-theoretic techniques and thermal-rc modeling for accurate and localized dynamic thermal management," in *Proc. High-Performance Computer Architecture*, feb. 2002, pp. 17–28.

[21] H. Zumbahlen, *Linear circuit design handbook*. Newnes, 2008.

[22] University of Michigan. Mibench version 1.0.[Online]. http://www.eecs.umich.edu/mibench/

[23] Y. Hua and T. Sarkar, "Generalized pencil-of-function method for extracting poles of an em system from its transient response," *Antennas and Propagation, IEEE Transactions on*, vol. 37, no. 2, pp. 229–234, feb 1989.

[24] L. Thiele, S. Chakraborty et al., "Design space exploration of network processor architectures," in *8th International Symposium on High-Performance Computer Architecture (HPCA8)*, Cambridge MA, USA, 2002, pp. 30–41.

[25] F. Singhoff, J. Legrand et al., "Cheddar: a flexible real time scheduling framework," in *Proc. annual ACM SIGAda international conference on Ada*, SIGAda '04. ACM, 2004, pp. 1–8.

[26] J. Wang and F.-y. Hu, "Thermal hotspots in cpu die and its future architecture," in *Intelligent Computing and Information Science*, Vol. 134.Springer Berlin Heidelberg, 2011, pp. 180–185.

[27] S. Hanumaiah, The magma thermal simulator. Arizona State University. [Online]. http://vrudhula.lab.asu.edu/magma/index.php

[28] P. Bourgos, A. Basu et al., "Rigorous system level modeling and analysis of mixed hw/sw systems," in *Formal Methods and Models for Codesign (MEMOCODE), 9th IEEE/ACM International Conference on*, july 2011, pp. 11–20.

Scenario-Based Design Flow for Mapping Streaming Applications onto On-Chip Many-Core Systems

Lars Schor[1], Iuliana Bacivarov[1], Devendra Rai[1], Hoeseok Yang[1], Shin-Haeng Kang[2], and Lothar Thiele[1]

[1]Computer Engineering and Networks Laboratory, ETH Zurich, CH-8092 Zurich, Switzerland
[2]School of Electrical Engineering and Computer Science, Seoul National University, Seoul, South Korea
firstname.lastname@tik.ee.ethz.ch

ABSTRACT

The next generation of embedded software has high performance requirements and is increasingly dynamic. Multiple applications are typically sharing the system, running in parallel in different combinations, starting and stopping their individual execution at different moments in time. The different combinations of applications are forming system execution scenarios. In this paper, we present the distributed application layer, a scenario-based design flow for mapping a set of applications onto heterogeneous on-chip many-core systems. Applications are specified as Kahn process networks and the execution scenarios are combined into a finite state machine. Transitions between scenarios are triggered by behavioral events generated by either running applications or the run-time system. A set of optimal mappings are precalculated during design-time analysis. Later, at run-time, hierarchically organized controllers monitor behavioral events, and apply the precalculated mappings when starting new applications. To handle architectural failures, spare cores are allocated at design-time. At run-time, the controllers have the ability to move all processes assigned to a faulty physical core to a spare core. Finally, we apply the proposed design flow to design and optimize a picture-in-picture software.

Categories and Subject Descriptors

C.3 [**Special-purpose and application-based systems**]: Real-time and embedded systems; C.1.4 [**Parallel architectures**]: Distributed architectures

General Terms

Algorithm, Design, Performance

Keywords

On-chip many-core systems, design flow, scenario-based model of computation, MPSoC, mapping optimization

1. INTRODUCTION

Real-time physics, artificial intelligence, or 3D rendering effects will soon be state-of-the-art in embedded devices and have in common that they have high performance requirements, are highly parallelizable, and increasingly dynamic. The demand for a high degree of visual realism in multimedia applications has driven system architects to use on-chip many-core systems [16]. Intel's SCC processor [10] is a prominent example of such an on-chip many-core architecture. By incorporating 48 cores into a single processor, the SCC processor is a prototype of future embedded platforms. Even more, the next generation of on-chip many-core systems is supposed to have hundreds of heterogenous cores [3]. Thus, traditional methods to design multiprocessor system-on-chips are not anymore appropriate to many-core systems that are architecturally more complex.

The software of future embedded systems is composed of a set of applications and only a fraction of all applications is running in parallel. We call a scenario a certain system state with a predefined set of running or paused applications. Typically for embedded systems, the number of possible scenarios is restricted and the scenarios are known at design time. Consequently, a design flow for mapping dynamic streaming applications onto on-chip many-core systems has to provide three key features to the system architect. First, a high-level specification model that hides unnecessary implementation details but provides enough flexibility to specify dynamic interactions between applications. Second, an optimal mapping of the application onto the architecture in a transparent manner. Third, run-time support to dynamically change the workload of the system.

This paper proposes the distributed application layer (DAL), a scenario-based design flow that supports design, optimization, and simultaneous execution of multiple applications targeting heterogenous many-core systems. Applications are specified as Kahn process networks (KPNs) [11]. KPNs are suitable for a general description of a high-level design flow as they are determinate, provide asynchronous execution, and are capable to describe data-dependent behavior. In case a higher predictability is required, the application model can be restricted, e.g., to synchronous data flow (SDF) graphs [15]. To coordinate the execution of different applications, we use a finite state machine (FSM), where each scenario is represented by a state. Transitions between scenarios are triggered by behavioral events generated by either running applications or the run-time system.

The design flow that we propose in this paper is illustrated in Fig. 1. During design-time analysis, a set of opti-

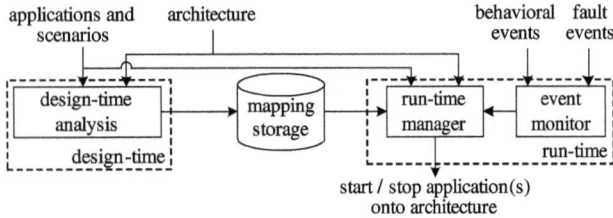

Figure 1: Overall structure of the scenario-based design flow.

mal mappings is calculated. Later, at run-time, the run-time manager monitors behavioral events, and applies the precalculated mappings to start, stop, resume, and pause applications according to the FSM. As the number of scenarios is restricted, an optimal mapping could be calculated for each scenario. However, assigning each scenario a different mapping might lead to bad performance due to reconfiguration overhead. For example, the user does not want to experience an interruption of the music when starting a different application. Therefore, processes are assumed resident, i.e., an application has the same mapping in two connected scenarios. The result of this approach is a scalable mapping solution where each application has assigned a set of mappings that are individually valid for a subset of scenarios.

The run-time manager is made up of hierarchically organized controllers that follow the architectural structure and handle the behavioral and architectural dynamism. In particular, behavioral dynamism leads to transitions between scenarios, and architectural dynamism is caused by temporary or permanent failures of the platform. The controllers monitor for behavioral events, change the current scenario, and start, stop, resume, or pause certain applications. Whenever they start an application, they select the mapping assigned to the new scenario. To handle failures of the platform, spare cores are allocated at design-time so that the run-time manager has the ability to move all processes assigned to a faulty physical core to a spare core. As no additional design-time analysis is necessary, the approach leads to a high responsiveness to faults.

The contributions of this paper can be summarized as follows:

- The considered scenario-based model of computation for streaming applications is formally described.
- We propose a novel hybrid design-time / run-time strategy for mapping software specified by the scenario-based model of computation onto heterogeneous on-chip many-core platforms.
- We formally describe a hierarchically organized run-time manager to handle the behavioral and architectural dynamism of on-chip many-core systems.
- Extensive experiments are carried out to show the effectiveness of the proposed approach. In particular, the scenario-based design flow is used to design and optimize a picture-in-picture software.

The remainder of the paper is organized as follows: First, related work is discussed. Afterwards, the considered class of on-chip many-core platforms is discussed in Section 3. In Section 4, the proposed model of computation is detailed. Section 5 describes the hybrid design-time / run-time mapping optimization strategy. Finally, in Section 6, case studies are shown to illustrate the presented concepts.

2. RELATED WORK

Programming paradigms for many-core systems have to tackle various new challenges. Techniques that worked well for systems with just a few cores will become the bottleneck in the next few years [25]. The KPN model of computation [11] is the basis of several frameworks for designing multi-processor systems, such as Daedalus [19], DOL [24], Koski [12], or SHIM [7]. As they provide a single mapping, they are only able to handle dynamism by over-provisioning the system.

To capture the increasing dynamism in future embedded applications, mapping strategies are proposed that generate a set of mappings at design-time [9, 17, 23]. Then, a run-time mechanism selects the best fitting mapping depending on the actual resource requirements of all active applications. The concept of system scenarios is introduced in [9] by automatically analyzing a system for similarities from a cost perspective. It has been applied in [23] to comprehend the dynamic behavior of an application as a set of scenarios. Each scenario is specified as an SDF [15] graph. In contrast, our work just specifies the running and paused applications per scenario, and each application is separately specified as a KPN. We think that the KPN model of computation is better suited to describe a high-level design flow and the individual specification of each application enables a better resource usage. Finally, multiple mappings that differ from each other in terms of power consumption and performance are generated in [17], but the approach is not scalable due to the centralized run-time manager.

The concept of hybrid mapping strategies has already been investigated in various other works. In [1], it is proposed to compute various system configurations and to calculate an optimal task allocation and scheduling for each of them. At run-time, the decision whether a transition between allocations is feasible, is based on precalculated migration costs. In our work, we assume that processes are resident. This makes design-time analysis more complex, but eliminates undesired disruption due to process migration. Similarly, process migration is prohibited in [21]. They use statistical methods to compute mappings for different interconnected usage-scenarios. As the approach evaluates a large number of mappings, it might not scale with the size of the platform. A hybrid mapping strategy is proposed in [22] that calculates several resource-throughput trade-off points at design-time. At run-time, it selects the best point with respect to available resources. However, the approach is restricted to homogeneous platforms and the schedulability of the system is only known at run-time.

In order to tolerate run-time processor failures, a multi-step mapping strategy is proposed in [14]. After calculating a static mapping for all possible failure scenarios, a processor-to-processor mapping is performed at run-time. As analyzing and storing a mapping scenario for each failure scenario is not scalable, we allocate spare cores at design-time.

Various options to design a run-time manager have been discussed in literature. On the one hand, a fully centralized approach can be seen as a broker running on its own core. While centralized approaches are widely used in multi-core systems [17, 20], they impose a performance bottleneck on many-core systems. On the other hand, a fully distributed approach [4, 13] leads to a high complexity. Therefore, we

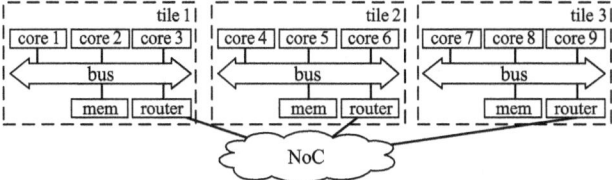

Figure 2: Sketch of a hierarchical on-chip many-core platform.

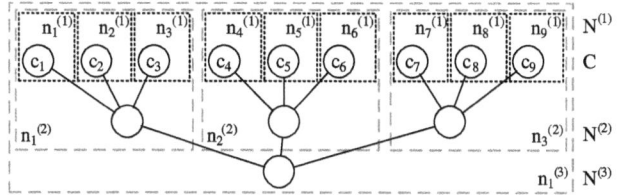

Figure 3: Abstract representation of the many-core platform sketched in Fig. 2.

propose a hierarchical centralized approach, that takes system scalability into account at a low complexity.

The KPN model of computation has been extended in [8] with the ability to support sporadic control events. However, the work includes neither concrete execution semantics nor mapping strategies. By separately specifying the execution scenarios as an FSM, we are able to formally define an execution semantic and to propose a hybrid design-time / run-time mapping strategy to efficiently execute multiple dynamic KPNs on a many-core platform. Finally, we define the semantics of a scenario change and propose a high-level interface for behavioral and fault events.

3. ARCHITECTURE MODEL

In this section, the architecture model is introduced. In order to describe the considered architecture in an abstract manner, we use a hierarchical representation. The on-chip many-core architecture $\mathcal{A} = \{C, D, N^{(1)}, \ldots, N^{(\eta)}, z\}$ consists of a set of cores C, a set of core types D, η sets of networks $N^{(1)}$ to $N^{(\eta)}$, and a function z. The function $z : C \rightarrow D$ assigns each core $c \in C$ its type $z(c) \in D$. The set of core types might be used to differ between DSP and RISC components or to distinguish between different operating frequencies. Each set of networks corresponds to a communication layer so that the architecture consists of η communication layers. A network $n^{(k)} \in N^{(k)}$ is defined as a subset of C. In particular, a network $n^{(1)} \in N^{(1)}$ represents the intra-core communication, i.e., $|N^{(1)}|=|C|$ and for each $c \in C$, there is a network $n^{(1)} \in N^{(1)}$ with $n^{(1)} = \{c\}$. The second set of networks $N^{(2)}$ partitions the cores into tiles so that each core is assigned to exactly one tile, i.e., we have $\bigcup_{n^{(2)} \in N^{(2)}} = C$ and $n_i^{(2)} \cap n_j^{(2)} = \emptyset$ for all $n_i^{(2)}, n_j^{(2)} \in N^{(2)}$ and $i \neq j$. Similarly, every other set of networks $N^{(k)}$ partitions the cores so that each network $n^{(k)} \in N^{(k)}$ contains multiple subordinate networks, i.e., there exists a $n^{(k)} \in N^{(k)}$ with $n^{(k-1)} \subseteq n^{(k)}$ for all $n^{(k-1)} \in N^{(k-1)}$, $\bigcup_{n^{(k)} \in N^{(k)}} = C$, and $n_i^{(k)} \cap n_j^{(k)} = \emptyset$ for all $n_i^{(k)}, n_j^{(k)} \in N^{(k)}$ and $i \neq j$. Finally, $N^{(\eta)} = \{n^{(\eta)}\}$ contains a single network hierarchically connecting all processors, i.e., $n^{(\eta)} = C$. Furthermore, the type of a network is defined as concatenation of all core types of the network.

The hierarchical representation of the architecture is a generalization of the well-known tile-based multiprocessor model [6]. First prototypes of future on-chip many-core systems typically consist of three sets of networks, i.e., $\eta = 3$, which correspond to the three communication layers intra-core, intra-tile, and inter-tile communication [10, 18, 26]. A shared bus is often used for intra-tile communication and a NoC for inter-tile communication. Figure 2 sketches a typical on-chip many-core system with $\eta = 3$ and its abstract representation is illustrated in Fig. 3.

Due to high power densities, on-chip many-core systems are prone to failures. In this work, we restrict ourselves to a failure of a core or a router. In case that a router fails, the tile is not anymore available. In any case, we suppose that either the failed component or any other component detects the failure and sends a fault event to the run-time manager. In order to handle architectural failures at run-time, spare cores and tiles are allocated at design-time. We call the abstract representation of the architecture without spare cores and tiles virtual architecture $^\mathcal{V}\mathcal{A}$. $^\mathcal{V}\mathcal{A} = \{^\mathcal{V}C, D, ^\mathcal{V}N^{(1)}, \ldots, ^\mathcal{V}N^{(\eta)}, ^\mathcal{V}z\}$ consists of a set of virtual cores $^\mathcal{V}C$, the set of core types D of architecture $\mathcal{A}$, η sets of virtual networks $^\mathcal{V}N^{(1)}$ to $^\mathcal{V}N^{(\eta)}$, and a function $^\mathcal{V}z$. The function $^\mathcal{V}z : ^\mathcal{V}C \rightarrow D$ assigns each core $^\mathcal{V}c \in ^\mathcal{V}C$ its type $^\mathcal{V}z(^\mathcal{V}c) \in D$. It is the system architect's task to specify the spare components at design-time. One possibility to generate $^\mathcal{V}\mathcal{A}$ is to remove from each network $n^{(i)} \in N^{(i)}$ one subordinate network $n^{(i-1)} \in N^{(i-1)}$ per network type so that each network is able to correct one failure. Finally, each virtual network $^\mathcal{V}n^{(i-i)}$ can be mapped onto any physical network $n^{(i-1)}$ that belongs to the same superior network $n^{(i)}$ and has the same type as $^\mathcal{V}n^{(i-1)}$. Consider for example the system illustrated in Fig. 2. Suppose that all cores are of the same type and the system architect selects $n_3^{(1)}$ as spare network of $n_1^{(2)}$. Then the virtual networks $^\mathcal{V}n_1^{(1)}$ and $^\mathcal{V}n_2^{(1)}$ can be mapped onto the physical networks $n_1^{(1)}$, $n_2^{(1)}$, and $n_3^{(1)}$, but not on $n_4^{(1)}$ as it belongs to a different tile.

4. MODEL OF COMPUTATION

In this section, we formally define the scenario-based model of computation for streaming applications. We first discuss the specification of individual applications as KPNs. Afterwards, the dynamic behavior of the system is captured by a set of scenarios.

4.1 Application Specification

The KPN [11] model of computation is considered in this paper to specify the application behavior. In particular, an application $p = (V, Q)$ consists of autonomous processes $v \in V$ that can only communicate through unbounded point-to-point FIFO channels $q \in Q$. A process $v \in V$ is a monotonic and determinate mapping F from one (or more) input streams to one (or more) output streams. As every process $v \in V$ is monotonic and determinate, there is no notion of time and the output just depends on the sequence of tokens in the individual input streams [8].

Conceptually, a KPN is non-terminating, i.e., once the process network has started it does not stop running. As this is not in accordance with the specification of a dynamic system, we extend the definition of a KPN with the ability to terminate and pause. To this end, we first propose the high-level API illustrated in Listing 1 to specify KPN processes. Roughly speaking, the INIT procedure is responsible for the initialization and is executed once at the startup of the application. Afterwards, the execution of a process is split into individual executions of the FIRE procedure, which is repeatedly invoked by the system scheduler. Once an application is stopped, the FINISH procedure is called for cleanup. Communication is enabled by calling high-level read and write procedures and each process has the ability to request a scenario change by calling the send_event procedure.

Listing 1: Implementation of a KPN process using the proposed API.

```
01 procedure INIT(ProcessData *p) // process initialization
02   initialize();
03 end procedure
04
05 procedure FIRE(ProcessData *p) // process execution
06   fifo->read(buf, size); // read from fifo
07   if (buf[0] == eventkey)
08     send_event(e); // send event e
09   end if
10   manipulate();
11   fifo->write(buf, size); // write to fifo
12 end procedure
13
14 procedure FINISH(ProcessData *p) // process cleanup
15   cleanup();
16 end procedure
```

Now, we are able to introduce and specify the four generic actions START, STOP, PAUSE, and RESUME of a KPN $p = (V, Q)$. The semantic of those four actions is summarized in Table 1. Stopping an application p might be problematic. Therefore, the FIRE method of all processes $v \in V$ is aborted only at predefined points such as when process v is calling a read or write procedure, or the execution of the FIRE procedure is finished. In the case that a process is blocked, i.e., the process attempts to read from an empty channel, the blocking is resolved before the fire method can be aborted. Finally, the finish procedure is executed to perform cleanup operations.

4.2 Scenario Specification

The dynamic behavior of a system can be captured by a set of scenarios. Each scenario represents a set of concurrently running or paused applications. Scenario transitions are triggered by behavioral events generated by either running applications or the run-time system. Consider, for

Table 1: Description of the four generic action types of a KPN $p = (V, Q)$.

Action	Description
START	All processes $v \in V$ and all FIFO channels $q \in Q$ are installed, and the INIT procedure of all processes $v \in V$ is executed once. Afterwards, all processes $v \in V$ are started and the FIRE method is continuously called by the scheduler.
STOP	The FIRE method of all processes $v \in V$ is aborted and the FINISH method of all processes $v \in V$ is executed. Afterwards, all processes $v \in V$ and all FIFO channels $q \in Q$ are removed.
PAUSE	The FIRE method of all precesses $v \in V$ is interrupted and all processes $v \in V$ are temporary detached from scheduler.
RESUME	All processes $v \in V$ are restarted and the FIRE method is continuously called by the scheduler.

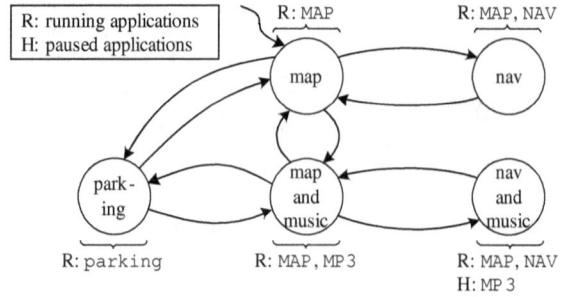

Figure 4: Example scenario specification of a (simplified) car entertainment system.

example, the (simplified) car entertainment system shown in Fig. 4. The software has five scenarios, with one to three applications. After startup, the system enters the *map* scenario where the MAP application is running and displaying the current position of the car on a map. Depending on the situation, the scenario might change. For example, the driver starts to drive backwards so that the parking assistant is started (scenario *parking*), the voice navigation notifies the driver to take the next exit (scenario *nav*), or the driver start listening to some music (scenario *map and music*). In addition, the voice navigation might notify the driver to change the driving direction while listening to music. To this end, the system switches to the scenario *nav and music*, and pauses the MP3 application.

Formally, we define the above described dynamic behavior of a system by an FSM $\mathcal{F} = (S, E, T, P, s_0, a, r, h)$ that consists of the set of scenarios S, the set of events E, the set of directed transitions $T \in S \times S$, the set of applications P, an initial scenario $s_0 \in S$, and three functions a, r, and h. The function $a : T \to E$ maps a transition $t \in T$ to a set of triggering events $a(t) \subseteq E$ for all $t \in T$. The function $r : S \to P$ assigns each scenario $s \in S$ a set of running applications $r(s) \subseteq P$ and the function $h : S \to P$ assigns each scenario $s \in S$ a set of paused applications $h(s) \subseteq P$. As we suppose that there is only one instance of an application, $r(s) \cap h(s) = \emptyset$ for all $s \in S$. Figure 5 presents an example of an FSM $\mathcal{F} = (S, T, E, P, s_0, a, r, h)$ with four scenarios s_0, s_1, s_2, and s_3 among which s_0 is initially active. The scenarios are linked by the set of transitions $T = \{t_1, t_2, t_3, t_4, t_5\}$ such that $t_1 = (s_0, s_1)$, $t_2 = (s_1, s_2)$, $t_3 = (s_2, s_3)$, $t_4 = (s_3, s_1)$, and $t_5 = (s_3, s_0)$. The function a assigns each transition its triggering events. For example, the transition t_2 from scenario s_1 to scenario s_2 happens when the events e_2 or e_3 are detected in scenario s_1. Finally, the functions r and h assign each scenario a list of running and paused applications.

4.3 Execution Semantics

The above introduced model of $\mathcal{F}$ is a Moore machine, i.e., each scenario has a list of running and paused applications, and each transition between scenarios has a set of events that trigger the transition. However, in terms of execution, each transition is associated with a set of actions. For example, transition t_1 of the FSM $\mathcal{F}$ illustrated in Fig. 5 is associated with the action {*pause application p_1*}, and transition t_4 is associated with the actions {*stop application p_3*, *start application p_2*}.

Therefore, in terms of execution, we map the system evolution to a Mealy machine and transform $\mathcal{F}$ into a new

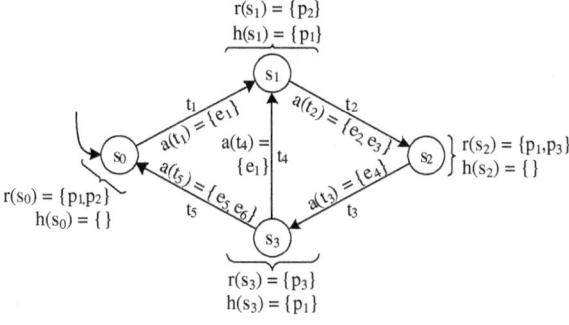

Figure 5: Example of an FSM $\mathcal{F} = (S, T, E, P, s_0, a, r, h)$.

FSM $\widetilde{\mathcal{F}} = (S, E, \widetilde{T}, P, t_0, a, u^s, u^t, u^p, u^r)$ that consists of the set of scenarios S, the set of events E, the set of directed transitions $\widetilde{T} \in S \times S$, the set of applications P, an initial transition $t_0 \in T$, and six functions a, u^s, u^t, u^p, and u^r. S, E, P, and $a : T \to E$ are defined as in Section 4.2 and $\widetilde{T} = T \cup t_0$. The functions u^s, u^t, u^p, and u^r assign each transition $t \in \widetilde{T}$ the set of applications to be started, stopped, paused, and resumed. Suppose that transition $t = (s_x, s_y)$, then $u^s(t)$, $u^t(t)$, $u^p(t)$, and $u^r(t)$ are formally defined as:

$$\text{START:} \quad u^s(t) = r(s_y) \setminus (r(s_x) \cup h(s_x)) \quad \subseteq P$$
$$\text{STOP:} \quad u^t(t) = (r(s_x) \cup h(s_x)) \setminus (r(s_y) \cup h(s_y)) \quad \subseteq P$$
$$\text{PAUSE:} \quad u^p(t) = h(s_y) \cap r(s_x) \quad \subseteq P$$
$$\text{RESUME:} \quad u^r(t) = r(s_y) \cap h(s_x) \quad \subseteq P$$

In other words, whenever transition $t \in \widetilde{T}$ is triggered, all applications $p \in u^s(t)$ are started, all applications $p \in u^t(t)$ are stopped, all applications $p \in u^p(t)$ are paused, and all applications $p \in u^r(t)$ are resumed.

In terms of execution, the initial transition t_0 takes place after startup so that the FSM enters scenario s_0. Whenever an event $e \in E$ is received that corresponds to one of the outgoing transitions of the current scenario, the transition takes place. In other words, an event $e \in E$ triggers a transition $t \in T$ if and only if $e \in a(t)$, $t = (s_x, s_y)$, and s_x is the current scenario of the FSM.

Conceptually, the reaction of the system to an event is immediate, i.e., the actions listed in Table 1 are performed in zero time. However, as the production and execution of these actions take a certain amount of time, we have to come up with additional rules, which preserve the described semantics. In particular, we assume that a transition is only triggered if the system is in a stable scenario. A stable scenario is reached if the execution of all actions triggered by the previous transition is completed. This rule is required as events might arrive faster than they can be processed. If the system is not yet in a stable scenario, the execution of new actions might cause the system to move to an unknown or wrong scenario. Practically, this requirement can be realized by storing all incoming events in a FIFO queue so that the events are processed in a First-Come-First-Served (FCFS) manner. If the current scenario has an outgoing transition that is sensitive to the head event of the FIFO queue, the transition takes place and the event is removed from the FIFO queue. Otherwise, the event is removed without changing the active scenario.

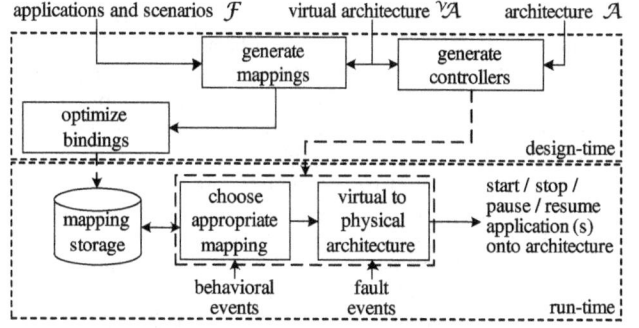

Figure 6: Overall mapping optimization approach with design-time and run-time component.

5. HYBRID MAPPING OPTIMIZATION

In this section, we present a hybrid design-time / run-time strategy for mapping streaming applications onto on-chip many-core platforms. The design-time component calculates an optimal mapping for each application and scenario where the application is either running or paused. At run-time, the dynamic mapping of the applications onto the architecture is controlled by a run-time manager, which monitors events, chooses an appropriate mapping, and finally executes the required actions, see Fig. 6.

5.1 Design-Time Analysis and Optimization

In this subsection, we introduce the proposed approach for design-time optimization. We minimize the maximum core utilization subject to utilization and communication constraints so that we obtain a system with a balanced workload.

5.1.1 Motivational Example

We start with an example. Consider the car entertainment system outlined in Fig. 4. As the workload of scenario *nav* is different from the workload of scenario *map and music*, different mappings should be used in both scenarios to optimize the performance. However, changing the process to core assignment with each scenario transition might lead to bad performance due to reconfiguration overhead. Therefore, the approach proposed in this paper assumes that processes are resident, i.e., once a process is mapped onto a core, it will not be remapped to another core. In other words, if an application is active in two connected scenarios, it has the same mapping in both scenarios. We think that this restriction is well suited for embedded systems where process migration leads to non-negligible costs in terms of time and system overhead. For example, consider again the car entertainment system. The MAP application will have the same mapping in all active scenarios. However, the mapping of the NAV application might be different in the scenarios *nav* and *nav and music* as they are not connected by a direct transition.

5.1.2 Mapping Specification

The design-time component calculates an optimal mapping for each application and scenario where the application is either running or paused. Thus, the output of the design-time analysis is a collection M of optimal mappings and exactly one mapping m of M is valid for a pair of an application and a scenario.

Formally, a mapping $m \in M$ is a triple (p, S^m, B^m) where p is an application, $S^m \subseteq S$ is a subset of scenarios, and $B^m \in V \times {}^VC$ the set of binding relations. S^m denotes the set of scenarios for which mapping m is valid. As processes are resident, the same mapping might be valid for more than one scenario. Finally, a binding relation $(v, {}^vc) \in B^m$ denotes that process v is bound to the virtual core ${}^vc$.

In the following, we propose a two-step procedure to calculate the mappings $m \in M$. First, we calculate pairs $<p, S^m>$ of an application p and a subset of scenarios S^m so that the size of each subset is minimized and no process migration is required if application p is using the same mapping in all scenarios $s \in S^m$. At the end of the first step, we allocate for each pair $<p, S^m>$ a mapping $m \in M$. Afterwards, in a second step, we calculate for each mapping $m \in M$ a set of optimized binding relations B^m so that an objective function is minimized and additional architectural constraints are fulfilled.

5.1.3 Mapping Generation

In a first step, we calculate pairs $<p, S^m>$ of an application p and a subset of scenarios S^m so that the size of each subset is minimized and additional constraints are fulfilled. The additional constraints ensure that no process migration is required if application p is using the same mapping in all scenarios $s \in S^m$. In particular, we can identify the following three constraints:

Constraint 1: Each application is mapped:

$p_\ell \in (r(s) \cup h(s))$
$\Rightarrow \exists\, m = (p, S^m, B^m) \in M : p_\ell = p \text{ and } s \in S^m.$

Constraint 2: Two mappings do not overlap:

$m_1 = (p, S^{m_1}, B^{m_1})$ and $m_2 = (p, S^{m_2}, B^{m_2})$
$\Rightarrow S^{m_1} \cap S^{m_2} = \emptyset.$

Constraint 3: Process migration is not allowed:

$p_\ell \in ((r(s_1) \cup h(s_1)) \cap (r(s_2) \cup h(s_2)))$ and $t = (s_1, s_2) \in T$
$\Rightarrow \exists\, m = (p, S^m, B^m) \in M : p_\ell = p \text{ and } s_1, s_2 \in S^m.$

The mapping generation problem can be solved by calculating for each application p the maximally connected components of a subgraph that just contains all scenarios where p is either running or paused. Then, we can generate a new pair $<p, S^m>$ for each component of this subgraph. Algorithm 1 presents the pseudocode to calculate all pairs $<p, S^m>$. The algorithm generates the pairs $<p, S^m>$ by sequentially analyzing all applications. First, a subgraph $\mathcal{G} = (S^{sub}, T^{sub})$ is determined by removing all scenarios $s \in S$ in which application p is neither running nor paused. Then, we determine the maximally connected components $\mathcal{G}_i^{conn} = (S_i^{conn}, T_i^{conn}) \in \mathcal{G}^{conn}$ of subgraph $\mathcal{G}$. In other words, the scenarios are partitioned into non-overlapping sets such that there is no transition between nodes in different subsets $\mathcal{G}_i^{conn}$ and the subsets are as large as possible. Finally, a new pair $<p, S_i^{conn}>$ is generated for all maximally connected components. By relying on a breadth-first search algorithm to calculate the set of all maximally connected components, the calculation of all pairs has a computational complexity of $O\left(|P| \cdot (|T| + |S|)\right)$.

Finally, as application p uses the same mapping in all scenarios $s \in S^m$, we can allocate for each pair $<p, S^m>$ a mapping $m = (p, S^m, \cdot) \in M$.

Algorithm 1: Pseudocode to generate all pairs $<p, S^m>$ of an application p and a subset of scenarios S^m so that the number of elements per subset is minimized and the constraints specified in Section 5.1.3 are fulfilled.

Input: FSM $\mathcal{F} = (S, T, E, P, s_0, a, r, h)$
Output: set of pairs $<p, S^m>$
01 **for all** applications $p \in P$ **do**
02      $S^{sub} \leftarrow (s \in S | p \in (r(s) \cup h(s)))$.
         $\triangleright$ *all scenarios where p is running or paused*
03      $T^{sub} \leftarrow (t = (s_1, s_2) \in T |$
         $p \in (r(s_1) \cup h(s_1))$ and $p \in (r(s_2) \cup h(s_2)))$
         $\triangleright$ *all transitions that affect p*
04      $\mathcal{G} \leftarrow (S^{sub}, T^{sub})$
05      $\mathcal{G}^{conn} \leftarrow$ set of all maximally connected components of $\mathcal{G}$
06   **for all** $\mathcal{G}_i^{conn} \in \mathcal{G}^{conn}$ **do** $\triangleright$ *gen. pairs for each component*
07   add $<p, S_i^{conn}>$ $\triangleright$ *add to the set of pairs*
08   **end for**
09 **end for**

5.1.4 Mapping Optimization

In the second step, we calculate for each mapping $m \in M$ the set of binding relations B^m so that the objective function, i.e., the maximum core utilization, is minimized and a set of predefined architectural constraints are fulfilled. The number of firings of process v per time unit is $f(v)$ and the maximum execution time of process v on a core of type d is $w(v, d)$. Furthermore, $M^s \subseteq M$ denotes the subset of all mappings with $s \in S$ and $p \in r(s)$, i.e., $M^s = \{(p, S^m, B^m) \in M | p \in r(s) \text{ and } s \in S^m\}$. The binding relations B^m are calculated so that the maximum core utilization is minimized, and the utilization and communication constraints are met in each scenario:

Objective function: The optimization goal of this problem is to minimize the maximum core utilization. In order to incorporate the different scenarios into a single objective function, we assign each scenario $s \in S$ an execution probability χ_s [21] so that the object function can formally be stated as:

$$\min\left(\max_{{}^vc \in {}^VC} \sum_{\{s \in S\}} \sum_{\{m \in M^s\}} \sum_{\{v \in V : (v, {}^vc) \in B^m\}} \chi_s \cdot f(v) \cdot w(v, {}^vz({}^vc)) \right).$$

Constraint 4: In order to make sure that the cores are able to handle the processing load, the following relation has to be satisfied for all cores ${}^vc \in {}^VC$ and all states $s \in S$ of the FSM $\mathcal{F}$:

$$\sum_{\{m \in M^s\}} \sum_{\{v \in V : (v, {}^vc) \in B^m\}} f(v) \cdot w(v, {}^vz({}^vc)) \leq 1.$$

Constraint 5: Similarly, we can formulate the bandwidth requirement for each network by adding the data volume per time unit of each channel. Then, the aggregated data volume for each network n must be smaller than its supported rate. As the applications are mapped onto a virtual architecture, one has to consider all possible separations between the processes. However, due to the hierarchical structure of the architecture, a virtual network is only mapped onto a physical network within the same superior network so that the maximum separation is bounded.

5.2 Run-Time Manager

In this subsection, we discuss the required run-time support to execute a set of applications P on an on-chip many-

Algorithm 2: Pseudocode to calculate the process network p^c for the hierarchical control mechanism.

```
01  function ComputeController(architecture A)
02      V ← V∪ MASTER                          ▷add MASTER controller
03      ComputeLayer(v, η − 1, A, V, Q)
04      p^c = (V, Q)
05      return p^c
06  end function
07
08  function ComputeLayer(v^p, l, A, V, Q)
09      for all n ∈ N^(l) do
10          if l == 2 then
11              V ← V∪ SLAVE                    ▷add SLAVE controller
12          else
13              V ← V∪ INTERLAYER               ▷add INTERLAYER controller
14              ComputeLayer(v, l − 1, A, V, Q)
15          end if
16          Q ← Q ∪ (v, v^p) ∪ (v^p, v)   ▷add channels between contr.
17      end for
18  end function
```

core architecture $\mathcal{A}$. The required run-time support is provided by a run-time manager that has the task to generate commands towards the operating system to ensure the execution semantics described in Section 4.3. Traditionally, run-time managers are either centralized or distributed. However, as a centralized approach comes with a performance bottleneck and a distributed approach leads to a high complexity, both approaches do not fulfill the requirements of embedded many-core systems. In this paper, we propose to split the workload among hierarchically organized controllers. In the following, we first discuss the general ideas of a hierarchical control mechanism and then describe the functionality of each individual controller.

5.2.1 Hierarchical Control Mechanism

The general idea of the hierarchical control mechanism is to assign each network $n \in \{N^{(2)}, \ldots, N^{(\eta)}\}$ its own controller $v^c \in V^c$ that handles all inner-network dynamism. In particular, the controller assigned to a network $n \in N^{(2)}$ monitors for behavioral and fault events. Whenever such a controller receives an event, it handles the event if it just affects the controller's network, and otherwise it sends the event to the controller of its superior network.

As the controllers communicate via FIFO channels $q^c \in Q^c$, the hierarchical control mechanism can be represented as a process network $p^c = (V^c, Q^c)$. Algorithm 2 shows the pseudocode to generate the process network p^c for architecture $\mathcal{A}$. To provide bidirectional communication, two FIFO channels connect each controller with its superior controller.

Figure 7 illustrates the process network p^c for the architecture shown in Fig. 3. The controllers can be categorized into three different types:

- A SLAVE controller is responsible for a tile, i.e., for a network $n^{(2)} \in N^{(2)}$. All architectural units in network $n^{(2)}$ and all processes v assigned to a core $c \in n^{(2)}$ are able to send events to the SLAVE controller. In order to control the execution of a process, a SLAVE controller is also able to send commands to the underlying operating system.

- A INTERLAYER controller is responsible for a network $n^{(i)} \in N^{(i)}$ with $i = [3, \eta - 1]$ and η the number of communication layers. It receives all events that cannot be handled by its subordinates. The INTERLAYER controller processes an event if it only affects its own

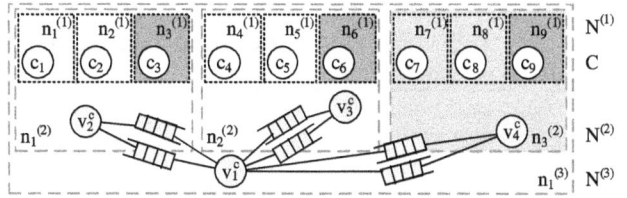

Figure 7: Run-time manager for the architecture illustrated in Fig. 3. v_2^c, v_3^c, and v_4^c are slave controllers and v_1^c is the master controller. $n_3^{(1)}$, $n_6^{(1)}$, $n_7^{(1)}$, and $n_3^{(2)}$ are spare networks.

network. Otherwise, it sends the event to its superior controller.

- The MASTER controller is responsible for network $n^{(\eta)} \in N^{(\eta)}$. It processes all events that cannot be handled by any other controllers.

Nowadays, all cores of a tile often share the same operating system so that one SLAVE controller can dynamically allocate processes to all cores of the tile. In case that each core has its dedicated operating system, we assign each core its own SLAVE controller to ensure the interaction between control mechanism and the operating system.

5.2.2 Hierarchical Event Processing

A controller of the hierarchical control mechanism only handles events that just affect the controller's network. Otherwise, the controller sends the event to the controller of its superior network. In the following, we detail this procedure for an INTERLAYER controller.

So far, we have seen that events can be categorized into two groups that cause different behavior. The first group contains behavioral events that trigger a scenario change. The second group contains fault events that are of the form (tag, n), where tag denotes the fault type, and n the affected network. Fault events only change the mapping of the virtual architecture $^{\mathcal{V}}\mathcal{A}$ onto the physical architecture $\mathcal{A}$, but not the mapping of the applications onto the virtual architecture $^{\mathcal{V}}\mathcal{A}$. Consequently, each controller consists of two components, see Fig. 6. The first component is responsible to handle behavioral events and ensures the execution semantics. It is just aware of the virtual architecture $^{\mathcal{V}}\mathcal{A}$, i.e., it generates commands towards $^{\mathcal{V}}\mathcal{A}$. The second component processes the fault events and redirects the commands to the corresponding physical network.

Next, we detail the procedure of an INTERLAYER controller when it receives a fault event. To this end, we suppose that controller v^c belongs to network $n^{(k)}$. Once it receives a fault event of the form $(fault, n^{(l)})$, it executes the procedure outlined in Algorithm 3. If $n^{(l)}$ is not a subordinate network of $n^{(k)}$, i.e., $l \neq k - 1$, v^c has only to reinstall the affected channels (Lines 9–11). Otherwise, if $n^{(l)}$ is a subordinate network of $n^{(k)}$, i.e., $l = k - 1$, v^c has handle the fault by migrating all processes mapped onto the faulty network $n^{(l)}$ to a spare physical network (Lines 2–8).

As a fault can be handled without additional mapping optimization, the system has a high responsiveness to faults. In case that a network $n^{(l)}$ is not anymore faulty, it sends a reintegration event of the form $(available, n^{(l)})$ to the controller, which marks $n^{(l)}$ as a spare network.

Algorithm 3: Pseudocode to handle a fault event $(fault, n^{(l)})$ **under the assumption that controller** v^c **belongs to network** $n^{(k)}$.

Input: fault event $(fault, n^{(l)})$
01   $^v n \leftarrow$ virtual network mapped onto $n^{(l)}$
02   **if** $l == k - 1$ **then** $\triangleright n^{(l)}$ *is subordinate of* $n^{(k)}$
03   **if** $n^{(k)}$ has a spare subordinate network $n_s^{(l)}$ of the same
           type as $n^{(l)}$ **then** $\triangleright v^c$ *handles the fault*
04   migrate $^v n$ to $n_s^{(l)}$
05   **else** $\triangleright v^c$ *is unable to handle the fault, reports* $n^{(k)}$ *as faulty*
06   send $(fault, n^{(k)})$ to superior network and **return**
07   **end if**
08   **end if**
09   **for all** $q \in Q$ that connect a v mapped onto $^v n$ with a v
           mapped onto a physical core $c \in n^{(k)}$ and $c \notin n^{(l)}$ **do**
10   reinstall q
11   **end for**
12   **if** $\exists q \in Q$ that connects a v mapped onto $^v n$ with a v mapped
           onto a physical core $c \notin n^{(k)}$ **then**
13   send $(fault, n^{(l)})$ to superior network
14   **end if**

6. EXPERIMENTAL RESULTS

In this section, we provide evaluation results by means of a prototype implementation of DAL. The goal is to demonstrate that *a*) the hierarchical control mechanism has low overhead, *b*) the proposed scenario-based model of computation enables the design of complex embedded systems, and *c*) the proposed hybrid mapping optimization strategy outperforms static mapping approaches and results in a maximum utilization that is close to the one of the optimal (local) mapping.

6.1 Control Mechanism

To measure the overhead of the hierarchical control mechanism, we developed a prototype implementation of DAL targeting an Intel i7-2720QM processor with four cores running Linux. The system is configured to form an architecture with three communication layers and only one tile so that the hierarchical control system consists of two controllers. The workload between the two controllers is split so that the MASTER controller is aware of the applications and the SLAVE controller is responsible for installing and removing processes and FIFO channels. We selected a different splitting as described in Section 5.2 to individually measure the overhead generated by the behavioral dynamism and by the interaction with the operating system.

The application set consists of the `fullload` application and the `pulse` application. The `fullload` application computes a predefined set of operations before stopping. Therefore, its execution time only depends on other processes running on the same core. The `pulse` application sleeps for a certain time interval, the so-called switching time. Then it sends an event to the run-time manager that tells the controller to stop and restart the `pulse` application. Each application is mapped onto a POSIX thread and scheduled by the operating system's scheduler. The overhead of the control mechanism is estimated by comparing the absolute execution times of the `fullload` application for different mappings, see Table 2 for the detailed mapping configurations.

In Fig. 8, the absolute time to execute the `fullload` application is compared for four mapping configurations and different switching times. The switching time defines the

Table 2: Mapping configurations to measure the overhead of the control mechanism. M denotes the master and S the slave controller.

	core 0	core 1	core 2	core 3
A)	M	S	fullload	pulse
B)	M	S, fullload	-	pulse
C)	M, fullload	S	-	pulse
D)	M, S, fullload	-	-	pulse

interval between each scenario change request. As the `fullload` application is running independent of the scenario changes, its absolute execution time only depends on the workload of the other processes that are running on the same core. Therefore, we can use the absolute execution time of the `fullload` application as an indicator for the overhead generated by the controllers.

While the MASTER controller generates no overhead, running the `fullload` application on the same core as the SLAVE controller increases the absolute execution time of the `fullload` application. If the SLAVE controller and the `fullload` application are running on the same core, the execution time of the `fullload` application is extended by 1.3 % if the switching time is set to 64 ms and by 8.1 % if the switching time is set to 1 ms.

6.2 System Specification and Optimization

To evaluate the performance of the proposed optimization strategy, we design a multistage picture-in-picture (PiP) software for embedded video processing systems targeting Intel's SCC processor [10].

6.2.1 Example System

We extended the Eclipse SDK with the ability to visually specify the FSM, the topology graph of an application, and the abstract model of the architecture. Figure 9 shows a screenshot of the extended Eclipse SDK with the FSM of the considered PiP software. The software is composed of eight scenarios and three different video decoder applications. The HD application processes high-definition, the SD application standard-definition, and the VCD application low-resolution video data. The software has two major execution modes, namely watching high-definition (scenario *HD*) or standard-definition videos (scenario *SD*). In addition, the user might want to pause the video or watch a preview of another video by activating the PiP mode (i.e., starting the VCD application). Due to resource restrictions, the user is only able to activate the PiP mode when the SD application is running or paused, or the HD application is paused. For illustration purpose, we use different motion JPEG (MJPEG) decoders as applications. The process net-

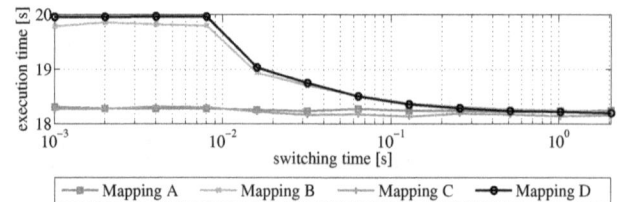

Figure 8: Comparison of the time to execute the `fullload` application in different mapping configurations. The different mapping configurations are detailed in Table 2.

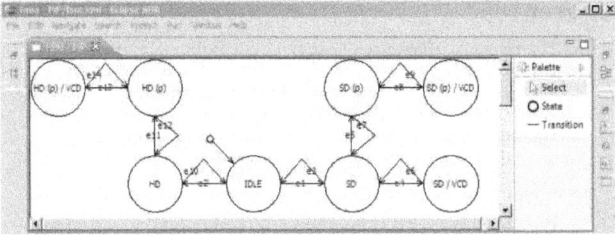

Figure 9: FSM of the PiP software. Paused applications are indicated by a (p) following the application's name.

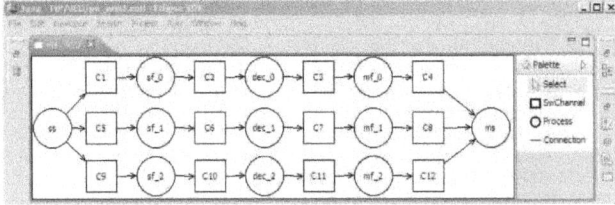

Figure 10: Process network of the VCD application.

work of the VCD application is depicted in Fig. 10 and the three different video decoder applications are summarized in Table 3. The motion JPEG (MJPEG) decoder is able to decode a certain number of frames in parallel. In particular, the ss ("split stream") process reads the video stream from a playout buffer and dispatches single video frames to subsequent processes. The sf ("split frame") process unpacks and predicts DCT coefficients so that the dec ("decode") process can decode one DCT block per activation. Finally, the mf ("merge frame") process collects the DCT blocks, and the ms ("merge stream") process collects the decoded frames.

All three video decoders read their playout buffers at a constant rate of 25 frames/second. The maximum execution time of a process, and the data volume per time unit and channel has been determined by running the applications on Intel's SCC processor with as in Section 6.3.

6.2.2 Mapping Optimization

Next, we show how the hybrid mapping optimization strategy compares to other mapping strategies. To this end, we extended the PISA framework [2] to solve the mapping optimization problem proposed in Section 5.1. In particular, PISA is extended to calculate the collection M of optimal mappings so that exactly one mapping m of this collection is valid for each pair of an application and a scenario. Violations of the bandwidth constraints are avoided by imposing a big penalty on the maximum utilization. PISA solves the mapping optimization problem by either generating 1000 random solutions and selecting the best of them as overall solution, or using the evolutionary algorithm (EA) SPEA2 [27].

In the following, we compare the performance of four dif-

Table 3: Configuration of the three video decoder applications of the PiP software.

app	resolution	pixels / frame	# processes	# chan.
HD	1280 × 720	921600	98	128
SD	720 × 576	414720	50	64
VCD	320 × 240	76800	11	12

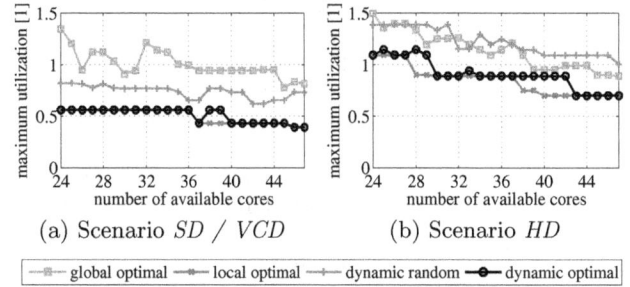

(a) Scenario SD / VCD (b) Scenario HD

global optimal — local optimal — dynamic random — dynamic optimal

Figure 11: Comparison of the maximum core utilization for different numbers of available cores and different optimization strategies. The dynamic optimal mapping strategy represents the hybrid scenario-based mapping optimization strategy proposed in this paper.

ferent mapping strategies when minimizing the maximum core utilization for different numbers of available cores:

- The DYNAMIC OPTIMAL mapping strategy represents the hybrid design-time / run-time mapping optimization strategy solved using EAs.
- The DYNAMIC RANDOM mapping strategy represents the hybrid design-time / run-time mapping optimization strategy solved by selecting the best of 1000 random solutions.
- The GLOBAL OPTIMAL mapping strategy calculates a single static mapping for the system, i.e., it does not make use of the different execution scenarios. The GLOBAL OPTIMAL strategy is solved using EAs.
- The LOCAL OPTIMAL mapping strategy calculates a single mapping for each scenario. Individually calculating a single mapping for each scenario might lead to the situation where an application has a different mapping in two connected scenarios, thus, the LOCAL OPTIMAL strategy requires run-time support for process migration. EAs are used to solve the LOCAL OPTIMAL strategy.

The results of this comparison are plotted in Fig. 11 for the scenarios SD / VCD and HD. Utilizations larger than one imply that the mapping strategy is unable to find a schedulable mapping for the considered number of available cores.

As expected, the LOCAL OPTIMAL mapping strategy reduces the maximum utilization the most as it calculates the local optimal mapping for just one scenario. However, the unavoidable run-time support for process migration leads to non-negligible costs in terms of time and system overhead. The hybrid design-time / run-time mapping optimization strategy, i.e., the DYNAMIC OPTIMAL mapping strategy, results for the SD / VCD and HD scenarios in a utilization that is on average 0.01 and 0.05 larger than the utilization calculated by the LOCAL OPTIMAL mapping strategy.

PISA is unable to find a valid mapping for the HD scenario when the GLOBAL OPTIMAL mapping strategy is used and less than 39 cores are available. On the other hand, PISA is already able to find a valid mapping for 30 cores and the HD scenario when the DYNAMIC OPTIMAL mapping strategy is used. Compared to the GLOBAL OPTIMAL mapping strategy, the DYNAMIC OPTIMAL mapping strategy reduces the utilization on average by 0.51 for the SD / VCD scenario and 0.16 for the HD scenario.

As the DYNAMIC OPTIMAL mapping strategy does not only optimize a single scenario, the utilization might be increased with the number of available cores. For example, the maximum utilization of scenario *HD* is slightly increased when moving from 32 to 33 available cores. Finally notice that the selection of the solver has a high influence on the performance of hybrid design-time / run-time mapping optimization strategy. Selecting the best of 1000 random solutions might even result in a performance that is worse than the GLOBAL OPTIMAL mapping strategy.

6.3   Real World Deployment

Based on Intel's SCC processor, we discuss a prototype implementation of the scenario-based model of computation. The goal is to evaluate the effort of a real world deployment of both the hierarchical control mechanism and KPNs according to the presented semantics. As a Linux operating system is running on each core of the SCC processor, a separate SLAVE controller is assigned to each core to ensure the communication between the hardware, the operating system, and the run-time manager. In addition, the MASTER controller is running on a dedicated core. Processes are mapped onto POSIX threads and scheduled by the operating system's scheduler. Inner-core communication is realized by local FIFO buffers and the RCKMPI library [5] is used for inter-core communication. Depending on the mapping, the controllers decide at run-time which communication type is suitable. As controllers are just KPN processes, no additional software is required to run them. All KPN processes are stored as shared objects and loaded on request of a SLAVE controller. In addition, SLAVE controllers have the ability to destroy running processes, and to install and remove communication channels.

The compiled code requires about 26 KB and 275 KB of static memory for the SLAVE and MASTER controller on Intel's SCC processor. This shows that the run-time system only introduces a small overhead in terms of memory usage.

7.   CONCLUSION

In this paper, we proposed the distributed application layer (DAL), a scenario-based design flow for mapping streaming applications onto heterogeneous on-chip many-core systems. Applications are modeled as Kahn process networks and a finite state machine is used to specify different execution scenarios. Behavioral events generated by either running applications or the run-time system trigger transitions between scenarios. The proposed mapping optimization strategy consists of two components. The design-time component calculates for each application a set of optimized mappings individually valid for a subset of scenarios. At run-time, hierarchically organized controllers monitor events, choose an appropriate mapping, and finally execute the required actions. We demonstrated that the hybrid design-time / run-time mapping optimization strategy outperforms global mapping optimization strategies and that the proposed scenario-based model of computation enables the design of complex embedded systems.

Acknowledgments

This work was supported by EU FP7 project EURETILE under grant number 247846.

References

[1] L. Benini et al. Resource Management Policy Handling Multiple Use-Cases in MPSoC Platforms Using Constraint Programming. In *Logic Programming*, volume 5366 of *LNCS*, pages 470–484. Springer, 2008.

[2] S. Bleuler et al. PISA – A Platform and Programming Language Independent Interface for Search Algorithms. In *Evolutionary Multi-Criterion Optimization*, volume 2632 of *LNCS*, pages 494–508. Springer, 2003.

[3] S. Borkar. Thousand Core Chips: A Technology Perspective. In *Proc. DAC*, pages 746–749, 2007.

[4] J. Cao et al. ARMS: An Agent-Based Resource Management System for Grid Computing. *Scientific Programming*, 10(2):135–148, 2002.

[5] I. Comprés Ureña et al. RCKMPI – Lightweight MPI Implementation for Intel's Single-chip Cloud Computer (SCC). In *Recent Advances in the Message Passing Interface*, volume 6960 of *LNCS*, pages 208–217. Springer, 2011.

[6] D. Culler et al. *Parallel Computer Architecture: A Hardware/Software Approach*. Morgan Kaufmann, 1999.

[7] S. A. Edwards and O. Tardieu. SHIM: A Deterministic Model for Heterogeneous Embedded Systems. *IEEE Trans. VLSI Syst.*, 14(8):854–867, 2006.

[8] M. Geilen and T. Basten. Reactive Process Networks. In *Proc. EMSOFT*, pages 137–146, 2004.

[9] S. V. Gheorghita et al. System-Scenario-Based Design of Dynamic Embedded Systems. *ACM Trans. Des. Autom. Electron. Syst.*, 14(1):3:1–3:45, 2009.

[10] J. Howard et al. A 48-Core IA-32 Message-Passing Processor with DVFS in 45nm CMOS. In *Proc. ISSCC*, pages 108–109, 2010.

[11] G. Kahn. The Semantics of a Simple Language for Parallel Programming. In *Proc. of the IFIP Congress*, volume 74, pages 471–475, 1974.

[12] T. Kangas et al. UML-Based Multiprocessor SoC Design Framework. *ACM Trans. Embedd. Comput. Syst.*, 5:281–320, 2006.

[13] S. Kobbe et al. DistRM: Distributed Resource Management for On-Chip Many-Core Systems. In *Proc. CODES/ISSS*, pages 119–128, 2011.

[14] C. Lee et al. A Task Remapping Technique for Reliable Multi-Core Embedded Systems. In *Proc. CODES/ISSS*, pages 307–316, 2010.

[15] E. Lee and D. Messerschmitt. Synchronous Data Flow. *Proc. IEEE*, 75(9):1235–1245, 1987.

[16] J. Manferdelli et al. Challenges and Opportunities in Many-Core Computing. *Proc. IEEE*, 96(5):808–815, 2008.

[17] G. Mariani et al. An Industrial Design Space Exploration Framework for Supporting Run-Time Resource Management on Multi-Core Systems. In *Proc. DATE*, pages 196–201, 2010.

[18] D. Melpignano et al. Platform 2012, a Many-Core Computing Accelerator for Embedded SoCs: Performance Evaluation of Visual Analytics Applications. In *Proc. DAC*, pages 1137–1142, 2012.

[19] H. Nikolov et al. Systematic and Automated Multiprocessor System Design, Programming, and Implementation. *IEEE T. Comput. Aid. D.*, 27(3):542–555, 2008.

[20] G. Sabin et al. Moldable Parallel Job Scheduling Using Job Efficiency: An Iterative Approach. In *Job Scheduling Strategies for Parallel Processing*, volume 4376 of *LNCS*, pages 94–114. Springer, 2007.

[21] A. Schranzhofer et al. Dynamic Power-Aware Mapping of Applications onto Heterogeneous MPSoC Platforms. *IEEE Trans. Industrial Informatics*, 6(4):692–707, 2010.

[22] A. K. Singh et al. A Hybrid Strategy for Mapping Multiple Throughput-constrained Applications on MPSoCs. In *Proc. CASES*, pages 175–184, 2011.

[23] S. Stuijk et al. A Predictable Multiprocessor Design Flow for Streaming Applications with Dynamic Behaviour. In *Proc. DSD*, pages 548–555, 2010.

[24] L. Thiele et al. Mapping Applications to Tiled Multiprocessor Embedded Systems. In *Proc. ACSD*, pages 29–40, 2007.

[25] A. Vajda. *Programming Many-Core Chips*. Springer, 2011.

[26] S. Vangal et al. An 80-Tile Sub-100-W TeraFLOPS Processor in 65-nm CMOS. *IEEE Journal of Solid-State Circuits*, 43(1):29–41, 2008.

[27] E. Zitzler, M. Laumanns, and L. Thiele. SPEA2: Improving the Strength Pareto Evolutionary Algorithm for Multiobjective Optimization. In *Proc. EUROGEN*, pages 95–100, 2002.

The RACECAR Heuristic for Automatic Function Specialization on Multi-core Heterogeneous Systems

John Robert Wernsing, Greg Stitt, and Jeremy Fowers
University of Florida
Department of Electrical & Computer Engineering
Gainesville, FL 32611
wernsing@ufl.edu, gstitt@ece.ufl.edu, jfowers@ufl.edu

ABSTRACT

Embedded systems increasingly combine multi-core processors and heterogeneous resources such as graphics-processing units and field-programmable gate arrays. However, significant application design complexity for such systems caused by parallel programming and device-specific challenges has often led to untapped performance potential. Application developers targeting such systems currently must determine how to parallelize computation, create different device-specialized implementations for each heterogeneous resource, and then determine how to apportion work to each resource. In this paper, we present the RACECAR heuristic to automate the optimization of applications for multi-core heterogeneous systems by automatically exploring implementation alternatives that include different algorithms, parallelization strategies, and work distributions. Experimental results show RACECAR-specialized implementations can effectively incorporate provided implementations and parallelize computation across multiple cores, graphics-processing units, and field-programmable gate arrays, improving performance by an average of 47x compared to a CPU, while the fastest provided implementations are only able to average 33x.

Categories and Subject Descriptors

D.2.2 [**Software Engineering**]: Design Tools and Techniques – *computer-aided software engineering (CASE)*

General Terms

Algorithms, Design, Measurement, Performance

Keywords

Elastic Computing, execution time, FPGA, GPU, heterogeneous, optimization, performance prediction, RACECAR

1. INTRODUCTION

Over the past decade, computing architectures have started on a clear trend towards increased parallelism via multi-core processors. More recently, this trend has focused on increased heterogeneity, with devices such as graphics-processing units (GPUs) and field-programmable gate arrays (FPGAs) commonly being used to improve embedded application performance [9][15][29].

Although such *multi-core heterogeneous systems* have significant potential for performance and low energy, increased application design complexity commonly prevents designers from reaching this potential. In extreme cases, such as for FPGAs, this complexity has prevented designers without low-level device expertise from even using the devices [22]. Such complexity is primarily caused by three challenges: 1) creating parallel implementations to exploit multiple cores or devices, 2) creating device-specialized implementations, often requiring different algorithms, optimizations, and programming languages, and 3) partitioning and load balancing work across numerous resources.

Although in the ideal case, compilers would automatically solve these challenges by optimizing a given function to utilize all of a system's resources, decades of studies have been unable to achieve this goal. Compilers are effective at optimizing code for an individual resource, but generally do not consider optimizations across multiple, heterogeneous resources. Even for compilers/tools that do consider multiple resources, these tools cannot transform code to use different algorithms to more effectively exploit the features of a heterogeneous device [32].

The current inability of compilers and operating systems to effectively optimize applications for multi-core heterogeneous systems is largely caused by a fundamental problem: *no single implementation of a function is optimal across all different devices, resource amounts, and input parameters.* For example, a sorting function running on a microprocessor would likely use a quick-sort algorithm, whereas on an FPGA, a bitonic-sort algorithm would be more efficient. Furthermore, implementation efficiency extends beyond just algorithmic choices and also requires considering the input parameters, numbers of devices/cores, work partitioning, etc.

To address these issues, we introduce the RACECAR heuristic for automatic function specialization on multi-core heterogeneous systems. Function specialization is traditionally a compiler optimization that creates custom (i.e., specialized) implementations of a function for known function invocations. For multi-core heterogeneous systems, we extend function specialization to explore algorithmic and implementation alternatives, different parallelization strategies, and different work partitionings, which we refer to as *multi-core heterogeneous function specialization (MHFS)*. Given a knowledge base of implementation alternatives, RACECAR creates specialized implementations by exploring and combining these possibilities. We present results showing RACECAR-specialized implementations automatically partitioned across multi-core microprocessors, GPUs, and FPGAs, achieving an average function speedup of 47x compared to a CPU, while the fastest single implementations were only able to average 33x. In some cases, RACECAR enabled implementations up to 16x faster than the fastest single implementation.

We envision several usage scenarios for RACECAR. First, compilers could use the heuristic for multi-core heterogeneous systems, or even for individual devices where specialization using different algorithms for different input parameters would be beneficial. Furthermore, runtime optimizations tools (e.g. [32]) could use the heuristic to make dynamic optimization decisions. The knowledge base required by the heuristic could be realized in function libraries by including multiple implementations provided by device/system vendors, domain experts, or open-source efforts.

2. PREVIOUS WORK

Decades of compiler research has focused on optimizing applications for multi-core heterogeneous systems via automatic parallelization [10][14] and adaptive optimization [8][19] of high-level code. Similarly, high-level synthesis tools for FPGAs have focused on automatic translation of high-level code into parallel circuits [4][17][30]. RACECAR complements these approaches by enabling optimization possibilities that include different algorithmic alternatives, while also enabling the possibility of runtime function specialization.

Numerous studies have simplified parallel programming via new languages [5][6][7][11][18]. The FPGA community has introduced numerous C-based languages for high-level synthesis tools [17]. Similarly, GPU vendors have introduced frameworks such as CUDA [24], Brook [3], and OpenCL [18] that enable compilation onto both CPUs and GPUs. Although new languages have reduced application design complexity, compilers/synthesis tools currently cannot effectively optimize code for significantly different devices, at least not without significant changes to the source code [27]. Also, the effectiveness of these languages is limited by the single algorithm specified in the code, which may not be efficient for all targeted devices. RACECAR enables these tools to explore algorithmic alternatives, in addition to other transformations, while potentially supporting any language.

Elastic computing [32] is conceptually similar to RACECAR. Elastic computing uses a function library defined with multiple implementations to dynamically choose efficient implementations for different runtime conditions. RACECAR complements elastic computing by providing implementation decisions for different parallelization approaches and work distributions. Furthermore, elastic computing requires low overhead for determining appropriate implementations, which RACECAR provides via a fast lookup into its output data structures.

PetaBricks [1] is a similar approach that consists of a language and compiler featuring algorithmic choice, but restricts parallelizing decisions to static choices. Qilin [20] dynamically determines an effective partitioning of work across heterogeneous resources, but only targets data-parallel operations. RACECAR is more transparent, supporting functions written in any language, compiled with any compiler, for any set of resources.

Adaptable software libraries are also related to RACECAR. FFTW [12] is an adaptive FFT implementation that composes blocks of functionality to specialize the execution for a particular architecture. OSKI [31] and ATLAS [34] are similar adaptive libraries for sparse matrix kernels and linear algebra, respectively. SPIRAL [26] is a similar framework but explores algorithmic and implementation choices to optimize DSP transforms. RACECAR enables more general adaptability by not being limited to a specific function, domain, or device.

RACECAR is also related to performance prediction, estimation, and analysis approaches, which are widely studied topics. Existing techniques evaluate architectural amenability for certain applications [16][25], assist in design space exploration [21] and verification [28], and help identify performance bottlenecks [23]. Recent work has introduced similar techniques for FPGA

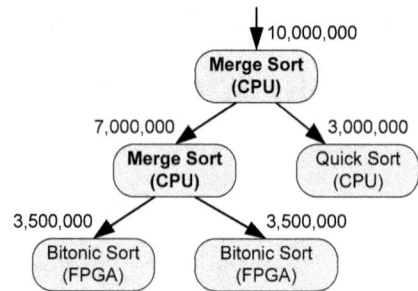

Figure 1. An example implementation tree for sorting 10,000,000 elements with labels specifying the implementation, resource, and apportioning of computation.

applications [16]. RACECAR extends these techniques by predicting performance for different devices, parallelization approaches, work partitionings, and input parameters.

3. MHFS PROBLEM DEFINITION

There are typically numerous ways to implement a function on a multi-core heterogeneous system, which include functionally equivalent algorithmic alternatives (e.g., quick sort, bitonic sort), language and compiler alternatives, and executing resource alternatives (e.g., CPU, FPGA, GPU). We refer to each possibility as an *implementation* of the function, each of which may be more efficient for different runtime conditions such as input parameters, available resources, etc. Therefore, the goal of the MHFS problem is to find the best implementation for a set of runtime conditions.

In addition to these common implementation possibilities, some implementations might support parallelizing computation across multiple resources, which we refer to as *parallelizing implementations*. Parallelizing implementations may use a variety of techniques, but in this paper we focus on those based on divide-and-conquer algorithms. Divide-and-conquer algorithms first divide an input into subsets, recursively perform the same computation independently on the multiple subsets (referred to as sub-executions), and then combine the sub-executions' output to form the overall result. For example, a parallelizing implementation of a sort function could use the divide-and-conquer merge-sort algorithm, which first splits its input into two subsets, sorts the subsets independently, and then merges the sorted subsets. As the algorithm specifies sets of computation which may execute independently, parallelizing implementations may utilize multiple resources for each of the sub-executions improving overall performance. Additionally, some divide-and-conquer algorithms allow arbitrary apportioning of work to each sub-execution, providing a means to enhance load-balancing.

As parallelizing implementations define computation recursively, each recursive call provides another opportunity for function specialization. In fact, the best implementation for a recursive call may be another parallelizing implementation, allowing for multiple levels of parallelism and numerous independent sub-executions, potentially utilizing up to all of the resources in a system. For example, Figure 1 illustrates how a sorting function may sort 10,000,000 elements on a system with two FPGAs and CPUs by nesting parallelizing implementations.

Therefore, by combining implementations and parallelizing implementations, every potential specialized function implementation may be illustrated as a tree-like structure that we refer to as an *implementation tree*. For example, the implementation tree illustrated in Figure 1 specifies which implementation to use for each call to the sort function, including the recursive function calls (illustrated as child nodes), and how

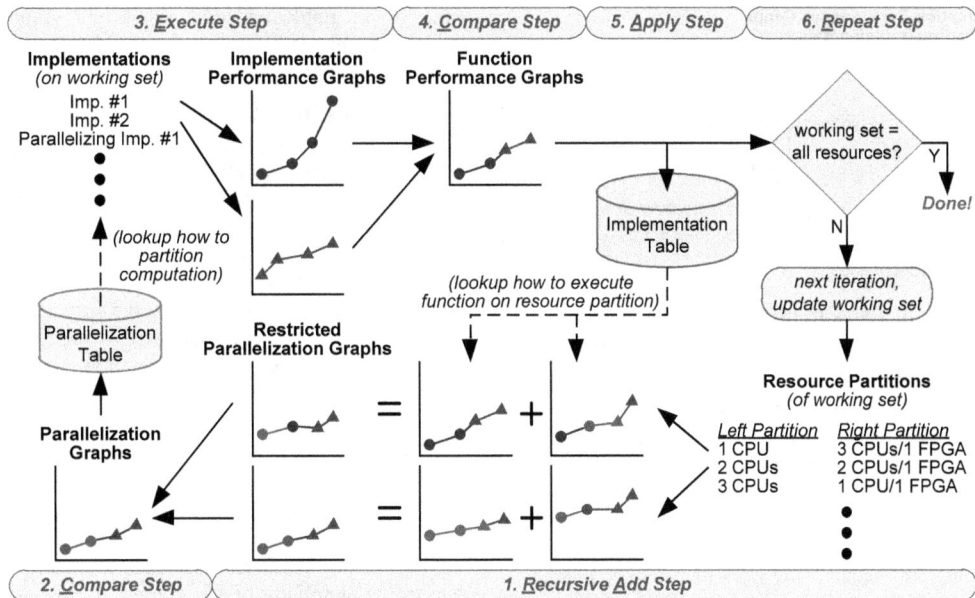

Figure 2. The high-level steps of the RACECAR heuristic.

much work to apportion to each call. From these definitions, we define the MHFS problem as follows:

Given a set of implementations for a function, input parameters for a call to the function, and the subset of system resources which the implementations may utilize, determine the implementation tree which requires the least execution time.

4. THE RACECAR HEURISTIC

RACECAR is a heuristic for multi-core, heterogeneous function specialization. The inputs to the heuristic are a set of implementations, parallelizing implementations, and additional information describing the function and resources available on a system. Note that the heuristic is not required to know the specific values for input parameters to the function beforehand. Instead, the heuristic analyzes the performances of the different implementations and iteratively builds data structures that specify how to efficiently execute the function for *any* set of input values. The heuristic saves the resulting data structures for use by compilers or runtime tools to make efficient implementation decisions for any specific call to the function.

The output of RACECAR is not an explicit implementation tree, but instead two data structures called the *implementation table* and the *parallelization table*. The implementation table, when provided with input parameters and an optional restriction on available system resources, returns the implementation that RACECAR estimates to provide the best performance. Any executing parallelizing implementations may then use the parallelization table to determine how to efficiently partition their computation. Note that an implementation tree could be generated from these data structures for known input parameters.

RACECAR consists of six iterative steps, illustrated in Figure 2, that correspond to letters in the RACECAR acronym – Recursive Add, Compare, Execute, Compare, Apply, and Repeat. These steps are listed in order, but the first two steps only occur after the first iteration, and therefore are not described until the end of the section. For each iteration, the heuristic optimizes for a specified subset of the system's resources, called the iteration's *working set*. Initially, the working set is a single CPU, but at the end of each iteration, the heuristic gradually grows the working set until it comprises of all system resources. The "execute" step (Section

4.1) considers all implementations that may execute on the current working set and measures their execution times, which it uses to generate a performance-estimation data structure called an *implementation performance graph*. Following which, the "compare" step (Section 4.2) combines the created implementation performance graphs into a *function performance graph*, which stores information on only the most efficient implementations of the function. The "apply" step then saves the function performance graph into the implementation table. If the working set does not comprise of all system resources, then all six steps will "repeat" using a larger working set. Using the new working set, the "recursive add" step (Section 4.3) then considers all possible ways to partition the resources for the current working set, looks up the corresponding function performance graphs, and performs an "adding" operation to generate a *restricted parallelization graph*, which specifies how to partition computation for that division of resources. Following which, the "compare" step (Section 4.4) then combines the restricted parallelization graphs into a *parallelization graph*, which may inform a parallelizing implementation of how to efficiently partition resources and computation. All six steps iterate until RACECAR evaluates a working set comprising of all resources.

4.1 Implementation Performance Graphs

The "execute" step of RACECAR determines the performances of each implementation executable in the current working set by generating an *implementation performance graph*. Each implementation performance graph specifies the estimated execution time of an implementation invoked with different *work metrics*, which are abstractions of the function's input parameters. Generation of implementation performance graphs is based on previous work in performance prediction [33].

RACECAR is, by design, not specific for any type of function, and therefore can make no assumptions about the structure of the input/output parameters or the performance characteristics of the implementations. As a result, abstraction is required to represent and interpret the analyzed function's input parameters.

The work metric is an abstraction of the input parameters that maps the potentially complex input parameter space of a function into a single numeric value. The mapping also allows for a comparative measure of the amount of work required to process

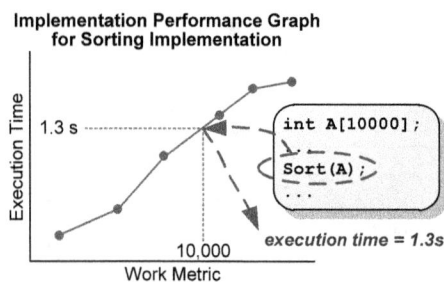

Implementation Performance Graph for Sorting Implementation

Figure 3. Example of a lookup into an implementation performance graph returning the estimated execution time for the implementation to sort 10,000 elements.

the parameters and, likewise, effectively groups together collections of parameters that exhibit similar performances. For example, most sorting implementations have an execution time that is related to the number of elements to sort (i.e., sorting more elements requires more time). As a result, an effective mapping is to set the work metric equal to the number of elements to sort. Note that the mapping only requires the work metric to be related, but not necessarily proportional, to the execution time.

In some cases, functions may require more complicated work metric mappings. For example, a matrix multiply function uses two input matrices, both of which significantly affect execution time. However, even in these cases, an asymptotic analysis of the performance of the function typically allows for the creation of an effective work metric. For matrix multiply, the asymptotic analysis reveals that the execution time is proportional to the product of specific dimensions of the input matrices, allowing for the calculated product to be a work metric. Previous work [33] describes other examples of work metric mappings. Although we have been able to find work metrics for many complex scenarios, there will be situations where an effective work metric does not exist. This limitation is discussed in Section 4.5.

To create an implementation performance graph for an implementation, RACECAR utilizes the *planner heuristic* from [33], which relies on sampling the execution time of the implementation at different work metrics to extrapolate the relationship between work metric and execution time. Note that by relying on actual execution time measurements, the planner heuristic captures all aspects of the execution time. For heterogeneous implementations, this includes the communication overhead of reading and writing to the device. For parallelizing implementations, this also includes the time spent partitioning the computation and merging the results.

An implementation performance graph, as illustrated in Figure 3, may be visualized as a two-dimensional piece-wise linear graph that maps work metric to execution time. Estimating the execution

time of an implementation using this graph simply requires calculating the work metric corresponding to the input parameters and looking up the corresponding execution time.

4.2 Function Performance Graphs

The "compare" step of RACECAR compares the implementation performance graphs of all the implementations that are executable within the current iteration's working set, and then combines them to create a *function performance graph*, which stores information about only the most efficient implementation for executing the function at different work metrics. Any implementation performance graph created during the current iteration's "execute" step must be considered, as well as any previously generated implementation performance graphs that correspond to implementations executing within proper subsets of the working set's resources. The order in which the working set is incremented guarantees that RACECAR would have already iterated through all subsets of the resources beforehand, allowing the heuristic to simply retrieve those implementation performance graphs.

Creating a function performance graph from a set of implementation performance graphs is a straight-forward process due to the simplicity of the graphs. As the mapping from input parameters to work metric is consistent for all of the graphs, the interpretation of the x-axis is also consistent, and locating the best performing implementation requires only locating the graph with the lowest execution time at a work metric. As illustrated by Figure 4, RACECAR performs this process for all work metric values by overlaying the implementation performance graphs and saving only the collection of segments and intersection points that trace the lowest boundary, which is called the *lowest envelope* of the graph. To perform this process, RACECAR uses a modified Bentley-Ottmann computational geometry algorithm [2] that starts at the lowest work metric value, determines which implementation performance graph is the best performing, and then proceeds with a sweep-line that checks for when another graph might outperform the current best by locating intersection points between the segments of the graphs. In addition to the lowest envelope, the algorithm also saves information about which implementation sourced the corresponding segment. For example, in Figure 4, implementation 3 was best for low work metric values, implementation 2 was best for middle values, etc.

Unlike the implementation performance graphs, which are associated with individual implementations, a function performance graph is associated with the function. A lookup of a work metric within the function performance graph returns the most efficient implementation of the function, using any of the provided implementations executing within the associated resources. The heuristic then saves the function performance graph in the "apply" step as part of the implementation table.

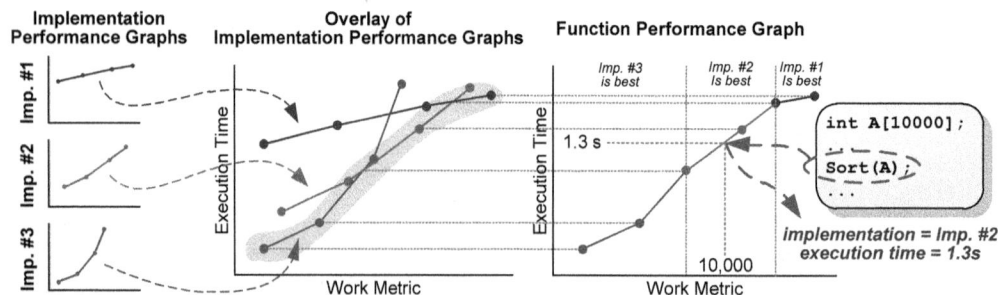

Figure 4. Example of creating a function performance graph from a set of implementation performance graphs. The illustrated lookup within the function performance graph returns the best implementation and estimated time for sorting 10,000 elements.

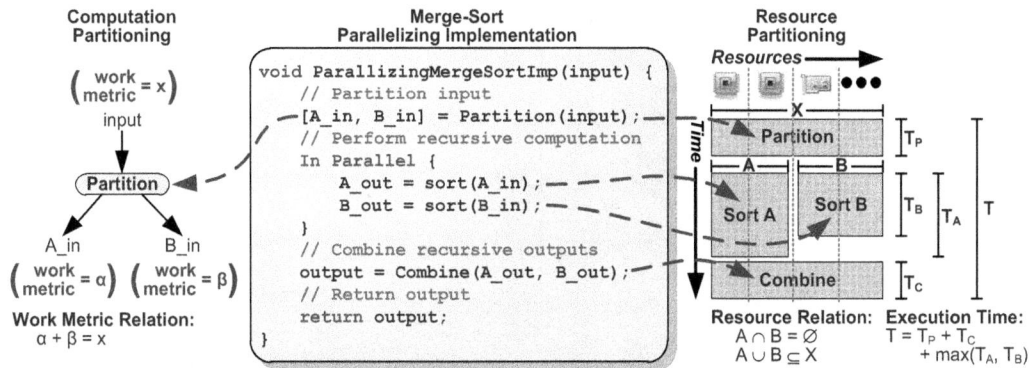

Figure 5. Computation partitioning, resource partitioning, and execution time for a merge-sort parallelizing implementation.

4.3 Restricted Parallelization Graphs

The "recursive add" and "compare" steps of RACECAR inform the parallelizing implementations of how to efficiently partition their computation across different resources by generating a *parallelization graph*. The parallelization graph informs the parallelizing implementations of what resources to use and how much computation to apportion for each of their recursive function calls. RACECAR creates the parallelization graph in two steps. First, the "recursive add" step creates a *restricted parallelization graph*, which answers only how much computation to apportion for a fixed partitioning of resources. Second, the "compare" step then combines the restricted parallelization graphs to form the parallelization graph.

All parallelizing implementations are assumed to adhere to the following parallelization strategy, as illustrated with a merge-sort example in Figure 5. The implementation must partition the input into two subsets and then perform two parallel recursive sub-executions of the function to independently process those subsets. After the sub-executions complete, the implementation must then combine the outputs to form the overall result. Divide-and-conquer, data-parallel, and other algorithms all support structuring their computation in this way.

Determining the best partitioning of computation for a parallelizing implementation requires first specifying a computation's permitted partitionings. For most types of parallelizing implementations, a valid partitioning of the computation may be specified by relating the input parameters of the two recursive function calls to the overall invocation parameters of the parallelizing implementation. As RACECAR uses the abstraction of a work metric, this partitioning specification can be represented as an equation, called a *work metric relation*, relating the work metrics of the two recursive calls to the work metric of the invocation parameters. For example, a merge-sort parallelizing implementation requires that the sum of the input sizes for its recursive sorts to equal the overall input size of the sort. Likewise, the corresponding work metric relation would equivalently state that the sum of the recursive function call work metrics must equal the work metric of the invocation parameters, as illustrated in Figure 5. In fact, any parallelizing implementations that set the work metric proportional to the amount of computation and follows the structure of dividing computation (without overlap) between the two recursive function calls, would also adhere to this work metric relation, making it very prevalent in common parallelizing implementations. As a result, we refer to this as the *standard work metric relation* and assume that the parallelizing implementations support this relation for the upcoming discussion. A discussion of handling other relations is presented at the end of the subsection.

In addition to restricting the partitioning of computation, a restriction must also be placed on the partitioning of the resources. RACECAR requires that the apportioning of resources to the recursive calls must be from the same subset of resources allocated for the overall parallelizing implementation. As the recursive calls must also execute in parallel, the two calls must use distinct proper subsets of the parallelizing implementation's resources. We refer to this restriction as the *resource relation*.

As illustrated in Figure 5, the execution time of a parallelizing implementation equals the time required by the partitioning and combining steps plus the maximum of the execution times of the two recursive calls. If it is assumed that the execution times of the partitioning and combining steps are relatively constant regardless of how the computation is apportioned, then minimizing the overall execution time is equivalent to minimizing the maximum execution time of the two recursive calls. Additionally, as the recursive calls must execute within a proper subset of the resources in the working set, function performance graphs already exist from previous iterations to estimate the execution time of the calls. As a result, determining efficient parallelizing decisions is an optimization problem, which we call the *parallelizing optimization problem (POP)*:

Given a work metric relation and resource relation for a parallelizing implementation, the set of execution resources allocated for that parallelizing implementation, function performance graphs for all proper subsets of the allocated resources, and the work metric of the input parameters, determine the apportioning of work metric and resources that adheres to the relations and minimizes the maximum estimated execution time of the recursive function calls.

RACECAR does not solve the POP problem for individual work metrics, but instead creates the parallelization graph to inform parallelizing implementations of how to partition computation for any work metric. Specifically, a parallelizing implementation may perform a lookup within the parallelization graph based on the invocation parameter's work metric to determine how to efficiently apportion the computation and resources between the implementation's recursive function calls.

As mentioned previously, RACECAR simplifies the creation of the parallelization graph by answering the questions of how to apportion resources and computation in two steps. The first step answers the question of how to partition the computation for a fixed partitioning of resources by creating a restricted parallelization graph. The heuristic creates a separate restricted parallelization graph for every possible resource partitioning. For example, if the working set of the current iteration was 4 CPUs/FPGA, then the heuristic would create restricted parallelization graphs for 1 CPU in parallel with 3 CPUs/FPGA, 2

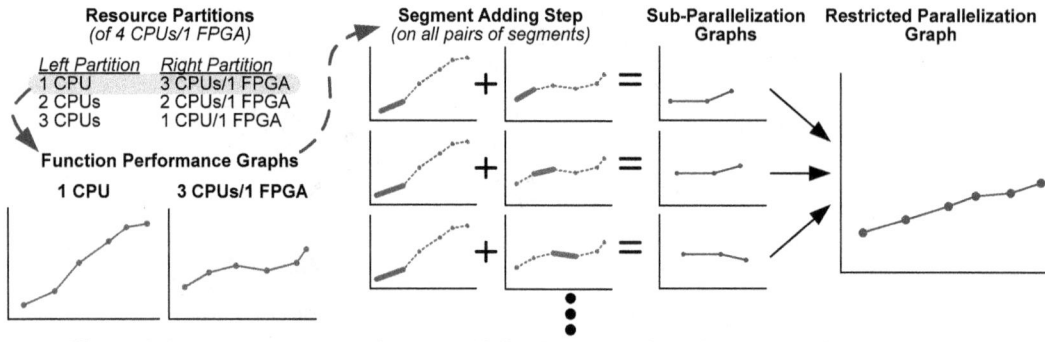

Figure 6. Steps to create a restricted parallelization graph from function performance graphs.

CPUs in parallel with 2 CPUs/FPGA, etc. After creating all of the restricted parallelization graphs, the second step then combines the restricted parallelization graphs to form the overall parallelization graph, as discussed in Section 4.4. The remainder of this subsection focuses on the creation of the restricted parallelization graphs for a specific partitioning of resources.

For each specific partitioning of resources, RACECAR creates the restricted parallelization graph by performing several steps, as illustrated in Figure 6. First, the heuristic retrieves the function performance graphs corresponding to the two partitions of the specified partitioning of resources. Second, the heuristic breaks up the function performance graphs into their constituent segments. Third, the heuristic processes all possible pairings of the segments from the two graphs individually in a process called *segment adding*. The output of segment adding is a *sub-parallelization graph*, which is identical in purpose to the restricted parallelization graph, but represents the optimal solution to the POP problem given only the information provided by the pair of segments. Lastly, the heuristic then combines all of the sub-parallelization graphs to form the restricted parallelization graph, which is the globally optimal solution for the POP problem given all of the information provided by the two function performance graphs. Note that optimality is defined here only in terms of the POP problem, which specifies minimizing the maximum execution time as estimated by the function performance graphs.

Segment adding generates a sub-parallelization graph by determining the optimal way to partition computation given only the information provided by two segments. To understand the operation of segment adding, first assume that x_1, y_1, x_2, y_2, etc. correspond to the coordinates of the endpoints of the two segments, as specified by Figure 7. By applying the standard work metric relation, those two segments can only create valid partitions for computation with work metrics ranging from x_1+x_2 to x_3+x_4. Likewise, the optimal way (as it is the only way) to partition the computation with a work metric of x_1+x_2 would be to partition the computation into recursive calls with work metrics of x_1 and x_2 respectively, resulting in an estimated execution time of $max(y_1, y_2)$. Similarly, this same fact applies at the two opposite endpoints of the segments with an execution time of $max(y_3, y_4)$ and work metrics of x_3 and x_4 being the optimal way to partition computation that has a work metric of x_3+x_4. Optimally partitioning the work metrics between the two endpoints may be described by first visualizing two fictitious *pointers* that initially start at the left endpoints of the two segments and then trace the sub-parallelization graph as the pointers move towards the right endpoints of their segments. Specifically, if the pointers are assumed to have coordinates (x_1', y_1') and (x_2', y_2'), then the corresponding point in the sub-parallelization graph would have coordinates with a work metric of $x_1'+x_2'$ and an execution time of $max(y_1', y_2')$. As the pointers start at the left endpoint of the two

segments, they are initially optimal, but then the problem becomes determining which of either (or both) of the pointers to move towards the right at each step in such a way to preserve optimality. As the POP problem requires minimizing the maximum estimated execution time, the pointers undertake movements that first lower the execution time of the sub-parallelization graph as early as possible and secondly postpone increasing the execution time of the parallelization graph until as late as possible. All possible cases for how to move the pointers are listed in Table I, with an example illustrated in Figure 7. Once both pointers reach the right endpoints of their respective segments, this situation also corresponds to the right endpoint of the sub-parallelization graph, and therefore the entire sub-parallelization graph would have been specified during the movements of the pointers.

An informal proof of optimality may be made by induction by noting that the pointers are initially at an optimal partitioning of the computation and every move of the pointers preserves this optimality, therefore the overall result is also optimal. Note that simply applying the movements described in Table I on the two function performance graphs themselves would not guarantee

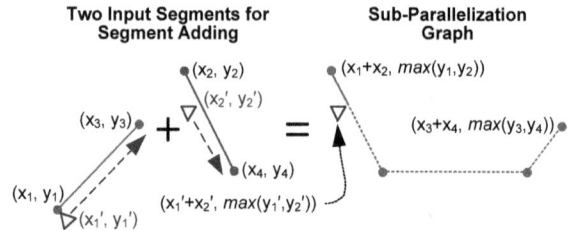

Figure 7. Example of creating a sub-parallelization graph.

Table I. The pointer movement rules used by segment adding.

Priority	Rule
1	If both pointers are at their right endpoints, then segment adding is complete.
2	If only one pointer is not at its right endpoint, then move that pointer to the right.
3	If both pointers have negative slopes and equal y's, then move both pointers to the right.
4	If the pointer with the larger y has negative slope, then move that pointer to the right.
5	If the pointers have unequal y's, then the pointer with the larger y must have a positive slope (or else it would have been handled previously), so move the pointer with the smaller y to the right.
6	The only remaining case would be if both pointers have positive slopes and equal y's, so move both pointers to the right.

optimality, as the process requires that the execution time changes consistently with the movement of the pointers.

As segment adding works by moving pointers through two straight segments, the resulting sub-parallelization graph is also a piece-wise linear graph, allowing for efficient storage and processing. Additionally, the movements of the pointers through the segments do not require a complex continuous movement, but may instead be implemented by only considering when the movements of the pointers should change. Likewise, each individual movement would correspond to the creation of a new segment in the sub-parallelization graph, and allows for an efficient implementation of the segment adding process.

The sub-parallelization graphs may be visualized as a two-dimensional graph relating the work metric of the invocation parameters to the maximum execution time of the recursive calls. Additional information about the work metrics of the recursive calls, the execution time of each call, and the implementations to use for each call is also saved in the graph. As the x-axes are consistent for all of the sub-parallelization graphs, the graphs may be combined in a process identical to the "compare" step described in Section 4.2. As each sub-parallelization graph specifies the optimal partitioning of computation restricted to the information of only two segments, and the heuristic combines sub-parallelization graphs for all possible pairings of the segments, the resulting graph, called the restricted parallelization graph, specifies how to optimally partition computation given all of the information in the two function performance graphs.

The previous discussion assumes that the standard work metric relation applies to the parallelizing implementations. The more general case of simply a linear relationship between the work metrics of the recursive calls and the invocation parameters could be represented as a work metric relation in the form of $C_1\alpha + C_1\beta + C_2 = x$, where C_1 and C_2 are restricted to being constant for a specified invocation parameter's work metric. Note that this form supports the case where the computation may overlap between the two recursive calls. Even in these cases, creating the restricted parallelization graph using the standard work metric relation is still valid as the parallelizing implementations can instead integrate the constants into their lookups, corresponding to a lookup of $y = (x - C_2)/C_1$. More complicated non-linear forms of the work metric relation are currently not supported by the RACECAR heuristic, but are planned as future work.

4.4 Parallelization Graphs

The "compare" step of RACECAR considers all of the restricted parallelization graphs, corresponding to the optimal parallelization with different fixed partitionings of resources, and then combines them to create the parallelization graph. As the x-axes are consistent for all of the restricted parallelization graphs, the graphs may be combined in a process identical to the "compare" step described in Section 4.2. As each restricted parallelization graph specifies the optimal partitioning for a specific partitioning of resources, and the heuristic combines restricted parallelization graphs corresponding to all possible resource partitionings, the resulting graph, called the parallelization graph, specifies how to optimally partition computation and resources given all of the information in all of the supplied function performance graphs.

When a parallelizing implementation is invoked, it only needs to perform a lookup within the parallelization graph, based on the work metric of the input parameters, to return all of the information required to efficiently partition the computation and execute the recursive calls. For example, Figure 8 illustrates a merge-sort parallelizing implementation performing a lookup of

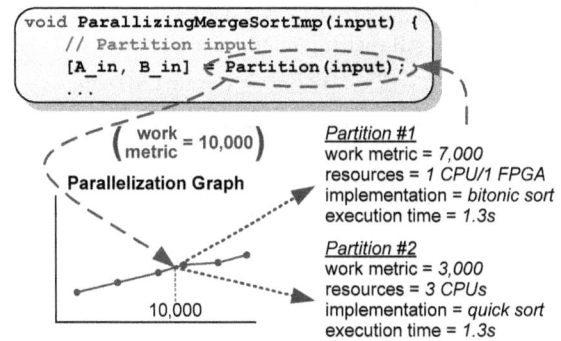

Figure 8. Example of a parallelizing implementation performing a lookup in a parallelization graph.

10,000, corresponding to the work metric of the invocation's input parameters. The lookup returns the work metric, resources, and implementation to use for each of the recursive calls, which corresponds to the optimal selection for minimizing the maximum execution time as estimated by the function performance graphs. The parallelizing implementation may then use this information to partition the computation accordingly and invoke the recursive calls using the corresponding resources and implementations.

4.5 Limitations

There are three main limitations of RACECAR. The first limitation is that the heuristic's implementation decisions will be less efficient if it cannot accurately create an implementation performance graph for an implementation. As described in Section 4.1, creating an implementation performance graph requires determining a relationship between the work metric and execution time. If an accurate mapping of the function's input parameters to work metric does not exist, or if the relationship between work metric and execution time have a large variance, then the resulting implementation performance graph will not accurately reflect the performance of the implementation for different input parameters, and likewise the heuristic will make less efficient decisions. Fortunately, even for cases when the implementation performance graph is less accurate, the heuristic will still operate correctly and output implementation decisions that work, albeit with reduced performance. For cases when the actual prediction error is small percentage-wise, the reduction in performance is typically negligible.

The second limitation of RACECAR is due to the required structure for parallelizing implementations, as described in Section 4.3. For implementations that do not adhere to this structure, the parallelization graphs may have less efficient parallelizing decisions. Fortunately, many parallelizing implementations can be written to adhere to this structure and implementations which do not may still gather useful information from the parallelization graphs.

The third limitation of RACECAR is due to potentially inaccurate assumptions made about the performance of parallelizing implementations. As described in Section 4.3, the heuristic assumes the most efficient way to partition computation is to minimize the maximum estimated execution time of the recursive calls. In reality, several more factors affect the performance of a parallelizing implementation. For example, the partitioning and combining steps of the parallelizing implementation may change depending on how the computation is apportioned, and therefore should also be taken into account. Note that simply having time-consuming (but consistent) partitioning and combining steps would not reduce the accuracy. Additionally, the heuristic

Table II. Speedup of RACECAR-determined implementations versus speedup of the fastest single implementation on the three systems. All speedup numbers are relative to a single-threaded CPU implementation executing on the same system.

Function	Gamma System Fastest Imp.	Gamma System RACECAR	Marvel System Fastest Imp.	Marvel System RACECAR	Novo-G System Fastest Imp.	Novo-G System RACECAR
1D Convolution	55.10	86.15	1.00	14.08	72.38	72.38
2D Convolution	41.20	69.75	1.00	14.03	84.78	84.78
Circular Convolution	32.67	107.99	1.00	12.99	1.00	90.80
Inner Product	1.00	2.47	1.00	2.06	1.00	2.64
Matrix Multiply	1.92	6.83	1.00	15.84	1.00	4.02
Mean Filter	24.66	44.19	1.00	15.37	1.00	4.35
Optical Flow	173.85	174.69	1.00	15.71	227.03	233.22
Prewitt	1.00	4.34	1.00	12.05	1.00	4.32
SAD	114.60	124.70	1.00	16.23	153.64	156.59
Sort	1.00	3.22	1.00	3.09	1.00	3.61
Average	**44.70**	**62.43**	**1.00**	**12.15**	**54.38**	**65.67**

assumes the function performance graphs accurately reflect the performance of the recursive calls, but this does not include the interaction between the two functions when they execute simultaneously. Resource contention, caching affects, and system scheduling may all affect the performance of the functions. Despite these limitations, the resulting error is typically small percentage-wise, and the implementation decisions still yield significant speedups as demonstrated by the results.

5. EXPERIMENTS

To assess RACECAR, we selected ten functions and created a total of thirty-seven alternate heterogeneous implementations of those functions to use as inputs for the RACECAR heuristic. Ideally, such implementations would be provided as part of a standard function library.

We evaluated RACECAR on three diverse systems, two of which contain heterogeneous resources. The first system, referred to as Gamma, consists of a 2.8 GHz quad-core Intel Xeon W3520, 12 GB of RAM, an Altera Stratix-III L340 FPGA located on a GiDEL PROCe III board, and a dual-chip Nvidia GTX-295 graphics card. The second system, referred to as Marvel, consists of eight 2.4 GHz AMD Opteron 880 dual-core processors and 32 GB of RAM. The third system, referred to as Novo-G, is a node of the Novo-G supercomputer [13] and consists of a quad-core Intel Xeon E5520, 6 GB of RAM, and four Altera Stratix-III E260 FPGA's located on a GiDEL PROCStar III board.

The ten functions come from a variety of problem domains and consist of: *1D convolution, 2D convolution, circular convolution, inner product, matrix multiply, mean filter, optical flow, Prewitt, sum-of-absolute differences image retrieval* (SAD), and *sort*. The convolution functions perform one-dimensional or two-dimensional discrete convolution on two input operands. *Inner product* calculates the inner product of two input arrays. *Matrix multiply* multiplies two input matrices of compatible dimensions. *Mean filter* applies an averaging filter to an input image. *Optical flow* processes an input image to locate a feature. *Prewitt* performs Prewitt edge detection on an input image. *SAD* performs the sum-of-absolute differences image processing algorithm on an input image. Lastly, *sort* sorts an input array.

The thirty-seven implementations consist of microprocessor and heterogeneous implementations. All ten functions contain a single-threaded microprocessor implementation except for *sort*, which contains three microprocessor implementations corresponding to different sorting algorithms (insertion sort, heap sort, quick sort). We created Gamma FPGA implementations for the *1D convolution, 2D convolution, optical flow*, and *SAD* functions. We created Gamma GPU implementations for the *1D*

convolution, 2D convolution, circular convolution, matrix multiply, mean filter, optical flow*, and *SAD* functions. We created Novo-G FPGA implementations for the *1D convolution, 2D convolution, optical flow*, and *SAD* functions. While ideally all functions would have heterogeneous implementations, time constraints required us to create implementations for only those functions we predicted significant speedup. Lastly, all ten functions also contain a parallelizing implementation.

RACECAR and the implementations were created in a variety of programming languages depending on the targeted execution resource. The heuristic itself and all microprocessor implementations were written in C++ and compiled using g++ 4.1.2. The GPU implementations were written in CUDA and compiled using Nvidia's CUDA compiler version 3.2. Lastly, the FPGA implementations were written in VHDL and compiled using Altera Quartus II version 9.1 or Xilinx ISE 9.1, depending on the targeted FPGA. RACECAR does not analyze compilation and place-and-route times as those are only one-time overheads.

5.1 RACECAR Function Speedup

We evaluated RACECAR by measuring the effectiveness of RACECAR's execution decisions to improve performance beyond that of the provided implementations. For each function and system, we provided RACECAR with the subset of implementations that supported the hardware of that system.

Table II lists the RACECAR-enabled speedup of each function on each system. All speedup numbers are relative to a single-threaded implementation of that function executing on the same system. To provide a fair comparison for what a developer might normally create to take advantage of a heterogeneous system (e.g., a single efficient FPGA or GPU implementation), the table also lists the speedup achieved by the fastest single implementation provided as an input for that function to RACECAR. RACECAR can achieve an overall speedup faster than its implementation inputs by parallelizing computation across multiple resources.

The speedup of each function was highly dependent on the implementations supported by the executing system. For functions executing with only microprocessor implementations, RACECAR was typically able to approach linear speedup with the number of microprocessors. For example, the Marvel system, which contains 16 microprocessors, was able to achieve greater than 14x speedup on 8 out of the 10 functions. For functions that contained a single very fast heterogeneous implementation (e.g., the functions with Novo-G FPGA implementations), the speedup was largely dictated by the single implementation. This result is due to the heterogeneous implementation dwarfing any speedup possible by parallelizing the computation across multiple, slower resources.

The Gamma system provided the most interesting results as it contains multiple fast heterogeneous resources. The fast GPU and FPGA implementations provided as inputs to RACECAR were able to, by themselves, achieve speedup averaging 45x when compared to a microprocessor implementation. Despite the already fast implementations, RACECAR was able to further increase speedup by having the GPU and FPGA implementations execute in parallel. For the fastest implementation of *1D convolution*, which uses the FPGA, RACECAR was able to increase speedup from 55x to 86x by determining how to parallelize computation across both the GPUs and FPGAs. Similarly, *mean filter* was able to increase speedup from 25x to 44x by taking advantage of the additional resources. Nearly all the functions on Gamma also follow this trend, as shown in Table II. Prior to RACECAR, determining how to effectively utilize multiple heterogeneous resources in a system was a laborious manual process. By using RACECAR, the heuristic automatically incorporates multiple fast individual implementations to make them even faster.

Figure 9 illustrates the average speedup achieved on each system by both the fastest single implementation and the RACECAR-determined implementation. On all systems, RACECAR was able to effectively utilize the parallel resources to significantly improve performance beyond any single implementation by itself. For both Gamma and Novo-G, the faster heterogeneous resources already provided a large speedup over the microprocessor implementations. None the less, RACECAR was still able to average a 1.3x improvement over the single implementations. For Marvel, all of the implementations were microprocessor implementations, allowing RACECAR to further increase performance by an average of 12x by parallelizing computation over the numerous CPUs. *Overall, RACECAR was able to achieve an average function speedup of 47x, while the fastest single implementations were only able to average 33x.*

5.2 Case Study: 1D Convolution on Gamma

In this section, we look more into the details of the RACECAR decisions for the *1D convolution* function executing on Gamma. This function and system were chosen as they provide a demonstration of RACECAR leveraging the performance of multiple heterogeneous implementations.

Figure 10 illustrates the partitioning of computation between resources for different work metric values. At smaller work metric values, which correspond to quick executions, the RACECAR-determined implementation relies solely on the microprocessor to perform convolution. As the amount of computation grows (i.e., larger work metric values), RACECAR partitions more and more computation onto the FPGA implementation. This partitioning is due to the FPGA having superior performance to both the CPU and GPU implementations, but also having a large latency that prevents any benefit when the amount of computation is small. As the work metric continues to increase, the computation becomes sufficiently large to justify the latency of using the two GPUs. Towards the upper-bound of the work metric range, the partitioning approaches 52% FPGA, 46% GPUs, and 2% CPUs.

Figure 11 lists the implementation tree of one specific convolution invocation with a work metric of 2.048 billion. As the *1D convolution* adapter calculates the work metric value to equal the product of the two input operands, this work metric value equates to convolving a 1,000,000 length vector with a 2,048 length vector. The figure repeats the results from the right-end of Figure 10 with the computation allocated to 52% FPGA, 23% to each GPU, and 0.5% to each of the four microprocessors.

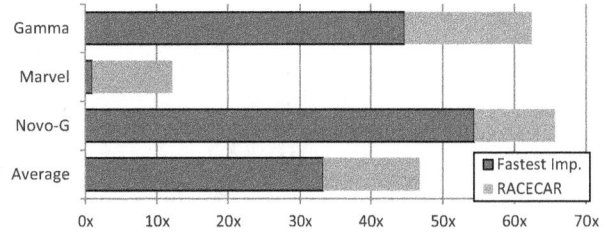

Figure 9. Average speedup of the functions on each system as compared against the fastest single implementation.

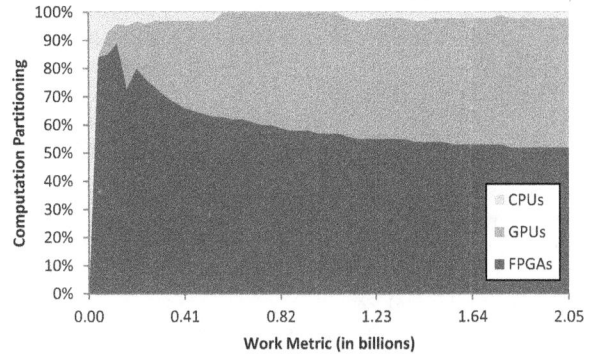

Figure 10. Partitioning of computation between resources at different work metrics for the RACECAR-determined convolution implementation executing on Gamma.

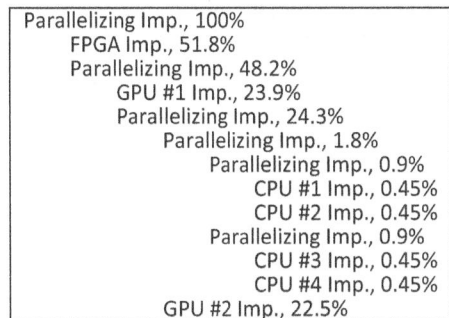

```
Parallelizing Imp., 100%
   FPGA Imp., 51.8%
   Parallelizing Imp., 48.2%
      GPU #1 Imp., 23.9%
      Parallelizing Imp., 24.3%
         Parallelizing Imp., 1.8%
            Parallelizing Imp., 0.9%
               CPU #1 Imp., 0.45%
               CPU #2 Imp., 0.45%
            Parallelizing Imp., 0.9%
               CPU #3 Imp., 0.45%
               CPU #4 Imp., 0.45%
         GPU #2 Imp., 22.5%
```

Figure 11. RACECAR-determined implementation tree showing work partitioning for a convolution implementation invoked at a work metric of 2.048 billion on Gamma.

6. CONCLUSIONS

In this paper, we introduce the RACECAR heuristic to create specialized function implementations for multi-core, heterogeneous systems. From a set of provided implementations, the heuristic evaluates different alternatives and builds data structures that may inform compilers and runtime optimization tools of how to efficiently execute the function for any input parameters. In addition to specifying the best implementation for a function, the heuristic also determines how to efficiently partition computation across parallel resources.

We evaluated the performance of RACECAR-specialized implementations on three diverse systems with various combinations of microprocessors, GPUs, and FPGAs, using a set of ten functions and thirty-seven implementations. For these experiments, RACECAR achieved an average function speedup of 47x, while the fastest single implementations were only able to average 33x.

Future work includes addressing limitations by supporting different structures for the parallelizing implementations and making better execution time approximations for parallel function calls. We additionally plan to enable RACECAR to efficiently share resources for multiple simultaneously executing functions. Lastly, we plan to extend RACECAR to clusters by supporting the partitioning of computation across multiple nodes, allowing for both intra- and inter-node optimization.

7. ACKNOWLEDGEMENTS

This work was supported by the National Science Foundation, grant CNS-0914474.

8. REFERENCES

[1] J. Ansel, C. Chan, Y. L. Wong, M. Olszewski, Q. Zhao, A. Edelman, S. Amarasinghe, "Petabricks: a language and compiler for algorithmic choice", in *PLDI '09: Proceedings of the 2009 ACM SIGPLAN conference on programming language design and implementation*, pp. 38–49, 2009.

[2] J. Bentley and T. Ottmann, "Algorithms for reporting and counting geometric intersections," *IEEE Transactions on Computers*, vol. C-28, pp. 643 –647, sep. 1979.

[3] I. Buck, T. Foley, D. Horn, J. Sugerman, K. Fatahalian, M. Houston, and P. Hanrahan, "Brook for gpus: stream computing on graphics hardware," in *SIGGRAPH '04: ACM SIGGRAPH 2004 Papers*, (New York, NY, USA), pp. 777–786, ACM, 2004.

[4] A. Canis, J. Choi, M. Aldham, V. Zhang, A. Kammoona, J. H. Anderson, S. Brown, and T. Czajkowski, "LegUp: high-level synthesis for FPGA-based processor/accelerator systems," in *FPGA'11: Proceedings of the 19th ACM/SIGDA International Symposium on Field programmable Gate Arrays*, pp. 33–36, 2011.

[5] B. Chamberlain, D. Callahan, and H. Zima. "Parallel programmability and the Chapel language". *International Journal of High Performance Computing Applications*, Vol. 21, Issue 3, August 2007, pg. 291-312.

[6] P. Charles, C. Grothoff, V. Saraswat, C. Donawa, A. Kielstra, K. Ebcioglu, C. von Praun, and V. Sarkar. "X10: an object-oriented approach to non-uniform cluster computing," in *Proceedings of the ACM SIGPLAN Conference on Object Oriented Programming, Systems, Languages, and Applications*, pp. 519-538, 2005.

[7] W. Chen, D. Bonachea, J. Duell, P. Husbands, C. Iancu, and K. Yelick. "A performance analysis of the Berkeley UPC compiler," in *ICS: Proceedings of the International Conference on Supercomputing*, pp. 63-73, 2003.

[8] K. D. Cooper, D. Subramanian, and L. Torczon, "Adaptive optimizing compilers for the 21st century," *J. Supercomput.*, vol. 23, no. 1, pp. 7–22, 2002.

[9] A. DeHon, "The density advantage of configurable computing," *Computer*, vol. 33, no. 4, pp. 41–49, 2000.

[10] A. Eichenberger, K. O'Brien, P. Wu, T. Chen, P. Oden, D. Prener, J. Shepherd, B. So, Z. Sura, A. Wang, T. Zhang, P. Zhao, and M. Gschwind, "Optimizing compiler for the cell processor, 2005," in *Parallel Architectures and Compilation Techniques, 2005. PACT 2005. 14th International Conference on*, pp. 161–172, Sept. 2005.

[11] A. Fin, F. Fummi, and M. Signoretto. "SystemC: a homogenous environment to test embedded systems." In *CODES'10: Proceedings of the International Workshop on Hardware/Software Codesign*, pp 17-22, 2001.

[12] M. Frigo and S. G. Johnson, "The design and implementation of FFTW3," *Proceedings of the IEEE*, vol. 93, no. 2, pp. 216–231, 2005. Special issue on "Program Generation, Optimization, and Platform Adaptation".

[13] A. George, H. Lam, and G. Stitt. "Novo-g: at the forefront of scalable reconfigurable supercomputing". *IEEE Computing in Science and Engineering Magazine* (Jan/Feb 2011), pp. 82–86, 2011.

[14] M. Girkar and C. D. Polychronopoulos, "Extracting task-level parallelism," *ACM Trans. Program. Lang. Syst.*, vol. 17, no. 4, pp. 600–634, 1995.

[15] Z. Guo, W. Najjar, F. Vahid, and K. Vissers, "A quantitative analysis of the speedup factors of FPGAs over processors," in *FPGA '04: Proceedings of the 2004 ACM/SIGDA 12th international symposium on Field programmable gate arrays*, pp. 162–170, 2004.

[16] B. Holland, K. Nagarajan, and A. D. George, "Rat: Rc amenability test for rapid performance prediction," *ACM Trans. Reconfigurable Technol. Syst.*, vol. 1, no. 4, pp. 1–31, 2009.

[17] Impulse Accelerated Technologies. 2010. http://www.impulseaccelerated.com/.

[18] Khronos Group. OpenCL 1.0. 2010. http://www.khronos.org/opencl/.

[19] P. M. W. Knijnenburg, T. Kisuki, and M. F. P. O'Boyle, *Iterative compilation*, pp. 171–187. New York, NY, USA: Springer-Verlag New York, Inc., 2002.

[20] C.-K. Luk, S. Hong, H. Kim, Qilin: Exploiting parallelism on heterogeneous multiprocessors with adaptive mapping, in *MICRO '09: Proceedings of the IEEE/ACM International Symposium on Microarchitecture*, pp. 45–55, 2009.

[21] G. Madl, N. Dutt, and S. Abdelwahed, "Performance estimation of distributed real-time embedded systems by discrete event simulations," in *EMSOFT '07: Proceedings of the 7th ACM & IEEE international conference on Embedded software*, pp. 183–192, 2007.

[22] B. Nelson, M. Wirthlin, B. Hutchings, P. Athanas, and S. Bohner. "Design productivity for configurable computing," in *ERSA '08: Proceedings of the International Conference on Engineering of Reconfigurable Systems and Algorithms*, pp. 57–66, 2008.

[23] G. R. Nudd, D. J. Kerbyson, E. Papaefstathiou, S. C. Perry, J. S. Harper, and D. V. Wilcox, "Pace–a toolset for the performance prediction of parallel and distributed systems," *Int. J. High Perform. Comput. Appl.*, vol. 14, no. 3, pp. 228–251, 2000.

[24] Nvidia. CUDA Programming Guide. 2008. http://www.nvidia.com/object/cuda_develop.html.

[25] W. Pfeiffer and N. J. Wright, "Modeling and predicting application performance on parallel computers using hpc challenge benchmarks," in *22nd IEEE International Parallel and Distributed Processing Symposium*, 2008.

[26] M. Puschel, J. Moura, J. Johnson, D. Padua, M. Veloso, B. Singer, J. Xiong, F. Franchetti, A. Gacic, Y. Voronenko, K. Chen, R. Johnson, and N. Rizzolo, "Spiral: Code generation for dsp transforms," *Proceedings of the IEEE*, vol. 93, pp. 232–275, Feb. 2005.

[27] S. Sirowy, G. Stitt, and F. Vahid, "C is for circuits: capturing FPGA circuits as sequential code for portability," in *FPGA '08: Proceedings of the 16th international ACM/SIGDA symposium on Field programmable gate arrays*, pp. 117–126, ACM, 2008.

[28] Y. tsun Steven Li, S. Malik, and A. Wolfe, "Performance estimation of embedded software with instruction cache modeling," in *ACM Transactions on Design Automation of Electronic Systems*, pp. 380–387, 1995.

[29] P. Trancoso and M. Charalambous, "Exploring graphics processor performance for general purpose applications," in *Proceedings of the 8th Euromicro Conference on Digital System Design*, pp. 306–313, 2005.

[30] J. Villarreal, A. Park, W. Najjar, and R. Halstead, "Designing Modular Hardware Accelerators in C with ROCCC 2.0," in *FCCM: Proceedings of the IEEE International Symposium on Field-Programmable Custom Computing Machines*, pp. 127–134, 2010.

[31] R. Vuduc, J. Demmel, and K. Yelick, "Oski: A library of automatically tuned sparse matrix kernels," *Journal of Physics*, vol. 16, pp. 521–530, 2005.

[32] J. R. Wernsing and G. Stitt, "Elastic computing: a framework for transparent, portable, and adaptive multi-core heterogeneous computing," in *LCTES '10: Proceedings of the ACM SIGPLAN/SIGBED 2010 conference on Languages, compilers, and tools for embedded systems*, pp. 115–124, 2010.

[33] J. Wernsing and G. Stitt, "A scalable performance prediction heuristic for implementation planning on heterogeneous systems," *in ESTIMedia'10: 8th IEEE Workshop on Embedded Systems for Real-Time Multimedia*, pp. 71 –80, 2010.

[34] R. C. Whaley, A. Petitet, and J. J. Dongarra, "Automated empirical optimization of software and the ATLAS project," *Parallel Computing*, vol. 27, no. 1–2, pp. 3–35, 2001.

SiblingRivalry: Online Autotuning Through Local Competitions

Jason Ansel   Maciej Pacula   Yee Lok Wong   Cy Chan   Marek Olszewski

Una-May O'Reilly   Saman Amarasinghe

Computer Science and Artificial Intelligence Laboratory
Massachusetts Institute of Technology
{jansel,mpacula,ylwong,cychan,mareko,unamay,saman}@csail.mit.edu

ABSTRACT

Modern high performance libraries, such as ATLAS and FFTW, and programming languages, such as PetaBricks, have shown that autotuning computer programs can lead to significant speedups. However, autotuning can be burdensome to the deployment of a program, since the tuning process can take a long time and should be re-run whenever the program, microarchitecture, execution environment, or tool chain changes. Failure to re-autotune programs often leads to widespread use of sub-optimal algorithms. With the growth of cloud computing, where computations can run in environments with unknown load and migrate between different (possibly unknown) microarchitectures, the need for online autotuning has become increasingly important.

We present SiblingRivalry, a new model for always-on online autotuning that allows parallel programs to continuously adapt and optimize themselves to their environment. In our system, requests are processed by dividing the available cores in half, and processing two identical requests in parallel on each half. Half of the cores are devoted to a known safe program configuration, while the other half are used for an experimental program configuration chosen by our self-adapting evolutionary algorithm. When the faster configuration completes, its results are returned, and the slower configuration is terminated. Over time, this constant experimentation allows programs to adapt to changing dynamic environments and often outperform the original algorithm that uses the entire system.

Categories and Subject Descriptors

I.2.5 [**Artificial Intelligence**]: Programming Languages and Software; D.3.4 [**Programming Languages**]: Processors—*Compilers*

Keywords

Autotuning, Evolutionary Algorithm, Genetic Algorithm

1. INTRODUCTION

Autotuning is becoming one of the most effective methods for gaining efficient performance on complex applications which run on modern hardware systems. Libraries such as Atlas [35], FFTW [19], and SPARSITY [24]; frameworks such as PERI [36], SPIRAL [28], and Green [7]; and languages such as PetaBricks [3], allow the programmer to set up an application to be autotuned for a given microarchitecture.

However, while offline autotuning provides great performance gains, it has two major problems. First, it adds an additional step to the software installation and upgrade process. Second, offline autotuning is unable to construct programs that respond to dynamically changing conditions. As we will show, changes to machine load can substantially degrade an application's performance. When such changes occur, an offline autotuned algorithm may no longer be the best choice. This situation is further exacerbated in the emerging cloud and data center computing environments, where in addition to sharing a machine with varying load, applications may be transparently migrated between machines, and thus potentially between microarchitectures. Such changes to computer architectures and microarchitectures have been shown to lead to significant performance loss for autotuned applications [3].

In response to some of these challenges, there is a growing body of work [7, 9, 12, 22, 23, 25] focused on creating applications that can monitor and automatically tune themselves to optimize a particular objective (e.g. meeting response time goals by trading quality of service (QoS) for increased performance or lower power usage). In order to provide stability, convergence and predictability guarantees, many of these systems construct (either by hand, or automatically) a linear model of their application and employ control theory techniques to perform dynamic tuning. The success of such techniques depends on the degree to which the configurable choices can be mapped to a linear system, a task that can be difficult when tuning large complex applications with interdependent configuration choices.

In contrast, offline evolutionary (a.k.a. genetic) autotuning techniques, such as the one used in PetaBricks [3], are model-free. They adaptively sample the search space of candidate solutions and take advantage of both large and small moves in the search space. Thus, they are able to find global optima regardless of how non-linear or interdependent the choice space and can do so without a model. Their selection component allows them to improve execution time even though they generate random variations on current solutions with unpredictable performance. When a specific variation is extremely slow, in an offline setting, it can be killed and prevent a sampling bottleneck. Unfortunately, this characteristic has meant that evolutionary techniques are generally considered to be unsuitable for use in the online setting. Executing multiple generations of a sizable population at runtime (even at periodic intervals) is too costly to be feasible. Additionally, the alternative approach of continuously replacing the components being executed by different experimental variations, offered by an autotuner, is also a poor choice as there is no execution standard to compare the variation against. Thus, the learning system has no way of knowing whether a particular variation is performing particularly poorly and thus should be aborted.

In this paper, we take a novel approach to online learning that enables the application of evolutionary tuning techniques to online autotuning. Our technique, called *SiblingRivalry*, divides the available processor resources in half and runs the current best algorithm on one half and a variation on the other half. If the current best finishes first, the variation is killed, the failure of the variation is reported to the online learning algorithm which controls the selection of both configurations for such "competitions" and the application continues to the next stage. If the variation finishes first, we have found a better solution than the current best. Thus, the current best is killed and the results from the variation are used as the program continues to the next stage. Using this technique, SiblingRivalry produces predictable and stable executions, while still exploiting an evolutionary tuning approach. The online learning algorithm is capable of adapting to changes in the environment and progressively identifies better configurations over time without resorting to experiments that might deliver extremely slow performance. As we will show, despite the loss of resources, this technique can produce speedups over fixed configurations when the dynamic execution environment changes. To the best of our knowledge, SiblingRivalry is the first attempt at employing evolutionary tuning techniques to online autotuning computer programs.

We have implemented a prototype of the SiblingRivalry algorithm within the context of the PetaBricks language [3, 4]. Our results show that SiblingRivalry's always-on racing technique can lead to an autotuned algorithm that uses only half the machine resources (as the other half is used for learning) but that is often faster than an optimized algorithm that uses the entire processing resources of the machine. Furthermore, we show that SiblingRivalry dynamically responds and adapts to changes in the runtime environment such as system load.

1.1 Contributions

SiblingRivalry makes the following contributions:

- To the best of our knowledge, the first general technique to apply evolutionary tuning algorithms to the problem of online autotuning of computer programs.

- A new model for online autotuning where the processor resources are divided and two candidate configurations compete against each other.

- A multi-objective, practical online evolutionary learning algorithm for high-dimensional, multi-modal, and non-linear configuration search spaces.

- A scalable learning algorithm for high-dimensional search spaces, such as those in our benchmark suite which average 97 search dimensions.

- Support for meeting dynamically changing time or accuracy targets which are in response to changing load or user requirements.

- Experimental results showing a geometric mean speedup of 1.8x when adapting to changes in microarchitectures and a 1.3x geometric mean speedup when adapting to moderate load on the system.

- Experimental results showing how, despite accomplishing more work, SiblingRivalry can actually reduce average power consumption by an average of 30% after a migration between microarchitectures.

1.2 Use cases

We envision a number of common use cases for our online learning techniques:

- *Adapting to dynamic load*: Production code is usually run not in isolation but on shared machines with varying amounts of load. Yet it is impossible for offline training to pre-compute a best strategy for every type of load. SiblingRivalry enables programs to dynamically adapt to changing load on a system. It ensures continual good performance and eliminates pathological cases of interference due to resource competition.

- *Migration in the cloud:* In the cloud, the type of machine on which a program is running is often unknown. Additionally, the virtual machine executing a program can be live migrated between systems. SiblingRivalry allows programs to dynamically adapt to these circumstances as the architecture changes underneath them.

- *Dynamically changing accuracy targets:* Depending on the situation, a user may need varying levels of accuracy (or quality of service) from an application. SiblingRivalry allows the user to dynamically change either the accuracy or performance target of an application. It supports trading-off execution time with accuracy.

- *Deploying to a wide variety of machines:* SiblingRivalry greatly simplifies the task of deploying an application to a wide variety of architectures. It enables a single centralized configuration, perhaps on a shared disk, to be deployed. This is followed by online customization for each machine on the network.

- *Reducing over-provisioning requirements hardware resources:* Data centers must often over-provision resources to handle rare load spikes. By supporting dynamic changes to desired accuracies during load spikes, SiblingRivalry can reduce the amount of required over-provisioning.

2. PETABRICKS LANGUAGE

The PetaBricks language provides a framework for the programmer to describe multiple ways of solving a problem while allowing the autotuner to determine which of those ways is best for the user's situation [3]. It provides both algorithmic flexibility (multiple algorithmic choices) as well as coarse-grained code generation flexibility (synthesized outer control flow).

At the highest level, the programmer can specify a *transform*, which takes some number of inputs and produces some number of outputs. In this respect, the PetaBricks transform is like a function call in a procedural language. The major difference is that we allow the programmer to specify multiple pathways to convert the inputs to the outputs for each transform. Pathways are specified in a dataflow manner using a number of smaller building blocks called *rules*, which encode both the data dependencies of the rule and C++-like code that converts the rule's inputs to outputs.

One of the key features of the PetaBricks programming language is support for variable accuracy algorithms, which can trade output accuracy for computational performance (and vice versa) depending on the needs of the user. Approximating ideal program outputs is a common technique used for solving computationally difficult problems, adhering to processing or timing constraints, or optimizing performance in situations where perfect precision is not necessary. Algorithmic methods for producing variable accuracy outputs include approximation algorithms, iterative methods, data resampling, and other heuristics. A detailed description of the variable accuracy features of PetaBricks is given in [4].

2.1 The PetaBricks Autotuning Setup

Choices are represented in a configuration file that contains three types of structures. The first type is selectors which allow the autotuner to make algorithmic choices. Selectors can make different decisions when called with different input sizes dynamically. Using this mechanism, selectors can be used by the autotuner to construct poly-algorithms that dynamically switch techniques at recursive call sites. Formally, a selector s consists of $\vec{C_s} = [c_{s,1}, \ldots, c_{s,m-1}] \cup \vec{A_s} = [\alpha_{s,1}, \ldots, \alpha_{s,m}]$ where $\vec{C_s}$ are the ordered interval boundaries (cutoffs) associated with algorithms $\vec{A_s}$. During program execution the runtime function $SELECT$ chooses an algorithm depending on the current input size by referencing the selector as follows:

$$SELECT(input, s) = \alpha_{s,i} \text{ s.t. } c_{s,i} > size(input) \geq c_{s,i-1}$$

where $c_{s,0} = 0$ and $c_{s,m} = \infty$. The components of $\vec{A_s}$ are indices into a discrete set of applicable algorithmic choices available to s, which we denote $Algorithms_s$.

The synthesized functions in the configuration file define continuous functions that specify a transform parameter that varies with input size. Each synthesized function is defined by a series of points $\vec{S_g} = [s_{g,0}, \ldots, s_{g,31}]$ which define the value of the synthesized function at exponentially increasing sample points with linear interpolation between the defined points. The value of the parameter at any dynamic transform call is defined by the function:

$$SYNTHFUNC(input, g) = \frac{s_{g,a}(2^b - n) + s_{g,b}(n - 2^a)}{2^b - 2^a}$$

where $n = size(input)$ and $a = \lfloor \lg_2 n \rfloor$ and $b = \lceil \lg_2(n+1) \rceil$.

In addition to these algorithmic choice selectors and synthesized functions, the configuration file contains many other discrete tunable parameters. These tunable parameters include things such as blocking sizes for local memory, sequential/parallel cutoffs, and user defined parameters. Each tunable parameter is an integer with a positive bounded range.

3. COMPETITION EXECUTION MODEL

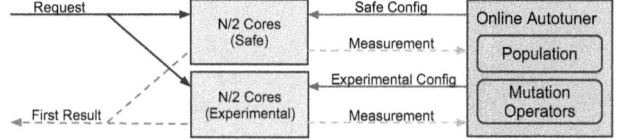

Figure 1: High level flow of the runtime system. The data on dotted lines may not be transmitted for the slower configuration, which can be terminated before completion.

Figure 1 shows the high level flow of how requests are processed by the PetaBricks runtime system. The cores on our system are split in half into two groups. One group of cores is designated to run safe configurations, while the other group runs experimental configurations. When a request is received, the autotuner runs the same request on both groups of cores in parallel using a safe configuration on one group and an experimental configuration on the other group. When the first configuration completes (and provides a satisfactory answer) the system terminates the slower one. The output of the better algorithm is returned to the user, and timing and quality of service measurements are sent to the autotuner so that it may update its population of configurations and mutation operator priorities.

3.1 Other Splitting Strategies

Our racing execution model requires that there be two groups of cores, one that executes an experimental configuration, while the other executes a safe configuration. While we have chosen to divide our resources in a 50/50 split, other divisions (such as 60/40 or 75/25) are possible.

We do not consider splits where we devote fewer cores to the experimental group than the safe group since doing so would prevent some superior configurations from completing (they would be killed immediately after the safe strategy completes). Further, tuning for fewer than half of the cores limits the potential benefits from autotuning.

One of the reasons we chose a 50/50 split over other possible splits was to minimize the gap between best-case and worst-case overheads that result from splitting. Splits that devote very few resources to the safe configuration will incur larger costs when the experimental configuration fails compared to when it succeeds.

Another major advantage of the 50/50 split is that it provides more data to the autotuner, since the performance of both tests can be compared directly. In uneven configurations, very little is learned about the configuration on the smaller part of the chip, since even if it is a better configuration it still may be aborted before completion. This means that the online learner is expected to converge more quickly in the 50/50 case.

3.2 Time Multiplexing Races

Another racing strategy is to run the experimental configuration and the safe configuration in sequence rather than in parallel. This allows both algorithms to utilize the entire machine. It also provides a way to, in some cases, avoid running the safe configuration entirely. These types of techniques are also the most amenable to at some point switching off online learning, if one knows that the dynamic execution environment has stabilized and the learner has converged.

There are two variants to this type of technique:

- *Safe configuration first.* In this variant, the safe configuration is run first, and is always allowed to complete, using the entire machine. Then the experimental configuration is allowed an equal amount of time to run, to see if it would have completed faster. Unfortunately, this method will incur a $2x$ overhead in the steady state, which is the same as the expected worst case for running the races in parallel (assuming linear scalability). For this reason this technique is only desirable if one plans to disable online learning part way through an execution.

- *Experimental configuration first.* In this variant, a model is required to predict the performance of a configuration given a specific input and current dynamic system environment. The model predicts the upper bound performance of the safe configuration. The experimental configuration is given this predicted amount of time to produce an answer before being terminated. If the experimental configuration produces an acceptable answer, then the safe configuration is never run, otherwise the system falls back to the safe configuration.

The efficacy of this technique depends a lot on the quality of the model used and the probability of the learning system producing bad configurations. In the best case, this technique can have close to zero overhead. However, in the worst case, this technique could both fail to converge and produce overheads exceeding 2x. If the performance model under-predicts execution time, superior configurations will be terminated prematurely and autotuning will fail to make improvements. If the performance model over-predicts execution time, then the cost of exploring bad configurations will grow. For our problem, the probability of a bad configuration is high enough that this type of technique is not desirable, however, with search spaces with more safer configurations this technique may become more appealing.

4. SIBLINGRIVALRY ONLINE LEARNER

The online learner is an evolutionary algorithm (EA) that is specially designed for the purpose of identifying, online, the best configuration for the program. It has a multitude of exacting requirements: It must be lightweight because it is always running. It cannot add significant computational or memory overhead to the application or it will diminish the overall value of autotuning. It must conduct its search in accordance with the structure of the pairwise competition execution model as described in Section 3. Accordingly, it must effectively search and adapt candidate solutions by offering competition configurations and integrating the feedback from their measurement results. Because the competition execution model is processing real requests, it must provide at least one configuration that is sufficiently safe to ensure quality of service. Despite the search space of candidate configurations being very large, it must converge to a high quality configuration quickly. It must not assume the underlying environment is stationary. It must converge in the face of high execution time variability (due to load variance) and react to system changes in a timely way without being notified of them.

To meet its convergence goals, the online learner, in effect, must ideally balance exploration and exploitation in its search strategy. Exploitation should investigate candidates in the "neighborhood" of currently high performing configurations. Exploration should investigate candidates that are very different from the current population to ensure no route to the optimum has been overlooked by the greedy nature of exploitation. This final required property of the online learner motivates one of its key capabilities. The online learner performs "adaptive mutator selection" which we explain in more detail in Section 4.5.

4.1 High Level Function

In the process of tuning a program, the online learner maintains a population of candidate configurations. The population is relatively small to minimize the computational and memory overhead of learning.

The online learner keeps two types of performance logs: per-configuration and per-mutator. Per-configuration logs record runtime, accuracy, and confidence for a given candidate, and are used by the learner to select the "safe" configuration for each competition, and to prune configurations which are demonstrably worse. Per-mutator logs record performance along the three objectives for candidates generated by a given mutator. This information allows the online learner to select mutators which have a record of producing improved solutions, using a process called Adaptive Operator Selection (see Section 4.5 for more information).

Whenever the program being tuned receives a request, the online learner selects two configurations to handle it: "safe" and "experimental". The safe configuration is the configuration with the highest value of the fitness function (see Section 4.3) in the current population, computed using per-configuration logs. The fitness value captures how well the configuration has performed in the past, and thus the safe configuration represents the best candidate found by the online learner so far. The experimental configuration is produced by drawing a "seed" configuration from the current population and transforming it using a mutator. The probability of a configuration being selected as a seed is proportional to its fitness.

Once the safe and experimental configurations have been selected, the online learner uses both to process the request in parallel, and returns the result from the candidate that finishes first and meets the accuracy target (the "winner"). The slower candidate (the "loser") is terminated. If the experimental configuration is the winner, it is added to the online learner's population. Otherwise, it is discarded. The safe configuration is added back to the population regardless of the result of the race, but might be pruned later if the new result makes it worse than any other candidate.

4.2 Online Learner Objectives

The online learner optimizes three objectives with respect to its candidate configurations:

- *Execution time:* the expected execution time of the algorithm.

- *Accuracy:* the expected value of a programmer metric measuring the quality of the solution found.

- *Confidence:* a metric representing the online learner's confidence in the first two metrics. This metric is 0 if there is only one sample and

$$Confidence = \frac{1}{stderr(\text{timings})} + \frac{1}{stderr(\text{accuracies})}$$

if there are multiple samples. This takes into account any observed variance in the objective. If the observed variance were constant, the metric would be proportional to $sqrt(T)$ where T is the number of times the candidate has been used.

Confidence is an objective because we expect the variance in the execution times and accuracies of a configuration (as it performs more and more competitions) to be significant. Confidence allows configurations with reliable performance to be differentiated from those with highly variable performance. It prevents an "outlier run" from making a suboptimal configuration temporarily dominate better configurations and forcing them out of the population.

Taken together, these objectives create a 3-dimensional space in which each candidate algorithm in the population occupies a point. In this 3-dimensional space, the online learner's goal is to push the current population towards the Pareto-optimal front.

4.3 Selecting the Safe and Seed Configuration

Each configuration of the population is assigned a fitness, m, that is updated every time it competes against another configuration. Fitness depends upon how well the configuration is meeting a target accuracy, m_a, and its execution time, m_t:

$$m_{config} = \left\{ \begin{array}{ll} \frac{-m_t}{\sum_{n \in P} n_t} - z \frac{g - m_a}{\sum_{n \in P} n_a} & \text{if } m_a < g \\ \frac{-m_t}{\sum_{n \in P} n_t} & \text{if } m_a \geq g \end{array} \right\}$$

where g is a target accuracy, z is a scalar weight set based on how often the online learner has been meeting its goals in the past, and P is the population of all candidates. Fitness prioritizes meeting the accuracy target, but gives no reward for accuracy exceeding the target.

To select the safe configuration, the online learner picks the algorithm in the population that has the highest fitness. When the online learner is not producing configurations that meet the targets, the weight of z is adaptively incremented to put more importance on accuracy targets when it calculates m.

To select a seed configuration, the online learner first eliminates any configuration that has an expected running time that is below the 65th percentile running time of the safe configuration. Then, it randomly draws a configuration from the remaining population using the fitness of each configuration to weight the draw. In evolutionary algorithm terminology, this type of draw is called "fitness proportional selection".

4.4 Mutation Operators

The online learner changes configurations of candidate algorithms though a pool of mutation operators that are generated automatically from information outputted by the PetaBricks compiler. Mutators create a new algorithm configuration from an existing configuration by randomly making changes to a specific target region of the configuration.

One can divide the mutators used by our online learner into the following categories:

- **Selector manipulation mutators** randomly either add, remove, or change levels of a selector decision tree. A decision tree is an abstract hierarchically ordered representation of the selector parameters in the configuration file. It enables the dynamic determination of which algorithm to use at a specific dynamic point in program execution. Each level of the tree has a cutoff value and an algorithmic choice. Each decision tree in the configuration results in 5 mutation operators: one operator to add a level, one operator to remove a level, one operator to make large random changes, and two operators to make small random changes.

- **Log-normal random scaling mutators** scale a configuration value by a random number taken from a log-normal distribution with scale of 1. This type of mutator is used to change cutoff values that are compared to data sizes. Examples of this are blocking sizes, cutoffs in decision trees, and cutoffs to switch between sequential and parallel code.

- **Uniform random mutators** replace an existing configuration value with a new value taken from a discrete uniform random distribution containing all legal values for the configuration item. This type of mutator is used for choices where there are a relatively small number of possibilities. An example of this is deciding the scheduling strategy for a specific block of code or algorithmic choices.

- **Synthesized function manipulation mutators** change the underlying parameter of a function that is used to decide a value that must change dynamically based on input size. For example, the number of iterations in a `for_enough` loop. These functions are represented by $\lg n$ points in the configuration value with runtime interpolation find values lying between the specified points.

4.5 Adaptive Mutator Selection (AMS)

The evolutionary algorithm of the online learner uses different mutators. This provides it with flexibility to generate experimental configurations that range from being close to the seed configuration to far from it, thus controlling its exploration and exploitation. However, the efficiency of the search process is sensitive to *which* mutators are applied and *when*. These decisions cannot be hard coded because they are dependent on what program is being autotuned. Furthermore, even for a specific program, they might need to change over the course of racing history as the population changes and converges. Mutators that cause larger seed-experiment configuration differences should be favored in early competitions to explore while ones that cause smaller differences should be favored when the search is close to the best configuration to exploit.

For this reason, the online tuner has a specific strategy for selecting mutators on the basis of how well they have performed. The performance of mutators is the extent to which they have generated experimental configurations of better fitness than others. In general, this is called "Adaptive Operator Selection" (AOS) [14, 15, 31] and our version is called "Adaptive Mutator Selection" (AMS).

There are two parts to AMS: credit assignment to a mutator, and mutator selection. AMS uses *Fitness-based Area-Under-Curve* for its credit assignment and a *Bandit* decision process for mutator selection. We use *Fitness-based Area-Under-Curve* because it is appropriate for the comparison (racing) approach taken by the online learner. We use the AUC version of the *Dynamic Multi-Armed Bandit* decision process because it matches up with the online learner's dynamic environment. Our descriptions are adapted and implemented directly from [29].

Credit Assignment

After each competition the AOS stops and assigns credit to operators based on their performance over the interval. *Fitness-based Area-Under-Curve* adapts the Area Under the ROC Curve criteria [11] to assign credit to comparison-based assessment of mutators by first creating a ranked list of the experimental configurations generated in any time window according to a fitness objective. The ROC (Receiver Operator Curve) associated to a given mutator, μ, is then drawn by scanning the ordered list, starting from the origin: a vertical segment is drawn when the current configuration has been generated by μ, a horizontal segment is drawn otherwise, and a diagonal one is drawn in case of ties. Finally, the credit assigned to mutator, μ, is the area under this curve (AUC).

Bandit Mutator Selection

The bandit-based mutator selection deterministically selects the mutator based on a variant of the Upper Confidence Bound (UCB) algorithm [5]:

$$\text{Select } \arg\max_i \left(AUC_{i,t} + C \sqrt{\frac{2 \log \sum_k n_{k,t}}{n_{i,k}}} \right)$$

where $AUC_{i,t}$ denotes the empirical quality of the i-th mutator during a user-defined time-window W (exploitation term), $n_{i,t}$ the total number of times it has been used since the beginning of the process (the right term corresponding to the exploration term), and C is a user defined constant that controls the balance between exploration and exploitation. Bandit algorithms have been proven to optimally solve the exploration vs. exploitation dilemma in a stationary context. The dynamic context is addressed in this formulation by using AUC as the exploitation term. See [29] for more details.

4.6 Population Pruning

Each time the population has an experimental configuration added, it is pruned. Pruning is a means of ensuring the experimental configuration should appropriately stay in the population and removing any configuration wholly

Acronym	Processor Type	Operating System	Processors
Xeon8	Intel Xeon X5460 3.16GHz	Debian 5.0	2 (×4 cores)
Xeon32	Intel Xeon X7560 2.27GHz	Ubuntu 10.4	4 (×8 cores)
AMD48	AMD Opteron 6168 1.9GHz	Debian 5.0	4 (×12 cores)

Table 1: Specifications of the test systems used and the acronyms used to differentiate them in results.

inferior to the experimental configuration. The experimental configuration should stay if, for any weighting of its objectives, it is better than any other configuration under the same weighting. This condition is expressed as:

$$\arg\max_{m \in P} \left(\frac{w_a}{\sum_{n \in P} n_a} m_a - \frac{w_t}{\sum_{n \in P} n_t} m_t + \frac{w_c}{\sum_{n \in P} n_c} m_c \right)$$

where P is the population and w defines a weight. The subscripts a, t, and c of w represent the accuracy, time, and confidence objectives for each configuration.

If the experimental configuration results in an extant configuration no longer being non-dominated, the extant configuration is pruned. We set $w_t = 1 - w_a$ and sample values of w_a and w_c in the range $[0, 1]$. We sample the time-accuracy trade-off space more densely than the confidence space, with approximately 100 different weight combinations total.

5. EXPERIMENTAL RESULTS AND DISCUSSION

We evaluate SiblingRivalry with two experimental scenarios. In the first scenario, we use a single system and vary the load on the system. In the second scenario we vary the underling architecture, to represent the effects of a computation being migrated between machines. In both cases we compare to a fixed configuration found with offline tuning that utilizes all cores of the underlying machine.

We performed our experiments on three systems described in Table 1. We refer to these three systems using the acronyms Xeon8, Xeon32, and AMD48. Power measurements were performed on the AMD48 system, using a WattsUp device that samples and stores the consumed power at 1 second intervals.

5.1 Sources of Speedups

The speedups achieved for different benchmarks can come from a variety of sources. Some of these sources of speedup can apply even to the case where the environment does not change dynamically. Different benchmarks obtained speedups for different reasons in different tests.

- Algorithmic improvements are a large source of speedup, and the motivation for this work. When the dynamic environment changes, the optimal algorithmic choices may be different and SiblingRivalry can discover better algorithms dynamically.

- For the variable accuracy benchmarks, additional speedup can be obtained since the online tuner receives runtime feedback on how well it is meeting its accuracy targets. If it observes that it is over delivering on its quality of service target it can opportunistically change algorithms, enabling it to be less conservative than offline tuning. For all tests, both SiblingRivalry and the baseline met the required quality of service requirements.

- SiblingRivalry benefits from a "dice effect," since it is running two copies of the algorithm it has an increased chance of getting lucky and having one configuration complete faster than its mean performance. External events, like I/O interrupts, have a lower chance of affecting both algorithms. This leads to a small speedup, which is a function of the variance in the performance of each algorithm.

- As the number of processing cores continues to grow exponentially, the amount of per core memory bandwidth is decreasing dramatically since per-chip memory bandwidth is growing only at a linear rate [8]. This fact, coupled with Amdahl's law, makes it particularly difficult to write applications with scalable performance. On our AMD48 machine, we found that some benchmarks with high degree of available parallelism exhibit limited scalability, preventing them from fully utilizing all available processors. In cases where the performance leveled off before half of the available processors, the cost of our competition strategy becomes close to zero.

5.2 Load on a System

To test how SiblingRivalry adapts to load on the system, we simulated system load by running concurrently with a synthetic CPU-bound benchmark competing for system resources. We allowed the operating system to assign cores to this benchmark and did not bind it to specific cores. For the different tests, we varied the number of threads in this benchmark to utilize between 0 and 100% of the processors on the system. Combined with the PetaBricks benchmarks, this creates an overloaded system where the number of active threads is double the number of cores. In all cases we compared SiblingRivalry to a baseline of a fixed configuration found with offline tuning on the same machine, without the additional load. We measure average throughput over 10 minutes of execution, which includes all of the learning costs.

We observed different trends of speedups on the two machines tested. On the Xeon8 (Figure 2(a)), the geometric mean cost of running SiblingRivalry (under zero new load) was 16%. This cost is largest for Matrix Multiply, which scales linearly on this system. For other benchmarks, the overheads are lower for two reasons. For the non-variable accuracy benchmarks, some benchmarks do not scale perfectly (These benchmarks exhibit an average speedup of 5.4x when running with 8 threads [3]). For variable accuracy benchmarks, the online autotuner is able to improve performance by taking advantage of using a number of candidate algorithms to construct an aggregate QoS that is closer to the target accuracy level than would be otherwise possible with a single algorithm.

Figure 2(b) shows the performance results on the AMD48 machine. In the zero load case, SiblingRivalry achieves a geometric mean speedup of 1.12x. This speedup comes primarily because of the way the autotuner can dynamically adapt the variable accuracy benchmarks (the same way it did on Xeon8). Additionally, while AMD48 and Xeon8 have very similar memory systems, AMD48 has six times as many cores, and thus 6 times less bandwidth per core. Thus, we found that in some cases, using additional cores on this system did not always translate to better performance.

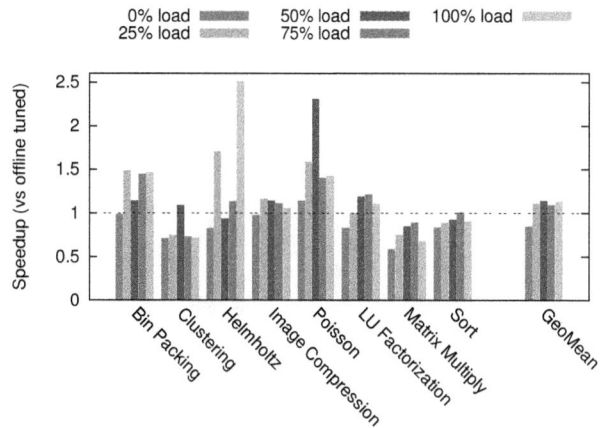

(a) Xeon8

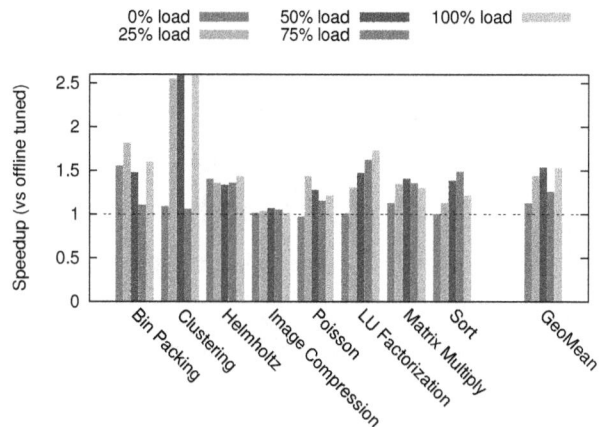

(b) AMD48

Figure 2: Speedups (or slowdowns) of each benchmark as the load on a system changes. Note that the 50% load and 100% load speedups for Clustering in (b), which were cut off due to the scale, are 4.0x and 3.9x.

For example, while some fixed configurations of our matrix multiply benchmark scale well to 48 cores, our autotuner is able to find a less scalable configuration that provides the same performance using only 20 cores. Once load is introduced, SiblingRivarly is able to further adapt the benchmarks, providing geometric speedups of up to 1.53x.

5.3 Migrating Between Microarchitectures

In a second group of experiments we test how SiblingRivalry can adapt to changes in microarchitecture. We first train offline on a initial machine and then move this trained configuration to a different machine. We compare SiblingRivalry to a baseline configuration found with offline tuning on the original machine. The offline configuration is given one thread per core on the system. Figure 3 shows the speedups for each benchmark after such a migration. SiblingRivalry shows a geometric mean speedup of 1.8x in this migration experiment.

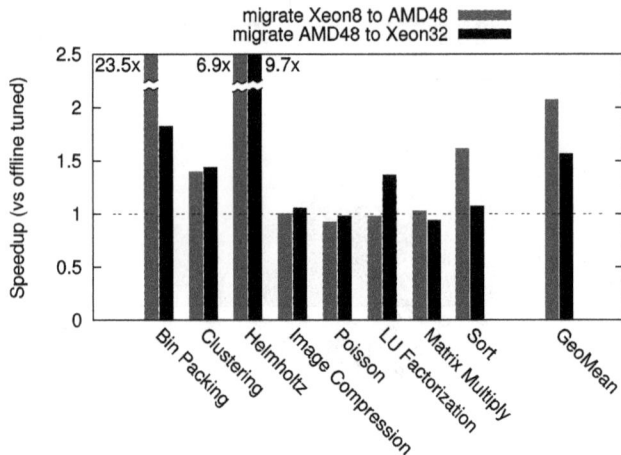

Figure 3: Speedups (or slowdowns) of each benchmark after a migration between microarchitectures. "Normalized throughput" is the throughput over the first 10 minutes of execution of SiblingRivalry (including time to learn), divided by the throughput of the first 10 minutes of an offline tuned configuration using the entire system.

Starting Configuration.

Figure 4 shows how using an offline tuned configuration affects the rate of convergence of SiblingRivalry. We show three starting configurations: a random configuration, a configuration tuned on a different machine, and a configuration tuned on the same machine. As one would expect, convergence time increases as the starting point becomes less optimal. Convergence times are roughly 5 minutes, 1 minute, and 0 for the configurations tried, though since changes are constantly being made it is difficult to mark a point of convergence.

Power Consumption.

Figure 5 shows the energy used per request for each of our benchmarks. While one might initially think that the techniques proposed would increase energy usage since up to twice the amount of work is performed, SiblingRivalry actually reduces energy usage by an average of 30% for our benchmarks. The primary reason for this decreased energy usage is the increased throughput of SiblingRivalry, which results in the machine being used for a shorter period of time. The benchmarks that saw increased throughput also saw decreased power consumption per request.

6. RELATED WORK

A number of offline empirical autotuning frameworks have been developed for building efficient, portable libraries in specific domains. PHiPAC [10] is an autotuning system for dense matrix multiply, generating portable C code and search scripts to tune for specific systems. ATLAS [35] utilizes empirical autotuning to produce a cache-contained matrix multiply, which is then used in larger matrix computations in BLAS and LAPACK. FFTW [18] uses empirical autotuning to combine solvers for FFTs. Other autotuning systems include SPARSITY [24] for sparse matrix computations, SPIRAL [28] for digital signal processing, and OSKI [34] for sparse matrix kernels.

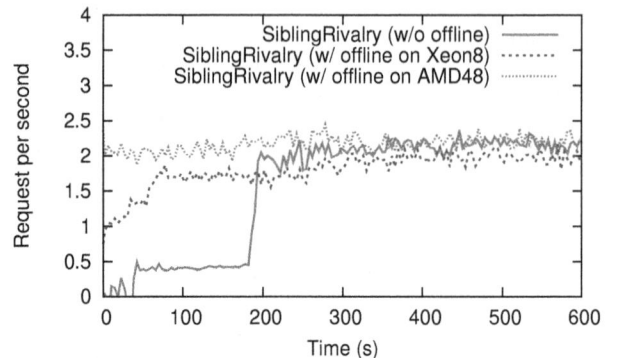

Figure 4: The effect of using an offline tuned configuration as a starting point for SiblingRivaly on the Sort benchmark. We compare starting from a random configuration ("w/o offline") to configurations found through offline training on the same and a different architecture.

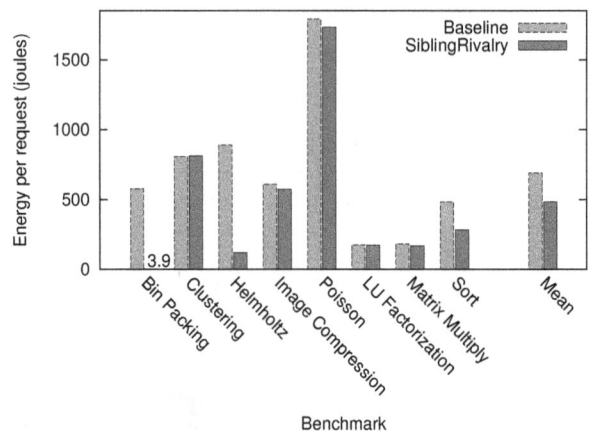

Figure 5: Average energy use per request for each benchmark after migrate Xeon8 to AMD48.

In the dynamic autotuning space, there have been a number of systems developed [7,9,12,22,23,25,30] that focus on creating applications that can monitor and automatically tune themselves to optimize a particular objective. Many of these systems employ a control systems based autotuner that operates on a linear model of the application being tuned. For example, PowerDial [23] converts static configuration parameters that already exist in a program into dynamic knobs that can be tuned at runtime, with the goal of trading QoS guarantees for meeting performance and power usage goals. The system uses an offline learning stage to construct a linear model of the choice configuration space which can be subsequently tuned using a linear control system. The system employs the heartbeat framework [21] to provide feedback to the control system. A similar technique is employed in [22], where a simpler heuristic-based controller dynamically adjusts the degree of loop perforation performed on a target application to trade QoS for performance.

The area of iterative compilation contains many projects that use different machine learning techniques to optimize lower level compiler optimizations [1, 2, 20, 26]. These projects change both the order that compiler passes are applied and the types of passes that are applied. These projects do not explore the type of algorithmic choices that the PetaBricks language exposes and these systems operate at compile time not runtime.

Additionally, there has been a large amount of work [6, 17, 32, 33] in the dynamic optimization space, where information available at runtime is used combined with static compilation techniques to generate higher performing code. Such dynamic optimizations differ from dynamic autotuning because each of the optimizations is hand crafted in a way that makes it likely that it will lead to an improvement in performance when applied. Conversely, autotuning searches the space of many available program variations without a priori knowledge of which configurations will perform better.

Evolutionary Algorithms Related Work.

There is one evolutionary algorithm, named Differential Evolution (DE) [27], that takes a comparison-based approach to search like our online learner. However DE compares a parent to its offspring, while we compare a safe configuration to the experimental configuration. These two configurations (safe and external) are not related. Further, DE does not generate offspring using mutators.

Our approach to multi-objective optimization is a hybrid of a pareto-based EA [16, 37] and a weighted objectives EA. Our approach avoids the O(nlogn) computational complexity of pareto-based EAs such as the very commonly used NSGA-II [16]. In the latter, these are incurred to identify successive Pareto-fronts and to compute the distance between the solutions on each front. Our approach of using multiple weight combinations and preserving dominating configurations for each is more robust than using only one.

7. CONCLUSIONS

This paper demonstrates that it can sometimes be more effective to devote resources to learning the smart thing to do, than to simple throw resources at a potentially suboptimal configuration. Our technique devotes half of the system resources to trying something different, to enable online adaption to the system environment. The geometric mean speedup of SiblingRivalry was 1.8x after a migration between microarchitectures. Even in comparison to an offline-optimized version on the same microarchitecture that uses the full resources, SiblingRivalry showed a geometric mean performance increase of 1.3x when moderate load was introduced on the machine. These results show that continuously adapting the program to the environment can provide a huge boost in performance that easily overcame the cost of splitting the available resources in half.

In addition, we have showed that an intelligent machine learning system can rapidly find a good solution even when the search space is extremely large. Furthermore, we demonstrated that it is important to provide many algorithmic and optimization choices to the online learner as done by the PetaBricks language and compiler. While these choices increase the search space, they make it possible for the autotuner to obtain the performance gains observed.

SiblingRivalry is able to fully eliminate the offline learning step, making the process fully transparent to

users, which is the biggest impediment to the acceptance of autotuning. For example, while Feedback Directed Optimization (FDO) can provide substantial performance gains, the extra step involved in the programmers workflow has stopped this promising technique from being widely adopted [13]. By eliminating any extra steps, we believe that SiblingRivalry can bring autotuning to the mainstream program optimization. As we keep increasing the core counts of our processors, autotuning via SiblingRivalry help exploit them in a purposeful way.

8. ACKNOWLEDGMENTS

This work is partially supported by DOE Award DE-SC0005288.

9. REFERENCES

[1] F. Agakov, E. Bonilla, J. Cavazos, B. Franke, G. Fursin, M. F. P. O'boyle, J. Thomson, M. Toussaint, and C. K. I. Williams. Using machine learning to focus iterative optimization. In *International Symposium on Code Generation and Optimization*, pages 295–305, 2006.

[2] L. Almagor, Keith D. Cooper, Alexander Grosul, Timothy J. Harvey, Steven W. Reeves, Devika Subramanian, Linda Torczon, and Todd Waterman. Finding effective compilation sequences. In *LCTES'04*, pages 231–239, 2004.

[3] Jason Ansel, Cy Chan, Yee Lok Wong, Marek Olszewski, Qin Zhao, Alan Edelman, and Saman Amarasinghe. PetaBricks: A language and compiler for algorithmic choice. In *PLDI*, Dublin, Ireland, Jun 2009.

[4] Jason Ansel, Yee Lok Wong, Cy Chan, Marek Olszewski, Alan Edelman, and Saman Amarasinghe. Language and compiler support for auto-tuning variable-accuracy algorithms. In *CGO*, Chamonix, France, Apr 2011.

[5] Peter Auer, Nicolò Cesa-Bianchi, Yoav Freund, and Robert E. Schapire. The nonstochastic multiarmed bandit problem. *SIAM Journal on Computing*, 32(1), 2003.

[6] Joel Auslander, Matthai Philipose, Craig Chambers, Susan J. Eggers, and Brian N. Bershad. Fast, effective dynamic compilation. In *PLDI*, 1996.

[7] Woongki Baek and Trishul Chilimbi. Green: A framework for supporting energy-conscious programming using controlled approximation. In *PLDI*, June 2010.

[8] K. Bergman, S. Borkar, D. Campbell, W. Carlson, W. Dally, M. Denneau, P. Franzon, W. Harrod, J. Hiller, S. Karp, S. Keckler, D. Klein, R. Lucas, M. Richards, A. Scarpelli, S. Scott, A. Snavely, T. Sterling, S. Williams, and K. Yelick. Exascale computing study: Technology challenges in achieving exascale systems, 2008.

[9] V. Bhat, M. Parashar, . Hua Liu, M. Khandekar, N. Kandasamy, and S. Abdelwahed. Enabling self-managing applications using model-based online control strategies. In *International Conference on Autonomic Computing*, Washington, DC, 2006.

[10] Jeff Bilmes, Krste Asanovic, Chee-Whye Chin, and Jim Demmel. Optimizing matrix multiply using PHiPAC: a portable, high-performance, ANSI C

coding methodology. In *Supercomputing*, New York, NY, 1997.

[11] Andrew P. Bradley. The use of the area under the ROC curve in the evaluation of machine learning algorithms. *Pattern Recognition*, 30(7), 1997.

[12] Fangzhe Chang and Vijay Karamcheti. A framework for automatic adaptation of tunable distributed applications. *Cluster Computing*, 4, March 2001.

[13] Dehao Chen, Neil Vachharajani, Robert Hundt, Shih-wei Liao, Vinodha Ramasamy, Paul Yuan, Wenguang Chen, and Weimin Zheng. Taming hardware event samples for FDO compilation. In *CGO*, New York, NY, 2010.

[14] Luis DaCosta, Alvaro Fialho, Marc Schoenauer, and Michèle Sebag. Adaptive operator selection with dynamic multi-armed bandits. In *GECCO*, New York, NY, 2008.

[15] Lawrence Davis. Adapting operator probabilities in genetic algorithms. In *ICGA*, San Francisco, CA, 1989.

[16] Kalyanmoy Deb, Samir Agrawal, Amrit Pratap, and T. Meyarivan. A fast elitist non-dominated sorting genetic algorithm for multi-objective optimization: NSGA-II. In Marc Schoenauer, Kalyanmoy Deb, Günter Rudolph, Xin Yao, Evelyne Lutton, Juan Julian Merelo, and Hans-Paul Schwefel, editors, *PPSN*, Berlin, 2000.

[17] Pedro C. Diniz and Martin C. Rinard. Dynamic feedback: an effective technique for adaptive computing. In *PLDI*, New York, NY, 1997.

[18] Matteo Frigo and Steven G. Johnson. FFTW: An adaptive software architecture for the FFT. In *IEEE International Conference on Acoustics Speech and Signal Processing*, volume 3, 1998.

[19] Matteo Frigo and Steven G. Johnson. The design and implementation of FFTW3. *IEEE*, 93(2), February 2005. Invited paper, special issue on "Program Generation, Optimization, and Platform Adaptation".

[20] Grigori Fursin, Cupertino Miranda, Olivier Temam, Mircea Namolaru, Elad Yom-Tov, Ayal Zaks, Bilha Mendelson, Edwin Bonilla, John Thomson, Hugh Leather, Chris Williams, Michael O'Boyle, Phil Barnard, Elton Ashton, Eric Courtois, and Francois Bodin. MILEPOST GCC: machine learning based research compiler. In *Proceedings of the GCC Developers' Summit*, Jul 2008.

[21] Henry Hoffmann, Jonathan Eastep, Marco D. Santambrogio, Jason E. Miller, and Anant Agarwal. Application heartbeats: a generic interface for specifying program performance and goals in autonomous computing environments. In *ICAC*, New York, NY, 2010.

[22] Henry Hoffmann, Sasa Misailovic, Stelios Sidiroglou, Anant Agarwal, and Martin Rinard. Using code perforation to improve performance, reduce energy consumption, and respond to failures. Technical Report MIT-CSAIL-TR-2209-042, Massachusetts Institute of Technology, Sep 2009.

[23] Henry Hoffmann, Stelios Sidiroglou, Michael Carbin, Sasa Misailovic, Anant Agarwal, and Martin Rinard. Power-aware computing with dynamic knobs. In *ASPLOS*, 2011.

[24] Eun-jin Im and Katherine Yelick. Optimizing sparse matrix computations for register reuse in SPARSITY. In *International Conference on Computational Science*, 2001.

[25] Gabor Karsai, Akos Ledeczi, Janos Sztipanovits, Gabor Peceli, Gyula Simon, and Tamas Kovacshazy. An approach to self-adaptive software based on supervisory control. In *International Workshop in Self-adaptive software*, 2001.

[26] Eunjung Park, L.-N. Pouche, J. Cavazos, A. Cohen, and P. Sadayappan. Predictive modeling in a polyhedral optimization space. In *IEEE/ACM International Symposium on Code Generation and Optimization*, pages 119 –129, April 2011.

[27] Kenneth Price, Rainer Storn, and Jouni Lampinen. *Differential Evolution: A Practical Approach to Global Optimization*. Natural Computing Series. Springer-Verlag, Berlin, Germany, 2005.

[28] Markus Püschel, José M. F. Moura, Bryan Singer, Jianxin Xiong, Jeremy R. Johnson, David A. Padua, Manuela M. Veloso, and Robert W. Johnson. Spiral: A generator for platform-adapted libraries of signal processing alogorithms. *IJHPCA*, 18(1), 2004.

[29] Robert Schaefer, Carlos Cotta, Joanna Kolodziej, and Günter Rudolph, editors. *Parallel Problem Solving from Nature*, volume 6238 of *Lecture Notes in Computer Science*, 2010.

[30] Cristian Tapus, I-Hsin Chung, and Jeffrey K. Hollingsworth. Active harmony: Towards automated performance tuning. In *In Proceedings from the Conference on High Performance Networking and Computing*, pages 1–11, 2003.

[31] Dirk Thierens. Adaptive strategies for operator allocation. In Fernando G. Lobo, Cláudio F. Lima, and Zbigniew Michalewicz, editors, *Parameter Setting in Evolutionary Algorithms*, volume 54 of *Studies in Computational Intelligence*. 2007.

[32] Michael Voss and Rudolf Eigenmann. Adapt: Automated de-coupled adaptive program transformation. In *International Conference on Parallel Processing*, 2000.

[33] Michael Voss and Rudolf Eigenmann. High-level adaptive program optimization with adapt. *ACM SIGPLAN Notices*, 36(7), 2001.

[34] Richard Vuduc, James W. Demmel, and Katherine A. Yelick. OSKI: A library of automatically tuned sparse matrix kernels. In *Scientific Discovery through Advanced Computing Conference*, Journal of Physics: Conference Series, San Francisco, CA, June 2005.

[35] Richard Clint Whaley and Jack J. Dongarra. Automatically tuned linear algebra software. In *Supercomputing*, Washington, DC, 1998.

[36] S. Williams, K. Datta, J. Carter, L. Oliker, J. Shalf, K. Yelick, and D. Bailey. PERI - auto-tuning memory-intensive kernels for multicore. *Journal of Physics Conference Series*, 125(1), July 2008.

[37] Eckart Zitzler, Marco Laumanns, and Lothar Thiele. SPEA2: Improving the strength pareto evolutionary algorithm for multiobjective optimization. In K. Giannakoglou, D. Tsahalis, J. Periaux, K. Papailiou, and T. Fogarty, editors, *Evolutionary Methods for Design, Optimisation and Control*. Barcelona, Spain, 2002.

Function Inlining and Loop Unrolling for Loop Acceleration in Reconfigurable Processors

Narasinga Rao Miniskar*   Pankaj Shailendra Gode*
Soma Kohli*   Donghoon Yoo†

*SAIT, Samsung India Software Operations Pvt. Ltd, Bengaluru, 560093, India
(nr.miniskar, p.gode, soma.k)@samsung.com
†SAIT, Samsung Electronics, Giheung 446-712, Korea
say.yoo@samsung.com

ABSTRACT

The next generation SoCs for consumer electronics need software solutions for faster time-to-market, lower development cost and higher performance while maintaining lower energy consumption and area. As a result, reconfigurable processors (RPs) have become increasingly important, which enables just enough flexibility of accepting software solutions and providing application-specific hardware reconfigurability. Samsung Electronics has developed a reconfigurable processor called Samsung Reconfigurable Processor (SRP), which is the basis of our work. Though, the SRP is a powerful processor, it requires a smart and intelligent compiler to compile the application software while exploring its reconfigurable architecture. The existing compiler for the SRP does not support functional inlining and loop unrolling, and no study has yet been done on these optimizations for the RPs. In this paper, we study the impact of these optimizations on the performance of applications for the SRP processor and we also show how these optimizations are supported in the SRP compiler. We analyze the performance improvement due to these optimizations on various benchmarks namely Sobel Edge filter, JPEG decoder, and Luma Deblocking filter of the H.264 standard. Our experimental results have shown about 83% gain on performance with the functional inlining optimization and the loop unrolling optimization when compared to the original code for Sobel filter and JPEG encoder, and 11% gain on performance for Luma Deblock filter.

Categories and Subject Descriptors

D3.4 [**Programming Languages**]: Processors-code generation,optimization,performance analysis

General Terms

Experimentation, Measurement, Performance, Algorithms

Keywords

Coarse Grained Reconfigurable Arrays, Compilers, VLIW, Optimizations, Performance Analysis

1. INTRODUCTION

The Samsung Reconfigurable Processor (SRP) is a proprietary lower-power and high performance DSP core developed by Samsung Electronics, Ltd., as an elaboration on ADRES [1], which has two modes for running applications. The computationally code-critical sections of application software run on the Coarse Grain Reconfigurable Array (CGRA) mode of SRP and the non-code critical sections of software run on Very Large Instruction Word (VLIW) mode of SRP. The VLIW engine is useful for general purpose computations such as function invocation and branch selection. The CGRA makes full use of the software pipeline technique via modulo scheduling to allow loop acceleration. The use of such an architecture to perform graphics processing has been demonstrated in [2].

Though the SRP has multiple Functional Units (FUs) (in 4x4 matrix), the maximal performance of the application depends on the ILP (Instruction Level Parallelism) possible in the application and modulo scheduling to exploit the LLP (Loop Level Parallelism) [1]. Application developers write software which is composed of separate interchangeable components by breaking down program functions into modules to represent the separation of concerns and to improve the maintainability and readability of the source code. This code needs to be optimized further for effectively utilizing the processor resources to increase the performance of an application. Function inlining and loop unrolling are well known optimizations applied for this purpose in the embedded application domain.

Loop unrolling is a well known loop transformation to optimize application performance at the expense of increased code size. It duplicates the body of the loop multiple times. Loop unrolling speeds up the execution by increasing the ratio of compute to control instructions and thus avoid branch penalties. In VLIW processors (Example: TI-C64x+), it also increases the ILP of a loop body to effectively utilize the multiple FUs. In the case of SRP, the CGRA-mapped loops (The loops which are intended to map to run in CGRA mode in SRP) will explore the software pipelining of operations inside the loop body to map the operations to functional units and provide the customized connections between the functional units. Hence, the CGRA mapping exploits the

LLP (Loop Level Parallelism) inside the loops. Loop unrolling will further enhance the opportunity of exploring the software pipelining on a larger unrolled loop body, which provides more effective utilization of FUs to increase the performance of the application.

Function inlining is also a well known optimization to inline the most frequently called functions inside a loop at the expense of increased code size. As the application software is becoming more modular, there tend to be more and more function calls for sets of operations. However, if the loop has function calls inside, it will be disqualified for the CGRA mapping due to software pipelining exploration limitations in SRP. Hence, the functional calls inside innermost loop bodies have to be inlined to enable the CGRA mapping.

Though, the effect of these optimizations are well studied for the DSP processors like RISC and VLIWs [3, 4], it is not studied yet for the CGRA based processor like SRP. In this paper, we study not only the individual effects of these optimizations but also the combined effects of these optimizations on the SRP. We also show how these optimizations are supported in the SRP compiler. We study these optimizations on the Sobel filter, Luma Deblock filter of H.264 and JPEG encoder benchmarks. Our experimental results have shown the cycle reductions of 83% for the Sobel filter and 93% of cycle reductions for the JPEG encoder when compared to their original uninlined versions.

This paper is organized as follows. Section 2 provides the details of the target SRP architecture used for our study. Section 3 studies the effect of function inlining and loop unrolling optimizations on SRP. Section 4 explains how the function inlining and loop unrolling optimizations are supported in the SRP compiler. Section 5 shows the results of these optimizations on the SRP benchmark applications. Section 6 explains the related work of these optimizations and past SRP work. Finally, Section 7 discusses the conclusions.

2. TARGET SRP ARCHITECTURE

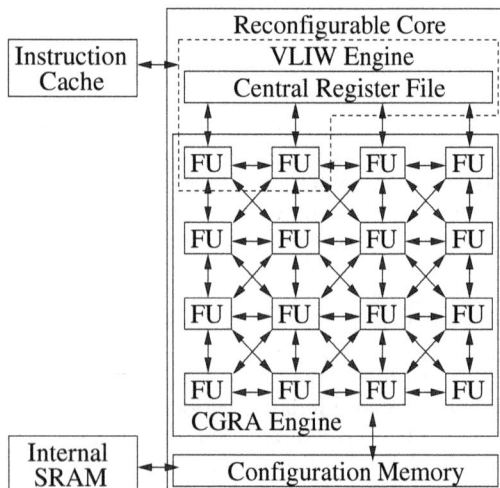

Figure 1: SRP Architecture

The Figure 1 shows a SRP core which has 16 Functional Units (FUs) arranged in 4x4 array [5]. Each functional unit is capable of performing either a single operation (e.g., ad-

dition, subtraction, load-store, etc.), or multiple ALU operations(e.g., multiply-accumulate operation). For efficiency and scalability, these units are connected with a sparse interconnection network. The VLIW and CGRA modes of executions in SRP share the common central register file. In the VLIW mode of execution, it uses 2 FUs as it is shown in **VLIW engine**. Both FUs support load-store instructions. In the CGRA mode, it can use all 16 FUs, but only the first column of FUs (adjacent to the VLIW engine) can support load-store instructions. Hence, the core can issue up to two load-store requests at every cycle in the VLIW mode and four load-store requests in the CGRA mode.

For the CGRA mode, the compiler applies software pipelining [6] to the innermost loops to exploit high ILP for the multiple functional units. The code outside the loop will run in the VLIW mode. The program execution begins with the VLIW mode of SRP core. When the CGRA-mapped loop is invoked, the processor stores the live-in values for the loop in the shared central register file. The loop kernel is repeatedly executed in CGRA mode. After the completion of loop execution, the control will be returned back to VLIW mode.

3. STUDY OF FUNCTION INLINING AND LOOP UNROLLING OPTIMIZATIONS FOR SRP

We have two kinds of benefits with the function inlining and loop unrolling optimizations. These two optimizations will (1) enable and (2) enhance the CGRA mapping opportunity for the desired loops to be mapped to the CGRA array of FUs in SRP.

3.1 Enable CGRA Mapping

In SRP compiler, only innermost loops containing no function calls are candidates for CGRA mapping on the SRP. However, this limitation can be quite severe as most application programmers prefer a modular style of coding. Let us consider a small example, a Sobel filter from image processing to perform the edge detection in the image [7]. The code of Sobel filter is shown in Figure 2. In this code we traverse through each pixel of image with x and y-loops. At each pixel in the image, the result of the Sobel operator is applied to convolve the 3x3 kernel of pixel neighbors, which is defined in $get\_pixel\_from\_image$.

If we want to map this filter to run in a CGRA mode to gain the performance with the parallel execution of FUs in CGRA mode, we can direct the compiler with the pragma of //#**pragma rpcc cgra** to map the x-loop to CGRA. The **rpcc** stands for *Reconfigurable Processor Compiler Collection*. However, the SRP compiler disqualifies this loop as it has the function call $get\_pixel\_from\_image$. Moreover, the CGRA-mappable loop should be the innermost loop due to the limitation of SRP compiler modulo scheduling exploration. Hence, it forces the developers to inline the function $get\_pixel\_from\_image$. The resultant code can be seen in Figure 3. However, the $x - loop$ is still not CGRA-mappable as it has $i\&j$-loop nests. The result of manually unrolled $i\&j$-loops are shown in Figure 4. Now, the x-loop is CGRA-mappable. The conditional statements in the loop body are converted into SRP predicated instructions. This example is sufficient enough to motivate us that, the function-inlining and loop unrolling optimizations to enable the CGRA-mappable opportunity for the loop bodies.

```
int get_pixel_from_image(int x, int y, int weight[3][3])
{
   int i,j;
   int pixel_value=0;
   for( j=-1; j<=1; j++ ) {
      for( i=-1; i<=1; i++ ) {
         pixel_value += weight[j+1][i+1] * image[y+j][x+i];
      }
   }
   return pixel_value;
}
void sobel_filter( )
{
   ....
   for(y=1; y<M-1; y++) {
      #pragma rpcc cgra
      for(x=1; x<N-1; x++) {
         pixel_value = get_pixel_from_image(x,y,weight);
         if( pixel_value < min )
            min = pixel_value;
         if( pixel_value > max )
            max = pixel_value;
      }
   }
   ....
}
```

Figure 2: Sobel filter C code

```
void sobel_filter( )
{
   ....
   for(y=1; y<M-1; y++) {
      #pragma rpcc cgra
      for(x=1; x<N-1; x++) {
         int pixel_value=0;
         for( j=-1; j<=1; j++ ) {
            for( i=-1; i<=1; i++ ) {
               pixel_value += weight[j+1][i+1] * image[y+j][x+i];
            }
         }
         if( pixel_value < min )
            min = pixel_value;
         if( pixel_value > max )
            max = pixel_value;
      }
   }
   ....
}
```

Figure 3: Function Inlining Optimization

3.2 Enhance the CGRA optimization with Loop Unrolling

Loop unrolling can be used to improve the performance of the loops either to increase the ILP of loops to run in VLIW mode or to increase LLP opportunity of loops to run in CGRA mode to explore the modulo scheduling on a larger loop body. If the intra iteration of the loop doesn't have sufficient ILP, the ILP can be exploited with inter-iterations either through software pipelining or through loop unrolling. The case in Figure 5 shows how loop unrolling can provide better performance than software pipelining.

For the example shown in Figure 5(a), the "for" loop iteration requires three memory operations, two loads and 1 store to complete. If there are only two memory functional units available, the resource bound will be two cycles, which means that at least two cycles are required per iteration in steady cycle. The Figure 5(b) shows the need of 8 cycles to produce four output results with software pipelining and the unrolling (by factor two) result in Figure 5(c) shows the

```
void sobel_filter( )
{
   ....
   for(y=1; y<M-1; y++) {
      #pragma rpcc cgra
      for(x=1; x<N-1; x++) {
         int pixel_value=0;
         pixel_value += weight[0][0] * image1[y-1][x-1];
         pixel_value += weight[0][1] * image1[y-1][x+0];
         pixel_value += weight[0][2] * image1[y-1][x+1];
         pixel_value += weight[1][0] * image1[y-0][x-1];
         pixel_value += weight[1][1] * image1[y-0][x+0];
         pixel_value += weight[1][2] * image1[y-0][x+1];
         pixel_value += weight[2][0] * image1[y+1][x-1];
         pixel_value += weight[2][1] * image1[y+1][x+0];
         pixel_value += weight[2][2] * image1[y+1][x+1];
         if( pixel_value < min )
            min = pixel_value;
         if( pixel_value > max )
            max = pixel_value;
      }
   }
   ....
}
```

Figure 4: Loop Unrolling Optimization

need of 6 cycles for four output results. The IPC of (c) is higher than (b).

```
for( i=0; i<N; i++ ) {
   output[i] = input1[i] + input2[i]
}
```
(a) Example Code

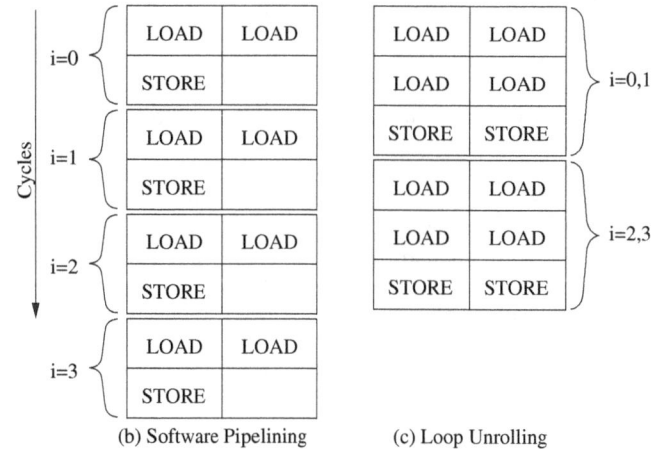

(b) Software Pipelining   (c) Loop Unrolling

Figure 5: Software Pipelining Vs Loop Unrolling

In SRP, the compiler explores the software pipelining to the CGRA-mapped loop. If the ILP is still not sufficient inside the software pipelining kernel, we can unroll the loop before the compiler applies the software pipelining. This can provide the combined gains of software pipelining and loop unrolling and can improve the performance in those cases where ILP is no sufficient in the loop bodies [8]. For the same example code in Figure 5(a), if we have six memory functional units in the architecture, the software pipelining for the unrolled code (by factor two) can utilize all six memory units for the load and stores in one cycle for every two iterations of i in steady cycle. The standalone software pipelining technique can utilize only three memory units in one cycle for every one iteration of i in steady cycle. The standalone loop unrolling technique can utilize maximum four memory units but in two cycles (due to load to store dependency) for every two iterations of i.

4. COMPILER OPTIMIZATIONS

We have extended the SRP compiler with the automatic function inlining and loop specific unrolling optimization passes. In this section, we will show how these two optimizations are supported in SRP compiler.

4.1 Function Inlining

Major components in the design are the three algorithms used to augment the Inliner pass to consider inlining call sites which can be mapped to CGRA. The implementation is hooked to the Inliner pass responsible for inlining function. A LLVM analysis pass collects the primary elements i.e. the required call sites (**CallSites** module), while **IsCalleeLeaf** and **InlineCostCalc** modules process the information to result in **CallSite** being identified for inlining.

There were two major challenges to overcome for SRP specific inlining, in order to gain considerable improvement through function inlining. The first challenge is, to consider the loops which contain call site, which adhere to the constraints imposed, for mapping loops to CGRA, such as innermost loop. The second challenge is to map the inlined code to CGRA. SRP compiler uses the LLVM infrastructure as front-end to leverage on the optimizations supported by LLVM.

4.1.1 Design

Function inlining uses the inlining infrastructure available with LLVM. A new LLVM pass is created specific to SRP specific function inlining. It considers all call sites but filters call sites, which on inlining, will still satisfy constraints for CGRA mapping.

Our approach starts by considering all callsites in input code. SRP applicable callsites are selected for inlining, if callee is a leaf function and if the call site is in innermost loop. Cost corresponding to these, SRP applicable callsites, is calculated and compared with the threshold limit identified for inlined function. The selected callsites are finally inlined using the LLVM inlining utility. The design flow for the SRP function inlining pass is shown in Figure 6.

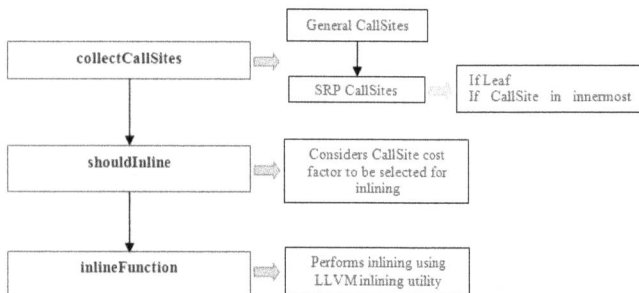

Figure 6: Design flowchart of Function Inlining

Inlining is performed with the following limitations, (1) inlining across multiple compilation units, (2) inlining on

recursive procedures, (3) indirect calls using function pointers and (4) callee definitions, which calls a function, which is not recursive.

4.2 Loop Unrolling Optimization

4.2.1 Inputs & Output

The loops to be unrolled is defined with the pragma //#**pragma unroll count=<count>** in its source code. An example loop to be unrolled is shown in Figure 7 for the Sobel filter.

```
int get_pixel_from_image(int x, int y, int weight[3][3])
{
    int i,j;
    int pixel_value=0;
    #pragma unroll count=3
    for( j=-1; j<=1; j++ ) {
        #pragma unroll count=3
        for( i=-1; i<=1; i++ ) {
            pixel_value += weight[j+1][i+1] * image[y+j][x+i];
        }
    }
    return pixel_value;
}
void sobel_filter( )
{
    ....
    for(y=1; y<M-1; y++) {
        #pragma rpcc cgra
        #pragma unroll count=2
        for(x=1; x<N-1; x++) {
            pixel_value = get_pixel_from_image(x,y,weight);
            if( pixel_value < min )
                min = pixel_value;
            if( pixel_value > max )
                max = pixel_value;
        }
    }
    ....
}
```

Figure 7: Loop Unrolling Optimization for Sobel filter

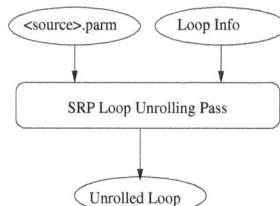

Figure 8: Inputs & Output

The inputs and output of SRP Loop unrolling optimization are shown in Figure 8. The <*source*>.*parm* file is required for the SRP loop unrolling pass to get the information about Loop unrolling pragmas written in source code. We have written a small script to read this pragma information from the source file to generate the <*source*>.*parm* file. The generated <*source*>.*parm* file for a small example code is shown in Figure 9.

4.2.2 Design

We have provided this SRP loop unrolling feature as a new pass to LLVM due to the following reasons.

```
15:    #pragma unroll count=4
16:    for( i=0; i<1000; i++ ) {
17:      A[i] = A[i] + 2 * B[i];
18:    }
<section name="loopTransformations">
    <section name="unroll">
      <section name="line_16">
        <!--Loop unrolling factor-->
        <property name="unroll_count" type="int" value="4"/>
        <!--Indicates for loop starting line no.-->
        <property name="loopStart" type="int" value="16"/>
      </section>
    </section>
</section>
```

Figure 9: Sample Code & Loop Unrolling Configuration

- The existing LLVM loop unrolling pass will apply the loop unrolling with flat unrolling count(or factor) for all loops. It is evident from the state-of-the-art loop unrolling that, the loop unrolling factor is very loop specific [9].

- Moreover, it is threshold based. If the loop size is big (150 instructions), it couldn't unroll the loop by default. But, the SRP have more number of functional units and it can support more operations than the number of functional units in its configuration memory. Hence, this restriction is not applicable for the SRP. The impact of loop size on the configuration memory of CGRA is very minimal when compared to the instructions mapped to VLIW processor. Even if we configure the threshold limit to the maximum value using **-unroll-threshold**, it is still not useful due to its flat unrolling factor for all loops.

- If the loop is not rotated, the present loop unrolling pass ignores the loop to unroll. This behavior needs to be extended.

- At present SRP is using LLVM 2.9 version, which has a major bug in updating the PHY nodes incoming values after unrolling. This bug fix is available in LLVM 3.0 version. Hence, we have to consider and reuse the LLVM 3.0 loop unrolling as much as possible.

- As we are supporting the loop unrolling feature with //**#pragma unroll count** pragma, we have to provide suitable mechanism to match the loops with this pragma information for taking the unrolling decision.

The Loop unrolling pass for the SRP is integrated with the LLVM 2.9 version. The **opt** tool of LLVM calls our loop unrolling pass for each loop. In the process of unrolling, we first identify whether the loop is to be unrolled or not by matching the pragma information which is defined in the source file, with the intermediate representation (IR) of Loop information line numbers. If both line numbers match, we apply the loop unrolling for the identified loop.

The Figure 10 explains our design flow for SRP loop unrolling. The **Identify the Loops to be Unrolled** component will match the line number information captured in <source>.parm file with the IR representation of loop information. If the loop is defined with the unrolling pragma, that loop will be passed to next stages in the design for

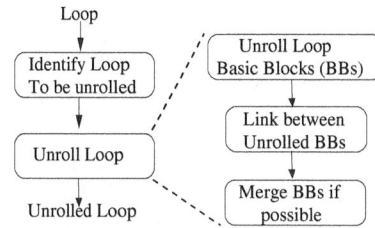

Figure 10: Loop Unrolling Design for SRP

the unrolling. The **Unroll Loop** component is the actual component to unroll the loops. The loop unrolling step is a straight forward method in the existing LLVM. We have used LLVM 3.0 loop unrolling implementation as there is a bug in LLVM 2.9 implementation. It first unrolls all basic blocks inside the loop as shown in **Unroll Loop Basic Blocks** component. The **Link between the Unrolled Basic Blocks** component will establish the control flow links between unrolled basic blocks based on the type of loop whether it is rotated or not and also based on the trip count (unrolling factor) values. We have shown four variations of loops and their unrolling results in Figure 11. Each loop is represented in IR with four basic blocks. The **%for.cond** basic block has the statements for the loop condition. The output of **%for.cond** has two control flow paths, but the selection of control flow based on the predicate value of **%for.cond** either **True:T** or **False:F**. The **%for.body** basic block has the statements for the loop body. The **%for.inc** basic block has the statements for the loop increment. The **%for.end** basic block has the statements for the loop exit statements. The control flow among the basic blocks is represented with arrows.

- If the loop is **not rotated** in its previous pass and its trip count (number of iterations) is either unknown or it is not exactly multiple of unrolling factor, our loop unrolling pass will unroll the loop, but the unrolled loop will have multiple exits as it is shown in Figure 11(a). However, as SRP supports predicate instructions, the multiple exits can be handled with conditional predicate instructions and the loop still qualifies for CGRA mapping.

- If the loop is **not rotated** in its previous pass and its trip count (number of iterations) is known and is exactly multiple of unrolling factor, our loop unrolling pass will unroll the loop and the unrolled loop will have a single exit as shown in Figure 11(b). Such a loop qualifies for CGRA mapping.

- If the loop is **rotated** in its previous pass and its trip count (number of iterations) is either unknown or it is not exactly multiple of unrolling factor, our loop unrolling pass will unroll the loop, but the unrolled loop will have multiple exits as it is shown in Figure 11(c). However, the SRP supports predicate instructions, the multiple exits can be handled with conditional predicate instructions and the loop still qualifies for CGRA mapping.

- If the loop is **rotated** in its previous pass and its trip count (number of iterations) is known and is exactly multiple of unrolling factor, our loop unrolling pass will unroll the loop and the unrolled loop will have a single exit as it is shown in Figure 11(d). Such a loop qualifies for CGRA mapping.

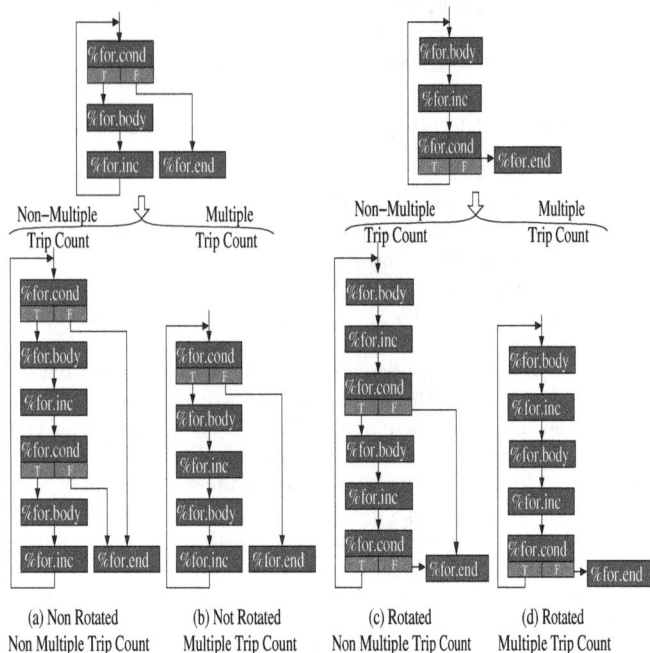

Figure 11: Loop Unrolling Variations

(a) Non Rotated Non Multiple Trip Count
(b) Not Rotated Multiple Trip Count
(c) Rotated Non Multiple Trip Count
(d) Rotated Multiple Trip Count

5. RESULTS

As SRP is a reconfigurable processor, we have considered the SRP architecture with 16 function units in 4x4 array to show the effects of these optimizations on the performance. The first row of two FUs are used in the VLIW mode execution of the SRP. The 4x4 array of FUs are used for CGRA mode execution of the CGRA-mapped loops in the application on the SRP. We have used an architecture simulator for our target SRP system [5]. This architecture simulator provides the functional correctness of an application and also provides the performance in cycles for the VLIW and CGRA mapped code. We have considered the Sobel filter, Luma Deblock filter of H.264 and JPEG encoder benchmarks to show our study and discuss the effects of function inlining and loop unrolling optimizations for SRP.

5.1 Sobel Filter

We have shown the performance results of Sobel filter in Figure 12, for the original code shown in Figure 2 and also after the optimizations applied. In the original code of Sobel filter, the x-loop is not CGRA-mappable due to the function call inside. After the inline operation, the SRP compiler has mapped the innermost loop, which is i-loop to CGRA. The i-loop iterates only for three times. Hence, we do not see much gain with the CGRA mapping. However, we observe a 24% reduction in cycle count when compared to the original code, due to the effect in the reduction of function call overhead in the innermost loop. When we have unrolled both the i and j-loops inside the function $get\_pixel\_from\_image$ with an unroll pragma, we observe the huge gain of 93% reduced

cycles when compared to the original code and 91% reduced cycles when compared to the inlined code. The unrolled code has enabled the x-loop to be mappable to the CGRA and the operations inside the x-loop are effectively utilized the CGRA functional units efficiently.

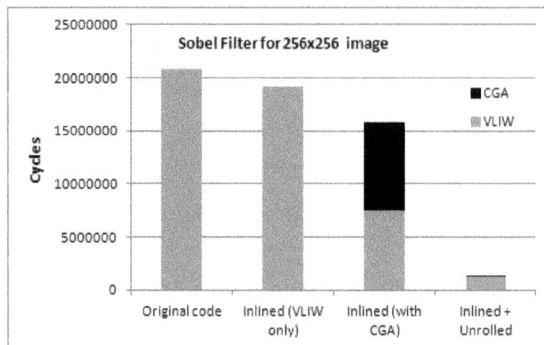

Figure 12: Sobel filter performance results

5.2 Luma Deblock filter

The performance results of Luma Deblock filter of H.264 is shown in Figure 13. We can see the cycle reductions of 1% after inlining (**Inlined VLIW only**) when compared to the original code. The complete code runs in the VLIW mode of SRP in its unoptimized form. However, the inlined innermost function call in the Luma Deblock filter has provided the opportunity to map its loop to CGRA. Hence, the **inlined code with CGRA mapping** shows the cycle reductions of 6%. In order to further reduce the CGRA cycles, we have unrolled the innermost loop to the factor of two and we have seen the CGRA cycles reduction of 11% when compared to the inlined with CGRA, though we do not see much gains in the total cycles. The gains are less when compared to the Sobel filter, because the innermost loop of Luma filter already has too many operations to fill the CGRA's 4x4 array.

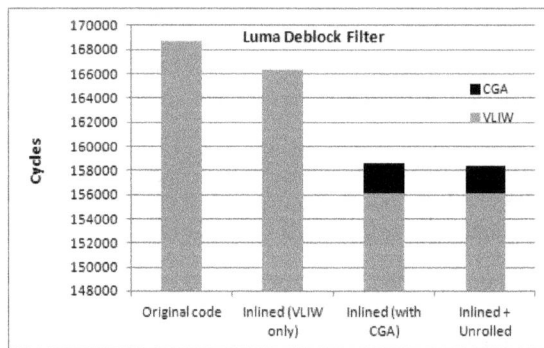

Figure 13: Luma Deblock filter performance results

5.3 JPEG Encoder

The performance results of JPEG encoder is shown in Figure 14. The JPEG encoder has the modules DCT, Quantize, ZigZag, RLE and Huffman encoding to encode the image into JPEG format. The inlining optimization has inlined all these modules inside the column loop of the image. However, we do not see much gain when we run this inlined code in a VLIW mode of SRP as the DCT, RLE and Huffman modules computation are dominated by function call overhead.

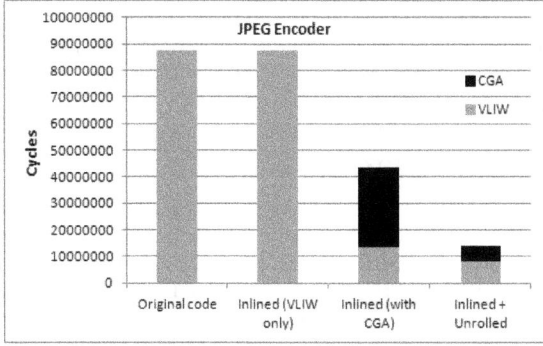

Figure 14: JPEG Encoder performance results

When we map the innermost loop of DCT and Quantize to run on CGRA array, we have seen a 50% reduction in cycles when compared to the original code. The DCT is performed on the 8x8 block of image as shown in Figure 15. Before unrolling, we are able to map only the innermost y-loop of DCT to CGRA. After unrolling the x-loop of DCT by 8 times and y-loop of DCT by 8 times (complete unroll), we have the opportunity now to map the v-loop of DCT to the CGRA. If we observe, the innermost two loops (x and y) of DCT are completely unrolled. The Quantize block is performed on the 8x8 block of image. We have also unrolled the innermost column loop of Quantize block by 8 times to map the row traverse loop of it to CGRA. Hence, we have seen the cycle reductions of 83% after unrolling the DCT and Quantize modules, when compared to the original code. The code of ZigZag, RLE and Huffman modules are not suitable for unrolling as the loops are not regular. One can also explore to make them regular with rewriting and can explore more performance gains of entire JPEG with other loop optimizations like loop coalescing, loop merging, etc., which is the out of the scope of this paper.

```
for(UBYTE u=0;u<8;u++) {
    for(UBYTE v=0;v<8;v++) {
        a = 0.0;
        for(UBYTE x=0;x<8;x++) {
            for(UBYTE y=0;y<8;y++) {
                a += f[x][y] *
                    cos((2.0*x+1.0)*u*3.14/16.0)*
                    cos((2.0*y+1.0)*v*3.14/16.0);
            }
        }
        F[u][v] = (int)(0.25*C(u)*C(v)*a);
    }
}
```

Figure 15: DCT code

5.4 Loop Unrolling Factor Exploration for SRP

We have performed another experiment to see the impact of unrolling factor on the performance for the loops mapped to the CGRA mode of SRP. We have considered a sample piece of code for this experiment, which is shown in Figure 16. The i-loop upper-bound N is set to 1000 and the *result* variable is initialized to 0. The performance results of this

```
for (i=0; i<N; i++) {
    result += i*10;
    A[i] = result;
}
```

Figure 16: Example code for unroll exploration

code for the different unrolling factors are given in Figure 17. We have shown these results when we have mapped this unrolled code to run in the VLIW mode of SRP (**VLIW Mapping of Loop**) and the results when we have mapped this unrolled code to run in the CGRA mode of SRP (**CGRA Mapping of Loop**). The **CGRA Mapping of Loop** includes both the cycles of CGRA which actually runs the i-loop and the cycles of VLIW which runs for the rest of the application code. We have obtained the performance gain in reduction of cycles with the unrolling factors of 2, 4, 8, 10, 12, 15, 18, 22, and 42.

In the **VLIW Mapping of Loop**, the unrolled loop shows the improved performance gains upto the unrolling factor of 15. From the unrolling factor 18 onwards, it shows the negative gains. This is due to the sub-optimal selection of VLIW instructions by the compiler when the unrolled code becomes too huge. In our experiment, the maximum performance for this loop is obtained with an unrolling factor of 15.

In the **CGRA Mapping of Loop**, if the unrolling factor is 1 (means original code), we have the cycle reductions of 6% with **CGRA Mapping of Loop** when compared to original code of **VLIW Mapping of Loop**. In Figure 17, we have shown the reduction percentage of **CGRA Mapping of Loop** when compared to **VLIW Mapping of loop** for the same unrolling factor. We have also shown the reduction percentage of **CGRA Mapping of Loop** when compared to original code. With the unrolling factor of two, we have 20% cycle reductions when compared to the original code. However, we do not see any significant gains after the unrolling factor of 8 upto 18. The maximum performance gain is obtained with the unrolling factor 42. We were unable to explore this further due to the code size limitation of CGRA due to the size of the unrolled code size.

In the **CGRA Mapping of Loop**, we have seen increase in the performance gain for all experimented unrolling factors unlike the VLIW Mapping of Loop, where it has shown negative gains after the unrolling factor of 15 as discussed before. It is known that the increasing unroll factor will affect the number of stages in the software pipelining of CGRA loop's data flow graph of operations and also on the initiation interval selected by the modulo scheduling algorithm for the CGRA mapping of loop. The initiation interval is also high for the higher unrolling factors, which is shown in the figure. It will affect the size of prologue and epilogue of software pipeline. If the unroll factor becomes large, the performance can be degraded and it depends on the size of prologue and epilogues, and the loop iterations. In this case, we have always seen the performance gains for the experimented unrolling factors in the CGRA mapping of loop due to the high loop iterations 1000 and the initiation interval is less than 82. The effect of prologue and epilogue are dominated by the high loop iterations.

We have also shown the effect of unrolling factor for the small loop iterations fixed to 100, which is shown in Figure 18. In the case of **CGRA Mapping of Loop**, the higher prologue and epilogue sizes for the higher unrolling factor are dominating the software pipeline kernel execution due to the less number of loop iterations. Hence, we have seen negative performance gains after the unrolling factor of 10, though it is not significant performance loss. We have also seen that the **VLIW Mapping of Loop** have lesser number of cycles when compared to **CGRA Mapping of Loop** after the unrolling factor 12. This is also due to the prologue and epilogue effects for the smaller loop iterations.

We can conclude that, the CGRA-mapped loops will not give negative gains even if we unroll the loop with higher unrolling factors for higher loop iterations. However, the effects of higher unrolling factor can give negative gains for the smaller loop iterations. The higher unrolling factor also increases the complexity of CGRA mapping due to larger loop body. Hence, it may provide sub-optimal results for the loop with higher unrolling factor. In this experiment, we are unable to get the results for unrolling factors beyond 42 for the **CGRA Mapping of Loop**, due to the CGRA mapping exploration limitation of SRP compiler.

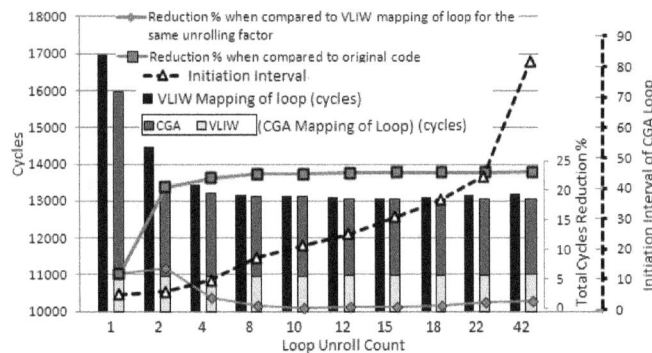

Figure 17: Unrolling factor exploration for N=1000

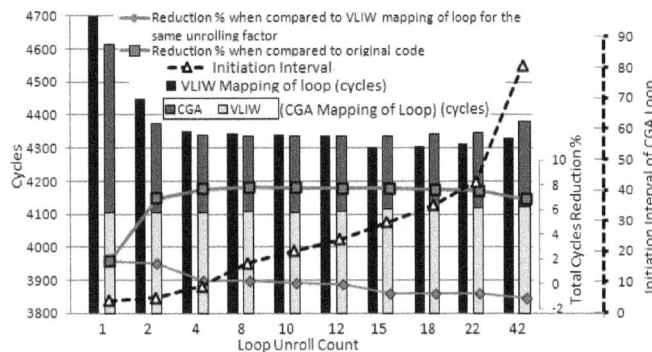

Figure 18: Unrolling factor exploration for N=100

6. RELATED WORK

The SRP is a proprietary lower-power DSP core developed by Samsung Electronics, Ltd, as an elaboration on ADRES [1] CGRA architecture. Mei has proposed a compiler framework for the ADRES CGRA architecture [10] and it is extended for the energy aware exploration in [11]. The SRP has its own compiler tool chain on the base of LLVM.

In the present compiler work of CGRA, we do not have any study of functional inlining and loop unrolling optimizations on the CGRA architectures. This is also because due to the lack of support in the compiler. Even though, if the application optimizers have applied these optimizations manually, this is very error prone and there is no study on the effects of these optimizations on the SRP. In this paper, we have studied the performance effects of these optimizations and we have also shown how these optimizations are supported in SRP compiler.

7. CONCLUSION

In this paper we have studied the impact of function inlining and loop unrolling optimizations on the performance of application for SRP. We have performed our analysis on the Sobel filter and the performance results are shown on the Sobel filter, Luma Deblock filter of H.264 and JPEG encoder benchmarks. The function inlining and loop unrolling optimizations on SRP have shown cycle reductions of 93%, 6% and 83% for the benchmarks Sobel filter, Luma Deblock and JPEG encoder respectively, when compared to their original code. We have also shown how these optimizations are supported in SRP compiler. The function inlining optimization is enabling the CGRA mapping of the innermost loops if they have any function calls inside. The loop unrolling optimization are enabling and enhancing the CGRA mapping opportunities with an increased ILP inside the loops.

8. REFERENCES

[1] B. Mei, A. Lambrechts, J.-Y. Mignolet, D. Verkest, and R. Lauwereins, "Architecture exploration for a reconfigurable architecture template," *Design Test of Computers, IEEE*, vol. 22, no. 2, pp. 90 – 101, march-april 2005.

[2] W. J. Lee, S.-O. Woo, K.-T. Kwon, S.-J. Son, K.-J. Min, G.-J. Jang, C.-H. Lee, S.-Y. Jung, C.-M. Park, and S.-H. Lee, "A scalable gpu architecture based on dynamically reconfigurable embedded processor," Aug 2011.

[3] S. Sair, D. Kaeli, and W. Meleis, "A study of loop unrolling for vliw-based dsp processors," in *Signal Processing Systems, 1998. SIPS 98. 1998 IEEE Workshop on*, oct 1998, pp. 519 –527.

[4] K. Heydemann, F. Bodin, P. M. W. Knijnenburg, and L. Morin, "Ufs: a global trade-off strategy for loop unrolling for vliw architectures: Research articles," *Concurr. Comput. : Pract. Exper.*, vol. 18, pp. 1413–1434, September 2006.

[5] C. Jang, J. Kim, J. Lee, H.-S. Kim, D.-H. Yoo, S. Kim, H.-S. Kim, and S. Ryu, "An instruction-scheduling-aware data partitioning technique for coarse-grained reconfigurable architectures," in *Proceedings of the 2011 SIGPLAN/SIGBED conference on Languages, compilers and tools for embedded systems*, ser. LCTES '11. New York, NY, USA: ACM, 2011, pp. 151–160.

[6] B. R. Rau, "Iterative modulo scheduling: an algorithm for software pipelining loops," in *Proceedings of the 27th annual international symposium on Microarchitecture*, ser. MICRO 27. New York, NY, USA: ACM, 1994, pp. 63–74.

[7] H. Myler and A. Weekes, *Computer Imaging Recipes in C.* Prentice Hall, NJ, 1993.

[8] J. Sanchez and A. Gonzalez, "The effectiveness of loop unrolling for modulo scheduling in clustered vliw architectures," in *Parallel Processing, 2000. Proceedings. 2000 International Conference on*, 2000, pp. 555 –562.

[9] S. Kurra, N. K. Singh, and P. R. Panda, "The impact of loop unrolling on controller delay in high level synthesis," in *Proceedings of the conference on Design, automation and test in Europe*, ser. DATE '07. San Jose, CA, USA: EDA Consortium, 2007, pp. 391–396.

[10] B. Mei, S. Vernalde, D. Verkest, H. De Man, and R. Lauwereins, "Adres: An architecture with tightly coupled vliw processor and coarse-grained reconfigurable matrix," vol. 2778, pp. 61–70, 2003.

[11] P. Raghavan, A. Lambrechts, J. Absar, M. Jayapala, F. Catthoor, and D. Verkest, "Coffee: compiler framework for energy-aware exploration," in *Proceedings of the 3rd international conference on High performance embedded architectures and compilers*, ser. HiPEAC'08. Berlin, Heidelberg: Springer-Verlag, 2008, pp. 193–208.

A Low-Overhead Interconnect Architecture for Virtual Reconfigurable Fabrics

Aaron Landy, Greg Stitt
University of Florida
Department of Electrical & Computer Engineering
Gainesville, FL, USA

landy@hcs.ufl.edu, gstitt@ece.ufl.edu

ABSTRACT

Field-programmable gate arrays (FPGAs) have been widely shown to have significant performance and power advantages compared to microprocessors and graphics-processing units (GPUs), but remain a niche technology due in part to productivity challenges. Although such challenges have numerous causes, previous work has shown two significant contributing factors: 1) prohibitive place-and-route times preventing mainstream design methodologies, and 2) limited application portability preventing design reuse. Virtual reconfigurable architectures, referred to as intermediate fabrics (IFs), were recently introduced as a potential solution to these problems, providing 100x-1000x place-and-route speedup, while also enabling application portability across potentially any physical FPGA. However, one significant limitation of existing intermediate fabrics is area overhead incurred from virtualized interconnect resources. In this paper, we perform design-space exploration of virtual interconnect architectures and introduce an optimized virtual interconnect that reduces area overhead by 48% to 54% compared to previous work, while also improving clock frequencies by 24% with a modest routability overhead of 16%.

Categories and Subject Descriptors

J.6 [**Computer-Aided Enginering**]: Computer-aided Design

General Terms

Performance, Design

Keywords

FPGA, intermediate fabrics, overlay networks, placement and routing, virtualization

1. INTRODUCTION

Field-programmable gate arrays (FPGAs) are reconfigurable devices capable of implementing application-specific circuits that can provide orders of magnitude improvements in performance, power, and energy compared to mainstream microprocessors and graphics-processing units (GPUs) [2][9][12][27]. Although these

advantages potentially advance the state-of-the-art for many applications, application designers often only use FPGAs when mainstream technologies cannot meet power and size constraints.

This mainstream resistance to FPGAs has resulted in part from low designer productivity, which previous work has shown to be an order of magnitude worse than other devices [24]. Although the main contributor to low FPGA productivity is an ASIC-prototyping-focused design methodology [24], advances in high-level synthesis from mainstream languages such as CUDA [26] and OpenCL [25] have enabled design flows similar to other devices. However, even with perfect compilers and synthesis tools (hereafter referred to collectively as *compilation*), FPGA productivity still suffers from prohibitive compilation times, often requiring many hours or even days for place-and-route [8], which prevents mainstream design methodologies. Furthermore, the lack of FPGA application portability prevents design reuse that is a common source of improved productivity on other devices.

To address these problems, previous work introduced application-specialized virtual devices, referred to as *intermediate fabrics (IFs)* [8][31]. Through abstraction of fine-grained resources, intermediate fabrics speed up place-and-route by several orders of magnitude while also enabling application portability across any physical FPGA that can implement the virtual fabric. Figure 1 illustrates a simple example of an intermediate fabric specialized

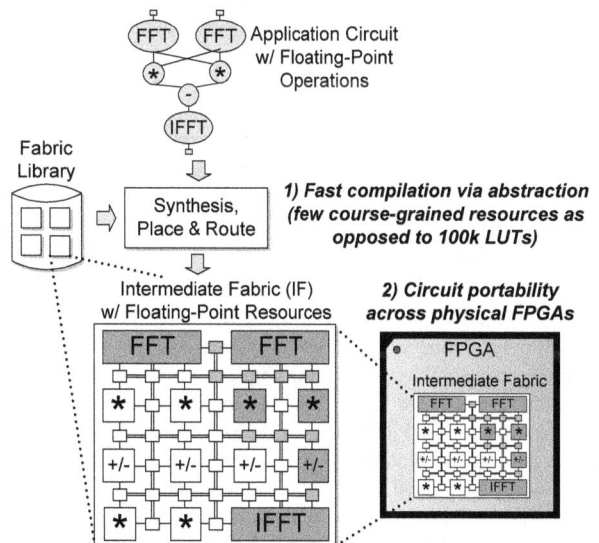

Figure 1: Intermediate fabrics (IFs) are virtual application-specialized fabrics implemented atop FPGAs that hide physical device complexity to achieve fast place-and-route and application portability.

for frequency-domain signal processing by providing coarse-grained, floating-point Fast-Fourier Transforms (FFTs) and arithmetic resources. By compiling a circuit to this intermediate fabric, the compiler avoids decomposing the circuit into tens-of-thousands of lookup tables (LUTs), enabling fast compilation on commercial FPGAs.

Although intermediate fabrics provide significant productivity improvements, previous fabric implementations have limited applicability due to area overhead incurred by the virtual interconnect, which prohibits many usage cases. Although this overhead can be reduced via specialization [8], previous intermediate fabrics can still use 2.5x the area of a circuit directly implemented on a physical FPGA [31].

To address the limitations of previous intermediate fabrics, in this paper we perform design-space exploration of virtual interconnect architectures to determine tradeoffs between area overhead, clock overhead, place-and-route time, bit file size, and reconfiguration time, among others. Such issues have been widely studied for FPGAs over the past two decades [4][28], but conclusions drawn for physical FPGAs are not necessarily applicable to virtual, application-specialized fabrics. Therefore, we revisit fundamental exploration in the context of virtual fabrics to identify key tradeoffs. Based on this exploration, we present an optimized virtual fabric that reduces LUT requirements by 48%-54% and flip-flop requirements by 46%-59%, while improving clock frequencies by an average of 24%. To achieve these improvements, the new interconnect has a modest routability overhead of 16%, which could be addressed by sacrificing a small amount of area savings to include more virtual routing resources.

The paper is organized as follows. Section 2 discusses related work. Section 3 provides an overview of previous intermediate fabrics and their interconnect. Section 4 describes the optimized virtual interconnect. Section 5 presents experimental results.

2. PREVIOUS WORK
Numerous previous studies have focused on overlay networks, which are conceptually similar to intermediate fabrics and implement a virtual network atop a physical FPGA. For example, Kapre et al. [15] compared tradeoffs between packet-switched and time-multiplexed overlay networks implemented on an FPGA. Intermediate fabrics differ from these overlay networks by providing a virtual interconnect capable of implementing register-transfer-level (RTL) circuits at different levels of granularity as opposed to arbitrary communication between abstract processing elements. By this definition, an intermediate fabric is an overlay network, but an overlay network is not necessarily an intermediate fabric.

Previous work has also investigated fine-grained overlay networks for virtual FPGAs [5][18]. Virtual FPGAs are conceptually similar to intermediate fabrics, which also provide virtual reconfigurable fabrics for implementing digital circuits. However, overlays for virtual FPGAs closely imitate fine-grained FPGA architectures [5][18] (e.g. LUTs as resources). Intermediate fabrics can also implement LUT-based architectures, but instead are usually specialized for specific domains and even individual applications using a resource granularity uncommon to FPGAs, which provides fast place-and-route. Previous virtual FPGAs can be viewed as specific, low-level instances of an intermediate fabric. One key difference is that because intermediate fabrics can be specialized, interconnect requirements differ from fine-grained virtual FPGAs, and also vary between specializations.

Numerous previous studies have introduced reconfigurable, coarse-grained physical devices for different application domains [3][7][10][13][14][21][29][30][32]. Although those devices provide good performance for their targeted applications, the disadvantage of such an approach is that specialized physical devices generally have high costs due to limited economy of scale. Intermediate fabrics can provide the same architectures implemented virtually atop common commercial-off-the-shelf FPGAs, which has significant cost advantages and an acceptable overhead for some use cases.

Several studies have also considered virtual coarse-grained architectures for specific domains [30][34]. These approaches are complementary and represent individual instances of intermediate fabrics.

Much previous work has also focused on fast place-and-route using both coarse-grained architectures [6][16][30][35] and specialized algorithms [1][17][23], in some cases combined with a place-and-route-amenable fabric [19][20][33]. Intermediate fabrics are complementary to these approaches and could potentially use these algorithms for place-and-route.

3. INTERMEDIATE FABRICS
This section overviews intermediate fabrics in Section 3.1 and then discusses the virtual interconnect architecture used by previous intermediate fabrics in Section 3.2.

3.1 Overview
As shown in Figure 1, an intermediate fabric is a virtual reconfigurable device, implemented atop a physical FPGA, which implements circuits from HDL or high-level code via synthesis, placement, and routing. Intermediate fabrics, like overlay networks [15] and virtual FPGAs [5][18], provide a fabric capable of implementing numerous circuits. However, unlike those techniques, intermediate fabrics tend to be specialized for the requirements of a specific set of applications, while providing enough routability to support similar applications or different functions in the same domain.

The example in Figure 1 illustrates an intermediate fabric specialized for a frequency-domain signal-processing circuit, and provides corresponding floating-point resources for FFTs and arithmetic computation. When directly compiling this circuit to an FPGA, place-and-route is likely to require hours due to the compiler decomposing the circuit into tens-of-thousands of LUTs. However, when targeting the intermediate fabric, the compiler decomposes the circuit into several coarse-grained resources, which reduces the place-and-route input size by orders of magnitude and provides 100x to 1000x place-and-route speedup [8][31].

A complete discussion of intermediate fabric usage models and their implementations is outside the scope of this paper; we instead summarize two basic models. The library model provides a large, pre-implemented set of intermediate fabrics that a designer or synthesis tool can choose from based on the requirements of the application. For the example in Figure 1, a designer or tool could choose the selected fabric from one of many fabrics that provide different fabric sizes, different combinations of resources, different precisions, etc. An alternative is the synthesis model, during which the synthesis tool creates a specialized fabric based on the application requirements. The advantage to the synthesis model is reduced area overhead. However, the disadvantage is that the application designer must

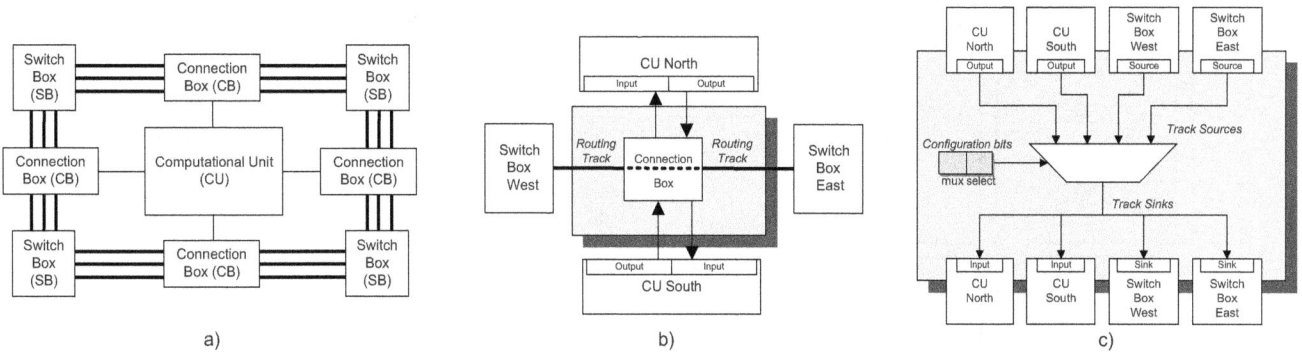

Figure 2: (a) Previous intermediate fabric interconnect architecture, where (b) routing tracks between resources were implemented as (c) multiplexors based on the number of track sources.

wait for place-and-route to implement the intermediate fabric on the physical FPGA. Although such place-and-route may require hours, the compilation time is amortized over the lifetime of the fabric because the physical place-and-route is only needed once.

3.2 Previous Interconnect Architecture

Figure 2(a) illustrates the basic island-style fabric used in previous intermediate fabrics [8][31]. Such a fabric closely imitates the widely studied structure of physical FPGAs consisting of switch boxes, connection boxes, and bidirectional routing tracks, but replaces LUTs with application-specific resources (e.g., floating-point units, FFTs) referred to as *computational units* (CUs). Note that because intermediate fabrics can be specialized, the CUs and virtual routing tracks can potentially be any width. For example, a fabric with floating-point CUs might provide 32-bit routing tracks. Intermediate fabrics also contain specialized regions for control and memory operations. However, in this paper, we focus on the areas of a circuit that contribute the most to long place-and-route, which for many applications are coarse-grained, pipelined datapath operations (e.g., FFTs).

The main limitation of previous intermediate fabrics is area overhead incurred by implementing the virtual fabric atop a physical FPGA (i.e., synthesized VHDL for the virtual fabric). Such overhead results from several sources. The largest source of overhead comes from mux logic in the virtual interconnect. Previous intermediate fabrics use virtual bidirectional routing tracks [8][31], whose register-transfer-level (RTL) implementation is shown in Figure 2(b) and (c). For an m-bit track with n possible sources, the RTL implementation uses an m-bit,

n:1 mux, in some cases with a register or latch on the mux output. For example, Figure 2(b) shows a common configuration of a bidirectional track with four sources: two switch boxes and two CUs, with the corresponding RTL implementation shown in Figure 2(c) as a 4:1 mux, with a select value stored in a 2-bit virtual configuration register. Considering the large number of tracks found in most fabrics, this mux-based implementation of virtual tracks uses numerous LUT resources in the physical FPGA, and is responsible for over 50% of the total LUT usage in many intermediate fabrics.

Similarly, virtual switch boxes and connection boxes implement various topologies using additional muxes between virtual tracks. The exact percentage of LUT usage for switch/connection boxes varies depending on the box topology and flexibility, but is also a significant contributor to area overhead. When combining all interconnect resources (tracks, switch boxes, and connection boxes), we determined that the virtual interconnect is commonly responsible for over 90% of LUT requirements.

In addition to the mux overhead, intermediate fabrics also require physical flip-flop resources for any storage. Virtual registers are technically not overhead because synthesis tools can directly implement virtual registers on physical flip-flops in the FPGA. However, virtual configuration flip-flops and any pipelined interconnect is overhead because the resulting physical flip-flops would not be used by a circuit directly targeting the FPGA.

4. OPTIMIZED INTERCONNECT

Based on the significant overhead caused by the virtual interconnect described in the previous section, in this paper we

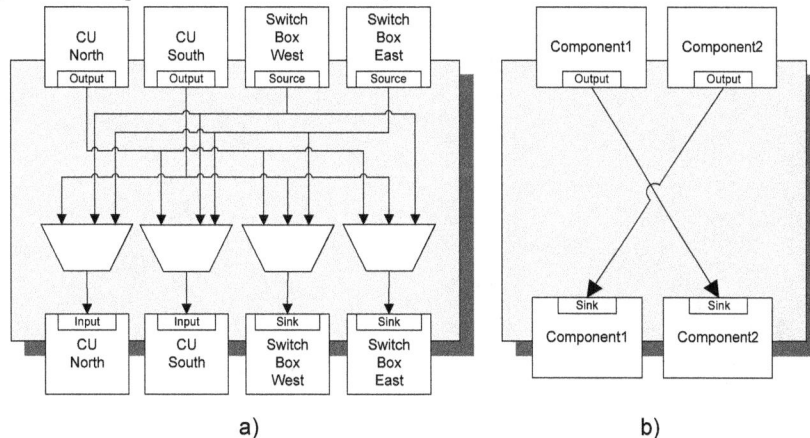

Figure 3: (a) A virtual-track implementation to reduce routing redundancy, which eliminates muxes when (b) tracks have two sources.

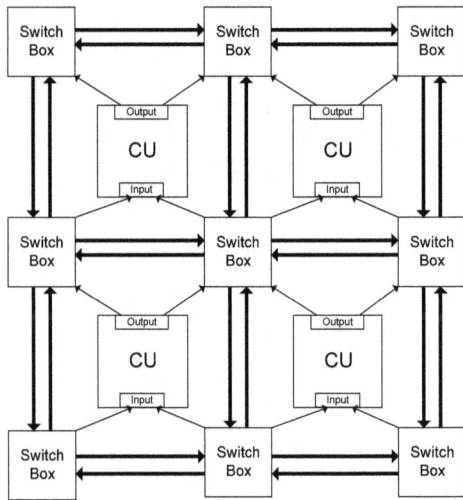

Figure 4: Layout of intermediate fabric using optimized interconnect with CU I/O connected directly to adjacent switch boxes.

focus on virtual interconnect optimizations to reduce muxes, with the goal of retaining high routability.

During an initial attempt at optimizing virtual tracks, we observed that the RTL implementation shown in Figure 2(c) contains some redundancy that could potentially be removed. Specifically, a physical track would never have a common source and sink, which results in an unnecessary input to the mux. For example, a physical FPGA would never route a signal out of a switch box and back into the same switch box using the same track. Therefore, we can eliminate the redundant routes and replace the n:1 mux with n different, $n-1$:1 muxes, where each mux defines one of the possible track destinations. Figure 3(a) shows an example for the previous track in Figure 2(c), where $n=4$. Despite eliminating routing redundancy, such an approach does *not* save area because in most cases, n separate $n-1$:1 muxes require more LUTs than a single n:1 mux.

However, we have observed there is a special case where the track implementation in Figure 3(a) can achieve reduced area. For any virtual track with exactly two possible sources, this implementation simplifies into two directional wires as shown in Figure 3(b). In other words, a 2-source virtual track requires two separate 1:1 muxes, but a 1:1 mux is just a wire.

Therefore, by using only 2-source virtual tracks throughout the entire intermediate fabric, we can potentially replace all mux logic and wires in Figure 3(a) with two wires for each track. Such an optimization has significant potential due to virtual tracks contributing to over 50% of area overhead. Furthermore, this optimization saves a significant amount of wires per track, while simultaneously improving routability by enabling routing in two directions. An additional advantage is that by reducing muxes, the fabric requires less configuration registers to store the corresponding select values, which reduces flip-flop overhead while also improving reconfiguration times.

Although using 2-source virtual tracks reduces area, replacing the 3- and 4-source tracks used in previous fabrics is a significant challenge. In a traditional island-style architecture, a track typically has 3-4 possible sources: 2 switch boxes and 1-2 CUs. If we eliminate the switch box connections, the track can only route between adjacent resources, which significantly limits routability. Similarly, if we remove the CU connections, then there is no way for routing to reach CUs.

To address this problem, we considered several significant modifications to traditional fabrics. First, we started with 2-source tracks between adjacent switch boxes, with each switch box as a possible source. However, that interconnect configuration does not provide a mechanism for connecting CUs to the routing tracks. We could have added connection boxes, but that would violate the 2-source restriction. Therefore, we considered adding additional channels to each switch box with direct connections to the CU I/O. The overall fabric layout for this optimized virtual interconnect is shown in Figure 4. As illustrated, in this unconventional fabric, no virtual track has more than 2 sources, which eliminates all muxes previously needed to implement tracks.

One challenge in designing this optimized interconnect is that although we eliminated track muxes, we added additional muxes inside of the switch boxes to support the additional CU channels. Unless the switch boxes add fewer muxes than we removed from the tracks, this optimization does not reduce area.

To ensure that the optimized interconnect reduces LUT usage, we exploit the internal characteristics of the switch box to handle the additional routing requirements with minimal logic. Previous intermediate fabric switch boxes use a planar topology, where each output from the switch box uses a 3:1 mux that selects an

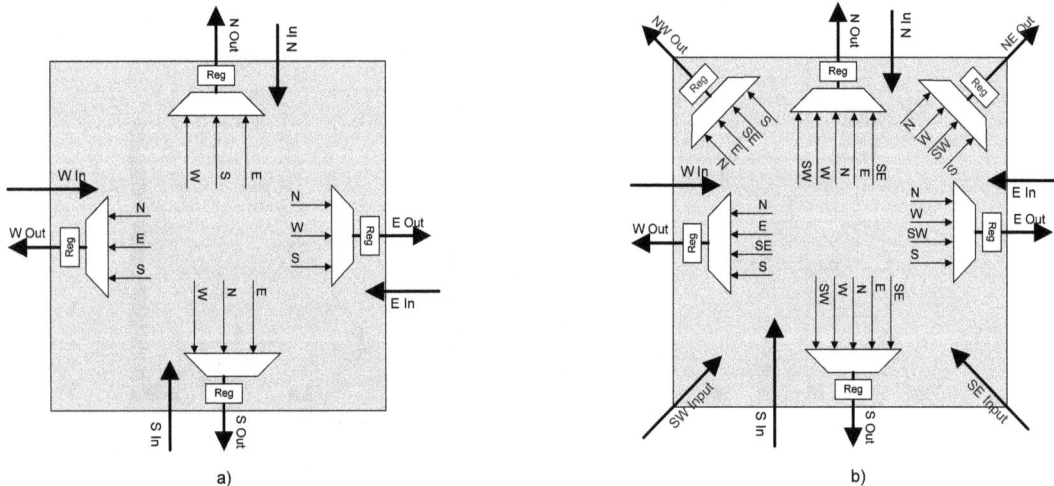

Figure 5: Switch box topology for (a) previous intermediate fabric interconnect and (b) the presented interconnect with diagonal CU channels.

114

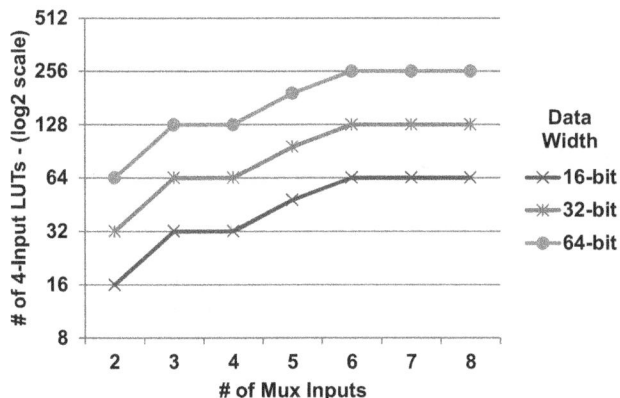

Figure 6: Virtex 4 LX100 LUT usage for different MUX input amounts. The plateaus provide opportunities for switch boxes to add more connections without an area penalty.

input from one of the three other channels, as shown in Figure 5(a). For the new interconnect, these multiplexors could potentially require four more inputs to handle routing of the four adjacent CUs, which would significantly outweigh track savings. However, we can exploit the fact that increasing mux inputs does not always increase LUT requirements. As shown in Figure 6, FPGAs have different area "plateaus" where additional mux inputs have the same LUT requirements as lesser inputs (e.g., 3-4 inputs and 6-8 inputs). The optimized interconnect exploits this characteristic by adding CU I/O connections to the muxes until reaching the largest input size of a plateau, which maximizes routability without any increase in area. Interestingly, the presented interconnect can be specialized for different physical FPGAs, which have different mux plateaus due to varying LUT sizes.

Although the optimized interconnect switch boxes are not restricted to a specific topology, we choose a planar-like topology for evaluation and target the mux plateaus for 4-input muxes. Therefore, the switch boxes increase 3-input muxes to 4 inputs wherever possible. The switch boxes also use 5-input muxes, but do not increase the inputs to 6 or more, despite the plateau between 6 and 8 inputs. Increasing the mux inputs to 8 may improve routability with additional overhead, but we defer such analysis to future work. An example topology is shown in Figure 5(b), where the switch box provides a planar topology for the north, east, south, and west channels, which correspond to virtual tracks. In this example, the CU channels (southeast, southwest, northwest, northeast) connect to the other channels in customizable ways. Note that we are not proposing a specific switch box topology for the optimized interconnect. Instead, like any intermediate fabric, we expect the topology to change based on application and routability requirements. For the applications we evaluated, using a highly directional fabric was beneficial due to pipelined, feed-forward datapaths. However, the switch box can easily be customized for other topologies. In the experiments, we use a fabric generation tool that allows specification of the exact switch box topology in a fabric description file.

5. EXPERIMENTS

In this section, we compare intermediate fabrics using the presented virtual interconnect with previous work [8][31]. Section 5.1 describes the experimental setup. Section 5.2 compares area requirements, clock speedups, and routability of both approaches

for unspecialized, uniform fabrics. Section 5.3 presents similar experiments for application-specialized fabrics.

5.1 Experimental Setup

This section describes the intermediate fabric tool flow used for the experiments (Section 5.1.1), along with the routability measurements (Section 5.1.2), and the tools used for evaluating the different interconnects (Section 5.1.3).

5.1.1 Tool flow

To implement applications on the intermediate fabrics, we manually synthesize circuits by creating technology-mapped netlists. We plan to convert open-source synthesis tools to target intermediate fabrics, including OpenCL high-level synthesis, but such a project is outside the scope of this paper. For place-and-route, we use the algorithm previously described in [8] to ensure that the comparison between the new and previous interconnect is not unfairly skewed by improved placement. In fact, the place-and-route results for the new interconnect are likely pessimistic because we did not modify the placer cost function for the new interconnect. The place-and-route algorithm is a variation of VPR [4], and uses simulated annealing for placement with a cost function that minimizes bounding box size. Routing uses the well-known PathFinder [22] negotiated-congestion algorithm. Both the new and previous interconnect have varying amounts of pipelining in switch boxes or on tracks. Instead of using pipelined routing algorithms (e.g., [11]), both approaches use realignment registers in front of each CU to balance the routing delays of all inputs. Because this pipelining strategy only works for pipelined datapaths that can be retimed without affecting correctness, we limit the evaluation to fabrics with coarse-grained resources commonly needed by datapaths in signal processing.

To configure the intermediate fabric for different applications, the place-and-route tool outputs a configuration bit file that we store in a block RAM on the targeted FPGA. Each intermediate fabric includes a programmer which loads the bitfile from the block RAM by shifting bits into virtual configuration registers that control the CUs and virtual switch boxes.

5.1.2 Routability Metric

To fairly compare tradeoffs between interconnects, it is necessary to measure routability. To perform these measurements for a given intermediate fabric, we place-and-route a large number of randomly generated netlists of varying sizes, and determine the 'routability score' of the interconnect based on the percentage of netlists that route successfully. Due to the fast place-and-route time for intermediate fabrics we were able to test 1,000 netlists for each fabric to obtain a high-precision metric.

The random netlist generator creates directed acyclic graph structures representative of pipelined datapaths. Based on the CU composition of each individual fabric tested, the generator creates a random number of datapath stages, each consisting of a random number of technology-mapped cells, and creates random connections between each stage. Each stage contains at minimum enough cells, and enough connections are made between stages, such that each cell has at least one path to the next stage. This method results in netlists containing one or more disjoint pipelines of one or more stages each.

5.1.3 Interconnect Evaluation

To evaluate different interconnects, we developed a tool capable of generating VHDL for intermediate fabrics using the new

Table 1: A comparison between the presented virtual interconnect (*New*) and previous uniform virtual interconnect (*Prev*). The presented interconnect had significant area savings and a clock speedup of 24%, with a modest 16% decrease in routability.

FPGA	Fabric Size (# of CUs)	LUT Usage			Flip-Flop Usage			Routability			Clock		
		Prev	New	Savings	Prev	New	Savings	Prev	New	Overhead	Prev	New	Speedup
Xilinx V4LX200	3x3	2%	1%	**71%**	1%	0.2%	**72%**	100%	78%	**22%**	173 MHz	175 MHz	**1%**
	4x4	5%	2%	**64%**	1%	0.4%	**65%**	100%	95%	**5%**	163 MHz	172 MHz	**6%**
	5x5	8%	3%	**60%**	2%	1%	**62%**	100%	87%	**13%**	152 MHz	172 MHz	**13%**
	6x6	12%	5%	**55%**	3%	1%	**59%**	100%	85%	**15%**	144 MHz	171 MHz	**19%**
	7x7	17%	8%	**53%**	5%	2%	**57%**	100%	84%	**16%**	123 MHz	170 MHz	**38%**
	8x8	23%	11%	**52%**	6%	3%	**56%**	100%	85%	**16%**	125 MHz	170 MHz	**36%**
	9x9	30%	15%	**51%**	8%	4%	**55%**	99.7%	84%	**16%**	115 MHz	168 MHz	**46%**
	12x8	36%	20%	**46%**	10%	5%	**55%**	99.2%	79%	**20%**	113 MHz	160 MHz	**42%**
Xilinx V5LX330	13x13	37%	20%	**46%**	18%	9%	**53%**	98%	80%	**18%**	125 MHz	162 MHz	**30%**
	14x14	44%	24%	**46%**	21%	10%	**52%**	94%	83%	**12%**	131 MHz	148 MHz	**13%**
Altera S4E530	15x15	n/a*	14%	**n/a***	n/a*	18%	**n/a***	90%	71%	**21%**	n/a*	175 MHz	**n/a***
	16x16	n/a*	16%	**n/a***	n/a*	21%	**n/a***	90%	70%	**22%**	n/a*	177 MHz	**n/a***
	Average	21%	11%	**54%**	8%	3%	**59%**	98%	82%	**16%**	136 MHz	167 MHz	**24%**

*n/a corresponds to examples that failed to synthesize for the corresponding device, which are excluded from the averages

interconnect. The tool takes as inputs a fabric-description file that defines the parameters of the fabric, such as size, aspect ratio, bit-width and the makeup of the fabric, including CU composition, and row and column channel descriptions. Channel descriptions include number of tracks, direction of each track, and switchbox topology.

To obtain physical FPGA utilization and timing results, we synthesized the intermediate fabric VHDL using Xilinx ISE 10.1, Synopsys Synplify Pro 2012, and Altera Quartus II 10.1, depending on the targeted FPGA. To evaluate the effects of FPGA variation on each virtual interconnect, we implemented intermediate fabrics on Xilinx Virtex 4 LX100 and LX200, Xilinx Virtex 5 LX330, and Altera Stratix IV E530 FPGAs. The intermediate fabric HDL synthesized for each test case uses the fixed-logic multipliers available on each physical device for all CUs (Xilinx DSP48s and Altera 18x18 Multipliers); therefore all device utilization represents the LUT and flip-flop overhead of implementing the target application via an intermediate fabric rather than a direct HDL implementation.

5.2 Interconnect Comparison for Uniform Intermediate Fabrics

In this section we compare area, routability, and maximum clock speed of intermediate fabrics using the presented interconnect to intermediate fabrics using interconnect previously presented in [8] and [31]. We evaluate each interconnect using different fabric sizes, implemented on several different physical FPGAs. Although intermediate fabrics can be specialized to an application, in this section we evaluate fabrics independently of targeted applications by using a uniform fabric consisting of 16-bit DSP CUs with various dimensions (e.g., 5x5 = 5 rows and 5 columns of I/O and CUs).

Table 1 compares LUT and flip-flop utilization (as a % of total device resources), routability of 1000 randomly generated netlists, and maximum clock speed for identical intermediate fabrics using the new and previous interconnects. We implemented fabric sizes between 3x3 and 12x8 on a Virtex 4 LX200, where an NxM fabric is composed of one row of *M* inputs, N-2 rows of *M* CUs, and one row of *M* outputs. We evaluated larger fabric sizes of 13x13 and 14x14 on a Virtex 5 LX330, and sizes 15x15 and 16x16 on a large Stratix IV E530. For fabrics using the previous interconnect, we used 3 16-bit tracks per channel with specialized connection boxes from [8], as previous work indicated this configuration to be an effective tradeoff between routability and overhead. For fabrics using the new interconnect, we used 2 16-bit tracks per row and 4 tracks per column with the switch box topology described in Section 4 optimized for 4-input muxes.

These results show the LUT and flip-flop utilizations of the new interconnect are significantly less than the previous interconnect, with an average LUT savings of 54% and flip-flop savings of 59% for the fabrics evaluated. Note that we were unable to synthesize the old interconnect on the Stratix IV device. We tried three different version of Quartus, but the old interconnect would cause a crash during the retiming stage of synthesis. For this reason, we exclude the Stratix IV results from the averages.

Additionally, the new interconnect showed significant maximum clock frequency speedup for larger fabrics. When implemented on the Virtex 4, new interconnect clock speeds decreased only 6.3% between fabrics of size 3x3 to 12x8, whereas the previous interconnect suffered from a 34.7% decrease in clock speed over the same range. Overall, the new interconnect averaged 167 MHz compared to 136 MHz.

The new interconnect did incur a routability penalty, with a average decrease of 16% compared to the previous interconnect. While this overhead is a potential limitation of the new interconnect, especially when applied to a general-purpose fabric, we believe this overhead to be an acceptable tradeoff when compared to the significant area savings provided by the new interconnect. Routability overhead can also be easily compensated for when designing the CU composition of a fabric. Because the placer algorithm used in these experiments is unchanged from that used for the old fabric, it is likely that an appropriately customized placer cost function would significantly improve the routability of the new interconnect. Similarly, fabrics using the new interconnect could account for decreased routability by including many more routing resources while still saving area. Routability decreased monotonically with increased fabric size due to the increased difficulty of routing larger netlists. The one exception was the 3x3 fabric with the new interconnect, which had lower routability than the larger fabrics. We identified the source of this problem as limited connections between I/O and CUs for very small fabrics using the new interconnect. Because we expect 3x3 to be an unusually small size for actual usage, this overhead is not a significant limitation.

	Place-and-Route Time					Area and Routability			Clock Speed		
	IF Prev	IF New	FPGA	Speedup Prev	Speedup New	LUT Savings	Flip-Flop Savings	Routability Overhead	IF Prev	IF New	Clock Overhead
Matrix multiply FXD	0.6s	0.6s	1min 08s	112x	112x	56%	60%	1%	170 MHz	186 MHz	-9%
Matrix multiply FLT	0.6s	0.6s	6min 06s	602x	602x	59%	59%	1%	184 MHz	222 MHz	-21%
FIR FXD	0.6s	0.6s	0min 33s	54x	58x	45%	41%	5%	174 MHz	158 MHz	9%
FIR FLT	0.6s	0.6s	4min 36s	454x	484x	35%	35%	5%	203 MHz	215 MHz	-6%
N-body FXD	0.5s	0.2s	0min 57s	126x	300x	40%	32%	1%	185 MHz	165 MHz	11%
N-body FLT	0.5s	0.2s	3min 42s	491x	1168x	37%	26%	1%	218 MHz	200 MHz	8%
Accum FXD	0.1s	0.02s	0min 26s	280x	1733x	52%	53%	0%	186 MHz	187 MHz	-1%
Accum FLT	0.1s	0.02s	0min 30s	323x	2000x	52%	50%	0%	225 MHz	241MHz	-7%
Normalize FXD	0.2s	0.3s	1min 10s	299x	241x	66%	71%	-63%	178 MHz	162 MHz	9%
Normalize FLT	0.2s	0.3s	6min 44s	1726x	1393x	43%	54%	-63%	197 MHz	222 MHz	-13%
Bilinear FXD	0.3s	0.3s	1min 08s	230x	213x	51%	47%	0%	184 MHz	165 MHz	10%
Bilinear FLT	0.3s	0.3s	8min 48s	1784x	1650x	41%	42%	0%	206 MHz	200 MHz	3%
Floyd-Steinberg FXD	0.1s	0.1s	1min 27s	621x	926x	53%	50%	2%	182 MHz	169 MHz	7%
Floyd-Steinberg FLT	0.1s	0.1s	5min 37s	2407x	3585x	48%	44%	2%	196 MHz	179 MHz	9%
Thresholding	1.4s	1.3s	0min 33s	24x	26x	44%	36%	5%	167 MHz	181MHz	-8%
Sobel	0.3s	0.4s	2min 28s	500x	344x	44%	31%	2%	181MHz	162 MHz	10%
Gaussian Blur	3.3s	2.2s	3min 19s	60x	90x	39%	41%	-42%	170 MHz	181MHz	-6%
Max Filter	0.2s	0.03s	1min 16s	444x	2533x	48%	41%	0%	186 MHz	176 MHz	5%
Mean Filter 3x3	0.2s	0.01s	2min 30s	962x	10714x	52%	52%	10%	185 MHz	187 MHz	-1%
Mean Filter 5x5	1.9s	1.9s	3min 25s	110x	108x	64%	65%	-1%	169 MHz	161MHz	5%
Mean Filter 7x7	8.9s	4.7s	5min 03s	34x	64x	39%	40%	-38%	157 MHz	183 MHz	-17%
Average	1.0s	0.7s	2min 56s	554x	1350x	48%	46%	-8%	186 MHz	186 MHz	0%

These results also show decreased LUT overhead savings of only 46% in fabrics implemented on the Virtex 5 device. This smaller improvement is likely due to different CLB configuration used by that device, with slightly altered mux-area plateau characteristics, whereas the optimizations used by the evaluated interconnect were optimized for 4-input muxes. Despite being optimized for a different LUT configuration, the new interconnect still had significant savings.

Flip-flop usage on the Altera device was significantly higher than both Xilinx devices, which resulted from the Xilinx FPGAs implementing the realignment registers as SRL16 primitives, in contrast to the Altera FPGA which used flip-flops. As future work, we will investigate optimizations for Altera FPGAs.

One additional advantage of reducing muxes throughout the interconnect is the corresponding elimination of configuration registers to store the select values. The fewer registers reduce flip-flops, which was shown in Table 1, but also reduces configuration bitfile size, which correspondingly reduces configuration times and block RAM overhead of the fabric. For the examples in this section, the new interconnect improved configuration times by an average of 55% compared to the previous interconnect.

5.3 Interconnect Comparison for Specialized Intermediate Fabrics

One advantage of intermediate fabrics is that a designer or tool can specialize the architecture and interconnect for a given domain or even an individual application. In this section, we compare intermediate fabrics using application-specialized interconnect presented in [8] with the new interconnect. To enable a fair comparison, we evaluate the same application circuits from [8] using the same specialized fabrics as previous experiments. Specialization used in the previous experiments included varying fabric sizes and non-uniform interconnects. For the new interconnect, we limit specialization to fabric sizes, making the results pessimistic. For all specialized fabrics, we used the smallest fabric and interconnect that could successfully route the target application netlist. For these experiments, the physical FPGA is a Virtex 4 LX100, which we chose to match the previous experiments.

To perform the comparison, we used the twelve applications from [8], seven of which were implemented using both 16-bit fixed point arithmetic and 32-bit floating point arithmetic, indicated with a FXD or FLT suffix respectively. All track widths matched the CU widths. All circuits without a suffix used 16-bit fixed-point CUs. We briefly summarize the previous applications as follows. *Matrix multiply* performs the kernel of a matrix multiplication, calculating the inner product of two 8-element vectors using 7 adders and 8 multipliers. *FIR* implements a 12-tap finite impulse response filter in transpose form with symmetric coefficients using 11 adders and 12 multipliers. *N-body*, representing the kernel of an N-body simulation, calculates the gravitational force exerted on a particle due to other particles in two-dimensional space using 13 adders, multipliers, and a divider. *Accum* monitors a stream, counting the number of times the value is less than a threshold. It is the smallest netlist, consisting of 4 comparators and 3 adders. *Normalize* normalizes an input stream using 8 multipliers and 8 adders. *Bilinear* performs bilinear interpolation on an image, requiring 8 multipliers and 3 adders. *Floyd-Steinberg* performs image dithering using 6 adders and 4 multipliers. *Thresholding* performs automatic image thresholding using 8 comparators and 14 adders. *Sobel* uses a 3x3 convolution to perform Sobel edge detection with 2 multipliers and 11 adders. *Gaussian blur* uses a 5x5 convolution to perform noise reduction using 25 multipliers and 24 adders. *Max filter* performs a 3x3 sliding-window image filter with 8 comparators. *Mean filter* similarly calculates the average of a sliding window, which we vary from 3x3 to 7x7, requiring a maximum of 48 adders and 1 multiplier.

Table 2 compares the interconnects for each case study. The first major column, *Place-and-Route Time*, compares place-and-route execution times for an intermediate fabric with the previous interconnect (*IF Prev*), an intermediate fabric with the new interconnect *(IF New)*, and when synthesizing VHDL for each example directly to the FPGA. The table also shows the resulting place-and-route speedup for the new and previous interconnects. The results show comparable place-and-route times for both the old and new interconnect. However, because the previous interconnect already achieves a place-and-route speedup of 554x compared to an FPGA, the further improvement by the new interconnect provided a 1350x place-and-route speedup. The place-and-route speedup was larger for the floating-point examples due to longer place-and-route times for the physical FPGA. Furthermore, these place-and-route speedups are highly pessimistic because the specialized examples from [8] do not include common board logic such as PCIe and memory controllers. Other studies have shown that including these controllers with tight timing constraints can add up to 20 minutes to FPGA place-and-route time, but have no effect on intermediate fabric place-and-route time [31].

The second major column in Table 2 reports area savings of the new interconnect in terms of FPGA LUTs and flip-flops, along with the routability overhead incurred to achieve these savings. On average, the new interconnect significantly reduced LUT usage by 48% and flip-flop usage by 46%, despite the significant specialization by the previous fabrics. On average, routability slightly improved by 8% with the new interconnect. However, this average is skewed by three outliers, *normalize*, *Gaussian*, and *mean7x7*, which had very low routability due to significant specialization in the previous fabrics. Excluding these outliers, the new interconnect had a 2% routability overhead. The smaller routability overhead compared to the previous section is due to the specialized versions of the previous interconnect, which used just enough routing resources to route the targeted application, and therefore lowered general routability.

The final column of table 2 compares the maximum clock speed of the specialized fabrics using both the new and old interconnect.

For specialized fabrics, these experiments show a negligible average impact on clock speed, with both interconnects showing an average clock frequency of 186 MHz. However, there was significant variation as high as 21% between specialized fabrics. It should be noted that these results are contrary to the results for larger fabrics presented in the previous section, which showed a clear trend of faster clock speeds for larger fabrics using the new interconnect. The reason for the smaller clock improvement compared to the previous section is due to the higher specialization of the previous interconnect, as opposed to using a uniform interconnect.

6. LIMITATIONS AND FUTURE WORK

Even with a 50% reduction in LUT utilization, intermediate fabrics will still have prohibitive overhead for use cases where an FPGA is close to being fully utilized. Fortunately, the trends towards multi-million-LUT FPGAs will lessen this problem over time. In addition, we plan to investigate virtual interconnect that directly targets the physical FPGA interconnect without using muxes. Such an approach could map virtual switch boxes directly onto physical switch boxes, potentially eliminating much of the remaining overhead. However, such an approach requires knowledge of proprietary routing architectures, and is therefore deferred to future work.

7. CONCLUSIONS

Previous work introduced intermediate fabrics to address FPGA problems related to lengthy place-and-route times and a lack of application portability. Although previous intermediate fabric approaches achieve both application portability and significant place-and-route speedup, the area overhead of those approaches prohibits important use cases. To address this problem, we identified the virtual interconnect as the main source of the overhead, and performed design-space exploration to identify unconventional alternatives that could achieve effective Pareto-optimal tradeoffs between overhead and routability. Based on this analysis, we introduced an optimized virtual interconnect architecture that reduces area requirements by approximately 50% and improves clock frequencies by 24%, with a modest 16% reduction in routability.

8. ACKNOWLEDGMENTS

This work was supported in part by the I/UCRC Program of the National Science Foundation under Grant Nos. EEC-0642422 and IIP-1161022. The authors gratefully acknowledge vendor equipment and/or tools provided by Altera and Xilinx.

9. REFERENCES

[1]   P. Athanas, J. Bowen, T. Dunham, C. Patterson, J. Rice, M. Shelburne, J. Suris, M. Bucciero, and J. Graf, "Wires on demand: Run-time communication synthesis for reconfigurable computing," in *FPL '07: International Conference on Field Programmable Logic and Applications*, Aug. 2007, pp. 513–516.

[2]   Z. Baker, M. Gokhale, and J. Tripp. "Matched filter computation on fpga, cell and gpu," In *Field-Programmable Custom Computing Machines, 2007. FCCM 2007. 15th Annual IEEE Symposium on*, 2007, pp. 207–218.

[3]   J. Becker, T. Pionteck, C. Habermann, and M. Glesner, "Design and implementation of a coarse-grained dynamically reconfigurable hardware architecture," in *VLSI '01: Proceedings of IEEE Computer Society Workshop on VLSI*, May 2001, pp. 41–46.

[4]   V. Betz and J. Rose, "VPR: A new packing, placement and routing tool for FPGA research," in *FPL '97: Proceedings of the 7th*

International Workshop on Field-Programmable Logic and Applications. London, UK: Springer-Verlag, 1997, pp. 213–222.

[5] A. Brant and G. Lemieux. "XUMA: An open FPGA overlay architecture", In *FCCM '12: Proceedings of the IEEE Symposium on Field-Programmable Custom Computing Machines*, 2012.

[6] T. J. Callahan, P. Chong, A. DeHon, and J. Wawrzynek, "Fast module mapping and placement for datapaths in FPGAs," in *FPGA '98: Proceedings of the 1998 ACM/SIGDA sixth international symposium on Field programmable gate arrays*. New York, NY, USA: ACM, 1998, pp. 123–132.

[7] K. Compton and S. Hauck, "Totem: Custom reconfigurable array generation," in *FCCM'01: Proceedings of the the 9th Annual IEEE Symposium on Field-Programmable Custom Computing Machines* 2001, pp. 111–119.

[8] J. Coole and G. Stitt. "Intermediate fabrics: Virtual architectures for circuit portability and fast placement and routing." In *CODES/ISSS '10: Proceedings of the IEEE/ACM/IFIP international conference on Hardware/Software codesign and system synthesis*, 2010, pp. 13–22.

[9] A. DeHon, "The density advantage of configurable computing," *Computer*, vol. 33, no. 4, pp. 41–49, 2000.

[10] C. Ebeling, D. C. Cronquist, and P. Franklin, "Rapid - reconfigurable pipelined datapath," in *FPL '96: Proceedings of the 6th International Workshop on Field-Programmable Logic,Smart Applications, New Paradigms and Compilers*. London, UK: Springer-Verlag, 1996, pp. 126–135.

[11] K. Eguro and S. Hauck, "Armada: timing-driven pipeline-aware routing for FPGAs," in *FPGA '06: Proceedings of the 2006 ACM/SIGDA 14th international symposium on Field programmable gate arrays*, 2006, pp. 169–178.

[12] J. Fowers, G. Brown, P. Cooke, and G. Stitt. "A performance and energy comparison of FPGAs, GPUs, and multicores for sliding-window applications", In *FPGA '12: Proceedings of the ACM/SIGDA international symposium on Field Programmable Gate Arrays*, FPGA'12, 2012, pp. 47–56.

[13] D. Grant, C. Wang, and G. G. Lemieux. "A CAD framework for Malibu: an FPGA with time-multiplexed coarse-grained elements", In *Proceedings of the 19th ACM/SIGDA international symposium on Field programmable gate arrays*, FPGA '11, 2011, pp. 123–132.

[14] M. Hammerquist and R. Lysecky, "Design space exploration for application specific FPGAs in system-on-a-chip designs," in *SOC '08: Proceedings of the IEEE International SOC Conference*, Sept. 2008, pp. 279–282.

[15] N. Kapre, N. Mehta, M. deLorimier, R. Rubin, H. Barnor, M. J. Wilson, M. Wrighton, and A. DeHon, "Packet-switched vs. time-multiplexed FPGA overlay networks," in *Proceedings of the IEEE Symposium on Field-Programmable Custom Computing Machines*, 2006.

[16] A. Koch, "Structured design implementation: a strategy for implementing regular datapaths on FPGAs," in *FPGA '96: Proceedings of the 1996 ACM fourth international symposium on Field-programmable gate arrays*, 1996, pp. 151–157.

[17] C. Lavin, M. Padilla, J. Lamprecht, P. Lundrigan, B. Nelson, and B. Hutchings. "HMFlow: Accelerating FPGA compilation with hard macros for rapid prototyping", In *Field-Programmable Custom Computing Machines (FCCM), 2011 IEEE 19th Annual International Symposium on*, 2011, pp. 117 –124.

[18] R. Lysecky, K. Miller, F. Vahid, and K. Vissers. "Firm-core virtual fpga for just-in-time fpga compilation", In *Proceedings of the 2005 ACM/SIGDA 13th international symposium on Field-programmable gate arrays*, FPGA '05, 2005, pp. 271–271.

[19] R. Lysecky, F. Vahid, and S. X.-D. Tan, "Dynamic fpga routing for just-in-time FPGA compilation," in *DAC '04: Proceedings of the 41st Annual Conference on Design Automation*, 2004, pp. 954–959.

[20] R. Lysecky, F. Vahid, and S. X. D. Tan, "A study of the scalability of on-chip routing for just-in-time FPGA compilation," in *FCCM '05: Proceedings of the 13th Annual IEEE Symposium on Field-Programmable Custom Computing Machines*, 2005, pp. 57–62.

[21] A. Marshall, T. Stansfield, I. Kostarnov, J. Vuillemin, and B. Hutchings, "A reconfigurable arithmetic array for multimedia applications," in *FPGA '99: Proceedings of the 1999 ACM/SIGDA Seventh International Symposium on Field Programmable Gate Arrays*, 1999, pp. 135–143.

[22] L. McMurchie and C. Ebeling, "Pathfinder: a negotiation-based performance-driven router for FPGAs," in *FPGA '95: Proceedings of the 1995 ACM Third International Symposium on Field Programmable Gate Arrays*, 1995, pp. 111–117.

[23] C. Mulpuri and S. Hauck, "Runtime and quality tradeoffs in FPGA placement and routing," in *FPGA '01: Proceedings of the 2001 ACM/SIGDA Ninth International Symposium on Field Programmable Gate Arrays*, 2001, pp. 29–36.

[24] B. E. Nelson, M. J. Wirthlin, B. L. Hutchings, P. M. Athanas, and S. Bohner, "Design productivity for configurable computing," in *ERSA '08: Proceedings of the International Conference on Engineering of Reconfigurable Systems and Algorithms*, 2008, pp. 57–66.

[25] M. Owaida, N. Bellas, K. Daloukas, and C. Antonopoulos. "Synthesis of platform architectures from opencl programs", In *Field-Programmable Custom Computing Machines (FCCM), 2011 IEEE 19th Annual International Symposium on*, 2011, pp. 186–193.

[26] A. Papakonstantinou, K. Gururaj, J. Stratton, D. Chen, J. Cong, and W.-M. Hwu. "FCUDA: Enabling efficient compilation of cuda kernels onto fpgas", In *Application Specific Processors, 2009. SASP '09. IEEE 7th Symposium on*, 2009, pp. 35–42.

[27] K. Pauwels, M. Tomasi, J. Diaz Alonso, E. Ros, and M. Van Hulle. "A comparison of fpga and gpu for real-time phase-based optical flow, stereo, and local image features", *Computers, IEEE Transactions on*, PP(99):1, 2011.

[28] J. Rose, J. Luu, C. W. Yu, O. Densmore, J. Goeders, A. Somerville, K. B. Kent, P. Jamieson, and J. Anderson. "The VTR project: architecture and cad for fpgas from verilog to routing", In *Proceedings of the ACM/SIGDA international symposium on Field Programmable Gate Arrays*, FPGA '12, 2012, pp. 77–86.

[29] L. Sekanina, *Evolvable Systems: From Biology to Hardware*. Springer Berlin / Heidelberg, 2003, ch. Virtual Reconfigurable Circuits for Real-World Applications of Evolvable Hardware, pp. 116–137.

[30] S. Shukla, N. W. Bergmann, and J. Becker, "Quku: A two-level reconfigurable architecture," in *ISVLSI '06: Proceedings of the IEEE Computer Society Annual Symposium on Emerging VLSI Technologies and Architectures*, 2006, p. 109.

[31] G. Stitt and J. Coole. "Intermediate fabrics: Virtual architectures for near-instant FPGA compilation", *Embedded Systems Letters, IEEE*, 3(3):81 –84, sept. 2011.

[32] W. Tsu, K. Macy, A. Joshi, R. Huang, N. Walker, T. Tung, O. Rowhani, V. George, J. Wawrzynek, and A. DeHon, "HSRA: high-speed, hierarchical synchronous reconfigurable array," in *FPGA '99: Proceedings of the 1999 ACM/SIGDA seventh international symposium on Field programmable gate arrays*, 1999, pp. 125–134.

[33] F. Vahid, G. Stitt, and R. Lysecky, "Warp processing: Dynamic translation of binaries to FPGA circuits," *Computer*, vol. 41, no. 7, pp. 40–46, July 2008.

[34] J. Wang, Q. Chen, and C. Lee, "Design and implementation of a virtual reconfigurable architecture for different applications of intrinsic evolvable hardware," *Computers & Digital Techniques, IET*, vol. 2, no. 5, pp. 386–400, September 2008.

[35] P. Yiannacouras, J. G. Steffan, and J. Rose. "Vespa: portable, scalable, and flexible fpga-based vector processors," In *Proceedings of the 2008 international conference on Compilers, architectures and synthesis for embedded systems* (CASES), 2008, pp. 61–70.

119

Energy Efficient Hybrid Display and Predictive Models for Embedded and Mobile Systems

Yuanfeng Wen[1], Ziyi Liu[1], Weidong Shi[1], Yifei Jiang[2], Albert M.K. Cheng[1], Khoa Le[1]

1.Department of Computer Science, University of Houston, Houston, TX 77004, U.S.A
2.Department of Computer Science, University of Colorado at Boulder, CO 80309, U.S.A.
{ wyf,ziyiliu, larryshi,cheng,ktle}@cs.uh.edu, yifei.jiang[2]@colorado.edu

ABSTRACT

Electrophoretic displays (EPDs) and organic light emitting diode (OLEDs) are two key technologies used in mobile devices. In this paper, we propose the design of an integrated hybrid display combining a transparent OLED (TOLED) and a low power EPD, which is adaptive to show contents of a frame partially on either the TOLED or the EPD. A windows-based predictive model and a calibration algorithm on TOLED are introduced to decide how frame contents can be split between the two displays for achieving the best tradeoff between power reduction and user experiences. A simulation environment that can estimate both the energy consumption and optical properties of the proposed hybrid display is set up based on actual physical measurements. Simulation results show that the predictive model can make right decisions on choosing proper displays in over 90% of the test cases, and this new display design can save over 70% power under many mobile application contexts and still support contents that require fast update rates.

Categories and Subject Descriptors

B.4.2 [**INPUT/OUTPUT AND DATA COMMUNICATIONS**]: Input/Output Devices–Image display

General Terms

Algorithms, Design, Experimentation, Performance

Keywords

EPDs, OLEDs, Hybrid Display, Predictive Model, Calibration

1. INTRODUCTION

Mobile electronic devices, especially smartphones, e-reader, tablets, and netbooks are powered from batteries which are limited in size and capacity. Thus power management has been and will continue to be an essential aspect of technology for designing mobile electronic devices. Today, high-end mobile gadgets are rich devices that can support a wide range of functionality and experiences such as voice communication, audio and video playback, email communication and online chat, web browsing, social networking, gaming, and more. With the popularity of mobile applications, more functionality will be integrated with mobile devices and increase the pressure on the battery life, and exacerbate the need for efficient power management. As mobile devices need to provide more PC-like capabilities, many of them integrate a large color display for supporting mobile applications. A high-end smartphone can provide the same screen resolution as workstations a few years back. The large mobile displays play an important role as human-machine interface and support media-rich applications. At the same time, they are energy-hungry components, often consuming significant percentage of total battery power.

OLEDs are envisaged to offer more brilliant images with higher levels of contrast than LCD panels and at the same time provide a significant reduction in energy consumption. The electrophoretic display has the advantages of being the best candidate for electronic paper. With the properties of being invariably reflective and bistable, it is more comfortable to read than conventional displays. EPD has no need to be refreshed constantly and it reflects ambient light rather than emitting its own light such as OLEDs. Moreover, the power supply of an EPD can be turned off after updating images. As a result, EPD consumes an order of magnitude less power than LCD panels and OLEDs. However, EPD has a very low refresh rate compared with other low-power display technologies. Therefore, EPD is unsuitable for certain application contexts such as playing a video.

The concept of hybrid mobile display is to integrate multiple displays of different techniques in one system to support display adaptation based on the usage context and contents. The result is improved trade-off between user experiences and energy management. In this paper, we propose and evaluate a mobile hybrid display design that integrates transparent see-through OLED with EPD in a stack structure. The hybrid display allows context based display adaptation by supporting two operation modes. In switch mode, a mobile system or user can adaptively switch between OLED and EPD based on the application context. In hybrid mode, both the EPD and the OLED can be turned on at the same time, in different display areas, with slow contents displayed on the EPD and fast contents on the OLED. When used in the hybrid mode, OLED can be adapted to the color space of EPD, thus creating consistent viewing experiences. Trans-

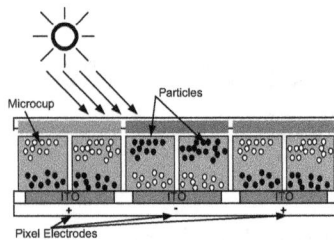
Figure 1: EPD

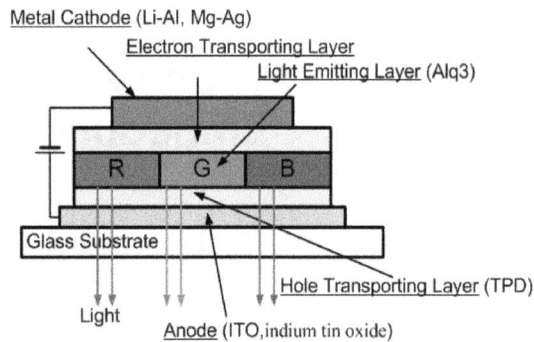

(a). OLED Device Structure (Pixel)

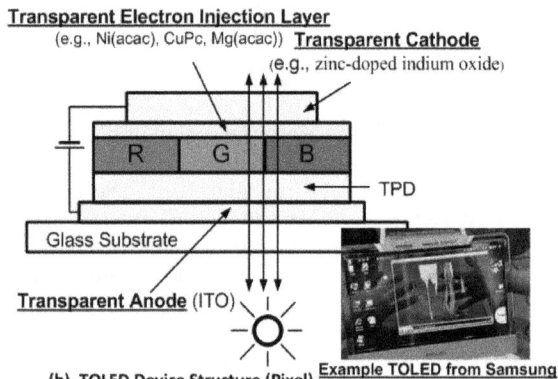

(b). TOLED Device Structure (Pixel)

Figure 2: OLED

parent OLED is a key technique that makes such a hybrid display a reality. If switched off, a transparent OLED display may appear as an ordinary window which allows a clear view on everything behind it.

However, designing such a hybrid display is a challenging task because it is hard to decide which parts of the displayed contents should be shown on the OLED panel and which parts should be shown on the EPD, which can achieve energy reduction and guarantee user experience at the same time. Users should not notice that two displays are being used. To further study energy reduction and user experience, we need to establish both a power model and optical model to evaluate the design of the proposed hybrid display.

The main contributions of our work include: (i) design of an integrated hybrid display stack combining TOLED and EPD for supporting context−based display adaptation; (ii) introducing a windows-based predictive model and a calibration algorithm on TOLED that allow frame contents to be shown on both TOLED and EPD at the same time for supporting improved trade-off between energy reduction and user experience; and (iii) energy and optical evaluation of the hybrid display using models exhibiting physical characteristics resembling measurements of actual EPDs, an actual OLED, and fabricated transparent OLED devices.

The rest of this paper is organized as follows. Section 2 describes background on mobile display technologies and motivates the research. The design of the hybrid mobile display is presented in Section 3. Section 4 shows the windows-based predictive model. Section 5 describes the hybrid display calibration. Section 6 details the power model of EPD and TOLED. The power simulation results and analysis are in Section 7. Some related works are discussed in Section 8, and the final conclusions of the paper are presented in Section 9.

2. BACKGROUND AND MOTIVATION

Display technology plays a critical role in the mobile industry. Most mobile devices own a screen with a specific display technology. Currently, handheld electronics have increased demand for displays in multiple areas, such as picture quality, size, and power consumption. The most common display technologies used in mobile devices are LCD and OLED screens which consume about half the amount of the battery power. A new trend in handheld devices like the Kindle, is to integrate an electrophoretic display that offers possibility for significant energy savings.

2.1 EPD

Electrophoretic display is a display technology design which imitates the ordinary ink on paper. This technology works by using millions of tiny microcapsules that are held between two arrays of electrodes as shown in Figure 1. The micro-

capsule contains positively charged color pigment particles and negatively charged color pigment particles suspended in a specific liquid layer. Since the particles are of opposite charge, the color pigment particles will switch between front and bottom of the film, allowing users to see different views of color.

The most important feature of these capsules is that the individual microcapsule is stable in its state. Even with the power turn-off, the display content remains visible. This bistate nature benefits some applications with low refresh rate such as reading books. Once the display is shown to the user, it can last a couple of hours with very little leakage power consumption. However the EPD technique has limitation for the device's refresh rate, thus only few reading devices utilize this technology.

2.2 OLED

When compared to the narrow usage of electrophoretic display, OLED displays dominant the recent smartphone display market. In figure 2(a), we can see that a typical OLED display consists of multiple layers, a cathode layer, an electron transport layer, an organic layer made of light emitting materials (e.g., Alq3), a hole transporting layer, an anode layer, and a substrate layer. When the voltage supplies to the OLED display, an electrical current flow is generated from the cathode to the anode. The cathode gives electrons to the organic layers. At the same time, the anode removes electrons from the organic layers. The photons, which are generated when the electrons move across the different organic layers, provide the light for the OLED display. Since OLEDs can emit light, without the need for a backlight, the OLED technique requires less power than the conventional LCD technique. However, displays using OLEDs

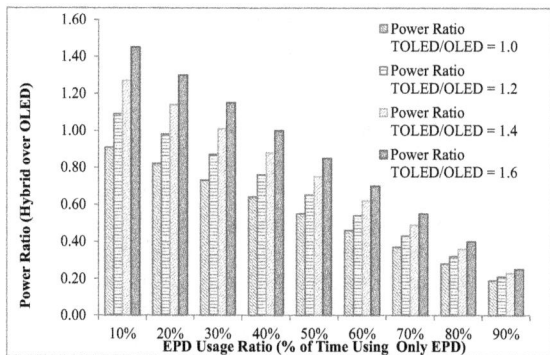

(a) Switching Between EPD and TOLED

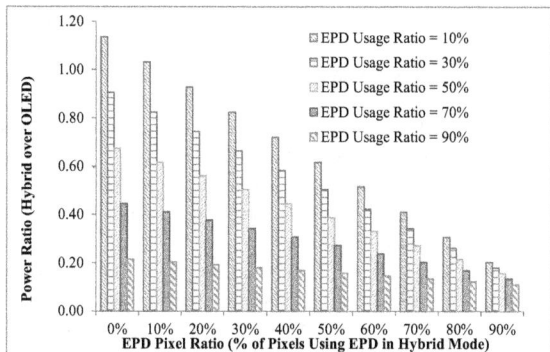

(b) Switch Plus Using Both Displays at the Same Time

Figure 3: Power Saving Estimation

consume order of magnitude of more power than the EPD based displays.

2.3 Transparent OLED

A unique property of many organic molecules is that most OLEDs are highly transparent over their own emission spectrum, and throughout most of the visible region of the spectrum. This property enables a new type of organic electroluminescent display (TOLEDs) that are greater than 80% transparent when turned off. TOLEDs [19, 16, 18, 13] use only transparent components as substrate, cathode and anode. A TOLED structure is shown in figure 2(b), in comparison with the conventional OLED structure. The high transparency of the device is achieved by replacing the nontransparent cathode (e.g., thick MgAg alloy) with a thin layer of transparent electrode. A transparent OLED display can be either active or passive-matrix. However, sometimes TOLED panels may require slightly higher voltage bias than the nontransparent ones for attaining the same current level or brightness.

2.4 Motivation

Our work is motivated by the observation that in the OLED and TOLED system, some applications require a high refresh rate to be functional (e.g., video player) but some applications do not require that (e.g., book reader). In addition, the applications that require high refresh rate may only need frequent changes in subareas of a screen instead of the whole screen. For example, the video area of a movie player requires a higher refresh rate but the area of the playlist does not.

We further explore the energy benefits in, (i) switch mode where entire screen is switched to a low refresh rate display

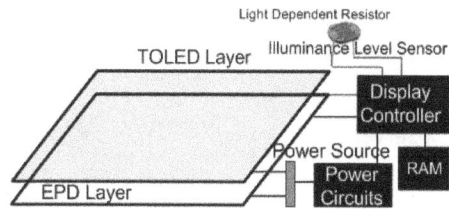

Figure 4: TOLED-EPD Hybrid Display

technique (e.g., EPD), when displayed content does not require frequent updates; and (ii) hybrid mode where subareas of a screen are switched to EPD when they do not require high refresh rates.

Figure 3(a) illustrates the potential energy savings for a mobile device that supports switch between the two displays based on the display contexts. The X-axis shows hypothetical percentage of display time where content is displayed on the EPD panel and the Y-axis indicates power consumption ratio using the TOLED and EPD hybrid display over a conventional OLED only display. As shown in the figure, even in an unlikely pessimistic case, when the TOLED consumes 1.4 times more power than an equivalent OLED, a TOLED−EPD hybrid display can still attain the same overall power consumption if around 32% display usage can be done using the EPD panel. Figure 3(b) shows power consumption ratio of the TOLED-EPD hybrid display over an OLED only display when both the switch mode and the hybrid mode are used. The X-axis shows the percentage of the pixels of an image that can be displayed on the EPD panel in a hybrid usage mode. The Y-axis indicates the power consumption ratio of the hybrid + swtich mode over an OLED only display. In addition, figure 3(b) includes data of five application scenarios where the average EPD usage in the switch mode is 10%, 30%, 50%, 70%, and 90%. We assume that power consumption of the TOLED itself is about 1.25 times of an equivalent OLED display using materials and fabrication process as close as possible. Figure 3(b) suggests that we can achieve even greater power savings using a TOLED−EPD hybrid on top of the switch mode by supporting selectively showing image content on both displays at the same time. For instance, counting the total amount of time spent by a person running applications that require a display, if half amount of the total time is spent on the applications whose contents can be displayed exclusively on the EPD panel using the switch mode, the maximum power saving is about 38% under the switch mode. For the rest amount of time, when the TOLED is used, if on average, for each frame, 40% of displayed contents can be further displayed on the EPD panel, additional 14% power can be saved.

3. EPD–TOLED HYBRID DISPLAY DESIGN

A mobile hybrid display can be realized by overlaying a TOLED module layer over an EPD module. Generally a TOLED display can be as thin as 1.5mm. The thickness of a color EPD film is 1.5mm or even less in future. As a result, the hybrid display can be only 3mm thick. Each display has its own active matrix TFT backplane. To support the hybrid mode, the EPD and the TOLED module must have the same pixel density. This would not be an issue because EPD display today can exceed pixel density of 200DPI and the pixel density continues to improve. Transparent AMOLED (active matrix OLED) with 200DPI was

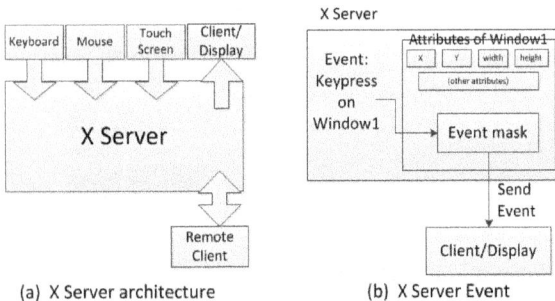

(a) X Server architecture   (b) X Server Event

Figure 5: X windows system

Table 1: Selected Events

Event Category	Event Type
Keyboard events	KeyPress, KeyRelease
Pointer events	ButtonPress, ButtonRelease
Exposure events	Expose, GraphicsExpose
Structure control events	ConfigRequest, ResizeRequest
State notification events	CreateNotify, DestroyNotify

demonstrated. Some high-end non-transparent AMOLED can support up to 300DPI pixel density. Over time, technology scaling will support a hybrid display with both high resolution EPD and TOLED of the exact same size and pixel density.

Figure 4 shows the design of the EPD-TOLED hybrid display. Instead of having two controllers, one for the EPD module and the other one for the TOLED module, one combined controller can be employed to control both the EPD and the TOLED module. This combined controller sends signals to drive both the EPD module and the TOLED module. When using a combined controller, we can easily support the hybrid display mode. The combined controller connects to a local RAM where images/frames, lookup tables, and signal waveform data can be stored. The displayer controller determines where to show each part of images/frames. This decision is made by a predictive model. The predictive model is discussed in section 4. A light dependent resistor is equipped in the design. The resistor, functioning as an illuminance level sensor, is connected to the display controller. Because contents shown on EPD and TOLED displays may look different, the display controller is responsible for calibrating the TOLED and EPD modules to let them have similar visual appearances so that users can use the hybrid display as a whole without being aware parts are shown on different displays. Section 5 details this design. A power circuit controls both the TOLED and the EPD. Typically, an EPD display module requires 15V power input. For evaluating power reduction, power models for EPD and TOLED displays are constructed in section 6.

4. PREDICTIVE MODEL

A predictive model, as a component of the display controller, determines the display mode (EPD or TOLED) for each pixel of a display screen, e.g., one or several subareas of the screen be displayed on the EPD module and the rest subarea(s) be displayed on the TOLED module. The prediction is based on the facts: 1) parts that are likely to change should be displayed on the TOLED; 2) More recent update history (changed or unchanged) of a display region has more impacts on the prediction. We use X windows system [9], or simply called X, the most widely used protocol as the reference windows system for graphical user interfaces (GUIs). Subareas in our prediction model are referred as windows or sub-windows in X windows system, i.e., our model makes predictions on where each window is going to be displayed.

X windows system uses a client-server model and is device-independent. The current major version is X11. As shown in Figure 5(a), X server can collect user input from keyboards, mouses or touch screens, and send the changes of GUIs to clients, which can be either local or network connected as

long as target computers implement X. Events are the packets sent to a client indicating that some changes happened. The client first registers its interested events on the server. Table 1 lists selected events in X windows system. Once specified events occur, the X server will send event notifications to the client. Figure 5(b) shows the process. Notice that, even though some Unix-like systems doesn't use X for graphics, the principle of their graphics designs is similar. For example, Android uses a windows manager over Surface Manager. These systems all create a hardware abstraction layer (HAL). Display changes are notified by events. Therefore, our predictive model can be generalized and easily applied to other graphics systems other than X. In this paper, we state the predictive model based on X windows system.

Before stating the core prediction algorithm, the following things have to be mentioned.

1. Not all windows on X are visible. For example, Input-Only windows are not visible, neither are those fully covered by some others. They are not considered in our prediction.

2. The ambient illuminance is a dominant factor. If the ambient illuminance is low, all the windows are shown on the TOLED. Because EPD can only reflect lights, EPD is barely visible under this situation. Therefore, all windows of current frame are shown on the TOLED.

3. Some programs have a direct access to the frame-buffer to update graphics. For example, Direct Graphics Access (DGA) is an extension for X Windows System, which makes client programs can manipulate frame-buffer directly. Those client programs usually need high refresh rate, such as video players, or games. Windows of this kind of program are shown on TOLED.

4. If users/developers set a preference on where to show a program, windows of the program are shown on the user-specified display.

5. Newly created windows are always shown on TOLED.

The prediction is based on histories. Let $P(t)$, be the estimated probability that a window is going to change at frame t, where $0 \le P(t) \le 1$; the bigger P(t), the more likely that the window will change; at the beginning, P(1) is set to 1.

Let $A(t)$, be the actual status whether the window is changed or not between frame $t-1$ and frame t, where $A(t) \in \{0,1\}$, and A(t) = 1 means that the window at frame t is different from that at frame $t-1$, i.e. specified events are received;

$P(t+1)$ is synthesis of the most recent status and historical prediction by using exponentially weighted moving average (EWMA): $P(t+1) = \alpha * A(t) + (1-\alpha) * P(t), 0 \le \alpha \le 1$ The coefficient α is an influence factor that indicates how the most recent status impacts on the prediction. A higher α discounts older statuses faster.

To determine which display to use, let θ_1 and θ_2 be the lower and upper threshold respectively, then

• if $P(t) \le \theta_1$, predict that the window is shown on the EPD;

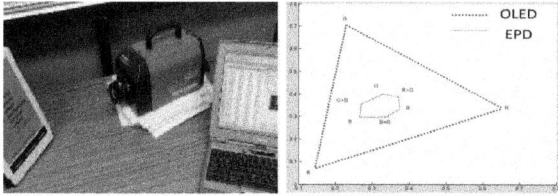

(a) Konica Minolta Spectroradiometer and Color EPD

(b) Color gamut

Figure 6: Color gamut for OLED and Color EPD

- if $P(t) \geq \theta_2$, predict that the window is shown on the TOLED;
- if $\theta_1 < P(t) < \theta_2$, predict that the window remains on the same display as it was at the previous frame.

$\alpha, \theta_1, \theta_2$ can be determined in this way:

- The k-step-back status has a relative small weight, δ, such as 0.0001, on P(t), then α is estimated by $(1 - \alpha)^k \leq \delta$. In our model, α is set to 0.85.
- If a window is shown on the EPD and it keeps changing in the next m contiguous frames, it is moved to the TOLED. Therefore, θ_2 is chosen by considering $\theta_2 \geq \alpha * \sum_{i=0}^{m-1}(1-\alpha)^i$. In our model, to get better user experience, that is, the system can rapidly reflect the changes. Once there is a change in a certain window, the window is switched to TOLED. θ_2 is chosen by setting $m=1$, i.e., $\theta_2 = 0.85$.
- If a window is shown on the TOLED and it remains the same in the next n contiguous frames, it is moved to the EPD, therefore θ_1 can be determined by $\theta_1 \leq (1-\alpha)^n$. In our model, θ_1 is chosen by setting $n=5$, i.e., $\theta_1 = 0.00007$.

The meta data, $P(t)$ and other information associated with each window, w, is stored in display controller RAM indexed by windows ID. $P(t)$ is either updated from frame to frame regularly, or updated immediately if events of changes are received. Algorithm 1 shows the prediction algorithm. Algorithm 2 shows the event-driven update process of the meta data.

5. HYBRID DISPLAY CALIBRATION

Calibrations are used to make contents displayed on the EPD and TOLED modules to have similar visual appearances. There are three modes in the hybrid display, i.e. EPD-only mode, TOLED-only mode, and hybrid mode. Calibrations are needed in the hybrid mode, because i) TOLEDs can present more colors than EPDs, i.e. TOLEDs have a larger gamut; and ii) unlike TOLEDs, EPDs only reflect lights. Contents shown on the EPDs are usually less colorful and darker than those shown on the OLEDs. Therefore, for better user experiences, the calibration is mainly performed for the TOLEDs so that they will show contents as close as possible to the EPDs. When calibration is applied, factors including gamut mapping between EPDs and OLEDs, EPDs' reflectance, TOLEDs' transmission, and ambient luminance have to be taken into consideration.

5.1 Color Gamut

To compare the color gamut of TOLEDs and color EPDs, we conducted measurements using real AMOLED and color AMEPD devices. The AMEPD can support 4096 colors. The measurement of the mono colors of the AMEPD and

---

Algorithm 1 History Based Prediction

```
 1: for each frame_t to display do
 2:     /* prediction*/
 3:     if the ambient illuminance is low then
 4:         Show all the windows on TOLED
 5:         CONTINUE
 6:     end if
 7:
 8:     for each window,w, in current X do
 9:         if w is INPUT-ONLY windows or INVISIBLE
            then
10:             CONTINUE
11:         end if
12:         if w has a user preference then
13:             Show w on user-specified display
14:             CONTINUE
15:         end if
16:         if w is using DGA extension then
17:             Show w on TOLED
18:             CONTINUE
19:         end if
20:         if w.P(t) ≤ θ_1 then
21:             Show w on the EPD
22:         else if w.P(t) ≥ θ_2 then
23:             Show w on the TOLED
24:         else
25:             Show w on the same display as it was at the previous frame.
26:         end if
27:         /* regular update*/
28:         if No events related to w are received between current frame and previous frame then
29:             SET w.P(t) = (1 − α) * w.P(t) + α * 0
30:         end if
31:     end for
32: end for
```

AMOLED was conducted by using the Konica Minolta Spectroradiometer, CS-1000. CS-1000 gives the measurement of spectral power distribution, luminance, chromaticity and correlated color temperature of light sources, display devices and the non-contact measurement of reflective subjects. It can be used for absolute measurement of TFT displays, LED's, reflective displays, etc. A ring light source was used as light source. The measured data were tristimulus values for a two-degree observer under D65. Figure 6 shows the color gamut of an AMOLED vs. a color AMEPD based on measurements of the primary (R, G, B). The color gamut is shown on device-independent stand color space, CIExyY color space. The color gamut area of the measured color EPD is much less the color gamut of the measured OLED panel. Note that the color EPD gamut is covered by the OLED color gamut. This means that it is plausible to simulate the color appearance of a color EPD panel using an OLED display panel by adapting gamut mapping [7].

Given a color (R, G, B) in RGB color space, we can use a conversion matrix to transform it to the standard CIExyY color space. The conversion for RGB to XYZ can use the matrix in [8]. Then, $x = \frac{X}{X+Y+Z}$ and $y = \frac{Y}{X+Y+Z}$. Different devices have different conversion matrix. To minimize the conversion computation cost, a color profile file [7] is maintained. A color profile file contains a transformation

Algorithm 2 Event Driven Update

1: **while** TRUE **do**
2: **if** an event in the selected event list is received **then**
3:   Retrieve window id, wID, and other information from event message
4:   **if** the window is newly created **then**
5:    Add new meta data w_{new}
6:    $w_{new}.P(t) = 1, w_{new}.id = wID$
7:   **else if** the window is destroyed **then**
8:    Remove the meta data, whose windows id is wID
9:   **else**
10:    Find the window, w, where $w.id = wID$
11:    SET $w.P(t) = (1 - \alpha) * w.P(t) + \alpha * 1$
12:   **end if**
13: **end if**
14: **end while**

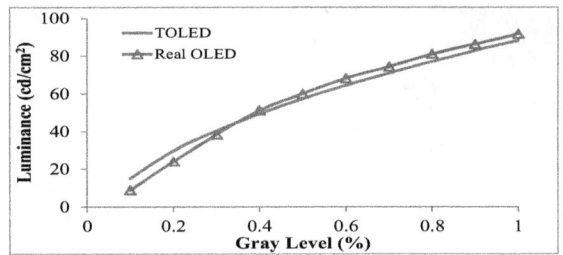

Figure 8: Gray Level - Luminance Characteristics (Actual OLED Measurement vs. Our Simulated TOLED Model)

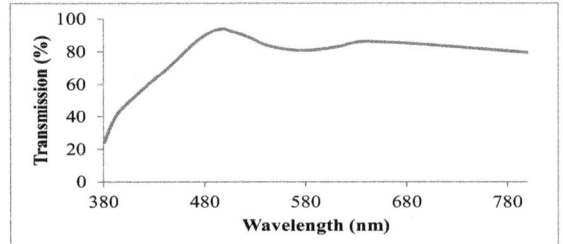

Figure 9: Transmission Rate of an Actual TOLED Device)

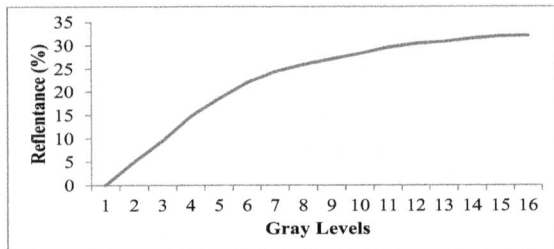

Figure 7: EPD Reflectance at Room Temperature

from EPD or TOLED color space to the standard CIExyY color space, which makes the transform with a small constant time. We have built the color profile file for the EPD and TOLED based on our measurement.

In figure 6, it already shows that TOLED has a larger color gamut than EPD does. We use perceptual rendering intents [7] to handle the outrange gamut. That is, compress the full CIExyY color space into the EPD gamut [7]. This can be also implemented by using a lookup table, which only cost O(1) to finish the compression.

By using the color profile file and perceptual colorimetry, the hybrid display can show the contents similar in colorfulness. Next, we need to adjust the brightness by considering the EPD reflectance and OLED transmission rate, both of which are modeled in the next two subsections.

5.2 EPD Reflectance

The optical reflectance of an EPD device is a non-linear function of gray levels [11, 15]. The number of gray levels is determined by the frame scan rate and the response time, which is the time to change the optical state from black to white or from white to black. The response time is sensitive to the ambient temperature. The higher the temperature is, the faster the EPD updates, which results in the reduction of selectable gray levels that is defined as the number of scanning frames in the time duration of one response. For example, if the response time is about 240ms at the temperature of $25°C$ and the frame scanning rate is 66 frames/s, the selectable gray levels are at most $\frac{240}{1000/66} = 16$. Usually, to achieve 16 gray levels, it needs more time than 240ms. In our model, we set it to 300ms. Consequently, our EPD takes total 1.2s to update (300ms * 4 for the four required steps to drive an EPD pixel to a new gray level, [12, 15]). Furthermore, in our color EPD model, reflectance at different color is based on real measurements. Figure 7 shows

the EPD reflectance function curve at different gray levels at room temperature($25°C$). For an EPD device, to update a pixel to a new gray level, it takes four steps [12]: 1) pulling back the pixel to full white state; 2) changing the pixel from full white to full black, 3) changing the pixel from full black to full white; and 4) setting the pixel to the given gray level. Those four steps are performed by the EPD controller via sending corresponding waveforms to the TFT driver. The steps of resetting a pixel to full white and black are necessary because they prevent particles from sticking. Therefore, for supporting 16 gray levels for each color dimension and the above four steps, updating a pixel takes 1.2s.

5.3 TOLED Transmission Rate

The modeled TOLED exhibits an average transmittance rate of over 70% the visible spectral region. According to [19], TOLED has a relatively low transmission rate when the wavelength is less than 450nm, and reaches the peak at around a wavelength of 500nm. With a wavelength larger than that, the transmission rate remains above 80%. The visible red, green, and blue light has a wavelength of about 650 nm, 510nm, and 475nm. The transmittance rate of RGB in our model are set to 84%, 90% and 86% separately. Further, to model how an image displayed on the EPD appears under the TOLED, we have to estimate the impact of EPD's reflectance and TOLED's transmission rate on the luminance of color. For this purpose, a model of EPD reflectance under different gray levels based on the actual measurement [11] is combined with the TOLED transmittance model [19]. The CIE XYZ color space is designed for color evaluation, the Y parameter of which is a measure of the luminance. The conversion for RGB to XYZ can use the matrix in [8]. Contributions of RGB components to the luminance level can be evaluated using $Y_L = 0.2126 * R^{2.2} + 0.7152G^{2.2} + 0.0724B^{2.2}$. The coefficients are valid for using D65 white point.

5.4 Illuminance Level Sensing and Calibration

The hybrid display controller can sense the ambient luminance, which determines EPD's brightness. The hybrid display controller can adjust the TOLED's luminance level

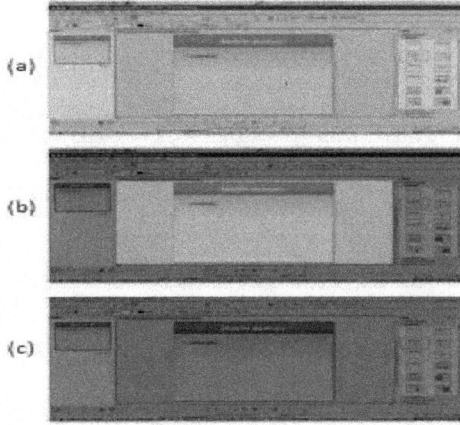

Figure 10: Calibration Results (Contents shown on EPD may look darker when printed)

according to the ambient light, which completes the calibration process. The calibration algorithm is shown in Alg 3

Algorithm 3 Hybrid Display Calibration

1: Convert $I = (R, G, B)$ in RGB color space to (x, y, Y) in xyY color space;
2: Compress (x, y, Y) to (x', y', Y) using perceptual rendering intent if necessary, where (x', y') is within the EPD gamut;
3: SET L_{EPDmax} = the max luminance (under full white), which the EPD can have under the current ambient illuminance;
4: SET $L_{TOLEDmax}$ = the max luminance the TOLED can emit;
5: SET $Y' = Y * (L_{EPDmax}/L_{TOLEDmax})$
6: Show (x', y', Y') on the TOLED;

Figure 10 shows examples of display appearances using the hybrid display. Figure 10(a) shows frame displayed on the TOLED; figure 10(b) shows the same frame displayed on both the TOLED and the EPD panel but without TOLED calibration. Therefore the pixels on the TOLED panel are brighter than those displayed on the EPD panel; figure 10(c) shows the appearance after TOLED adjustment. Contents on both displays look similar. Note that calibration is only used in the hybrid mode.

5.5 Prediction and Calibration Overhead

The overhead of our design comes from two sources, i.e. to determine on which display panel a window should be shown and calibration of these pixels shown on the TOLED panel. Both of them are small. Firstly, the total number of windows in one frame is usually less than 20. The overhead for tracking these components is minimal. Secondly, according to our measurement, in the hybrid display mode, the percentage of frame contents shown on the TOLED is typically less than 20%. The cost of calibration is also reduced by using color profile file. Our study shows that the predictor only has an energy cost of 3.4 miliwatts.

6. POWER MODEL

In order to evaluate the power efficiency of the hybrid display, power models for EPD and TOLED are discussed in this section.

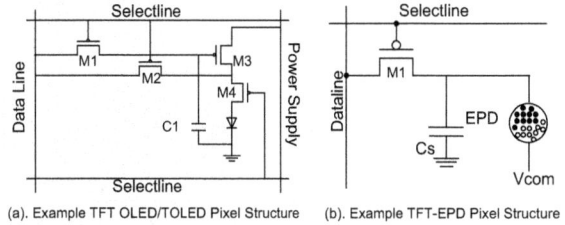

(a). Example TFT OLED/TOLED Pixel Structure   (b). Example TFT-EPD Pixel Structure

Figure 11: EPD and OLED Equivalent Circuit Models

6.1 EPD Power Model

Figure 11(b) shows an equivalent circuit model for driving an EPD pixel. According to [3, 2], the total power consumption for an EPD pixel consists of three parts, capsule switching power, capsule leakage power, and storage capacitor charge power.

Capsule switching power is the power cost for pigment particles moving through the capsule. The power consumption for each particle could be estimated by multiplying the force imposed on the particle (N) with the particle travel distance (s) [3, 2]. We can determine the force F by Newtons Law: $N = qE$ where q stands for the particle's charge, and E is the electric field inside the capsule. Electric field equals to Voltage divided by capsule diameter. In this case, for each capsule switching, it will cost 3.24E-9W power [2].

A small amount of current will leak through the fluid when the power supplies the capsule. The capsule leakage power can be calculated using the supply voltage and resistance of the capsule: $P = V^2/R$. By applying the capsules height, radius and resistivity, we get resistance of the capsule: $R = \rho h / \pi r^2$. Each subpixel leaks 8.84E-13W power which is negligible because it is several thousands of times smaller than the capsule switching power.

In order to store the required energy for switching color states, we need a storage capacitor shorted to ground shown in figure 11. The charged capacitor will provides electric field which enables the color pigment particles to move through the fluid. The storage capacitor will be charged during the row-write stage. Multiplying the row-write time with the capsule switching power, we get the capacitor storage energy lost for an entire row. Normally by dividing the row number of screen from frame-write rate, the row-write time is relatively small. As calculated, this energy loss is much smaller as well when compared with the switching power.

For our TOLED−EPD hybrid display, we use a subpixel based color EPD with 4K colors. In this color EPD, each pixel consists of three basic capsules with R,G,B filter covered respectively (see figure 2(a)). The structure for these subpixels are the same, but filled with different color pigment. Each capsule displays one of the 16 graylevels using a driving waveform [15].

6.2 TOLED Power Model

OLED power consumption models have been studied recently [1, 17, 5]. As shown in figure 2, TOLEDs have similar structure with the OLEDs but made of transparent components (e.g., transparent anode and cathode). Both of them use light emitting materials. Typically, electrical and optical characteristics of the OLEDs and TOLEDs can be specified using the current density−voltage characteristic (J-V) and current density−luminance characteristic (J-L). Given these electrical and optical characteristics of an OLED film, one

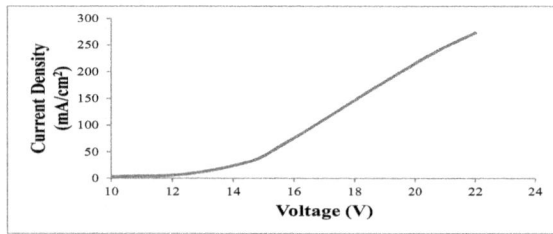

(a) V-J Characteristic

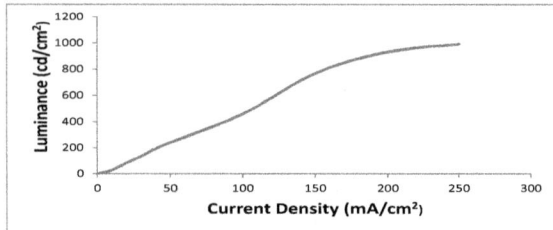

(b) J-L Characteristic

Figure 12: Physical Characteristics of an Actual TOLED Device

Table 2: Simulation Parameters

EPD parameters	Value	Unit
microcapsule diameter (d) [2, 4]	50	μm
particles per capsule [2]	1300	—
pigment particle charge (q) [3]	4.8E-16	Coulomb
supply voltage [2]	15	Volts
suspension resistivity [2]	1.0E12	Ωm
particle concentration [2]	$2*10^8$	m^{-3}
EPD TFT Rate	66	frames/s
EPD Color Levels	16*16*16	
EPD response time	300	ms
EPD update time	1.2	s
Capsule leakage power [2]	8.84E-13	Watts
Steady-state power consume [2]	3.24E-9	Watts
TOLED parameters	**Value**	**Unit**
TOLED Vdd	13.8	Volts
TOLED Max Luminace	90	cd/m^2
TOLED transmission rate	80%	
TOLED pixel area	15028	μm^2

can estimate its energy efficiency. Due to differences in materials and fabrication process, different OLED devices may have different electrical and optical characteristics. In the past several years, a great deal of efforts have been spent on searching solutions that can lead to increase in device efficiency (obtaining the same luminance by using less energy).

In [1], the authors described a detailed model and design for active matrix OLED display based on organic TFT. According to [1], the current across each pixel, I_{pix}, is proportional to the luminance, L_{pix}, and to the area of the pixel,A_{pix}, i.e., $I_{pix} = KL_{pix}A_{pix}$. Using measured electrical optical characteristics of an actually fabricated TOLED device [19] and [1], we create a TOLED model that has the same current density−voltage characteristic and current density−luminance characteristic as the actual TOLED reported in [19], see figure 12. We use the TOLED in [19] because it requires low input voltage and has good voltage − luminance performance, more suitable to be used as mobile device display. The coefficient, K, is set to $2.5A/cd$ according to the published results in [19]. The pixel area is $15028\mu m^2$ ($221\mu m * 68\mu m$). The device has six layers consisting of glass-ITO-TPD-Alq3-Ni (acac)2-IDIXO (transpar-

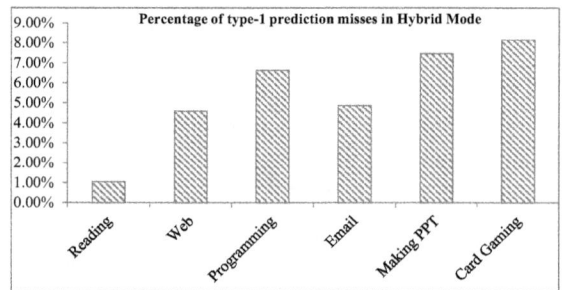

Figure 13: Percentage of type1 prediction misses

ent cathode). It has close to 90% transparency in the visible region.

For TOLEDs and OLEDs, luminance level changes with pixel gray level. Since luminance is proportional to the current value, we validate our TOLED model by calculating luminance level at different gray levels. The result luminance−gray level relationship is plotted in figure 11(a) together with the luminance−gray level results from the actual measurements of a real OLED device [17]. The blue curve corresponds to the modeled TOLED and the red one is based on the reported results of actual measurements [17]. The figure indicates that our TOLED model has an input−luminance profile consistent with the profile of an actual OLED device.

7. EVALUATION

7.1 Simulation Setup

We simulate our hybrid display approach using the models described in section 4−6 and study its performance. For the proposed TOLED−EPD hybrid display, we model both its power and optical behavior. Models of the EPD panel is described in section 5.2 and section 6.1. Section 5.3 and section 6.2 contain a reference TOLED model. The EPD model parameters are based on real physical measurement. The TOLDE model parameters are based on physical measurements obtained from a fabricated TOLED and cross-validated by measured results from an actual OLED device. The simulation parameters are listed in Table 2. In our simulation, we assume size of a pixel on the OLED panel is around 15k μm^2. The color pixel on the EPD panel contains 6 capsule, the diameter of the capsule is $50\mu m$. Thus the area of the pixel on the OLED panel is same as on the EPD panel. Since we have the same DPI and the same size, the user wouldn't feel resolution difference by using our hybrid display. In order to calculate the display power consumed in the hybrid display mode, we collect data from different usage scenarios using a netbook running Ubuntu Linux system with X windows server installed. The netbook has an Intel Atom N450 processor at 1.66GHz and 1 GB memory. Six video segments of one hour and a half are recorded, corresponding to reading books, web browsing, programming in Eclipse, email, making PPT, and card gaming (without DGA extension). Those video segments are used as data set for display test.

7.2 Prediction Miss

There are two types of prediction misses in our model. One corresponds to the case that a window that should be placed on the TOLED panel is predicted to be shown on the EPD panel. This is called a *type*1 miss. The other corresponds to the case that a window should be placed on the

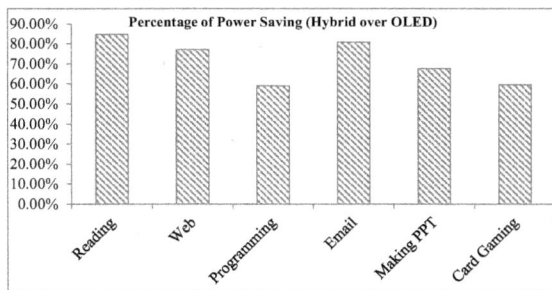

Figure 14: Power Saving in Different Contexts

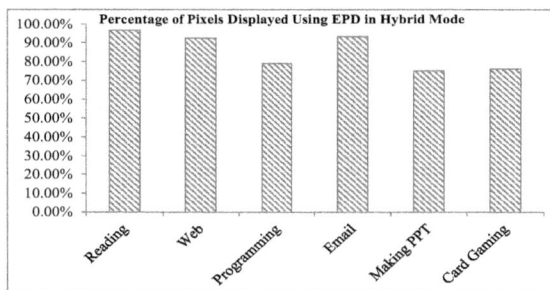

Figure 15: Percentage of Pixels Using EPD in Hybrid Mode

EPD panel is predicted to be shown on the TOLED panel. This is called a *type*2 miss. The *type*2 miss will not bother users, because the TOLED panel is more powerful than the EPD in terms of both color space and update rate. However, the *type*1 miss has a more significant negative impact on the user experiences because the refresh rate of the EPD·panel is much lower. The *type*1 miss of the hybrid display is evaluated in figure 13. Reading has the lowest *type*1 misses, which is less than 1%, while card gaming and PPT−making has the highest, which are over 7%. However, the average percentage of *type*1 miss in the prediction model is only 5.46%, which means the predictive mode can make the right decisions on choosing a proper display in over 90% of the cases. Furthermore, according to our prediction model, windows with updates are going to be switched to the TOLED panel one frame right after update events are detected. Therefore, user experiences can be guaranteed.

7.3 Energy Simulation

The six application scenarios are studied to show performance of the hybrid display mode. We compare with the results of a traditional OLED. Notice that card games are written without DGA extensions. Games using DGA extensions are to be shown on the TOLED directly. Figure 14 shows the results. Overall, when using the hybrid mode, the results show at least 60% savings in power consumption. Reading books has the most power reduction, which saves 84.61%. While programming and card gaming only save 59.04%. This is because that the contents are static during most reading time. By contrast, more frequent changes are expected during programming (constantly compiling and testing) and playing games. Energy reduction in the cases of web browsing, Email,and PPT creation are 77.11%, 80.68%, and 67.62% respectively. The average is 71.44% for the six application contexts. In those cases, one can achieve significant amount of energy savings.

To further study how the frame contents are actually displayed, we collect percentage of pixels shown on the EPD panel. We count the usage at the pixel level instead of at the windows level. This is because sizes of windows vary from each other. Pixel display statistics at the pixel level are more accurate. Our results in figure 15 show that about 97% of the displayed contents are shown on the EPD panel during reading, compared with 79% of the contents during programming and 75% of the contents during playing games shown on the EPD panel. Web browsing, Email and PPT creation have percentages of 92.49%, 93.38% and 75.11%, respectively.

The results in figure 14 and figure 15 also indicate that energy reduction is dependent of the displayed pixel contents. Since white pixels consume the most power on the

OLED panel, when they are relocated to be shown on the EPD panel in the hybrid mode, the amount of energy reduction is larger than moving colored pixels to the EPD panel. This explains why when comparing energy reduction of PPT creation test against tests of programming and card gaming, PPT creation has slightly less percentage of pixels shown on the EPD panel but has the most energy reduction. When creating PPT, the display background has more background pixels in white than other tested scenarios.

8. RELATED WORK

In this section, we survey works that are most related to ours, focusing on approaches of power consumption reduction for different display technologies, including LCD, EPD, and OLED. We also discuss the existing hybrid display technologies that aim to reducing the power usage and maintaining high display quality at same time.

Display power reduction for mobile devices has been actively researched in the recent years. In [6], the authors find that the display idle time is following certain distribution. For reducing LCD power consumption, they proposed two schedules to turn the LCD screen dim or off. One is called deterministic schedule and the other one is called probabilistic schedule. Either algorithm contributes 50% energy savings of the default schedule on E71.

For EPD, in [2], the authors present a smart driver approach for saving EPD energy. The driver only updates changed pixels between frames, ignoring the ones with only minor changes. Furthermore, a lazy driver is also proposed, which sets a threshold on the changes of pixel colors. Only those with changes exceeding the threshold are updated.

In [5], the authors provide three-level models for power consumption for OLED displays. The three levels are pixel level, image level, code level respectively. Their models can achieve over 90% accuracy in estimation for 300 benchmark images. They also provided power modeling and optimization for OLED displays, which helps energy-efficient GUI design on the OLED.

For reducing OLED power consumption, in [10], the authors studied OLED power modeling and power consumption optimization. A partial screen darken method, namely dark windows, is proposed to save power and in the meanwhile preserving the quality of user experiences. In [17], the authors present a dynamic voltage scaling based technique for OLEDs. Their method reduces the power consumption by scaling down the supply voltage.

Recently, mobile device companies have started to explore ways to mix different display technologies. Apple Inc. filed a patent about hybrid display by incorporating EPD technology into iPhone, iPad and iPod touch [14]. In their model, the hybrid system would switch different modes by displaying the content either on an EPD device or on an OLED device, but not both. Samsung also implemented a prototype that combines e-paper and a LCD screen. The display panel can switch between the two display modes: the "memory mode", which is similar to the Kindle; the "dynamic mode", which can playback color video. Our design distinguishes from those works by being able to show frame contents on both transparent OLED and EPD at the same time. In addition, we propose an adaptive control approach that can take into account content update rates and decide at window or subframe level which display should be used for attaining the best tradeoff between energy reduction and support for contents. Furthermore, we evaluate performance of the proposed hybrid display system using high fidelity simulations derived from reported measurements of actual EPD and TOLED devices.

9. CONCLUSIONS

In this paper, we describe the design and evaluation of an integrated hybrid display for mobile devices, which combines a transparent OLED (TOLED) module and a color EPD module. In addition to EPD only and OLED only display mode, the TOLED−EPD display supports a hybrid display mode where both the EPD module and the TOLED module are used for displaying contents of a frame at the same time. Display contents that need to be refreshed quickly are shown on the OLED module while slow update or static contents are displayed over the low power color EPD module. This hybrid display uses a window-based predictive model to choose which display should be used for a piece of display content for achieving energy reduction. A calibration approach for the TOLED pixels is also applied to make sure that the hybrid display can present visually consistent views on both display modules simultaneously. Based on actual measurements of the physical characteristics of fabricated TOLED devices, published EPD and OLED power models, and reflectance measurements of actual color EPDs, we set up a simulation environment that can estimate both the energy consumption and optical properties of the proposed hybrid display. Simulation results show that in the hybrid mode, the predictive mode can make correct decisions on choosing the proper displays in over 90% of the cases. The results also show that the average power saving is 71.44% for many mobile application contexts.

10. ACKNOWLEDGEMENT

The authors are grateful to anonymous reviewers for providing many valuable comments to improve the quality of this paper. The authors would also like to thank Dr. Heidi Hofer at College of Optometry, University of Houston, for providing Konica Minolta Spectroradiometer.

11. REFERENCES

[1] AERTS, W., VERLAAK, S., AND HEREMANS, P. Design of an organic pixel addressing circuit for an active-matrix oled display. *Electron Devices, IEEE Transactions on* (2002), 2124 – 2130.

[2] BAKER, M. A., SHRIVASTAVA, A., AND CHATHA, K. S. Smart driver for power reduction in next generation bistable electrophoretic display technology. CODES+ISSS '07, ACM, pp. 197–202.

[3] BERT, T., SMET, H. D., BEUNIS, F., AND NEYTS, K. Complete electrical and optical simulation of electronic paper. *Displays 27*, 2 (2006), 50 – 55.

[4] DALISA, A. Electrophoretic display technology. *Electron Devices, IEEE Transactions on 24*, 7 (1977), 827 – 834.

[5] DONG, M., CHOI, Y.-S. K., AND ZHONG, L. Power modeling of graphical user interfaces on oled displays. DAC '09, ACM, pp. 652–657.

[6] FALAKI, H., GOVINDAN, R., AND ESTRIN, D. Smart screen management on mobile phones.

[7] FRASER, B., MURPHY, C., AND BUNTING, F. *Real World Color Management*. Real World. Pearson Education, 2004.

[8] HOFFMANN, G. Cie color space. *Brain* (2010), 1–30.

[9] ISRAEL, E., AND FORTUNE, E. *The X-Window system server: X version 11, release 5*. X and Motif Series. Digital Press, 1992.

[10] IYER, S., LUO, L., MAYO, R., AND RANGANATHAN, P. Energy-adaptive display system designs for future mobile environments. In *Proceedings of the 1st international conference on Mobile systems, applications and services* (2003), MobiSys '03, ACM, pp. 245–258.

[11] KAO, W.-C., LIU, J.-J., AND CHU, M.-I. Integrating photometric calibration with adaptive image halftoning for electrophoretic displays. *Display Technology, Journal of 6*, 12 (2010), 625 –632.

[12] KAO, W.-C., YE, J.-A., LIN, F.-S., LIN, C., AND SPRAGUE, R. Configurable timing controller design for active matrix electrophoretic display with 16 gray levels. In *ICCE '09* (2009), pp. 1 –2.

[13] LEWIS, J., AND GREGO, S. Highly flexible transparent electrodes for organic light-emitting diode-based displays. *Applied Physics Letters 85*, 16 (2004), 3450–3452.

[14] LIN, GLORIA, HODG, AND ANDREW. US Patent NO. US572204 Systems And Methods For Switching Between An Electronic Paper Display And A Video Display , 10 2009.

[15] LU, C.-M., AND WEY, C.-L. A Controller Design for Color Active-Matrix Displays Using Electrophoretic Inks and Color Filters. *Journal of Display Technology 7* (Sept. 2011), 482–489.

[16] PFEIFFER, M., FORREST, S., ZHOU, X., AND LEO, K. A low drive voltage, transparent, metal-free nip electrophosphorescent light emitting diode. *Organic Electronics 4*, 1 (2003), 21 – 26.

[17] SHIN, D., KIM, Y., CHANG, N., AND PEDRAM, M. Dynamic voltage scaling of oled displays. In *Proceedings of the 48th Design Automation Conference* (2011), DAC '11, ACM, pp. 53–58.

[18] WEI, BIN, YAMAMOTO, AND SAYAKA. High-efficiency transparent organic light-emitting diode with one thin layer of nickel oxide on a transparent anode for see-through-display application. *Semiconductor Science and Technology*, 7 (2007), 788–792.

[19] YAMAMORI, A., H. Transparent organic light-emitting diodes using metal acetylacetonate complexes as an electron injective buffer layer. *Applied Physics Letters 78*, 21 (2001), 3343-3345.

Energy Efficient Special Instruction Support in an Embedded Processor with Compact ISA

Dongrui She
Eindhoven University of
Technology, The Netherlands
d.she@tue.nl

Yifan He
Eindhoven University of
Technology, The Netherlands
y.he@tue.nl

Henk Corporaal
Eindhoven University of
Technology, The Netherlands
h.corporaal@tue.nl

ABSTRACT

The use of special instructions that execute complex operation patterns is a common approach in application specific processor design to improve performance and efficiency. However, in an embedded generic processor with compact instruction set architecture (ISA), such instructions may lead to large overhead as: i) more bits are needed to encode the extra opcodes and operands, resulting in wider instructions; ii) more register file (RF) ports are required to provide the extra operands to the function units. Such overhead may increase energy consumption considerably.

In this paper, we propose to support flexible operation pair patterns in a processor with a compact 24-bit RISC-like ISA using: i) a partially reconfigurable decoder that exploits the locality of patterns to reduce the requirement for opcode space; ii) a software controlled bypass network to reduce the requirement for operand encoding and RF ports. We also propose an energy-aware compiler backend design for the proposed architecture that performs pattern selection and bypass-aware scheduling to generate energy efficient codes. Though proposed design imposes extra constraints on the operation patterns, the experimental results show that the average dynamic instruction count is reduced by over 25%, which is only about 2% less than the architecture without such constraints. Due to the low overhead, the total energy of the proposed architecture reduces by an average of 15.8% compared to the RISC baseline, while the one without constraints achieves almost no energy improvement.

Categories and Subject Descriptors

B.1.4 [**Control Structures and Microprogramming**]: Microprogram Design Aids; C.1 [**Processor Architectures**]; D.3.4 [**Programming Languages**]: Processors

General Terms

Algorithms, Design

Keywords

Reconfigurable architecture, special instruction, low power, code generation

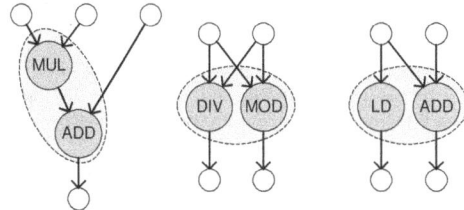

Figure 1: Special operation patterns

1. INTRODUCTION

Embedded systems, especially the ones in mobile devices like smart phones, are becoming more and more important in everyday life. The rapid development in embedded processors enables such devices to run high performance applications like wireless communication and high definition video codecs. However, power efficiency is becoming the bottleneck in high performance embedded system design, especially for those ones that run on limited power sources like batteries. Moreover, high power dissipation makes the chip's thermal design more difficult.

Many applications contain frequently executed operation patterns in the data-flow graphs (DFGs), like the ones shown in Fig. 1. In this work, *special instructions* are defined as instructions that execute such patterns. When properly utilized, special instructions are able to dramatically reduce the number of instructions and communication in the datapath, which have great impact on both performance and energy consumption. In application specific instruction set processor (ASIP) design, it is common to synthesis instruction sets that support such patterns in the targeted applications to achieve better performance and energy efficiency [15, 18, 23]. In this paper, we tackle the problem of integrating flexible special instruction support in an embedded generic processor with a compact instruction set architecture (ISA). Most previous works focused on improving the performance [18, 19]. Apart from performance improvement, the main focus of this work is on energy efficiency of the processor for different types of applications. In most mainstream processor architectures, only few number of such patterns are supported, as supporting arbitrary operation patterns in a generic processor incurs large overhead. From an energy efficiency point of view, the overhead is mainly caused by:

- More bits in the instruction to encode opcodes for all possible patterns and extra operands in the special instructions. It results in wider instruction, and the instruction fetch consumes more energy, even when a normal instruction is fetched. In a compact RISC ISA like the ARM Thumb [5], this problem is more serious as the number of bits in the instruction is very limited.

- More ports in the register file (RF) to provide sufficient data bandwidth for the special function units. A RF with more ports is much less energy efficient. Also, even the normal instructions need to pay the extra cost. Methods like register file clustering [14] or FU internal registers [23] are able to partially solve the problem. But such methods usually lack flexibility and often lead to very complex code generation.

To achieve high energy efficiency, the support for special instructions needs to have low overhead, while still being able to support applications from different domains. In this paper, we propose a schema for integrating special instruction unit (SFU) into a RISC-like embedded processor with 24-bit instruction width. The SFU supports flexible *operation pair* patterns. To integrate the SFU into the RISC datapath with minimum overhead, we use:

- A partially reconfigurable decoder that allows low overhead reconfiguration for each kernel to use its specific patterns. As a result, no extra bits are needed for the special instruction opcode.
- A bypass network in the datapath that is exposed to software, thereby reducing the requirement for both operand encoding and register file ports.

The use of a reconfigurable decoder and an explicit bypass network imposes some constraints on the special instructions the processor can execute, e.g., at least one of the operands of a three-input special instruction has to come form the bypass network. A compiler backend is designed to generate energy efficient code for the proposed architecture. The compiler selects patterns and performs bypass aware scheduling to utilize the SFU and explicit bypass network. A bypass aware DFG transformation is introduced to improve both bypassing and special instruction generation. Experimental results show that for a set of benchmarks form different domains, the proposed architecture achieves an average of 25% reduction in dynamic instruction count, which is only 2% worse than the architecture without constraints on the special instructions. As for energy consumption, the proposed architecture achieves an average reduction of 15.8%, while the unconstrained architecture only reduces 1%. The key contributions of this paper are:

- We propose an architecture that supports flexible operation pairs in a processor with a compact 24-bit RISC-like ISA. The proposed architecture has a partially reconfigurable decoder and a software-controlled bypass network, allowing the processor to support operation pairs without increasing the instruction width or number of register file ports. The proposed architecture is implemented in synthesizable Verilog RTL.
- A compiler backend is designed for the proposed architecture. It is capable of utilizing the SFU and the explicit bypass network to generate energy efficient target code. A complete compiler for the target architecture is implemented based on the LLVM framework.
- Comprehensive and detailed experimental results demonstrate that the proposed architecture and compiler are able to improve the energy efficiency significantly.

The remainder of this paper proceeds as follows: Section 2 describes the DFG patterns we consider in this work and the design of the SFU that executes such patterns. The proposed integration of SFU into the processor datapath with explicit bypass is depicted in Section 3. Section 4 introduces the compiler backend design for the proposed architecture. Detailed and comprehensive results that demonstrate the

effectiveness of the proposed design are given in Section 5. Section 6 discusses related work. Finally, Section 7 concludes our findings and discusses future work.

2. OPERATION PATTERNS AND SPECIAL FUNCTION UNIT

Each basic block of a program can be represented by a data-flow graph (DFG) $G(V, E_d, E_f)$, where:

- V is a set of nodes. Each node in V represents either an actual operation or a live-in variable (register file or immediate). In this work, we assume that the operations in V can be directly mapped to a function unit (FU) in a typical RISC processor.
- E_d is a set of directed edges. An edge $e = (u, v)$ represents that node v consumes the output of u, i.e., there is true data dependency between u and v.
- E_f is a set of directed edges. An edge $e = (u, v)$ represents that there is false/output dependency between node v and u.

For a basic block, the DFG is a directed acyclic graph (DAG). A *special operation pattern* is defined as a subgraph of a DFG that contains more than one basic operation. Fig. 1 shows some examples of these patterns. Compared to a combination of basic operations that performs the same computation, executing a special operation pattern using a special instruction has a few advantages:

- Fewer instructions are needed to execute the operations, resulting in less control overhead.
- The communication between operations can be done within the FU, which is usually much more efficient.

For a certain application, some special operation patterns appear frequently. In application specific instruction-set processor (ASIP) design, a common approach for improving performance as well as energy efficiency is to synthesize special function units that support these patterns [15, 18, 23, 26]. Different from the work of ASIP design, the goal of this work is to support special operation patterns in a RISC-like generic processor, without introducing heavy modification to existing architecture and code generation framework. Instead of trying to support arbitrary operation patterns, we focus on a specific type of operation pattern, namely, operations pairs. The definition of the operation pair pattern, as well as motivation of choosing such patterns are given in Section 2.1. The design of a special function unit (SFU) that provides flexible support for these patterns is depicted in Section 2.2. In Section 2.3, we analyze a set of kernels based on the patterns supported by the proposed SFU.

2.1 Operation Pair Patterns

In this work, we want to integrate the support for special operation patterns without major modification to the original RISC architecture. A RISC processor typically has two read ports and one write port (2R1W). Though there are some other possible sources for input operands, like immediate field and bypass network, the number of source operands cannot grow dramatically without heavy modification to the instruction format. The same holds for the destination operand. In addition, the number of arbitrary operation patterns in different applications is huge. The FU that supports all these patterns is likely to be very complex and inefficient. So in this work, we focus on *operation pair* patterns, i.e., patterns with two operations a and b that meet the following criteria:

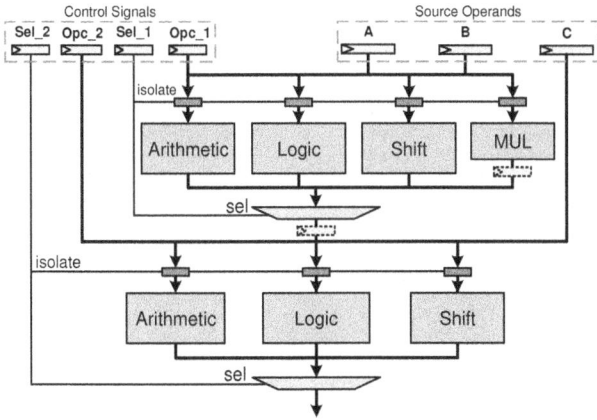

Figure 2: Special function unit

Kernel	Description	Domain
FIR	5-tap finite impulse response filter	Image
Histogram	256-bin histograming	Image
YUV2RGB	YUV to RGB color space conversion	Image
IDCT	2D 8x8 Inverse cosine transformation	Image /Coding
MatVec	Matrix vector multiplication	General
CRC	Cyclic redundancy check code calculation	Network/Storage
DES	The Data Encryption Standard algorithm	Security

Table 1: Kernel description

- There is true dependency between a and b: $(a,b) \in E_d$.
- There are at most three input operands. More formally, for a set of edges P that contains all edges to a or b in E_d except (a,b), we have $|P| \le 3$;
- At most only one of a and b has consumer outside the pattern, i.e., at least one of the following holds:
  - The result of a is only consumed by b: $\{(a,c)|(a,c) \in E_d, c \neq b\} = \emptyset$. If this constraint is met, only b may have consumers outside the pair pattern.
  - b has no consumer: $\{(b,c)|(b,c) \in E_d\} = \emptyset$. If this constraint is met, only a may have consumers outside the pair pattern.
- There is no path from a to b in G other than (a,b). So combining them does not create cycles in G.

Integrating such patterns in a RISC processor is relatively easy: we only need to supply one more source operands than for a normal operation.

2.2 Special Function Unit Design

The design of our special function unit is shown in Fig. 2. The SFU supports two levels of basic operations. To avoid introducing large area and timing overhead, only one multiplier is included in the SFU, which is put in the first level. The design of the SFU allows almost arbitrary combinations of operation pairs that satisfy the constraints in Section 2.1. When fully decoded, an 18-bit control signal is needed for the SFU to execute one special operation. To improve the energy efficiency of the SFU, *operand isolation* is used to isolate each sub-function-unit. So a unit only toggles when it actually needs to perform computation, thereby reducing unintended circuit activities.

As shown in Fig. 2, the SFU can be pipelined, or partially pipelined, which allows architectures with SFUs to reach high frequency if necessary.

2.3 Application Analysis

We analyzed seven kernels listed in Table 1, which come from various application domains. In total, 35 distinct pair

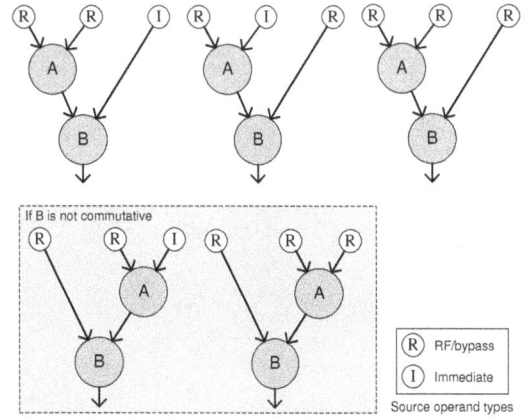

Figure 3: Cases for the same pattern that need different coding

Total	Hist	FIR	IDCT	Y2R	MatVec	CRC	DES
35	2	3	9	9	11	9	12

Table 2: Kernel pattern statistics

patterns that can be supported by the SFU are needed for these kernels. The number of patterns can grow much larger if more applications from different domains are included. In addition, to generate a valid special instruction from an operation pattern, more information needs to be encoded, e.g., if there is immediate and whether the immediate is for the first or the second operation. Fig. 3 shows an example of a three input operation pair that requires different control coding. When all these factors are considered, the total number of different special instruction patterns can easily grow to way over one hundred.

However, if we look into each individual kernel, we can see that the number of patterns used in one kernel is much smaller than the number of total patterns. Table 2 shows the statistics of pattern matches in the seven representative kernels from different domains. The statistics show that it is possible to exploit the *temporal locality of patterns* to reduce the number of patterns a processor needs to support during the execution of an application or a kernel. Findings in [17, 26] also lead to similar conclusion. This observation can be used to guide the design of efficient special instruction support in processors, which is discussed in Section 3.

3. INTEGRATING SFU INTO PROCESSORS WITH COMPACT ISA

In this work, a 4-stage RISC processor with a 24-bit instruction set architecture (ISA) is used as the baseline. The key features of the baseline architecture are described in Table 3. Most instructions are three-address instructions: two source operands and one destination are encoded. Fig. 4 depicts the datapath of the baseline processor.

In the baseline architecture, the major limiting factors of integrating the SFU introduced in Section 2.2 are:

Instruction width	24 bits
Pipeline stages	4
Register file	32b×32, 2R1W
Opcode	6 bits
Immediate	8 bits

Table 3: Key features of the baseline ISA

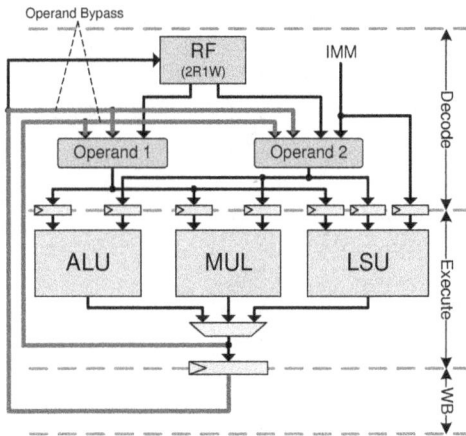

Figure 4: A typical RISC datapath

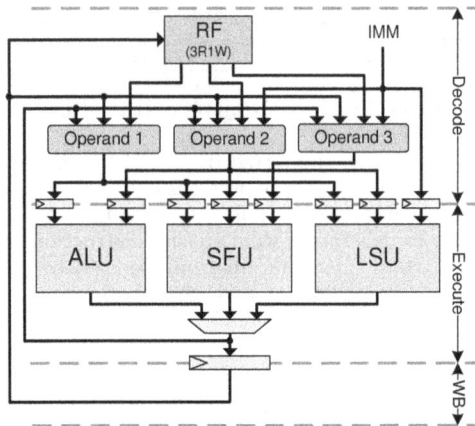

Figure 5: SFU datapath without constraints

- After adding the basic integer and control operations, only less than 16 opcodes are left in the opcode space.
- At most 3 bits can be used for encoding the extra operand in three-input instructions, which are not enough for a register index.
- The 2R1W RF cannot provide enough operand bandwidth for the SFU.

A straightforward solution to these problems is to increased instruction width and number of RF ports. To accommodate the extra opcodes and register index, at least additional 7 bits are needed (5 bits for the third register operand, 2 bits for extra opcodes). As a result, the width of the instruction memory increases to 32 bits. In addition, the RF needs to have three read ports (3R1W) in order to provide sufficient bandwidth for the SFU. The resulting datapath is shown in Fig. 5. To avoid high area overhead, the multiplier is absorbed into the SFU. Based on the estimation of CACTI [6], the energy consumption of each access to the instruction memory is increased by 10% to 30% depending on the size and configuration. And based on the implementation result, the energy consumption of the RF is also increased by 12% due to the extra read port. Since both instruction memory and register file are among the most frequently used components in a processor, an architecture with such large overhead is unlikely to be energy efficient.

To improve the energy efficiency, such overhead have to be mitigated. In this work, we propose an energy efficient support for the SFU by using: *i*) a partially reconfigurable

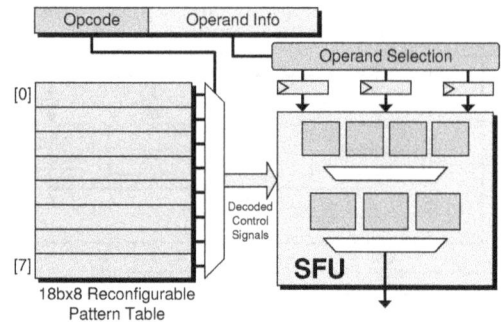

Figure 6: Partially reconfigurable SFU decoder

decoder that exploit the locality of the operation patterns to reduce the opcode encoding requirement; *ii*) a software-controlled bypass network that exploit the processor pipeline to reduce the operand encoding and RF port requirement. Section 3.1 and Section 3.2 describe the details of the partially reconfigurable decoder and the software-controlled bypass network, respectively. Section 3.3 depicts how the SFU is integrated into the baseline processor.

3.1 Partially Reconfigurable Decoder for SFU

As discussed in Section 2.3, a key observation is that although a large number of patterns are needed to cover the operation patterns in different applications, only a small number of such patterns are active in one kernel, i.e., in most kernels, the operation patterns have good locality. To utilize such locality, this work introduces a partially reconfigurable decoder for the SFU.

Fig. 6 depicts the structure of the reconfigurable decoder for the SFU. The center of the decoder is a look-up-table with eight entries, called *pattern table*. Each entry in the pattern table stores an 18-bit control signal required by a special instruction. Since the table only has eight entries, the free opcodes in the opcode space can be used to address it. When a special instruction is fetched, the decoder reads a pattern table entry and uses it to control the SFU; when a normal instruction is fetched, the decoder proceeds as a normal RISC decoder, and the pattern table is clock gated to eliminate unnecessary accesses.

The pattern table is visible to the software. So when different operation patterns are needed, the software can reconfigure the SFU decoder by writing extra control signal needed by these operations into the pattern table. By enabling the reconfiguration of the pattern table, the processor is able to use all the operation patterns supported by the SFU. And since in most cases the operation patterns have good locality, the overhead of reconfiguration is very low.

3.2 Explicit Bypass

In a typical pipelined datapath of a processor, like the one in Fig. 4, there is a bypass/forwarding network, whose primary function is to avoid pipeline stalls caused by data dependencies. A side effect of such a network is that many operands can be read from the pipeline registers instead of the RF. There are two types of RF access elimination:

- *Bypassing*: the result of an operation can be read from the pipeline register before it is written back to RF;
- *Dead writeback elimination*: if all uses of a variable are bypassed, its writeback is no longer necessary.

However, in conventional processor architectures, such bypassing network is invisible to software, which makes it difficult to eliminate RF accesses: *i*) bypassing requires RF

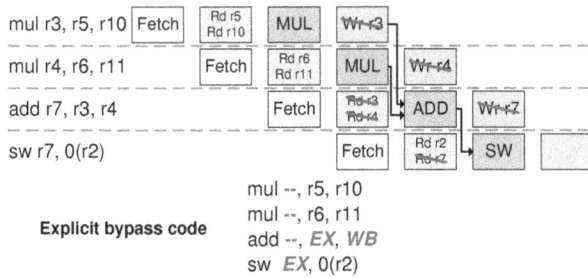

Figure 7: Reduce RF accesses via explicit bypass

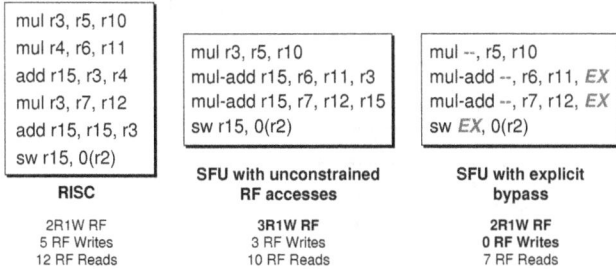

Figure 8: Special instruction example

indexes to be checked before decode stage, which may increase the critical path of fetch stage or results in an extra pipeline stage; *ii*) dead writeback elimination is impossible unless liveness information is explicitly encoded in instructions. In this work, we propose to use a bypass network that is controlled by software, i.e., the bypassing information is statically encoded in the instructions. Fig. 7 shows an example of reducing RF accesses via explicit bypassing. Apart form reducing the total number of register accesses, explicit bypassing helps integrating the SFU without increasing instruction width and RF ports in two ways:

- Encoding a bypass source uses fewer bits than an RF index, as the number of bypass sources are much fewer than the number of registers in RF (4 vs. 32).
- Fewer RF ports are required when some operands are bypassed.

By imposing the constraint that at least one of the source operands in a three-input special instruction has to come from the bypass network, the special instructions can be encoded in the 24-bit instruction, and there is no need to increase the number of RF ports. Fig. 8 shows an example of special instructions. In processor with unconstrained SFU, the number of instructions is reduced from 6 to 4, at the cost of increasing the number of read ports of the RF from 2 to 3. In a processor with explicit bypassing, the same code size improvement can be achieved even when there is a constraint that at least one of the operands comes from the bypass network. And with such a constraint, the requirements for the instruction bits and RF port are reduced.

3.3 Integrating SFU into Processor Datapath

We propose an architecture that is able to support all the operation pair patterns of the SFU described in Section 2.2, by employing the partially reconfigurable decoder and explicit bypass network introduced in previous subsections. Fig. 9 shows the datapath of the proposed processor architecture. Note that because there are input registers for each FU, the result of one operation is stable at the output port of the FU until the next operation that uses the same FU comes. So it is possible to use the output of each FU as

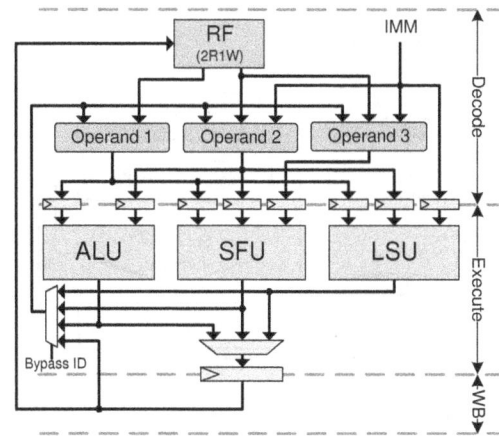

Figure 9: SFU datapath with constraints

a separate bypass source, which increases the possibility of bypassing. Compared to the one with direct SFU support (Fig. 5), the proposed architecture imposes extra constraints on the special instructions it can execute:

- For a three-input special instruction, at least one of the source operands has to come from the bypass network.
- At most eight special instruction patterns are active at the same time. To support different patterns, the program needs to reconfigure the pattern table.

With these constraints, the proposed architecture is much more energy efficient: instruction width remains 24 bits instead of 32 bits and the RF is 2R1W instead of 3R1W. To use explicit bypass without changing the normal instruction format, part of the RF address space is used for the bypass source. As a result, the number of registers in the RF reduces from 32 to 28. The effect of a smaller RF is mitigated by the explicit bypassing, as it eliminates the necessity of allocating registers for short-live variables in many cases.

The introduction of a pattern table and an explicit bypass results in extra context when exceptions happen. The pattern table can be handled in a similar fashion as general purpose registers. For explicit bypass, it is required that the processor saves the complete state for the execute and writeback stages of the pipeline. This can be done using a scan-chain that automatically saves/restores the registers when exceptions happen. Since the number of registers is small, the overhead in area and response time is small.

4. CODE GENERATION FOR SPECIAL INSTRUCTIONS

The compiler in this work is implemented based on the open-source LLVM framework [3]. Fig. 10 shows the backend compilation flow for the proposed architecture. The input of the backend is a low-level intermediate representation (IR), which is basically RISC assembly with virtual registers, embedded with control-flow and data-flow information. Since the proposed architecture only has small modification to the original RISC architecture, most part of the compiler can simply reuse the same passes as a compiler for RISC architecture. The main difference is that the backend needs to be aware of the explicit bypass network and has to utilize the special function unit (SFU). The selection of pair patterns for generating special instructions is described in Section 4.1. Section 4.2 discusses the changes in instruction scheduler and register allocator due to explicit bypass. A transparent DFG transform that improves bypassing and

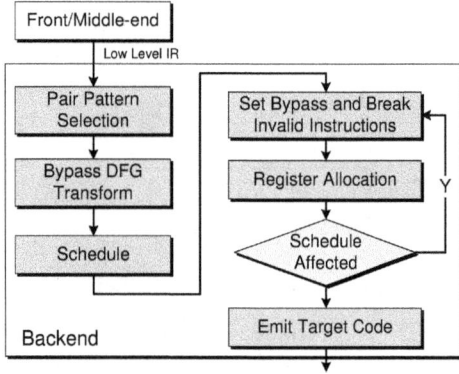

Figure 10: Compiler backend flow

helps the selected patterns to meet the architectural constraints, is described in Section 4.3.

4.1 Pair Pattern Selection

To use the SFU, the compiler needs to choose pairs of DFG nodes that can be used to generate special instructions, i.e., the pair pattern selection. The first step of pair pattern selection is to find all the node pairs whose patterns are supported by the SFU in the data-flow graph (DFG) under the constraints described in Section 2.1. A set containing all these node pairs is obtained by a scan through all nodes in the DFG, M. Each pair in M is called a *match*. The matches that are obviously not going to meet the operand bypass constraint, e.g., the ones with three non-constant live-in variables, are excluded from M.

The next step is to choose a subset S of M for generating special instructions. Obviously each DFG node should only be used by one pattern in S, as duplicating DFG nodes only results in extra energy consumption in the pair patterns. A match interference graph $G_I(V, E)$ can be built:

- V is a set of nodes representing all possible matches.
- E is a set of undirected edges. $(u, v) \in E$ means that match u and match v share a common DFG node. So u and v cannot be selected simultaneously.

An example of match interference graph is given in Fig. 11: on the left is a DFG with four possible matches; on the right is the match interference graph of the four possible matches. S should be an *independent set* of G_I, i.e., nodes in S are pair-wise non-adjacent in G_I. The objective here is to find as many pairs as possible, which is essentially to get the *maximum independent set* (MIS) of G_I, i.e., the independent set with maximum cardinality.

Though MIS is NP-complete in general, the minimum degree heuristics performs very well for sparse and bounded degree graph [2]. In the DFG pair pattern selection, many nodes in the match interference graph have the same degree, which results in many ties in minimum degree selection Since in the proposed architecture, only limited number of operation patterns are supported without reconfiguration, the pattern frequency is used to break the ties. The algorithm used for pattern selection is depicted in Algorithm 1. The algorithm yields $\{1, 3\}$ for the example in Fig. 11, which is the MIS of the interference graph.

4.2 Instruction Scheduling and Register Allocation

A list scheduler is used to perform basic block level scheduling. In the proposed architecture, the total number of physical registers are reduced as part of the RF address space is

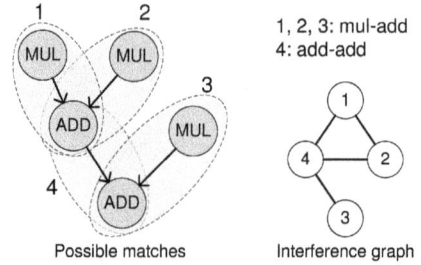

Figure 11: Operation patterns matches

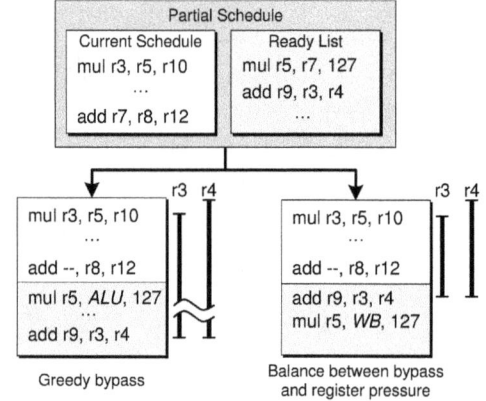

Figure 12: Bypass and register pressure trade-offs

used by bypass sources. So although explicit bypass eliminates the need for many temporary registers, it is still very important for the compiler to make sure that register pressure stays low. When the list scheduler greedily chooses the node with maximum number of bypass, the register pressure may go up. Fig. 12 shows an example of how a greedy bypass scheduler may increase the register pressure. In this work we use a scheduling algorithm which is similar to the integrated prepass scheduling (IPS) [1]. Depending on the register pressure of the current partial schedule, The scheduler switches between between two policies: *i*) choose the node that maximizes bypassing, or *ii*) choose the node that minimizes register pressure. The details of the scheduling algorithm is given in Algorithm 2. The register pressure threshold can be chosen based on the estimation of available registers for the basic block. The register allocation is done with a graph-coloring algorithm. The register allocation is almost the same as the one used for a RISC processor, except that small constant values (ones that can fit in the

---

Algorithm 1: Pattern Selection

Input : Match interference graph of the basic block $M(V, E)$ and pattern frequency F_p

Output : Set of pattern matches S in which nodes do not interfere with each other

1 $S \leftarrow \emptyset$
2 **while** $M \neq \emptyset$ **do**
3    $D \leftarrow \{d | d \in V, \nexists u \in V : degree(u) < degree(d)\}$
4   **if** $|D| = 1$ **then**
5      $n \leftarrow D[0]$
6   **else**
7      $Q \leftarrow \{q | q \in D, \nexists u \in D : F_p(Pat(u)) > F_p(Pat(q))\}$
8   // Pick the first one if Q has more than one node
9      $n \leftarrow Q[0]$
10   **end**
11   $S \leftarrow S \cup \{n\}$
12   Remove n from M, along with all its edges and neighbors
13 **end**

---

instruction immediate field) in special instructions are not always re-materialized to immediate filed when it results in an instruction with two immediate values, which is invalid.

After the scheduling, a scan through all instructions is preformed to check for invalid special instructions, i.e., the instructions that do not meet the constraints given in Section 3.3. If a special instruction is found to be invalid, the checker decomposes it into normal instructions. Due to the nature of explicit bypassing, this transformation does not increase register usage. Then the compiler collects pattern informations and decides where to insert the reconfiguration codes. In this work, there are two possible scenarios:

- If the number of patterns used in a function is less than or equal to the pattern table size, all patterns are loaded at the entry block of the function.
- If the number of patterns used in a function exceeds the pattern table capacity, the compiler tries to perform reconfiguration before entering each intensive loop. The loop information can be obtained through static estimation or profiling.

When both ways fail to accommodate all used patterns, the compiler selects the most frequently used patterns. And a special instruction whose pattern is not in the pattern table is decomposed to two normal instructions. When there is a function call, the pattern table becomes part of the context, and needs to be saved like the general purpose registers. When compiler optimization is enabled, the frequently called simple functions usually get in-lined. So we expected the reconfiguration overhead to be negligible in most cases.

As shown in Fig. 10, whenever a code transformation changes the schedule, the bypass status of each instruction needs to be updated, so the same check needs to be performed. The process terminates: in the worst case, the loop stops when all special instructions are decomposed to normal instructions. In practice only one or two iterations are sufficient in most cases.

Algorithm 2: Basic Block Scheduling

Input : DFG $G(V, E_d, E_f)$ and register pressure threshold t_r
Output : The schedule of the DFG $T : V \mapsto \mathbb{N}$

```
 1 // Set number of cycles based on conservative estimation
 2 R ← ∅                              // Ready set
 3 L ← ∅                              // Live variable set
 4 S ← ∅                              // Set of scheduled operations
 5 c ← 0
 6 while |S| ≠ |V| do
 7     if |L| < t_r then
 8         | o ← find_node_with_max_bypass (R, T)
 9     else
10         | o ← find_node_reduces_max_register_pressure (R,
              T, L, G)
11     end
12     for s ∈ {u|u ∈ V, (o, u) ∈ E_d ∪ E_f} do
13         | if s is enabled by o then
14         |     | R ← R ∪ {s}
15         | end
16     end
17     for p ∈ {u|u ∈ V, (u, o) ∈ E_d} do
18         | if o is last use of p then
19         |     | L ← L \ {p}
20         | end
21     end
22     if o has value output then
23         | L ← L ∪ {o}
24     end
25     S ← S ∪ {o}
26     T[o] ← c
27     R ← R \ {o}
28     c ← c + 1
29 end
```

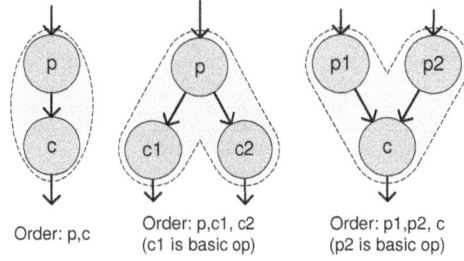

Figure 13: DFG clustering for explicit bypass

4.3 Bypass-Aware Graph Clustering

Whether an operand is bypassed or not depends on the schedule distance between the producer operation and the consumer. In the proposed architecture, bypassing not only affects the number of RF accesses, but also decides whether a special instruction is valid. To better utilize the explicit bypass, and more importantly, to reduce the number of special instructions invalidated by the scheduling, we introduce a bypass aware DFG transformation before the scheduling. The basic idea is to cluster a set of nodes if the nodes can be scheduled in such a way that:

- All the intermediate results are bypassed.
- Register pressure does not increase.
- Combining these nodes does not result in a cyclic dependency.

However, to find arbitrary subgraphs that meet these constraints is difficult as the number of possible subgraphs grows exponentially with the number of nodes. In this work, we introduce fixed patterns that meet the constraints and can be scheduled easily. We choose the patterns shown in Fig. 13, as they are easy to match and common in DFGs from different applications. The order in of each pattern in Fig. 13 represents the internal order of the nodes in the cluster, which satisfies the afore-mentioned constraints. The clustering can be done iteratively until no more transform is possible.

The transformation described in this subsection is transparent to the scheduler. After the graph clustering, the scheduler can schedule the resulting graph as if it is a normal DFG. After the scheduling, a valid schedule of the original DFG can be produced by expanding each clustered node to the internal list of DFG nodes.

5. EVALUATION AND ANALYSIS

Table 4 presents the architectures used in the experiments. The proposed architecture, i.e., with partially reconfigurable decoder, explicit bypass network, and constrained special instruction patterns (see Section 3.3), is called *SFU-24*. And the architecture that integrates SFU without the constraints in *SFU-24* is called *SFU-32*. The datapaths of the baseline, SFU-32 and SFU-24 are shown in Fig. 4, Fig. 5 and Fig. 9, respectively. All three cores are implemented in Verilog RTL and synthesized with TSMC 90nm low power library at 1.2V and typical case. Clock gating is used to minimize dynamic power consumption. The core energy consumption is estimated with the backend information and real toggle rate generated by post-synthesis simulation. The area and energy consumption of the memory are estimated with CACTI [6], using 90nm low operating power technology. Table 5 shows the energy model of the memory used in the experiments.

5.1 Area and Frequency

The implementation results of the three architectures are shown in Table 6. The increase in the core area is under-

Architecture	Baseline (Base)	Unconstrained SFU (SFU-32)	Proposed (SFU-24)
Instruction Width	24 bits	32 bits	24 bits
Instruction Memory	12kB 24-bit	16kB 32-bit	12kB 24-bit
		4k words	
Data Memory		16kB 32-bit	
Register File	32b×32 2R1W	32b×32 3R1W	32b×28 2R1W
SFU Patterns	0	128	8

Table 4: Configuration of different architectures

Memory	16kB 32-bit	12kB 24-bit
Energy per access (pJ)	15.38	11.62

Table 5: Memory energy consumption

standable and expected, as the SFU, as well as its decoding part, are much more complex compared to simple FUs in RISC. The core area of SFU-32 is slightly larger than SFU-24 as it needs to support more patterns in the decoder. The difference in memory area between SFU-32 and SFU-24 is significant. This is caused by the instruction memory since SFU-32 uses 32-bit instructions, while SFU-24 uses 24-bit instructions. In all, the SFU-32 pays a very high price in terms of area. In contrast, the proposed SFU-24 realizes the special instruction support with a relatively small overhead. In particular, it does not increase the memory area, which is the dominant part in many modern processors.

The reduced maximum frequency of SFU-32 and SFU-24 is mainly caused by the un-pipelined SFU, which has two levels of sub-function-units. It can be mitigated by introducing a pipeline stage in the SFU, though the trade-offs are out of the scope of this work. In this work, we use the un-pipelined SFU in both SFU-32 and SFU-24.

5.2 Energy Consumption

Table 1 lists the benchmarks used in the experiments. These kernels are from various application domains. The code for the proposed SFU-24 is generated by the compiler described in Section 4. For SFU-32, the code generation process is almost the same as SFU-24, except that all the constraints on operand bypassing and opcode space are removed, and no reconfiguration code is generated. All benchmark programs are compiled with maximum optimization enabled (-O3). Table 7 shows the absolute results of the baseline processor. The memory energy in the table includes both instruction memory and data memory. The energy consumption of each kernel is calculated by multiplying the number of cycles with the average energy (i.e., core + mem-

Architecture	Base	SFU-32	SFU-24
Normalized Core Area	1	1.309	1.268
Normalized Memory Area	1	1.154	1
Maximum Frequency	450MHz	325MHz	325MHz

Table 6: Implementation result comparison

Kernel	Simulated Cycles	Average Core Energy per Cycle	Average Memory Energy per Cycle
Histogram	21547	11.05pJ	16.10pJ
FIR	40973	18.41pJ	16.24pJ
IDCT	2303	17.93pJ	14.56pJ
YUV2RGB	43032	17.88pJ	13.82pJ
MatVec	3729	13.27pJ	14.00pJ
CRC	162017	12.73pJ	11.82pJ
DES	857130	14.89pJ	14.64pJ

Table 7: Results of the baseline architecture

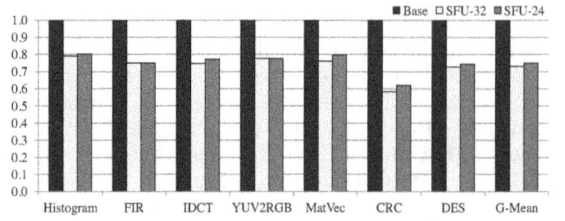

Figure 14: Dynamic instruction count (overhead included)

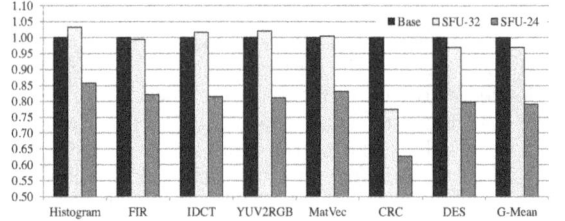

Figure 15: Normalized memory energy consumption

ory) per cycle. In the remainder of this sub section, we normalize all results to the baseline.

Fig. 14 shows the normalized dynamic instruction count of the three different cores. Including the overhead of reconfiguration, SFU-24 achieves a reduction of 25%, which is only 2% worse than SFU-32. When the instruction width is factored in, as shown in Fig. 15, the memory energy consumption of SFU-24 is much less than SFU-32. Though the number of fetches is reduced dramatically, SFU-32 only achieves 3.5% average memory energy reduction due to increased instruction width. In 4 out of 7 benchmarks the energy consumption actually goes up. In contrast, the proposed SFU-24 is able to directly convert the reduction in instruction count into memory energy saving. An average of 21% saving is observed.

Fig. 17 shows the normalized core energy consumption. Comparing to the baseline processor, the proposed SFU-24 reaches a maximal core energy reduction by 21.5% in the FIR case, and by 11.2% on average. The main contributions of energy reduction are from: 1) reduced RF access energy; 2) reduced datapath and control path overhead due to merged operations.

On the other hand, the SFU-32 increases the average core energy by 0.3%. And it performs very bad in two cases: FIR and IDCT, in which the core energy increases by over 8%. The explicit bypass network is an important contributing factor in this huge difference. As show in Fig. 16, the number of accesses to the RF in SFU-24 is significantly reduced. In addition, the RF in SFU-24 has less ports than the one in SFU-32. As a result, the core of SFU-24 consumes much less energy compared to SFU-32, for which in both FIR and IDCT, a degradation of over 5% is observed.

Fig. 18 shows the normalized total energy consumption. The proposed SFU-24 reduces both the memory and core energy, and it achieves an average saving of 15.8%. It reaches a maximal of 33.1% energy saving in CRC. While the total energy saving of SFU-32 is only 1.1%.

These results show that although the use of SFU is able to significantly reduce the dynamic instruction count, directly putting the SFU into a generic processor without any constraint does not result in an energy efficient architecture. The proposed architecture with a partially reconfigurable decoder and an explicit bypass network is able to reach a balance between the energy efficiency and the flexibility of

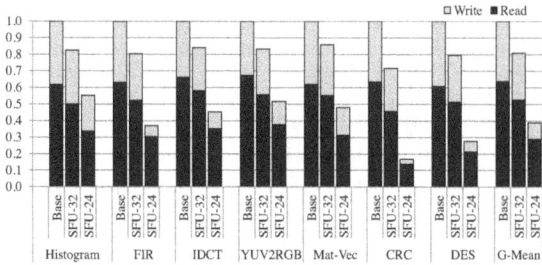

Figure 16: Normalized number of RF accesses

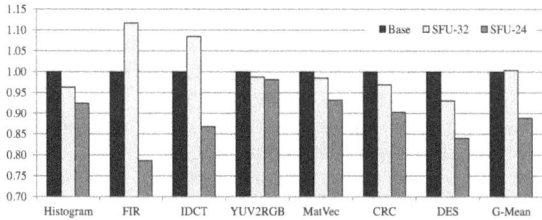

Figure 17: Normalized core energy consumption

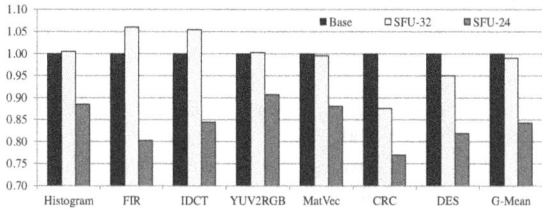

Figure 18: Normalized total energy consumption

the SFU, and it results in an architecture with high energy efficiency and good performance.

6. RELATED WORK

The use of complex operation patterns, called instruction set extension (ISE), is common in instruction set synthesis for ASIP design [15, 18, 23]. There are also studies trying to integrate such ISE in general purpose architectures [19, 20, 21], most of which focus on improving the performance.

The data bandwidth from the register file to the FUs is an important constraint in ISE design [13]. Leupers et al. introduced special register file called *internal registers* (IR) for the special instruction units [23]. The IR is an effective way of implementing application specific special instruction, but it lacks flexibility and complicates the code generation as the registers and FUs are no longer orthogonal, i.e., an FU cannot accesses arbitrary registers. Karuri et al. proposed RF clustering in single issue processor to mitigate the register file port pressure in ISE in ASIP design [14]. While reducing port pressure, the RF clustering, which is similar to what is used in clustered VLIW architectures, also makes the code generation much more complex. Pozzi and Ienne exploited the fact that pipelined SFUs do not need all operands in the same cycle to distribute register file accesses across multiple cycles [4]. This cannot be applied to the SFUs that are similar to the one used in this work. Utilizing the bypass network has been proven to be an efficient way to increase operand bandwidth and reduce register file energy in different types of architectures [7, 10, 12, 24]. Jayaseelan et al. proposed explicit forwarding to reduce register file port pressure and operand encoding cost for application specific ISE in a RISC-like datapath, which resembles the idea of explicit bypass in this work [21]. However the power model

used in [21] only considers the consumption of the register file, which is over-simplified for a complete processor design. The overall energy efficiency of the proposed architecture is not clear. Cong et al. proposed shadow registers to solve the operand bandwidth issue for supporting special instructions in a configurable processor [11]. The shadow registers are similar to explicit pipeline registers, but have more flexibility. To avoid dramatical increase of control bits, the shadow registers are hash-mapped, which may be less efficient in terms of energy. In this paper, we explored the trade-offs in utilizing bypass network for energy efficient ISE in a generic processor with compact ISA and presented detailed and realistic results. The proposed solution achieved high energy efficiency while maintaining the generality of the baseline.

In ASIP designs, dynamic instruction set configuration is often used to optimize the resource usage. The rotating instruction set processing platform (RISPP) uses a run-time reconfigurable instruction set to enable the reuse of resources for special instructions in ASIP [16]. Huynh et al. proposed dynamic instruction set configuration for a flexible reconfigurable custom instruction unit, addressing the trade-offs between area, performance and reconfiguration cost [9]. Some recent works proposed integration of special instructions for a relative wide range of applications. Clark et al. proposed integration of a configurable compute accelerator (CCA) into a general-purpose processor [19, 20]. The architecture of CCA is relatively complex and it requires up to 4 inputs and 2 outputs, as its main objective is improving performance. The control part of CCA is designed to be transparent such that the code can be executed with or without CCA. Woh et al. proposed AnySP, a wide SIMD signal processor targeting wireless and multimedia applications [17]. In AnySP the idea of operation pairs is similar to the SFU design in this work, and the operand problem is partially solved by introducing an extra small RF. In PEPSC, an architecture designed for efficient scientific computing, Dasika et al. proposed a FPU that is capable of executing up to five back-to-back operation [8]. In this work we exploited the locality of the special operation patterns in designing a partially reconfigurable decoder to achieve energy efficient integration of SFU into a RISC processor with compact ISA, which allowed the proposed architecture to improve energy efficiency substantially in different domains.

Selection and scheduling for special instructions is one of the most important parts in code generation for ASIP and many reconfigurable architectures. Kastner et al. proposed an algorithm for generating special instructions in a system with reconfigurable fabrics [22]. Guo et al. proposed a graph covering algorithm for code generation of Montium reconfigurable processor [25]. Park et al. presented a greedy algorithm for increasing the bypassing in a RISC processor [24]. In [21], integer linear programming (ILP) is used to perform bypass aware scheduling in a processor with application specific ISE. The proposed algorithm inserts register copying instructions to meet the special instruction constraints.

In this work, we proposed a novel architecture that uses special instructions to improve the energy efficiency of a generic processor with a compact ISA. Two major issues: *i)* opcode and operand encoding; *ii)* operand bandwidth to SFU are solved by using a partially reconfigurable decoder and explicit bypass network.

7. CONCLUSIONS AND FUTURE WORK

Integrating a special function unit (SFU) that executes complex operations into a generic processor for energy efficiency is not easy, as special instructions may incur large overhead, especially when the ISA is a compact one. This paper introduced an architecture for integrating SFU that supports flexible operation pair patterns in a generic processor with a compact ISA. A partially reconfigurable decoder and a software-controlled explicit bypass network are used to: i) encode extra opcodes and operands in the limited instruction coding space; ii) supply sufficient data to the special instructions without increasing the number of register file ports. We presented a compiler backend design for the proposed architecture. The compiler is able to utilize the SFU and the explicit bypass network to generate energy efficient code. Results including benchmarks from different domains demonstrate that the proposed architecture and compiler are effective: average dynamic instruction count is reduced by over 25%. The total processor energy consumption is reduced by 15.8%.

Further trade-offs between performance, energy and area are possible when extra pipeline stages in the SFU are introduced. Future work also includes supporting more complex patterns, and exploring the trade-offs between the complexity of the SFU and the energy efficiency of the processor.

8. ACKNOWLEDGMENTS

This work is supported by the Dutch Technology Foundation STW, project NEST 10346, and the Ministry of Economic Affairs of the Netherlands, project EVA PID07121.

9. REFERENCES

[1] J. R. Goodman and W. Hsu. Code scheduling and register allocation in large basic blocks. In *Proceedings of the 2nd International Conference on Supercomputing*, pages 442–452, 1988.

[2] M. Halldórsson and J. Radhakrishnan. Greed is good: approximating independent sets in sparse and bounded-degree graphs. In *Proceedings of the 26th Symposium on Theory of Computing*, pages 439–448, 1994.

[3] C. Lattner and V. Adve. LLVM: A compilation framework for lifelong program analysis & transformation. In *Proceedings of the 2004 International Symposium on Code Generation and Optimization*, pages 75–86, 2004.

[4] L. Pozzi and P. Ienne. Exploiting pipelining to relax register-file port constraints of instruction-set extensions. In *Proceedings of the 2005 International Conference on Compilers, Architectures and Synthesis for Embedded Systems*, pages 2–10, 2005.

[5] ARM Ltd. ARM Thumb Instruction Set. http://www.arm.com/.

[6] CACTI. cacti 5.3, rev 174. http://quid.hpl.hp.com:9081/cacti/.

[7] D. She et al. Scheduling for register file energy minimization in explicit datapath architectures. In *Design, Automation Test in Europe Conference Exhibition 2012*, 2012.

[8] G. Dasika et al. PEPSC: A power-efficient processor for scientific computing. In *Proceedings of the 2011 International Conference on Parallel Architectures and Compilation Techniques*, pages 101–110, 2011.

[9] H. P. Huynh et al. An efficient framework for dynamic reconfiguration of instruction-set customization. In *Proceedings of the 2007 International Conference on Compilers, Architecture, and Synthesis for Embedded Systems*, pages 135–144, 2007.

[10] J. Balfour et al. An energy-efficient processor architecture for embedded systems. *Computer Architecture Letters*, 7(1):29–32, 2007.

[11] J. Cong et al. Architecture and compilation for data bandwidth improvement in configurable embedded processors. In *Proceedings of the 2005 International Conference on Computer-Aided Design*, pages 263–270, 2005.

[12] J.Balfour et al. Operand registers and explicit operand forwarding. *Computer Architecture Letters*, 8(2):60–63, 2009.

[13] K. Atasu et al. Automatic application-specific instruction-set extensions under microarchitectural constraints. In *Proceedings of the 40th Design Automation Conference*, pages 256–261, 2003.

[14] K. Karuri et al. Increasing data-bandwidth to instruction-set extensions through register clustering. In *Proceedings of the 2007 International Conference on Computer-Aided Design*, pages 166–171, 2007.

[15] K. Karuri et al. A generic design flow for application specific processor customization through instruction-set extensions. In *Proceedings of the 9th International Workshop on Embedded Computer Systems*, pages 204–214, 2009.

[16] L. Bauer et al. Rispp: Rotating instruction set processing platform. In *Proceedings of the 44th Design Automation Conference*, pages 791 –796, 2007.

[17] M. Woh et al. AnySP: anytime anywhere anyway signal processing. In *Proceedings of the 36th International Symposium on Computer Architecture*, pages 128–139, 2009.

[18] N. Clark et al. Processor acceleration through automated instruction set customization. In *Proceedings of the 36th International Symposium on Microarchitecture*, pages 129–140, 2003.

[19] N. Clark et al. Application-specific processing on a general-purpose core via transparent instruction set customization. In *Proceedings of the 37th International Symposium on Microarchitecture*, pages 30–40, 2004.

[20] N. Clark et al. An architecture framework for transparent instruction set customization in embedded processors. In *Proceedings of the 32nd International Symposium on Computer Architecture*, pages 272–283, 2005.

[21] R. Jayaseelan et al. Exploiting forwarding to improve data bandwidth of instruction-set extensions. In *Proceedings of the 43rd Design Automation Conference*, pages 43–48, 2006.

[22] R. Kastner et al. Instruction generation for hybrid reconfigurable systems. *ACM Trans. on Design Automation of Electronic Systems*, 7(4):605–627, 2002.

[23] R. Leupers et al. A design flow for configurable embedded processors based on optimized instruction set extension synthesis. In *Design, Automation and Test in Europe, 2006*, pages 581–586, 2006.

[24] S. Park et al. Bypass aware instruction scheduling for register file power reduction. In *Proceedings of the 2006 Conference on Language, Compilers, and Tool Support for Embedded Systems*, pages 173–181, 2006.

[25] Y.Guo et al. A graph covering algorithm for a coarse grain reconfigurable system. In *Proceedings of the 2003 Conference on Language, Compiler, and Tool for Embedded Systems*, pages 199–208, 2003.

[26] P. Yu and T. Mitra. Characterizing embedded applications for instruction-set extensible processors. In *Proceedings of the 41st Design Automation Conference*, pages 723–728, 2004.

When Less Is MOre (LIMO): Controlled Parallelism for Improved Efficiency

Gaurav Chadha, Scott Mahlke, Satish Narayanasamy
Advanced Computer Architecture Laboratory, University of Michigan
Ann Arbor, MI, USA
{gauravc, mahlke, nsatish}@umich.edu

ABSTRACT

While developing shared-memory programs, programmers often contend with the problem of how many threads to create for best efficiency. Creating as many threads as the number of available processor cores, or more, may not be the most efficient configuration. Too many threads can result in excessive contention for shared resources, wasting energy, which is of primary concern for embedded devices. Furthermore, thermal and power constraints prevent us from operating all the processor cores at the highest possible frequency, favoring fewer threads. The best number of threads to run depends on the application, user input and hardware resources available. It can also change at runtime making it infeasible for the programmer to determine this number.

To address this problem, we propose LIMO, a runtime system that dynamically manages the number of running threads of an application for maximizing peformance and energy-efficiency. LIMO monitors threads' progress along with the usage of shared hardware resources to determine the best number of threads to run and the voltage and frequency level. With dynamic adaptation, LIMO provides an average of 21% performance improvement and a 2x improvement in energy-efficiency on a 32-core system over the default configuration of 32 threads for a set of concurrent applications from the PARSEC suite, the Apache web server, and the Sphinx speech recognition system.

Categories and Subject Descriptors

D.4.1 [**Operating Systems**]: [Scheduling]; D.4.8 [**Operating Systems**]: [Modeling and prediction]

Keywords

Dynamic Multi-threading, Dynamic Voltage and Frequency Scaling

1. INTRODUCTION

Due to limited success in improving efficiency of a single core and continuous technology scaling, chip multiprocessors (CMPs) have become the standard in providing greater computational power.

With CMPs, architects place together many simpler cores on a single chip instead of a single large complex core, while still working within the same power envelope. Running many cores at a lower voltage/frequency expends less energy. So much so that, even phones, tablets and other embedded devices today use multicore processors (e.g. Qualcomm Snapdragon, Apple A5, Samsung Exynos, NVIDIA Tegra 3 - all have quad-core processors). This trend, however, requires programmers to create applications with sufficient thread level parallelism (TLP) to extract performance efficiently from the CMPs.

Efficient parallel programming is a difficult task. Many mature parallel programming paradigms like OpenMP, MPI, Nvidia's CUDA, OpenCL, Intel's Ct, TBB, are now available which make this job more feasible and help programmers effectively divide their applications into many threads. However, a very important problem faced by programmers is how many threads should an application be divided into for the best performance and energy-efficiency. Spawning too few threads might lead to underutilization of CMP resources, making the application inefficient. Having too many threads, on the other hand, runs the risk of over-subscribing the resources which again causes performance and energy losses. This problem is magnified by the presence of many different CMPs with varied numbers of cores and configurations (e.g. OMAP 5 vs NVIDIA Tegra 3).

We observe that technology imposed constraints will further shift the scales in favor of running fewer threads than the number of available processor cores. One study found that with a 45 nm TSMC process, less than 7% of a 300mm^2 chip can be operated at the highest possible frequency for a constant power budget of 80W [34]. Commercial processors allow operating systems to perform Dynamic Voltage and Frequency Scaling (DVFS) [11] to increase the frequency of some cores when others are disabled while still working within a fixed power budget. This strengthens the case for using less cores for applications where a higher number of threads does not give a significant performance boost.

A common solution is to set the number of threads equal to the number of available cores. To improve upon this scheme, previous work has proposed techniques that profile applications statically to choose an appropriate number of threads [17,21,22] to improve performance by reducing communication and contention for shared resources (however, they did not consider power constraints and DVFS which would further favor running fewer threads, nor were they looking to increase energy-efficiency of the application). Unfortunately, static solutions are limited due to several reasons:

- **Different Inputs**: The same application can exhibit varying degrees of parallelism and performance scalability for different inputs. A static solution would be unsuccessful in pre-

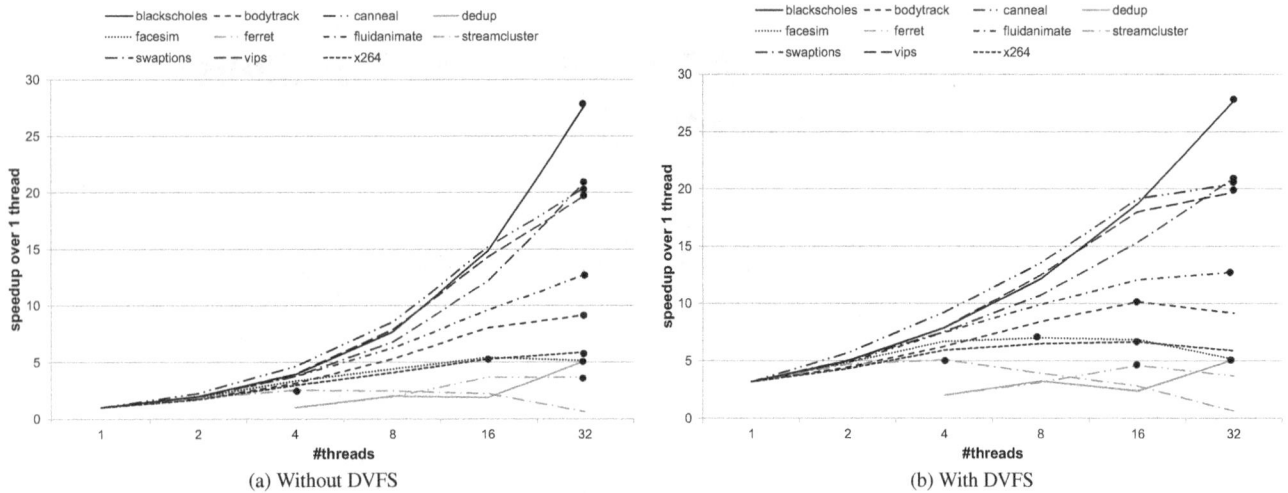

Figure 1: Speedup of Parsec benchmarks with different number of threads over their single threaded runs. These benchmarks were run on a 32 core system.

dicting the optimal number of threads for any input it has not profiled before.

- **Changing available system resources**: The amount of cache capacity and bandwidth available to an application's threads can change as other applications running in the system consume more or less of these resources. A static solution would be completely oblivious of these changes and thus incapable of adapting to these.

- **Different hardware configurations**: Many different CMPs exist with varied number of cores and cache/bandwidth configurations. A static solution will have to have profiling data on all such hardware configurations to be effective which might quickly become intractable.

- **Changing program characteristics during execution**: All of the above remaining constant, an application in itself can have many different execution phases with significantly different characteristics with regards to cache usage, bandwidth utilization, degree of parallelism available, etc. leading to different numbers of optimal threads for different phases.

For the above reasons, static solutions leave much room for improvement. In this work, we propose a lightweight run-time system, *Less Is MOre* or LIMO, which changes the number of running threads of an application dynamically, thus adapting to fine-grained changes in the best number of threads to run. The objective of LIMO is to use DVFS and variable active core count to run an application as efficiently as possible. When many threads exist and resources are not constrained, maximal threads are run at lower frequency. However, when hardware (e.g., shared L2 cache space) or software (e.g., lock variables) resources limit parallel performance, fewer threads are kept active at a higher frequency. For example, if a thread goes into a spin loop waiting on a shared variable, this thread is not doing any useful work and can be disabled by clock-gating or power-gating the core. The power saved from this core is used to boost the voltage and frequency of the remaining cores which are doing useful work. The best number of threads to use for an application particularly those with heterogeneous threads can change frequently as threads move through different code regions.

Traditional OS scheduler level techniques employing DVFS only look for CPU utilization, which if low, the core's frequency / voltage is stepped down to save power. Intel Turbo Boost goes a step

further, and apart from disabling cores as requested by the OS, it increases the frequency / voltage of the remaining active cores. This, though, is a purely reactive mechanism, coming in to effect after detecting low CPU utilization on some cores. Distinct from the above and other related works (Section 5), our work takes measures to reduce shared resource contention, employ DVFS and increase performance aggressively and pro-actively. LIMO not only disables cores with inactive / stalled threads, but also those with active threads doing useful work, when it determines that fewer threads running at higher frequency are better for performance. No prior work ever shuts down a core doing useful work. LIMO also monitors contention in shared resources (shared L2 cache and bandwidth) and pro-actively reduces the number of active cores, if they start getting oversubscribed. Detection of spin loops (such cores are disabled by LIMO) also sets this work apart. Detecting these is important as these keep the CPU utilization high without making progress in program execution, subverting the OS' attempt at shutting down cores running unproductive threads.

2. ROADBLOCKS TO SCALABILITY

It is common for programmers to create as many threads as the number of processor cores available to execute their program. If a programmer expects that some threads could block for any reason, then she might create more threads than the number of available processor cores in the hope that the operating system scheduler would help her achieve higher performance.

The motivation for our work is that greedily executing as many threads as the system permits may not always yield the best performance.

In this section, we discuss performance scalability issues for shared-memory programs and motivate our work by illustrating how executing fewer threads in some instances can yield better performance using micro-benchmarks and PARSEC benchmarks [4]. The experiments discussed in this section were conducted on a 32-core system containing four 8-core Intel Xeon X7560 processors each with 24 MB last level L3 shared cache, and 32 GB of main memory.

2.1 Lack of Parallelism

Depending on the program input, the amount of parallelism available in an application can vary. As a result, it is possible that a

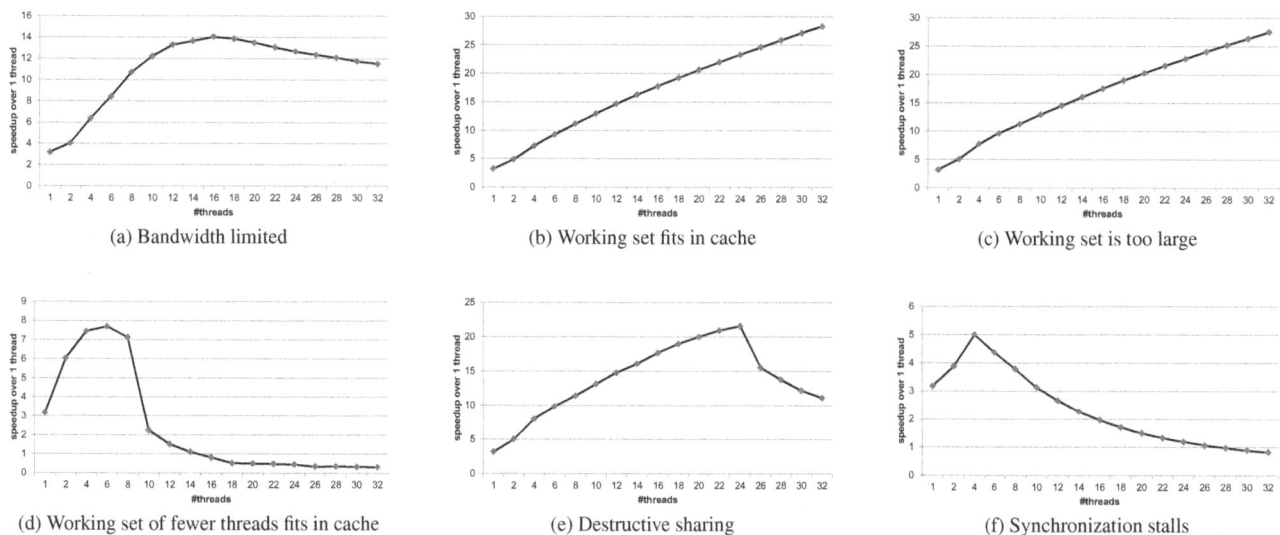

Figure 2: Speedups (with DVFS) of micro-benchmarks over their single threaded runs on a 32 core system.

programmer creates more threads than necessary to expose parallelism, which could lead to contention for shared-data, resulting in decreased performance. There are two ways in which contention for shared-data could hurt performance. One is due to the cost of synchronization waits, and the other is due to the frequent transfer of data from one processor core to another.

Lack of parallelism leads to increased synchronization wait time. If a synchronization operation is implemented as a busy-wait (e.g. using a spin loop), it causes the processor core executing the busy-wait operation to waste power which could have been utilized to increase the frequency of the other cores performing useful work. If a synchronization operation yields a processor core on wait, there is the cost of context switching that thread in and out. Thus, when more threads contend for synchronization resources, performance of the application can degrade. Figure 2(f) shows the performance of a micro-benchmark that exhibits this behavior. All the threads of the program concurrently compute factorial of a number and add it to a shared variable protected by a single lock. Performance drops when we increase the number of threads beyond four while executing on a 32-core system. When we slightly modified the same program by removing the lock, we observed the behavior shown in Figure 2(e). Performance scales slightly better, but eventually starts decreasing after 24 threads. The reason for this performance drop is not due to contention to synchronization variable, but due to the contention to shared-data that tracked the sum of all the factorials. Thus, in addition to synchronization cost, frequent transfer of shared-data between threads could also degrade performance as it could cause frequent coherence invalidations of the cache block containing the shared-data.

If parallelism in an application varies based on input, a programmer would not be able to determine the optimal number of threads to achieve the best performance. Thus, it is important for a runtime system to observe these above effects and control the number of concurrently executed threads to achieve higher performance.

2.2 Lack of Sufficient Shared System Resources

Concurrent threads contend for shared physical resources in a system. Shared caches, on-chip network and memory bandwidth are some of the heavily contended shared resources.

2.2.1 Shared Cache

To study the effects on the shared last level cache (24 MB L3 in our 32-core system), we created a micro-benchmark where each thread walks over its private array with a stride of one cache line size and summed over the elements. The working set (WS) size of a thread was controlled by fixing the maximum array index while keeping the total size of the array constant across all three cases discussed below.

- **Working set fits in cache** (Figure 2(b)): Not considering other scalability limiting factors, if the WS of an application fits in the shared cache, executing the maximum number of threads would yield best performance.

- **Working set is very large without data reuse** (Figure 2(c)): If one thread's WS size exceeds that of the last level cache (LLC) or there is no data reuse (e.g. streaming applications such as video decoders), more threads could yield higher performance by initiating more memory requests in parallel and thereby exploit memory level parallelism (MLP).

- **Working set with fewer threads fits into the shared-cache** (Figure 2(d)): It's a common case where the WS of fewer threads fits in the shared cache, but not of too many threads. It is important to have a runtime mechanism that can adapt the number of concurrent threads to attain high performance.

2.2.2 Memory Bandwidth

Applications with poor locality (such as streaming applications) require high memory bandwidth. As we had discussed earlier, these applications tend to benefit from more threads to exploit MLP. However, as their demand increases to a point when the on-chip network and memory bandwidth are saturated, then we may start to see performance degradation due to destructive interference between memory requests. Figure 2(a) shows the performance of a program that sums the values of elements spread over a very large array.

2.3 Dark Silicon Favors Fewer Threads

While it is true that with shrinking device sizes, more and more transistors can be integrated on a chip, increasing the number of

143

cores on a processor, multicore scaling has become thermal and power limited. What this means is that though manufacturers can still increase the number of cores in a processor, not all of them can be turned on at their maximum frequency at the same time [9, 34], leading to the term *dark silicon*. This limitation can be seen in commodity processors today, such as the quad-core Intel Core-i7 systems. These processors employ Intel Turbo Boost Technology [11]. However, the frequency / voltage and the number of cores active can only be changed in discrete steps.

In this work we start with disabling cores not doing useful work. The power "saved" from such cores can be used to boost the frequency of the remaining active cores, thus helping improve the performance of applications that do not show good scalability. Frequency scaling is done according to the following power equation:

$$P = ACV^2F \qquad (1)$$

where P is power, A is the activity factor, i.e. the fraction of the circuit that is switching, C is the switched capacitance, V is the supply voltage and F is the clock frequency. A is a constant, and assuming we scale voltage and frequency together,

$$P \propto F^3 \qquad (2)$$

Thus for every reduction in the number of active cores by half the frequency can be boosted by a factor of $2^{\frac{1}{3}}$. Figure 1(a) shows the performance scalability of PARSEC benchmarks for `sim-large` input on our 32-core system. The optimal number of threads that yields the best performance for an application is indicated using a black dot. We observe that only two programs, `streamcluster` and `facesim` perform better when executed with fewer than 32 threads. However, when we assume DVFS to increase the frequency of the configuration that runs fewer than 32-threads (2.268 GHz for 4-cores, 1.8 GHz for 8-cores, 1.429 GHz for 16-cores), five out of eleven applications perform better with fewer than 32-threads.

However, it is difficult to know apriori the best number of threads to execute for a given application, as it also depends on the program input and system configuration. Also, the same number of threads may not be the best answer throughout the execution of an application as it could have different phases exhibiting varied characteristics. In this paper, we propose a scheme that dynamically varies the number of active cores and their frequencies depending on parallelism available in the application and also application's demand for the shared-cache resource.

3. LIMO

LIMO is a runtime system that dynamically changes the number of running threads of an application to deliver higher performance and energy-efficiency when compared to running threads on all available processor cores. Section 2 listed in detail the different factors that affect a multi-threaded application's scalability. LIMO monitors synchronization stalls, demand for shared cache and off-chip memory bandwidth to determine the number of threads to execute. If LIMO decides to execute fewer threads than the number of available processor cores, it applies DVFS to boost the frequency of the active cores.

3.1 Design Overview

The application is allowed to create as many threads as the programmer had specified (for the applications we analyze, we create as many threads as the number of available processor cores). Thus, one thread is created per processor core. For example, in a 32-core CMP, the application starts out by running 32 threads, one on each core.

```
activeThreads ():
    for each thread t that stalls:
        disableCore (t)
        activeThreadsCount--
    for each thread t that is now ready:
        add t to readyThreadsSet
```

Figure 3: Algorithm for determining the number of threads that can do useful work

```
wsThreads ():
    if quantum instructions executed since last call:
        wsSize = WSEstimator ()
        maxWSSize = wsThreshold x L2CacheSize
        wsSizePerThread = wsSize/avgNumActiveCores
        wsThreadsCount = maxWSSize/wsSizePerThread
    else:
        wsThreadsCount is not updated
```

Figure 4: Algorithm for determining the maximum number of threads that can run without causing thrashing in the L2 cache

```
runningThreads ():
// This is called if
// 1. one or more threads are stalled or are ready
// 2. quantum instructions executed since last call
    activeThreads ()
    wsThreads ()
    maxThreadsCount =
        min (activeThreadsCount, wsThreadsCount)
    if maxThreadsCount < activeThreadsCount:
        disable (activeThreadsCount -
            maxThreadsCount) cores
        if maxThreadsCount <= thresholdLower:
            increase frequency
    else if maxThreadsCount > activeThreadsCount:
        if maxThreadsCount >=
            (activeThreadsCount +
                readyThreadsSet.size):
            enable all threads in readyThreadsSet
        else:
            enable (maxThreadsCount -
                activeThreadsCount) threads
        if maxThreadsCount >= thresholdUpper:
            decrease frequency
```

Figure 5: Algorithm for determining the number of threads to run and the frequency

LIMO monitors the threads' progress (Figure 3). If any thread stalls (in a synchronization function, blocking I/O call or is suspended), the core on which this thread was running is disabled and the number of active threads (*activeThreadsCount*) is reduced. Since this thread is clearly not making any forward progress, disabling that core saves power and leaves room in the fixed power budget to increase the voltage and frequency of the remaining cores. Similarly, when previously stalled threads can now do useful work, they are added to a set keeping track of all ready but not executing threads (*readyThreadsSet*).

To reduce contention over the shared cache, LIMO uses estimates of the working set (WS) size of the application [8] (*WSEstimator*) and keeps it from oversubscribing the cache (Figure 4). After every *quantum* of 100 million instructions, the WS of the application evaluated over the last period is used in the decision of how many threads to run over the current period. If the WS of the application is too big to fit in the shared L2 cache causing thrashing and reducing efficiency, estimates of the WS size of configurations with lower number of threads are calculated using simple linear scaling of the WS size with the number of threads (our algorithm does not need the exact WS size, and thus this estimate is adequate). We found out empirically that even a configuration whose estimated WS size exceeds the L2 cache capacity by 40% (*wsThreshold*) can deliver good performance. Using this, the algorithm calculates the maximum number of threads to run (one whose estimated WS size does not exceed the L2 cache capacity by more than *wsThreshold*), *wsThreadsCount*.

As detailed in Figure 5, at the end of each *quantum* of instructions or when a thread either gets stalled or becomes ready, the algorithm uses the minimum of *wsThreadsCount* and *activeThreadsCount* as the maximum number of threads that can run (*maxThreadsCount*). Employing DVFS, we can boost the frequency / voltage when fewer cores are active and get better performance and energy-efficiency.

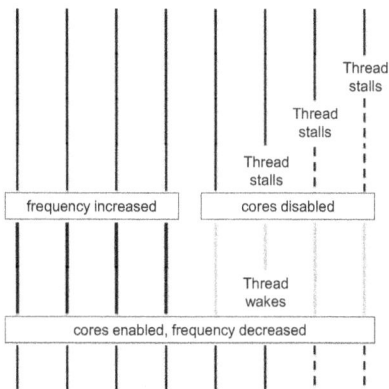

Figure 6: An example of varying the number of running cores in the case of 8 threads.

As discussed in section 2.3 in current systems voltage, frequency and the number of active cores can only be changed in discrete steps and not continuously. In our system we assume 4, 8, 16 or 32 cores can be active at a time (active core levels). This gives three core number thresholds at which the frequency and voltage can be stepped up or down. Assuming IPC/core remains constant while decreasing the number of active cores (a rather conservative assumption since the strain on shared resources decreases), and that performance scales linearly with frequency (an approximate assumption, which is adequate here since we use this only to obtain core number thresholds for our heuristic and not for any actual performance evaluation), we find out the core number thresholds using $n_1 f_1 = n_2 f_2, n_2 = \lfloor \frac{n_1 f_1}{f_2} \rfloor$ where n_i is the number of active cores and f_i the frequency at which they are run. If *maxThreadsCount* is below the next lower core number threshold for the current number of active cores (*thresholdLower*), some active or ready cores are disabled and the frequency is increased. A similar approach is employed if *maxThreadsCount* is greater than *thresholdUpper*.

For example, suppose initially all 32 threads were doing useful work. After some time, 12 of those threads are stalled, leaving only 20 threads that are doing useful work (*activeThreadsCount* = 20). If the frequency at which 32 cores run is 1.134 GHz, keeping the power budget constant and assuming we scale both voltage and frequency together and linearly, 16 cores can run at a maximum frequency of 1.429 GHz following 2. 16 cores running at 1.429 GHz will perform better than 20 cores running at 1.134 GHz. This is because, let's say IPC/core at 1 Ghz is *a*. 16 cores running at 1.429 GHz give a performance of 16 x 1.429 x a = 22.864*a*, whereas 20 cores running at 1.134 GHz give a performance of 20 x 1.134

GHz x a = 22.68*a*. Figure 6 shows an example of the mechanism for 8 threads.

We have designed and used distinct mechanisms to detect different roadblocks to scalability, because as shown in Section 2 the action to be performed (increase or decrease the number of active cores) varies with the cause of reduced performance.

3.2 Implementation

LIMO assumes support from the operating system (OS), hardware and compiler to gather required information and make decisions on the number of active cores that can achieve high performance.

LIMO relies on two specific pieces of runtime information. First, we need hardware support to determine the working set size of a thread, which would allow LIMO to determine the number of threads that can be executed without degrading the performance due to shared-cache capacity constraints.

Second, we need to know the number of threads that can make progress. The operating system already has information about threads that block by invoking a system call. If a synchronization operation is implemented as a blocking wait, then when a thread needs to stall waiting for a synchronization operation to succeed it invokes an operating system call to block itself (e.g. `sys_futex()`). However, we need additional support for detecting threads that block due to busy-wait (spin loop).

Instead of assuming runtime support to detect spin loops, we propose to use static analysis to conservatively determine loops that are likely to be spin loops. The analysis finds loops where the conditional variables can be guaranteed to be not modified within the loop body. Once the compiler finds a spin loop in an application, it transforms it to include a check in the spin loop that checks how many times the loop has iterated. If the number of iterations exceeds a threshold (three in our experiments), the compiler inserts a special system call to yield the thread to the operating system, which would inform the operating system that the thread has blocked due to a spin loop. The thread is scheduled back by the operating system after one time quantum has expired.

Thus, the OS has access to information about how many threads are in a state where they can make useful progress. Also, the OS reads from our performance counter that keeps track of the estimated working set size of the application. Based on this information, the operating system decides to activate the appropriate number of cores (based on the algorithm discussed in Section 3.1). Either when the current interval (used for WS estimation) ends, or when a thread's state changes, OS recalculates the number of cores that should be activated. It signals the hardware specifying the number of cores and the frequency they can operate at. When more threads are in the active state where they can make useful progress, the OS applies its baseline scheduling policies to ensure fairness between the threads.

We assume on-chip switching regulators [15] for DVFS, which can change a processor's power state in 30ns. We also use the working set estimator described in [8]. The memory addresses accessed (at cache line granularity) are hashed into n-buckets, represented by an n-bit vector, using a randomizing hash function. Given the fraction (f) of buckets filled, the working set size can be estimated as $\frac{log(1-f)}{log(1-\frac{1}{n})}$. This calculation is done afer every period of 100 million executed instructions. This information can be stored in special registers and read by the OS when executing the scheduling algorithm.

3.3 Fine grained monitoring

With the ability of fast change of processor power states, LIMO adapts to fine-grained changes in program characteristics. By disabling (clock-gating) the cores it exploits even small windows of energy saving opportunities and boosts performance by reducing contention in shared resources. Since the cores are clock-gated, they preserve their state and there is no need of a context switch. This facilitates fast wake up of cores (30 ns), and thus the overhead of this scheme is very low (even so, it is included in our results).

4. EXPERIMENTAL EVALUATION

We used full system simulators to design and evaluate our scheme, capturing and negotiating the effects of our scheme on the entire system.

4.1 Methodology

We used a modified timing simulator FeS2 [28], with support for shared L2 caches, that uses the full system simulator Simics [25]. FeS2 is a cycle-accurate x86 simulator with support for running multi-threaded programs. It includes a detailed processor core model. Ruby from the gem5 project [5], is used to model the memory subsystem including non-blocking caches, memory controllers, main memory, etc. We simulated the effects of the design presented in section 3 with our simulation infrastructure. Hardware modifications are proposed in our design, necessitating the use of simulators for this study.

We evaluate our scheme on benchmarks from the PARSEC benchmark suite [4], Apache HTTP server program (httpd) and Sphinx (speech recognition) from the ALP benchmark suite [20]. Blackscholes, dedup, facesim, ferret, fluidanimate, streamcluster, swaptions and vips from Parsec were run with the input simlarge. Apache server was benchmarked using Surge [2].

While we have not evaluated our scheme with multiprogram workloads, for such scenarios we propose that each application be allotted a fixed number of maximum cores that it can use, partitioning the total number of cores among applications. Within each such partition, our scheme presented in this paper can be used as it is.

Our design monitors and is capable of detecting oversubscription of shared resources (bandwidth, L2 cache) and synchronization stalls. Other factors limiting scalability were discussed in section 2. However, we did not observe all those scalability limiting factors in real benchmarks, and hence this section discusses only the ones we did.

The full system simulator used is too slow to simulate these benchmarks for the entire duration of their executions. So, first we executed the benchmarks in their entirety on Simics. Using stores as an execution progress metric, we took checkpoints at regular intervals during these runs. Thereafter, starting from these checkpoints, we ran timing simulations with FeS2 for 80 million *useful* instructions (dynamic instructions executed in user mode, excluding the ones executed in a spin loop). All statistics were cleared after 20 million such instructions, giving sufficient time for the caches to warm up. The benchmarks were sampled in this way so that we would observe different phases of execution of the program showing different characteristics. (Note: Working set estimation may not occur a second time in our simulation window of a single checkpoint. This is fine since working sets don't change significantly in shorter execution spans.)

The hardware configuration parameters are modelled after a Core-i7 system, with private L1 caches and shared L2 cache. Simics simulated a 32 core machine, running unmodified Fedora 5, kernel 2.6.15-1. While 32 cores might seem excessive for embedded devices today, the market trend shows that this might not be a distant possibility. ARM Cortex A15 (to be released this year) will have 8

cores, which is an eight fold increase in the number of cores in the last 3 years.

Following equation 2 we ran 4, 8, 16, 32 cores at 2.268, 1.8, 1.429, 1.134 GHz respectively. The simulated machine had 32 cores for all configurations simulated. To simulate 4, 8 and 16 cores, the remaining cores are simply not simulated in Simics.

4.2 Results

In this section we present our findings regarding the performance of the proposed scheme (LIMO) for the benchmarks discussed above.

We measure performance of the benchmarks in terms of *useful* instructions committed per nano second. *Useful* instructions are dynamic instructions executed in user mode, excluding the ones executed in a spin loop. Henceforth, in this paper we will refer to useful instructions as instructions. *Synchronization stalls* is the total amount of time spent by all the threads stalled in synchronization functions (e.g. waiting on a lock). If $sync_{tot}$ is the total time spent by all threads stalled in synchronization functions aggregated across all threads, $useful_{tot}$ is the total time spent by all threads doing useful work aggregated across all threads, then

$$\% sync \; stall = \frac{sync_{tot}}{useful_{tot} + sync_{tot}} \times 100$$

The benchmark ferret performs image similarity search. It has been parallelized using the pipeline model with six stages. The first and the last stage for input and output of data respectively. The middle four parallel stages are for image segmentation, feature extraction, indexing of candidate sets and ranking. The distinctively different tasks need to be done by threads from different stages makes them highly heterogeneous. Figure 7(a) shows the performance of different thread configurations for ferret in terms of instructions committed per nanoseconds (IPS). Each line in the plot has nine discrete points (nine checkpoints) representing progressing execution on the x-axis. The different configurations are 8 threads active (8t), 16 threads active (16t), 32 threads active (32t), 64 threads in the system (64t), variable number of threads active with hardware managed DVFS like Turbo Boost (TB_DVFS) and our scheme (LIMO). For all configurations except 64t, number of threads active equals number of cores active. 64t has 64 threads running on 32 cores. LIMO has a variable number of cores active varying dynamically over the course of execution of the application, and has a maximum of 32 threads in the system.

As can be seen from Figure 7(a), except LIMO, no one configuration performs the best always. 16t is best for checkpoint 5, whereas 8t performs the best for checkpoint 3. LIMO does very well and performs better than all the others for most checkpoints and as good as 8t for the remaining (checkpoints 4 and 8). Figure 7(e) shows %sync stall for ferret. For checkpoints 1, 2, 5, 6 and 7, in configurations 16t and 32t a large number of threads spend a considerable amount of time stalled because of synchronization constructs. LIMO recognizes this and disables some cores (almost all of whose threads are stalled and not doing any useful work), letting fewer cores (which can do useful work) run at a higher frequency, while still working within the same constant power budget. Figure 8 clearly shows the average number of cores active is much lower than 32 for LIMO. It can thus deliver better performance than any other configuration.

However, as discussed in section 2 synchronization stalls is just one of many factors affecting scalability. 8t performs particularly well on checkpoints 3, 4 and 9. Figure 7(c) shows 8t having markedly fewer L2 load misses on precisely those checkpoints. The working set for 8 threads fits better in the L2 cache, whereas for configurations with higher thread numbers, the working set be-

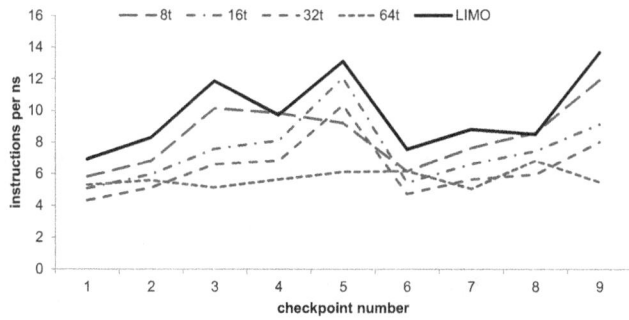

(a) Performance of ferret

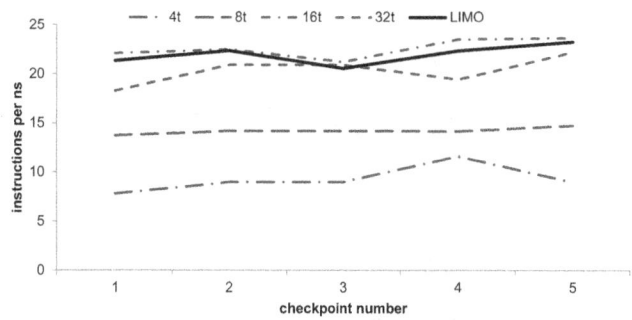

(b) Performance of httpd

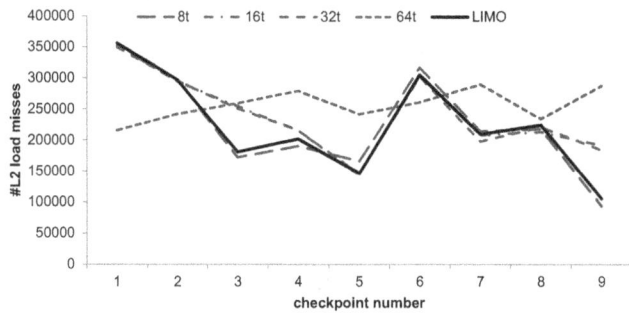

(c) L2 load misses for ferret

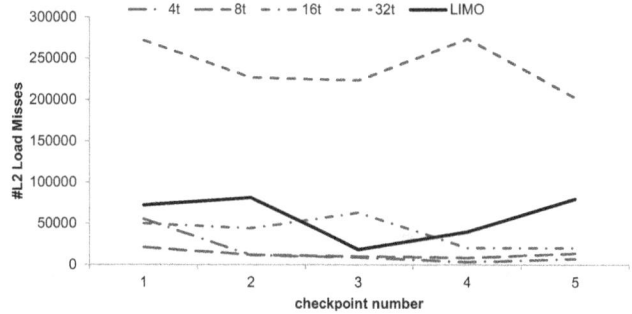

(d) L2 load misses for httpd

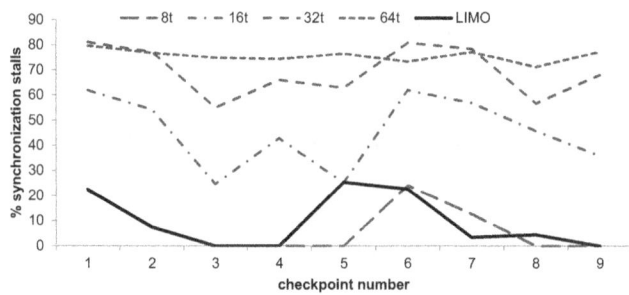

(e) Synchronization stalls for ferret

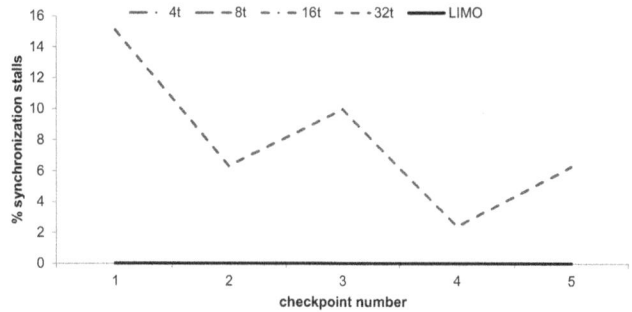

(f) Synchronization stalls for httpd

Figure 7: Execution statistics of different numbers of threads and LIMO on a 32 core system for ferret and httpd

comes too large, significantly decreasing the efficacy of the L2 cache. LIMO, having information on the working set size for one configuration, estimates that the working set of 8 threads can fit much better in the L2 cache. It, thus picks 8 threads almost all the time for these three checkpoints thus delivering high performance. Further proof of the analysis just presented can be found in the fact that high performance of LIMO accompanies very low percentage of synchronization stalls and close to the lowest number of L2 load misses among all configurations.

The Apache httpd server benchmark shows very different characteristics than ferret. It uses a work pool parallelization model, where each incoming request is handled by a different free thread. The number of threads that Apache can spawn thus limits the number of requests it can serve concurrently. For a heavy load of incoming requests, there is always work for the threads to do and consequently there are few synchronization stalls (Figure 7(f)). 16t is mostly the answer for best performance (Figure 7(b)), performing better than 32t but, unlike ferret it is not because of synchronization stalls. L2 load misses (Figure 7(d)), on the other hand,

are significantly higher for 32t compared to other configurations. The penalty imposed by such a high number of L2 load misses eclipses the benefit obtained from parallel computation with more threads. 16 threads with a higher frequency and a smaller working set are able to make much better use of the L2 cache and deliver higher performance. On an average LIMO picks close to 16 threads throughout the execution of the application and thus gets performance that is very close to 16t. However, it still tries to disable cores and increase the frequency whenever the number of active cores goes below a threshold. This ends up hurting performance slightly, compared to always keeping as many cores active as can do useful work with a maximum of 16 cores (essentially what 16t does).

In Figure 9, we show the performance of TB_DVFS, 64t and LIMO relative to 32t for all benchmarks. A system with an Intel Turbo Boost like hardware is represented by TB_DVFS. As expected, it is not able to capture the benefits of pro-active and low latency disabling of threads and subsequent change in voltage and frequency levels. However, it does well for streamcluster, since

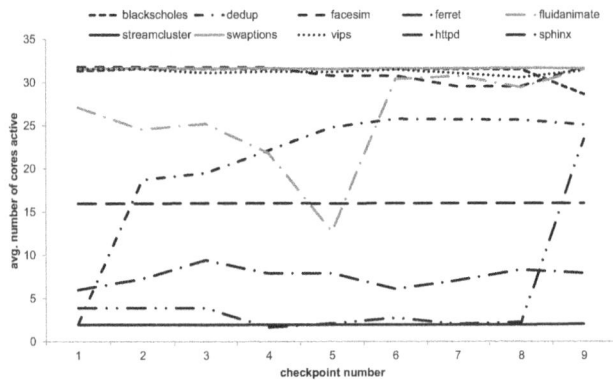

Figure 8: Number of cores active on average during the execution.

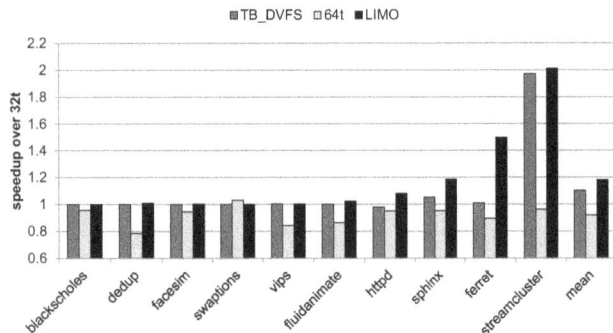

Figure 9: Speedup for all benchmarks over 32t.

this benchmark does not exhibit varying characteristics during its execution. 64t represents what the operating system could do to address synchronization stalls. In this configuration there are 2 threads per core. If a thread stalls, the OS will always have a thread that is not running anywhere else to schedule on this core. However, this can be beneficial only if the application performs better with 64 threads compared to 32, and if threads don't stall too frequently, since otherwise the context switch overhead can outweigh the benefits of switching threads on cores. However, as can be seen from Figure 9, 64t is unable to deliver any performance benefits, and in fact hurts performance in most cases. Lack of scalability, as shown in Figure 1, provides a compelling reason for this trend. While this might indicate 32 cores is over-kill for the benchmarks chosen in this study, we argue that lack of scalability is a real problem which will get exposed, if not at 32 cores with a different set of benchmarks, but definitely at a higher number of cores. For instance, if we had limited our study to a maximum of 8 cores, most of the benchmarks wouldn't have shown a problem with scalability, which gets exposed at 32 cores.

LIMO is the best performing configuration for all checkpoints (Figure 9). The benefits of this scheme get explored specially in cases where there is high variability in the execution characteristics of benchmarks, like ferret and sphinx. However, even for benchmarks like streamcluster, httpd and fluidanimate, LIMO shows benefits. The performance characteristic of streamcluster portrays an important use-case for LIMO, where the programmer is unaware of the best number of threads to run. LIMO recognizes that it runs best with 2 threads, even if there are 32 cores available.

Figure 11 shows that not only does LIMO improve performance of multi-threaded applications, but it is also highly energy efficient. Here energy efficiency is defined as (energy consumed by running 32 threads)/(energy consumed by LIMO). All energy numbers were obtained using McPat [24].

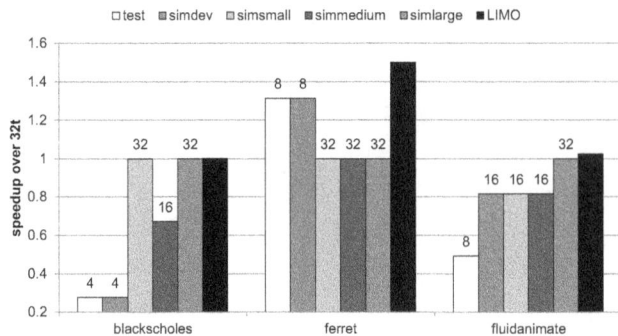

Figure 10: Speedup for blackscholes, ferret and fluidanimate over 32t. test, simdev, simsmall and simmedium are sample inputs to the benchmarks that a static profiler could be trained on. simlarge is the actual input used for final performance measurements. The numbers over corresponding bars represent the best number of threads chosen.

Figure 10 compares LIMO with possible static profiling schemes. We ran each of the parsec benchmarks with five different inputs, for 4, 8, 16 and 32 threads. Possible static profiling schemes would choose the number of threads that performed the best, as the right number of threads to run for best performance. As can be seen from Figure 10, different inputs give different answers for the right number of threads to run for best performance. LIMO performs the best regardless of the profile-guided answers. Blackscholes shows good scalability at least up to 32 threads and does not show variation in the right number of threads to run even during the course of execution of the program. Therefore, LIMO picks 32 threads to run almost all the time and performs as well as 32t. Ferret, as shown earlier shows significant variations due to both synchronization stalls and cache capacity problems. LIMO exploits the opportunities presented due to such variations and outperforms all other thread configurations. The performance of LIMO is also significant in the case of fluidanimate. Fluidanimate shows good scalability up to 32 threads, like blackscholes. However, unlike blackscholes, it exhibits variations in execution characteristics and thus the best number of threads to run, which is exploited by LIMO delivering better performance than any static choice of active threads.

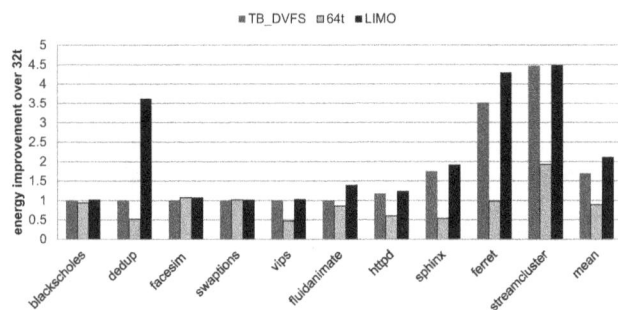

Figure 11: Energy efficiency for all benchmarks over 32t.

5. RELATED WORK

More threads do not always lead to better performance is the cornerstone of the motivation for this work. Other researchers have also observed this fact. Table 1 summarizes notable differences between LIMO and selected previous related works.

Previous works related to ours can be categorized in the following three categories.

Work	Choose optimal #threads	Variable #threads at runtime	DVFS	Heterogeneous threads	No initial/apriori profiling	Heterogeneous resources
LIMO	✓	✓	✓	✓	✓	
Li and Martinez [23]	✓	✓			✓	
Suleman, et. al. [32]	✓					
Jung, et. al. [12]	✓	✓		✓	✓	
Lee, et. al. [21]	✓					
Lee, et. al. [22]				✓		
Suleman, et. al. [31]						✓
Bhattarjee, Martonosi [3]			✓		✓	

Table 1: Comparison with related work

5.1 Variable number of threads

These previous works vary the number of active threads to run for an application.

Li and Martinez proposed a system in [23] which optimized power consumption of an application given a performance target. The optimization space is two-dimensional - varying the frequency / voltage and the number of cores. A combination of binary search algorithm along with a hill-climbing heuristic is employed to determine the best number of threads and frequency. The number of threads is varied during the execution of the program, but only to achieve the performance target with minimum power consumption on average. LIMO does not need to do a space search and varies the number of active threads during runtime to adapt to changing program characteristics and over the course of execution of the program. [23] sets a performance target to meet, which is hard to estimate. LIMO, on the other hand, tries to deliver the best performance possible while working within a constant power budget (dictated by TDP).

Feedback driven threading by Suleman, et. al. [32] presents solutions for two cases manifested by multi-threaded applications, one where the performance is limited by off-chip bus bandwidth and the other when it is limited by synchronization. They have built models to predict the right number of threads to run, which are trained through profiling initial few iterations of the loop in the application. The models used assume data parallel, homogeneous threads in the application. Similarly, Jung, Han, et. al. [12] propose a solution to mitigate shared resource contention in SMT architectures. Even though, they change the number of threads dynamically for performance, they rely on OpenMP library to automatically adjust thread decomposition and their scheme only works on data-parallel loops. These works, addressing data-parallel applications, are limited in scope compared to LIMO, which is applicable for applications with heterogeneous threads. Also, LIMO employs DVFS to boost frequency when fewer cores are active.

There has been a recent work by Lee and Kim [21], which works on a similar problem as LIMO. However, LIMO differs from their work as theirs does not employ DVFS, is for applications running on GPUs, involves exhaustive exploration of search state space and it does not change the number of threads dynamically.

Additionally, an important point that separates LIMO from the above works is that it does not assume anything about the nature of the multi-threaded application. It could be a data-parallel application with identical threads or a pipeline parallel one with heterogeneous threads, etc.

5.2 Scheduling constant number of threads

There is a large body of work concerned with thread scheduling on multi-core architectures for reducing data communication costs and contention for shared resources: caches, off-chip memory bandwidth, etc.

Thread Tailor [22] by Lee and Clark assumes there are many threads per core in a system. It colocates threads on cores such that data communication among them is minimized. Thereafter, they are run just like an OS schedules threads in an oversubscribed system. Kumar, et. al. [17] propose mechanisms (to reduce data communication costs) to be included in the compiler that helped overlap communication of data with computation by identifying the pattern of communication in the algorithm.

A significant body of work has devised schemes dictating partitioning of shared cache among cores, assigning / scheduling of threads to cores as well as frequency throttling of cores to minimize contention for the shared cache, front-side bus (FSB) and prefetching units [6, 13, 14, 16, 26, 29, 30, 33, 35].

This body of work addresses a similar problem as LIMO - reducing contention in shared resources for improved performance or energy efficiency. But they assume that all threads need to run. LIMO differs from them in that it tries to improve performance through changing the number of active threads (often running fewer than maximal threads) and boosting frequency working within a constant power budget.

5.3 Heterogeneous hardware resources

There is still other work concerned with thread scheduling and mapping to cores on heterogeneous CMPs. The work by Bhattacharjee and Martonosi [3] designs thread criticality predictors. These are used to pick the thread most critical for performance, which can then be sped up through DVFS, load shedding or allocating more resources for that thread. Suleman, et. al. [31] assumed a CMP with one big core and many smaller cores. They proposed executing all critical sections in an application on the big core, speeding up critical section execution and essentially reducing synchronization stalls. Similarly, [1, 7, 10, 18, 19, 27] propose schemes for intelligent thread scheduling and mapping on heterogeneous CMPs.

LIMO differs from these works in that it runs fewer threads with increased frequency whenever it is beneficial for performance. It also changes the active thread count dynamically.

6. CONCLUSIONS

Applications today need to be multi-threaded to take advantage of the multi-core processors seen everywhere in computing. Even though mature programming methodologies have made the difficult task of writing efficient and correct parallel programs easier, programmers still have to face the hard task of determining the number of threads to create for best performance. Too many threads can saturate shared resources, degrading performance. Too few threads might make insufficient use of the resources available making the application inefficient. In an attempt to solve the problem of finding the best number of threads to run for an application for peformance, we propose LIMO - a dynamic runtime system that monitors threads' progress, dynamically changes the number of running threads adapting to fine grained changes in application characteristics and employs DVFS to boost frequency of the active cores when some others are disabled while still working within a constant power budget.

Through this system, we aim to relieve the programmer from the job of determining the best number of threads to run. An application can be simply started with as many threads as the number of cores on any hardware and our scheme strives to deliver the best performance in so far as the number of running threads is concerned. Using mutlithreaded applications from the Parsec benchmark suite, Apache httpd server and Sphinx from ALP benchmark suite we show an average performance improvement of 21% and a 2x improvement in energy-efficiency over the default configuration of running 32 threads on a 32 core system.

7. ACKNOWLEDGMENTS

We would like to thank the anonymous reviewers for their valuable comments. This research was supported by National Science Foundation grants CNS-0964478 and CCF-0916770 and funding from Intel Corporation.

8. REFERENCES

[1] M. Annavaram, E. Grochowski, and J. Shen. Mitigating amdahl's law through epi throttling. In *Proceedings of the 32nd annual international symposium on Computer Architecture*, ISCA '05, pages 298–309, Washington, DC, USA, 2005. IEEE Computer Society.

[2] P. Barford and M. Crovella. Generating representative web workloads for network and server performance evaluation. In *Proceedings of the 1998 ACM SIGMETRICS joint international conference on Measurement and modeling of computer systems*, SIGMETRICS '98/PERFORMANCE '98, pages 151–160, New York, NY, USA, 1998. ACM.

[3] A. Bhattacharjee and M. Martonosi. Thread criticality predictors for dynamic performance, power, and resource management in chip multiprocessors. In *Proceedings of the 36th annual international symposium on Computer architecture*, ISCA '09, pages 290–301, New York, NY, USA, 2009. ACM.

[4] C. Bienia, S. Kumar, J. P. Singh, and K. Li. The parsec benchmark suite: Characterization and architectural implications. Technical Report TR-811-08, Princeton University, January 2008.

[5] N. Binkert, B. Beckmann, G. Black, S. K. Reinhardt, A. Saidi, A. Basu, J. Hestness, D. R. Hower, T. Krishna, S. Sardashti, R. Sen, K. Sewell, M. Shoaib, N. Vaish, M. D. Hill, and D. A. Wood. The gem5 simulator. *SIGARCH Comput. Archit. News*, 39(2):1–7, Aug. 2011.

[6] D. Chandra, F. Guo, S. Kim, and Y. Solihin. Predicting inter-thread cache contention on a chip multi-processor architecture. In *Proceedings of the 11th International Symposium on High-Performance Computer Architecture*, pages 340–351, Washington, DC, USA, 2005. IEEE Computer Society.

[7] L. De Giusti, E. Luque, F. Chichizola, M. Naiouf, and A. De Giusti. Amtha: An algorithm for automatically mapping tasks to processors in heterogeneous multiprocessor architectures. In *Proceedings of the 2009 WRI World Congress on Computer Science and Information Engineering - Volume 02*, pages 481–485, Washington, DC, USA, 2009. IEEE Computer Society.

[8] A. S. Dhodapkar and J. E. Smith. Managing multi-configuration hardware via dynamic working set analysis. In *Proceedings of the 29th annual international symposium on Computer architecture*, ISCA '02, pages 233–244, Washington, DC, USA, 2002. IEEE Computer Society.

[9] H. Esmaeilzadeh, E. Blem, R. St. Amant, K. Sankaralingam, and D. Burger. Dark silicon and the end of multicore scaling. In *Proceeding of the 38th annual international symposium on Computer architecture*, ISCA '11, pages 365–376, New York, NY, USA, 2011. ACM.

[10] A. Fedorova, J. C. Saez, D. Shelepov, and M. Prieto. Maximizing power efficiency with asymmetric multicore systems. *Commun. ACM*, 52:48–57, December 2009.

[11] Intel. Intel turbo boost technology in intel core microarchitecture (nehalem) based processors, 2008.

[12] C. Jung, D. Lim, J. Lee, and S. Han. Adaptive execution techniques for smt multiprocessor architectures. In *Proceedings of the tenth ACM SIGPLAN symposium on Principles and practice of parallel programming*, PPoPP '05, pages 236–246, New York, NY, USA, 2005. ACM.

[13] D. Kaseridis, J. Stuecheli, J. Chen, and L. John. A bandwidth-aware memory-subsystem resource management using non-invasive resource profilers for large cmp systems. In *High Performance Computer Architecture (HPCA), 2010 IEEE 16th International Symposium on*, pages 1 –11, jan. 2010.

[14] D. Kaseridis, J. Stuecheli, and L. K. John. Bank-aware dynamic cache partitioning for multicore architectures. In *Proceedings of the 2009 International Conference on Parallel Processing*, ICPP '09, pages 18–25, Washington, DC, USA, 2009. IEEE Computer Society.

[15] W. Kim, M. S. Gupta, G. yeon Wei, and D. M. Brooks. Enabling onchip switching regulators for multi-core processors using current staggering. In *In Proceedings of the Work. on Architectural Support for Gigascale Integration*, 2007.

[16] R. Knauerhase, P. Brett, B. Hohlt, T. Li, and S. Hahn. Using os observations to improve performance in multicore systems. *Micro, IEEE*, 28(3):54 –66, may-june 2008.

[17] R. Kumar, G. Agrawal, and G. Gao. Compiling several classes of communication patterns on a multithreaded architecture. In *Parallel and Distributed Processing Symposium., Proceedings International, IPDPS 2002, Abstracts and CD-ROM*, pages 18 –23, 2002.

[18] R. Kumar, D. Tullsen, N. Jouppi, and P. Ranganathan. Heterogeneous chip multiprocessors. *Computer*, 38(11):32 – 38, nov. 2005.

[19] R. Kumar, D. M. Tullsen, and N. P. Jouppi. Core architecture optimization for heterogeneous chip multiprocessors. In *Proceedings of the 15th international conference on Parallel architectures and compilation techniques*, PACT '06, pages 23–32, New York, NY, USA, 2006. ACM.

[20] M. lap Li, R. Sasanka, S. V. Adve, Y. kuang Chen, and E. Debes. The alpbench benchmark suite for complex multimedia applications. In *In Proc. of the IEEE Int. Symp. on Workload Characterization*, pages 34–45, 2005.

[21] J. Lee, V. Satish, K. Compton, M. Schulte, and N. S. Kim. Improving the throughput of power-constrained gpus through adaptive voltage, frequency, and core scaling. In *PACT'11*, 2011.

[22] J. Lee, H. Wu, M. Ravichandran, and N. Clark. Thread tailor: dynamically weaving threads together for efficient, adaptive parallel applications. In *Proceedings of the 37th annual international symposium on Computer architecture*, ISCA '10, pages 270–279, New York, NY, USA, 2010. ACM.

[23] J. Li and J. F. Martinez. Dynamic power-performance adaptation of parallel computation on chip multiprocessors. In *HPCA'06*, pages 77–87, 2006.

[24] S. Li, J. H. Ahn, R. D. Strong, J. B. Brockman, D. M. Tullsen, and N. P. Jouppi. Mcpat: an integrated power, area, and timing modeling framework for multicore and manycore architectures. In *Proceedings of the 42nd Annual IEEE/ACM International Symposium on Microarchitecture*, MICRO 42, pages 469–480, New York, NY, USA, 2009. ACM.

[25] P. S. Magnusson, M. Christensson, J. Eskilson, D. Forsgren, G. Hallberg, J. Hogberg, F. Larsson, A. Moestedt, and B. Werner. Simics: A full system simulation platform. *Computer*, 35:50–58, 2002.

[26] A. Merkel, J. Stoess, and F. Bellosa. Resource-conscious scheduling for energy efficiency on multicore processors. In *Proceedings of the 5th European conference on Computer systems*, EuroSys '10, pages 153–166, New York, NY, USA, 2010. ACM.

[27] T. Y. Morad, U. C. Weiser, A. Kolodny, M. Valero, and E. Ayguade. Performance, power efficiency and scalability of asymmetric cluster chip multiprocessors. *IEEE Comput. Archit. Lett.*, 5:4–, January 2006.

[28] N. Neelakantam, C. Blundell, J. Devietti, M. M. K. Martin, and C. Zilles. Fes2: A full-system execution-driven simulator for x86, 2008.

[29] M. K. Qureshi and Y. N. Patt. Utility-based cache partitioning: A low-overhead, high-performance, runtime mechanism to partition shared caches. In *Proceedings of the 39th Annual IEEE/ACM International Symposium on Microarchitecture*, MICRO 39, pages 423–432, Washington, DC, USA, 2006. IEEE Computer Society.

[30] G. E. Suh, S. Devadas, and L. Rudolph. A new memory monitoring scheme for memory-aware scheduling and partitioning. pages 117–128, 2002.

[31] M. A. Suleman, O. Mutlu, M. K. Qureshi, and Y. N. Patt. Accelerating critical section execution with asymmetric multi-core architectures. In *Proceeding of the 14th international conference on Architectural support for programming languages and operating systems*, ASPLOS '09, pages 253–264, New York, NY, USA, 2009. ACM.

[32] M. A. Suleman, M. K. Qureshi, and Y. N. Patt. Feedback-driven threading: power-efficient and high-performance execution of multi-threaded workloads on cmps. *SIGPLAN Not.*, 43:277–286, March 2008.

[33] D. K. Tam, R. Azimi, L. B. Soares, and M. Stumm. Rapidmrc: approximating l2 miss rate curves on commodity systems for online optimizations. In *Proceeding of the 14th international conference on Architectural support for programming languages and operating systems*, ASPLOS '09, pages 121–132, New York, NY, USA, 2009. ACM.

[34] G. Venkatesh, J. Sampson, N. Goulding, S. Garcia, V. Bryksin, J. Lugo-Martinez, S. Swanson, and M. B. Taylor. Conservation cores: reducing the energy of mature computations. In *Proceedings of the fifteenth edition of ASPLOS on Architectural support for programming languages and operating systems*, ASPLOS '10, pages 205–218, New York, NY, USA, 2010. ACM.

[35] S. Zhuravlev, S. Blagodurov, and A. Fedorova. Addressing shared resource contention in multicore processors via scheduling. In *Proceedings of the fifteenth edition of ASPLOS on Architectural support for programming languages and operating systems*, ASPLOS '10, pages 129–142, New York, NY, USA, 2010. ACM.

Lazy Cache Invalidation for Self-Modifying Codes

Anthony Gutierrez   Joseph Pusdesris   Ronald G. Dreslinski   Trevor Mudge
Advanced Computer Architecture Laboratory
University of Michigan
Ann Arbor, MI, USA
{atgutier, joemp, rdreslin, tnm}@umich.edu

ABSTRACT

Just-in-time compilation with dynamic code optimization is often used to help improve the performance of applications that utilize high-level languages and virtual run-time environments, such as those found in smartphones. Just-in-time compilation introduces additional overhead into the instruction fetch stage of a processor that is particularly problematic for user applications—instruction cache invalidation due to the use of self-modifying code. This software-assisted cache coherence serializes cache line invalidations, or causes a costly invalidation of the entire instruction cache, and prevents useful instructions from being fetched for the period during which the stale instructions are being invalidated. This overhead is not acceptable for user applications, which are expected to respond quickly.

In this work we introduce a new technique that can, using a single instruction, invalidate cache lines in page-sized chunks as opposed to invalidating only a single line at a time. Lazy cache invalidation reduces the amount of time spent stalling due to instruction cache invalidation by removing stale instructions on demand as they are accessed, as opposed to all at once. The key observation behind lazy cache invalidation is that stale instructions do not necessarily need to be removed from the instruction cache; as long as it is guaranteed that attempts to fetch stale instructions will not hit in the instruction cache, the program will behave as the developer had intended.

Categories and Subject Descriptors

B.3.2 [**Memory Structures**]: Design Styles—*Cache memories*; C.0 [**Computer Systems Organization**]: Hardware/software interfaces; C.1.3 [**Processor Architectures**]: Other Architecture Styles—*High-level language architectures*

General Terms

Design, Performance

Keywords

Architecture, Self-Modifying Code, Software-Assisted Coherence, Instruction Caching

1. INTRODUCTION

Instruction fetch is a critical component for achieving high performance in modern microprocessors, if there are no instructions to execute, progress cannot be made and the complex structures of out-of-order processors will not be efficiently utilized. Nearly two decades ago it was shown that real-world applications suffer from excessive instruction cache miss rates and fetch stalls [23]. More recent studies have shown that, for both smartphone and server workloads, instruction fetch performance has not improved, despite increasing instruction cache sizes and improved branch predictor accuracy [13, 18]. Real-world applications have become increasingly reliant on high-level languages, shared libraries, OS support, just-in-time (JIT) compilation and virtual machines. And, while the use of these modern programming constructs has made programmers more efficient and applications more portable, their use has led to increased code size and complexity, which stresses instruction fetch and memory resources.

Smartphone application developers in particular rely on portability and rapid development to ensure their applications are relevant and profitable. Similarly, smartphone manufacturers rely on the most popular applications being available on their platform to drive sales. This symbiotic relationship has led both application developers and smartphone manufacturers to rely on platforms that support high-level languages and virtual machines. Google's Android platform [12], which is currently the most popular smartphone OS on the market today [10], relies on the Dalvik virtual machine [9]. Android applications are written in Java and the Dalvik virtual machine now supports JIT compilation [5].

To overcome some of the performance loss incurred by the use of high-level programming constructs, JIT compilation with dynamic code optimization is often used [2]. JIT compilation uses dynamic code profile information to optimize and recompile code as it runs. This use of self-modifying code requires that the instruction cache be kept explicitly coherent. However, most systems, particularly mobile systems, do not support hardware coherence in the instruction cache. The cost of allowing the instruction cache to snoop the bus on every memory write is inefficient, because most memory writes are data, not instruction writes. To ensure that the instruction cache is kept coherent, and that stale instructions are not fetched, JIT compilers use software-assisted coherence. In other words, the JIT compiler is responsible for managing the invalidation and writeback of the affected cache lines. There are two mechanisms by which stale instructions can be invalidated in the instruction cache:

- **Invalidate the entire instruction cache.** The benefit of this approach is that all stale instructions are invalidated with a single instruction, making this a very simple approach. The downside is that many useful instructions will be needlessly invalidated from the instruction cache, thus increasing instruction miss rates.

- **Invalidate a single line at a time.** This approach has the benefit of keeping most of the useful instructions in the instruction cache, which prevents excessive instruction cache miss rates. The downside of this approach is that the invalidations are serialized, which prevents useful work from being performed for the period during which invalidation occurs.

The pseudo code shown in listing 1 shows how software-assisted cache coherence is performed on most modern architectures that have Harvard caches and no hardware coherence for the instruction cache. Each instruction cache line in the range is invalidated in serial. Each invalidate also accesses the cache and performs tag lookups for each line in the range. No useful instructions can be fetched or executed during this period, primarily because of the possibility of fetching an instruction that is meant to be invalidated.

Listing 1: **Serial invalidation algorithm.**

```
invalidate_range(start, end) {
    addr = start

    while(addr < end) {
        dcache_clean(addr)
        addr += line_size
    }

    //ensure dcache_clean() completes
    barrier()

    addr = start
    while(addr < end) {
        icache_inv(addr)
        addr += line_size
    }

    //ensure icache_inv() completes
    barrier()

    //flush pipeline to remove any
    //stale instructions
    flush_pipeline()

    return
}
```

As noted above, both of these approaches have their strengths and weaknesses. Invalidating the entire instruction cache trades off invalidation precision for simplicity and very fast invalidation. Single line invalidation trades off simplicity

and fast invalidation for very precise instruction invalidation. As shown in [14] evicting blocks from the code cache in medium sized chunks often leads to the best performance for the systems hardware caches. Thus, it is desirable to have a technique that can provide very fast invalidation, e.g., by using a single instruction, and that can do so without invalidating the entire instruction cache. However, it should be noted that we are not proposing to replace single line or full cache invalidation; we are proposing a new technique that gives more flexibility when choosing the granularity at which to invalidation cache lines.

In this work we make the following contributions:

- We analyze several benchmarks that make heavy use of JIT compiled code: the DaCapo benchmarks [4], a suite of open-source Java benchmarks, as well as BBench [13, 11], a web-page rendering benchmark. We show that these benchmarks invalidate a large number of cache lines and that they do so frequently.

- We develop a technique that provides the speed of entire instruction cache invalidation (it can be done with a single instruction), but gives much better precision (invalidations are on a per-page basis as opposed to invalidating the entire instruction cache), thus preventing long periods when useful work cannot be completed because cache maintenance operations are being performed.

Our analysis of BBench and the DaCapo benchmarks reveals that cache line invalidations frequently come in large bursts, always in multiples of an entire page, and that they happen frequently; a burst can happen as frequently as every 1,100 instructions for some benchmarks. We show that the fraction of time during which cache line invalidations occur can be decreased significantly ,which allows the CPU to more quickly resume doing useful work.

In section 2 we detail the design of our lazy cache invalidation hardware. In section 3 we discuss our experimental methodology. Section 4 outlines our experimental results. Finally, section 5 discusses related works and section 6 concludes and discusses future work.

2. LAZY CACHE INVALIDATION

In this section we outline our lazy cache invalidation technique. In particular, we describe a new instruction, which we call *pginv*, that can be used to invalidate an entire memory page instantaneously. We also describe the baseline hardware on which our design is implemented, as well as the additional hardware we introduce to support the *pginv* instruction.

2.1 Code Version Numbering

Lazy cache invalidation associates a version number with each piece of instruction data. Whenever new code is written its version is incremented. The version number is stored both per cache line and per TLB entry. The version number of a cache line is compared with the version number in its corresponding TLB entry in parallel with its tag lookup, and if the versions do not match, the access is considered a miss and the line will be fetched from memory.

The version number is maintained in the TLB; any time a new cache line is brought into the cache it is given the

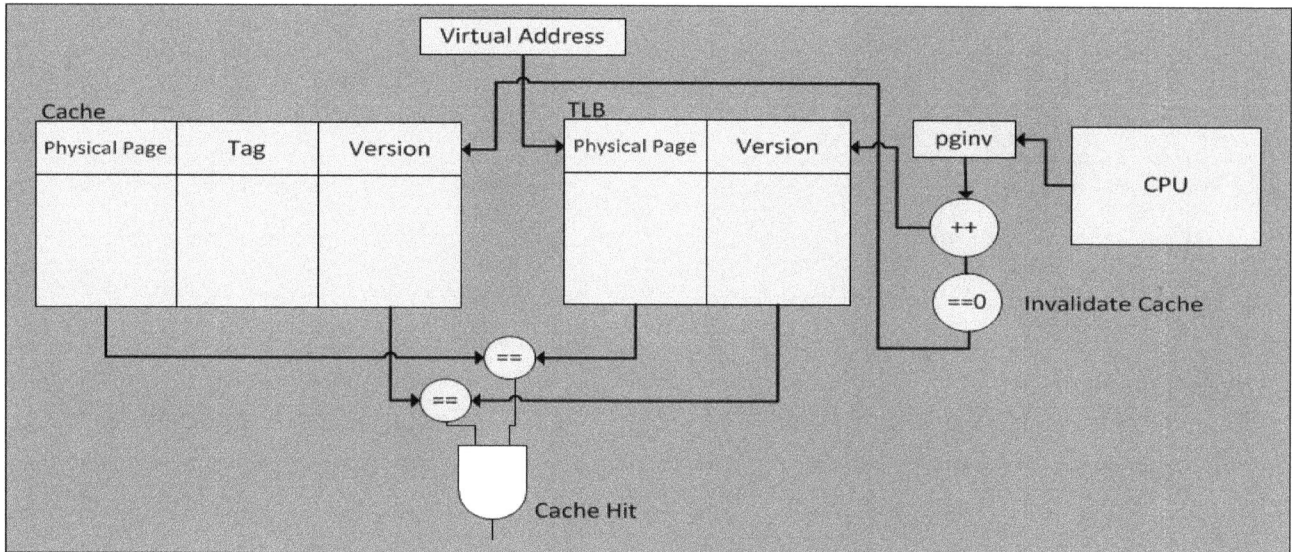

Figure 1: **Lazy cache invalidation hardware and implementation.** The CPU writes the virtual address to the *pginv* register. This increments the version in the TLB. If a page fault occurs the system waits until the new entry is loaded in the TLB before incrementing the version. If the version number overflows, the entire instruction cache will be invalidated.

version number of its corresponding TLB entry. If the version number rolls over the entire cache must be invalidated; this is to prevent the version number from rolling over to a version that matches a stale cache line. It is possible to avoid flushing the entire cache when the version number rolls over by using the existing page invalidate methodology, i.e., by invalidating each line serially. However, this option is not explored in this work because version number rollover is rare, even for small version number sizes as we will show in section 4.

The use of a TLB entry allows for more efficient instruction cache invalidation, primarily because each TLB entry is associated with an entire page of memory (typically 4kB). This allows a reasonable amount of code to be written without having to invalidate the entire cache or invalidate 4kB of data serially. Because JIT compilers often optimize at the granularity of basic blocks [2, 15], the instructions they write exhibit high spatial locality, making all lines written by self-modifying code likely to be on the same page.

Maintaining the version number in the TLB implies that the version number values do not need to be unique across TLB entries. Because physically tagged cache lines are assumed, each cache line maps to exactly one page thus, misreading stale data due to version aliasing is impossible. Storing the version number in the TLB has the added benefit of allowing the version number to be stored in the page table along with its corresponding TLB entry when it gets evicted; this prevents lazy cache invalidation from having to needlessly invalidate each line contained within the page pointed to by a new TLB entry, or in the worst case invalidate the entire cache.

2.2 Page Invalidate Instruction

To implement the lazy cache invalidation technique we propose a simple ISA modification, the introduction of a new instruction we call *pginv*, to perform page invalidation.

The *pginv* instruction operates in a similar fashion to an instruction that invalidates a single cache line, such as the ARM *mcr icimvau* [1] system control instruction, i.e., it takes as an argument the virtual address of a memory location to be invalidated. However, unlike the *mcr icimvau* instruction it is meant to invalidate the entire page that contains the line for the given address.

Because the *pginv* instruction is responsible for invalidating an entire page, the virtual address it receives must be aligned with a page boundary. It can be left up to the JIT compiler to ensure that the address it sends to the *pginv* instruction is page aligned but, for our implementation we make it the responsibility of the *pginv* instruction to align the address properly. This is typically done by masking off certain bits of the virtual address, making page alignment simple.

The instruction operates by accessing the TLB and, if the corresponding entry is present, it increments the version number in the TLB entry. If the TLB entry is not present a page fault is triggered, just as it would on any TLB miss, and once the fault is handled it attempts to increment the version number again. This effectively invalidates all cache lines contained within this page because their versions will no longer match. Note that existing invalidation techniques, such as using *mcr icimvau* also require a TLB lookup, and can also cause a page fault, because they also use the virtual address of a cache line.

2.3 Baseline Hardware

Lazy cache invalidation is most applicable when the base architecture uses Harvard style caches, separating data and instructions, with no hardware coherence for the instruction cache. In addition, the system should use virtual memory with physically tagged caches. TLBs must be used to cache virtual address translations. These features describe the vast majority of modern architectures. The JIT com-

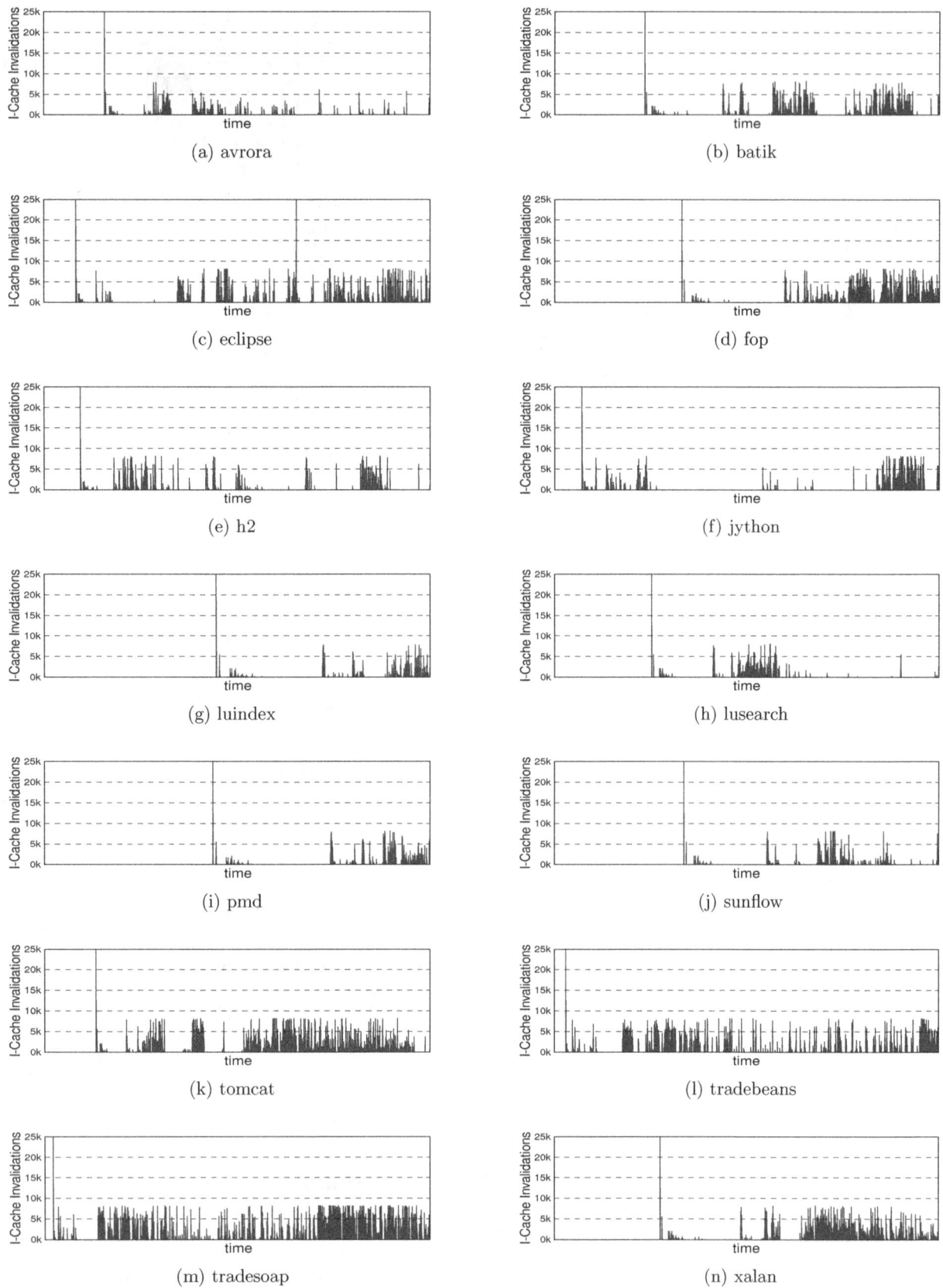

Figure 2: **Instruction cache invalidations in the DaCapo benchmarks.** The number of i-cache invalidation instructions are sampled every 100,000 instructions. Most of the DaCapo benchmarks perform cache invalidations throughout the entire course of the execution, and they do so in bursts.

154

Frequency	1GHz
Cache Line Size	32 bytes
L1 Cache Size	32kB split I/D
L1 Associativity	4-way set associative
L2 Cache Size	1MB shared L2
L2 Associativity	8-way set associative

Table 1: **Hardware parameters.** The memory system parameters for our simulation framework. The memory system is modelled after an ARM Cortex-A9 processor, a current state-of-the-art smartphone core.

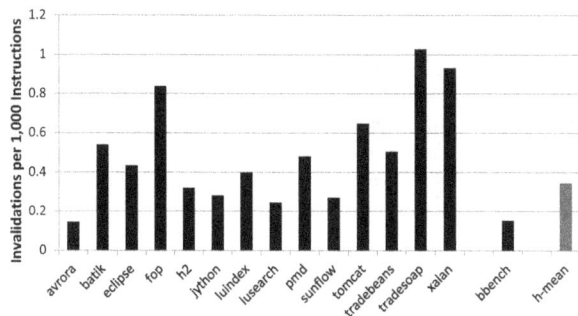

Figure 3: **Invalidation rates.** The rate of invalidate instructions per 1,000 instructions.

piler must issue invalidate instructions manually whenever it writes new code to the cache. This is typically how JIT compilers behave because most systems use Harvard caches with no hardware coherence in the instruction cache.

3. EXPERIMENTAL METHODOLOGY

In this section we describe our simulation framework and detail our experimental methodology. We first describe and analyze the benchmarks, in particular their use of cache invalidation instructions. Finally we describe the kernel modifications necessary to support lazy cache invalidation, as well as our implementation of lazy cache invalidation in the gem5 simulator.

3.1 Benchmarks

For our experiments we use several JIT compiled benchmarks. The DaCapo benchmarks [4] and BBench [13, 11], which we describe in further detail in the following sections. These benchmarks represent realistic and diverse user applications. They are primarily written in Java, make heavy use of shared libraries, OS support, JIT compilation, and state-of-the-art virtual machines.

3.1.1 BBench

BBench [13, 11] is a new web-page rendering benchmark that is designed to automate web browsing in such a way that makes a browser a useful interactive workload. It comprises several of the most popular web-pages, all of which utilize modern web technology such as CSS, HTML, flash, and multi-media. We run BBench on the native Android browser using Android version 2.3, Gingerbread [12], using version 2.6.35.8 of the Android kernel from Linux-ARM [17]. The version of Android we use has only simple modifications

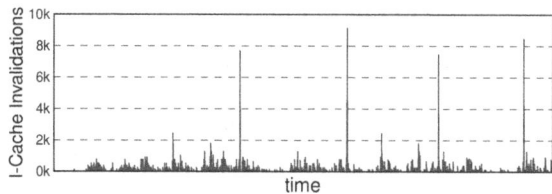

Figure 4: **Instruction cache invalidations in BBench.** The number of i-cache invalidation instructions are sampled every 100,000 instructions. BBench continuously performs cache invalidate operations and cache invalidations appear in repetitive bursts.

made to it, thus it is interactive and contains a full graphical user interface, which is accurately rendered by gem5.

Because the Android browser is part of the Android filesystem large portions of it are written in native C code; however, it still exhibits a fairly large amount of self-modifying code as we will show. Android applications are typically written entirely in Java and so we expect that most Android applications will exhibit even larger amounts of self-modifying code than our BBench results show.

3.1.2 DaCapo Benchmarks

The DaCapo benchmarks [4] are an open-source collection of realistic Java applications. We run all of the DaCapo benchmarks on Ubuntu 11.04 using version 2.6.38.8 of the Linux kernel. The Ubuntu disk image we used for our experiments is a modified version of a disk image created using the RootStock utility [22]. The disk image is *headless*, meaning it does not utilize a graphical user interface.

We installed the client side embedded Java runtime environment version 1.6.0.30 from Oracle [19] on our Ubuntu disk image and all DaCapo benchmarks were run on this virtual machine. We attempted to run the DaCapo benchmarks on the OpenJDK version of the Java virtual machine however, because of a known bug in OpenJDK for ARM, most of them were not able to run.

3.2 Simulation Environment

We use the gem5 [3] full-system simulator for all of our experiments. Our system parameters are shown in table 1. All of our experiments are run in full-system mode using the ARM ISA. We use the *simple timing* CPU model to obtain traces of all invalidation instructions executed. We use the ARM ISA because it is the most popular architecture used in modern smartphone and tablet devices. gem5 supports a large portion of the ARMv7 ISA; however, it does not currently provide support for the ARM *mcr icimvau* instruction, as well as several of the associated cache maintenance operations and registers. We first needed to provide support for the cache maintenance portions of the ARMv7 ISA relevant to our study. This includes the *mcr icimvau* instruction and the *mcr icialluis* instruction (these instructions invalidate a single cache line by its virtual address and the entire instruction cache respectively) as well as the cache size identification register *CCSIDR* and the cache type register *CTR* [1]. These registers provide information about cache line sizes in the system, which is necessary for the proper execution of the cache invalidation instructions.

3.3 Analysis of JIT Compiled Codes

We collected instruction traces from both the DaCapo benchmarks and BBench to determine how frequently they perform cache maintenance instructions. Figure 3 reports the overall number of invalidation instructions per 1,000 instructions executed. As can be seen in this figure some of the benchmarks execute cache line invalidate instructions as often as 1 for every 1,000 instructions executed, and on average 0.48 instructions per 1,000 are invalidations. This may not seem like a large number, but when you consider that these instructions are not performing useful work related to program execution this number is significant. And as we will see, these instructions often come in large bursts, which stall instruction fetch for a significant period of time.

In figure 2 we show the rate of invalidations per instruction sampled over time. The samples are taken for every 100,000 instructions executed. This graph shows that for many of the DaCapo benchmarks invalidations come in bursts, and that invalidation happens continuously throughout the entire run of the benchmark. Figure 4 shows the same data for BBench. Similar to the DaCapo benchmarks, BBench performs invalidations continuously throughout the entire run. However, unlike the DaCapo benchmarks, it happens less frequently (note the different y-axis values for the BBench graph).

From our analysis we discover that invalidations always happen in multiples of 128, which is exactly the size of a page. It is also shown that over 99% of the time invalidations occur in bursts of exactly 128, or one page. There are very few bursts of 2, 3, or more pages occurring. This shows that JIT compilers typically invalidate an entire page at a time, making lazy cache invalidation an ideal solution to speed up the invalidation process. Even if JIT compilers invalidate at granularities that are different than a page our technique is still useful; we are proposing that our technique offers a useful complement;

Figure 5 reports the median number of instructions between bursts of invalidations. This figure shows that for the DaCapo benchmarks bursts of invalidations occur as often as every 1,300 instructions, and for BBench every 20,000 instructions. We report the median, as opposed to the average, because a few very long periods without invalidations skew the average.

To quantify the effect that cache invalidation has on performance we define a segment of program execution we call a *work segment*, which we further divide into two segments, a *useful work* segment, and a *cache maintenance* segment. Based on our analysis we discover that for the DaCapo benchmarks the median size of a *cache maintenance* segment is roughly 30% of the *work segment*, and for BBench it is around 2.5%. As we will see in section 4, lazy cache invalidation reduces the fraction of time the *work segment* spends in a *cache maintenance* segment to almost nothing for both the DaCapo benchmarks and for BBench. In effect, lazy cache invalidation makes the effect of cache maintenance negligible.

3.4 Implementation of Lazy Cache Invalidation

The implementation of lazy cache invalidation required some modification to the Linux kernel source as well as gem5. In the following sections we describe the changes we made to our simulation framework to support lazy cache invalidation.

3.4.1 Kernel Source Modifications

We had to add support for our *pginv* instruction into the Linux kernel source. We profiled our benchmarks and discovered that all of the cache invalidation instructions executed were called from the *v7_coherent_user_range()* function. This function is defined in the ARM specific kernel assembly source and operates identically to the code shown in listing 1.

Because this function always invalidates a page at a time, we only needed to remove the loop around the i-cache invalidate instruction and insert our *pginv* instruction. We use the start address given to the *v7_coherent_user_range()* function as the input to the *pginv* instruction.

Although we never observed anything other than page-sized chunks being invalidated in the benchmarks we ran, it is possible for some codes to invalidate at some other granularity. There are two possibilities for ranges that do not invalidate only a single page:

- The range is less than a page and all lines in the range are contained within the same page.

- The range is greater than a page, or spans multiple pages.

In both cases we invalidate every page (using our lazy cache invalidation technique) touched by the range of addresses given. We do this by aligning the addresses to a page and calculating how many pages are touched by using the size of the range. This may cause needless invalidations, thereby increasing cache miss rates slightly, but it keeps implementation overhead low. Misaligned ranges are unlikely however, as is evident from the fact that we never observed a single occurrence of a misaligned range invalidation.

3.4.2 ISA Modification in gem5

To add support for lazy cache invalidation we needed to add a new instruction called *pginv* to the ISA. To do this we modified gem5 to add the functionality for the *pginv* instruction. We mimicked our implemenation of the *mcr icimvau* instruction by making *pginv* an ARM *mcr* system control register instruction [1].

When the instruction is encountered it triggers a write to the *pginv* control register. The value written to the register is the virtual address of the page being invalidated. Once the value is written the system control mechanism takes control and is responsible for aligning the virtual address to a page, looking up the corresponding TLB entry, and incrementing the version number of the page. If a page fault is encountered the instruction waits until it is handled and, once the proper entry is brought into the TLB, the version number is incremented. The *pginv* instruction automatically detects a version number overflow and is responsible for invalidating the entire instruction cache.

4. RESULTS

In this section we discuss the results of our lazy cache invalidation technique. In particular we discuss how lazy cache invalidation reduces the time spent performing *cache maintenance* segments. We also examine how frequently the entire instruction cache needs to be invalidated due to

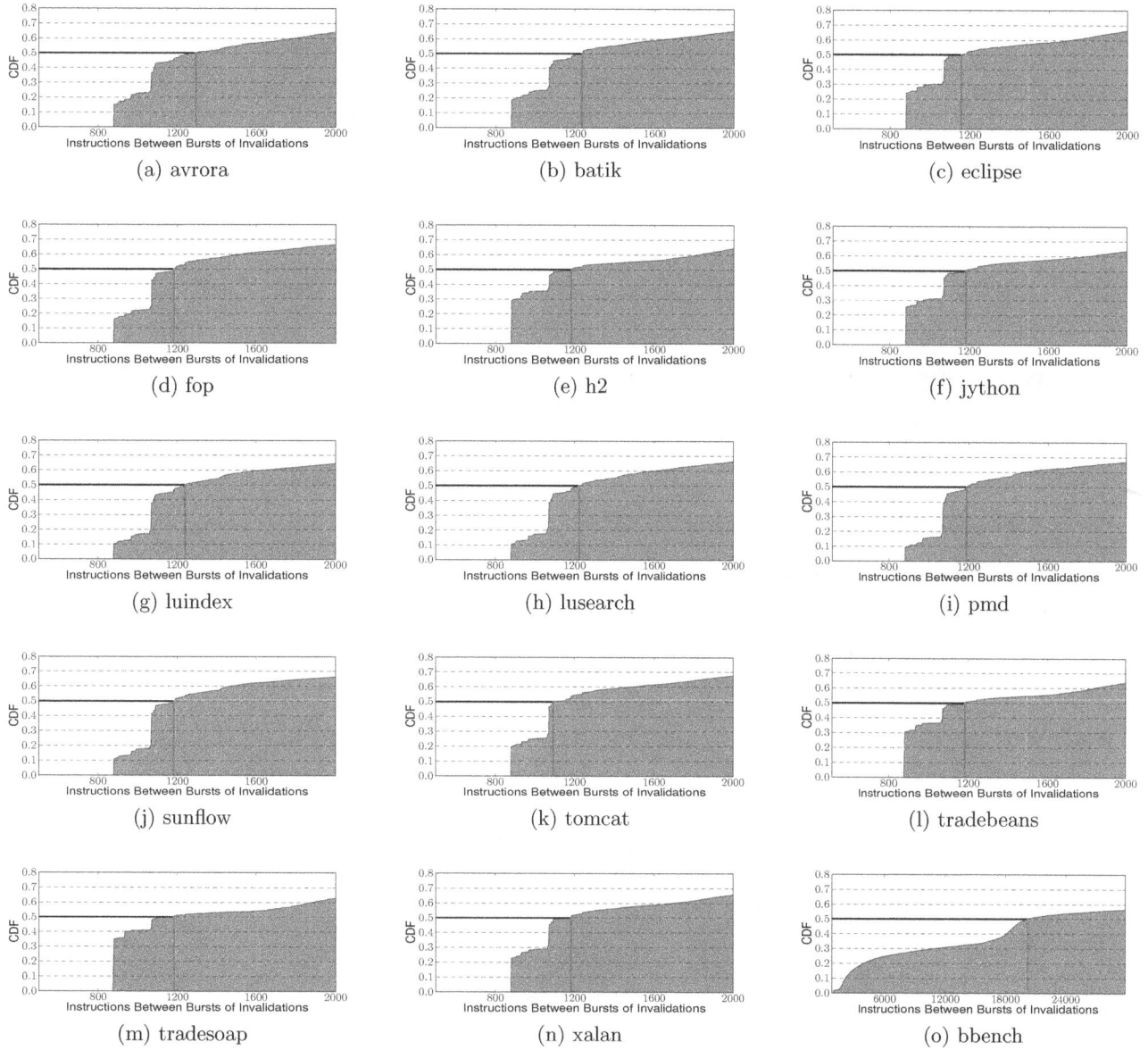

Figure 5: **Number of instructions between invalidation periods.** The CDF of the number of useful instructions executed between each invalidation period. The number of instructions between invalidation periods is small. In most cases fewer than 1,300 instructions are executed between *cache maintenance* segments for the DaCapo benchmarks. For BBench around 20,000 instructions are executed between *cache maintenance* segments.

(a) Number of Overflows

(b) Number of Instructions Between Overflows

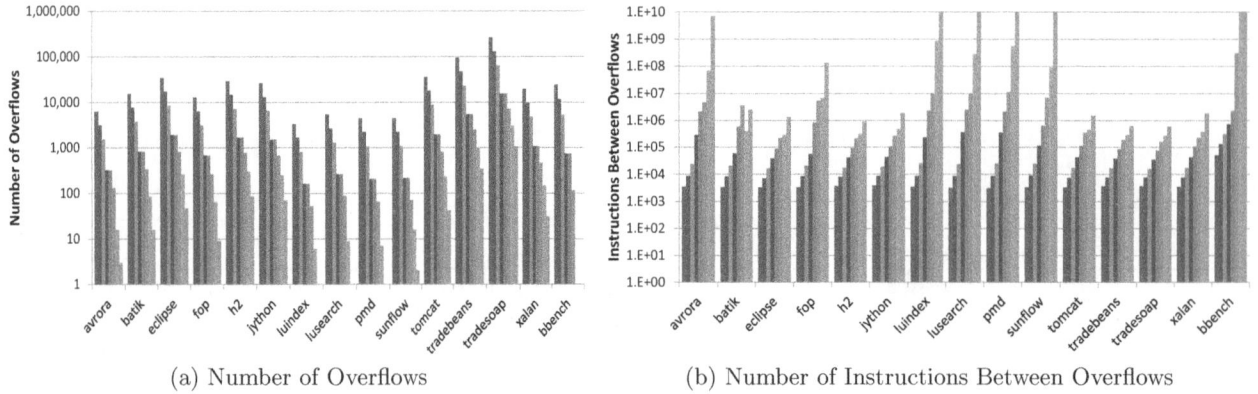

Figure 7: **Sensitivity of overflows to counter size.** The bars represent, from left to right, version counter sizes of one through eight bits respectively. Note that the y-axis is logarithmic. For BBench, overflows never occur for a version counter size of seven or eight bits, therefore the distance between overflows is essentially infinite. This figure shows that overflows do not occur often, even for modest sized version counters. When overflows occur they happen far apart.

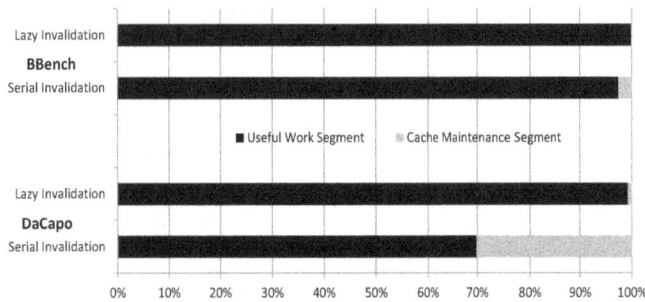

Figure 6: **Ratio of useful instructions to cache maintenance instructions.** The median size of a *cache maintenance* segment is reduced by around 30% for the DaCapo benchmarks, and around 3% for BBench.

version number overflow, as well as how close overflows occur in time.

4.1 Cache Invalidation Speedup

Figure 6 shows the fraction of time a *work segment* spends executing a *cache maintenance* segment. Again, we report the median segment sizes because a few very large data points skew the average. As can be seen from this figure the common case is to spend a significant fraction of time executing cache invalidate instructions. Because we are replacing segments of 128 instructions with a single instruction *cache maintenance* segments practically vanish.

During the *cache maintenance* segment the CPI for application instructions is essentially zero. Because the *cache maintenance* segments are always multiples of 128, and these periods are frequent, this can hinder the responsiveness of the application. As the authors in [20] have shown user satisfaction is highly correlated to application responsiveness. In [20] the authors used frequency as the metric by which to judge performance, but CPI and frequency are highly correlated.

4.2 Sensitivity of Overflows to Counter Size

One possible overhead of the lazy cache invalidation technique is forced invalidations caused by version number overflow, therefore the size of the version number counter is a critical design decision. Because of power and area constraints in smartphones, the version numbers cannot be too large. We measure how often each page is invalidated by a *pginv* instruction to determine how many times an overflow occurs. We also calculate how many instructions occur between version number overflows. If overflows occur too often, or if they occur in bursts, the benefits of lazy cache invalidation will be negated.

Figure 7a shows the median number of version number overflows for each benchmark and figure 7b reports the median number of instructions between version number overflows. For each benchmark the bars in the graph represent, from left to right, the results for counter values of one through eight bits respectively. As can be seen from these graphs, version number overflows are rare even for modest counter sizes. Forced cache invalidations are sparse, and infrequent enough that a version number size of five bits does not affect performance. Assuming 32kB caches with 32B lines, a five bit version counter would incur less than 2% overhead in the instruction cache.

5. RELATED WORK

This sections discusses previous work on software-assisted cache coherence. Techniques that propose efficient methods of cache coherence, as well as methods to speed up invalidation are discussed.

5.1 Software-Assisted Cache Coherence

Much of the previous work on software-assisted cache coherence focuses on using software as the primary means for maintaining cache coherence. This work was relevant in an era where hardware-based cache coherence was impractical and inefficient for large numbers of cores. However, modern technology scaling has led to multiple CPUs on a single chip and very fast and efficient busses, which makes snoopy-based hardware coherence the primary means for providing cache coherence in modern microprocessors. However, because data are not written to the instruction cache in Harvard architectures, and because instruction writes are not as common as data writes, snoopy-based coherence for instructions is still not efficient for instruction caches. Due to energy constraints, mobile systems in particular cannot afford to allow the instruction cache to snoop the bus on every write. The lack of efficiency for snoopy-based coherence in instruction caches makes software-assisted coherence ideal for self-modifying codes.

5.1.1 Compiler Directed Techniques and Reference Marking

Knowing which lines to invalidate, and when to invalidate is of particular interest in software-assisted cache coherence techniques. Reference marking [16] is a compile-time method that segments program into chunks called *epochs*. Each memory reference in an epoch is marked as uncacheable if it is read by more than one processor and it is written by by at least one processor. To ensure that no stale data are read the cache is flushed at the end of every epoch. The work in [6, 8] improves on this approach by selectively invalidating marked references, as opposed to indiscriminately invalidating all marked references. Compile-time information is used to determine whether or not a reference is guaranteed to be up-to-date. These techniques reduce the overhead of cache invalidation by removing unnecessary cache invalidations; however, they do not speed up cache invalidations when they must occur (invalidations will still be carried out serially in these implementations).

5.1.2 Coherence Based on Data Versioning

Versioning has also been used to speed up the invalidation process and to dynamically identify which cache lines need to be invalidated [7, 21]. In [7] the authors propose associating each cache line with two counters. One is called a *birth version number (bvn)* and is stored on the cache line, the other is called a *Current Version Number (CVN)*, which is a global (per CPU) counter that represents the current version of the line. The *bvn* counter is checked against the *CVN* on each access, if the *bvn* is less than the *CVN* the access misses.

The *bvn* is set to the *CVN* when it is loaded from global memory and is incremented on each write. Compile-time analysis is used to determine when a *CVN* can change and it is updated based on this analysis and with minimal hardware and CPU communication. The *CVN* values are stored in global storage called the *version manager* and are obtained by indexing into the *version manager* with a unique ID number that is associated with each cache line. If any single *CVN* overflows all *CVNs* must be reset and the cache must be flushed; this ensures that a *CVN* doesn't rollover and match an invalid *bvn*.

In [21] the authors proposed using a version number, called a *one time identifier (OTI)*, for each line and its associated TLB entry. They have a global counter called the *OTI register* that contains the current value of the *OTI*. Each time a TLB entry is loaded into the TLB it reads from the *OTI register* and the *OTI register* is incremented. On every cache access to a page marked as shared the *OTI* value for the line is compared with the *OTI* value for the associated TLB entry. If the *OTI* values do not match the access is considered a miss and the line is fetched from memory.

It is assumed that the OS provides functionality to detect when a page is write-shared and when control is passed, e.g., by marking a page as shared when a lock within it is acquired, and marking it as not shared when the lock is released. After a page is released, the corresponding TLB entry must be marked as invalid, which implicitly changes its *OTI* value, to ensure that all subsequent accesses to this page are fetched from memory; this guarantees that no stale data are read. If the *OTI register* ever rolls over the entire cache must be flushed to prevent stale data from being misread as valid.

Our lazy cache flushing technique differs from these versioning approaches in both how we control updating of the version and how the version affects invalidation. In particular [7] increments the counters much more frequently, i.e., any time it is possible that a shared variable is modified. It also requires significantly more storage dedicated to version counters because it requires two counters per cache line, and they are typically larger than the counter values we use (to prevent frequent overflows), whereas we require only one counter per cache line and one per each TLB entry (which typically has far fewer entries than the cache). This overhead is not efficient for the instruction cache because it is not written to nearly as much as the data cache.

In [21] an entire page is invalidated each time a new TLB entry is brought into the TLB. This does not necessarily happen due to writes to a shared region, it could also happen when a TLB entry is evicted due to a conflict with another TLB entry. This increases needless invalidations and also accelerates counter rollover. Because the counter is global it also gets updated more frequently, which requires it to be larger. Because lazy cache invalidation targets self-modifying code, we only need to invalidate a page when instruction data are being written. Also, because lazy cache invalidation allows each TLB entry to maintain its own counter, the counters need not be as large. With lazy cache invalidation the counter for each TLB entry gets incremented only when that specific page is touched and not when any TLB entry is touched.

6. CONCLUSIONS

Software developers often make use of high-level languages and other advanced features when designing their software. The use of these high-level constructs improves the entire software development design flow. Smartphone sales are driven by the availability of applications that users care about, so the use of these high-level features will become more prominent going forward. Because of this fact, it is important for architects to design their CPUs with support for such high-level features.

In this work we have profiled several realistic user applications and we have demonstrated that these applications perform frequent, lengthy bursts of cache maintenance instructions. We have developed a new technique for fast cache invalidation, which we call lazy cache invalidation, that is shown to reduce the fraction of time a JIT compiler spends performing cache maintenance operations, and it does so with negligible overhead. By allowing a JIT compiler to invalidate an entire page with a single instruction we reach a good balance between the selective invalidation of the single line invalidation approach, and the speed of the entire cache invalidate instruction. We complement single line and whole cache invalidation and provide JIT compiler developers another option for cache invalidation that is often more efficient.

There are areas where further optimizations can be made to support self-modifying code. One effect of cache line invalidation is increased cache misses. The JIT compiler is responsible for writing back the newly written instructions out of the data cache into the second level cache—or memory if there is no second level cache. One of the consequences of this is that instruction fetch will miss on these instructions. However, because these instructions are being rewritten by the JIT compiler it is likely that they are frequently executed and will be fetched in the near future. Instruction pre-fetching of lines frequently written by the JIT compiler could reduce some of these instruction fetch misses.

The writeback of new instructions from the data cache is a serial, two-step process. The JIT compiler first writes the new instructions to the data cache, then it writes them back. Because the JIT compiler knows when it is writing instruction data, one possible optimization to this process is to require that instruction writes be write-through. This would allow the the JIT compiler to avoid the second step in the process, i.e., writing the instructions back.

Acknowledgments

This work was supported by a grant from ARM Ltd. In particular we would like to thank Ali Saidi and Stuart Biles. Special thanks to Korey Sewell for his advice on gem5. We would also like to thank the anonymous reviewers for their feedback.

References

[1] ARM. *ARM Architecture Reference Manual*, ARM v7-A and ARM v7-R edition.

[2] J. Aycock. A Brief History of Just-In-Time. *ACM Computing Surveys*, 35(2):97–113, 2003.

[3] N. Binkert, B. Beckmann, G. Black, S. K. Reinhardt, A. Saidi, A. Basu, J. Hestness, D. R. Hower, T. Krishna, S. Sardashti, R. Sen, K. Sewell, M. Shoaib, N. Vaish, M. D. Hill, and D. A. Wood. The gem5 Simulator. *SIGARCH Computer Architecture News*, 39(2):1–7, Aug. 2011.

[4] S. M. Blackburn, R. Garner, C. Hoffmann, A. M. Khang, K. S. McKinley, R. Bentzur, A. Diwan, D. Feinberg, D. Frampton, S. Z. Guyer, M. Hirzel, A. Hosking, M. Jump, H. Lee, J. E. B. Moss, A. Phansalkar, D. Stefanović, T. VanDrunen, D. von Dincklage, and B. Wiedermann. The DaCapo Benchmarks: Java Benchmarking Development and Analysis. In *the Proceedings of the 21st annual ACM SIGPLAN conference on Object-Oriented Programming Systems, Languages, and Applications (OOPSLA)*, pages 169–190, 2006.

[5] D. Bornstein. Dalvik JIT.

[6] H. Cheong and A. V. Vaidenbaum. A Cache Coherence Scheme With Fast Selective Invalidation. In *the Proc. of the 15th Annual International Symposium on Computer Architecture (ISCA)*, pages 299–307, 1988.

[7] H. Cheong and A. Veidenbaum. A version control approach to cache coherence. In *the Proc of the 3rd International Conference on Supercomputing (ICS)*, pages 322–330, 1989.

[8] H. Cheong and A. Veidenbaum. Compiler-Directed Cache Management in Multiprocessors. *IEEE Computer*, 23(6):39–47, June 1990.

[9] D. Ehringer. The Dalvik Virtual Machine Architecture.

[10] Gartner. Market Share: Mobile Communication Devcies by Region and Country, 3Q11.

[11] gem5. BBench Source.

[12] Google. Android Source.

[13] A. Gutierrez, R. Dreslinski, T. Wenisch, T. Mudge, A. Saidi, C. Emmons, and N. Paver. Full-System Analysis and Characterization of Interactive Smartphone Applications. In *the Proc. of the 2011 IEEE International Symposium on Workload Characterization (IISWC)*, pages 81–90, 2011.

[14] K. Hazelwood and J. E. Smith. Exploring Code Cache Eviction Granularities in Dynamic Optimization Systems. In *the Proc. of the International Symposium on Code Generation and Optimization (CGO)*, pages 89–99, 2004.

[15] K. Ishizaki, M. Kawahito, T. Yasue, M. Takeuchi, T. Ogasawara, T. Suganuma, T. Onodera, H. Komatsu, and T. Nakatani. Design, Implementation, and Evaluation of Optimizations in a Just-In-Time Compiler. In *the Proc. of the ACM 1999 Conference on Java Grande*, pages 119–128. ACM, 1999.

[16] R. L. Lee, P. C. Yew, and D. H. Lawrie. Multiprocessor Cache Design Considerations. In *the Proc. of the 14th Annual International Symposium on Computer Architecture*, pages 253–262, 1987.

[17] Linux-Arm.org. Armdroid Kernel.

[18] D. Meisner. *Architecting Efficient Data Centers*. PhD thesis, University of Michigan, 2012.

[19] Oracle. Embedded java runtime environment.

[20] A. Shye, Y. Pan, B. Scholbrock, J. S. Miller, G. Memik, P. A. Dinda, and R. P. Dick. Power to the People: Leveraging Human Physiological Traits to Control Microprocessor Frequency. In *the Proc. of the 41st annual IEEE/ACM International Symposium on Microarchitecture (MICRO)*, pages 188–199, 2008.

[21] A. J. Smith. CPU Cache Consistency with Software Support and Using "One Time Identifiers". In *the Proc. of the Pacific Computer Communications Symposium*, pages 153–161, 1985.

[22] Ubuntu. Rootstock.

[23] R. Uhlig, D. Nagle, T. Mudge, S. Sechrest, and J. Emer. Instruction Fetching: Coping with Code Bloat. In *the Proc. of the 22nd annual International Symposium on Computer Architecture (ISCA)*, pages 345–356, 1995.

Static Task Partitioning for Locked Caches in Multi-Core Real-Time Systems *

Abhik Sarkar, Frank Mueller
North Carolina State University
mueller@cs.ncsu.edu

Harini Ramaprasad
Southern Illinois University
harinir@siu.edu

ABSTRACT

Locking cache lines in hard real-time systems is a common means to ensure timing predictability of data references and to lower bounds on worst-case execution time, especially in a multi-tasking environment. Growing processing demand on multi-tasking real-time systems can be met by employing scalable multi-core architectures, like the recently introduced tile-based architectures. This paper studies the use of cache locking on massive multi-core architectures with private caches in the context of hard real-time systems. In shared cache architectures, a single resource is shared among *all* the tasks. However, in scalable cache architectures with private caches, conflicts exist only among the tasks scheduled on one core. This calls for a cache-aware allocation of tasks onto cores. Our work extends the cache-unaware First Fit Decreasing (FFD) algorithm with a Naive locked First Fit Decreasing (NFFD) policy. We further propose two cache-aware static scheduling schemes: (1) Greedy First Fit Decreasing (GFFD) and (2) Colored First Fit Decreasing (CoFFD). This work contributes an adaptation of these algorithms for conflict resolution of partially locked regions. Experiments indicate that NFFD is capable of scheduling high utilization task sets that FFD cannot schedule. Experiments also show that CoFFD consistently outperforms GFFD resulting in lower number of cores and lower system utilization. CoFFD reduces the number of core requirements from 30% to 60% compared to NFFD. With partial locking, the number of cores in some cases is reduced by almost 50% with an increase in system utilization of 10%. Overall, this work is unique in considering the challenges of future multi-core architectures for real-time systems and provides key insights into task partitioning with locked caches for architectures with private caches.

Categories and Subject Descriptors

D.4.7 [**Operating Systems**]: Organization and Design—*real-time systems and embedded systems*; D.4.1 [**Operating Systems**]: Process Management—*scheduling*; B.3.2 [**Memory Structures**]: Design Styles—*cache memories*

---

*This work was supported in part by NSF grants CNS-0905181 and CNS-0905212.

General Terms

Design, Experimentation.

Keywords

Real-Time Systems, Multi-Core Architectures, Timing Analysis.

1. INTRODUCTION

Multi-core architectures have become prevalent in embedded system design. This is evident from the variety of multi-core processors available today, such as the 4-core MPCores and Cortex processors from ARM, the 8-core P4080 PowerPC from Freescale and the 64-core TilePro64 from Tilera [1], which find applications in power control systems, satellites and network packet processing. However, hard real-time system designers have been skeptical in adopting these architectures. Unpredictability of multi-core caches have been a significant contributing factor to this skepticism.

Research on cache contention has primarily considered shared caches. This simplifies the problem as all tasks are considered to be contending for the shared cache space. Most contemporary research aims at optimizing the analysis on aforementioned systems [6, 9]. Such schemes become inapplicable to scalable multi-cores, such as shown in Figure 1.

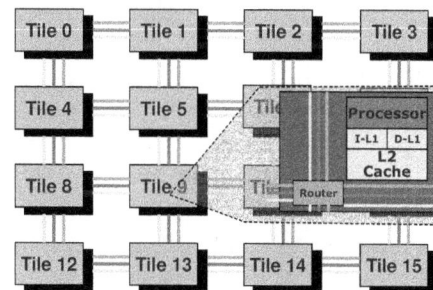

Figure 1: Tile-based Architecture

These architectures use private L1+L2 caches. Any task allocation algorithm on such architectures requires prior knowledge of each task's Worst Case Execution Time (WCET). However, the WCET of a task obtained by static cache analysis depends on cache analysis of all other tasks on a particular core. In this work, it is assumed that private L2 caches are large enough with high associativity (16-32 ways) to hold the data space and instructions of hard real-time tasks. This simplifies the analysis of L2 caches as any access to the L2 cache is a hit after a compulsory miss on warm-up. Thus, a tighter upper bound on the Worst Case Execution Time (WCET) can be established by modeling references resolved at the L2 level as hits after the warm-up phase of the first job execution in a periodic task system. Still, the access latency of L2 caches is an order of magnitude higher than that of L1 caches so that bounds on WCET are not as tight as they could be. To further tighten WCET bounds, cache locking of selected lines in L1 can be employed on scalable multi-core platforms.

In general, cache locking techniques provide predictability to a task's cache access behavior. Cache locking can be realized at various granularities. Studies on uni-processor cache locking have assumed the entire L1 cache to be locked [16, 17]. Another study on cache locking for shared caches has assumed locking individual cache lines [19]. Locked caches on uni-processors identify sets within a single cache way for a given task set to improve predictability and, indirectly, utilization/response time of tasks while ensuring schedulability on a single core. In contrast, our work extends to scalable multi-core architectures where tasks are statically partitioned. Our work focuses on distributing tasks over disjoint cores while considering their locked state. A real-time system developer may choose to lock a set of cache lines to tighten WCET bound. This work uses these tightened WCET bounds to statically allocate tasks on a disjoint set of cores.

Prior literature on uni-processor locking techniques focuses on filling a single cache way while reducing the overall utilization of a core. Reduction of the system utilization can be achieved by placing all tasks with conflicting locked cache regions on different cores on scalable architectures. However, such a scheme would consume a large number of cores and result in under-utilization of computing resources. Also, multiple cache ways per L1 cache can be dedicated to locking. Hence, the objective of allocating tasks on scalable multi-cores has to be balanced between the following objectives:

1. Reduction of the number of cores; and
2. Reduction of the overall system utilization.

Static task partitioning has been considered as a viable scheduling option for real-time tasks on multiple cores. Such scheduling schemes aim at minimizing the number of cores for a set of tasks with given worst-case execution time (WCET). However, partitioning tasks with locked cache regions involves resolving the conflicts between locked regions of different tasks.

One of the most commonly used partitioning algorithm is the First Fit Decreasing (FFD) algorithm. First, we extend this algorithm with an approach called Naive Locked FFD (NFFD). Prior to allocation, NFFD decides to use cache locking for tasks that have prohibitively high utilization without locking. It avoids conflict analysis among locked regions by placing each locked task on a different core before allocating unlocked tasks using FFD. We call this algorithm cache-unaware as it avoids any form of analysis on locked cache regions. Then, we develop and evaluate two cache-aware partitioning algorithms: (1) Greedy First Fit Decreasing (GFFD), and (2) Colored First Fit Decreasing (CoFFD). GFFD tries to allocate tasks onto a minimum number of cores [3]. This scheme lacks prior information on the number of cores of a concrete processor but rather reasons abstractly about the minimum number of cores of a hypothetical processor design. CoFFD, a more sophisticated scheme, exhibits a novel approach based on graph coloring that delivers task partitioning. In contrast to GFFD, CoFFD initially assumes a given number of cores for an architecture. The algorithm then tries to allocate a given task-set onto the fixed number of cores. In case of failure,

the number of cores is incremented and the attempt to allocate tasks to cores is repeated. If the objective is to achieve minimum utilization, tasks should be allocated with all candidate regions locked as this lowers their WCET.

Table 1 depicts a comparison of the number of allocated cores for different task sets of 32 tasks using FFD, NFFD, GFFD and CoFFD on an architecture that uses system parameters shown in Table 2. We consider two utilizations for each task: one with locking for all the regions specified by the developer (u_{locked}) and another without locking any of those regions ($u_{unlocked}$). A task is termed to be of high, medium and low utilization when ($0.55 > u_{locked} \geq 0.40$), ($0.40 > u_{locked} \geq 0.25$) and ($0.25 > u_{locked} \geq 0.15$), respectively. The first column depicts the number of tasks in the task sets. The remaining columns show the number of cores consumed by the task set under FFD, NFFD, GFFD and CoFFD, respectively. We observe that FFD fails to allocate high utilization task sets as $u_{unlocked}$ exceeds the utilization bound of 1 for such tasks. This is because it forces regions to be unlocked while the other policies allow locking. NFFD performs better than FFD for low utilization tasks as well. The table shows that the number of cores allocated by cache-aware schemes is significantly lower than the allocations performed by cache-unaware schemes. As the objective is to minimize the number of cores, the two algorithms are adapted to consider both u_{locked} and $u_{unlocked}$ during allocation. The algorithms select one of these versions to avoid lock conflicts while ensuring that utilization constraints are met. We observe that CoFFD consistently results in allocating fewer cores than GFFD. Task sets composed of high utilization tasks allocate fewer cores under CoFFD with at most 3% higher system utilization than GFFD. For low utilization task sets, CoFFD allocates fewer cores and lowers system utilization by up to 40% over GFFD.

Table 1: Locking and Conflict Analysis for 32 Tasks

Number of Tasks	Number of Cores Required			
	FFD	NFFD	GFFD	CoFFD
High util.	Failed	32	22	20
Med. util.	31	31	21	20
Low. Util.	23	22	14	12

We also propose a mechanism to resize locked regions so that they become partially unlocked. This scheme is applicable when the programmer can provide the maximum number of references to a locked cache line. The two algorithms, GFFD and CoFFD, were adapted to exploit this per-line reference frequency information, based on which they choose whether to retain the lock of a line or unlock it due to lock conflicts of lines between disjoint tasks. We observe that such a mechanism can further reduce the number of allocated cores. It may even allow GFFD to perform at par with CoFFD. Overall, we provide key insights into task partitioning with locked caches for large-scale multi-core architectures with private caches.

Summary of contributions: This research makes the following contributions in the context of hard real-time systems with cache locking:

1. This work is the first to employ locked caches on massive multi-core architectures for hard real-time systems.
2. We propose GFFD, an allocation scheme that partitions a given set of tasks with conflicts in their locked cache regions so that the number of allocated cores is kept low. This algorithm is further adapted to resolve

conflicts by (i) unlocking entire task or (ii) resizing locked regions.

3. We propose Colored First Fit Decreasing (CoFFD) that (i) derives task allocations for a given number of cores resulting in a feasible schedule, (ii) enhances a coloring algorithm to deliver balanced allocation and (iii) reduces the number of cores relative to Greedy First Fit Decreasing (GFFD).

4. We propose a novel mechanism that allows tasks to resolve conflicts by partially unlocking the locked regions and inflating their WCETs accordingly. This method aims at improving the schedulability of task sets on a given number of cores when resolution of conflicts by partial unlocking result in lower system utilization than unlocking an entire task.

2. RELATED WORK

In the past decade, there has been considerable research promoting locked caches in the context of multi-tasking real-time systems. Static and dynamic cache locking algorithms for instruction caches have been proposed to improve system utilization in [16, 15]. Several methods have been developed to lock program data that is hard to analyze statically [20]. Further techniques have been developed for cache locking that provide performance comparable to that obtained with scratchpad allocation [17]. Recently, cache locking has also been proposed for multi-core systems that use shared L2 caches [19]. This trend is a strong proponent of cache locking as a viable solution in future real-time system designs on multi-cores.

Choffnes et al. have proposed migration policies for multicore fair-share scheduling [7]. Their technique strives to minimize migration costs while ensuring fairness among the tasks by maintaining balanced scheduling queues as new tasks are activated. Calandrino et al. propose scheduling techniques that account for co-schedulability of tasks with respect to cache behavior [2, 4]. Their approach is based on organizing tasks with the same period into groups of cooperating tasks. All these methods improve cache performance in soft real-time systems. Li et al. discuss migration policies that facilitate efficient operating system scheduling in asymmetric multicore architectures [11, 12]. Their work focuses on fault-and-migrate techniques to handle resource-related faults in heterogeneous cores and does not operate in the context of real-time systems. Eisler et al. [8] develop a cache capacity increasing scheme for multicores that scavenges unused neighboring cache lines.

Paolieri et al. [14] have proposed TDMA-based bus and L2 cache access to improve predictability on multi-core architectures. Their work focuses on supporting hard real-time applications on multi-cores but assumes shared L2 caches with contention due to accesses by different tasks. Ouyang et al. [13] have proposed extending Quality of Service support to mesh-based interconnects but their study is limited to the on-chip network traffic.

3. SYSTEM DESIGN

In this section, we describe our system architecture and assumptions to WCET analysis for this study. The objective of this work is to best utilize a private cache architecture. This corresponds to the current trend in potentially mesh or tile-based multi-core designs. Tile-based architectures consist of a large number tile processors (cores). Each

tile consists of an in-order processor, a private L1, a private L2 cache and a router (see Figure 1). Each tile acts as a node on a mesh interconnect. Recent work has added Quality-of-Service (QoS) policies to mesh-interconnects [13]. We have identified these trends as the driving force for the simplification of our system. We assume an architecture that has private caches and has a QoS-based interconnect. We assume that the first level of cache allows a certain number of ways of the associative cache to be locked as shown in Figure 2. We also assume that the L2 caches are large enough with high associativity so that the address space of allocated hard real-time tasks on a core fit within the L2 cache. Thus, we assume that the off-chip references occur only while accessing sensory data, which accounts for a very small fraction of the total references. Also, these systems can have inclusive or non-inclusive L2 caches. With inclusive caches, the locked regions in L1 need to be locked in L2 as well.

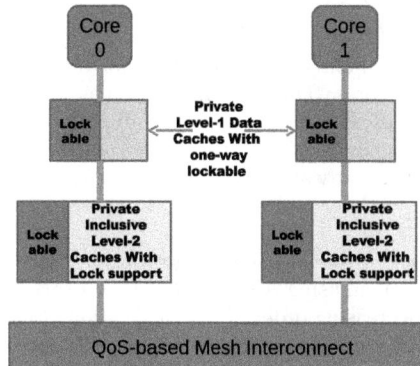

Figure 2: A Lock-based Architecture

Our algorithms are applicable to a system considering both data and instruction caches. However, for the simplicity of analysis we assume that instruction references for hard real-time tasks are all hits at the first level of cache. We also assume that loads to the lines that have not been locked in the L1 cache bypass the L1 cache (as in a previous research work [10]). This allows cores with lower core utilization to co-schedule non-real-time tasks along with hard real-time tasks without affecting the deterministic behavior of the latter. Such hybrid execution of application tasks has been considered in recent research [14]. We assume that a hard real-time task can only lock one cache line per set. Thus, for a 8KB L1 cache with an associativity of two, a hard real-time task can lock up to 4KB of cache content.

We assume that all hard real-time tasks are periodic. Each task's deadline is the same as its period, i.e., an invocation of a task's job has to finish before its next invocation. We further assume that the system runs a scheduler per core. Each of these schedulers independently schedules the tasks allocated to this core. We assume them to utilize Earliest Deadline First (EDF) scheduling. EDF optimally schedules tasks for uni-processor, i.e., the utilization bound for each core is defined by the following equation: $\sum_{i=1}^{n} \frac{C_i}{P_i} \leq 1$, where C_i and P_i are the WCET and the period of the ith task, respectively. Deadlines are assumed to be the same as the periods.

For the algorithms, each task needs to provide the following information: $<list_{locked-sets}, WCET_{locked}, WCET_{unlocked}>$. $list_{locked-sets}$ is the list of sets where the programmer intends to lock a cache line for the task. $WCET_{locked}$ and $WCET_{unlocked}$ are the WCETs of a task when all the lines of $list_{locked-sets}$ are locked and unlocked, respectively. $WCET_{locked}$ does not include the overhead of loading the contents of a task because it is a one-time cost incurred at system start-up.

We also assume that the real-time tasks are pairwise independent. Hence, these tasks do not cause any coherence traffic on the interconnect.

4. TASK PARTITION ALGORITHMS
4.1 Cache-Unaware Schemes

Static task partitioning algorithms for multi-core architectures have been widely studied. Most of these approaches consistently aim at minimizing the number of cores utilized [3]. They use bin-packing schemes considering a single utilization value per task. These algorithms for distributed systems are cache unaware. In the following section, we present two cache-unaware schemes, namely FFD and NFFD.

4.1.1 First Fit Decreasing (FFD)

FFD is a commonly used algorithm for allocating tasks on distributed cores. This implementation assumes that the tasks are unlocked, i.e., we consider all tasks with a utilizations of $u_{unlocked}$ using $WCET_{unlocked}$. This algorithm takes task (i), already allocated set of cores N_{procs} and a flag that decides whether task to be allocated in a locked state or unlocked state if it adds a new core to N_{procs}. The FFD algorithm picks tasks in decreasing order of their $u_{unlocked}$ and allocates them using Algorithm 1. Line 1 sorts the cores in N_{proc} in decreasing order of core utilization. Lines 3-8 iterate over the cores until the task is allocated or until all cores have been considered and task could not be allocated. A task is allocated to a core if a core's utilization does not exceed 1 (utilization bound for EDF). If a task could not be allocated to any core in N_{procs}, lines 9-13 add a new core to N_{procs} and the task is allocated to it in an unlocked state.

Input: i : task, N_{procs} : processors, $isLock$: boolean
Output: N_{procs} number of processors
1 N_{procs}.sort(decreasing utilization) ;
2 **foreach** N_{procs} j **do**
3   **if** $Success = false$ **then**
4   **if** $i.u_{unlocked} \leq 1 - j.u$ **then**
5   allocate task i to core j;
6        $j.u = j.u + i.u_{unlocked}$;
7        $Success :=$ true ;
8   break;
     end
   end
end
9 **if** $Success = false$ **then**
10   allocate New_{proc};
11    $N_{procs} := N_{procs} \cup New_{proc}$;
12   allocate task i to New_{proc};
13   **if** $isLock = true$ **then**
     $New_{proc}.u := i.u_{locked}$;
   end
   else
     $New_{proc}.u := i.u_{unlocked}$;
   end
end

Algorithm 1: FFD Task Allocation (baseFFD)

4.1.2 Naive Locked FFD (NFFD)

We extend FFD with a simple approach of using locked caches. Tasks are defined to be locked or unlocked prior to their allocation. Thus, all the tasks have a single WCET before allocation, which is $WCET_{locked}$ for a locked task or $WCET_{unlocked}$ otherwise. Bin packing has difficulties to co-locate multiple tasks with high utilization. Any task whose utilization is greater than 1 is deemed to be locked. Each of these locked tasks is allocated to a separate core as the algorithm is cache-unaware. The algorithm proceeds to allocate the set of unlocked tasks with an initial value of N_{procs}, the number of cores assigned to locked tasks.

4.2 Cache-Aware Task Partitioning

We next present two cache-aware mechanisms. Initially, our algorithms consider two values, $WCET_{locked}$ and $WCET_{unlocked}$. In Section 4.2.4, we discuss a mechanism with the objective of reducing the impact of conflicts. The $list_{locked-sets}$ item is used to deduce a conflict matrix M_{conf} for locked tasks. A conflict among the locked sets indicates the existence of common locked cache set(s). Each empty entry in $M_{conf}(i,j)$ signifies the absence of conflicts between tasks i and j while every filled entry signifies existence of a conflict.

4.2.1 Greedy First Fit Decreasing (GFFD)

We first illustrate GFFD by example using a conflict graph. An undirected conflict graph of four nodes/vertices is depicted in Figure 3.

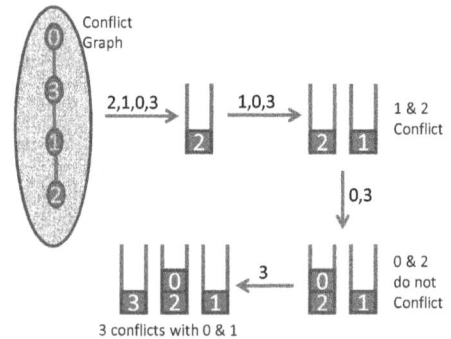

Figure 3: Greedy First Fit Decreasing in Operation

A conflict graph in the context of task partitioning is a graph $G = (V;E)$, where every vertex/node $v \in V$ corresponds uniquely to a task and an $edge(i;j) \in E$ indicates that tasks i and j are in conflict and cannot be allocated onto the same core. The objective is to map nodes into buckets while keeping the number of buckets low. The FFD algorithm arranges nodes in traversal order via heuristics before allocating them. In this example, the algorithm establishes an allocation order of nodes 2, 1, 0 and 3. At each step, the node in question checks if it can be placed within any of the existing buckets. A node can be allocated to a bucket if the bucket does not contain any node that conflicts with it. In the example, node 0 gets allocated to a bucket that contains node 2, which does not conflict with 0. In case all buckets conflict, a new bucket is created, e.g., during the allocation of nodes 1 and 3.

We developed a modified version of the FFD algorithm. We call this Greedy First Fit Decreasing (GFFD). Algorithm 2 presents the details of the algorithm. This algorithm takes a task set, the number of locked ways per cache and a conflict matrix M_{conf} as an input. If the number of

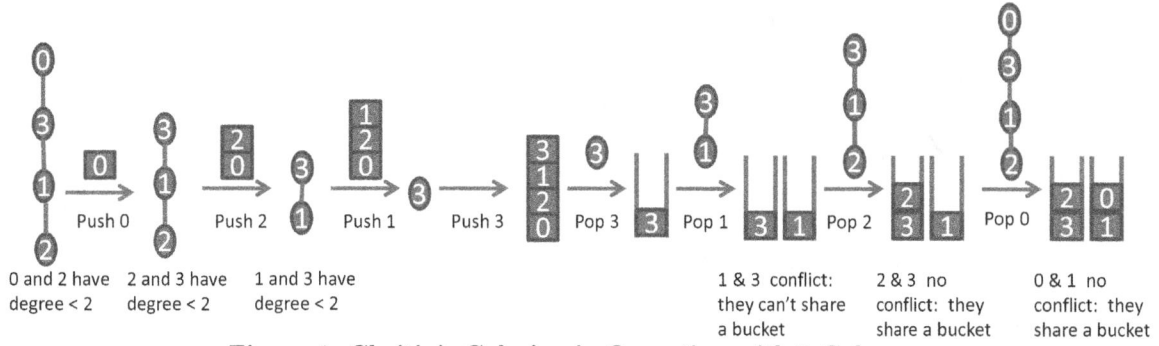

0 and 2 have   2 and 3 have   1 and 3 have   1 & 3 conflict: 2 & 3 no   0 & 1 no
degree < 2   degree < 2   degree < 2   they can't share   conflict: they conflict: they
                                                                a bucket   share a bucket share a bucket

Figure 4: Chaitin's Coloring in Operation with 2 Colors

tasks is N, then M_{conf} is a $N \times N$ matrix with each entry representing a conflict between two tasks. A value of 1 represents a cache conflict among locked regions of tasks, while a 0 represents otherwise. The idea is to incrementally add cores to the schedule starting with an initial number of cores, N_{procs}, of 1. Lines 3-13 proceed to allocate tasks in FFD fashion using u_{locked}. Line 8 uses a procedure IsAllocatable() that returns the cache way that is still unassigned to any locked lines of tasks that conflict with any locked lines of task i. In case a valid cache way is found and the allocation of the task with the locked region passes the schedulability test, the task is allocated to the core. If, however, all the lockable cache-ways of the core's L1 are in conflict or the schedulability test fails, the algorithm tries to allocate the task to another core until it runs out of cores in N_{procs}. If the task remains unallocated, line 15 uses Algorithm 1 to allocate the task. The value of *true* for the third parameter to $baseFFD$ forces the task to be allocated in locked state when a new core is added to N_{procs}.

Input: M : Set of Tasks, $Assoc$: Number of locked
  ways per cache, M_{conf} : conflict Matrix
Output: N_{procs} number of processors
1   $N_{procs} := 1$;
2   M.sort(decreasing u_{locked});
3   **while** M *is not empty* **do**
4     $Success :=$ false ;
5   N_{procs}.sort(decreasing utilization) ;
6     $i := M$.front;
7   **foreach** N_{procs} j **do**
8   **if** $k:=IsAllocatable(j,i,Assoc,M_{conf}) \neq -1$
        then
9   **if** $i.u_{locked} \leq 1 - j.u$ **then**
10   allocate task i to core j in kth way;
11          $j.u = j.u + i.u_{locked}$;
12          $Success :=$ true ;
13   break ;
          end
        end
      end
14   **if** $Success = false$ **then**
15       $N_{procs} := baseFFD$(i, N_{procs},true);
      end
    end

Algorithm 2: Greedy First Fit Decreasing (GFFD)

4.2.2   Colored First Fit Decreasing (CoFFD)

GFFD identifies task conflicts only after a task has been committed for allocation, even though a conflict matrix is already present. The algorithm does not have a prior notion of the number of cores available within the system. Furthermore, the order in which tasks are assigned to cores is still based on task utilization. We can do better. When tasks contend for cache regions, analysis of the cache conflict graph yields superior, conflict-guided allocations. Such analysis considers tasks in a conflict-conscious order that ensures they can co-exist with each other for a given number of cores. To this end, we adapted a graph coloring approach by Chaitin [5] that is widely used in register allocation, which is based on the following theorem:

CHAITIN'S THEOREM 1. *Let G be a graph and $v \in V(G)$ such that $deg(v) < k$, where $deg(v)$ denotes the number of edges of vertex v. A graph G is k-colorable if and only if G - v is k-colorable.*

This theorem provides the basis for graph decomposition by repeatedly deleting vertices with degree less than k until either the graph is empty or only vertices with degree greater than or equal to k are left. In the latter case, the graph cannot be colored. However, by removing a task from a conflict graph using some heuristic, a new coloring attempt can be made for the remaining of the graph. Figure 4 shows how Chaitin's theorem can be used in practice. In this example, the conflict graph is the same as in the FFD example in Figure 3. This new example shows how Chaitin's approach allocates the set of nodes to two buckets/colors. At first, the algorithm fills up a stack removing one node at a time. A node is a viable candidate for being pushed onto the stack if and only if the degree is less than 2. When a node is removed, it reduces the degree of its neighbor in the remainder of the graph. Since all nodes can be pushed onto the stack, the graph is two-colorable (cf. Chaitin's theorem). During the following steps, nodes are popped off the stack and associated with a color/bucket. In our example, Chaitin's algorithm successfully allocates nodes to two buckets. In contrast, three buckets were required by the FFD algorithm.

Algorithm 3 shows the task coloring mechanism, which is responsible for finding non-conflicting tasks that can be grouped together in a given number of colors. The number of colors is equal to the number of locked cache ways that can be filled within a given number of cores. Lines 4-13 fill up two data-structures, *colorStack* and *spilledList*. Every iteration of this loop finds a task that can be placed on either of these stacks. Line 5 searches through the list of unallocated tasks and finds the task with lowest degree. A task with minimum degree is pushed onto *colorStack* if and only if its degree is less than $NumOfColors$. Otherwise,

165

the algorithm finds a task using a heuristic that focuses on minimizing a metric. For example, in algorithm 3 the metric $u_{locked}/degree$ is minimized at line 10. The objective of this heuristic is to decrease the conflict degrees of as many tasks as possible and, at the same time, to pick a task that causes the minimum increase in the system utilization while remaining unlocked ($u_{unlocked}$). This task is then added to the *spilledList*. While removing the tasks from M, we decrease the conflict *degree* of neighbors.

Input: M : Set of Tasks, $NumOfColors$: Number of Cores × Number of locked ways per cache, M_{conf} : conflict Matrix
Output: $colorList$, $spilledList$, $rejectedTaskList$
1 $colorStack$:= empty;
2 $spilledList$:= empty;
3 $colorList$:= empty;
4 **while** M *is not empty* **do**
5 $\quad$ t := lowest degree task by linear search of M ;
6 $\quad$ **if** $t.degree < NumOfColors$ **then**
7 $\quad\quad$ push t onto $colorStack$;
8 $\quad\quad$ remove t from M and M_{conf} ;
$\quad$ **end**
9 $\quad$ **else**
10 $\quad\quad$ t := task with minimum ($u_{unlocked}/degree$) ;
11 $\quad\quad$ push t onto $spilledList$;
12 $\quad\quad$ remove t from M and M_{conf} ;
$\quad$ **end**
end
13 $aveCoreUtil = \frac{colorStack.u}{NumOfColors}$;
14 **while** $colorStack$ *is not empty* **do**
15 $\quad$ t := Pop $colorStack$;
16 $\quad$ repopulate M_{conf} ;
17 $\quad$ $curColor$:=0;
18 $\quad$ **for** $curColor = 0 \rightarrow NumOfColors - 1$ **do**
19 $\quad\quad$ **if** *None of the neighbors has this color* **then**
20 $\quad\quad\quad$ $curCore := curColor$ mod number Of Cores ;
21 $\quad\quad\quad$ **if** $curCore.u < aveCoreUtil$ and $curCore.u + t.u \leq 1$ **then**
22 $\quad\quad\quad\quad$ $t.color := curColor$;
23 $\quad\quad\quad\quad$ $colorList$[curColor] := t ;
24 $\quad\quad\quad\quad$ Add $t.u$ to $curCore.u$;
25 $\quad\quad\quad\quad$ break ;
$\quad\quad\quad$ **end**
$\quad\quad$ **end**
$\quad$ **end**
26 $\quad$ **if** *t.color is not a valid Color* **then**
27 $\quad\quad$ push t onto $rejectedTaskList$;
$\quad$ **end**
end

Algorithm 3: Task Coloring Algorithm

Once all tasks have been distributed among either of the stacks, lines 13-27 put the tasks in *colorStack* into different colorLists. Assigning a task from *colorStack* to a *colorList* is equivalent to allocating the task to a core as each color corresponds to a lockable cache way. The *colorLists* are associated with cores in a round robin manner, i.e., if the number of lockable cache ways per task is equal to two and the number of cores is three, then there are a total of six *colorLists*. The first, second and third *colorLists* are as-

sociated with the first cache way on cores one, two and three, respectively. The fourth, fifth and sixth *colorLists* are associated with the second cache way on cores one, two and three. Lines 15-16 pop a task from the *colorStack* and re-populate the conflict edges in the graph with the tasks that have already been colored. The algorithm then loops through all the colors until it finds a color that has not been allocated to any of its neighbors in the graph. Line 20 picks the core associated with that color. For a task to be assigned a color, the task has to pass the EDF schedulability test.

Furthermore, the current utilization of the core has to be less than $aveCoreUtil$, where $aveCoreUtil$ is computed at line 14. These conditions prevent *colorLists* from becoming unbalanced. Chaitin's algorithm in its purest form is

- unaware of the tasks in the *spilledList* and
- unable to deliver a balanced *colorList*.

E.g., if none of the tasks are conflicting then all tasks can be given the same color. Conditions at line 21 allow the tasks to be evenly distributed across cores. If either of the conditions fail, then the algorithm moves on to the next color until all the colors have been tried. If a task cannot be assigned a valid color, it is moved to *rejectedTaskList*.

Input: $rejectedTaskList$, $Assoc$: Number of locked ways per cache, M_{conf} : conflict Matrix,N_{procs} : number of cores
1 $rejectedTaskList$.sort(decreasing u_{locked});
2 **foreach** $rejectedTaskList$ i **do**
3 $\quad$ N_{procs}.sort(decreasing u); $Success$ = false;
4 $\quad$ **foreach** N_{procs} j **do**
5 $\quad\quad$ **foreach** $Assoc$ k **do**
6 $\quad\quad\quad$ **if** $IsAllocatable(j,i,Assoc,M_{conf}) \neq -1$ **then**
7 $\quad\quad\quad\quad$ allocate task i to core j in kth associativity;
8 $\quad\quad\quad\quad$ $j.u = j.u + i.u_{locked}$;
9 $\quad\quad\quad\quad$ $Success$ = true;
10 $\quad\quad\quad\quad$ goto line 11;
$\quad\quad\quad$ **end**
$\quad\quad$ **end**
$\quad$ **end**
11 $\quad$ **if** $Success==false$ **then**
12 $\quad\quad$ put task i on $spilledList$;
$\quad$ **end**
end
13 $spilledList$.sort(decreasing $u_{unlocked}$);
14 **foreach** $SpilledList$ i **do**
15 $\quad$ **if** $N_{procs} \neq baseFFD(i,N_{procs},false)$ **then**
16 $\quad\quad$ return Failed Allocation;
$\quad$ **end**
end
17 return Successful Allocation;

Algorithm 4: Colored First Fit Decreasing (CoFFD)—Uncolored Lists

The task coloring stage outputs partially filled cores and a list of tasks in *rejectedTaskList* and *spilledStack*. These are subsequently used by the second part of the allocation shown in Algorithm 4. Algorithm 4 first tries to allocate tasks from the *rejectedTaskList*. It sorts the tasks of *rejectedTaskList* in decreasing order of their u_{locked}. Each iteration of the loop starting at line 2 then picks a task in order and tries to allocate it in FFD fashion on N_{procs}. If a task cannot be allocated to a core, it is moved to the *spilledList*. Once the *rejectedTaskList* is empty, all the tasks in *spilledList* are allocated using *baseFFD*. If all the tasks in *spilledList* are allocated, the task set is deemed to be schedulable on a given number of N_{procs} cores. Otherwise, N_{procs} is incremented by the caller of CoFFD. This process repeats until a schedule has been found.

Figure 5 depicts a step-by-step working example:

(a) Tasks are grouped in a conflict graph. Our example has five tasks with u_{locked} utilizations of 0.5, 0.3, 0.4, 0.2 and 0.2. Each task conflicts with its neighboring task. Therefore, tasks form a chain of conflicts in the graph.

(b) Our graph coloring algorithm is applied to split the tasks in *ColorLists*. The task set is split into two colors alternating between adjacent tasks in the same *colorList*.

(c) We assume a multi-core system with single-way locking in the L1 cache. Since the aggregate utilization is 1.6, N_{procs} is initialized with the ceiling of system utilization, which is 2. The tasks in each *colorList* are sorted in decreasing order of u_{locked}. The cores are filled in a round-robin fashion. The green *colorList* fits within core zero. Tasks in the red *colorList* are allocated to core one. Tasks with higher utilization (0.5 and 0.4) are allocated to core one while the task with utilization 0.2 is moved to the *rejectedTaskList* as it exceeds the utilization bound of 1.

(d) The algorithm now tries to allocate the task from *rejectedTaskList* to core zero. It fails due to task conflicts with an already allocated task and due to the availability of only one cache way for locking.

(e) At this stage, the task is moved to the *spilledList*. The task's utilization is increased to $u_{unlocked}$ because the previous steps show that the task cannot be allocated on given cores without unlocking its locked regions. This changes its utilization from 0.2 to 0.4.

(f) The task is allocated on core 0 with this inflated utilization because such allocation does not violate the utilization bound on core 0.

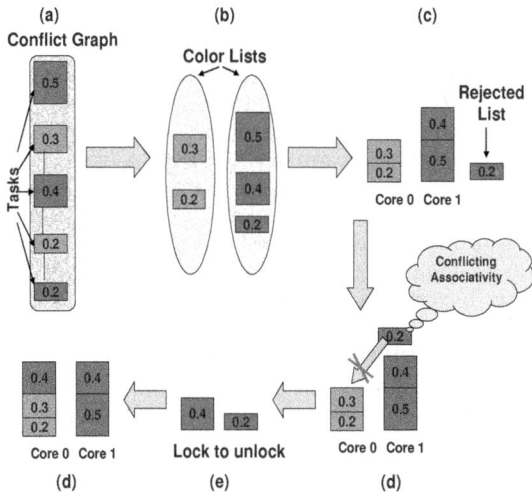

Figure 5: Task Coloring in Operation

4.2.3 Algorithmic Complexity

Bin packing is known to be NP-hard. Any known optimal solution is exponential in complexity. Besides experimental evaluations, it is important to assess the complexity of sub-optimal, heuristic approaches to assess their scalable in terms of number of tasks and cores. In the following, the algorithmic complexity of GFFD and CoFFD are assessed.

For the purpose of complexity analysis, let the number of tasks be X and the number of cores be Y. Let t be the task to be allocated next.

Algorithmic Complexity of GFFD: The outer loop in algorithm 2 iterates over all tasks. The inner loop from 8-13 iterates over all cores. The function *IsAllocatable* iterates over the task task conflict set, M_{conf}, bounded by the number of tasks, to detect if t conflicts with any of the tasks allocated to a core, i.e., *IsAllocatable* has an algorithmic complexity of $O(X)$. Thus, the combined algorithmic complexity of GFFD is $O(YX^2)$.

Algorithmic Complexity of CoFFD: CoFFD consists of algorithms 3 and 4. The former algorithm colors the tasks while allocating them to cores. It has two loops. The first loop between lines 4 and 12 iterates over all tasks. The nested computations of linear search at line 5, reduction of number of conflicts for tasks conflicting with t at line 8 and 12, and linear search at line 10 are bounded by the number of tasks, i.e., they have an algorithmic complexity of $O(X)$ for a combined complexity of $O(X^2)$ for the first loop. The second loop between lines 14 and 27 iterates over all tasks while pushing them onto a stack. The nested loop within iterates over the set of colors, which is bounded by the number of cores, Y. The nested conditional at line 19 iterates over the set of neighboring nodes in the repopulated graph whose cardinality is bounded by the number of tasks, X. This implies an algorithmic complexity of $O(YX^2)$ for the second loop, which dominates the complexity of the first loop, i.e., is the overall algorithmic complexity of algorithm 3. The algorithmic complexity of algorithm 4, sequentially invoked next, is $O(YX^2)$ following the same argument as for GFFD since their algorithmic structure are equivalent in terms of loop iterators, i.e., the rejected task list is bounded by the number of cores. The loop iterating over the spilled list is bounded by the number of tasks but its complexity is dominated by the previous loop. Thus, the algorithmic complexity of CoFFD is $O(YX^2)$.

Thus, both the cache-aware algorithms deliver us the task partitioning with algorithmic complexity of $O(YX^2)$.

4.2.4 Optimized Region Resizing for Multi-cores

So far, we have assumed that conflicting tasks can only share a resource either by locking all specified regions or keeping all of them unlocked. This is useful when locked regions should remain transparent to the programmer. We can improve on our results if programmers can accurately estimate the upper bound on the number of references to each locked cache line (e.g., based on upper loop bounds), which we later demonstrate by showing the effect of region resizing in the evaluation section. This requires the specification of the number of references (N_{refs}) for each locked cache line in $list_{locked\_set}$. We can then compute the reference frequency, R_f, of a locked cache line for task t as

$$R_f = \frac{N_{refs}}{Period_t}$$

When the allocation of a task with $WCET_{locked}$ has failed, we need not inflate the WCET of the task directly from

$WCET_{locked}$ to $WCET_{unlocked}$. Instead, we can resolve conflicts at a much finer granularity. If a task C has a conflict with another task A at set m, and if R_f for set m of task C is higher than R_f for set m of task A, then task C will retain its locked line while task A will lose one. If multiple cache ways are lockable, the locked cache line with the minimum R_f is replaced. This increases the utilization of the task with the newly locked line.

Optimization-induced changes to task allocation algorithms: Since a task will lock multiple cache lines, allocation of a task to a core may affect different tasks on different cache sets. Hence, the schedulability test has to use the temporary WCETs of all the affected tasks before making permanent changes. The *IsAllocatable* procedure performs a locked cache analysis and delivers the temporary WCETs along with a list of cache resizing specifications if the schedulability test succeeds. In case the test fails, the list of updates is rejected and no permanent changes are made to the WCETs. In Algorithm 3, the heuristic for selecting spilled tasks will change since partial locking of cache lines affects multiple tasks instead of dilating the WCET of just one. Thus, we spill the task whose $(Number\_of\_conflicting\_cache\_lines/degree)$ is minimal.

We can use the algorithms presented above in several ways. If tasks can meet their deadlines only under locking with $WCET_{locked}$, then these algorithms will allocate them with $WCET_{locked}$. If $WCET_{locked}$ and $WCET_{unlocked}$ are provided, then both fully locked and fully unlocked scenarios can be assessed by the algorithms. Dealing with execution times at coarser levels seems more attractive to the developers. This allows them to select lockable lines with rough estimate of the access patterns. Also, it may not be possible to deduce an accurate number of references or the estimates can be highly pessimistic, especially when data regions are being accessed sparsely. Conversely, if data regions are being frequently referenced and references are uniformly dense around locked regions, then the region resizing can be used in conjunction with GFFD and CoFFD.

5. TASK-SET GENERATION

Due to the unavailability of a full blown real-time application for massive multi-core architectures, we decided to utilize synthetic task sets in our experiments. This allows us to vary various parameters like the size of locked regions, number of tasks, and conflicts, which in turn test corner cases of our algorithms. The impetus towards massive multi-core architectures will allow such applications to be prevalent in the future. We assume that static analysis tools such as [18] deliver the $WCET_{locked}$, $WCET_{unlocked}$ and R_f, which is beyond the scope of this paper. Table 2 shows the architectural and task-set parameters of our experimental framework.

We generated the synthetic task-set values (period, locked execution time and unlocked execution time) as follows:

1. Task sets with varying number of locked sets were generated with 1 to 4 locked regions. Each locked region is given a random number of references. Every cache line is subjected to a uniform number of references to model spatial locality effects.

2. The total number of references were derived by aggregating the number of references incurred within the locked regions of the task. Since the programmer will be locking the regions in L1 (highest utilization benefit), we assume that these locked lines consume 80%

Table 2: System Parameters

Parameter	Value
Processor Model	in-order
Cache Line Size	32B
L1 Cache Size/Associativity	8KB/2-way
Lockable associativity	1/2
L1 Access latency	1 cycle
L2 Access Latency	10 cycles
External Memory Latency	100 cycles
Max. sets locked by a task	114/128
Min. sets locked by a task	8/128
Max. size of locked region	57 sets
Min. size of locked region	8 sets
Max. size of task sets	42
total tasks generated	126
Max. locked regions by a task	4
Min. locked regions by a task	1

of the total data loads. Out of the remaining 20%, we assume 18% are hits in the L2 cache and 2% are references to sensory data that goes off chip. We also assume that every 5th instruction is a load. This lets us infer number of instruction fetches that incur L1 cache hits (see Section 3). These assumptions allow us to derive a $WCET_{locked}$ for a task.

3. To derive the $WCET_{unlocked}$, we assume unlocked regions to hit in L2 cache. If two locked regions are accessed by two different paths, then the increase in WCET is due to just one region (the one that dominates the references), not both. Thus, we randomly select tasks to accommodate such behavior. This also results in varied increases in execution time between $WCET_{locked}$ and $WCET_{unlocked}$ across tasks.

4. Next, we assign periods to each task i to group them into different utilization categories: high utilization ($0.55 > u_i > 0.40$), medium utilization ($0.40 > u_i > 0.25$), and low utilization ($0.25 > u_i > 0.15$).

5. We assume that the tasks do not have any inter-task dependencies.

6. We assume a task utilization equal to a task's density, i.e., a task's deadline is equal to its period.

We present our experimental results for a system that supports single locked cache ways. Such a scheme is also applicable when considering horizontal cache partitioning, where all the lockable ways in each set are dedicated to a task.

Cache-unaware vs. Cache-aware: First, we compare the cache-unaware schemes (FFD, NFFD) against cache-aware ones (GFFD, CoFFD). Table 3 shows the best allocations produced by schemes within the two categories, i.e., NFFD (cache-unaware) and CoFFD (cache-aware). On average, the number of cores used by cache-aware schemes is 40% less than that of contemporary allocation schemes applicable for distributed core mechanisms. We also observe that the contemporary FFD fails to allocate high utilization task sets. It performs worse than NFFD for low utilization task sets as shown earlier in Table 1.

Allocations while retaining locked state: Table 4 depicts the results of our algorithms when tasks are allocated in locked state, i.e., with an execution time of $WCET_{locked}$. The first column shows the number of tasks in the task-set. The second and third columns show the number of cores allocated by GFFD and CoFFD, respectively, when a task-set is composed of high utilization tasks only. The fourth

Table 3: Allocated Cores: Cache-aware/-unaware

# of	high util.		med. util.		low util.	
tasks	unaware	aware	unaware	aware	unaware	aware
4	4	**3**	4	**2**	3	**2**
8	8	**5**	8	**4**	5	**3**
12	12	**8**	12	**5**	8	**4**
16	16	**10**	16	**8**	12	**6**
20	20	**13**	20	**11**	16	**8**
24	24	**15**	23	**15**	19	**10**
28	28	**19**	27	**19**	21	**11**
32	32	**20**	31	**21**	22	**12**
36	36	**21**	35	**22**	23	**15**
42	42	**25**	41	**24**	24	**17**

and fifth columns represent the same for medium utilization tasks, and the sixth and seventh columns for lower utilization tasks. Lower core allocations are depicted in bold font. In all cases, CoFFD results in fewer cores allocated than GFFD, especially as the number of tasks increases. As more tasks are added to the system, the conflict graph becomes denser. CoFFD avoids conflicts strategically due to its coloring scheme while the greedy scheme results in a less conflict-conscious allocation.

Table 4: Allocated Cores: CoFFD/GFFD, All Tasks Locked

# of	high util.		med. util.		low util.	
tasks	GFFD	CoFFD	GFFD	CoFFD	GFFD	CoFFD
4	**3**	**3**	3	**2**	3	**2**
8	6	**5**	5	**4**	4	**4**
12	9	**8**	6	**5**	5	**5**
16	11	**10**	9	**8**	8	**8**
20	**13**	**13**	12	**11**	12	**11**
24	16	**15**	16	**15**	16	**15**
28	20	**19**	20	**19**	20	**19**
32	22	**20**	22	**21**	22	**21**
36	24	**21**	24	**22**	23	**22**
42	27	**25**	25	**24**	24	**23**

Allocations with all or none: This experiment allows allocation of tasks either with locking of all regions or while leaving all of them unlocked. After a locked allocation with $WCET_{locked}$ is attempted, algorithms can fall back to an unlocked allocation with $WCET_{unlocked}$ for a given task in case conflicts have prevented the allocation on a given core. Table 5 depicts the results with best results in bold face. The first column shows the number of tasks in the task-set. The second and the third columns show the number of cores allocated by GFFD and CoFFD, respectively. Sets with higher/medium utilization tasks result in similar allocations. This is because it is difficult for the higher utilization tasks to be allocated under the inflated execution budget of $WCET_{unlocked}$. However, tasks with lower utilizations can be allocate tasks with $WCET_{unlocked}$. The fourth and the fifth columns depict the system utilization delivered under the allocations of the algorithms. The last column shows the decrease in system utilization achieved by CoFFD over GFFD. The results indicate that CoFFD beats GFFD not only in terms of allocating fewer cores but also in improving system utilization by over 18% for task-sets with large numbers of tasks. This is because GFFD inflates the execution budget of tasks that cannot be allocated to cores under locking. In addition, conflict analysis prior to allocation allows the algorithm to apply heuristics to reduce the number of tasks that remain unlocked. The results of CoFFD are due to combined heuristics for selecting spilled tasks. Heuristic 1 selects the task with the least $\frac{WCET_{unlocked}}{degree of Conflicts^2}$ value,

which emphasizes the task's degree. This prevents the number of cores to be increased when non-conflict placements are still feasible. Algorithmically, CoFFD avoids spills of tasks onto the stack (see Algorithm 4). Heuristic 2 selects the task with the least $WCET_{unlocked}$ value. Of the two heuristics, CoFFD selects the one that results in the allocation of fewer cores. For example, most task sets in Table 5 resulted in the allocation of fewer cores under heuristic 1, but the last task set would have resulted in the allocation of 18 cores whereas heuristic 2 reduced this allocation to 17. This behavior was also observed while allocating tasks with locked region resizing (see below).

Table 5: CoFFD vs. GFFD: Selected Tasks Unlocked

# of tasks	GFFD	CoFFD	GFFD Util.	CoFFD Util.	Util. decreased by CoFFD
4	**2**	**2**	1.48	0.88	**40.54 %**
8	**3**	**3**	2.05	2.027	**0.88 %**
12	5	**4**	3.77	3.06	**18.83 %**
16	7	**6**	5.07	4.13	**18.54 %**
20	9	**8**	7.33	5.86	**19.64 %**
24	11	**10**	8.6	7.04	**18.13 %**
28	12	**11**	10.2	8.65	**15.19 %**
32	14	**12**	11.57	9.7	**16.16 %**
36	15	**15**	12.67	10.27	**18.94 %**
42	17	**17**	14.04	11.87	**20.37 %**

Region Resized Locking: The next experiment assessed the optimization of resizing locked regions for conflicted tasks. We observed that sets with high utilization tasks result in dilation of WCET when locking fails, which reduces their chances of being allocated. In Table 6, we show the results for task-sets with low utilization tasks as they benefited the most from region resizing. The first column shows the number of tasks in the task-sets. The second and the third columns show the number of cores allocated when partial locking is used by GFFD and CoFFD, respectively. The fourth and fifth columns show the number of allocated cores when tasks are not allowed to unlock any of their regions. The results indicate that for higher number of tasks, partial locking after resizing reduces the number of required cores by 50%. It is interesting to note that the greedy algorithm performed as well as CoFFD with combined heuristics 1 and 2. This is due to the fine-grained arbitration of conflict regions under resizing. For task-sets with medium utilization tasks, CoFFD and GFFD allocate a similar number of cores for all task-sets. Yet, CoFFD results in 1%-14% reduced system utilization.

Table 6: Region Resizing

Number of Tasks	GFFD w/ Partial Locking	CoFFD w/ Partial Locking	GFFD w/ locks only	CoFFD w/ locks only
4	**2**	**2**	3	**2**
8	**3**	**3**	4	**4**
12	**4**	**4**	5	**5**
16	**6**	**6**	8	**8**
20	**7**	**7**	12	**11**
24	**8**	**8**	16	**15**
28	**10**	**10**	20	**19**
32	**10**	**10**	22	**21**
36	**12**	**12**	23	**22**
42	**13**	**13**	24	**23**

6. CONCLUSIONS

The use of multi-core architectures is not yet prevalent in real-time systems since guaranteeing predictability of hard real-time tasks on such architectures remains a challenge.

Cache locking is a technique that is commonly employed to improve the predictability of real-time task execution. This work is the first to study allocation of real-time tasks with locked caches on distributed cache systems. Contemporary static scheduling schemes may not use locked caches. However, this renders certain high utilization tasks unschedulable as their unlocked WCET is prohibitively high. A simplistic solution would be to allowing locking of such tasks and placing locked tasks onto different cores. We call this Naive locked FFD (NFFD) as it locks certain tasks with high utilizations and is cache-unaware.

This paper proposes two cache-aware algorithms for task allocation in a multi-core environment where tasks are allowed to lock cache lines in a specified subset of cache ways in each core's private L1 cache. The first algorithm, GFFD, is an enhanced version of the First Fit Decreasing (FFD) algorithm. The second, CoFFD, is based on a graph coloring method.Our best scheme, CoFFD, reduces the number of core requirements from 25% to 60% compared to NFFD with an average reduction of 40%. CoFFD consistently performs better than GFFD as it lowers both the number of cores and system utilization.

We also propose a mechanism that allows locked regions to be resized. This scheme is applicable when the programmer can accurately provide the number of references to a locked cache line, yet does not want to be concerned with fine-grained locking decisions. The two algorithms were further adapted to use task and reference information to choose whether to retain a line in locked or unlocked state for conflicting regions. With such partial locking, the number of cores in some cases is reduced by almost 50% with an increase in system utilization of 10%. Overall, this work is unique in considering the challenges of future multi-core architectures for real-time systems and provides key insights into task partitioning with locked caches for architectures with private caches.

7. REFERENCES

[1] Tilera processor family. http://www.tilera.com/.

[2] J. Anderson, J. Calandrino, and U. Devi. Real-time scheduling on multicore platforms. In *IEEE Real-Time Embedded Technology and Applications Symposium*, pages 179–190, Apr. 2006.

[3] A. Burchard, J. Liebeherr, Y. Oh, and S. Son. New strategies for assigning real-time tasks to multiprocessor systems. *IEEE Trans. on Computers*, 44(12):1429–1442, 1995.

[4] J. Calandrino and J. Anderson. Cache-aware real-time scheduling on multicore platforms: Heuristics and a case study. In *Euromicro Conference on Real-Time Systems*, pages 209–308, July 2008.

[5] G. J. Chaitin. Register allocation & spilling via graph coloring. In *ACM SIGPLAN Conference on Programming Language Design and Implementation*, pages 98–105, 1982.

[6] S. Chattopadhyay, A. Roychoudhury, and T. Mitra. Modeling shared cache and bus in multi-cores for timing analysis. In *Proceedings of the 13th International Workshop on Software & Compilers for Embedded Systems*, SCOPES '10, pages 6:1–6:10, New York, NY, USA, 2010. ACM.

[7] D. Choffnes, M. Astley, and M. J. Ward. Migration policies for multi-core fair-share scheduling. *ACM SIGOPS Operating Systems Review*, 42:92–93, 2008.

[8] N. Eisley, L.-S. Peh, and L. Shang. Leveraging on-chip networks for data cache migration in chip multiprocessors. In *International conference on Parallel architectures and compilation techniques*, pages 197–207, 2008.

[9] N. Guan, M. Stigge, W. Yi, and G. Yu. Cache-aware scheduling and analysis for multicores. In *Proceedings of the seventh ACM international conference on Embedded software*, EMSOFT '09, pages 245–254, New York, NY, USA, 2009. ACM.

[10] D. Hardy, T. Piquet, and I. Puaut. Using bypass to tighten wcet estimates for multi-core processors with shared instruction caches. In *Proceedings of the 30th Real-Time Systems Symposium*, pages 68–77, Washington D.C., USA, Dec. 2009.

[11] T. Li, D. Baumberger, D. A. Koufaty, and S. Hahn. Efficient operating system scheduling for performance-asymmetric multi-core architectures. In *In ACM/IEEE conference on Supercomputing*, pages 1–11, Nov. 2007.

[12] T. Li, P. Brett, B. Hohlt, R. Knauerhase, S. McElderry, and S. Hahn. Operating system support for shared-isa asymmetric multi-core architectures. In *Workshop on the Interaction between Operating Systems and Computer Architecture*, pages 19–26, June 2008.

[13] J. Ouyang and Y. Xie. Loft: A high performance network-on-chip providing quality-of-service support. *Microarchitecture, IEEE/ACM International Symposium on*, 0:409–420, 2010.

[14] M. Paolieri, E. Quiñones, F. J. Cazorla, G. Bernat, and M. Valero. Hardware support for wcet analysis of hard real-time multicore systems. In *ISCA*, pages 57–68, 2009.

[15] I. Puaut. Wcet-centric software-controlled instruction caches for hard real-time systems. In *ECRTS '06: Proceedings of the 18th Euromicro Conference on Real-Time Systems*, pages 217–226, Washington, DC, USA, 2006. IEEE Computer Society.

[16] I. Puaut and D. Decotigny. Low-complexity algorithms for static cache locking in multitasking hard real-time systems. In *In IEEE Real-Time Systems Symposium*, pages 114–123, 2002.

[17] I. Puaut and C. Pais. Scratchpad memories vs locked caches in hard real-time systems: a quantitative comparison. In *Proceedings of the conference on Design, automation and test in Europe*, pages 1484–1489, San Jose, CA, USA, 2007. EDA Consortium.

[18] H. Ramaprasad and F. Mueller. Tightening the bounds on feasible preemptions. *Transactions on Embedded Computing Systems*, Mar. 2008 (accepted).

[19] V. Suhendra and T. Mitra. Exploring locking & partitioning for predictable shared caches on multi-cores. In *Proceedings of the 45th annual Design Automation Conference*, pages 300–303, New York, NY, USA, 2008. ACM.

[20] X. Vera, B. Lisper, and J. Xue. Data caches in multitasking hard real-time systems. In *In IEEE Real-Time Systems Symposium*, pages 154–165, 2003.

Revisiting Level-0 Caches in Embedded Processors

Nam Duong, Taesu Kim, Dali Zhao and Alexander V. Veidenbaum
Department of Computer Science
University of California, Irvine
{nlduong, tkim15, daliz, alexv}@ics.uci.edu

ABSTRACT

Level-0 (L0) caches have been proposed in the past as an inexpensive way to improve performance and reduce energy consumption in resource-constrained embedded processors. This paper proposes new L0 data cache organizations using the assumption that an L0 hit/miss determination can be completed prior to the L1 access. This is a realistic assumption for very small L0 caches that can nevertheless deliver significant miss rate and/or energy reduction. The key issue for such caches is how and when to move data between the L0 and L1 caches. The first new cache, a *flow a he*, targets a conflict miss reduction in a direct-mapped L1 cache. It offers a simpler hardware design and uses on average 10 less dynamic energy than the victim cache with nearly identical performance. The second new cache, a *hit a he*, reduces the dynamic energy consumption in a set-associative L1 cache by 30 without impacting performance. A variant of this policy reduces the dynamic energy consumption by up to 50 , with 5 performance degradation.

Categories and Subject Descriptors

B.3.2 [**Memory Structures**]: Design Styles—*Ca he memories*

General Terms

Design, Performance

Keywords

cache design, level-0 cache, migration policy, conflict misses, dynamic energy

1. INTRODUCTION

The use of a small cache in conjunction with a level-1 data cache (L1 cache) has been proposed [11, 24, 13, 14, 21, 8]. They were used to reduce conflict misses in a direct-mapped L1 cache (the Miss cache, Victim cache [13]) or reduce accesses to the L1 cache (Filter cache [14], line buffers [21, 8],

HotSpot cache [24]. These caches are typically very small compared to the L1 cache, often with only a few lines. With the exception of the victim cache, these are L0 caches. Given the small size of L0 caches, this L0/L1 cache hierarchy can benefit from a different management policy. This paper proposes two such policies and evaluates their performance and impact on energy consumption.

Prior work mostly assumed that the L0 cache is accessed prior to the L1, thus either increasing the L1 access time or requiring a predictor and a recovery mechanism to access the desired cache level directly. This papers assumes that the L0 cache hit/miss determination is known prior to processor access to the L1 cache. This is enabled by decoupling the tag array and data array of the L0 cache and performing tag comparison in the address computation stage of the processor pipeline. This is only possible due to the very small size of the L0 cache and relatively low clock rates.

Fig. 1 shows several possible L0 cache organizations. The baseline L1 cache is shown in Fig. 1a. In Fig. 1b, a small filter cache is placed between the processor and the L1 cache. In Fig. 1c, the victim cache is used to buffer lines evicted from the L1 cache before they are written back to the L2 cache or the memory. Fig. 1d shows a general L0/L1 organization we are are exploring. Here data can be moved between two caches and/or the L2 cache or the memory.

The L0/L1 organization introduces different opportunities and options. The L0 cache can be used to filter accesses to the L1 cache, as in the filter cache. Using the L0 cache, lines can be kept longer avoiding early eviction from L1. This is similar to the victim cache in a direct-mapped L1 cache. In fact, both benefits can be exploited at the same time in the new organization. The management policy needs to manage the different data paths and data movement between the two caches and the memory. The number of concurrent reads/writes in each cache, the number of read/write ports, cache coherence, and modifications to the existing L1 cache should all be considered in designing such policies.

This paper first systematically studies data movement between two caches and the memory. Specifically, it explores a number of *pla ement* and *migration* policies, which manage data transfer between the L0 and L1 caches, on a hit to either cache or a miss in both. The policies decide in which cache to insert a line on a miss or where a line is moved ("promoted") on a hit. In particular, we investigate 4 insertion policies and 4 promotion policies. As the hit and miss events are independent, their combination results in 16 different policies. However, not all of them are meaningful or useful. The selected policies are empirically analyzed

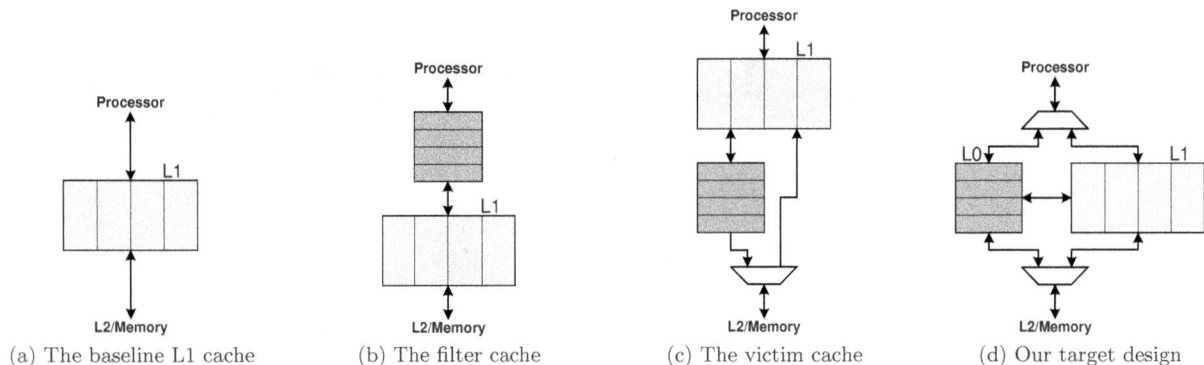

(a) The baseline L1 cache   (b) The filter cache   (c) The victim cache   (d) Our target design

Figure 1:　i erent cache organi ations.

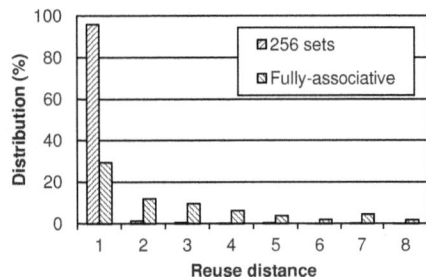

Figure 2:　euse distance distribution.

and compared to prior policies. While prior designs are effective, they can be further optimized to reduce the energy consumption.

Two new policies/organizations are proposed in this paper. A *flow a he* reduces conflict misses for a direct-mapped L1 cache. Compared to the modified victim cache it uses simpler hardware and less energy. A *hit a he*, is effective in filtering accesses to a set-associative L1 cache.

This paper makes the following contributions:

1. It studies possible migration policies between the L0 and L1 caches.
2. It proposes two new migration policies to enhance operations of the L0/L1 hierarchy.
3. It describes a practical design to support these policies.

The rest of the paper is organized as follows. In Sec. 2, by using distributions of reuse distances, we show design opportunities of a small L0 cache. Our exploration of migration policies is presented in Sec. 3. We also analyze potential applications of each design in this section. Evaluation framework is described in Sec. 4. Sec. 5 includes hardware designs and analysis of selected configurations. Sec. 6 differentiates our study to prior work, and finally Sec. 7 concludes.

2. BACKGROUND

When designing a cache, we can use reuse distance and its distribution as a guide to select the best cache organization [17, 6]. It can predict the hit rate of a cache with LRU replacement algorithm. In this paper, the reuse distance to a cache line is defined as the number of references to the same cache set since its insertion or promotion until it is accessed again. We study the distributions for 2 different cache configurations: a fully associative cache and a 256-set

cache to fully consider the effects of different cache mapping functions. The first configuration reflects the behavior of a fully associative L0 cache and the second corresponds to a direct-mapped or set-associative L1 cache. Using a simulator modeling a simple processor with the D-cache and I-cache, we collected memory traces of different benchmarks for each cache configuration for the D-cache. To simplify the calculation of reuse distance, we use a very large cache with very high associativity, so that no cache line will be evicted after its insertion. Distribution histograms are computed from the traces.

Fig. 2 shows the average distributions for different benchmarks using the methodology described in Sec. 4. As we can see, 96　of the accesses to a 256-set cache are immediate reuses. This implies high locality of accesses at the first level cache. L1 access latency is critical to processor performance, and a small increase in the miss rate can impact performance significantly. Therefore, a new L1 design should not increase the miss rate at this level.

Now let us consider the reuse distribution of the fully-associative cache. About 29　of the accesses are immediate reuses, while 41　and 57　of the accesses reuses lines that are 2 and 4 accesses ahead of time respectively. This means a small fully-associative L0 cache with 2 or 4 blocks would be beneficial if we store cache lines with small reuse distance in it. The benefits include filtering accesses to the L1 cache and keeping cache lines longer.

3. MIGRATION POLICY

As shown in Fig. 1d, the introduction of the L0 cache creates a non-trivial design space. There are several dimensions of this space as data can be moved among caches and/or the memory. Examples include which lines should be moved, when and how. This section explores this design space. Recall that a migration policy manages cache line movements between the L0 and the L1 cache. We focus on two independent events which happen during accesses from the processor: a miss in both caches or a hit in either cache. The miss results in an eviction and an insertion while the hit results in a promotion of the hit line. We first explore different individual migration policies during these two events. We do not aim to list all possibilities, but the potential policies only. We also leave the discussion of hardware design and optimizations to a later section. The only big constraint in this section is the L1 cache is set-associative, while the L0 cache is a fully-associative one. This implies that a line from

(a) Insertion

(b) Promotion

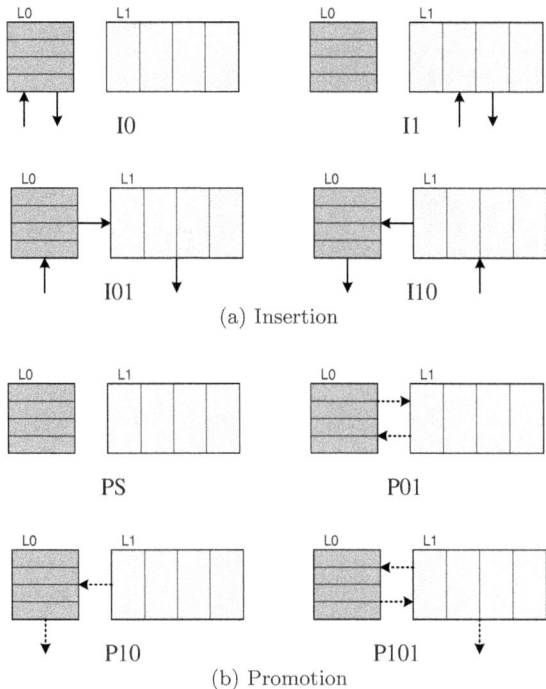

Figure : ndi idual migration policies.

the L1 cache can go to anywhere in the L0 cache, while an L0 line can be updated into a fixed set of the L1 cache only. Later in the section, we analyze selected combinations of policies and quantitatively compare them for their potential applications.

3.1 Migration During an Insertion

Fig. 3a shows 4 different migration policies due to a miss. During this event, the missed line is inserted into a cache and replaces another line, and the victim can be either written back to the other cache or other levels. The first two policies, I0 and I1, only insert the missed line into either the L0 or L1 cache, respectively. There is no migration between two caches. Because the missed lines are less likely to be reused than the reused lines [18, 12], by inserting them into a cache only, pollution of the other cache is reduced. In the other two policies, I10 and I01, after the missed line is inserted into one cache, the victim is written to the other cache, and victimizes a line from that cache. In contrast to the two former policies, the purpose of these two policies is to keep lines longer in the cache[1].

3.2 Migration During a Promotion

Fig. 3b shows different promotion policies. We classify them into 3 categories based on how the hit line is promoted and which cache should have higher priority.

Separated. The first and simplest policy is the separated promotion policy, PS in Fig. 3b. Upon a hit to each cache, the hit line is not promoted to the other cache, only state of the corresponding cache is updated.

$\rightarrow$ **1.** In this category, the L1 cache has a higher priority than the L0 cache, where a hit to a line in the L0

cache brings it to the L1 cache and swaps with a line there, while there is no data movement during a hit to the L1 cache. It is the P01 policy in Fig. 3b. The victim cache, which employs the L0 cache as a backup for victims from the L1 cache, uses this mechanism.

1 $\rightarrow$. This category emphasizes on the L0 cache, where the hit line in the L1 cache is *opied* to the L0 cache and replaces a line there[2]. A raising question at this point is how the evicted L0 line is treated. A simple solution, the P10 policy in Fig. 4d, is to write it back to other cache levels or the main memory. However, as the contents of lines in L0 may be modified by write hits, this policy must invalidate hit lines in the L1 cache once they are copied to the L0 cache to guarantee correctness.

While this policy is simple, as the L0 cache is very small, replacements happen frequently. Moreover, lines in L0 have short reuse distances as they are reused lines promoted from the L1 cache. This leads to degradation due to the eviction of reused lines in the L0 cache. The policy P101 in Fig. 4b is investigated as a solution for this issue. In this policy, an evicted line from the L0 cache is "saved" by writing back to the L1 cache. The closest study to this approach may be the filter cache [14] and the line buffers [21]. Later the multi-line buffer work [8] uses the L0 cache as a write-through cache, avoids this problem by writing back lines to the L1 cache which are modified during a write hit to the L0 cache.

3.3 Combined Migration Policies

In the previous sections we have described individually 4 insertion policies and 4 promotion policies. There are a total of 16 combinations. However, not all of them are meaningful or useful. In this section we analyze a selected number of policies and their names, as shown in Fig. 4. In the figure, each migration policy is shown with their insertion and promotion policies. For example, I10P01 is the policy of the insertion policy I10 and promotion policy P01. The baseline caches are shown in Fig. 4a. I1PS is the configuration with the L1 cache only, and I0PS corresponds to only L0 cache.

The combined migration policies described in this section are independent of replacement policy. A replacement policy changes the state of lines within a set of L1 or within L0, and is orthogonal to the migration policy. In our design, replacement state of a line is updated based on if a line is inserted to a cache or promoted within the cache, regardless if it is a hit to the D-cache. For example, a hit line from L1 being promoted to L0 is treated as an inserted line whereas it is a hit to L1. In this paper, we assume the LRU policy for both L0 and L1 caches.

This section also compares these combined policies in terms of hits and misses for both the D-cache using the simulation framework described in Sec. 4. For the purpose of comparison, the D-cache consists of a 4-way L0 and an 8KB direct-mapped L1 cache. Both L0 and L1 caches have line size of 32B and use LRU replacement policy. Fig. 5 compares them for two aspects. The first is the misses per kilo instructions (MPKIs) of the D-cache normalized to the baseline cache with L1 cache only (I1PS). The second is the hit rates to the L0 cache of different policies, including the L0 cache only configuration (I0PS), are shown. Here the hit rate is computed by the number of hits to L0 divided by

---

[1]Another possibility is inserting a missed line into both caches, as in the miss cache [13]. That work showed that the miss cache is less effective than the victim cache.

[2]Due to the difference in organizations of two caches, two lines can not be swapped as in the previous category.

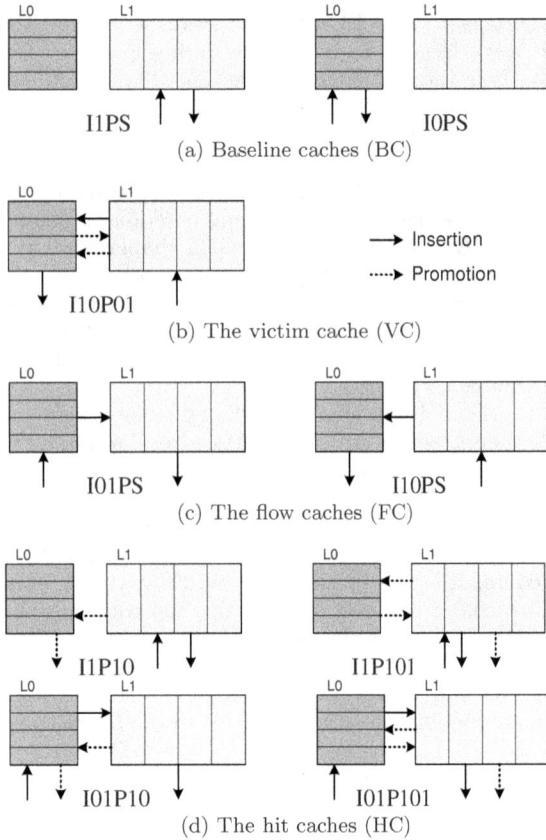

(a) Baseline caches (BC)

(b) The victim cache (VC)

(c) The flow caches (FC)

(d) The hit caches (HC)

Figure : Selected migration policies.

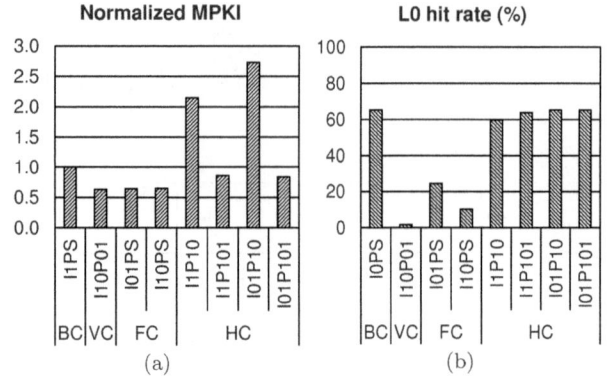

Figure : Comparing migration policies (See Fig. 4 for the abbreviations).

total number of *a esses to the D- a he*. This is also the bypass rate to the L1 cache.

3.3.1 The Victim Cache (VC)

Fig. 4b shows the policy I10P01 which is the configuration of the victim cache. In this policy the L0 cache is used as a backup cache for the L1 cache. A line evicted from L1 is stored in L0 for a few more accesses before is really evicted. In the case of a hit to L0, the hit line is swapped with a line in the L1 cache.

Fig. 5 shows that the victim cache is effective in reducing conflict misses for the direct-mapped L1 cache. Compared to the baseline L1, the victim cache removes up to 37 misses to the D-cache. This was also observed in the original work of the victim cache.

3.3.2 The Flow Caches (FC)

The flow caches are shown in Fig. 4c. Caches of this type have that name because a line inserted to the D-cache makes its way from a cache to another cache before is evicted to the main memory or other cache levels, hence they are kept longer before being evicted. Similar to the victim cache, the flow caches have potential application in a direct-mapped L1 cache. However, hardware design of the flow caches are simpler with no migration during a promotion. There are two caches of this type. In the first one, I01PS, missed lines are inserted into the L0 cache first, while in the other, I10PS, missed lines are inserted into the L1 cache first.

Now, let us compare them to the victim cache. In Fig. 5a, two flow caches have similar performance to the victim cache

for the D-cache. From the figure, the difference between their normalized MPKIs is negligible. Let us compare the victim cache and the I10PS configuration. Recall that their insertion policies are the same, and the difference is that the victim cache swaps lines between caches on an L0 hit, while the I10PS policy does not. This implies that a line in the L0 cache can provide as many hits as the ones in the L1 cache, and swapping them does not make much impact. This also explains a similar hit rate between I10PS and I01PS. Note that the victim cache is proposed for the high performance domain, and a simpler design as the flow cache can be achieved for the embedded domain without negatively impacting performance.

Besides, the L0 cache also has potential in reducing accesses to the L1 cache in the D-cache, as seen in Fig. 5b. In the victim cache, the L0 cache has a low hit rate, with only 1.6 . Meanwhile, these numbers for two flow caches are 24 and 10 , respectively. These numbers are the results of the fact that in the first configuration, I01PS, missed lines are inserted into the L0 cache first, and in the second one, I10PS, the data evicted from the L1 to the L0 cache stay in the L0 cache before being evicted. Because accessing the L0 cache requires less dynamic energy than the L1 cache, the flow caches have higher potential of reducing energy consumption.

As a result, a simple hardware design combined with energy saving opportunities makes the flow caches attractive in a D-cache with a direct-mapped L1 cache. Between two flow caches, I01PS has higher L0 hits compared to I10PS, thus we decide to use I01PS in design a flow cache.

3.3.3 The Hit Caches (HC)

As analyzed in Sec. 2, the L0 cache can be used to filter accesses to the L1 cache. This is done by storing high locality lines in this cache. One class of such line is the reused lines. First, missed lines are inserted into the L1 cache and upon a hit they are promoted to the L0 cache. For this purpose, the L0 cache is called the hit cache, as illustrated in the first two configurations, I1P10 and I1P101 in Fig. 4d. The different between the two policies is that in I1P10, the evicted line from the L0 cache is written back to the memory while in I1P101, it is written back to the L1 cache. For comparison purpose, we also include two other policies, I01P10 and I01P101, which are similar to the described ones, except that a missed line is inserted into the L0 cache first. Note

Cache	Migration policy			Potential application	
	Name	Insertion	Promotion	Target L1 cache	Description
Flow cache (FC)	I01PS	L0 → L1	Separated	Direct-mapped	Reducing conflict misses
Hit cache (HC)	I1P101	L1 only	L1 → L0 → L1	Set-associative	Reducing energy consumption

Table 1: Summary of selected migration policies.

that I01P101 is very similar to the filter cache [14] or block buffering work [21].

Performance of different hit caches are compared at the last 4 bars in Fig. 5 for the D-cache. Due to the fact that I1P10 and I01P10 evict lines from the L0 cache while invalidating lines in the L1 cache, frequent L0 replacements result in overall degradation. I01P10 even has higher misses than I1P10.

This issue is not seen in the other two policies, I1P101 and I01P101. As described previously, they save the evicted lines from L0 by writing them back to the L1 cache. In fact, they even have less misses compared to the baseline L1   I1P101 removes 14   misses while I01P101 removes 16 . So, where can they be applied? Let us consider the L0 hit rates (Fig. 5b). All 4 policies have high hit rates to the L0 cache, with at least 60 , and are similar to the baseline L0 cache only. This means that more than half of the accesses to the L1 cache are filtered, and I1P101 and I01P101 can be used to filter accesses to the L1 cache while not impacting performance. Compared to I01P101 which is similar to the filter cache, I1P101 will be more attractive because it has simpler hardware design. It can be concluded that the I1P101 policy is potential in filtering accesses to the L1 cache in the D-cache, especially when the L1 cache is large or has high associativities.

3.3.4 Summary

In this section, we have analyzed and compared different migration policies, and found two configurations which have potential enhancing L1 cache operations. Table 1 summaries their descriptions. Depending on the migration policy, each configuration has its own application for a specific target cache. The flow cache targets a direct-mapped data cache to reduce conflict misses. The hit caches are used to reduce energy due to the accesses to the L1 cache. We will describe in detail their designs and compare to prior designs in a later section.

3.4 Multi-core Environment

Until this point we have described different migration policies for the L0 cache. For the migration policies which do not have inclusiveness, this is achieved by also moving the state of a line state during the migration. In the other case, as in Fig. 4d, line state is also updated along with the update of a line's content. This helps make the design transparent to a multi-core configuration.

4. SIMULATION FRAMEWORK

We evaluate the parallel L0 cache and migration policies using the gem5 simulator [5]. For the purpose of comparing hit and miss rates of an in-order embedded processor, we model a simple single-stage in-order processor. The system has split D-cache and I-cache. There are no other levels of caches, but these two caches are connected directly to

Parameter	Configuration
Processor (in-order)	
Pipeline Depth	1
Issue Width	1 instruction/cycle
Width	32 bits
L1 cache (set-associative)	
Line size	32B
Cache size	4KB, 8KB, 16KB
Associativity	1 way, 2 ways, 4 ways
Interface ports	1 read, 1 write
L0 cache (fully-associative)	
Line size	32B
Associativity	2 ways, 4 ways, 8 ways
Interface ports	1 read, 1 write

Table 2: Processor con guration.

	Tag	Data	Total
64B (2-way)	1.12	1.77	2.89
128B (4-way)	1.92	2.33	4.25
256B (8-way)	3.55	3.46	7.01

(a) L0 cache

	1 way	2 ways	4 ways
4KB	4.14	7.24	12.46
8KB	5.17	10.83	19.44
16KB	7.36	18.90	27.33

(b) L1 cache

Table :   nergy consumption (p) of an access to the   and 1 cache.

the main memory. Various configurations are described in Table 2.

We study our design using benchmarks from the MiBench suite [10] (basicmath, qsort, susan, jpeg, lame, tiff, typeset, dijkstra, patricia, ghostscript, rsynch, stringsearch, blowfish, sha, adpcm, CRC32, FFT), the CommBench suite [23] (cast, drr, jpeg, reed, zip) and the MediaBench suite [15] (adpcm, epic, g721, gsm, jpeg, mpeg2). Some benchmarks are excluded due to compilation or runtime errors. Each benchmark was complied using a cross compiler for Alpha architecture and is run for 200M instructions or until completion. For each benchmark, all possible inputs are used. The resulting total number of executions is 46. We do not report results for individual benchmarks but their averages.

We use Cacti [22] to estimate energy consumption of accesses (read or write) to the L0 and L1 caches using the 65nm technology, as shown in Table 3. We do not use newer Cacti versions as they are not aimed to support small caches. For the L0 cache, because the tag and data arrays are decoupled, when checking for L0 hit, only the tags are accessed. The data array of the L0 cache only consumes energy during the real accesses to it. In Table 3a, energy for three L0 sizes are shown. Table 3b shows the energy consumption of the L1 cache with different sizes and associativities. The tag and data arrays of the L1 cache are accessed in parallel.

We use the following model to estimate energy consumption. Let us denote H_C and A_C as the number of hits and accesses in the cache C, where C is L , L or D (D-cache); and E_{L0T}, E_{L0D} and E_{L1} as the energy of one access to the L0 tag, L0 data and L1, respectively (Table 3). We have the following observations. First, the L0 tag array is accessed on every reference from the processor. Second, an L0 hit does not access the L1 cache and only the L0 data array is accessed. Third, an L0 miss results in an access to the L1 cache. Finally, let M_{L0} and M_{L1} denote the number of L0 and L1 accesses due to the migration between two caches. Energy accessing the D-cache is computed as:

$$E = A_D * E_{L0T} \quad H_{L0} * E_{L0D} \quad (A_D - H_{L0}) * E_{L1}$$
$$M_{L0} * (E_{L0T} \quad E_{L0D}) \quad M_{L1} * E_{L1}$$

Dividing by A_D we have the average energy of an access:

$$E_A = E_{L0T} \quad HR_{L0} * E_{L0D} \quad (1 - HR_{L0}) * E_{L1}$$
$$WB_{L0} * (E_{L0T} \quad E_{L0D}) \quad WB_{L1} * E_{L1}$$

Where HR_{L0} is the L0 hit rate; WB_{L0} and WB_{L1} are the fractions of writebacks to the destination L0 or L1 cache from the other cache, respectively. These factors are normalized to the number of D-cache accesses. In this model we do not include energy consumption of the control logic as it is negligible.

5. CACHE DESIGN AND APPLICATIONS

In this section we describe in detail hardware designs of each migration policy. This includes the interface between the processor and the caches, and the hardware design of each migration policy.

5.1 Processor-Cache Interface

In this section, we describe hardware design for the interface between the processor and the caches. This includes the accesses from the processor and the writeback of read data to the processor. For the first aspect, prior studies have shown that the addition of a L0 cache in between the L1 cache and the processor can degrade performance significantly if the hit rate at L0 is not enough to compensate the increased distance between L1 and the processor [14]. Various solutions were proposed to avoid such negative impact. In [24], mechanism to decide access to L0 or L1 at the instruction cache is integrated into the BTB. The block buffering work [21] implemented a write-through L0 cache, and decision to access L0 or L1 is known after the set IDs are decoded. In [16], the decision of which way to access is done in parallel with the access to the LS .

Our design is based on three observations. First, the number of L0 line tags to compare is very small and they are known early. Second, we target embedded domain, where the high-end processors are clocked at around 1GHz. And third, we observe that the address generation unit (AGU) is often assigned a stage as in ARM processors [1]. This stage takes place after the register read and before the memory access[3]. The AGU is just shift/addition of a base address with an offset, and is fast. The data cache organization with L0 and L1 caches is shown in Fig. 6.

[3]In ARM Cortex-M3 [2], while the AGU does not take a whole stage, its clock speed is low, around 100MHz [20]).

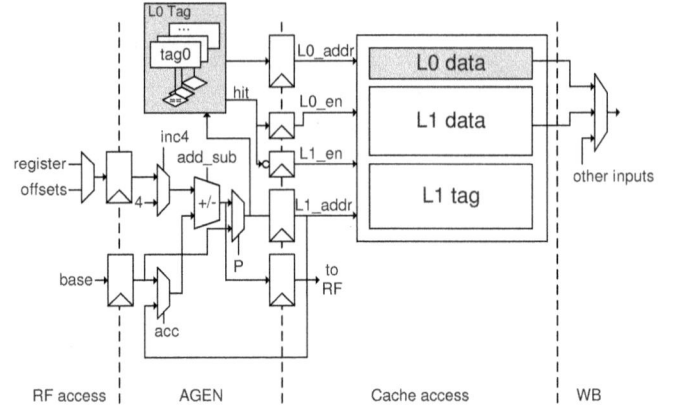

Figure : Processor-cache interface.

In this figure, the target architecture is the ARM11 processor [1]. Note that the cache access takes one or more cycles depending on the implementation. All memory instructions such as coprocessor load/store or load/store instructions use this AGU logic. In our design, the output of generated address is compared with all tags stored in L0 tag memory. The AGU was modeled using Verilog-HDL and synthesized using the TSMC 65nm TC library. The maximum clock speed for this block is 1GHz with 13 timing margin for place and route. This can be further reduced by overlapping the AGU and the tag comparison.

The outputs from the L0 and L1 caches are multiplexed with other sources, such as from coprocessors, at the writeback stage.

5.2 The Flow Cache – Reducing Conflict Misses

5.2.1 Hardware Design

Recall that the flow cache inserts a missed line into the L0 cache first, and upon eviction the line is migrated into the L1 cache. On a hit to either cache, no data movement happens, but the state of the cache which is hit is updated. In a conventional design, upon a miss to the L1 cache, a line is evicted and the missed line is inserted through the refill path. This can happen in one or more cycles depending on line size and bus width. With the introduction of the L0 cache, victim selection at the L0 and L1 cache are done in parallel, and the migration from L0 to L1 happens in parallel with the refill to L0 and writeback from L1. This implies that the L0 cache does not create any extra latency due to data migration, and the simplicity of hardware design makes it suitable in a low-end embedded processor.

5.2.2 Analysis

Fig. 7 compares different techniques to reduce conflict misses in different direct-mapped L1 caches. The techniques include increasing associativity, using modified victim caches and using flow caches. In the figure, three metrics are compared: misses per kilo instruction (MPKI) of the D-cache, the L0 hit rate of the victim caches and the flow caches, and energy consumption. The first and the last metrics are normalized to the baseline direct-mapped L1 cache. The second is the real hit rate computed by the number of L0 hits divided by the number of D-cache accesses. Note that this is also the L1 bypass rate.

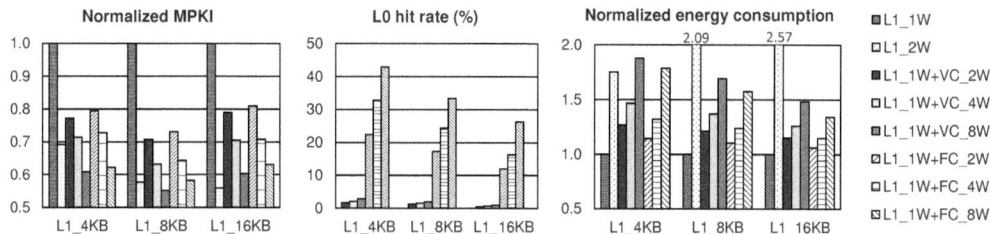

Figure : Comparing techni ues to reduce conflict misses (VC – victim cache, FC – flow cache).

First, increasing the associativity is known to be effective in reducing conflict misses. For example a 2-way 16KB L1 cache has around 40 fewer misses compared to the direct-mapped L1 cache of the same size. However, the performance improvement results in the increase of dynamic energy consumption. Doubling the associativity increases the dynamic energy by 1.7 to 2.5 times, meaning that increasing the associativity is not always a good choice.

Second, the victim caches are also effective in reducing conflict misses. A 2-way victim cache can remove around 20 while an 8-way one around 40 . Using victim cache requires less energy consumption compared to increasing associativity. For example, a 2-way victim cache increases the dynamic energy by 15 to 28 compared to the baseline. The numbers are higher for a 4- or 8-way victim cache. The reason of low energy consumption is a small L0 cache, which consumes much less energy compared to a large L1 cache.

While the victim cache has been more effective than increasing the associativity, our results also show that using a flow cache is a competitive choice to the two other methods due to two reasons. The first is performance. The flow cache, with simpler hardware design, achieves almost as much miss reduction as the victim cache of the same size. The second reason is dynamic energy consumption. Results show that a flow cache consumes less energy compared to a same-size victim cache. For a 4KB L1 cache, a 2-way L0 cache implemented as a flow cache consumes 14 more energy while 20 misses are removed, while a same size victim cache consumes 27 energy to remove a similar number of misses. Energy reduction is even more effective when the cache size is increased. A 2-way L0 cache increases only 6 more energy for a 16KB L1 cache to remove 20 misses. In general, the flow cache further optimizes energy consumption while still achieves similar performance. Note that the benefit does not simply come from having more data arrays. Our results (not shown here) confirm that a 4KB direct-mapped L1 plus an 8-way L0 perform as well as a 8KB direct-mapped L1 cache, while the size is only 53 .

To understand the effectiveness of the flow cache, let us compare the hit rates of the L0 cache. Fig. 7 also shows the L0 hit rates of different victim caches and flow caches. It is shown that the L0 cache used as a victim cache has a hit rate of less than 3 for all configurations, while for the flow caches it is much higher, from 10 to 40 . The L0 hit rate in the flow caches is high in a small L1 cache. By filtering accesses to the L1 cache, energy consumption is smaller than the victim cache.

In summary, the effectiveness in reducing conflict misses combined with simple hardware design and low energy consumption makes the flow cache attractive in enhancing oper-

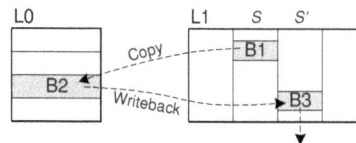

Figure : Migration during hit to the 1 cache in the hit cache.

ations of a direct-mapped L1 cache, especially in a low-end embedded processor.

5.3 The Hit Cache – Reducing Energy Consumption

5.3.1 Hardware Design

As shown in the previous section, the hit cache is used to reduce accesses to the L1 cache, hence is effective in reducing energy consumption for a set-associative cache. Unlike the filter cache, on a miss to both caches, it inserts a missed line into the L1 cache only. The L1 cache is bypassed on a hit to the L0 cache. During a hit to the L1 cache, the hit line is promoted to the L0 cache and replaces a line there. The evicted line is written back to the L1 cache, as illustrated in Fig. 8. In this figure, an access results in a hit to line B1 of a set S in the L1 cache, and victim selection finds a victim B2 in the L0 cache. B2 is written back to the L1 cache and replaces a line B3 in a set S' there. B1 is copied to the L0 cache in the place of B2. Now B1 and B2 become identical. It can be observed that if the access to B1 is a read, then the writeback of B3 can not be happen in the same cycle with reading B1 because we only allow 1 read and/or 1 write at any cycle. In this section, we describe a hardware implementation to support this policy. The hardware design must satisfy that the number of accesses to the L1 cache is minimized to save energy, while performance is not significantly impacted.

In [21, 8] the block buffers are used to store a cache line which are likely to be reused. This is enabled by placing the buffers close to the data array of the L1 cache, before the multiplexing to choose desired word. We also implement a similar mechanism to enable fast migration between the L0 and L1 cache, by moving the L0 data array close to the L1 data array, as depicted in Fig. 6. Note that the caches are also close to the AGEN unit, therefore while the tag and data arrays of the L0 cache are decoupled, the distance is short, allowing fast updates of the L0 cache. An alternative is to use the latches for buffering lines when migrating data between two caches. This is similar to the write buffers which are popular in multi-cycle pipelined caches.

We investigate two hardware implementations for the hit

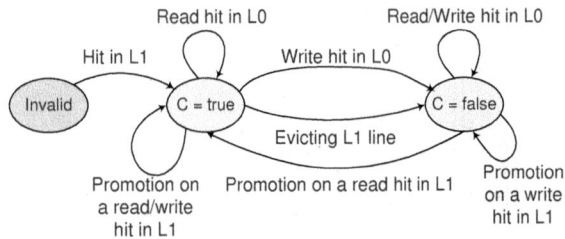

Figure : State transition of   lines.

cache, depending on when and how to write B2 back to the L1 cache, the *eager* and the *lazy* mechanisms, described as follows.

ager update. In this design, each valid line in the L0 cache always has a copy in the L1 cache, and a write hit into the L0 cache also updates line content in the L1 cache. There is no need to search for the victim B3 and a line B2 when evicted from the L0 cache is simply discarded. Also, the miss rate of this implementation does not change compared to the baseline L1 cache. In this design, the L0 cache operates as a write-through cache, and an eviction of the L1 line also invalidates its L0 copy, if existing. Note that the works in [14, 21, 8] also use this approach. Because this policy updates the L1 copy content of B2 every write hit, we call it the eager design.

a y update. An alternative design is the lazy design, which delays the update until B2 is evicted. Compared to the eager design, this design has more potential to reduce accesses to the L1 cache, especially when B2 is written multiple times before it is evicted from the L0 cache. In this design, it is not required to force B2 to have a copy. Instead, when the B2 line is modified, its copy in the L1 cache is *invalidated*, by updating the corresponding valid bit. B2 can only be written back to the L1 cache if and only if B3 is an invalid line. We also allow the replacement of the L1 copy without invalidating the L0 line as in the write-through cache.

To support this mechanism, each L0 cache line is instrumented with an extra *opy* bit, the **C** bit, to indicate whether it has a valid copy in the L1 cache. The state transition is shown in Fig. 9. When a line is hit in the L1 cache, it is copied to the L0 cache, and the **C** bit is set. This bit is unset if the L0 line is modified due to a write hit or the L1 copy is evicted (which does not happen frequently). Note that in a write hit the L1 line is invalidated. The state does not change if the access is a read hit in the L0 cache. When the line is evicted due to a promotion from the L1 cache, the **C** bit is updated for the *new* line and cache migration is performed. The migration is done with the awareness of hardware constraints. If the previous line has **C** set, then it is simply discarded and the new line has a copy in both caches (**C** is set). If the evicted line has **C** unset, a read hit in the L1 cache does the writeback of the line to the L1 cache, and the new line is read from the L1 cache and written into the L0 cache. In this case, there is 1 read and 1 write happening in each cache. Otherwise, if it is a write hit in the L1 cache, there are two writes happen in the L1 cache, one is the write access and the other is the writeback to the L1 cache. Due to the constraints, only the writeback to the L1 cache is done. The hit line is read from the L1, modified and written into the L0 cache without having a copy in the

L1 cache. In the figure, the promotion due to a write in the L1 cache results in the unset **C** bit.

---

lgorithm 1 Promotion during a hit to   1 in   1.

Note – *set(Bi)*: set ID in L1 of Bi, Bi.C: bit **C** of Bi.

```
 1: Find victim B2 in L0
 2: if B2 is invalid then
 3:    Copy (B1 → B2)
 4: else if B2.C = true then
 5:    Discard B2
 6:    Copy (B1 → B2)
 7: else if set(B1) = set(B2) then
 8:    Swap B1 and B2
 9: else
10:    Find victim B3 from set(B2)
11:    if B3 is invalid then
12:       Move B2 to the position of B3
13:    else
14:       Write back B2 to main memory
15:    end if
16:    Copy (B1 → B2)
17: end if
```

In Fig. 9 we have shown the state transition, including a promotion from the L1 cache. Let us describe how the migration is performed in this case. Using the notations in Fig. 8, the algorithm is shown in Alg. 1. There are 3 possibilities after B2 is already valid. First, if B2 has an L1 copy (bit **C** is set), it is simply discarded and B1 is copied to B2 (in the case of a write, data is written into both lines). Second, if B1 and B2 are in the same set, they are simply swapped. In these first two cases, because at most 1 read and 1 write happen to each cache, the read and write can be done in one cycle. In the last case, because L1 has only one read port then there is no available port to write back B3, hence B2 is written back to L1 only if B3 is invalid, and is written back to the main memory otherwise. This might degrade performance because of the discarded B2. Fortunately, the case of discarding B2 because B3 is valid is very rare.

Now, we describe hardware support for the case where B2 must be written back to the memory (other cases are similar or simpler). With the target L1 as a set-associative cache, then process is as follow:

Step : Calculate set S of L1 to access; find victim B2 from L0.

Step : Calculate way ID in S to access data (block B1); start writing back B2 to the memory.

Step 3: Copy hit data from B1 to B2; if the access is a write then update the content of B1 and B2.

In the case where the L1 lines are invalidated due to different reasons, such as due to coherence protocols, the invalid lines can be exploited to minimize writing back B2 to the memory. It can also be observed that this lazy mechanism lays between two promotion policies, P10 and P101. Recall that P10 never saves the evicted line in L0 while P101 always does, our real design saves lines which have a copy or can be written back to the L1 cache given the hardware constraints.

5.3.2 Analysis

In this section we analyze and compare two design described in the previous section. Fig. 10 shows the operations of the hit cache, including the hit rate in the L0 cache, misses per kilo instructions (MPKI) of the D-cache, fraction of writeback from L0 to L1, and energy consumption. The

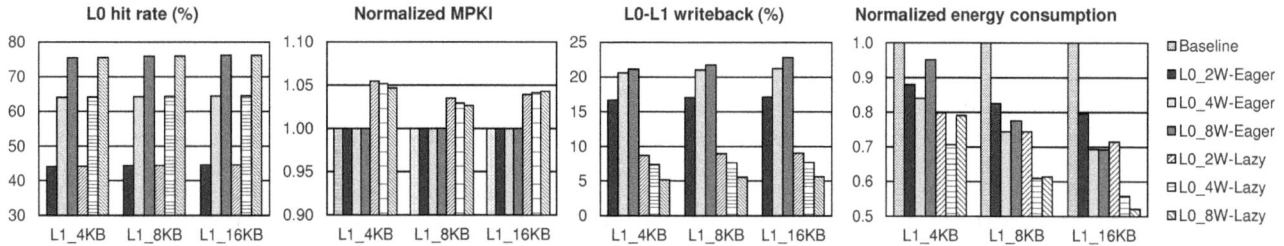

Figure 1 : it cache operations.

L0 hit rate and the writeback fraction are computed by dividing the number of L0 hits and writebacks by the total number of accesses to the D-cache, respectively. MPKI and energy consumption are normalized to the baseline L1 cache. For each eager and lazy design, we show the results for the L0 cache of 2, 4 and 8 ways, and the 4-way L1 cache of 4KB, 8KB, and 16KB.

First, the L0 hit rate is very similar with different L1 sizes and designs, and is similar to that in Fig. 5, with the difference less than 1 . For a 2-way L0 cache, the hit rate is about 45 while in a 8-way L0 cache it is around 75 . This confirms the importance of the L0 cache in reducing accesses to the L1 cache. Second, the MPKI of the eager design is the same with the baseline L1 design, while that of the lazy design is around 5 higher. It is interesting that for the L1 size of 4BK and 8KB, the misses decrease when the associativity of the L0 increases, while they increase for the 16KB L1 cache. Third, let us compare the fraction of L0-L1 writebacks. In general, with the same L0 and L1 sizes, the lazy design offers around 2 to 3 times less writebacks than the eager design. This confirms that a line can be updated multiple times while in the L0 cache.

For the eager design, a high L0 associativity creates more updates to the L1 cache, while in the lazy design, it saves more writebacks. For example, an 8-way L0 has around 20 writebacks with eager design, while it is only 5 with the lazy design.

Finally, let us analyze the saving of energy consumption. It is obvious that high L0 hit rate and low writeback fraction combined help save more energy due to less accesses to the L1 cache, especially when the L1 access energy is high. Due to this fact both the eager and lazy designs see the best energy savings with a 4-way L0 cache, but not a 2-way nor 8-way one with the L1 cache of 4KB and 8KB. For the 16KB L1 cache, the 8-way L0 cache saves more compared to the 4-way L0 cache. Compared to the eager design, the lazy design saves more energy, with around 10 more. For the target 16KB L1, the 8-way L0 energy saving of the eager design is30 while that of the lazy design is up to 50 .

In summary, the eager design saves about 30 access energy without impacting performance, while the lazy design saves 50 but with 5 more misses.

6. RELATED WORK

In the previous sections we have compared our study with several prior studies. This section summarizes them as well as discusses more related work. In the best or our knowledge, our work is the first to study data migration in a systematic way. From the exploration we find new opportunities to optimize the L0 cache design. Compared to the victim cache [13], the flow cache design is simpler and uses the L0

cache to filter accesses to the L1 cache, hence achieve similar conflict miss reduction, while requires less energy. We achieve our goals due to the victim cache targets high performance processors, while ours is the embedded processors. The hit cache may be closest to the filter cache [14] and the block buffering work [8, 21]. In [14], the filter cache is placed in between the processor and the L1 cache. In fact the filter cache can be considered another version of the buffering blocks in [21]. In these works, the L0 hit rate must be high enough to compensate the increased latency between the processor and the L1 cache. Later the work in [8] designs the L0 cache as a write-through cache, and it do not impact the system's performance. In our design, we further study the tradeoffs between performance and energy, and from that propose two configurations addressing the tradeoffs. Note that the filter cache is proposed for the embedded processors, and the block buffering work is proposed for high performance ones.

Besides these designs, other designs also exploit a small L0 cache [24, 3, 11, 4, 7, 9]. In the HotSpot cache [24] and its variant [3], the L0 cache is used in the I-cache to store "hot" loops which have high execution fraction, to reduce accesses to the L1 cache. It does so by using the BTB to identify fetch addresses which belong to the hot loops. A similar approach [7] stores basic instruction blocks in a Tagless Instruction Cache. It also uses the BTB to store block information. Another approach [11] is similar to our design in that the L0 cache is known to be hit or missed before real accesses from the processor. That work is targeted for the instruction cache. The loop cache [9] focuses on designing cache to store loops for special purposes. The Non-Temporal Streaming cache [19] improves the direct-mapped L1 cache by using a small cache to hold non-temporal lines and targeted numerical programs. The scratchpad memory [4] was proposed to store critical data to avoid long accesses to the memory. In terms for access determination from the processor, the study in [16] proposes to do the set determination in parallel with the load store queue access, hence saving time comparing set IDs. Our study is proposed for the data cache, where the L0 tag comparison is moved to the processor pipeline.

7. CONCLUSIONS

In this paper we show that a migration policy between an L0 cache and an L1 data cache is crucial in optimizing cache performance in an embedded processor. We systematically investigated different policies during an insertion and a promotion, and found two configurations which have potential applications. The first is the *flow a he*, which reduces conflict misses in a direct-mapped L1 cache. By comparing to the victim cache, we show that the flow cache is a suitable choice for the embedded system domain. The second is the *hit a he*, which reduces accesses to the set-associative L1 cache. Two hardware mechanisms were proposed for the hit cache. One does not impact performance, while the other has a slight degradation but further reduces energy consumption.

8. ACKNOWLEDGMENTS

This work is supported in part by NSF grant CISE-SHF 1118047. Nam Duong is also supported by the Dean's Fellowship, Donald Bren School of Information and Computer Sciences, UC Irvine. The authors would like to thank the anonymous reviewers for their useful feedback.

9. REFERENCES

[1] *ARM T -S Te hni al Referen e Manual*, 2005-2007.

[2] *Cortex-M3 Te hni al Referen e Manual*, 2005-2008.

[3] K. Ali, M. Aboelaze, and S. Datta. Modified hotspot cache architecture: A low energy fast cache for embedded processors. In *Em edded Computer Systems Ar hite tures, Modeling and Simulation, International Conferen e on*, 2006.

[4] R. Banakar, S. Steinke, B.-S. Lee, M. Balakrishnan, and P. Marwedel. Scratchpad memory: design alternative for cache on-chip memory in embedded systems. In *Pro eedings of the tenth international symposium on Hardware/software odesign*, 2002.

[5] N. Binkert, B. Beckmann, G. Black, S. K. Reinhardt, A. Saidi, A. Basu, . Hestness, D. R. Hower, T. Krishna, S. Sardashti, R. Sen, K. Sewell, M. Shoaib, N. Vaish, M. D. Hill, and D. A. Wood. The gem5 simulator. *ACM SIGARCH Computer Ar hite ture News*, 2011.

[6] C. Cascaval and D. A. Padua. Estimating cache misses and locality using stack distances. In *Pro eedings of the th annual international onferen e on Super omputing*, 2003.

[7] C.-W. Chen and C.- . Ku. A tagless cache design for power saving in embedded systems. *The Journal of Super omputing*, 2011.

[8] K. Ghose and M. B. Kamble. Reducing power in superscalar processor caches using subbanking, multiple line buffers and bit-line segmentation. In *Pro eedings of the international symposium on Low power ele troni s and design*, 1999.

[9] A. Gordon-Ross, S. Cotterell, and F. Vahid. Exploiting fixed programs in embedded systems: A loop cache example. *IEEE Computer Ar hite ture Letters*, 2002.

[10] M. R. Guthaus, . S. Ringenberg, D. Ernst, T. M. Austin, T. Mudge, and R. B. Brown. MiBench: A free, commercially representative embedded benchmark suite. In *Pro eedings of the Workload Chara terization*, 2001.

[11] S. Hines, D. Whalley, and G. Tyson. Guaranteeing hits to improve the efficiency of a small instruction cache. In *Pro eedings of the th Annual IEEE/ACM International Symposium on Mi roar hite ture*, 2007.

[12] A. aleel, K. B. Theobald, S. C. Steely, r., and . Emer. High performance cache replacement using re-reference interval prediction (RRIP). In *Pro eedings of the 3 th annual international symposium on Computer ar hite ture*, 2010.

[13] N. P. ouppi. Improving direct-mapped cache performance by the addition of a small fully-associative cache and prefetch buffers. In *Pro eedings of the th annual international symposium on Computer Ar hite ture*, 1990.

[14] . Kin, M. Gupta, and W. H. Mangione-Smith. The filter cache: an energy efficient memory structure. In *Pro eedings of the 3 th annual ACM/IEEE international symposium on Mi roar hite ture*, 1997.

[15] C. Lee, M. Potkonjak, and W. H. Mangione-Smith. Mediabench: a tool for evaluating and synthesizing multimedia and communicatons systems. In *Pro eedings of the 3 th annual ACM/IEEE international symposium on Mi roar hite ture*, 1997.

[16] D. Nicolaescu, A. Veidenbaum, and A. Nicolau. Reducing power consumption for high-associativity data caches in embedded processors. In *Pro eedings of the onferen e on Design, Automation and Test in Europe*, 2003.

[17] P. Petoumenos, G. Keramidas, and S. Kaxiras. Instruction-based reuse-distance prediction for effective cache management. In *Systems, Ar hite tures, Modeling, and Simulation, International Symposium on*, 2009.

[18] M. K. ureshi, A. aleel, . N. Patt, S. C. Steely, and . Emer. Adaptive insertion policies for high performance caching. In *Pro eedings of the 3 th annual international symposium on Computer ar hite ture*, 2007.

[19] . Rivers and E. Davidson. Reducing conflicts in direct-mapped caches with a temporality-based design. In *Pro eedings of the International Conferen e on Parallel Pro essing*, 1996.

[20] S. Sadasivan. *An Introdu tion to the ARM Cortex-M3 Pro essor*. ARM, 2006.

[21] C.-L. Su and A. M. Despain. Cache design trade-offs for power and performance optimization: a case study. In *Pro eedings of the international symposium on Low power design*, 1995.

[22] D. Tarjan, S. Thoziyoor, and N. ouppi. CACTI 4.0. Technical Report HPL-2006-86, HP Labs, 2006.

[23] T. Wolf and M. Franklin. CommBench-a telecommunications benchmark for network processors. In *Pro eedings of the IEEE International Symposium on Performan e Analysis of Systems and Software*, 2000.

[24] C.-L. ang and C.-H. Lee. HotSpot cache: joint temporal and spatial locality exploitation for i-cache energy reduction. In *Pro eedings of the international symposium on Low power ele troni s and design*, 2004.

Architectural Synthesis of Flow-Based Microfluidic Large-Scale Integration Biochips

Wajid Hassan Minhass
whmi@imm.dtu.dk

Paul Pop
pop@imm.dtu.dk

Jan Madsen
jan@imm.dtu.dk

Felician Stefan Blaga

DTU Informatics
Technical University of Denmark
DK-2800 Kgs. Lyngby, Denmark

ABSTRACT

Microfluidic biochips are replacing the conventional biochemical analyzers and are able to integrate the necessary functions for biochemical analysis on-chip. In this paper we are interested in flow-based biochips, in which the flow of liquid is manipulated using integrated microvalves. By combining several microvalves, more complex units, such as micropumps, switches, mixers, and multiplexers, can be built. The manufacturing technology, soft lithography, used for the flow-based biochips is advancing faster than Moore's law, resulting in increased architectural complexity. However, the designers are still using full-custom and bottom-up, manual techniques in order to design and implement these chips. As the chips become larger and the applications become more complex, the manual methodologies will not scale, becoming highly inadequate. Therefore, for the first time to our knowledge, we propose a top-down architectural synthesis methodology for the flow-based biochips. Starting from a given biochemical application and a microfluidic component library, we are interested in synthesizing a biochip architecture, i.e., performing component allocation from the library based on the biochemical application, generating the biochip schematic (netlist) and then performing physical synthesis (deciding the placement of the microfluidic components on the chip and performing routing of the microfluidic channels), such that the application completion time is minimized. We evaluate our proposed approach by synthesizing architectures for real-life applications as well as synthetic benchmarks.

Categories and Subject Descriptors

J.6 [**Computer-Aided Engineering**]: Computer-aided design (CAD)

General Terms

Design, Performance

Keywords

microfluidic, biochips, architecture, synthesis, flow-based

1. INTRODUCTION

Microfluidics-based biochips (also referred to as lab-on-a-chip) integrate different biochemical analysis functionalities (e.g., mixers, filters, detectors) on-chip, miniaturizing the macroscopic biochemical processes to a sub-millimetre scale [12]. These microsystems offer several advantages over the conventional biochemical analyzers, e.g., reduced sample and reagent volumes, faster biochemical reactions, ultra-sensitive detection and higher system throughput, with several assays being integrated on the same chip [15].

Microfluidics-based biochips have become an actively researched area in recent years. These chips can readily facilitate clinical diagnostics, especially immediate point-of-care disease diagnosis. In addition, they also offer exciting application opportunities in the realm of massively parallel DNA analysis, enzymatic and proteomic analysis, cancer and stem cell research, and automated drug discovery [12, 15]. Utilizing these biochips to perform food control testing, environmental (e.g., air and water samples) monitoring and biological weapons detection are also interesting possibilities.

There are several types of biochip platforms, each having its own advantages and limitations [11]. In this paper, we focus on the flow-based biochips in which the microfluidic channel circuitry on the chip is equipped with chip-integrated microvalves that are used to manipulate the on-chip fluid flow [12]. By combining several microvalves, more complex units such as mixers, micropumps, multiplexers can be built, with hundreds of units being accommodated on a single chip [11]. Analogous to its microelectronics counterpart, this approach is called microfluidic Large Scale Integration (mLSI) [12].

1.1 Related Work

During the last decade, a significant amount of work has been carried out on the individual microfluidic components as well as the microfluidic platforms [10, 11]. The manufacturing technology, soft lithography, used for the flow-based biochips has advanced faster than Moore's law [9]. Although biochips are becoming more complex everyday, Computer-Aided Design (CAD) tools for these chips are still in their infancy. Most CAD research has been focussed on device-level physical modeling of components [17].

Designers are using full-custom and bottom-up methodologies to implement these chips. Microfluidic components are designed and connected together to match the steps of the desired biochemical application using technical drawing tools such as AutoCAD [1]. In order to design a chip, the designer needs to have a complete understanding of the application requirements and at the same time, have the knowledge and skills of chip fabrication. The placement and routing is also done manually [2] and then the chip is fabricated using soft lithography techniques. Recent work has proposed automation techniques for the placement, routing and optimization

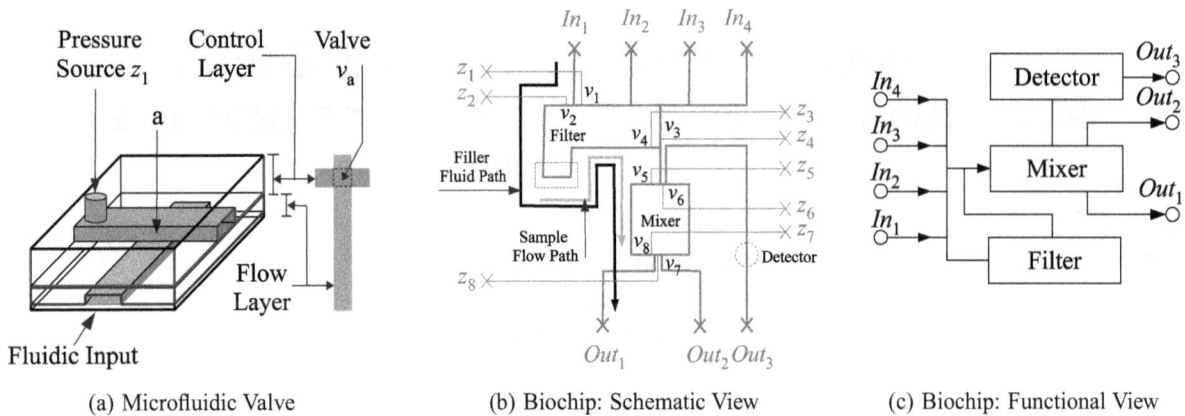

(a) Microfluidic Valve   (b) Biochip: Schematic View   (c) Biochip: Functional View

Figure 1: Flow-Based Biochip Architecture Model

for the channels that are used to control the microvalves [4]. However, this work is limited to the control part of the chip. In order to execute the application, designers manually map the operations to the valves of the chip using a customized interface (analogous to exposing the gate-level details).

As the chips grow more complex (commercial biochips are available which use more than 25,000 valves and about a million features to run 9,216 polymerase chain reactions in parallel [15]) and the need of having multiple and concurrent assays on the chip becomes more significant, the manual methodologies will not scale and will become highly inadequate. Therefore, new top-down methodologies and design tools are needed, in order to provide the same level of CAD support to the biochip designer as the one currently taken for granted in the semiconductor industry. Such an approach would also decouple the biochip architecture design from fabrication details, allowing users to focus on applications without requiring knowledge and skills of chip fabrication [12].

Significant work on top-down synthesis methodologies for droplet-based biochips has been proposed [6]. However, the architecture of the droplet-based chips differs significantly from the flow-based chips. In the flow-based biochips, components of different types (e.g., mixers, heaters) are physically designed on the chip and connected to each other using microfluidic channels. Once fabricated, the number and type of the components, their placement scheme on the chip and the routing interconnections cannot be modified. Droplet-based biochips (also referred to as digital biochips), however, use the idea of virtual components and are reconfigurable. A digital biochip consists of a two-dimensional array of identical electrodes on which the fluid is manipulated as discrete droplets. Adjacent set of electrodes can be combined together to form a virtual component, e.g., a mixer can be created by grouping adjacent electrodes and moving the droplet around on these electrodes to achieve mixing. Any set of electrodes can be used for this purpose and thus the chip is termed reconfigurable. The same electrodes can later be used for performing other operations as well, e.g., fluid transport, storage. Because of the architectural differences, the models and techniques proposed for the digital chips are not applicable to their flow-based counterparts.

1.2 Contribution

We propose a top-down architectural synthesis methodology for the flow-based microfluidic biochips. Given a biochemical application modeled as a sequencing graph, a microfluidic component library and the chip area, the architectural synthesis consists of the

following three steps: (i) *allocation* of components from a given library, (ii) performing the *schematic design* and generating the *netlist*, and the biochip (iii) *physical synthesis*, i.e., deciding the placement of the microfluidic components on the chip and performing routing of the microfluidic channels on the available routing layers creating component interconnections.

The synthesis problem is NP-complete. We use an approach similar to High-Level Synthesis [8] for performing allocation and netlist generation. The component placement is done using Simulated Annealing and we tailor the Hadlock's algorithm [16] from the Very Large-Scale Integrated (VLSI) circuits domain for performing the microfluidic channel routing. Synthesis is done in such a way that the application completion time is minimized and the imposed constraints (e.g., resource, dependency) are satisfied.

We build on our previous work in [14], where we consider that the architecture is given, and propose an approach for mapping a biochemical application onto the given architecture such that the application completion time is minimized. However, this paper is the first to present an approach for the automatic synthesis of a biochip architecture. The main contributions of this paper are the formulation of the architectural synthesis problem and the proposed synthesis framework, which show how the well-known algorithms from the High-Level Synthesis of VLSI circuits can be tailored to tackle the flow-based biochips.

The paper is organized in seven sections. The biochip architecture model and the biochemical application model are presented in Section 2. The problem is formulated in Section 3 and the synthesis steps are presented in Section 4. The proposed synthesis framework is discussed in Section 5 and is further evaluated in Section 6. We present our conclusions in Section 7.

2. SYSTEM MODEL

2.1 Biochip Architecture

Fig. 1b shows the schematic view of a flow-based biochip with 4 input ports and 3 output ports, 1 mixer, 1 filter and 1 detector. Fig. 1c shows the functional view of the same chip. The biochip is manufactured using multilayer soft lithography [12]. A cheap, rubber-like elastomer (polydimethylsiloxane, PDMS) with good biocompatibility and optical transparency is used as the fabrication substrate. Physically, the biochip can have multiple layers, but the layers are logically divided into two types: *flow layer* (depicted in blue) and the *control layer* (depicted in red). The liquid in the flow layer is manipulated using the control layer [12].

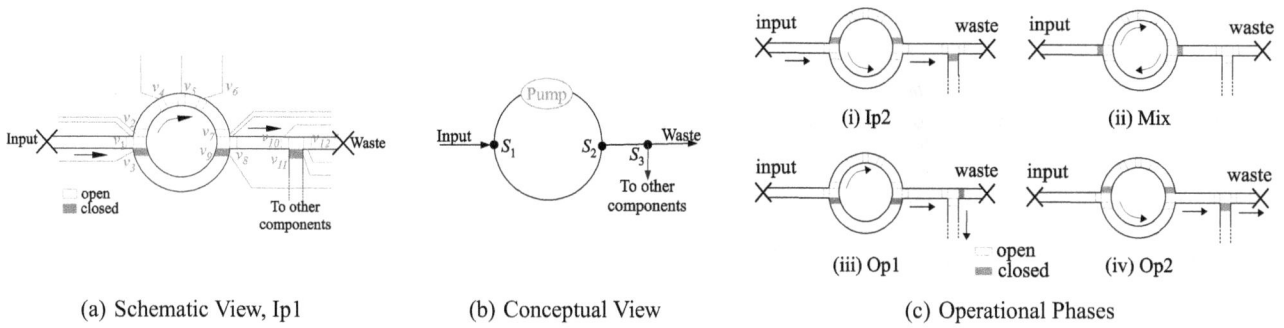

(a) Schematic View, Ip1   (b) Conceptual View   (c) Operational Phases

Figure 2: Microfluidic Mixer

The basic building block of such a biochip is a valve (see Fig. 1a), which is used to manipulate the fluid in the flow layer as the valves restrict/ permit the fluid flow. The control layer (red) is connected to an external air pressure source z_1. The flow layer (blue) is connected to a fluid reservoir through a pump that generates the fluid flow. When the pressure source is not active, the fluid is permitted to flow freely (open valve). When the pressure source is activated, high pressure causes the elastic control layer to pinch the underlying flow layer (point a in Fig. 1a) blocking the fluid flow (closed valve). Because of their small size ($100 \times 100 \ \mu m^2$), a biochip can accommodate thousands of valves. By combining these valves, more complex units, such as switches, multiplexers, micropumps, mixers, can be built [12]. For example, the valves can be combined to represent a switch. As shown in Fig. 3, a switch may consist of one valve (restricting/ allowing flow in a channel) or may consist of more than one valve. Multiple valve switches are present at the channel junctions and are used to control the path of the fluids entering the switch from different sides. The fluid flow can be generated using off-chip or on-chip pumps. The control layer can be placed both above and/ or below the flow layer, creating "pushdown" or "push-up" valves, respectively. Connections to the external ports (fluidic ports and pressure sources) are made by punching holes in the chip (gaining access to the flow and control layer) and placing external tubings (connected to the external fluidic reservoirs through pumps or pressure sources) into the punch holes [12]. All input ports are connected to off-chip pumps.

All fluid samples inside the chip occupy a fixed unit length (or a multiple of it) on the flow channel, i.e., the fluid samples have discretized volumes. Unit length samples are obtained by a process called *metering*, carried out by transporting the sample between two valves that are a fixed length apart [19]. In general, the chip is filled with a filler fluid (e.g., immiscible oil) and the fluid samples are emulsified in the filler fluid. As emulsions, the samples do not touch the channel walls directly (preventing cross-contamination) and can be moved over long channel lengths of any shape while retaining their content [19].

In order to make a fluid sample flow on the chip (e.g., *Filter* to the *Mixer* in Fig. 1b), (i) the point of fluid sample origin (*Filter*) needs to be connected to a pump (on-chip or off-chip) for generating the flow. As shown in Fig. 1b, the closest pump from the *Filter* is the off-chip pump connected to the input port In_1. We term the flow starting point as the *source* (In_1 in this case). (ii) The fluid sample destination point (*Mixer*) needs to be connected to a fluidic output port (*sink*, e.g., Out_1). Next, (iii) a path for the fluid flow needs to be established from the source to the sink using the microfluidic valves and then (iv) the desired flow (*Filter* to *Mixer*) can be achieved by activating the pump. For the *Filter* to *Mixer* flow in Fig. 1b, the path is established by closing the valve

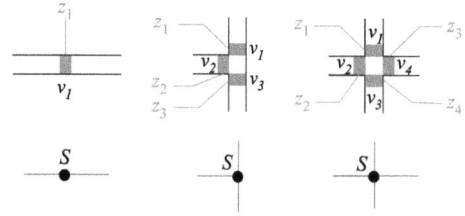

Figure 3: Switch Configurations

set v_1, v_3, v_6 and v_7, while the valve set v_2, v_4, v_5 and v_8 is kept open (the path is shown in black in Fig. 1b). The entire path already contains the filler fluid and the sample emulsified in the filler fluid is now present inside the *Filter*. A pumping action at the source (In_1) then creates a filler fluid flow towards the sink (Out_1). The emulsified sample flows with the filler fluid from the *Filter* towards the *Mixer*. The pumping action is stopped once the fluid sample reaches its destination (the green path in Fig. 1b shows the flow of the sample). While the sample flows from the *Filter* to the *Mixer*, the established path (including the source, sink points) is reserved and cannot be used for any other flows.

2.1.1 Component Model

We use our dual-layer component modeling framework proposed in [14] consisting of a *flow layer model* and a *control layer model*. The flow layer model ($\mathcal{P}, C, \mathcal{H}$) of each component M is characterized by a set of operational phases $\mathcal{P}$, execution time C and the component geometrical dimensions $\mathcal{H}$. The control layer model captures the valve actuation details required for the on-chip execution of all operational phases of a component. Table 1 shows the flow layer model library $\mathcal{L} = M(\mathcal{P}, C, \mathcal{H})$ of eight commonly utilized microfluidic components [10, 19].

Table 1: Component Library ($\mathcal{L}$): Flow Layer Model

Component	Phases (P)	Exec. Time (C)
Mixer	Ip1/ Ip2/ **Mix**/ Op1/ Op2	0.5 s
Filter	Ip/ **Filter**/ Op1/ Op2	20 s
Detector	Ip/ **Detect**/ op	5 s
Separator	Ip1/ Ip2/ **Separate**/ Op1/ Op2	140 s
Heater	Ip/ **Heat**/ Op	20°C/s
Metering	Ip/ **Met**/ Op1/ Op2	-
Multiplexer	Ip or Op	-
Storage	Ip or Op	-

183

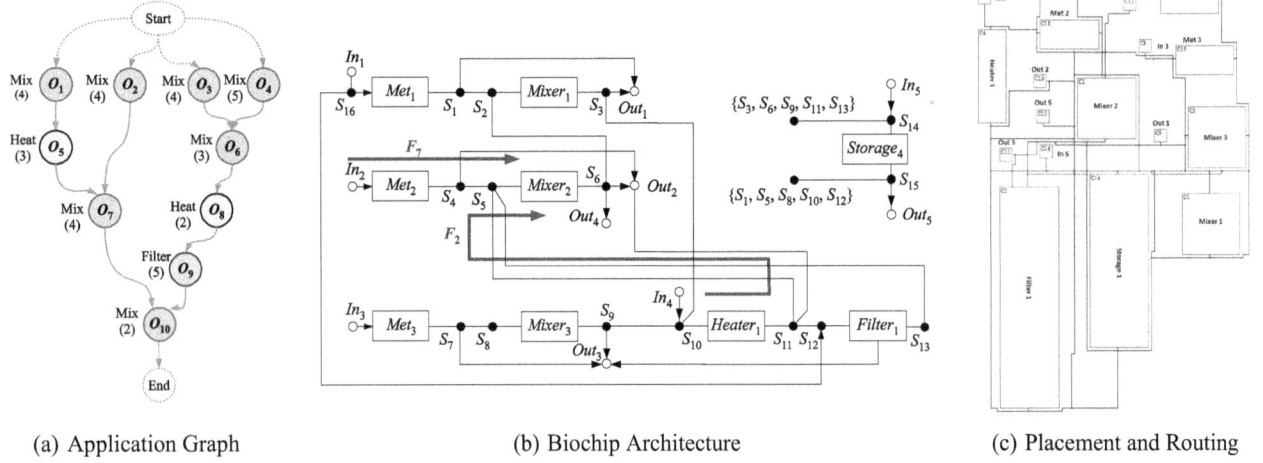

(a) Application Graph

(b) Biochip Architecture

(c) Placement and Routing

Figure 4: Biochip Application and Architecture Example

Table 2: Mixer: Control Layer Model

Phase	v_1	v_2	v_3	v_4	v_5	v_6	v_7	v_8	v_9
1. Ip1	0	0	1	0	0	0	0	0	1
2. Ip2	0	1	0	0	0	0	1	0	0
3. Mix	1	0	0	Mix	Mix	Mix	0	1	0
4. Op1	0	0	1	0	0	0	0	0	1
5. Op2	0	1	0	0	0	0	1	0	0

Consider the pneumatic mixer [7] in Fig. 2a which is implemented using nine microfluidic valves, v_1 to v_9. Fig. 2b shows the conceptual view of the same mixer. The valve set $\{v_4, v_5, v_6\}$ acts as an on-chip pump. The valve set $\{v_1, v_2, v_3\}$ is termed as switch S_1 and the valve set $\{v_7, v_8, v_9\}$ as switch S_2. The two switches facilitate the inputs and outputs, and the pump is used to perform the mixing. The mixer output can either be sent to the waste or to the other components in the chip using the switch S_3 (Fig. 2a).

The mixer has five operational phases. The first two phases represent the input of two fluid samples that need to be mixed, followed by the mixing phase. The mixed sample is then transported out of the mixer in the last two phases. For the first fluidic input (phase Ip1, depicted in Fig. 2a), valves v_1, v_2, v_7 and v_8 are opened (together with v_4, v_5, v_6), the pump at the *Input* is activated and the liquid fills in the upper half of the mixer.

In the next phase Ip2, the second fluid sample fills the lower half of the mixer (Fig. 2c-i). Once both halves are filled, the mixer input and output valves (v_1 and v_8) are closed while valves v_2, v_3, v_7, v_9 are opened and the mixing operation is initiated (Fig. 2c-ii). Valve set $\{v_4, v_5, v_6\}$ acts as a peristaltic pump. Closing valve v_4 inserts some pressure on the fluid inside the mixer, closing valve v_5 creates further pressure, then as valve v_6 is closed valve v_4 is opened again. This forces the liquid to rotate clockwise in the mixer. The valves are closed and opened in a sequence such that the liquid rotates at a certain speed accomplishing the mixing operation. Next, in phase Op1 (Fig. 2c-iii), half of the mixed sample is pushed out of the mixer towards the rest of the chip and in Op2 (Fig. 2c-iv), the other half is transported to the waste.

Table 2 presents the control layer model of the pneumatic mixer shown in Fig. 2, whose flow layer model is characterized by the first row in Table 1. In Table 2, the valve activation for each phase is shown, '0' representing an open and '1' a closed valve. The status

'Mix' shown for the valve set $\{v_4, v_5, v_6\}$ on row 4 of Table 2 represents the mixing step in which these valves are opened and closed in a specific sequence to achieve mixing. The control layer model of a component contains all the details that a biochip controller requires for executing the operational phases of that component.

The different operational phases may or may not be executable in parallel depending on how the component is implemented, e.g., the mixer presented here has only one input port to receive both the input fluids, thus only one input phase can be activated at a time.

2.1.2 Architecture Model

We use our previously proposed topology graph-based model [14] in order to capture the biochip architecture. The biochip architecture shown in Fig. 4b is captured by $\mathcal{A} = (\mathcal{N}, S, \mathcal{D}, \mathcal{F}, \mathcal{K}, c)$, where $\mathcal{N}$ is a finite set of vertices, S is a set of switches, $S \subseteq \mathcal{N}$, $\mathcal{D}$ is a finite set of directed edges, $\mathcal{F}$ is a finite set of flow paths and $\mathcal{K}$ is a finite set of routing constraints. A vertex $N \in \mathcal{N}$ has two types: a vertex $S \in S$ represents a switch (e.g., S_1 in Fig. 4b), whereas a vertex $M \in \mathcal{N}, \notin S$, represents a component or an input/output node (e.g., $Mixer_1$ and In_1, respectively, in Fig. 4b).

The set of *flow paths* $\mathcal{F}$ is the set of permissible flow routes on the biochip. Each flow path has an associated control layer model that contains the details required for its utilization, i.e., the switch sequence and the pump activation details. A directed edge $D_{i,j} \in \mathcal{D}$ represents a directed communication channel from the vertex N_i to vertex N_j, with $N_i, N_j \in \mathcal{N}$. For example, in Fig. 4b, D_{Filter_1, S_5} represents a directed link from vertex $Filter_1$ to vertex S_5. A flow path, $F_i \in \mathcal{F}$, is either a single directed edge or a subset of two or more directed edges of $\mathcal{D}$, $F_i \subseteq \mathcal{D}$, representing a directed communication link between any two vertices $\in \mathcal{N}$. In Fig. 4b, $F_2 = (D_{Heater_1, S_{11}}, D_{S_{11}, S_5}, D_{S_5, Mixer_2})$ represents a directed link from vertex $Heater_1$ to vertex $Mixer_2$. A routing constraint, $K_i \in \mathcal{K}$, is a set of flow paths that are mutually exclusive with the flow path $F_i \in \mathcal{F}$, i.e., none of the flow paths in the set can be activated in parallel. For example, F_2 and F_7 in Fig. 4b are mutually exclusive as they share the vertices S_5 and $Mixer_2$. The function $c(y)$, where y is either a directed edge $D \in \mathcal{D}$ or a flow path $F_i \in \mathcal{F}$, represents its routing latency (time required by a fluid sample to traverse y).

2.2 Biochemical Application Model

We model a biochemical application using a sequencing graph. The graph $\mathcal{G}(O, \mathcal{E})$ is directed, acyclic and polar (i.e., there is a

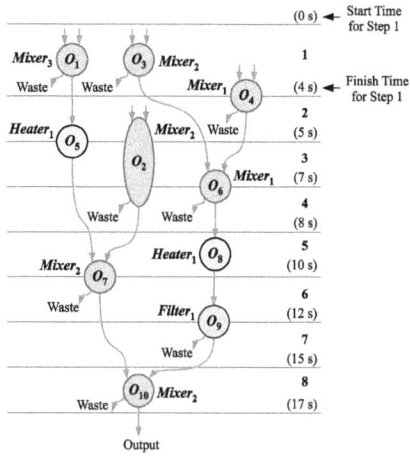

(a) Allocation Example for Fig. 4a

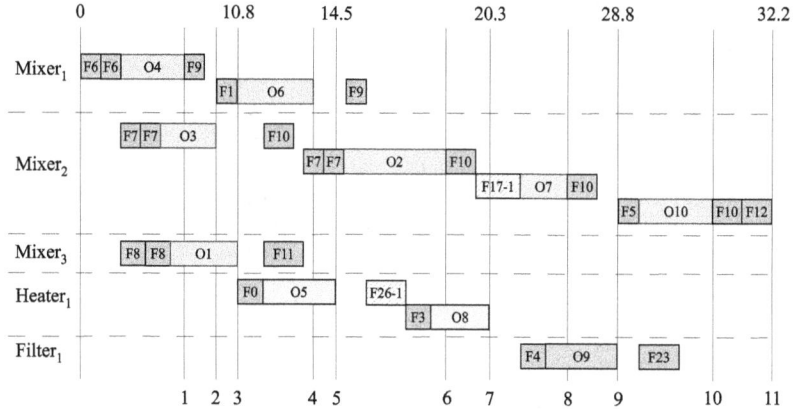

(b) Schedule

Figure 5: Illustrative Example

start vertex that has no predecessors and an *end* vertex that has no successors). Fig. 4a shows an example of a biochemical application. Each vertex $O_i \in O$ represents an operation that can be bound to a component using a binding function $\mathcal{B} : O \rightarrow M$. Each vertex has an associated weight $C_i(M_j)$, which denotes the execution time required for the operation O_i to be completed on component M_j. The execution times provided in Table 1 are of the actual functional phase (given in bold in the table, e.g., **Mix**). These execution times are taken as the typical execution times for the particular component types, i.e., typical mixing time is 0.5 s but a biochemical application description may specify a longer time (e.g., 5 s) if required for a certain operation. The edge set $\mathcal{E}$ models the dependency constraints in the assay, i.e., an edge $e_{i,j} \in \mathcal{E}$ from O_i to O_j indicates that the output of O_i is the input of O_j. An operation can start when all its inputs have arrived.

3. PROBLEM FORMULATION

The problem addressed in this paper can be formulated as follows: Given a biochemical application modeled as a sequencing graph $\mathcal{G}$ and a characterized component library $\mathcal{L}$, we are interested in synthesizing a biochip architecture $\mathcal{A}$ and a mapping Ψ of $\mathcal{G}$ onto $\mathcal{A}$, such that the application completion time is minimized and the imposed constraints are satisfied. The synthesis approach can handle several constraints, such as overall chip area, maximum number of components of a certain type and the external input and output ports. The number of external ports is also limited by the maximum number of punch holes possible on the chip under the given design rules [2]. As mentioned, the objective of the problem is to minimize the application completion time under the given constraints. However, other objectives can also be handled, such as the minimization of the architecture cost under a given timing constraint. The synthesis of the architecture $\mathcal{A}$ is the focus of this paper. The mapping of the application $\mathcal{G}$ onto the synthesized architecture is the focus of our previous work in [14].

Synthesizing an architecture $\mathcal{A}$ means deciding on (1) the allocation $\mathcal{U}$ of components from the component library $\mathcal{L}$, (2) the configuration for interconnection of these components (netlist), (3) placement $\mathcal{Z}_f$ of the components onto the chip layout area and interconnecting them by flow channel routing $\mathcal{R}_f$, and (4) placement $\mathcal{Z}_c$ of control valves and control ports on the chip and interconnecting them by control channel routing $\mathcal{R}_c$. The flow path set $\mathcal{F}$,

associated latencies and the corresponding routing constraints $\mathcal{K}$ also need to be extracted from the synthesized architecture. These are given as an input to the application mapping stage.

Synthesizing a mapping $\Psi = <\mathcal{B}, \mathcal{X}>$ means deciding on (5) the binding $\mathcal{B}$ of the operations and edges in the application $\mathcal{G}$ onto the components and flow paths in the synthesized architecture $\mathcal{A}$ and (6) generating the corresponding schedule $\mathcal{X}$ while satisfying all the constraints imposed by the synthesized architecture, such as routing constraints.

Other constraints can also be catered for in the synthesis flow (using the same set of models) by including additional optimization steps. For example, reliability of an mLSI biochip depends directly on the reliability of the valves (the valves can operate reliably only up to a few thousand actuations). Therefore, in order to achieve enhanced reliability, an optimization step can be added directed at balancing the load on the valves, i.e., each valve goes through approximately the same number of valve actuations during the application execution.

4. BIOCHIP SYNTHESIS

The following subsections explain the design tasks involved in the biochip synthesis using Fig. 4 as an illustrative example. Section 5 presents our proposed synthesis framework for these tasks.

4.1 Allocation and Schematic Design

In this step, the microfluidic components required for implementing the given biochemical application $\mathcal{G}$ are allocated from the component library $\mathcal{L}$, while taking into account the imposed

Table 3: Allocated Components ($\mathcal{U}$)

Function	Constraints	Allocated Units	Notations
Input port	5	5	$In_1 ... In_5$
Output port	5	5	$Out_1 ... Out_5$
Mixer	3	3	$Mixer_1 ... Mixer_3$
Heater	2	1	$Heater_1$
Filter	1	1	$Filter_1$
Metering Units	3	3	$Met_1 ... Met_3$
Storage Units	4	4	$Storage_x$

resource constraints. Next, based on the given application, a chip schematic is designed and the netlist is generated. For example, to implement the biochemical application from Fig. 4a under the constraints given in Table 3 columns 1 and 2, we could use an allocation $\mathcal{U}$ as captured by the last two columns in Table 3. The schematic design corresponding to such an application and allocation is presented in Fig. 4b. Note that the storage units are needed in order to save the output of a component so that it can be used at a later stage. The flow path set is also generated in this step. A flow path is the path starting from the point of fluid sample origin and ending at the fluid sample destination point, e.g., $Heater_1$ to $Mixer_2$ in Fig. 4b. Source-sink paths associated with each flow path are also defined, e.g., for the flow path $Heater_1$ to $Mixer_2$ in Fig. 4b, the source-sink path is (In_4, S_{10}, $Heater_1$, S_{11}, S_5, $Mixer_2$, S_6, Out_2). Routing constraints are also extracted at this stage. Two flow paths, whose corresponding source-sink paths have a common vertex are mutually exclusive and need to be listed under the routing constraints, e.g., F_7 and F_2 in Fig. 4b are mutually exclusive since they share common vertices (e.g., S_5) in their source-sink paths. Table 5 shows the flow path set, the source-sink set and the routing constraints associated with the architecture in Fig. 4b. Additional routing constraints may be imposed during the placement and routing phases, resulting in an updated routing constraints list.

4.2 Physical Synthesis

In this step, the allocated components are placed on a chip layout area and the interconnections between components are routed as channels on the chip such that the application completion time is minimized. The placement and routing phases are governed by design rules (see Table 4) imposed by the fabrication process carried out in a standard microfluidic foundry [2, 4]. During placement, the components are treated as fixed size blocks, represented by rectangles, each having a fixed length and width. The placement is done in such a way that all design rules are satisfied and no two components overlap on the chip.

For mLSI-based biochips, the placement and routing phases can be divided into two stages, one for each logical layer in the chip: the flow layer and the control layer (in Fig. 1b, the flow layer is shown in blue and the control layer in red).

4.2.1 Flow Layer

This stage involves determining the placement of microfluidic components and the fluidic inlet/ outlet ports Z_f on the chip layout area, and then routing the interconnecting nets $\mathcal{R}_f$ as microfluidic flow channels. Only one layer is available for performing the flow channel routing [12]. In VLSI chips, the intersection of nets is considered a short-circuit and is thus not permitted. However, net intersection is possible in the biochip flow layer. A switch is placed at the location of the intersection so that both nets (a net represents a microfluidic channel) can be used, at different points in time, without unintended fluid mixing. Considering that only one layer is available for routing all flow channel nets, the possibility of net intersection helps in achieving 100% routability. However, net intersections cause routing constraints, resulting in longer application completion times. Fig. 4c shows the placement and routing scheme for the flow layer of the biochip architecture shown in Fig. 4b. The entire placement and routing shown is done in one layer.

4.2.2 Control Layer

In this stage, the placement of the control valves and the control ports Z_c is decided, and then the valves are connected to the control ports through control channel routing $\mathcal{R}_c$. In Fig. 1b, the control layer is shown in red, with the control valves labelled as v_x and the

Table 4: Design Rules

Parameter	Suggested Value
Width of flow channel	100 μm
Minimum spacing between flow channels	40 μm
Width of control channel	30 μm
Width of control valve	100 μm
Minimum spacing between control channels	40 μm
Minimum spacing between external ports	1500 μm

control ports as z_y. Positions of the valves that are used inside a microfluidic component can be obtained directly from the component library. The positions of the valves that need to be placed on the flow channels are inferred from the flow routing information (e.g., valves need to be placed at all flow channel intersections). As explained in Section 2, one logical control layer can have two physical layers that can be used for placement and routing (above and below the flow layer) [12]. Contrary to the flow channels, control channels are not allowed to intersect.

After the placement is complete, the next step is to connect the valves to the ports using control channels. The control channels can be routed over/ under any flow channel/ component without forming a valve. The crossing of the control channel over a flow channel forms a valve only if the control channel has a large width (100 μm) [2]. The flow path channel lengths (used to calculate the routing latencies) and any additional routing constraints (imposed because of net intersections in the flow layer) can now be extracted from the layout and captured in the biochip architecture model $\mathcal{A}$. Table 5 shows the routing constraints and the list of flow paths for the biochip architecture in Fig. 4b together with their corresponding routing latencies.

4.3 Application Mapping

The next step is mapping the biochemical application $\mathcal{G}$ onto the synthesized architecture $\mathcal{A}$ such that the application completion time is minimized and the dependency, resource and routing constraints are satisfied. The binding $\mathcal{B}$ for the operations is the same as determined when generating the schematic. Binding of the edges and scheduling $\mathcal{X}$ for both the operations and the edges is generated in this step. Fig. 5b shows the schedule for the case when the application in Fig. 4a is scheduled on the architecture in Fig. 4b. The schedule is represented as a Gantt chart, where, we represent the operations and fluid routing phases as rectangles, with their lengths corresponding to their execution duration.

5. SYNTHESIS STRATEGY

Fig. 6 shows the block diagram of our proposed design methodology. In this paper, we focus on the "Architectural Synthesis" block which synthesizes the biochip architecture which is then given as input to the "Application Mapping" block. For the application mapping, we use our previously proposed approach in [14]. Microfluidic platforms are equipped with a controller that manages all on-chip control, i.e., issuing signals to on-chip components for executing a biochemical application, performing data acquisition and signal processing operations [10]. The mapping implementation (containing the binding and scheduling information), together with the component and biochip architecture models, can be used to generate the control sequence for a biochip controller ("Control Synthesis") in order to automatically execute the biochemical application onto the synthesized biochip.

The biochip synthesis problem presented in Section 3 is NP-complete (the scheduling step, even in simpler contexts is NP-com-

Table 5: Flow Path Set ($\mathcal{F}$), Source-Sink Set and Routing Constraints ($\mathcal{K}$)

Flow Path Set	Source-Sink Set	Routing Constraints
$F_0 = (Mixer_3, S_9, S_{10}, Heater_1)$, 0.7 s	$F'_0 = (In_3, Met_3, S_7, S_8, Mixer_3, S_9, S_{10}, Heater_1, S_{11},$ $Out_2)$	$K_0 : (F_1, F_2, F_3, F_4, F_5, F_6, F_7, F_8,$ $F_9, F_{10}, F_{11}, F_{12}, F_{13}, F_{14}$
$F_1 = (Mixer_2, S_6, S_2, Mixer_1)$, 0.4 s		$F_{15}, F_{16}, F_{17}, F_{18}, F_{19}, F_{20},$
$F_2 = (Heater_1, S_{11}, S_5, Mixer_2)$, 0.5 s	$F'_1 = (In_2, Met_2, S_4, S_5, Mixer_2, S_6, S_2, Mixer_1, S_3,$ $Out_1)$	$F_{21}, F_{24}, F_{25}, F_{26}, F_{27}, F_{28})$
$F_3 = (Mixer_1, S_3, S_{10}, Heater_1)$, 0.6 s		$K_1 : (F_0, F_2, F_3, F_4, F_5, F_6, F_7, F_8,$
$F_4 = (Heater_1, S_{11}, S_{12}, Filter_1)$, 2.1 s	$F'_2 = (In_4, S_{10}, Heater_1, S_{11}, S_5, Mixer_2, S_6, Out_2)$	$F_9, F_{10}, F_{12}, F_{13}, F_{14}, F_{15}, F_{16},$
$F_5 = (Filter_1, S_{13}, S_5, Mixer_2)$, 0.8 s	$F'_3 = (In_1, S_{16}, Met_1. S_1, S_2, Mixer_1, S_3, S_{10}, Heater_1,$	$F_{17}, F_{24}, F_{25}, F_{26})$
$F_6 = (In_1, S_{16}, Met_1, S_1, S_2, Mixer_1)$, 1.3 s	$S_{11}, Out_2)$	...
$F_7 = (In_2, Met_2, S_4, S_5, Mixer_2)$, 1.9 s	$F'_4 = (In_4, S_{10}, Heater_1, S_{11}, S_{12}, Filter_1, Out_3)$	...
$F_8 = (In_3, Met_3, S_7, S_8, Mixer_3)$, 2.1 s	$F'_5 = (In_1, S_{16}, S_{12}, Filter_1, S_{13}, S_5, Mixer_2, S_6, Out_2)$	$K_{28-x}: (F_0, F_3, F_4, F_5, F_6, F_7, F_9,$
$F_9 = (Mixer_1, S_3, Out_1)$, 1.2 s	$F'_6 = (In_1, S_{16}, Met_1, S_1, S_2, Mixer_1, S_3, Out_1)$	$F_{11}, F_{14}, F_{15}, F_{16}, F_{17},$
$F_{10} = (Mixer_2, S_6, Out_2)$, 0.3 s	$F'_7 = (In_2, Met_2, S_4, S_5, Mixer_2, S_6, Out_2)$	$F_{18}, F_{19}, F_{20}, F_{21}, F_{22},$
$F_{11} = (Mixer_3, S_9, Out_3)$, 0.6 s	...	$F_{23}, F_{25}, F_{26}, F_{27})$
...	$F'_{28-x} = (In_1, S_{16}, S_{12}, Filter_1, S_{13}, S_{14}, Storage, S_{15},$ $Out_5)$	
$F_{28-x} = (Filter_1, S_{13}, S_{14}, Storage)$, 0.5 s		

Figure 6: Design Methodology

plete [18]). Our synthesis strategy in this paper is to solve each design task separately, by adapting well-known heuristic algorithms from VLSI domain. The heuristics do not guarantee obtaining the optimal solution. Obtaining the optimal results (in terms of application completion time) is infeasible even for small examples. The following subsections present the chosen heuristics and describe our strategy using Fig. 4 as an example.

5.1 Allocation and Schematic Design

This stage receives the application graph G, component library $\mathcal{L}$ and the resource constraints as input and determines the allocation $\mathcal{U}$ and generates the netlist. All components of the architecture model $\mathcal{A}$ are captured here except the routing latency c.

5.1.1 Allocation

The most common approach for allocation in High-Level Synthesis (HLS) [8] is to use resource-constrained List-Scheduling and binding. We start off by topologically sorting the operations of the biochemical application based on their dependency constraints and then prioritizing them using an *urgency criteria* [8]. The urgency of an operation is specified by the length of the longest path from the operation to the end node in the application graph. An oper-

ation is considered *ready*, if all of its predecessors have finished execution. All the operations in the application are evaluated, the ready ones are found and are placed in a ready list RL. For example in Fig. 4a, operations O_1 to O_4 have no predecessors and are thus considered ready, whereas O_6 cannot be executed until O_3 and O_4 are complete. For each ready operation we allocate a component of the required type, considering the imposed constraints (see Table 3, column 2). The operation is bound greedily to the allocated component and scheduled.

Fig. 5a shows the allocation schedule for the application in Fig. 4a. The schedule is divided into 8 schedule steps. The start of an operation marks the start of a schedule step (O_1, O_3, O_4 start at time t = 0 s, thus starting schedule step 1) and an operation completion marks the end of a schedule step (schedule step 1 ends at 4 s as operations O_1 and O_3 finish, and schedule step 2 ends at 5 s when operation O_4 finishes). Unlike the control steps in HLS [8] (where all control steps represent a fixed time duration, a clock cycle), the schedule steps are of varying time lengths.

The binding of each operation is also shown in Fig. 5a, the component name is placed next to the operation (e.g., O_1 is bound to $Mixer_3$). If the number of ready operations exceeds the number of available components, then the least urgent operations (i.e., greedy binding based on the urgency criteria) are deferred, e.g., in Fig. 5a, O_2 is deferred to schedule step 2 as there are only three mixers available for usage in schedule step 1.

As soon as an operation completes, it marks the end of a schedule step. The operations are then re-evaluated to find the new list of ready operations and the process is repeated. Table 3 shows the list of allocated components. All imposed resource constraints have been fulfilled. All components have been used in their maximum allowed number except the heater. Only one heater has been allocated considering the requirement, compared to the 2 heater units that were allowed by the user. At this stage, the routing latencies are not yet known. The actual values of the routing latency are generated after the placement and routing is complete. A set of input and output ports is allocated for each component in order to serve as the source and sink point during flow path execution. Metering units are used to create discretized samples of unit volume. The number of metering units allocated depends on the maximum possible external inputs that can be executed in parallel. In the current case, a maximum of three external inputs are taken in parallel in schedule step 1 (Fig. 5a) and thus three metering units have been allocated.

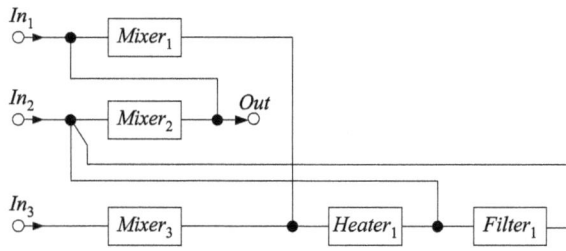

Figure 7: Schematic

5.1.2 Schematic Design

In the next step, we extract the schematic design from the generated binding and scheduling information (analogous to data path generation in HLS [8]). Each schedule step (Fig. 5a) is scanned to find the input source of the utilized components and a corresponding net is placed between the component and the input source. For example, $Heater_1$ in schedule step 5 gets an input from $Mixer_1$ and gives an output to $Filter_1$, therefore it is connected to both components. The extracted component interconnection scheme is shown in Fig. 7.

Next we connect input and output ports to each component to serve as the source and sink point. Metering units are placed at the fluidic sample input ports. Storage units are needed to store intermediate results of operations [19]. Unlike in HLS (where registers are required at every control step [8]), biochips require storage only under special conditions. Consider an operation O_x bound to a component M_y that finishes execution. If another operation gets bound to M_y in the next schedule step and the successor operation of O_x has not been scheduled yet, then the output of O_x will need to be moved to the storage. Each storage unit is capable of storing multiple fluid unit samples, depending on the number of storage channels inside the unit. Since the routing latencies are not yet known, it is not possible to accurately assess which components would require the storage unit usage. For now, the storage unit is is connected to all components and the designer specifies the maximum capacity of the unit. Unnecessary connections and extra storage channels are removed after the application mapping step. The final component interconnection configuration is shown in Fig. 4b.

The flow path set $\mathcal{F}$ and the corresponding routing constraints $\mathcal{K}$ are also generated in this step. The flow path set for the biochip architecture in Fig. 4 is shown in Table 5. The source-sink path for each flow path and the routing constraints are also shown.

5.2 Physical Synthesis

This stage takes the allocation $\mathcal{U}$, the netlist, component library L and the desired layout size as input and performs placement and routing ($\mathcal{Z}_f$, $\mathcal{R}_f$, $\mathcal{Z}_c$, $\mathcal{R}_c$), determining any additional constraints in the set $\mathcal{K}$ and the routing lengths of the flow paths (that are used to calculate the routing latencies c). We use a grid-based approach to perform physical synthesis. The grid size is dictated by the design rules and the component sizes on the grid are calculated accordingly using their dimensions given in the component library. The design rules imposed by the foundry and followed during the physical synthesis are summarized in Table 4. The placement and routing phases are divided into two stages, one for each logical layer.

5.2.1 Flow Layer

According to the problem formulation from Section 3, the placement and routing should be done such that the application com-

pletion time is minimized. However, this would require using the mapping and scheduling (Section 5.3) as the cost function, which is too time-consuming. Instead, we use the total channel length and the number of net intersections as the cost function. Minimizing the channel length minimizes the routing latencies, in turn minimizing the application completion time. Similarly, minimizing the number of net intersection minimizes the number of routing constraints, allowing more flow paths to be executed in parallel. This will not lead to the optimal result, but will reduce the application completion time. Furthermore, performing actual routing to compare various placement solutions is impractical as routing is a time-consuming process. Therefore, we perform placement and routing in separate steps and use an estimation method (Semi-Perimeter method, the most widely used approximation method [16]) to estimate the total channel length in order to judge the quality of the placement solution.

The placement of components such that the total channel length is minimized is an NP-complete problem, for which a number of good heuristic techniques have been developed [16]. Considering the problem at hand, we use Simulated Annealing (SA) (one of the most used methods for cell placement in VLSI [16]) for performing component placement on the chip. Various algorithms have been proposed for routing over the years. We use Hadlock's Algorithm (HA) [16] and extend it for the flow layer routing. HA is suitable for the current problem since it also uses a grid model approach, finds the shortest path between two vertices (if such a path exists) and is faster than the other algorithms in this category [16]. We extend HA to also consider the possibility of net intersections, ensuring a 100% routability. The quality of the solution is judged by the number of net intersections and the total channel length. Since HA is sensitive to the order in which the nets are routed, we iterate on HA, providing it a re-ordered netlist for every iteration in order to achieve a routing solution that minimizes the total channel length and net intersections.

The routing latency corresponding to each flow path is also generated in this step. Routing latencies are calculated by using the routing length of each flow path extracted from the architecture and the flow rate used on the chip. We consider a flow rate of 10 mm/s for all experiments in this paper. If the flow path length is 10 mm and the flow rate is set at 10 mm/s, then a unit volume of liquid (10 mm length on the channel) traverses this flow path in 2 s, i.e., from the time the tip of the 10 mm unit sample enters the flow path till the time the tail leaves from it. The latency values are required while performing application mapping. Latency values generated for each flow path are shown in Table 5.

Physical Synthesis Algorithm. Fig. 8 shows our algorithm for the physical synthesis of the flow layer. The algorithm takes the allocated component set M, the generated netlist *List* and the component library L as an input, and returns the placement and routing information of the flow layer. The objective is to place all the components on the chip and minimize the total channel length in order to reduce the routing latencies, while satisfying the design rules. Fig. 4c shows the flow layer placement and routing scheme that comes out of our algorithm.

Simulated Annealing [16] (lines $1-17$ in Fig. 8) is used for generating the placement scheme. SA is a metaheuristic, which, starting from a random initial placement of components (line 3), iteratively obtains a better placement scheme by performing *moves* (line 6), i.e., design transformations, (swapping, rotating or randomly changing component location on the chip) to modify the current solution. SA also accepts deteriorations in cost (lines $11-13$) to a limited extent in an effort to obtain global optimum, in terms of the cost function used. The placement generated by SA $\mathcal{Z}_f$ is given as

FlowPlaceAndRoute(*M*, *List*, $\mathcal{L}$***)**

```
1   // Phase I: Flow Layer Placement
2   Initialize T
3   Z_f^{now} = InitialPlacement(M, L)
4   repeat
5      for i=1 to TL do
6         Z'_f = moves(Z_f^{now})
7         δ = cost(Z'_f) - cost(Z_f^{now})
8         if δ < 0 then
9            Z_f^{now} = Z'_f
10        else
11           if random(0,1) < e^{-δ/T} then
12              Z_f^{now} = Z'_f
13           end if
14        end if
15     end for
16     T = α × T
17  until <stop criterion is met>
18  // Placement returns the best solution Z_f
19  // Phase II: Flow Channel Routing
20  R_f^{now} = RouteFlowLayer(Z_f, List)
21  c^{now} = cost(R_f^{now})
22  repeat
23     List = Re-order(List)
24     R'_f = RouteFlowLayer(Z_f, List)
25     c' = cost(R'_f)
26     if c' < c^{now} then
27        c^{now} = c'
28        R_f^{now} = R'_f
29     end if
30  until <stop criterion is met>
31  return <Z_f, R_f^{now}>
```

Figure 8: Physical synthesis algorithm for the flow layer

input to the Hadlock's Algorithm [16] (lines 20−30) to iteratively generate the routing. A re-ordered netlist is generated (line 23) in every iteration in order to cater for HA's sensitivity to the order in which the nets are routed. The best solution for the placement Z_f and the routing $\mathcal{R}_f^{now}$ is then returned (line 31).

5.2.2 Control Layer

Control layer placement and routing can be done using the same algorithms as described for the flow layer. We aim to target this step in our future research. Since the number of control valves on these chips can be extremely high (commercial chip having more than 25,000 valves [15]) and the number of punch holes that can be made on the chip for connecting the control ports is limited by the design rules [2], each valve cannot be connected to a separate control port. Different approaches aimed at sharing the control ports between valves have been proposed [12], which can be used to reduce the required number of control ports.

5.3 Application Mapping

Now since we have the biochip architecture $\mathcal{A}$, the biochemical application G and the characterized component library $\mathcal{L}$, we use our previously proposed binding and scheduling strategy [14] for mapping the given application onto the synthesized architecture such that the application completion time is minimized and all the imposed constraints are satisfied. Fig. 5b shows the schedule determined by our tool when the application in Fig. 4a is sched-

uled on the architecture in Fig. 4b. We use the same binding as the one generated during the schematic design (Fig. 5a). As shown in Fig. 5b, the application requires only one storage reservoir. The output of operation O_5 is moved to the storage since the heater needs to be reused for operation O_8 before the successor operation of O_5 (which is operation O_7) is released. The application execution is completed in 32.2 s.

6. EXPERIMENTAL EVALUATION

We evaluate our proposed approach by synthesizing biochip architectures for three real life assays and a set of four synthetic benchmarks. We implement these applications onto the synthesized chips and determine the application completion time. The algorithm was implemented in C#, running on a Pavilion laptop (HP dv6-2155dx) with Core i3, Dual Processors at 2.13 GHz and 4 GB of RAM.

Table 6 shows our experimental results. Column 1 presents the application and column 2 shows the list of allocated components, in the following format: (Input ports, Output ports, Mixers, Heaters, Filters, Detectors). Columns 3−6 present the desired chip area, total length of the flow channels, total number of net intersections and the total number of valves on the chip, respectively. Chip area represents the area given by the user as input. Chip area and total channel lengths are scaled, with a unit length being equal to 150 μm, i.e., a total length of 10 given in Table 6 corresponds to 1500 μm. The number of valves are calculated by considering 1 valve for each I/O port, 4 valves for each intersection (switch), 9 valves for each mixer, 6 valves for each metering unit and 2 valves each for all remaining components. This valve count can be further minimized by removing the valves which are never used. We plan to target this in our future research. The last column presents the completion time δ_G of the application, in seconds, on the synthesized architecture.

Real-life assays can be converted to our application model using [5]. The first real-life assay we use is the PCR (polymerase chain reaction) mixing stage that has 7 mixing operations and is used in DNA amplification. The architecture details and the corresponding application completion time are shown in row 1 of Table 6. Row 2 shows the architecture generated for Multiplexed IVD (in-vitro diagnostics) that has a total of 12 operations and is used to test different fluid samples from the human body. The third row shows a larger real-life application, a colorimetric protein assay (CPA, 55 operations), utilized for measuring the concentration of a protein in a solution. It uses a chip equipped with 295 valves to complete its execution in 72.7 s. The architectural details given in row 4 are for the example application (EA) given in Fig. 4a.

In the second set of experiments we have evaluated our proposed method using a set of four synthetic benchmarks. The benchmark applications are composed of 10, 30, 40 and 50 operations. Table 7 shows the details of the synthesized architectures considered and the respective application completion times achieved.

For each application in Table 7, two sets of architectures were synthesized. The first row presents results for the architecture syn-

Table 6: Real-Life Applications

Appl.	Allocated Units	Chip Area	Net Length	Total Inters.	Total Valves	δ_G
PCR	(3, 3, 3, 0, 0, 0)	250 × 250	198	4	67	19.7 s
IVD	(5, 5, 3, 0, 0, 3)	250 × 250	393	10	101	20 s
CPA	(5, 5, 5, 0, 0, 3)	250 × 250	1360	51	295	72.7 s
EA	(5, 5, 3, 1, 1, 0)	150 × 150	1917	63	311	32.2 s

Table 7: Synthetic Benchmarks

$|O|$	Allocated Units	Chip Area	Net Length	Total Inters.	Total Valves	δ_G
10	(2, 2, 1, 1, 1, 1)	150×150	1813	45	211	39.9 s
	(5, 5, 2, 1, 1, 1)	150×150	1926	68	324	35.7 s
30	(6, 6, 3, 2, 2, 1)	250×250	3575	122	573	64.5 s
	(15, 18, 6, 4, 3, 1)	350×350	5243	124	665	46.1 s
40	(8, 8, 4, 3, 1, 2)	350×350	4799	151	716	69.8 s
	(18, 20, 7, 5, 2, 3)	350×350	7452	171	889	59.5 s
50	(10, 10, 5, 2, 2, 2)	350×350	6522	177	839	81.25 s
	(21, 24, 10, 4, 3, 3)	400×400	9366	213	1109	60.1 s

thesized under designer-given constraints (maximum number of components of a certain type is constrained), whereas, the second row presents the results of an unconstrained architecture, i.e., no constraints were placed on the number of components to be used. Allocation step for the unconstrained architecture case can be considered similar to ASAP Scheduling [13]. For all applications, the unconstrained architecture produces a completion time that is smaller than that of the constrained architecture. All experiments presented in this section took between 3 to 30 minutes to complete, depending on the complexity of the application. All benchmarks and test files can be found here [3].

7. CONCLUSIONS

In this paper we have presented a top-down architectural synthesis approach for flow-based microfluidic biochips. The proposed approach synthesizes a biochip architecture for a given biochemical application, such that the application completion time is minimized. The synthesis process involves component allocation, design schematic generation, and the physical synthesis (placement and routing) of the chip. The approach has been evaluated by synthesizing biochip architectures for three real-life assays and a set of synthetic benchmarks. To the best of our knowledge, this is the first time an architectural synthesis framework has been proposed for the mLSI biochips. The proposed approach is expected to facilitate programmability and automation in the microfluidics domain, reducing human effort and minimizing the design cycle time.

8. ACKNOWLEDGMENTS

This work was supported by the Danish Agency for Science, Technology and Innovation, Grant No. 2106-08-0018 "ProCell".

9. REFERENCES

[1] AutoCAD Products. http://usa.autodesk.com/autocad-products/.

[2] Designing your own device: Basic design rules. http://www.stanford.edu/group/foundry/.

[3] mLSI Biochips. https://sites.google.com/site/mlsibiochips/.

[4] N. Amin, W. Thies, and S. Amarasinghe. Computer-aided design for microfluidic chips based on multilayer soft lithography. In *Proceedings of the IEEE International Conference on Computer Design*, 2009.

[5] V. Ananthanarayanan and W. Thies. Biocoder: A programming language for standardizing and automating biology protocols. *Journal of Biological Engineering*, 4(13), 2010.

[6] K. Chakrabarty and T. Xu. *Digital Microfluidic Biochips: Design Automation and Optimization*. CRC Press, Boca Raton, FL, 2010.

[7] H. Chou, M. Unger, and S. Quake. A microfabricated rotary pump. *Biomedical Microdevices*, 3, 2001.

[8] P. Coussy and A. Morawiec. *High-level synthesis: From algorithm to digital circuit*. Springer, 2008.

[9] J. W. Hong and S. R. Quake. Integrated nanoliter systems. *Nature Biotechnology*, 21:1179–1183, 2003.

[10] Y. C. Lim, A. Z. Kouzani, and W. Duan. Lab-on-a-chip: a component view. *Journal of microsystems technology*, 16(12), December 2010.

[11] D. Mark, S. Haeberle, G. Roth, F. von Stetten, and R. Zengerle. Microfluidic lab-on-a-chip platforms: requirements, characteristics and applications. *Chem. Soc. Rev.*, 39:1153–1182, 2010.

[12] J. Melin and S. Quake. Microfluidic large-scale integration: The evolution of design rules for biological automation. *Annual Reviews in Biophysics and Biomolecular Structure*, 36:213–231, 2007.

[13] G. D. Micheli. *Synthesis and optimization of digital circuits*. McGraw-Hill, New York, 1994.

[14] W. H. Minhass, P. Pop, and J. Madsen. System-level modeling and synthesis of flow-based microfluidic biochips. In *Proc. of the International Conference on Compilers, Architectures and Synthesis of Embedded Systems (CASES)*, 2011.

[15] J. M. Perkel. Microfluidics - bringing new things to life science. *Science*, November 2008.

[16] S. M. Sait and H. Youssef. *VLSI physical design automation: theory and practice*. World Scientific Publishing Co. Pte. Ltd., 1999.

[17] J. Siegrist, M. Amasia, N. Singh, D. Banerjee, and M. Madou. Numerical modeling and experimental validation of uniform microchamber filling in centrifugal microfluidics. *Lab Chip*, 10:876–886, 2010.

[18] D. Ullman. NP-complete scheduling problems. *Journal of Computing System Science*, 10:384–393, 1975.

[19] J. P. Urbanski, W. Thies, C. Rhodes, S. Amarasinghe, and T. Thorsen. Digital microfluidics using soft lithography. *Lab Chip*, 6:96–104, 2006.

DaaC: Device-reserved Memory as an Eviction-based File Cache

Jinkyu Jeong
Computer Science Dept.
Korea Advanced Institute of
Science and Technology
Daejeon, Rep. of Korea
jinkyu@calab.kaist.ac.kr

Hwanju Kim
Computer Science Dept.
Korea Advanced Institute of
Science and Technology
Daejeon, Rep. of Korea
hjukim@calab.kaist.ac.kr

Jeaho Hwang
Computer Science Dept.
Korea Advanced Institute of
Science and Technology
Daejeon, Rep. of Korea
jhhwang@calab.kaist.ac.kr

Joonwon Lee
College of ICE
Sungkyunkwan Univ.
Suwon, Rep. of Korea
joonwon@skku.edu

Seungryoul Maeng
Computer Science Dept.
Korea Advanced Institute of
Science and Technology
Daejeon, Rep. of Korea
maeng@calab.kaist.ac.kr

ABSTRACT

Most embedded systems require contiguous memory space to be reserved for each device, which may lead to memory under-utilization. Although several approaches have been proposed to address this issue, they have limitations of either inefficient memory usage or long latency for switching the reserved memory space between a device and general-purpose uses.

Our scheme utilizes the reserved memory as an eviction-based file cache. It guarantees contiguous memory allocation to devices while providing idle device memory as an additional file cache called *eCache* for general-purpose usage. Since the eCache stores only evicted data from in-kernel page cache, memory efficiency is preserved and allocation time for devices is minimized. Cost-based region selection also alleviates additional read I/Os by carefully discarding cached data from the eCache. The prototype is implemented on the Nexus S smartphone and is evaluated with popular Android applications. The evaluation results show that 50%-85% of flash read I/Os are reduced and application launch performance is improved by 8%-16% while the reallocation time is limited to a few milliseconds.

Categories and Subject Descriptors

D.4.2 [**Operating Systems**]: Storage Management—*main memory, allocation/deallocation strategies*

General Terms

Management, Performance

Keywords

memory management, memory reservation, contiguous memory allocation

1. INTRODUCTION

Recently, general-purpose embedded systems such as smartphones are increasing their market shares. Gartner expects that mobile phones will overtake PCs as the most common Web access device worldwide [11]. International Data Corporation also predicts that vendors will ship one billion smartphones in 2015 [16]. Since such embedded systems have lower computing power than general PCs, many hardware-implemented features complement CPU's insufficient computing capability. For example, video playback and camera functions are usually implemented by separate hardware. This computing delegation from CPU to those acceleration hardware devices not only unburdens CPU load but also decreases power consumption.

Such an acceleration hardware device usually needs contiguous memory space. For example, decoding one full-HD frame requires at least 6MB of memory, and the required memory size can increase depending on the implementation of decoding function. In addition, the required memory should be physically contiguous since those devices do not usually support scatter/gather I/Os [8]. Since an operating system (OS) manages the whole physical memory at page-granularity, it is not easy to allocate physically contiguous large memory chunks to those devices in runtime. Therefore, the necessary memory space for a device is usually reserved statically as *static reservation*. Many state-of-the-art smartphones reserve from 15% to 22% of its main memory for such acceleration hardware devices as shown in Table 1.

While the memory reservation guarantees exclusive use of a device, it leads to inefficient memory utilization since the memory region cannot be used for other purposes even when the device is idle. Many reports reveal that video playback or taking pictures are not dominant workloads in smartphone applications [10, 25]. Accordingly, the memory space for the dedicated use of the acceleration devices is wasted.

IOMMU (input/output memory management unit) [22, 1, 3], which provides on-demand mapping between I/O addresses and physical addresses, can eliminate the low memory utilization problem by providing *on-demand memory allocation* for devices. Since IOMMU provides virtually contiguous address spaces to devices, scattered pages allocated in on-demand manner becomes contiguous on a device's I/O address space. Additional cost of IOMMU hardware, however, can increase the unit cost of system. In addition, managing address mappings for devices increases burden on CPU [5, 4]. Finally, since this approach is hardware dependent [22], its deployment is limited.

Contiguous Memory Allocation [27] and Rental Memory [18] provide software-level approaches to increase the memory utilization. The two approaches allow kernel to use reserved memory for movable pages such as stack, heap and page cache pages while acceleration devices are idle. When a device becomes active, the device's reserved region can be exclusively used by the device because the movable pages in the region can migrate into other memory regions (e.g., normal memory). We denote this operation as *on-demand reservation* since this operation still provides physically contiguous regions to devices. As these schemes are implemented at software-level, many deployed devices can take advantage of those approaches via software update.

The two approaches, however, sacrifice either end-user latency or memory efficiency. When the movable pages are placed on the reserved memory, the dirty pages among them take long time to be placed in other location when the device becomes active. This additional delay directly increases the launch time of applications which depend on the acceleration devices. Accordingly, the degree of user satisfaction can be seriously compromised. If only clean data is placed on the reserved memory, returning the reserved memory to the device becomes simple and fast (hundreds of milliseconds) by discarding the clean data [18]. The simple discard operation can be, however, inefficient because it may cause additional page faults.

In this paper, we propose a novel device-reserved memory management scheme that provides on-demand memory reservation to devices while preserving the memory efficiency of system and minimizing the on-demand reservation time for devices. Our scheme uses Device-reserved memory as an eviction-based file Cache (DaaC). By gathering the reserved memory regions for each device, we build an eviction-based file cache (*eCache*). The eCache provides contiguous memory allocation (i.e., on-demand reservation) to acceleration devices while it stores file caches in memory to increase the memory utilization. Since the management of the eCache is eviction-based and exclusive, data stored in the eCache is guaranteed to be less important than those in upper-level cache (e.g., in-kernel page cache). Therefore, the on-demand reservation comes at a minimal cost by discarding data stored in the eCache.

In addition, cost-based memory region selection during the on-demand reservation is suggested to sustain the memory efficiency (or the caching efficiency of the eCache). Since the eCache consists of many devices' reserved memory regions, one device can utilize multiple regions for its memory provisioning when not all devices are active simultaneously. Accordingly, it is important to choose a device allocation region so that minimum number of page faults occurs after the on-demand reservation. In this regard, we assign the

Device	Total	Avail.	Reserved	Usage
Nexus One	512	379	81 (16%/23%)	Video, Camera
Desire HD	768	N/A	157 (20%/N/A)	"
Galaxy S	512	334	115 (22%/34%)	JPEG, Video, Camera
Nexus S	512	386	105 (21%/27%)	"
Galaxy S2	1024	816	154 (15%/19%)	"

Table 1: Memory reservation in many smartphones (in MB)

cost for each cached data of which the cost value reflects the LRU distance in the eCache. By aggregating the cost of the cached data in each predefined allocation region, our scheme can find a minimal cost region for device memory allocation. When all devices are activated, the eCache can still handle all on-demand reservation requests without external fragmentation.

Based on the proposed scheme, we implemented the prototype on Nexus S smartphone with Android Open Source Project 2.3.7_r1 and Linux kernel 2.6.35.7. The prototype is evaluated with various user workloads that comprise many well-known Android applications. When reserved memory regions, whose size is 21% of the total memory, are managed in our scheme, read I/O size is significantly reduced by 76%-85% when the workload contains only 5% of applications that depend on acceleration devices. The average application launch time is also reduced by from 8% to 16%. Even though a workload contains large portion of acceleration device-dependent applications, 50%-70% of read I/Os are still serviced by the eCache. While the eCache absorbs significant read I/O traffics, the on-demand reservation is still provided in a few of milliseconds, 10 ms for a video decoding device and 4 ms for a camera device. The two reservation time are only 2% of Movies application's launch time and 1% of Camera application's one, respectively. The device memory allocation delay is small enough that our scheme can be transparent.

The rest of this paper is organized as follows. The following section shows the background of this work and depicts the motivation. Section 3 presents the details of our scheme. Section 4 discusses implementation issues of our prototype. Section 5 shows the evaluation results of our scheme. Section 6 discusses the related work. We conclude this paper in Section 7.

2. BACKGROUND AND MOTIVATION

In this section, we first provide the fact that nontrivial portion of reserved memory could be wasted for most of the time by presenting the memory reservation status and by showing previous surveys on statistics of smartphone application usage. Then, we describe the motivation of our work with illustrating the limitation of previous approaches.

2.1 Background

Many state-of-the-art smartphones use memory reservation (static reservation) for their multimedia acceleration devices. Table 1 shows a total memory size, an OS-available memory size (in /proc/meminfo), and a reserved memory size in each smartphone; the reservation information is obtained by analyzing each device's source code. As shown in

Device	Region	Size	Usage
Video Decoder	mfc0(fw)	2MB	Firmware
	mfc0	34MB	Video decoding
	mfc1	36MB	Video decoding
Camera	fimc0	6MB	Taking pictures
	fimc1	9MB	Always
	fimc2	6MB	Taking pictures
JPEG decoder	jpeg	8MB	Taking pictures

Table 2: Detailed usages of reserved memory in Nexus S

the table, many smartphones reserve a number of large continuous memory regions for their multimedia acceleration devices such as a camera, a video decoder and a JPEG decoder. We note that some memory regions, which are used by other devices such as a radio device or a GPU device, are not taken into account in the table. In summary, the portion of the reservation is nontrivial, reaching from 15% to 22% compared to their total memory size.

In more detail of Nexus S [13], which is used in our prototype implementation, it has three devices that reserve six disjoint memory regions. As shown in Table 2, the video decoder (*s3c mfc*), reserves two 36MB-sized regions for its operation. The 2MB-sized region at the beginning of the first region stores the firmware code of the device. The camera device (*s3c fimc*) reserves three memory regions, whose sizes are 6MB, 9MB and 6MB, respectively. From our test, the first and the last regions are used while the camera device is working. The second region is always used regardless of whether the camera device is active; always-used regions are not our target. The JPEG decoder device (*s3c jpeg*) reserves 8MB of memory which is used when to change raw image data taken from the camera device to a JPEG-formatted file. Hence, the JPEG device works only while a picture is being taken. In summary, 70MB of memory for the video decoder is used only while the device is working (e.g., by a video playback application). The 12MB of the memory for the camera device is used only when a camera application is operating. The 8MB of the memory for the JPEG device is used only when the camera is used to take pictures.

Each device's memory region is exploited as a data exchange channel between a user-level application and its owner device. For example of the JPEG device, a camera application opens a /dev/s3c-jpeg file when a user presses the shutter button on the screen. After that, the application calls mmap system call to map the JPEG device's reserved memory region to the application's address space. The application puts raw image data taken from the camera device into the mmaped space and gets a JPEG-formatted image. After the application saves the picture into a JPEG-formatted file, the device file is closed.

2.2 Motivation

Smart devices, such as smartphones, tablets and smart TVs, are becoming general-purpose systems by adopting open platform environments. They provide not only their own functions, such as calling, sending SMS and watching TV, but also a variety of functions, such as web-browsing, taking pictures and accessing social networks. Falaki et al. [10] characterized smartphone users' application usage as shown in Table 3. Nielsen company [25] also reported statistics of smartphone applications based on more categories as shown in Table 4. From the two tables, mobile activities

Category	Popularity
Communication (email, SMS, IM, etc)	44%
Browsing (web browser, SNS apps, etc)	10%
System (file explorer, etc)	5%
Games	2%
Maps	5%
Media (pictures, music, videos, etc)	5%
Productive (office, PDF reader, etc)	5%
Others	11%

Table 3: Relative popularity of each application category in Android users in 2009 [10]

Category	Used portion	Category	Used portion
Games	65%	Sports	30%
Music	45%	Communication	25%
SNS	54%	Banking/Finance	31%
News/Weather	56%	Shopping/Retail	29%
Maps/Navi./Search	55%	Productivity	30%
Video/Movies	25%	Travel/Lifestyle	21%
Entertainment/Food	38%		

Table 4: Categories of applications used in the past 30 days [25] at Q4 2009

spread across diverse categories. The category that includes video playback or taking pictures is significantly low; the portion is less than 5% of the total application usage. Although some users could have higher usage of the multimedia applications, we believe that using smartphones only for multimedia activities is rare. Accordingly, the reserved memory regions for the multimedia acceleration devices are not fully utilized in smartphone activity.

Contiguous Memory Allocation [27, 8] reduces the reservation inefficiency by enabling the kernel to exploit reserved memory regions when devices are idle. The pages being able to reside in the reserved memory are limited to movable pages (e.g., anonymous pages, such as process stack and heap, and page cache pages). Because the movable pages can be migrated to other memory regions (e.g., normal memory), each reserved memory region is guaranteed to be reallocated to its owner device.

When on-demand reservation is available, the reserved memory is additional but temporal memory. For the memory efficiency [19], it is crucial to keep as many important (necessary) pages as possible in memory even if the reserved memory is reallocated to devices. Otherwise, additional I/Os to read the necessary pages could make system slower. The CMA approach spontaneously follows this principle by migrating all pages in the reserved region to other regions. For the page migrations, the page allocator in the kernel replaces page frames that store the least important data in the system. The reclaimed page frames are provided as destination pages of the page migrations.

The CMA approach, however, can compromise the end-user latency. The on-demand memory reservation time (or memory reallocation time for device) directly increases the launch time of applications that use the acceleration devices. Depending on the characteristics of pages in device-reserved memory, the on-demand reservation time can increase from a few seconds to tens of seconds [18]. The two upper lines in Figure 1(a) depict the time to migrate pages in a reserved memory region in the Nexus S smartphone. For example

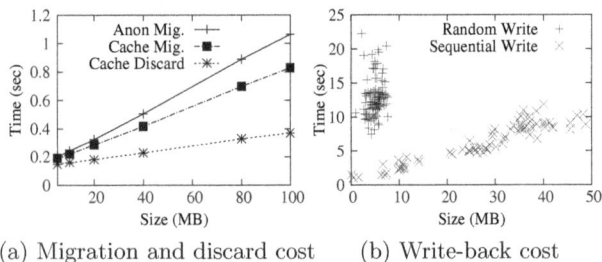

(a) Migration and discard cost   (b) Write-back cost

Figure 1: Time cost of on-demand reservation

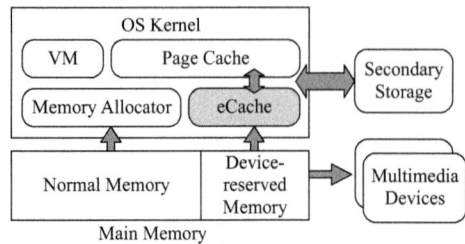

Figure 2: Memory Usage during the normal work-load running

of the mfc video decoder, migrating 70MB of the memory takes from 0.6 seconds (when the region is full of clean page caches) to 0.8 seconds (full of anonymous pages). As the time to launch a video application is approximately 0.3 seconds, the migration time makes the launch time increase by a factor of from three to four due to the on-demand reservation. The migration not only requires the explicit latency of memory copies but also incurs implicit overheads such as CPU cache pollution due to the memory copy operations.

The on-demand reservation time becomes more serious when the reserved region contains dirty pages. A write-back page, a dirty page being in the middle of write-back I/O, is neither movable nor discardable until the write-back I/O for the page is finished. Accordingly, if a reserved region is filled with many dirty pages, it could take much more time to complete the on-demand reservation operation. Figure 1(b) shows the time to reclaim a reserved memory region which contains the page cache pages for Sysbench file I/O benchmark's input files. Because the number of write-back pages in the region is the main culprit of increasing reclamation time, we varied the size of write-back pages in the x-axis. We ran 100 reclamations repetitively and measured the time of each operation. As shown in the figure, when the number of write-back pages increases, the reclamation latency increases ranging from 1 second (0.5KB of sequential write pages) to 22 seconds (2MB of random write pages). This additional delay can lead to user dissatisfaction with acceleration device-dependent applications.

The Rental Memory, our previous approach, minimizes the on-demand reservation time by limiting the types of pages to clean page caches among the movable pages [18]. When on-demand reservation occurs, it discards all clean pages in the reserved memory region. Since discarding clean page caches is less costly than migrating pages as shown in Figure 1(a), the on-demand reservation time can be reduced to hundreds of milliseconds. This approach, however, can degrade the memory efficiency of the system. Since the discard operation does not consider the importance of pages, such as the pages in current working set, in the reserved region, discarding the important pages in the region will cause read I/Os after the on-demand reservation completed. Accordingly, the additional read I/O operations become the expense of achieving the short launch time of applications that depend on the acceleration devices.

In summary, providing on-demand reservation to devices increases the available memory size in the system. However, the on-demand reservation time can compromise the end-user latency if the reserved memory is not carefully used. Meanwhile, minimizing the on-demand reservation time can

degrade the system's efficiency. Accordingly, we argue that the device-reserved memory should be managed differently in order to minimize the on-demand reservation time while preserving the memory efficiency of the system.

3. DEVICE-RESERVED MEMORY AS AN EVICTION-BASED FILE CACHE

The main goals of our scheme are (1) to lower the on-demand reservation cost for user's satisfaction, and (2) to provide on-demand reservation without degrading the memory efficiency by carefully managing on-demand reservation. In order to achieve our goal, we propose a scheme that uses the device-reserved memory as an eviction-based file cache. The eviction-based exclusive cache management scheme [7] is originally designed for storage cache management. The eviction-based cache resides between an upper-level cache (e.g., page cache) and lower level storage, and caches data evicted from the upper-level cache. Evicted data is data flushed from the upper-level cache by a page frame replacement. The main characteristic of the eviction-based cache management scheme is that it always stores less important data than those stored in the upper-level cache. In addition, an eviction-based cache increases the effective size of the upper-level cache by being exclusively managed [7, 6, 28].

Device-reserved memory is a good target of the eviction-based exclusive cache, which is referred to as *eCache* in the rest of this paper. The characteristic of storing less important data can contribute to preserving the memory efficiency. Since the eCache always stores less important data, on-demand reservation makes the less important data to be discarded from memory. Accordingly the on-demand reservation becomes simple, and the on-demand reservation time also can be minimized. When a device becomes idle again, the memory region provided to the device is returned to the eCache to cache evicted data. When all devices, which contribute their reserved memory regions to the eCache, become activated the system state is the same as when the static reservation approach is used. In addition, by managing the eCache exclusively, it increases the effective size of the in-memory file cache. The page frames in the eCache are still in the same memory chipset in the system. Accordingly, the cached data in the eCache can be accessed almost as fast as those in the kernel page cache. Since the kernel always synchronizes data in secondary storage with modified one in its page cache prior to evicting the data, discarding stored data in the eCache does not violate the consistency of data between the kernel page cache, the eCache and the secondary storage. Figure 2 depicts the overview of the eCache.

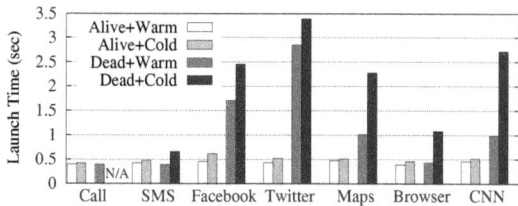

Figure 3: Slowdown of application launch time with absence of library page caches

3.1 Why File Cache?

As an answer to the question of which types of data can reside in the eCache, anonymous pages are out of the target. Since many embedded systems are not equipped with swap storage, anonymous pages cannot be evicted from the kernel page cache. Without considering the eviction-based placement, placing anonymous pages in the additional memory can incur additional overhead. As we described in Section 2.2, page migration itself is overhead in terms of the on-demand reservation time. In addition, when considering that the device-reserved memory is temporal memory, keeping anonymous pages in the eCache makes anonymous pages to be overcommitted against the normal memory size. When the size of anonymous pages is larger than the size of normal memory, killing low priority tasks lowers the availability of the system. Finally, we still have a large size normal memory that can allocate anonymous pages sufficiently. Even though the additional memory cannot be used for anonymous pages, the total anonymous page footprint is the same as those with the static reservation approach.

Meanwhile, allocating page caches on the additional memory can increase the performance of the system by absorbing more read I/O traffics. Practically, many commodity OSes provide as large page caches as possible if memory is sufficient. In addition, Android applications are well-known to be tightly coupled with the libraries since the framework libraries in Android provide diverse functions and the same look and feel [14]. Accordingly, the more library files are cached, the less major faults occur while applications are starting. In order to detail the impact of page caches to the launch performance of applications, we measured the slowdown of application launch time when page caches for an application are not in the memory. In the Android system, the application (*activity* in Android) can be started from two cases: when the application (or process) is dead, and when the application is alive. We evaluated the application launch time in the two cases. As shown in Figure 3, keeping page caches in memory significantly improves launch performance by from 19% to 175% when an application is dead. Even when an application is alive, the launch performance is improved by from 6% to 36%.

The following subsection describes how the eCache stores file data evicted from the kernel page cache and how the cached data is promoted to the page cache. The next subsection describes how a contiguous region of the eCache is provided to devices when an on-demand reservation occurs.

3.2 eCache Management

The eCache stores file data at page granularity that is the same management unit in the kernel page cache. Each file page is accessed by a unique key consisting of *file system*

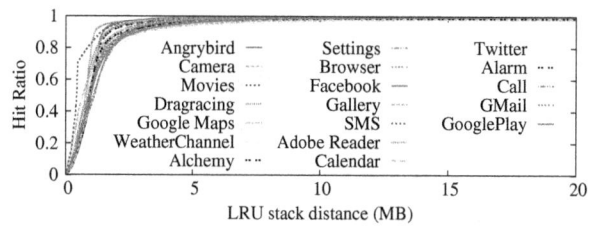

(a) Page cache miss ratio curve

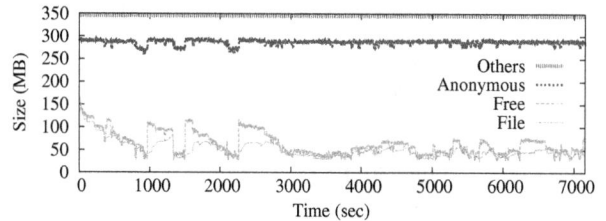

(b) Memory usage (stacked)

Figure 4: Page cache miss ratio curve and memory usage and in the Normal workload in Section 5.2

id, *inode* number and *offset* in the inode. During file page retrieval, the file system id and the inode number are hashed, and the corresponding hash entry points the root of a radix tree. The radix tree stores references to cached pages in the file by using each page's offset as an index.

In order to cooperate with the page cache in the kernel, the eCache provides four interfaces: `put_page()`, `get_page()`, `flush_page()`, and `flush_inode()`. When a file page in the page cache is a target of page replacement in the kernel, the `put_page()` is called. The function copies the evicted data in the page cache page into a free page frame in the eCache, and establishes indexing structures to the newly stored page. The `get_page()` function is called when the kernel requires to read a file page that is not in the page cache. When the required file page exists in the eCache, its data is copied to the page cache page. Since the eCache is managed exclusively to the kernel page cache, the cached page in the eCache is discarded (or removed). `flush_page()` and `flush_inode()` are invoked when some pages in a file or a whole file is removed from a file system. The two functions flush one or all of the cached data of the specified file in the eCache, respectively. Therefore, the data consistency is not violated between the page cache, the eCache and the secondary storage.

Among many replacement algorithms, we used LRU-based page replacement in the eCache. We believe that any other page placement algorithms can also be used. All page frames in the eCache are linked to form a single LRU list. When a new file page is evicted from the page cache, the page frame at the end of the list (or at the LRU position) is freed (if needed) and stores the content of the evicted file page. Then, the page frame is moved to the beginning of the list (or MRU position). When a page is accessed via the `get_page()` function, the cached data in the corresponding page frame is discarded and the page frame is moved to the LRU position. The LRU-based page replacement is well-known to be effective when the cache employs eviction-based placement and is exclusively managed [7].

As data in the eCache is indirectly accessed, thrashing problem can happen when a file page is frequently evicted from and promoted to the page cache. In Android environment, the thrashing phenomenon unlikely occurs for two reasons. First, many Android applications have less than 10MB of file cache working set sizes. Figure 4(a) shows the miss ratio curve of page cache accesses for various Android applications. The tested workloads are described in Section 5.2. We also added some realistic behaviors (e.g., playing games) after launching each application. The memory-mapped page cache accesses are sampled at every 20 ms. As shown in the figure, the hit ratios are saturated between 5MB and 10MB. Second, the *lowmemorykiller* in Android system preserves a certain amount of page cache in system. It starts killing background applications to reclaim memory when both free memory and cached pages are under 32MB, respectively, in usual configuration. Accordingly, the page cache size in the kernel is kept around 40MB as shown in the *file* line in Figure 4(b). Accordingly, most of the pages for a foreground application can be located in the page cache.

3.3 On-demand Reservation

From the perspective of device, the eCache is a memory allocation pool when on-demand reservation is needed for devices. It is important to note that the eCache consists of contiguous page frames and the size is the sum of each device's reserved memory size. When a device requests memory allocation using the `eCache_alloc()` function, a naive approach is to statically fix the location of each device's memory region for the contiguous memory allocation. When a device requests its on-demand reservation to the eCache, all of the cached data in its fixed region are discarded and the page frames comprising the fixed region are removed from the LRU list.

This naive approach, however, could degrade the local memory efficiency (or caching efficiency). A device-fixed region is always smaller than the size of the eCache when multiple regions of devices comprise the eCache. Accordingly, a device-fixed region could contain many important pages that have higher chances to be accessed than the other pages in the rest of the regions in the eCache. Accordingly, this static region selection approach will likely incur additional read I/O operations. As an alternative approach, dynamic region selection can avoid the additional read I/Os albeit the dynamic approach could lead to a slight increase of on-demand reservation time.

For this dynamic region selection, it is also important to avoid external fragmentation in the eCache region. Since the size of the eCache is static, an improper region selection will prevent another device's on-demand reservation when the reservation requests are issued in about the same time. For example, the eCache consists of two devices' memory regions whose sizes are two and three contiguous page frames. If the former device's memory allocation is done on the second and third page frames in the eCache, remaining page frames are separately located and non-contiguous. Because of the fragmentation, a future allocation request for three contiguous pages cannot be handled.

In order to eliminate this fragmentation problem, we restrict that the on-demand reservation can be handled on one of the predefined regions (candidate regions) for each device. For example, if we have three devices (mfc, fimc and jpeg), which requires six, four and three contiguous page frames, respectively, we have 6(=3!) memory allocation cases, the permutation of the three devices, as shown in the top side of

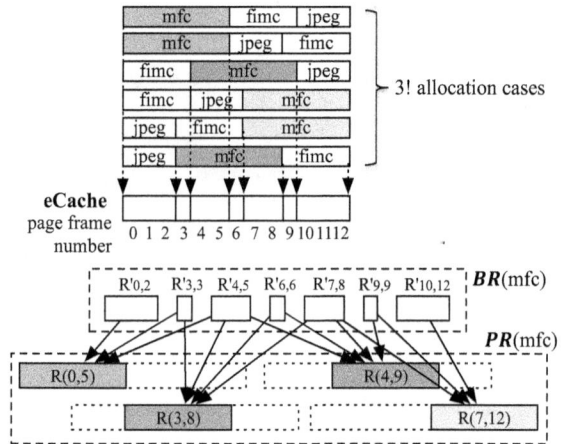

Figure 5: Cost calculation for mfc allocation case. mfc size is 6, fimc size 4 and jpeg 3.

Figure 5. We define predefined memory allocation regions for a device d as $\mathbf{PR}(d)$. $\mathbf{PR}(d)$ is a set of memory regions each of which is denoted as $R_{a,b}$ where $R_{a,b}$ denotes page frames whose indices are from a to b. Hence, the predefined memory allocation regions for the mfc device in the figure are:

$$\mathbf{PR}(\text{mfc}) = \{R_{0,5}, R_{3,8}, R_{4,9}, R_{7,12}\}$$

From the predefined regions for each device, it is important to choose a region that will expense minimal cost, when the region is allocated. In this regard, we define C_i that is a potential cost (e.g., probability for future read) when the data in the ith page in the eCache is discarded for device memory allocation. Then, the potential cost of one region $R_{a,b}$ is calculated by the following equation.

$$C(R_{a,b}) = \sum_{i=a}^{b} C_i \qquad (1)$$

Accordingly, a device d's memory allocation with minimal cost can be accomplished by finding a $R_{a,b}$ with minimum $C(R_{a,b})$ in $\mathbf{PR}(d)$. In order to avoid redundant calculation for the costs of overlapped page frames, each R in $\mathbf{PR}$ is divided into disjoint subregions. We define a base region of a device d as $\mathbf{BR}(d)$ that has an element $R'_{a,b}$, which is a set of pages from ath to bth, as an element. Then, a predefined region is divided into many subregions in the base region as shown in the bottom side of Figure 5. For example,

$$\mathbf{BR}(\text{mfc}) = \{R'_{0,2}, R'_{3,3}, R'_{4,5}, R'_{6,6}, R'_{7,8}, R'_{9,9}, R'_{10,12}\}$$

and, $R_{0,5} = \{R'_{0,2}, R'_{3,3}, R'_{4,5}\}, R_{3,8} = ...$

Then, the equation (1) can be transformed to:

$$C(R_{a,b}) = \sum_{R'_{a,b} \in R} C(R'_{a,b}) = \sum_{R'_{a,b} \in R} (\sum_{i=a}^{b} C_i) \qquad (2)$$

By calculating the $C(R'_{a,b})$ in $\mathbf{BR}(d)$, $C(R_{a,b})$ can be calculated without the redundant cost calculation. The time complexity for one device memory allocation becomes $O(n + pb + s)$. n is the size of the eCache and s is the size of requested region for a device. When m is the number of devices that require on-demand memory reservation from the eCache, p is $|\mathbf{PR}| = \sum_{i=0}^{m-1} \binom{m-1}{i}$ and b is $|\mathbf{BR}|$. The two values are dependent to m. In our prototype, m is 4, p is 8, and the maximum b is 8. In general, m is relatively small, and therefore, the term pb can be ignored. Therefore, the time complexity is $O(n + s)$.

The effectiveness of the algorithm shown above depends on how precisely C_i represents the probability to cause read I/O when the data in the page is discarded. The main property of C_i is that the important page should have larger value. An LRU distance, which is an offset from the LRU position in the LRU list, is a proper candidate for C_i. An LRU distance of ith page is denoted as l_i; this value is similar to the inverse of the stack distances in [21, 2]. When a page is recently added in the eCache, it is located on the MRU position; the recently added page has the highest probability to be accessed, and the page's LRU distance is the highest in the eCache. By using l_i, C_i can be determined as follows.

$$C_i = \begin{cases} \infty & \text{if } i\text{th page is allocated to other devices} \\ l_i & \text{otherwise} \end{cases}$$

By assigning infinity to the cost of pages that are allocated to other devices, the on-demand reservation does not choose predefined regions that already have one or more allocated pages for the other devices. Each page's LRU distance value is calculated by one traversal of the LRU list when device memory allocation is requested. Accordingly, the time complexity of device memory allocation is still linear.

Finally, When a device becomes idle, its allocated memory region is returned to the eCache through the `eCache_free()` function. The returned page frames are inserted in to the LRU list.

4. IMPLEMENTATION

We implemented our scheme in Linux Kernel 2.6.35.7 with the Nexus S smartphone on Android Open Source Project [12]. We modified the device drivers in the kernel to support runtime position changes of the base address of each device's reserved memory. The modification requires only a few lines of codes, which are in charge of notifying the base address of reserved memory to its device. We changed the sequence of each device's reserved memory in order to make the eCache one large contiguous region. Compared to Table 2, the reservation sequence becomes *mfc(fw)*, *mfc0*, *mfc1*, *fimc0*, *fimc2*, *jpeg* and *fimc1*. We regarded fimc0 and fimc2 as one *fimc* whose size is 12MB. The eCache size is 90MB for mfc0, mfc1, fimc and jpeg.

The implemented eviction interface is similar to Clean-Cache [20]. For device memory allocation, the two interfaces, `eCache_alloc()` and `eCache_free()`, are called when a device file is opened and when a device file is closed, respectively.

When `eCache_alloc()` occurs, the selected page frames for device memory allocation are freed from the eCache in a lazy manner. Hence, we only invalidate page frames that are allocated to devices. Subsequent operations accessing the page frames are in charge of freeing the page frames actually. By using this lazy discard operation, the cost of freeing device-allocated page frames is amortized to the cost of subsequent eCache access operations. Due to the exclusive management of the eCache, the lazy discard operation incurs minimal impact on the subsequent operations. For example, `get_page()` always tries to remove the index to a target page regardless of whether the target page is in the

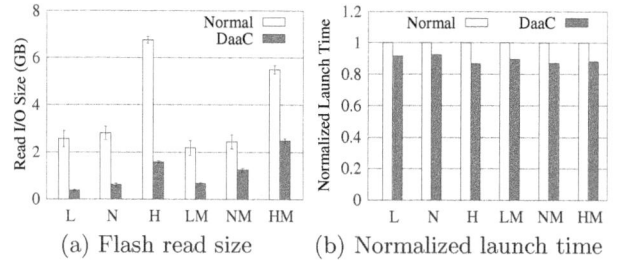

(a) Flash read size   (b) Normalized launch time

Figure 6: Flash read size and normalized application launch time in all workloads

eCache or not. Accordingly, even if the target page is invalid, the `get_page()` works the same as when the target page is valid, but returns failure instead of success.

5. EVALUATION

5.1 Environment

Nexus S, our target platform, is equipped with ARM Cortex A8 1GHz processor, 512MB RAM, and 16GB internal flash storage. We used custom firmware, which is built from Android AOSP 2.3.7_r1 with a *userdebug* configuration.

5.2 Methodology

We used six different types of workloads as described in a technical report [17]. Briefly, the light workload (L) consists of 12 essential applications and one game application. The normal workload (N) contains additional applications such as social network applications, additional games and a document reader. The heavy workload (H) includes other useful applications in addition to the normal workload. Since the on-demand reservation frequency depends on the portions of multimedia applications, such as Movies, YouTube and Camera, we added three workloads, light multimedia (LM), normal multimedia (NM), and heavy multimedia (HM), that intensively run the three multimedia applications.

We used read I/O size and application *launch time* [9] as our performance metrics. The application launch time is the time elapsed between when an *intent*, a message to invoke an application's activity, is initiated and when the application's main routine (i.e., onResume()) completes making the application window visible [23]. Only if an application is newly started, the launch time of the application is reported by *ActivityManager* through a *logcat* command. We modified a source code to make ActivityManager show the launch time even when an application is alive.

5.3 Performance

We first measured the basic performance of the eCache and the flash device in Nexus S. The performance of the eCache is the average time of completing `get_page()` in the all workloads. Flash read performance is measured by reading 4KB of page directly. Since the eCache is an in-memory cache, the average 4KB read response time in the eCache is 0.07 msec which is approximately 20 times faster than the flash read (1.51 msec).

Figure 6(a) shows the size of read I/O that occurred during each workload running. We ran each workload four times and depicted the average read I/O size. *Normal* denotes the static reservation approach for devices. *DaaC* is

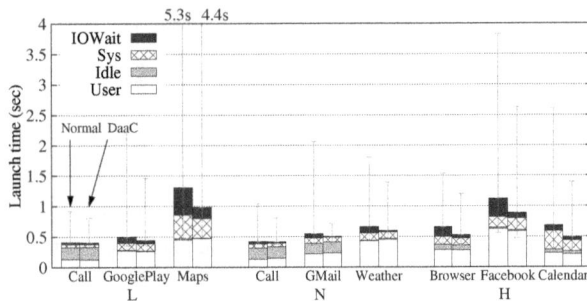

Figure 7: Breakdown of application launch time

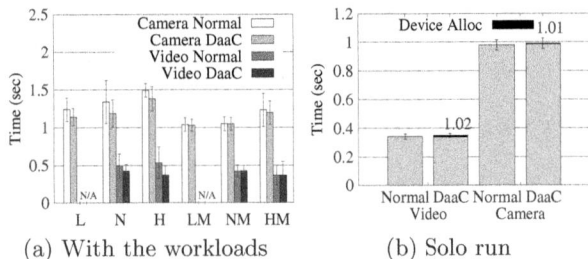

(a) With the workloads   (b) Solo run

Figure 8: Launch time of device-dependent applications

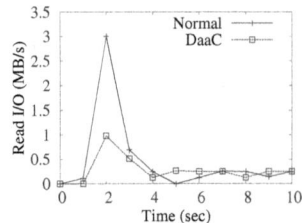

Figure 9: Read I/O occurred while the Movies application is launching

Get	Hit	Type
0.55	0.55	Dalvik Caches (framework, core, services, Gallery3D.apk, et al)
1.30	1.16	Libraries (libc, libdvm, libcutils, libcstageflight, libcaudioflinger, libOMX.SEC.AVC.Decoder, et al)
0.83	0.81	Framework Resource (framework-res.apk)
0.38	0.02	Etc. (sh, linker, mp4 file)

Table 5: The size of files hit in the eCache when Movies application is launching (in MB)

the on-demand reservation using our scheme. As shown in the figure, our scheme significantly reduces read I/O by from 76% to 85% compared to the normal case. Since the eCache stores a large amount of file caches, read I/O traffic is largely absorbed by the eCache. The multimedia-intensive workloads (LM, NM, and HM) performed relatively larger amount of read I/O operations than non-multimedia-intensive ones (L, N, and H). Because the acceleration device-dependent applications (i.e., Camera, Movies, and YouTube) are more frequently invoked, many cached data in the eCache is frequently invalidated due to the on-demand memory reservations. The eCache, however, is quickly refilled with evicted data when device-dependent applications are finished and a subsequent application is launched.

Figure 6(b) shows the geometric mean of the normalized launch times of all applications for each workload. As our scheme reduces many read I/O operations, the launch time is decreased by 8% to 16% compared to the normal case. The main benefit of the eCache during application launch comes from read I/O reduction. In order to show the time reduction in more detail, we break down the launch time of applications into *user*, *idle*, *system*, and *I/O-wait* time. The user and idle time denote how many CPU cycles an application spends in user and idle contexts, respectively. The system time shows how many CPU cycles used at the kernel context including I/O handling. The I/O-wait time indicates how many CPU cycles an application waits for read I/O operations to complete. Since the eCache contributes to the reduction in read I/O and I/O-related kernel operations, the system time and I/O-wait time are reduced from total launch time by the eCache. We selected three applications based on the frequency of executions from the three workloads (Light, Normal and Heavy) in Figure 7. The figure also includes the minimum and maximum launch time of the applications. Except for the Call application, the applications

showed reduced system and I/O-wait time by 22%-42% compared to those of the normal case. As the portion of system and I/O wait time varies across the applications, the launch time of the applications is reduced by 2%-29%.

Compared to the read I/O reduction, the launch performance improvement is not significant. The reason is that only less than half of read I/O reduction contributes to the application launch performance. Approximately 60% of read I/O operations occurred during the operations other than application launches. Accordingly, the other user interactive operations, such as menu changes, loading the other screen, will also benefit from the reduced I/O operations.

Since our scheme utilizes device-reserved memory for the eCache, we have tradeoff between the gains from caching files and expenses of on-demand reservation time. In order to reveal this tradeoff, we first show the activity time of Movies and Camera applications in each workload. The launch time of the two applications includes on-demand reservation of *mfc0* and *mfc1*, and *fimc*, respectively. Figure 8(a) shows the average launch time of each application. Note that the light workload does not include the Movies application. Interestingly, the launch performance with our scheme is better than those with the static reservation approach. The reason is that the device memory allocation occurs in the middle of launching the application. Therefore, many file accesses can be hit in the eCache.

Figure 9 shows the read I/O throughput (MB/s) while the Movies application is starting. We note that the previous Movies application launch was 2,000 seconds before this Movies application launch; hence the files for the application were likely to be evicted from the page cache and even from the eCache. As shown in the figure, the normal case shows more read I/O operations while the application is launching (the time period between 1 second and 3 second). Our scheme, however, exhibits less read I/O operations because many of those are absorbed by the eCache. Table 5 shows the summary of actual read requests to the eCache when the Movie application is starting. Not only commonly used files (i.e., framework dependent files and libraries) but also application-specific files (e.g., video decoder-dependent libraries) are retrieved from the eCache.

In order to expose the pure cost of the on-demand reservation in our scheme, we ran each of two applications without any other applications. Each application is executed 100 times, and we measured the average launch time. Figure 8(b) shows the breakdown of the launch time of the Movies and Camera applications. As shown in the figure, the additional time for device memory allocation slightly increases the application launch time by 2% and 1% respectively. As the unit cost of device memory allocation is extremely low, consisting of a linked list traversal, integer calculations and setting tombstones, the device allocation time for both $mfc0$ and $mfc1$ is 11ms (5.8ms + 4.8ms) and the time for $fimc$ is 4ms. Recall that the minimum cost to provide 70MB of memory using the on-demand reservation in the previous approaches is 0.3 seconds as shown in Figure 1(a). Accordingly, our scheme provides the on-demand reservation at least 30 times faster.

5.4 Policy Analysis

In this subsection, we analyze the LRU position-aware region selection during the on-demand memory reservation. Our policy is denoted as LRU that uses $C_i = l_i$ for the page cost function. For comparison, we added four different policies. $Static$ fixes the memory region for each device. In our prototype, we have 24(=4!) different static allocation cases. We provided the best case result among the 24 different cases. $Random$ randomly selects a region among the predefined regions for a device. $Count$ assigns the same cost (1) to pages which are in use in the eCache for caching. Hence,

$$C_i = \begin{cases} \infty & \text{if } i\text{th page is allocated to other devices} \\ 1 & \text{if } i\text{th page is allocated for caching} \\ 0 & \text{otherwise} \end{cases}$$

Finally, $Optimal$ shows an optimal case, which is practically impossible without knowing the future accesses to the eCache.

We evaluated each policy with trace-driven simulation in order to minimize runtime variation. A trace includes all accesses to the eCache through the interfaces described in Section 3. We gathered the trace from one of each real workload execution in the previous subsection. Figure 10 shows the normalized $read\ I/O\ size$ and $average\ utilization$ of the eCache. The read I/O size for each workload is calculated based on the number of `get_page()` misses and is represented in a normalized value to the normal case. The average utilization shows how many cached pages are in the eCache. The average utilization is the average of the number of valid pages divided by the number of page frames in the eCache at every second.

Across the workloads, multimedia intensive workloads (LM, NM, HM) have performed more read I/O operations because more frequent on-demand reservation requests for devices discard many cached files in the eCache as illustrated in Figure 10(a). This result is consistent to the result shown in Figure 6(a). The cost-based policies (count and LRU) perform less read I/O operations than static and random policies. The static and count policies show higher eCache utilization in workload L, N, and LM than the other policies in Figure 10(b). But, increasing the utilization of the eCache is not related to the efficiency of the eCache because the

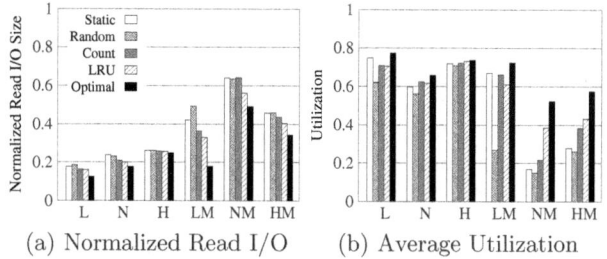

(a) Normalized Read I/O   (b) Average Utilization

Figure 10: Normalized read I/O size, and average eCache utilization with varying device memory allocation policy

static and count policies perform more read I/O operations than the LRU policy in Figure 10(a). Among the cost-based policies, our LRU policy performs better than the count policy by 2%-13% in terms of read I/O reduction. This result indicates that even though the LRU positions of contiguous pages are aggregated, the aggregated value is sufficient to represent the potential cost when the contiguous pages are chosen for the victim of on-demand memory reservation. Accordingly, our suggested policy performs better than the other policies in the tested workloads.

6. RELATED WORK

In this section, we discuss our work with related studies. The waste of reserved memory for device has been addressed previously. At the early stage of Contiguous Memory Allocation (CMA) [8], it tries to minimize reservation footprint by sharing reserved memory regions between devices. The rationale of this scheme is that not all devices are activated simultaneously. This scheme is orthogonal to our approach and we believe that our work can be complementary to this scheme. The later version of CMA [24, 27] increases the reserved memory's utilization by allowing kernel to use the page frames in the reserved memory region similarly to Hotplug Memory [26, 15]. Movable pages (e.g., page cache pages and anonymous pages) are allowed to be placed in the CMA region. As described in Section 2.2, this approach increases the memory efficiency of system but can sacrifice end-user latency.

In contrast, Rental Memory Management [18], our previous approach, utilizes device-reserved memory for clean page caches since keeping dirty page caches in the reserved memory causes unpredictable delay for device memory allocation. Although the additional memory is used for clean caches, its performance is almost comparable to the CMA approach while minimizing the on-demand reservation time under one second. This approach, however, compromises the memory efficiency of system as depicted in Section 2.2. We believe that our scheme will performs better than this approach for two reasons. First, both approaches have the same size of the file cache in memory. Based on the characteristics of applications depicted in Figure 4, the mostly accessed page caches are likely to be in the kernel page cache instead of the eCache because the eCache always contains the least important file caches than those in the page cache. Accordingly, the access of the eCache rarely occurs. Second, our scheme always discards the least important pages in system while this approach does not.

7. CONCLUSION

In resource-constrained embedded systems, such as smartphones, the under-utilized reserved memory is one of the major sources of inefficient resource management. On-demand reservation, which allows the system to exploit the reserved memory during an idle time of owner devices, sheds lights on the way of increasing the performance of the system while guaranteeing devices the use of reserved memory space.

We proposed a novel on-demand reservation approach, named *eCache*, that maximizes the memory efficiency of the system and minimizes the on-demand reservation time for end-user latency. By using the eCache, the system can greatly reduce the number of read I/O operations and increase the launch performance of applications by from 8% to 16%. With this performance improvement, the nature of eviction-based placement spontaneously maximizes the memory efficiency of the system. In addition, the on-demand reservation time can be minimized to millisecond level. This unrecognizable latency may make system more transparent in comparison to the system with the static-reservation approach.

8. ACKNOWLEDGMENTS

This work was supported by the IT R&D program of MKE/KEIT [10041244, SmartTV 2.0 Software Platform] and by the National Research Foundation of Korea(NRF) grant funded by the Korea government(MEST) (No. 2012-0000148)

9. REFERENCES

[1] D. Abramson, J. Jackson, S. Muthrasanallur, G. Neiger, G. Regnier, R. Sankaran, I. Schoinas, R. Uhlig, B. Vembu, and J. W. and. Intel virtualization technology for directed I/O. *Intel Technology Journal*, 10(3)(3), August 2006.

[2] G. Almási, C. Caşcaval, and D. A. Padua. Calculating stack distances efficiently. *SIGPLAN Not.*, 38(2 supplement):37–43, June 2002.

[3] AMD. IOMMU architectural specification. http:// support.amd.com/us/ProcessorTechDocs/48882.pdf, March 2011.

[4] N. Amit, M. Ben-Yehuda, and B.-A. Yassour. IOMMU: Strategies for mitigating the IOTLB bottleneck. In *Proc. of WIOSCA'10*, 2010.

[5] M. Ben-Yehuda, J. Xenidis, M. Ostrowski, K. Rister, A. Bruemmer, and L. Van Doorn. The price of safety: Evaluating IOMMU performance. In *Proc. of OLS '07*, pages 71–86, July 2007.

[6] Z. Chen, Y. Zhang, Y. Zhou, H. Scott, and B. Schiefer. Empirical evaluation of multi-level buffer cache collaboration for storage systems. In *Proc. of SIGMETRICS '05*, pages 145–156, 2005.

[7] Z. Chen, Y. Zhou, and K. Li. Eviction-based cache placement for storage caches. In *Proc. of USENIX ATC'03*, pages 269–282, Jun 2003.

[8] J. Corbet. Contiguous memory allocation for drivers. http://lwn.net/Articles/396702/, July 2010.

[9] W. Enck, P. Gilbert, B.-G. Chun, L. P. Cox, J. Jung, P. McDaniel, and A. N. Sheth. Taintdroid: an information-flow tracking system for realtime privacy monitoring on smartphones. In *Proc. of OSDI'10*, pages 1–6, 2010.

[10] H. Falaki, R. Mahajan, S. Kandula, D. Lymberopoulos, R. Govindan, and D. Estrin. Diversity in smartphone usage. In *Proc. of MobiSys'10*, pages 179–194, 2010.

[11] Gartner. Gartner highlights key predictions for it organizations and users in 2010 and beyond. http://www.gartner.com/it/page.jsp?id=1278413, January 2010.

[12] Google. Android open source project. http://source.android.com/, 2012.

[13] Google. Nexus s. http://www.android.com/devices /detail/nexus-s, 2012.

[14] A. Gutierrez, R. Dreslinski, T. Wenisch, T. Mudge, A. Saidi, C. Emmons, and N. Paver. Full-system analysis and characterization of interactive smartphone applications. In *Proc. of IISWC'11*, pages 81 –90, nov. 2011.

[15] D. Hansen, M. Kravetz, and B. Christiansen. Hotplug memory and the Linux VM. In *Proc. of OLS '04*, 2004.

[16] IDC. Worldwide smartphone market expected to grow 55% in 2011 and approach shipments of one billion in 2015, according to idc. http://www.idc.com/getdoc .jsp?containerId=prUS 22871611, June 2011.

[17] J. Jeong, H. Kim, J. Hwang, J. Lee, and S. Maeng. Device-reserved memory as an eviction-based file cache. Technical Report CS-TR-2012-360, Korea Advanced Institute of Science and Technology, July 2012.

[18] J. Jeong, H. Kim, J. Hwang, J. Lee, and S. Maeng. Rigorous rental memory management for embedded systems. *ACM Trans. Embed. Comput. Syst.*, accepted.

[19] G. S. Joachim. Memory efficiency. *J. ACM*, 6(2):172–175, Apr. 1959.

[20] D. Magenheimer, C. Mason, D. McCracken, and K. Hackel. Transcendent memory and linux. In *Proc. of OLS'09*, pages 191–200, 2009.

[21] R. Mattson, J. Gecsei, D. Slutz, and I. Traiger. Evaluation techniques for storage hierarchies. *IBM Systems Journal*, 9(2):78–117, 1970.

[22] R. Mijat and A. Nightingale. Virtualization is coming to a platform near you. http://www.arm.com/files /pdf/System-MMU-Whitepaper-v8.0.pdf, 2011.

[23] D. Morrill. Inside the Android application framework. In *Google I/O*, 2008.

[24] M. Nazarewicz. Contiguous memory allocator version 6. http://lwn.net/Articles/419639/, December 2010.

[25] Nielsen. The state of mobile apps. http://blog. nielsen.com/nielsenwire/online_mobile/the-state-of-mobile-apps/, June 2010.

[26] J. H. Schopp, D. Hansen, M. Kravetz, H. Takahashi, I. Toshihiro, Y. Goto, K. Hiroyuki, M. Tolentino, and B. Picco. Hotplug memory redux. In *Proc. of OLS '05*, 2005.

[27] M. Szyprowski and K. Park. Arm DMA-mapping framework redesign and IOMMU integration. In *Proc. of Embedded Linux Conference Europe*, 2011.

[28] T. M. Wong and J. Wilkes. My cache or yours? making storage more exclusive. In *Proc. of USENIX ATC'02*, pages 161–175, June 2002.

Integrating Software Caches with Scratch Pad Memory*

Prasenjit Chakraborty
Department of Computer Science & Engineering
Indian Institute of Technology Delhi
New Delhi, India
prasenjit@cse.iitd.ac.in

Preeti Ranjan Panda
Department of Computer Science & Engineering
Indian Institute of Technology Delhi
New Delhi, India
panda@cse.iitd.ac.in

ABSTRACT

Software cache refers to cache functionality emulated in software on a compiler-controlled Scratch Pad Memory (SPM). Such structures are useful when standard SPM allocation strategies cannot be used due to hard-to-analyze memory reference patterns in the source code. SPM data allocation strategies generally rely on compile-time inference of spatial and temporal reuse, with the general flow being the copying of a block/tile of array data into the SPM, followed by its processing, and finally, copying back. However, when array index functions are complicated due to conditionals, complex expressions, and dependence on run-time data, the SPM compiler has to rely on expensive DMA for individual words, leading to poor performance. Software caches (SWC) can play a crucial role in improving performance under such circumstances – their access times are longer than those for direct SPM access, but they retain the advantages (present in hardware caches) of exploiting spatial and temporal locality discovered at run-time. We present the first automated compiler data allocation strategy that considers the presence of a software cache in SPM space, and makes decisions on which arrays should be accessed through it, at which times. Arrays could be accessed differently in different parts of a program, and our algorithm analyzes such uses and considers the possibility of selectively accessing an array through the SWC only when it is efficient, based on a cost model of the overheads involved in SPM/SWC transitions. We implemented our technique in an LLVM based framework and experimented with several applications on a Cell based machine. Our technique results in up to 82% overall performance improvement over a conventional SPM mapping algorithm and up to 27% over a typical SWC-enhanced implementation.

Categories and Subject Descriptors

D.3.4 [**Programming Languages**]: Processors—*code generation, compilers, memory management, optimization*

---

*This research was partially supported by an IBM Faculty Award grant.

General Terms

Algorithm, Design, Performance

Keywords

Memory Allocation, Software Cache, Scratch Pad Memory, DMA

1. INTRODUCTION

Scratch Pad Memory (SPM) is an attractive memory architecture alternative in modern embedded systems processors because of better access time predictability and low power consumption compared to hardware caches. However, because the memory is explicitly managed by the compiler, a sophisticated analysis is necessary to discover and exploit spatial and temporal locality of reference, unlike in hardware caches where this happens transparently. The general approach is to attempt retaining frequently accessed data and instructions in the SPM. When arrays are large, blocks/tiles of the array are fetched into SPM from the background memory (which could be a standard memory hierarchy that includes caches), processed, and finally written back. This expands the scope of data mapping into SPM by creating a dynamic mapping of data into SPM space, but still requires a reasonable compile-time understanding of array reference patterns. However, when array index functions are complicated due to conditionals, complex expressions, and dependence on run-time data, the SPM compiler has to rely on expensive DMA operations for individual words, leading to poor performance and energy. On the other hand, a hardware cache naturally detects and exploits such locality at run-time. This situation can be addressed by a Software Cache (SWC), in which the hardware cache feature is emulated in software, on an SPM structure as shown in Figure 1. A part of the SPM address space is designated as SWC, and the Directory (tags and control) and data array are stored in different regions within the SWC. The respective start/base addresses are stored in registers.

The processing sequence of a typical READ (hit) operation is as follows. The corresponding data transfers and computations in each step are labelled 1, 2, 3, 4, and 5 in Figure 1, corresponding to the steps below.

1. The incoming address to be looked-up is separated into Tag, Index, and Offset fields. The address of the corresponding Directory entry is computed using the Index field and the base address of the Directory. This address is sent over the ADDR Bus.

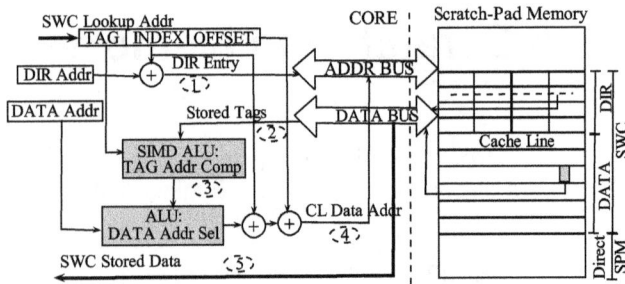

Figure 1: SWC – Cache emulated in software.

2. The information stored in the directory entry, consisting of Tags, Valid, Modified, and LRU bits, is read from the memory and sent over the DATA Bus.

3. The Tag field of the looked up address is compared with the stored tags fetched from the directory entry. The matching way number is determined and passed to the data address selector.

4. The matching Way number and the base address of the Data array determine the address of the matching Way of the SWC. The Index field is then added to determine the Cache Line (CL) address. The Offset field is finally added to generate the word address. This final address is sent over the ADDR bus.

5. The data read from memory is finally returned over the DATA bus.

While early implementations of SWC had a significant overhead due to the separate tag comparisons and multiple memory lookups, the SIMD features in modern architectures such as Cell [17], Fermi [24] and ARM [4] can be used to implement an efficient SWC using parallel fetches from all the tag arrays and simultaneous tag comparisons. The resulting design still has longer access latency than a direct SPM access, but is much faster than an explicit DMA initiated to fetch a word into SPM. Thus, the SWC could be an interesting candidate for mapping data whose run-time locality properties cannot be easily analyzed statically or are otherwise not amenable to standard SPM-based optimizations.

We present the first automated compiler data allocation strategy that considers the presence of a software cache in SPM space, and makes decisions on which arrays should be accessed through it, at which times. Arrays could be accessed differently in different parts of a program, and our algorithm analyzes such uses and considers the possibility of selectively accessing an array through the SWC only when necessary, based on a cost model of the overheads involved in SPM/SWC transitions.

We make the following specific contributions in this paper.

1. We develop an SWC-aware compiler algorithm for data mapping that attempts to perform a whole program optimization involving all array references throughout their life times. The algorithm is based on a prioritization of arrays, followed by a mapping phase that is aware of the array access patterns in different regions of a program.

2. Our data mapping strategy is able to seamlessly integrate existing SPM mapping techniques, and is structured as an enhancement to assign the SWC to data

arrays where it is considered to be more appropriate than SPM. Known techniques such as tiling/blocking, double buffering, and scatter-gather are integrated into our algorithm to ensure efficient DMA access in the SPM when necessary.

3. Our mapping algorithm assigns the mode of data access (SWC or Direct SPM) at different program points, based on a cost model that predicts the data transfer and cache flushing overheads. We build an access cost graph for each array, and use a shortest path formulation to determine the trajectory of mode changes during program execution.

We focus our attention on data mapping in this paper. Ideally, data and instructions compete for on-chip memory space and should be optimized together, but we assume a scenario with separate fixed SPM spaces available for data and instructions. The rest of the paper is organized as follows. In Section 2, we review related work in SPM and data mapping. In Section 3 we provide motivating examples to help understand the applicability of SWC. Sections 4 and 5 have the details of our compiler technique. In Section 6 we discuss our experimental evaluation and results. We summarize and conclude the paper in Section 7.

2. RELATED WORK

Compiler directed static data allocation has been well researched on both standalone SPM systems, as well those with both SPM and Data Cache [25, 26, 3, 16]. Numerous research efforts on compiler based dynamic management of SPM for regular array accesses are based on loop transformations to exploit spatial locality and block/tile management to maximize SPM accesses while minimizing memory traffic between main memory and SPM [18, 12, 33]. Li et al. [20] propose SPM management analogous to register allocation based on graph colouring. A recent work [10] proposes prefetching into the SPM well in advance to hide the transfer latency. Current research has been extended to support and augment software targeting multicore architecture that employs SPM [6, 22]. Compiler based approaches to use SPM for irregular array accesses revolve around the concept of exploiting the locality by transferring blocks of data to SPM and servicing accesses with such blocks in a predictable manner. The idea is to use a cost model to decide on the optimal migration point where a suitable range of the irregular array can be moved to SPM under the assumption that the range of certain array indices is known and small, which is sometimes the case in certain scientific and multimedia applications [1]. Techniques proposed in [13, 34] attempt to learn about locality dynamically and predict the presence of data blocks in SPM. Such techniques incur the overhead of training the engine at run-time for proper prediction, but are complementary to our proposed approach, and could also be integrated into the strategy. A general approach targeting all memory objects and whole program optimization is considered in [30], which uses a data program relationship graph to identify points where variables can be moved in and out of SPM; the actual transfer depends on a profile driven cost computation. Another recent work [11] proposes a method to map program's dynamic heap objects to SPM. Several research efforts target ILP formulation based strategies for assigning memory objects dynamically to SPM with the objective of reducing the overall energy consumption and minimize WCET of the application [28].

The other line of research involving SPM usage for irregular array accesses, has suggested SWC as a fall back mechanism [23, 9, 7]. Early work on design and use of SWC is described in [5, 15]. While the SWC could exploit locality better than other compiler direct schemes, the mechanism suffered from performance loss due to inherent lookup delays. Possible optimizations for reducing the overhead associated with SWC lookup were suggested in [23]. Due to the evolution of SIMD based multimedia enhancements in modern processors, a parallel cache tag lookup can be easily implemented, which improves the access time of SWCs significantly, in comparison to the earlier implementations. A novel SWC implementation proposed in [2] overlaps the communication with computation to minimize the lost cycles wasted due to waiting in the SWC. To improve upon the performance of SWC a recent work [9] proposed compiler transformations integrated with run-time library services for pre-fetching cache lines into SWC for irregular array references that otherwise perform poorly in SWC. To ease programmability of multi-cores a distributed coherent SWC been proposed in [19]. Access specific restructuring of SWC design has been proposed in [14] where the compiler maps the accesses to the most suitable cache structure. An SWC configurable as set- or fully associative and an adaptive line size and replacement policy was implemented in [27].

We propose a framework to integrate techniques for accessing different types of array accesses over the entire lifetime of the arrays in the program. Our work targets whole program optimization for array accesses, similar to [30], but considers the judicious usage of SWC for non-affine accesses. While our analysis could benefit from profiling, our default technique avoids the need for profile data by considering the most suitable method for a local region of the program based on a static cost analysis performed by the compiler. Other techniques on SPM and SWC targeting optimizations on individual loops, can be easily stitched into our data mapping framework. To our knowledge, this is the first proposal for an integrated data mapping framework for handling both SWC and SPM involving whole program optimization.

3. MOTIVATING EXAMPLES

In this section we present example array reference patterns that highlight the main features of our mapping technique. The formal algorithm targeting data mapping into an architecture that integrates SWC and SPM, is given in Section 5.

3.1 Blocking and Double Buffering

Simple loops with regular arrays accessed inside them can be optimized by blocking/tiling transformations. In double buffering, the execution of a block and DMA fetch of the next block proceed in parallel, hiding the transfer latency from main memory owing to compute-communication overlap. Wherever applicable, the use of double buffering can significantly reduce the pressure on SPM usage during whole program optimization in the presence of a large number of arrays; we only need to allocate sufficient buffer space in the SPM instead of the whole array. Consequently our technique assigns higher priority to such arrays. We use the analysis given in [8] to compute the cost of accessing an array in a loop using double buffer. Using SWC in such loops

with simple, analyzable and regular array accesses, yields no performance advantage.

3.2 Scatter-Gather Processing

It is common to have an array of structures in which a single field of the structure is accessed though the array is accessed regularly. The memory layout of the structure results in unused data being fetched from main memory to SPM. Techniques for converting Array-of-Structures to Structure-of-Arrays do not apply here, as multiple fields in the structure are also accessed together in other parts of the application, where fetching the whole structure is desirable. However, the scatter-gather fetch feature of modern DMA engines can be used to select only the desired elements scattered at fixed strides in main memory, and place contiguously in SPM. The DMA invocation copies data elements from a sequence of elements that are separated by a fixed stride, into the SPM. The compacted transformed loop would then access each element contiguously from SPM resulting in a better SPM utilization. Such DMA operations can also be used for multi-dimensional arrays accessed column-wise but stored in row-major order – which typically occurs in matrix operations. In our technique we identify all opportunities to use scatter-gather early in the program analysis, and estimate its usefulness by doing a whole program analysis.

3.3 Conditional Array Accesses

SWC has been suggested as a possible mechanism for data access when array index expressions are complex or data-dependent [9]. SWC is also a candidate when we have simple linear array index expressions, but the access is guarded by a condition. The example in Figure 2a is the cost updation loop used in Dijkstra's shortest path algorithm. We observe a regular (linear, affine) access to the *AdjMatrix* array (second dimension), but accesses to *rgnNodes* are regular but sporadic and dependent on *AdjMatrix* data. In an SPM-based implementation, if *NUM_NODES* is large, the *for*-loop is usually blocked, so that blocks of data from both *AdjMatrix* and *rgnNodes* arrays are fetched into the SPM before processing. However, this may lead to the redundant fetching and writing back of large chunks of the *rgnNodes* array, due to its conditional access —a sparse graph can cause a straightforward blocking procedure to be inefficient. SWC can exploit the inherent spatial locality of the accesses and can overcome such inefficiencies. Figure 2b shows the accessed elements of the two arrays (shaded squares represent accessed data). Standard SPM blocking methods fetch the entire blocks into SPM. If *rgnNodes* is fetched through SWC, then only the accessed words/lines are fetched into SWC. *AdjMatrix* is still accessed through SPM with similar results. If the condition evaluates to true infrequently, this reduces execution time even though the per-access memory latency is higher in SWC. We attempt to address this situation in our technique. A detailed analysis is presented in Section 4.6.3.

3.4 Temporal Locality

If a user hint is available about temporal locality existing in hard-to-analyze array access patterns, the SWC can be effectively utilized. For example, as observed during the heap building stage of HeapSort procedure, nodes closer to the root are visited more frequently by the algorithm. For

```
while(qcount() > 0) {
  dqueue(&iNode, &iDist, &iPrev);
  for(i=0;i<NUM_NODES;i++) {
    if((iCost==AdjMatrix[iNode][i]) != NONE) {
      if((NONE==rgnNodes[i].iDist) ||
        rgnNodes[i].iDist > (iCost+iDist)) {
        rgnNodes[i].iDist = iDist + iCost;
        rgnNodes[i].iPrev = iNode;
        enqueue(i,iDist+iCost,iNode);
      }
    }
  }
}
```

(a) rgnNodes accessed under a conditional

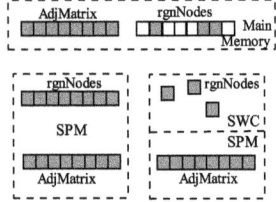

(b) Blocks fetched through SPM Vs SWC

Figure 2: Conditional but Regular Access. In an SPM-only solution (left), all elements of both arrays are fetched into SPM. In SWC (right), only the required elements of *rgnNodes* are fetched

```
for(i=0;i<num_blocks;i++) {        for(ipin=1;ipin<n_pins;ipin++) {
  num_conn = get_num_conn(i);        bnum = plist[ipin];
  if(block[i].type==CLB) {           x = block[bnum].x;
    ...                              y = block[bnum].y;
  }                                  ...
} // LOOP1                         } // LOOP2
```

(a) Regular Access   (b) Irregular Access

Figure 3: Multiple access modes for same array (block)

large heaps, conventional techniques would fetch the heap data element-by-element into the SPM through expensive DMA. However, the reuse can be naturally exploited if the array is fetched through the SWC. In our mapping strategy described later, we attempt to choose the mode (SWC or SPM) that would lead to overall best performance as estimated by an analysis of the costs involved.

3.5 Mode Transitions in Array Accesses

Since the same array may be accessed differently in different parts of a program, the appropriate mode of access —SWC or SPM —may also vary accordingly. The code snippet in Figure 3 is taken from the VPR program in the SpecInt 2000 suite. In LOOP1, the array *block* is accessed in a regular manner. In LOOP2 from another phase of the program, the same array is accessed irregularly due to the index *bnum* being data dependent. Our study of several large programs shows that such mode transitions in array accesses are common occurrences. When the possibility of mapping an array to SPM or SWC exists, a careful analysis is needed to decide the access modes at different program points in a whole-program optimization. To maintain consistency of data, operations such as cache flushing may be needed. For example, if an array's access mode changes from SWC to SPM, updated array elements present in the SWC need to be written back first before the array is accessed into the SPM; such overheads need to be accounted for.

4. FRAMEWORK FOR DATA MAPPING

In this section we outline our framework for analyzing array accesses in a program and mapping the arrays into the SPM or SWC. Heuristics are needed here because even the basic SPM mapping problem can be shown to be a variation of the Knapsack problem, which is NP-complete.

4.1 Deriving Regions in the Program

Since the SPM/SWC decisions for the same array can be different for different phases of the program, we first define Program Regions along the execution path. At the boundary of these regions we evaluate the allocation of the arrays depending on the access pattern in that region. In this work the region formation is similar to the proposal in [30], but also differs in several ways as explained below. We consider conditionals, loops, and function calls as candidates for region boundaries. We construct the Control Flow Graph (CFG) for each function in the program. We illustrate the region formation with the help of an example in Figure 4a. As we traverse the CFG for *main* we encounter loop L_1 and we define Region 0 comprising only this loop. Next we define Region 1 for the call to function A which has a solitary loop L_3. Similarly Regions 2 and 3 are defined for loops L_4 and L_5 respectively at the call to function B. Next we define Region 4 for the fork node representing the conditional C_1, which comprises both the *then* and *else* paths. Region 5 starts for the loop LC_1. This region has a conditional and a basic block after the join. Finally, we define Region 6 for loop L_2. Figure 4b shows the flow of the program divided into regions. The above procedure could be made more sophisticated in the future by introducing some automation that first quantifies the complexity of the code sections during region formation.

4.2 Array Access Graph

For each array, we build an Array Access Graph (AAG) that attempts to capture the cost of mapping the array to SWC or SPM in and between different program regions. The AAG is initialized with nodes S and E, corresponding to the Start and End of the program. We introduce nodes C_i and D_i (for Cache and Direct) representing the mapping of the array into SWC or SPM respectively, in region i. An edge from C_i to C_{i+1} (or D_i to D_{i+1}) denotes that the array continues to be accessed through the SWC (or SPM) in both regions i and $i+1$. An edge from C_i to D_{i+1} (or D_i to C_{i+1}) denotes that the mapping for the array changes from SWC in region i to SPM in region i+1 (or the other way around). In addition, edges are introduced from S to C_0 and D_0, and to E from C_{n-1} and D_{n-1}. A path in the AAG from S to E covers either C_i or D_i for every region i accessing the array, and denotes the set of mapping decisions taken for the array in all the regions, as shown in Figure 5.

4.3 Node Cost Estimates

Each node in the AAG is associated with a node cost, which represents the approximate number of cycles required for accessing all array data in the region through SPM or SWC. Within a region, the total cost for accessing an array directly from SPM is expressed as:

$$C_{dn} = A \times N_a \tag{1}$$

where A is the access latency for SPM and N_a is the number of accesses made to the array in the region. The cost to

```
void main () {
  // Region 0
  for (...) { // Loop : L_1
  }
  // Region 1
  Func_A ();
  // Region 2 & 3
  Func_B ();
  // Region 4
  if (x) { // Cond : C_1
    Access Array_A [];
    Access Array_B [];
  } else {
    Access Array_C [];
  }
  // Region 5
  while (...) { // LoopCond : LC_1
    if (x) {
      Access Array_M [];
    } else if (y) {
      Access Array_N [];
      Access Array_O [];
    } else {
      Access Array_M [];
      Access Array_O [];
      Access Array_P [];
    }
    Access Array_Q [];
  }
  // Region 6
  for (...) { // Loop : L_2
  }
}

void Func_A () {
  for (...) { // Loop : L_3
  }
}

void Func_B () {
  for (...) { // Loop : L_4
  }
  for (...) { // Loop : L_5
  }
}
```

(a) Example Code   (b) Divided into Regions

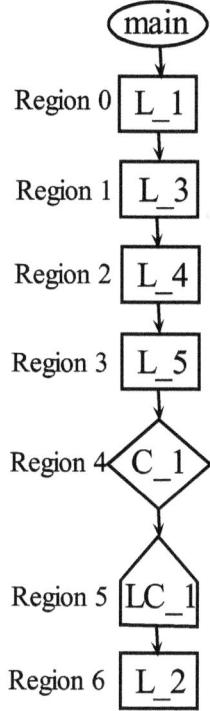

Figure 4: Execution flow with Regions and Timestamps

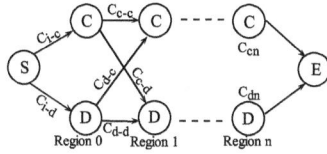

Figure 5: Array Access Graph

access an array through SWC is expressed as:

$$C_{cn} = (H + A) \times N_a \qquad (2)$$

where H is the latency for performing the operations to locate the accessed word in the SWC. The node costs for SWC access assume cache hits and the edge costs in the next section cover the cost to move the data into the SWC (misses) if needed.

4.4 Edge Cost Estimates

For each node in the AAG, there are two access choices for the array in the next region — either access it directly from SPM, or access using SWC. There are certain overheads incurred when changing the access mode. These overheads are captured as edge costs in the AAG. For each region's direct access node D, if the array is to be used by bringing it completely or partially into the SPM, we need to compute its edge cost. This would simply become the cost to setup the DMA and the cost to fetch the bytes into SPM:

$$C_{i-d} = (S + T_g \times B_{sz}) \times N_b \qquad (3)$$

where S is the latency for DMA setup, T_g is the latency to transfer a byte from main memory to SPM, B_{sz} is the size of the buffer allocated in SPM for the array in the region, and N_b is the number of times such a block is transferred. For an array that is transferred completely to SPM, N_b becomes 1, whereas for an irregularly accessed array not already present in SPM, B_{sz} becomes the size of the element type and N_b is the number of irregular accesses in the region. Similarly, compulsory SWC misses for array data to be used in a region's node C, would be reflected in a cost added to the incoming edge.

$$C_{i-c} = M \times N_l \qquad (4)$$

where M is the cache miss latency and N_l is the number of cache blocks in the array. At the start node S, the array has not been accessed yet, and at the end node E, it will never be accessed further. Hence, for both these, the array does not need to be present in either SPM or cache. The edge costs from S to D_0 and C_0 are given by Equations 3 and 4 respectively. If we access an array directly from SPM in the current region and will also access it from SPM in the next, then the transition/edge cost is 0, assuming that the array is not swapped out of SPM between these regions. However, the same cannot be said about SWC to SWC access between regions, due to the unpredictability of its content except for regular accesses in both regions. We assume that data fetched into the SWC, is present until it is explicitly flushed out due to SWC→SPM transitions in the AAG or the array is implicitly flushed out due to regular access in that region, which can be determined. Thus, we count the cost due to compulsory misses and capacity misses where it is deterministic. This is a simplification, but nonetheless, works well, since we consider SWC only for the special case of irregular accesses identified earlier. Hence, in the AAG, all cache to cache transition costs for irregular accesses are always 0. The transition cost when the access mode changes from SPM to SWC simply becomes C_{i-c} as in Equation 4, if the SPM contents are not dirty. If the SPM contents are dirty, an additional cost is incurred to write back the contents to main memory. The cost is given as:

$$C_{d-c} = (S + T_p \times B_{sz}) \times N_b + C_{i-c} \qquad (5)$$

where T_p is the latency to transfer a byte from SPM to main memory. Similarly the transition cost when the access mode changes from SWC to SPM is given as:

$$C_{c-d} = I_c \times N_l + C_{i-d} \qquad (6)$$

if the cache contents are not dirty, and

$$C_{c-d} = F_d \times N_l + C_{i-d} \qquad (7)$$

if the cache contents are dirty. I_c is the latency to invalidate a line in the SWC and F_d is the latency to flush a cache block to memory.

4.5 Example AAG

An example AAG is illustrated in Figure 6, with a code snippet extracted from the Bzip2 application. The array *ftab* is accessed in 3 regions in different ways. As the size of *ftab* is larger than the SPM size, we construct an array access graph and compute the costs using Table 1 for each node and edge as described above and shown in Figure 6d assuming a buffer size of 16KB for direct SPM access. The value of *last* is taken as 20000 for the computation.

205

```
                                        c1 = block[−1];
                                        for(i=0;i<=last;i++) {
  for(i=0;i<65536;i++)                     c2 = block[i];
    ftab[i] = 0;                           ftab[(c1<<8)+c2]++;
                                          c1 = c2;
                                        }
        (a) Region 0                    (b) Region 1
```

```
  for(i=0;i<65536;i++)
    ftab[i] += ftab[i−1];
```

(c) Region 2   (d) AAG with costs ($\times 10^3$)

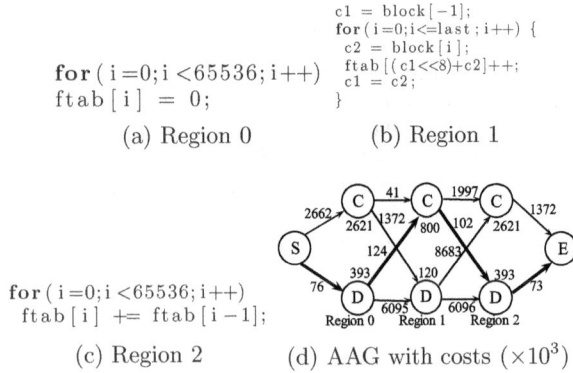

Figure 6: Allocation decision for *ftab* array in Bzip2

4.6 Special Cases

4.6.1 Scatter-Gather Costs

Similar to the edge cost defined in Equation 3, the edge cost representing fetch of N scattered elements to SPM can be represented as:

$$C_{e-sg} = S_{sg} + T_{sg} \times E_{sz} \times N \qquad (8)$$

where E_{sz} is the size of each element. Once elements are transferred to SPM, they are accessed contiguously just like any other array and hence the node cost can be the same as that given by Equation 1.

4.6.2 Double Buffering Costs

As double buffering overlaps the fetch and execution cycles for a loop we attribute the cost only to the node cost and assign the corresponding edge cost to 0. We use the analysis presented in [8] where cost of the general case of a non-DMA bound and non-compute bound loop is represented as:

$$C_{db-n} = (S/N_b + D + C) \times N/2 \qquad (9)$$

where N is the iteration count of the loop, N_b is the blocking factor, C is the compute cycles of the loop and D is the DMA transfer cycles for the loop. The compute cycles of the loop can be accurately estimated provided we have a detailed knowledge of the target platform. In this work we derive an approximation of C by using the latencies of the instructions (I_i) in the loop as published by CELL architecture and using the following equation:

$$C = \sum_i Lat(I_i) \times Loop\_Trip\_Count \qquad (10)$$

4.6.3 Cost for Accesses under Conditionals

In this section we derive the cost equations for the case where an array is accessed under a condition, as explained earlier. The fetch and access costs (i.e., edge and node costs) when the array is brought directly to SPM, is identical to the single buffer costs and given by Equations 3 and 1 respectively. As discussed in Section 3.3, entire blocks need to be fetched into the SPM even if the conditionals cause only a subset of the data to be accessed. The corresponding cost when the array is accessed through SWC, is computed using the probability of the condition being true, and an estimate of inherent spatial locality in the accesses. Assuming that the total number of cache lines accessed in the loop is N_c,

the total number of misses (edge cost) can be computed as:

$$M \times N_c \times (1 - f)$$

where f is the fraction of lines of the array already present in the cache. f is 0 if the cache is cold for the array. The node cost is given by Equation 2, where N_a is the number of actual accesses made to the array in the loop. If p is the probability of the condition being true, then $N_a = p \times N$, where N is the iteration count of the loop. Introducing another factor $q = N_c/N_a$, the measure of spatial locality in the accesses we can finally simplify the edge and node costs respectively for conditional accesses as:

$$C_{e-c} = M \times p \times q \times N \times (1 - f) \qquad (11)$$

$$C_{n-c} = (H + A) \times p \times N \qquad (12)$$

q captures the number of distinct cache lines fetched per access, and is a measure of the extent of spatial locality. Smaller q implies more spatial locality, and fewer misses. Static — and even, constant — values for p and q can provide useful estimates. In this work we assume default values for p and q. We have used relatively simple cost estimates in our formulation, which could be easily replaced by alternatives:

- A profile-based approach could be used to obtain key parameters such as p and q above. This could be very useful because the simulation for obtaining the parameters needs to be run only once, but our mapping strategy evaluates and selects the best mapping out of all SPM/SWC combinations in all regions.

- A more sophisticated cache miss estimation technique, such as [32], could be used. However, such procedures consume too much time, and are more exact when array accesses have well behaved index expressions. This makes such techniques unsuitable because such arrays will usually be mapped to SPM, not SWC. Most irregular accesses mapped to SWC are caused by data dependent conditionals, which are hard to predict by static estimates.

5. MAPPING STRATEGY

The important steps of our mapping strategy are: prioritizing the arrays, building the AAG, determining mapping decisions for individual arrays, and the overall algorithm for mapping all arrays.

5.1 Prioritization of Arrays

We attempt to capture the relative importance of the arrays in terms of their impact on program performance, through a priority scheme. We start first by prioritizing the regions, and then accumulating the priority of an array in the regions of its reference throughout its lifetime in the program. In programs where the loop count is not known statically we can use a profile driven approach or some technique that estimates the loop iteration count statically as described in [21]. In Algorithm 1, we calculate the priority of all the arrays accessed in the program as follows. We first compute the priority of each region as the ratio of array access count within the region to the total array accesses in the whole program (Lines 3–6). For each array A we iterate through the regions in which it is accessed, and determine the number of distinct elements of the array A

Algorithm 1: Prioritization of arrays

Input: List of arrays and accesses
Output: Ordered list of arrays

```
 1 begin
 2 │  Ref_tot ⟵ total array accesses in the program
 3 │  foreach region R in the program do
 4 │  │   Ref_R ⟵ total array accesses in region R
 5 │  │   Prio_R ⟵ Ref_reg / Ref_tot
 6 │  end
 7 │  foreach array A in the program do
 8 │  │   prio[A] ⟵ 0
 9 │  │   foreach region R in the program do
10 │  │   │   if A is not accessed in R then
11 │  │   │   │   continue              // go to next region
12 │  │   │   end
13 │  │   │   n ⟵ number of accesses of A in R
14 │  │   │   if is_double_buffer(A, R) then
15 │  │   │   │   m ⟵ double buffer size
16 │  │   │   else if is_scatter_gather(A, R) then
17 │  │   │   │   m ⟵ scatter gather size
18 │  │   │   else
19 │  │   │   │   m ⟵ size of array A
20 │  │   │   end
21 │  │   │   prio[A] ⟵ prio[A] + Prio_R × (n/m)
22 │  │   end
23 │  end
24 │  sort_descending(prio)
25 end
```

accessed in the region. This should be the highest number of accesses amongst all the paths in that region (Line 13). Next, we calculate the minimum space requirement m in SPM for the array to execute efficiently. For a regularly accessed array, this should be either the array size (Line 19), or if double buffering or scatter-gather is applicable, then the relevant buffer size needed (Lines 15,17). This ensures that if an array can always be double buffered, then, since its space requirement is relatively low, its priority would be high. For an irregularly accessed array the size m would always be the array size. In Line 21, we accumulate the priority of the array by the ratio n/m, weighted by that region's priority. The fraction n/m gives the access count per unit space occupied in the SPM, and is along the lines of the *value density* heuristic of the Knapsack problem used in [26]. Including the region's priority in the equation ensures that arrays accessed in important regions are assigned higher priority globally. Once the priorities of all the arrays are calculated, we sort them in descending order in Line 24.

5.2 Least Cost Path for an Array

As mentioned earlier, a path in the AAG from S to E denotes the set of mapping decisions for an array in all the relevant regions. The cost of a specific assignment (each region using SWC or SPM for the array) can be computed by first defining a Path Cost in the AAG., where the path cost between a pair of nodes v_i and v_j is defined as:

$$PathCost(v_i...v_j) = \sum_{v \in v_i...v_j} C_v + \sum_{e \in v_i,...,v_j} C_e$$

where C_v is the weight of node v and C_e is weight of edge e. Thus, the path cost includes the cost of all the nodes in the path, as well as the cost of all edges. Recall that the node cost captures the memory delay estimate for accessing the array in the SWC or SPM, in the region, and the edge cost

captures the additional delay as we move from one region to another —where, for example, flushing of the SWC may cause an additional delay. The optimal set of mapping decisions for an array corresponds to the Least Cost Path from S to E in the graph. We can use the specific structure of the AAG to arrive at an efficient linear-time algorithm for computing the least cost path, given in Algorithm 2. A simple dynamic programming formulation can be adopted because the problem exhibits the optimal substructure property. In iteration i of the loop, we compute the best path so far, for both SWC and SPM assignments to the array. If SWC is to be used in region i, then there are two possibilities:

1. SWC was assigned in region $i-1$, and the new cost C1 (Line 6) is obtained by adding the weight of node C_i to the cumulative cost C_{SWC}, and the data transfer cost, if any, between the accesses in regions $i-1$ and i, e.g., misses and writebacks.

2. SPM was assigned in region $i-1$, and new cost C2 (Line 7) is obtained by adding the weight of node C_i as well as the transition cost from SPM to SWC, to the cumulative cost C_{SPM}.

The lower of the two costs determines the selection for region i, and the corresponding edge that leads to this choice is noted in the PrevSWC array (Lines 10-16). If SPM is to be used in region i, then an analogous computation is used to choose and store the appropriate predecessor from region $i-1$ (Lines 17-23). The cumulative costs C_{SWC} and C_{SPM}, are combined with the edge weights of the final stage leading to edge E (Lines 25-26), and the smaller of the two costs is the cost corresponding to the least cost path from S to E. The actual path is obtained by just retracing the decisions captured in the two arrays PrevSWC and PrevSPM.

For the example AAG of Figure 6d, we have the initialization $C_{SWC} = 5283$ and $C_{SPM} = 469$. In the first loop iteration ($i = 1$), we have $C1 = 5283 + 800 + 41$, $C2 = 469+800+124$, $D1 = 5283+120+1372$, and $D2 = 469+120+6095$, leading to $C_{SWC} = 1393$, and $C_{SPM} = 6684$, with PrevSWC[1]=SPM and PrevSPM[1]=SPM. Continuing, we have $C_{SWC} = 6011$ and $C_{SPM} = 1888$ at $i = 2$, with PrevSWC[2]=SWC and PrevSPM[2]=SWC. The least cost path (highlighted in Figure 6d) is obtained from the PrevSPM array values as follows: $S \rightarrow SPM \rightarrow SWC \rightarrow SPM \rightarrow E$, implying that it is best to assign array *ftab* to SPM in Region 0; access it through SWC in Region 1; and switch back to SPM in Region R2.

5.3 Mapping All Arrays

The overall strategy for mapping all arrays into SPM or SWC, is outlined in Algorithm 3. The first step (Line 2) is to divide the program into statically determined regions as described in section 4.1. Each such region is assigned a global time-stamp starting from 0, which determines the execution order. In Line 3, we sort the arrays accessed in these regions in order of their importance, as given in Algorithm 1. Each array is considered in decreasing order of priority for SPM/SWC mapping, iterating through the program regions (Lines 4–28). In Line 6 we build the array access graph from the program regions where the array is accessed (Section 4.2). From the weighted array access graph we determine the least cost path to ascertain how the array should be mapped in each region (Line 7). Our final

---

Algorithm 2: Least Cost Path

Input: AAG with costs
Output: Least cost nodes and edges

```
1  begin
2  |  C_SWC ← wt(C_0) + wt(S, C_0)
3  |  C_SPM ← wt(D_0) + wt(S, D_0)
4  |  PrevSPM[0] ← PrevSWC[0] ← S
5  |  for i ← 1 to n − 1 do
6  |  |  C1 ← C_SWC + wt(C_i) + wt(C_{i−1}, C_i)
7  |  |  C2 ← C_SPM + wt(C_i) + wt(D_{i−1}, C_i)
8  |  |  D1 ← C_SWC + wt(D_i) + wt(C_{i−1}, D_i)
9  |  |  D2 ← C_SPM + wt(D_i) + wt(D_{i−1}, D_i)
10 |  |  C_SWC ← min(C1, C2)
11 |  |  C_SPM ← min(D1, D2)
12 |  |  if C1 < C2 then
13 |  |  |  PrevSWC[i] ← SWC
14 |  |  else
15 |  |  |  PrevSWC[i] ← SPM
16 |  |  end
17 |  |  if D1 < D2 then
18 |  |  |  PrevSPM[i] ← SWC
19 |  |  else
20 |  |  |  PrevSPM[i] ← SPM
21 |  |  end
22 |  end
23 |  C_SWC ← C_SWC + wt(C_{n−1}, E)
24 |  C_SPM ← C_SPM + wt(D_{n−1}, E)
25 |  if C_SWC < C_SPM then
26 |  |  PrevSWC[n] ← SWC
27 |  |  Retrace path from PrevSWC[n]
28 |  else
29 |  |  PrevSPM[n] ← SPM
30 |  |  Retrace path from PrevSPM[n]
31 |  end
32 end
```

Algorithm 3: SPM Array Allocation

Input: Program Source Code
Output: SPM/SWC Allocation for all arrays in all regions

```
1  begin
2  |  Divide the program into regions and assign timestamps
3  |  PrioritizeArrays()
4  |  foreach array A in sorted list do
5  |  |  regList ← list of regions where A is accessed
6  |  |  G ← BuildArrayAccessGraph(A, regList)
7  |  |  LCP ← LeastCostPath(G)
8  |  |  foreach node n ∈ LCP do
9  |  |  |  r ← getRegion(n)
10 |  |  |  m ← n.access_mode
11 |  |  |  if m = SWC then
12 |  |  |  |  Allocate[r].swc(A)
13 |  |  |  else
14 |  |  |  |  s ← n.size
15 |  |  |  |  if m = DoubleBuffered then
16 |  |  |  |  |  Allocate[r].db(A, s)
17 |  |  |  |  else if m = ScatterGather then
18 |  |  |  |  |  Allocate[r].scg(A, s)
19 |  |  |  |  else if m = Buffered then
20 |  |  |  |  |  Allocate[r].sb(A, s)
21 |  |  |  |  else if n.swapin = true then
22 |  |  |  |  |  Allocate[r].swapin(A)
23 |  |  |  |  else
24 |  |  |  |  |  Allocate[r].preserve(A)
25 |  |  |  |  end
26 |  |  |  end
27 |  |  end
28 |  end
29 |  GenerateCode(Allocate, RegionList)
30 end
```

objective is to transform the code by inserting data transfer DMA calls and modifying the array accesses in each region as dictated by the least cost path. The *for*-loop in Lines 8–27 iterates through each node in the path, and collects information about the array access mode (SWC, Double-Buffer, ScatterGather, etc.), which is used to generate the transformed code. If the array is accessed through SWC in a region (Line 11), then the appropriate library call is generated for the array access. Otherwise, one of several SPM access transformations is applied (Lines 15-25). For single buffered, double buffered, and scatter-gather modes, we need to allocate suitable space in SPM, the information about which is extracted from the AAG (Line 14). Finally, if the array is to be completely resident in SPM, then it is either swapped-in at this region boundary (Line 21), or if it is already resident in SPM due to accesses in the previous region, then it is marked appropriately to avoid being swapped out before this region (Line 24). Once the mapping decisions are made for all arrays, we initiate the code transformation process in Line 29.

6. EXPERIMENTS

In this section we evaluate the impact of our approach on several example applications by comparing the performance against other approaches, on a CELL BE system.

6.1 Setup

We implemented the front end of the compiler pass in LLVM [31] to transform the workloads to run on the Cell BE Processor. The front end parses the source code and ex-

Table 1: Latencies in cycles of Cell BE

DMA Setup	300	SWC Miss Clean Evict	700
Transfer	0.26 c/b	SWC Miss Dirty Evict	1300
SPM Access	6	Cache Block Flush	670
SWC Hit	34	Cache Block Invalidate	70

tracts the features necessary to derive the regions and identify the array access patterns, which are passed as input to the mapping algorithm. Using the detailed annotation produced by the mapping module we manually insert the appropriate DMA swap-in/swap-out and SWC calls to the original source code resulting in a source to source transformation. For the sake of brevity we have omitted the checks to maintain coherency between the SPM buffers and SWC — similar to the work in [7, 29] except we don't employ any runtime disambiguation. The transformed source was compiled using Cell BE *gcc*. We evaluated the results on a Cell BE machine using a single SPE with 256 KB local store. Cycles were measured using the *SPU Decrementer* hooks provided by the SPU timer library contained within the SPU Runtime Library Extensions in SDK 3.1. We used the built-in SWC for Cell in GCC toolchain 4.4 and integrated it into the applications. The DMA and SWC metrics were gathered using software counters instrumented in the appropriate libraries. Table 1 lists the parameters and latency of Cell BE architecture measured by us.

6.2 Benchmark Selection

We evaluated the performance of our approach using 2 benchmarks from SPEC2000 INT, one from SPEC2006 FP suite, and a Sparse Matrix-Vector multiplication (*SpMV*) kernel. The benchmarks (*VPR and Bzip2*) from the SPEC 2000 suite are large, with several complex loops/conditionals

Table 2: Benchmark Characteristics

Benchmark	Num Reg	Num Arrays	SCG	DB	Transitions
VPR Route	82	59	Medium	Medium	High
VPR Place	52	27	Medium	Medium	High
Bzip2	36	13	No	Low	Medium
Bwaves	11	14	No	High	No
SpMV	3	5	No	No	No

and a large number of directly and indirectly accessed arrays over many phases of the program. *Bwaves* from SPEC2006 is a benchmark with more regular accesses. Table 2 lists the characteristics of the benchmarks in terms of number of regions, and presence of patterns namely scatter gather (SCG), double buffer (DB), and array mode transitions.

6.3 Results

We measured the performance improvement of our algorithm by comparing it against an SPM-only implementation and against traditional SW cache based techniques. We implemented two versions involving SW cache. In one version (*Cache-Crude*), an array is always accessed through SWC if there is at least one region where it is irregularly accessed. In the second version (*Region-Best*), we used the most beneficial technique (direct or SWC) for array mapping, restricting the analysis to individual regions closely resembling the implementation in [7]. This implementation gives an indication of the importance of performing a whole program optimization rather than a local best effort.

We maintained the total SPM size of 64 KB for all our experiments. This includes the Cache Tag size of 4 KB & Cache Data size of 16 KB for the SWC. For SPM-only, we used the entire 64 KB as SPM size. The SPM size is chosen to induce reasonable contention for the scarce SPM resource amongst the competing arrays. The size is also representative of the SPM in embedded systems such as Fermi. The rest of the SPM space is shared by scalar data, stack, and application code. The results are collected for 4 different techniques to access the arrays as described. We present the results normalized to 1.0 for our algorithm (*Integrated*). We show the performance improvement by measuring the cycle count and improvement in memory traffic comprising implicit DMA transfers, cache misses and writebacks. For Bzip2, the result is averaged over 4 representative input files.

Figure 7 compares the number of cycles for each implementation normalized to the cycle count of our technique. Comparing our technique with SPM-only (first and last bars), we notice an improvement by a factor of 1.5 to 5 times (except Bwaves), owing largely to the use of SWC for irregular accesses prevalent in these benchmarks. SPM-only incurs a large fetch latency for each irregular access if the array is not resident in SPM. For Bwaves, which is devoid of irregular patterns, SPM-only outperforms our technique due to a larger SPM (64KB) at its disposal compared to ours (44KB). Further, for Bwaves, our technique maps none of the arrays to SWC, and hence, the difference in performance was because of an empty, unused 20KB space allocated for the SWC. As a simple future enhancement, we could just de-allocate the SWC when we establish that it is not necessary for a significant program duration. When compared to the Cache-Crude and Region-Best, we obtain a speed-up of 1.19 and 1.27 times for VPR Place; and 1.06 and 1.04 times for Bzip2 respectively. This is achieved mainly by the judicious use of SWC and SPM for the arrays transitioning between regular and irregular access patterns across regions. We perform at par for VPR Route, even though there is

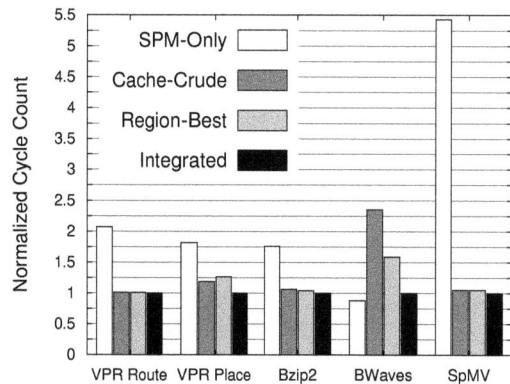

Figure 7: Normalized cycle count for each benchmark for different mapping techniques on Cell BE

a high density of pattern transitions due to fact that our technique converges towards mapping irregular accesses to SWC, for the dominant phase of the application. Cache-Crude and Region-Best incur higher penalties for Bwaves because the decision to map arrays with a strided access into SWC, turned out to be inefficient.

Figure 8 shows the memory traffic between SPM and main memory for all the techniques. We observe that SPM-only transfers substantially smaller volume for VPR Place and Bzip2, compared to the other techniques. This is largely attributed to fetching irregular accesses through DMA, whereas extra bytes (corresponding to full cache lines) are fetched when these accesses are mapped to SWC. However, the setup cost for smaller-sized DMAs results in significant performance penalties for SPM-only. Further, the results show that even though we do not reduce the overall data movement significantly as compared to other techniques, our technique exploits the knowledge of fetch latencies and results in overall performance improvement.

Overall, the results show that our technique is able to perform better for benchmarks where there is significant scope of mapping arrays differently for different phases of the program. In the cases where an application is naturally more amenable to either regular (SPM) or irregular (SWC) patterns, our results are similar to those of the best among the other techniques. Since we are able to effectively exploit the combined presence of SPM and cache, our technique is also obviously applicable to architectures such as NVIDIA Fermi, where part of the on-chip SPM space can be configured through hardware, to function as a cache.

7. CONCLUSION

We presented a data mapping technique that takes into consideration the presence of an SWC within a scratch pad memory. For every array, we decide on whether to access it through SPM or SWC in each program region, using a cost estimate that accounts for the overheads involved in access mode transitions between SPM and SWC. Our experiments on a Cell processor based architecture showed that our technique resulted in performance improvements of up to 82% over SPM-only and up to 27% over previous SWC-based strategies. Handling other constructs causing uncertainty in data access, such as pointers, in the SWC data mapping strategy, requires more careful attention, and is a topic of future research. We plan to extend the formulation to in-

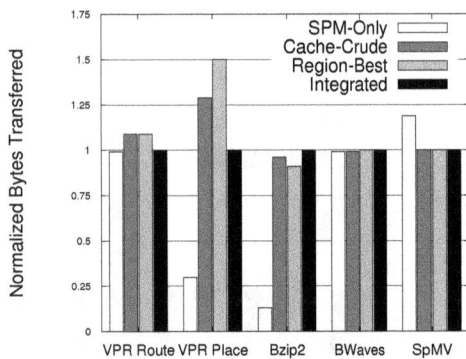

Figure 8: Normalized transfer of bytes between SPM & MM for each benchmark on Cell BE

corporate both instructions and data, and also investigate a more sophisticated handling of the cost estimates used in the algorithm.

8. REFERENCES

[1] M. J. Absar and F. Catthoor. Compiler-based approach for exploiting scratch-pad in presence of irregular array access. In *DATE*, 2005.

[2] J. Balart, M. Gonzalez, X. Martorell, and et al. A novel asynchronous software cache implementation for the Cell-BE processor. In *LCPC*, 2007.

[3] R. Banakar, S. Steinke, B. Lee, M. Balakrishnan, and P. Marwedel. Scratch-pad memory: A design alternative for cache on-chip memory in embedded systems. In *CODES*, 2002.

[4] D. Brash. The ARM architecture version 6 (ARMv6). Technical report, January 2002.

[5] M. C. Carlisle and A. Rogers. Software caching and computation migration in olden. *Parallel and Distributed Computing*, 38(2):248–255, 1996.

[6] W. Che and K. S. Chatha. Compilation of stream programs onto scratchpad memory based embedded multicore processors through retiming. In *DAC*, 2011.

[7] T. Chen, H. Lin, T. Zhang, and et al. Orchestrating data transfer for the Cell/B.E. processor. In *ICS*, 2008.

[8] T. Chen, Z. Sura, K. O'Brien, and K. O'Brien. Optimizing the use of static buffers for DMA on a CELL chip. *LCPC*, 2006.

[9] T. Chen, T. Zhang, Z. Sura, M. G. Tallada, K. O'Brien, and K. O'Brien. Prefetching irregular references for software cache on Cell. In *CGO*, 2008.

[10] J. Cong, H. Huang, C. Liu, and Y. Zou. A reuse-aware prefetching scheme for scratchpad memory. In *DAC*, 2011.

[11] A. Dominguez, S. Udayakumaran, and R. Barua. Heap data allocation to scratch-pad memory in embedded systems. *J. Embedded Computing*, 1(4):521–540, 2005.

[12] P. Francesco, P. Marchal, D. Atienza, L. Benini, F. Catthoor, and J. M. Mendias. An integrated hardware/software approach for runtime scratchpad management. In *DAC*, pages 238–243, 2004.

[13] M. K. G. Chen, O. Ozturk and M. Karakoy. Dynamic scratch-pad memory management for irregular array access patterns. In *DATE*, 2006.

[14] M. Gonz'alez, N. Vujic, X. Martorell, and et al. Hybrid access-specific software cache techniques for the Cell BE architecture. In *PACT*, 2008.

[15] A. Iyengar. Design and performance of a general-purpose software cache. In *IPCC99*, 1999.

[16] A. Janapsatya, S. Parameswaran, and A. Ignjatovic. Hardware/software managed scratchpad memory for embedded system. In *ICCAD*, 2004.

[17] J. A. Kahle, M. N. Day, H. P. Hofstee, C. R. Johns, T. R. Maeurer, and D. Shippy. Introduction to the Cell multiprocessor. Technical report, IBM, July/September 2005.

[18] M. Kandemir, J. Ramanujam, M. Irwin, N. Vijaykrishnan, I. Kadayif, and A. Parikh. Dynamic management of scratch-pad memory space. In *DAC*, June 2001.

[19] J. Lee, S. Seo, C. Kim, and et al. Comic: a coherent shared memory interface for Cell BE. In *PACT*, 2008.

[20] L. Li, L. Gao, and J. Xue. Memory coloring: A compiler approach for scratchpad memory management. In *PACT*, 2005.

[21] P. Lokuciejewski, D. Cordes, H. Falk, and P. Marwedel. A fast and precise static loop analysis based on abstract interpretation, program slicing and polytope models. In *CGO*, 2009.

[22] D. Lu, A. Shrivastava, and K. Bai. Vector class on limited local memory (LLM) multi-core processors. In *CASES*, pages 215–224, 2011.

[23] C. A. Moritz, M. Frank, and S. Amarasinghe. Flexcache: A framework for flexible compiler generated data caching. In *IMS*, November 2000.

[24] NVIDIA. NVIDIA's next generation CUDA compute architecture: FERMI. Technical report.

[25] P. R. Panda, F. Catthoor, N. D. Dutt, K. Danckaert, E. Brockmeyer, A. V. C. Kulkarni, and P. G. Kjeldsberg. Data and memory optimization techniques for embedded systems. *TODAES*, 6(2):149–206, 2001.

[26] P. R. Panda, N. D. Dutt, and A. Nicolau. Efficient utilization of scratch-pad memory in embedded processor applications. In *EDTC*, pages 7–11, 1997.

[27] S. Seo, J. Lee, and Z. Sura. Design and implementation of software-managed caches for multicores with local memory. In *HPCA*, 2009.

[28] V. Suhendra, T. Mitra, A. Roychoudhury, and T. Chen. WCET centric data allocation to scratchpad memory. In *RTSS*, 2005.

[29] L. Tao, L. Haibo, and et al. Dbdb: Optimizing dma transfer for the Cell BE architecture. In *ICS*, 2009.

[30] S. Udayakumaran and R. Barua. An integrated scratch-pad allocator for affine and non-affine code. In *DATE*, 2006.

[31] UIUC. *The LLVM Reference Manual (Version 2.6)*.

[32] X. Vera and J. Xue. Let's study whole-program cache behaviour analytically. In *HPCA*, 2002.

[33] M. Verma, S. Steinke, and P. Marwedel. Data partitioning for maximal scratchpad usage. In *ASP-DAC*, 2003.

[34] T. Yemliha, S. Srikantaiah, M. Kandemir, and O. Ozturk. SPM management using markov chain based data access prediction. In *ICCAD*, 2008.

Analytical Approaches for Performance Evaluation of Networks-on-Chip

Abbas Eslami Kiasari
KTH Royal Institute of
Technology, Sweden
kiasari@kth.se

Axel Jantsch
KTH Royal Institute of
Technology, Sweden
axel@kth.se

Marco Bekooij
University of Twente,
The Netherlands
marco.bekooij@nxp.com

Alan Burns
University of York,
United Kingdom
alan.burns@york.ac.uk

Zhonghai Lu
KTH Royal Institute of
Technology, Sweden
zhonghai@kth.se

ABSTRACT

This tutorial reviews four popular mathematical formalisms – *dataflow analysis, schedulability analysis, network calculus,* and *queueing theory* – and how they have been applied to the analysis of Network-on-Chip (NoC) performance. We review the basic concepts and results of each formalism and provide examples of how they have been used in on-chip communication performance analysis. The tutorial also discusses the respective strengths and weaknesses of each formalism, their suitability for a specific purpose, and the attempts that have been made to bridge these analytical approaches. Finally, we conclude the tutorial by discussing open research issues.

Categories and Subject Descriptors

C.4 [Performance of Systems]: Design studies, Modeling techniques, Performance attributes

General Terms

Design, Performance

Keywords

System-on-Chip, Network-on-Chip, Design methodology, Performance evaluation, Analytical modeling

1. INTRODUCTION

In modern system-on-chip (SoC), the on-chip communication infrastructure or network-on-chip (NoC) is a dominant factor for design, validation and performance analysis. SoC designers are interested in NoC performance evaluation since their goal is either to provide a minimum level of performance at lowest possible cost, or to provide the highest performance at a given cost. In both cases a reliable measure of performance is indispensible. However, in the first case the focus is typically on *worst-case performance*, while in the latter case the *average-case performance* is the main metric [8]. In real-time systems such as automotive or avionic applications, the worst-case execution time is of particular concern since it is important to know how much time might be needed in the worst-case to guarantee that the task will always finish its jobs before the predetermined deadline. However, the worst-case-based design results in resource over-dimensioning. Therefore, the average-case-based design methods are usually used for non-time critical applications to have a more efficient system.

Performance estimation tools can be classified in *simulation models* and *analytical models*. SoC designers have tackled performance analysis by exploring the design space using detailed simulations. Simulation tools are flexible and accurate, but often have to be complemented by an analytical performance modeling approach. In particular, analytical models can analyze the worst-case. An appropriate analytical model can estimate very early in the design phase the desired performance metrics in a fraction of time that simulation would take. Although the use of high-level models conceals a lot of complex technological aspects, it facilitates fast exploration of the NoCs design space. Also, the analytical models provide not only the timing properties of the system, but also useful feedback about the system behavior. Hence, it can be invoked in any optimization loop for NoCs for fast and accurate performance estimations.

2. OVERVIEW OF THE TUTORIAL

This tutorial reviews the applicability and the application of dataflow models, schedulability analysis, network calculus, and queueing theory to NoC performance analysis. The key message of each presentation is described in the following subsections.

2.1 Dataflow Models (Marco Bekooij)

Timed dataflow models have been successfully applied to the derivation of the minimum throughput and maximum latency of network-on-chips [5]. Furthermore, these models are used to compute trade-offs between allocated bandwidth of the network connections and the required capacity of the buffers in the network [11]. Flow-control on the network connections results in cyclic dependencies in these dataflow models. However, such cyclic dependencies do not complicate dataflow analysis significantly. Also, the effects of starvation free arbitration are included in the dataflow models [13].

Dataflow models of networks can be created at different levels of abstraction depending on the required conciseness and accuracy of the model. Conservativeness of these levels of abstraction can be shown by making use of the earlier-the-better refinement relation and its transitivity property [4]. This refinement relation also implies that for proving the temporal requirements of a network, it suffices to show that an admissible schedule exists that adheres to these requirements. Approximation algorithms have been developed that compute these admissible schedules in polynomial time [12]. These algorithms are based on convex programming.

2.2 Schedulability Analysis (Alan Burns)

Scheduling analysis (SA) is a mathematical formalism used to confirm that all deadlines will be met in a real-time system. SA is usually applied to application tasks running on one or more CPUs/cores; but it is a general framework that allows the worst-case behavior of systems to be evaluated. Usually within SA, tasks are repetitive and are either released periodically or sporadically. Tasks can also suffer release jitter.

In this section we introduce a form of SA known as Response-Time Analysis (RTA) for analyzing resources that are scheduled by the common fixed priority dispatching policy. We then show how this analysis can be applied to determine the worst-case latencies for messages on a SoC. The analysis is then used to minimize the number of priority levels (and hence virtual channels) needed to deliver a system in which all messages are delivered by their deadlines. Background on the techniques to be introduced in this section can be found in standard textbooks [1]. The application of RTA to NoC message scheduling is described in [10].

2.3 Network Calculus (Zhonghai Lu)

Network calculus dealing with queuing systems is a formalism for design, analysis and implementation of performance guarantees in communication networks. The research was pioneered by Cruz in his seminal paper [3]. Chang systematically studied this subject [2]. In [6], stochastic network calculus generalizes the deterministic network calculus. Network calculus has been very successful when applied to achieve per-node and end-to-end QoS guarantees in Asynchronous Transfer Mode (ATM) networks, and Internet for both differentiated and integrated services. Recently it is applied to embedded real-time systems, off-chip networks such as wireless sensor networks, and on-chip networks [9].

This tutorial introduces the basics of network calculus within the context of on-chip networks. We begin by introducing the basic concepts such as arrival and service curves of network calculus to uncover the foundation for its elegance. Afterwards, we explain how closed-form formulas for calculating packet delay and backlog bounds can be obtained. With a clear-box approach on an example, we then orient our attention to its application to on-chip networks, analyzing service curves of an on-chip router and a concatenation of routers and further deriving per-flow end-to-end delay bound formula. Finally we give a short summary, reviewing its strength and pointing out future perspectives.

2.4 Queueing Theory (Abbas Eslami Kiasari)

Queueing theory is a branch of probability theory which is concerned with the mathematical modeling and analysis of systems that provide service to stochastic demands. Typically, a queueing model represents a system by probability models of customers' arrival time and service time. Since queueing theory deals with probability models, it is used to compute average-case performance metrics such as average packet latency, average throughput, average energy and power consumption, and average resource utilization.

This section starts with an introduction to queueing theory which demonstrates how to model events and resources in packet-switched networks. Then, we continue the tutorial by briefly reviewing related research where queueing theory is used for performance evaluation and optimization of NoCs. Using a state-of-the-art queueing model [7], we give a numerical example to estimate the average latency of packets in NoCs.

2.5 Bridging the Formalisms (Axel Jantsch)

The general trade-off between abstraction and accuracy can be observed in the comparison between these four formalisms. Since each of the reviewed formalisms has different advantages and difficulties, and since they also partially differ in purpose, none of them can easily replace all others. There are definitely point problems for each formalism that are worthy for further studies, but research on integrated approaches to the problems of system performance analysis is most urgent. Although each formalism can be extended in various directions, these extensions typically run into problems of complex mathematics or they are perceived to be unnatural and cumbersome. Therefore, we believe that comprehensive frameworks that combine two or more formalisms would be most desirable.

3. REFERENCE

[1] A. Burns and A. Wellings. *Real-Time Systems and Programming Languages*. Addison-Wesley, 4th Ed., 2009.

[2] C. S. Chang. *Performance Guarantees in Communication Networks*. Springer-Verlag, 2000.

[3] R. L. Cruz. A calculus for network delay, part I: network elements in isolation; part II: network analysis. *IEEE Transactions on Information Theory*, 37(1):114-141, 1991.

[4] M. Geilen, S. Tripakis, and M. Wiggers. The earlier the better: a theory of timed actor interfaces. In *Proceedings of the ACM International Conference on Hybrid Systems: Computation and Control*, pages 23-32, 2011.

[5] A. Hansson, M. Wiggers, A. Moonen, K. Goossens, and M. Bekooij. Enabling application-level performance guarantees in network-based systems on chip by applying dataflow analysis. *IET Computers & Digital Techniques*, 3(5):398-412, 2009.

[6] Y. Jiang and Y. Liu. *Stochastic Network Calculus*. Springer, 2008.

[7] A. E. Kiasari, Z. Lu, and A. Jantsch. An analytical latency model for networks-on-chip. *IEEE Transactions on Very Large Scale Integration (VLSI) Systems*, Jan. 2012. doi: 10.1109/TVLSI.2011.2 178620

[8] A. E. Kiasari, A. Jantsch, and Z. Lu. Mathematical formalisms for performance evaluation of networks-on-chip. *Accepted for publication in the ACM Computing Surveys*.

[9] Y. Qian, Z. Lu, and W. Dou. Analysis of worst-case delay bounds for on-chip packet-switching networks. *IEEE Transactions on Computer-Aided Design of Integrated Circuits and Systems*, 29(5):802-815, 2010.

[10] Z. Shi and A. Burns. Real-time communication analysis for on-chip networks with wormhole switching. In *Proceeding of the IEEE International Symposium on Networks-on-Chip (NoCS)*, pages 161-170, 2008.

[11] M. Wiggers, M. Bekooij, M. Geilen, and T. Basten. Simultaneous budget and buffer size computation for throughput constraint task graphs. In *Proceedings of the Design, Automation and Test in Europe Conference and Exhibition (DATE)*, pages 1669-1672, 2010.

[12] M. Wiggers, M. Bekooij, and G. Smit. Efficient computation of buffer capacities for cyclo-static dataflow graphs. In *Proceedings of the Design Automation Conference (DAC)*, pages 658-663, 2007.

[13] M. Wiggers, M. Bekooij, and G. Smit. Monotonicity and run-time scheduling. In *Proceedings of the International Conference on Embedded Software*, pages 177-186, 2009.

Embedded Reconfigurable Architectures

Stephan Wong
Delft University of Technology
The Netherlands
J.S.S.M.Wong@tudelft.nl

Luigi Carro
Universidade Federal do Rio
Grande do Sul
Brazil
carro@inf.ufrgs.br

Stamatis Kavvadias
University of Siena
Italy
kavadias@dii.unisi.it

Georgios Keramidas
Industrial Systems Institute
Greece
keramidas@isi.gr

Francesco Papariello
ST Microelectronics
Italy
francesco.papariello@st.com

Claudio Scordino
Evidence s.r.l.
Italy
claudio@evidence.eu.com

Roberto Giorgi
University of Siena
Italy
giorgi@dii.unisi.it

Stefanos Kaxiras
Uppsala University
Sweden
stefanos.kaxiras@it.uu.se

ABSTRACT

In current-day embedded systems design, one is faced with cut-throat competition to deliver new functionalities in increasingly shorter time frames. This is now achieved by incorporating processor cores into embedded systems through (re-)programmability. However, this is not always beneficial for the performance or energy consumption. Therefore, adaptable embedded systems have been proposed to deal with these negative effects by reconfiguring the critical sections of an embedded system. In these proposals, we are clearly witnessing a trend that is moving from static configurations to dynamic (re)configurations.

Consequently, the proposed embedded systems can adapt their functionality at run-time to meet the application(s) requirements (e.g., performance) while operating in different environments (e.g., power and hardware resources). Besides processor cores, we have to deal with memory hierarchies and network-on-chips that should also be (dynamically) reconfigurable. Furthermore, the interplay of these components is increasing the design complexity that can be only alleviated if they can self-optimize.

In this tutorial, we will present and discuss several strategies to perform the mentioned dynamic reconfiguration of the processor, memory, and NoC components - together with their interaction. We will review and present the state-of-the-art for the design of each component that allows for a gradual selection of design points in the trade-off between performance and power. Finally, we will highlight an open-source project that incorporates many approaches for dynamic reconfiguration in both actual hardware and simulation accompanied by the necessary tools.

Categories and Subject Descriptors

C.3 [**Special-Purpose and pplication-based Systems**]:
Real-time and embedded systems

General Terms

Design, Performance, Reliability

Keywords

Compilers, Dynamic Reconfiguration, Embedded Systems and Applications, Memory Hierarchies, NoC, Processor Design, Simulation

1. LIST OF TOPICS

In this tutorial, we will discuss the following topics:

- **ntroduction: eed for (dynamic) adaptability?** This part will provide a general introduction to adaptability within embedded systems from the applications and hardware design perspectives. It will be argued that dynamic reconfigurability is the next stage in embedded systems design.

- **eterogeneous beha ior of the applications and systems** This part will show, using examples, how the behavior of even a single thread execution is heterogeneous, and how difficult it is to distribute heterogeneous tasks processes among the components in a SOC environment, reinforcing the need for adaptability. This is furthermore complicated when considering multiple threads and the existence of an embedded operating system.

- **dapti e and recon gurable processor architectures** This part will present an overview of adaptive and reconfigurable processors and their basic functioning. We will also discuss those which present some level of dynamic adaptability.

- **econ gurable memory hierarchies** This part will present the need for sophisticated memory hierarchies to deal with varying applications and present techniques how the organization of these memory components can be "morphed" when switching applications without much performance loss.

- **Communication architectures - oCs** This part will discuss how important NoCs are for future embedded systems, which will have more heterogeneous applications being executed, and how the communication pattern might aggressively change, even with the same set of heterogeneous cores, from application to application.

- **Tools (compilers and simulators)** This part will discuss the need for a new breed of tools that are needed to support the earlier mentioned approaches.

- **Putting it all together** An analysis on the aforementioned techniques: how they can work together and what will be the impact of their use in future embedded systems. What is the price to pay for adaptability, and for which kind of applications it is well suited. This part will also present a working implementation of the software infrastructure to select and trigger the best reconfiguration of the architecture at run-time.

- **Conclusions** A summary of the research discussed and the road ahead.

2. ADDITIONAL AUTHOR INFORMATION

The following persons were involved in building this tutorial:

- Stephan Wong (Delft University of Technology - TUD) is an associate professor at Computer Engineering laboratory at TUD. He is the co-inventor of the MOLEN processor architecture and has considerable experience with reconfigurable architectures. He is coordinator of the ERA project (an European funded FP7 project) that is focusing on many topics described in this tutorial.

- Luigi Carro (Universidade Federal do Rio Grande do Sul - UFRGS) is a full professor at the Institute for Informatics at UFRGS. He has considerable experience with computer engineering with emphasis on hardware and software design for embedded systems focussing on: embedded electronic systems, processor architecture dedicated test, fault-tolerance, and multi-platform software development.

- Stamatis Kavvadias (University of Siena - UNISI) is a research associate at the Department of Information Engineering at UNISI. His main research area is memory hierarchy microarchitecture, communication, synchronization, cache coherence, and task scheduling in CMPs.

- Georgios Keramidas (Industrial Systems Institute - ISI) is a post-doctoral fellow at ISI and a visiting assistant professor at the University of Patras, Greece. His research interests include computer architecture, in particular, the design of memory subsystems of single core and multicore systems.

- Francesco Papariello (ST Microelectronics - STMICRO) is a researcher in the Advanced Systems Technology R&D group at STMICRO. He has been involved in the design and development of simulation and design space exploration tools, among them the Lx (ST2xx family) simulation models and the xSTreamISS, the simulation infrastructure for the xSTream platform (streaming multi-core heterogeneous system).

- Claudio Scordino (Evidence s.r.l. - EVI) is a project manager within EVI and his research activities include operating systems, real-time scheduling, energy saving and embedded devices.

- Roberto Giorgi (University of Siena - UNISI) is an associate professor at the Department of Information Engineering at UNISI. His main research area is in computer architecture with emphasis on multiprocessor/multicore issues (processor, coherence, and programmability).

- Stefanos Kaxiras (Uppsala University - UU) is a full professor at the Department of Information Technology at UU. He has considerable experience in memory systems (highly scalable cache coherence, cache management using reuse distances), power (decay), instruction-based prediction, network processors (IPstash IP-lookup memories), memory/processor integration (datascalar/distributed vector architectures).

3. ACKNOWLEDGMENTS

The research leading to the results presented in this tutorial has received funding from the European Community's Seventh Framework Programme (FP7/2007-2013) under grant agreement nr. 249059. The information presented is provided as is and no guarantee or warranty is given that the information is fit for any particular purpose. The user thereof uses the information at its sole risk and liability. The opinions expressed in the document are of the authors only and I no way reflect the European Commission's opinions.

Author Index